Variorum Reprints:

ANDRÉ GRABAR
L'empereur dans l'art byzantin
Strasbourg 1936 edition

LOUIS BRÉHIER
La sculpture et les arts mineurs byzantins
Paris 1936 edition

In the Collected Studies Series:

W.H.C. FREND
Religion Popular and Unpopular in the Early Christian Centuries

FRANÇOIS HALKIN
Saints moines d'Orient

FRANÇOIS HALKIN
Martyrs Grecs. IIe-VIIIe s.

PAUL J. ALEXANDER
Religious and Political History and Thought in the Byzantine Empire

MILTON V. ANASTOS
Studies in Byzantine Intellectual History

A. H. ARMSTRONG
Plotinian and Christian Studies

ANDRÉ GRABAR
L'art paléochrétien et l'art byzantin

VESELIN BEŠEVLIEV
Bulgarisch-Byzantinische Aufsätze

PHILIP GRIERSON
Dark Age Numismatics

KARL FERDINAND WERNER
Structure politiques du monde franc (VIe-XIIe siècles)

BERNHARD BLUMENKRANZ
Juifs et Chrétiens — Patristique et Moyen-Age

PAUL MEYVAERT
Benedict, Gregory, Bede and Others

Town and Country
in the Early Christian Centuries

Professor W. H. C. Frend

W.H.C. Frend

Town and Country in the Early Christian Centuries

VARIORUM REPRINTS
London 1980

British Library CIP data

Frend, William Hugh Clifford
　Town and country in the early Christian
　centuries. — (Collected studies series; CS110).
　1. Church history — Primitive and early church,
　ca.30-600
　I. Title　II. Series
　270.1　　　　　BR162.2

ISBN 0-86078-055-4

Published in Great Britain by　Variorum Reprints
　　　　　　　　　　　　　　　　20 Pembridge Mews London W11 3EQ

Printed in Great Britain by　Kingprint Ltd
　　　　　　　　　　　　　　　Richmond Surrey TW9 4PD

VARIORUM REPRINT CS110

CONTENTS

Preface i—ii

HISTORY AND ARCHAEOLOGY

I   Town and Countryside in Early Christianity   25—42
*Studies in Church History XVI (ed. D. Baker).
Oxford, 1979*

II   The Winning of the Countryside   1—14
*The Journal of Ecclesiastical History XVIII.
London, 1967*

III   The Gospel of Thomas.
Is Rehabilitation Possible?   13—26
*The Journal of Theological Studies N.S. XVIII.
Oxford, 1967*

IV   The Ecology of the Early Christianities   15—28
*Christianity in its Social Context, ed. Gerard
Irvine (= Lectures to the Society of St. Anne's,
1965). S.P.C.K. Theological Collections, 8.
London, 1967*

V   The Archaeologist and Church History   259—265
*Antiquity XXXIV.
Newbury, 1960*

VI   Ecclesiastical History:
Its Growth and Relevance   38–51

The Philosophical Journal 8.
Glasgow, 1971

VII   Review of T. Klauser, *Henri Leclercq*
1869-1945: vom Autodidacten zum
Kompilator Grossen Stils   320–324

The Journal of Theological Studies N.S. XXX.
Oxford, 1979

THE CHURCH AND THE ROMAN EMPIRE

VIII   The Church of the Roman Empire, 313-600   57–87

The Layman in Christian History, ed. Stephen
Neill and Hans-Ruedi Weber.
SCM Press, London, 1963

IX   A Severan Persecution?
Evidence of the "Historia Augusta"   470–480

Forma Futuri. Studi in onore del
Cardinale Michele Pellegrino.
Bottega D'Erasmo, Turin, 1975

X   The Failure of the Persecutions in the
Roman Empire   263–287

Studies in Ancient History, ed. M.I. Finley.
Past and Present Series.
Routledge and Kegan Paul, London & Boston, 1974

XI   Eastern Attitudes to Rome during the
Acacian Schism   69–81

Studies in Church History XIII (ed. D. Baker).
Oxford, 1976

THE WEST

| XII | *Ecclesia Britannica:* Prelude or Dead End? | 129–144 |

The Journal of Ecclesiastical History 30.
Cambridge, 1979

| XIII | A Note on the Influence of Greek Immigrants on the Spread of Christianity in the West | 125–129 |

Mullus. Festschrift Th. Klauser = Jahrbuch für Antike und Christentum. Ergänzungsband I.
Münster, 1964

| XIV | Paulinus of Nola and the Last Century of the Western Empire | 1–11 |

The Journal of Roman Studies LIX.
London, 1969

| XV | Blandina and Perpetua: Two Early Christian Heroines | 167–175 |

Les Martyrs de Lyon (177). Colloques internationaux du CNRS, no.575.
Paris, 1978

NORTH AFRICA

| XVI | The Early Christian Church in Carthage | 21–40 |

Excavations at Carthage in 1976, conducted by the University of Michigan, iii.
University of Michigan, Ann Arbor, 1977

| XVII | Jews and Christians in Third Century Carthage | 185–194 |

Paganisme, Judaïsme, Christianisme. Influences et affrontements dans le monde antique. Mélanges offerts à Marcel Simon.
Boccard, Paris, 1978

XVIII	The *Memoriae Apostolorum* in Roman North Africa	32–49
	The Journal of Roman Studies XXX. *London, 1940*	
XIX	Circumcellions and Monks	542–549
	The Journal of Theological Studies N.S. XX. *Oxford, 1969*	
XX	The Revival of Berber Art	342–352
	Antiquity XVI. *Gloucester, 1942*	
XXI	North Africa and Europe in the Early Middle Ages	61–80
	Transactions of the Royal Historical Society, 5th series, 5. *London, 1955*	

NUBIA

XXII	The Mission to Nubia: an Episode in the Struggle for Power in Sixth Century Byzantium	10–16
	Travaux du Centre d'archéologie méditerranéenne de l'Académie Polonaise des Sciences, tome 16. *Etudes de Travaux VIII.* *Warsaw, 1975*	
XXIII	The Cult of Military Saints in Christian Nubia	155–163
	Theologia Crucis – Signum Crucis. *Festschrift für Erich Dinkler, ed. Carl Andresen and Günter Klein.* *J. C. B. Mohr (Paul Siebeck), Tübingen, 1979*	

| XXIV | Recently Discovered Materials for Writing the History of Christian Nubia | 19–30 |

Studies in Church History XI, ed. D. Baker. Oxford, 1975

| XXV | Review of Erich Dinkler (Ed.): *Kunst und Geschichte Nubiens in christlicher Zeit* | 336–339 |

Zeitschrift für Kirchengeschichte II/III. Stuttgart, 1973

Index   1–11

This volume contains a total of 372 pages.

PREFACE

This second volume of Collected Studies is concerned largely with the different interpretations of Christianity among Christians in town and countryside, and also the relation between text and field research as means of study. In the United Kingdom, Patristic studies have always been literary-oriented, and since the works of the Fathers have survived more often than those of their schismatic and heretical opponents, the bias has tended to be towards the study of Christian orthodoxy. My interest has leant in the other direction — to seek to understand the origins, development and the strengths and weaknesses of movements which have lain outside the mainstream of orthodox belief. This, of course, has involved new methods of approach, particularly those of the field archaeologist, whose role is to discover and to relate his discoveries on the ground with information derived from the texts.

The Donatist Church in North Africa has been a case in point. It was represented on the ground by numbers of small, roughly built churches and chapels in the Romano-Berber villages of Numidia (Central Algeria) where literary sources attested its strength. What did its adherents believe? How long did the Church survive? What clues does archaeology provide for the North African Circumcellions? When did Islam supplant Christianity as the religion of the people? The two early works included in this collection (No. XVIII and XX), discussing the association of Saints Peter and Paul with local (Donatist?) martyrs, and the association of a vigorous artistic movement with the rise of Donatism illustrate my researches in some of these fields. Since they were written (in 1939), the study of early Christianity and particularly of its lost traditions, has been aided by a continuous series of archaeological discoveries. The scholar is now far better equipped to study Gnosticism, Manichaeism, and Monophysitism than he was forty years ago. And, in areas such as Roman Britain where textual evidence for early Christianity is sparse, archaeological work is enabling some of the main lines of the progress of the new faith to be traced.

The present studies cover many of my interests, the Donatists and Monophysites, ideas of martyrdom and persecution, the layman's contribution to the Church's teaching and order, the different theologies that divided eastern and western Christendom, and the ascetic movement and its contribution to the fall of the Roman Empire in the west.

There are many organisations and individuals that I would like to thank at the end of forty years' research and writing. I am particularly grateful to the Craven Committee of Oxford University for giving me an early opportunity in 1937 of studying the remains of the Donatist Church in North Africa. Similarly, but for the Egypt Exploration Society, I would never have interested myself in Nubian Christianity. My work at Q'asr Ibrim in 1963-4, 1972 and 1974 is represented in the last four studies. I am particularly grateful also to the University of Michigan for re-kindling an interest in Byzantine Africa, and the transition to Islam, through their invitation to me to join their "Save Carthage" project in 1976 and 1977, and having provided me with the chance of helping (with French colleagues) in September 1977, to launch the Tunisian "Projet paléochrétien". Tunisia thus became the first Mediterranean Moslem country to embark officially on early Christian studies.

The field open to British scholars is a wide one. Some opportunities have not been taken up, others, such as the establishment of Christian archaeology as a discipline as it is understood on the continent have failed to appeal to senior academic institutions. As Britain enters increasingly into the realm of European scholarship it may be expected that some existing gaps will be filled. These studies are published in the hope that they may encourage a new generation of scholars to continue their author's work.

W. H. C. FREND

Glasgow University
September, 1979

HISTORY AND ARCHAEOLOGY

I

TOWN AND COUNTRYSIDE IN EARLY CHRISTIANITY

A VISITOR to the Greco-Roman world about the year 350 AD would have found himself confronted by one of the great 'sea changes' in the lives of its peoples. The structure of city, farm and village that had persisted for centuries would appear to be intact. The market-places of the towns would be lined with altars and statues of long-dead benefactors. Temples to the gods of Rome and perhaps to a native deity duly Romanised, would dominate the scene. Wherever one stood in the city the temples in the forum would be the landmark. Nearby, would be the amphitheatre and great bath-building, the social centres of the old community, and near the entrance to the town the triumphal arch, marking perhaps the unification of Roman citizen and native inhabitant into one community.

By 350, however, this civilisation was passing away. In the west, for every Bordeaux with its fine classical schools and antiquarian interests, the home of the poet and politician, Ausonius, there was an Aventicum, a one-time *colonia* and cantonal town of the Helvetii described by the historian, Ammianus Marcellinus as abandoned and full of half-ruined buildings.[1] In the east, Antioch could live up to Libanius's description of its magnificence, its wealth based on its customs dues and busy trade, and could afford to supply lavish amusements,[2] but many other once famous cities, even Diocletian's capital, Nicomedia, and Carnuntum, the one-time Danube citadel, were impoverished, their walls 'a heap of ashes'.[3] Moreover, such rebuilding as there was going on, was mainly of a different type. Big new halls of assembly and worship were springing out of the ground. At the dedication of one, the church of the Golden Dome at Antioch, the emperor Constantius had held a council attended by nearly one hundred

---

[1] A[mmianus] M[arcellinus, *Res Gestae*], ed J. C. Rolfe (London/Cambridge, Mass., 1935) bk 15 cap 11 para 12.
[2] Libanius, *Antiochikos, Orationes* 11, 196, ed R. Förster (Leipzig 1903) 1 p 504, and compare A. J. Festugière, *Antioche païenne et chrétienne*, Bibliothèque des écoles françaises d'Athènes et Rome 194 (Paris 1959) pp 23–7.
[3] AM bk 22 cap 9 para 4 (Nicomedia) and bk 30 cap 5 para 2 (Carnuntum).

bishops in 341[4] At Aquileia at the nothern end of the Adriatic, Athanasius had watched another large church being built in 345.[5] Even more impressive, outside some of the old towns entire quarters dedicated to the needs of the new all-conquering Christian religion were making their appearance. At Djemila and Timgad in north Africa and at Salona in Dalmatia these were the new centres of urban life.[6] The leaders of this new civilisation, the bishops, presbyters and the host of administrative underlings had supplanted the old city councils in all but name as the rulers of the community. Theirs was the power and the wealth. The magistrates merely administered the law and paid the taxes. Our visitor would have seen the Mediterranean in a state of transition, when the old cities, their fierce local patriotism, and their religion based on the traditional gods of the locality were giving way to a world-wide faith whose leaders could impose a common teaching on their believers from one end of the Mediterranean to the other.

In the countryside a similar transition was taking place, but in a different form. Our visitor, if he was a bishop and had been provided with a diploma to use the public posting service[7] to travel, let us say, from Constantine to Timgad in Numidia, would have encountered a distinctive form of Christianity as he would have found a different style of life. In the dry climate that prevailed in an inhospitable landscape, he would have seen fewer towns until he reached the zone of military cantonments that guarded the Aures passes. His journey would have taken him through villages, thickly but untidily spaced and he would have noticed how each family had its olive press and silo for storing grain and, above all, the numerous small whitewashed churches that could be found at every corner. If he had stopped to enter, he would have perceived a similarity in design, a raised apse at the east end, and in front a roughly constructed square enclosure for the altar, beneath which would lie the sacred relics of the martyrs.[8] An inscription proclaiming that here 'the just shall enter',[9] or a snatch

---

[4] Sozomen, *HE* bk 3 cap 5 para 2, ed J. Bidez and G. C. Hansen, *GCS* (Berlin 1960) p 105.
[5] By bishop Fortunatianus. See H. Leclercq, 'Aquilée', *DACL* 1.2 col 2661. For Athanasius's presence with Fortunatianus at Aquileia see *Apologia ad Constantium* 3, *PG* 25 (1884) col 599B.
[6] See J. Lassus, 'Les edifices du culte autour de la basilique', *Atti del 6 Congresso Internazionale di archeologia cristiana, Ravenna 1962* (Rome 1965) pp 581–610.
[7] Compare AM bk 21 cap 16 para 18.
[8] These churches are described by A. Berthier and his colleagues in his *Le christianisme antique dans la Numidie centrale* (Algiers 1942) pp 39 seq.
[9] For example, see P. Monceaux, *Histoire littéraire de l'Afrique chrétienne* (Paris 1912) pp 444–84.

Town and countryside in early Christianity

from the Psalms, 'Praise ye the Lord and rejoice, ye righteous, and let us glory in the Lord with a true heart' (Ps 30.12), or merely the expressive, 'Praise to God' (*Deo Laudes*) would have caught his attention,[10] and perhaps, too, the traditional native geometric designs, based on the wood-carver's art cut on the pillars that supported the roof either side of the apse. Outside, his attention could have been attracted to a group of men carrying clubs, whose language amongst themselves he might not have understood, ostensibly on pilgrimage from one martyr's shrine to another but (if he could understand Berber) expressing contempt for the church in the city,[11] and vowing that if they saw one of the local landowners riding in his carriage, they would pitch him out, put a slave in his place and give him a taste of what servitude meant.[12] These were the 'saints', the circumcellions for whom Christianity involved dramatic reversal of fortunes of this world and the glory reserved for the martyr in the next. Our friend would have reached Timgad a puzzled but a wiser man.

In Egypt and Syria he would have found similar differences between Christianity in town and countryside, but without some of the violence of sentiment against the institutions of the empire and the personalities of the urban bishops. Monasticism, however, in both these areas was largely a native movement. In Egypt, its founder, *c*270 had been Antony (251–356) who, despite his Greek name, was the son of a relatively wealthy Coptic farmer. In contrast to the urban episcopate, the vast majority of whose members were Greek, or Jewish-Christian by origin,[13] Antony's colleagues and imitators were Egyptians such as Amoun and Pachomius, men who struggled with Greek as a second language. Moreover, the way they understood scripture differed from that of their urban and Greek-speaking superiors. 'If thou wilt be perfect, go, sell all that thou hast', and other similar Domenical commands were to be taken literally and not allegorised away into moral

---

[10] See [W. H. C.] Frend, [*The Donatist Church*] (Oxford 1952) p 318.
[11] On the circumcellions see Frend pp 172–7; Frend, 'Circumcellions and monks', *JTS*, ns 20 (1969) pp 542–9; and for their contempt even for Donatist bishops see Optatus, [*De Schismate*], bk 3 cap 4, ed C. Ziwsa, *CSEL* 26 (1893)—'Dicuntur [episcopi] huiusmodi homines in ecclesia corrigi non posse'.
[12] Optatus p 82, and in the early fifth century see Augustine *Ep* 185.4.15, ed A. Goldbacher, *CSEL* 57 (1911) p 14.
[13] See A. Martin, 'L'Eglise et la Khora egyptienne au IVe siècle', *Les Transformations dans la société chrétienne au IVe siècle, Actes du Congrès à Varsovie du CIHEC*, 1978 (to be published).

platitudes.¹⁴ Antony's monks accepted 'the whole yoke of the Lord'. They 'took no thought for the morrow' (Mt 6.34).¹⁵ They believed in solitary prayer and fasting. In the deserts, beyond the boundaries of city and village, they fought the demons with the weapon of asceticism, self mortification, martyrdom in intent if not in deed. They were, like the circumcellions, men of the bible. For up to twenty years, between 284-304 while living in an abandoned fort on the east side of the Nile, Antony and his followers could not have received eucharist from the hands of a priest.¹⁶ The communal, or coenobitic monastic movement, inspired and organised by Pachomius, a generation later, was scarcely less un-hierarchic. Pachomius resisted strenuously Athanasius's wishes to ordain him presbyter,¹⁷ and though his monastic settlements were eventually under episcopal control, the emphasis of his teaching lay on the ascetic life, on work with one's hands, literal application of the bible, and alleviation of all forms of suffering and distress in the community on an individual basis. His outlook recalled the spirit of the gospel rather than that of the ordered churches that had established themselves in the Egyptian towns. In Syria, the monastic movement was even more given to extremes of individual asceticism. The *boskoi*, or grass-eaters, symbolised their rejection of urban civilization.¹⁸

One major aspect of Egyptian and Syrian monasticism differed from the rural Christianity of the north African circumcellions. Though they disliked judges and tax-collectors,¹⁹ and confronted economic and social conditions as bad as those prevailing in north Africa, they were not even implicitly revolutionaries against secular authority.²⁰ By superb tact, Constantine had won the allegiance of the native Egyptian confessors at Nicaea.²¹ A few years later, Athanasius

---

[14] Such as by Clement of Alexandria in *Quis dives salvetur?*, ed G. W. Butterworth (London/Cambridge, Mass., 1953).
[15] See [*Athanasius, Life of*] *Antony* cap 3 *PG* 26 (1887) col 844, and compare *ibid* cap 20.
[16] The point made by L. Duchesne, *The History of the Early Church* (Eng trans London 1931) 2, p 390.
[17] Theodore, *Vita Pachomii* cap 28, ed T. Lefort, *CSCO, Scriptores Coptici*, III.7 (Paris 1924, Louvain 1936).
[18] On the *boskoi* see Sozomen, *HE*, bk 6 cap 33, also A. Vööbus, 'A History of Asceticism in the Syrian Orient', *CSCO Subsidia* 17 (1960) pp 24-5.
[19] *Antony* cap 44, col 907B.
[20] For instance, see John Chrysostom, *Homilia in Matt* 61.3, *PG* 58 (1862) col 591. Syrian landowners were described as 'more cruel than the barbarians because they imposed intolerable and unending taxes and corvées on the working population on their lands'.
[21] His reception of Paphnutius who had been terribly mutilated in the persecution, for instance; see Socrates *HE* bk 1 cap 11, *PG* 67 (1864) col 101C.

Town and countryside in early Christianity

was to begin a series of tours and visitations that consolidated the friendship of the Coptic monastic leaders into a lasting loyalty. From that time on the monks were the staunch allies of the see of Alexandria. In Syria they acted as God-inspired intermediaries between people and authorities.[22] They were never to be a destructive force within the eastern Roman empire.

Yet for all that, Christianity in town and countryside in east and west was developing on different lines, separate in one part of the empire, complementary in the other. Our friend bumping along the uneven roadways from one *mansio* to the next might well be asking himself why this should be so.

Even to sketch an answer for him, one must go back to two different elements in the background of the history of the early church. First, there are the contrasts that existed within Israelite society which affected the earliest Christian message, and secondly, the structure of society that confronted the Christian mission in the Greco-Roman world.

As is well known, the old testament tells the social as well as the religious history of the Jewish people. From the earliest moment in creation there were to be conflicts of interests. The story of Cain and Abel, the one 'the tiller of the ground', the other, 'the keeper of sheep' (Gen 4.2) reflects the age-old rivalry between the two basic communities in the evolution of primitive society. Later, one can detect the thinly disguised tensions between the priestly and the prophetic parties in Israel. The priests served the temple of the Lord in an orderly, urbanised environment. The prophets, as Elijah and Elisha or Amos, were countrymen (see 1 Kings 19.19 on Elisha), often itinerant, moving from place to place, even living in caves (1 Kings 19.9), warning kings against backsliding from the strict worship of the Lord, or denouncing the crimes of the rich. And grave were the penalties for ignoring the commands of 'the sons of the prophets', even if these seemed ridiculous (see 1 Kings 20.35–7). The wilderness and the heroic age of Israel rather than Jerusalem and Solomon's temple inspired them. Wandering about 'in sheepskins and goatskins' in deserts, persecuted by those who thought they knew better, was how romantics of the time of Christ depicted them (Hebs 11.37–8).

The prophetic tradition hardened and steeled the Jews against possible absorption into surrounding alien cultures. In the growing

---

[22] See the excellent study by P. R. L. Brown, 'The Rise and function of the Holy Man in Late Antiquity', *JRS* 61 (1971) pp 80–101.

crisis that followed the annexation of Judaea by Antiochus III after the battle of Panium in 198 BC, the country districts stood firm for uncompromising Judaism whereas the high priests and Jewish aristocracy in Jerusalem were prepared to move a long way towards hellenisation. In the great war against the Seleucids that lasted between 165 and 141 BC, the Maccabees triumphed. They represented the conservative country areas and enforced their will on Jerusalem. Their successful revolt was aimed as much against apostate Jews—mainly in Jerusalem—as against the Seleucids.[23]

Another century passed in which the pattern of events tended to repeat itself. The Hasmonaean, that is, the dynasty of Judas Maccabaeus, was a bad neighbour to surrounding states, but it also imitated many of their ways. The court of Alexander Jannaeus resembled that of a Syrian princeling and his aggressive wars were fought with mercenaries like those employed by his neighbours. At some point, a group of pious Jews accepted the leadership of one whom they called 'The Righteous Teacher' and went out into the wilderness with the set intention of separating themselves 'from the abode of perverse men' and from the Temple itself.[24] As in the great days of Israel, they prepared themselves to fight the final war of Jahwe, and expected his kingdom to descend, not in Jerusalem, but in the wilderness, as prophesied in Is. 40.3. In the monastery established at Q'mran, the Dead Sea covenanters maintained themselves, observing the letter of the law and separating completely from idolatrous society, including that of Jerusalem itself. Property they regarded as sin. Some of the aims of the sect expressed in unity through the Spirit—love for one's fellows in the brotherhood, and the breakdown of all social barriers—foreshadowed those of the primitive church.

There can be little doubt that John the Baptist had some affinity with these covenanters,[25] even if the supposition that his aged parents committed him to the sect instead of the Temple, can never be proved. The baptism he proclaimed, however, was not a proselyte baptism but a ceremony of purification such as those undertaken by the

---

[23] See the short but invaluable account of the decisive years 167–4 BC, by Fergus Millar, 'The Background to the Maccabaean Revolution; Reflections on Martin Hengel's "Judaism and Hellenism",' *Journal of Jewish Studies* 29, 1 (Oxford 1978) pp 1–21.

[24] The Sectarian Rule of the Community from Q' mran, Cave 1 (= IQS) 8, 12–13. See also J. T. Milik, *Ten years of Discovery in the Wilderness of Judaea* (London 1959) pp 115–16, and F. Moore Cross, *The Ancient Library of Q'mran* (London 1958) p 55.

[25] I accept the view put forward by [J. A. T.] Robinson ['The Baptism of John and the Q'mran community'], *HTR* 50 (July 1957) pp 175–90, (references to work by Brownlee, Bo Reicke and A. S. Geyser).

Town and countryside in early Christianity

covenanters. For our purpose, however, one should notice that John's message was that of a prophet who emerged from the desert. He proclaimed in fearsome terms the imminent arrival of the kingdom of God, and, like the covenanters, he believed it would arrive 'in the wilderness'. 'Prepare ye the way of the Lord: make his paths straight', found in all four gospels (Mt 3.3, Mk 1.3, Lk 3.4 and Jn 1.23), are probably his own words. He, too, has severe things to say to the representatives of the urban religion associated with the Temple, who visited him. 'You viper's brood', he addressed the pharisees and sadducees, 'who warned you to escape from the coming retribution? Then prove your repentance by the fruit it bears, and do not presume to say to yourselves, "We have Abraham for our father", for I tell you, God is able to raise up from these stones children to Abraham' (Mt 3.2–9). The end was near; the fire would purge thoroughly and drastically. John's irruption from the desert boded ill for even the nationally minded pharisees and indeed, to all Jews who believed that Jahwe could best be served through the Temple cult.[26]

Jesus accepted John's baptism and His first mission was carried out —I can see no reason to disbelieve the fourth gospel here—in association with his cousin in the Jordan valley (Jn 3.22–3, 4.2).[27] Though Jesus frequently visited and had a deep affection for Jerusalem, the main area of His mission was rural Palestine. It was among the villages of Galilee that the lepers were cleansed, the blind received their sight, and the sick were healed (see Mt 11.5). Satan's kingdom was attacked there in the first place. Towns he seems to have avoided. There is no evidence he went to Sepphoris, Antipas's capital a bare four miles from Nazareth, and it was to the villages round about Caesarea Philippi, not to that centre itself, that he took his disciples after the end of the Galilean ministry (Mk 8.27). Though Jesus did not dress or behave like an ascetic prophet—the pharisees pointed out early in His mission (Luke 6.1 *seq*) that John's disciples fasted often but 'yours do not fast' (Mt 9.14), the way of life that he demanded of his followers was rigorous in the extreme. 'Foxes have holes and the birds of the air have nests, but the Son of Man hath not where to lay his head' (Lk 9.58). The tradition which he allowed those who heard him to believe he represented, was that of the prophet. The crowds in Jerusalem hailed

---

[26] On the eschatological character of John's ministry, see Robinson p 189. 'The purpose of John's baptism, we may say, was precisely to force the eschatological issue.'
[27] See C. H. Dodd, *Historical Tradition in the Fourth Gospel* (Cambridge 1963) compare pp 279 *seq*, 300–1.

him as 'the prophet from Nazareth' (Mt 21.10). Earlier, at the outset of his mission, Jesus had opened his sermon in the town of his upbringing, with the words of Second Isaiah (61.1-2) and when roused by the growing hostility of his audience reminded them of the words of the great prophets of the past, Elijah and Elisha (Lk 4.25-8). His message that blessed poverty and equated piety with humility, that preached the practical impossibility of the salvation of the rich, and associated wealth or Mammon with unrighteousness, stood within the prophetic tradition of Israel. The question he posed to his generation was whether he was the prophet who would be 'raised up from among you' who must be heeded (Deut 18.15) or a false prophet 'who presumes to speak a word in my name which I have not commanded him to speak', and so be worthy of death (Deut 18.20). Jesus's complete reversal of current values and absolute commands for purity, self-sacrifice and selfless love for one's neighbour were too much for the Jewish high-priesthood in Jerusalem.

Jesus's mission had been rural and his parables and examples of conduct worthy of the kingdom of God were drawn mainly from rural life. Within a very short time from the crucifixion, however, His followers were giving a different emphasis to his message. Long before Paul appeared on the scene, Christianity had concentrated on the towns of Palestine, on Caesarea, Joppa, Damascus and distant Antioch. These centres and even Samaria rather than Galilee became the focus of the first Christian mission.

The point is worth making, for the contrast is too often drawn as simply one between Jesus and Paul. In fact, Paul merely continued the work, with brilliant success, that had already been begun by the disciples themselves. With Paul, of course, the Christian message was transformed from a rural Palestinian to an urban Jewish dispersion setting with incalculable results. Only with reservations can Paul be called the interpreter of Jesus's religion. Like his Master, he believed that the end was approaching, but he preached no gospel of repentance, nor did he attempt to explain Jesus's teaching to his urban audiences. He did not disavow Jesus 'born of woman' (Gal 4.4), but for him and his hearers the heavenly being, the Lord Christ had replaced the prophet of Nazareth.[28] His medium was Greek and not Aramaic. For Jews and proselytes in the towns of Asia Minor and the Aegean coasts his message was, that the first-born of creation familiar to them in their

[28] See W. L. Knox, *St Paul and the Church of the Gentiles* (Cambridge 1961) pp 163 *seq* for the development in Paul of the equation of Jesus with the heavenly Wisdom of God.

Town and countryside in early Christianity

reading of Proverbs and the Book of Wisdom had indeed come in flesh, and that through the cross salvation was available to all believers. Paul's mission was not to the outcasts of the highways and byeways outside the cities but to town-dwellers who already knew their septuagint and debated the law. Just as he himself moved easily among the upper reaches of provincial society, so his audience was drawn from the urban middle classes, not from the rural multitudes to whom Jesus had spoken. Indeed, his words would have meant nothing to the Lycaonians who if they had understood them (Acts 14.11-17), might have retorted, 'Why should this benevolent God you preach want to destroy his creation?'.[29] A God of Jewish history was hardly intelligible to those who looked for a saving god in nature.

To the God-fearers, however, who heard him, Paul was a deliverer. There can be no doubt that in city after city of Asia Minor and Greece, Paul's message was heard with rapture.[30] This was a revolutionary religion based on personal commitment to Christ, a new exodus based on a new torah. In ten years, between 47 and 57 Paul turned the Jewish dispersion upside down. The Jewish communities were irretrievably split and never returned to unity.

Paul's revolution, however, was religious, not social. Himself respectful to the authorities, loyal to the empire, he was not the man to draw out the implications of Jesus's social teaching. Relations between Christian and Christian were indeed to be characterised by 'love towards the brethren', but the institutions of the empire were sacrosanct. Slavery remained unassailable. There is no word of sympathy for the lot of the scarcely less unfree cultivator.[31]

In 70 AD Jerusalem fell and with it the link that bound Pauline to Palestinian Christianity. For the next three centuries, Christianity was to be primarily a western, a Greek-speaking, religion. Its organisation was based on the urban community, led first by presbyter-bishops and after the end of the first century by bishops, who were assisted by presbyters and deacons. It was the organisation of the hellenistic synagogue adapted to the needs of Christianity. Prophets and teachers gradually faded out of reckoning as the Coming with which their message was primarily concerned was even further delayed.

---

[29] See M. Dibelius, *Studies in the Acts of the Apostles* (Eng trans London 1956) p 71 n; E. Haenchen, *The Acts of the Apostles: a Commentary* (Eng trans London 1971) pp 431-4.
[30] For instance, the Galatians, 'received me as an angel of God, as Jesus Christ', Gal 4.15.
[31] For Paul's social teaching see G. E. M. de Ste. Croix, 'Early Christian attitudes towards Property and Slavery', SCH 12 (1975) p 19.

Moreover, though the lordship of Jesus was assumed and the gospels were increasingly read alongside the septuagint, the prevailing interpretation of His teaching was either Pauline or a Christianised pharisaism which emerged towards the end of the first century.[32] It has often been noted that the writer of 1 Clement quotes Paul without appearing to discuss specific Pauline doctrines. It seems that the dispersion communities, including Rome, grafted the personality of Jesus on to what they had accepted in Judaism, namely, the predominantly pharisaic religion of the last two centuries BC and a Judaised stoic ethic. It is interesting that even in the *Didache*, that owes much to Matthew's gospel, the writer does not insist that the way of life was marked through carrying out the precepts of the sermon on the mount, but rather by a generalised formula of benevolence towards one's neighbour.[33] Not surprisingly, the Christian communities of the first half of the second century, such as Polycarp's at Smyrna, were small, self-contained and introspective. Being 'blameless before the Gentiles' was more important than going out to convert them.[34]

The church's progress during the second century committed it even further to an urban environment. The first great intellectual movement within Christianity, namely gnosticism, could not have been more city-based. Though still accepting many of the pre-suppositions of Judaism, the gnostics attempted to fuse all current religious knowledge whether pagan, Jewish or Christian, round the person of Christ portrayed as the divine saviour.[35] Though they failed, their orthodox rivals found in their turn that they could not express themselves adequately without recourse to the language of philosophy. It was part of the church's strength at this time, that it could absorb philosophical ideas without abandoning its uncompromising opposition to idolatry. Sect and great church alike were finding a place for the active and inquiring gentile mind dissatisfied with the inability of philosophers to find answers to religious questions. Justin Martyr, Tatian, and for a short time Proteus Peregrinus were typical recruits. To the outside observer, Christianity was an opposition urban cult, whose members

---

[32] I refer in particular, to the long moralising passages in 1 *Clement* which have no reference either to the gospels or Paul and yet reflect Christian teaching of the day.

[33] Thus *Didache* 1 and 4, with the emphasis on selective almsgiving rather than drastic self-denial.

[34] Polycarp to the *Philippians* 10.2, with the emphasis also on general philanthropy and good works as the Christian's task.

[35] See Hans Jonas's fine work, *The Gnostic Religion* (Boston 1963); John Dart, *The Laughing Saviour*, (The Discovery and significance of the Nag Hammadi Library) (San Francisco 1976) part 2.

Town and countryside in early Christianity

having 'rejected the Greek gods', formed an 'illegal association' bound together by oaths, who sought to subvert tradition and family for the sake of the deluded worship of the 'crucified sophis'.[36] With few exceptions, the Christian groups in the second century were found in cities where Judaism was strong, as in Sardes in the east, or among merchant colonies, such as at Lyon. Traders and artisans made up their numbers.[37]

Episcopal government, too, was based on the city. This put its bishops and clergy willy-nilly among the privileged orders of ancient society. The persecutions of the Christians in the second century related to their status and influence within that society. We hear of no organisation of country parishes at this time, and certainly no rejection of urban institutions. The church had settled down as a radically-minded Judaistic sect, whose members believed that the world had been created for their sake, and who debated lengthily who amongst them would be most worthy to be saved from its coming destruction.[38] Their heroes were recognisably urban, like Attalus, the Phrygian physician and stalwart among the martyrs of Lyon in 177, and Justin Martyr himself. Their enemies were local philosophers who feared Christian rivalry[39] or urban mobs always ready to lay local disasters at their door.

There was one major exception, however, to this second century urban Christianity. Parts of Phrygia may have been a 'special case'. Certainly, there were many Jewish inhabitants, including, it would seem, Jews on the land, the descendants of colonists given land there by Antiochus III. There may have been something that could be termed a rural Dispersion, but whatever the causes, Christianity there retained a prophetic basis, which burst into the open in 172 with the preaching of a converted priest of Cybele, Montanus and his two female companions, Priscilla and Maximilla. Their message was dynamic and uncompromising. They claimed to be inspired by the Holy Spirit and announced the Coming was at hand and would take place near the villages of Tymion and Pepuza some fifteen miles west of the city of Philadelphia. This was a revival of the wilderness doctrine

---

[36] The accusations of Celsus in [Origen], C[contra] C[elsum] 1.1 and 3.55; for 'rejection of the gods' see Lucian, On the Death of Peregrinus 13.
[37] Note, for instance, the immigrant merchant character of the community of Lyon as shown by the account of the martyrs of Lyon, preserved by Eusebius, HE bk 5 caps 1–2.
[38] Celsus, in Origen, CC bk 4 cap 23.
[39] Such as the Cynic Crescens, who appears to have denounced Justin to the authorities in Rome. See Justin 2 Apologia 2.2.

of the Coming. People summoned by the prophets to attend the inauguration of the millenium abandoned their families and work to stream into the countryside. Wars, rumours of wars, and other messianic woes were prophesied, and death by martyrdom prepared for by fasting and continence was enjoined on Montanus's followers as the command of the Spirit.[40]

Originally, Montanus found support in the cities of Asia Minor as well as in the countryside, but his movement was resisted strongly by the urban episcopate who tried to convict him and his prophetesses of being false prophets.[41] The women in particular were persecuted. Montanism remained primarily a rural movement, its most lasting influence was in up-country Phrygia, in the Tembris valley for instance, in the north of the province. Inscriptions from the imperial estate that included a large part of the area, dated 249–79 proclaim an open confession of 'Christians to Christians', shunning 'neutral' or 'concealed' Christian formulae used by urban congregations at the time and rejoicing in the title of 'soldier of Christ'.[42]

So, where we have evidence for a rural Christianity in the late second and early third century, we find its characteristics much different from those of its urban contemporary. Its basis is prophecy, and its hope is eschatological: its emphasis is on martyrdom. There is no tendency to compromise with secular society. The faith is not to be concealed but to be proclaimed from the roof tops. Here, the second factor which was mentioned at the beginning of this paper may be taken into account. The ancient world was a severely hierarchical and structured society. The towns were the exclusive organs of government, taxation, policing and culture. The village had no identity of its own apart from its existence within the territory of a city. Romans, Greeks and Jews might contest for supremacy in the cities, but beyond the city walls was barbarism, represented by a succession of conquering and conquered races, retaining their own customs, crafts and languages, but all now subservient to the rulers in the towns, supported if needed by the authorities of the empire itself. The persistence of languages, such as Phrygian, Lycaonian, Aramaic, Coptic, Neo-Punic, Berber, and Celtic remind us that the Roman empire in the first two centuries was divided

---

[40] Eusebius's account based on anti-Montanist sources, *HE* bk 5 caps 16–18. For assessments of the evidence, see P. de Labriolle's classic, *La Crise Montaniste* (Paris 1913); J. Massingberd Ford, 'Montanism a Jewish-Christian Heresy?' *JEH* 17.2 (1966) pp 145–58.
[41] Eusebius, *HE* bk 5 cap 16, 12–16.
[42] See W. M. Calder, 'Philadelphia and Montanism', *BJRL* 8 (1923) pp 309–46.

Town and countryside in early Christianity

by class and caste, and that these divisions had often resulted from military conquest and/or economic dispossession. Between town and countryside, citizen and barbarian, there was little love lost. If the countryside was to be converted to Christianity, it was likely to be to the uncompromising religion of Jesus and not the salvation-theology of Paul. Montanism was a warning of things to come.

The third century continued developments already discernible in the late-second. In the first half of the century, the church emerged from the shadows of Judaistic cult to become one of the major religions of the Greco-Roman world. Its urban character, however, was emphasised to an even greater degree than before. The bishop was the head of an urban community, with a staff of clergy resembling a civil service with a career structure based on service, experience and age. Presbyters, at least in Carthage, were paid a monthly stipend.[43] The congregations over which they presided were becoming as institutional as themselves; people were seeking office, Origen tells us c240, for 'the sake of a little prestige'.[44] A major reason why the Decian persecution of 250 so nearly succeeeded was that it fell on almost exclusively urban communities, which, when put to the test of obeying either church or empire, still instinctively obeyed the orders of the emperor.

Nonetheless, protest and opposition, within the framework of urban society was maintained by Christians. One has only to read the story of Perpetua and her companions at Carthage in 202/3, to realise how deep could be the sense of alienation from pagan society in the Severan era and how attractive the martyr ideal. Perpetua had everything in life, wealth, good Carthaginian family, well educated, fluent in Greek and Latin and married with a child and her own establishment.[45] Yet she turned her back on all this, defied her father and the provincial authorities alike, strode into the amphitheatre as though she owned it, and after one encounter with a heifer had the strength to summon catchumens together and tell them, 'You must all stand fast in the faith, and love one another, and do not be weakened by what we have gone through'.[46]

There were martyrdoms in this period in other parts of the empire, notably in Rome, Antioch and Alexandria. Behind a common bravery and devotion to Christianity there were beginning to emerge

---

[43] Cyprian, *Ep* 34.4.2, ed [W.] Hartel, *GSEL* 3, 2 (1881) p 571.
[44] Origen, *CC* bk 3 cap 9, Eng trans H. Chadwick (Cambridge 1953) p 134.
[45] See the *Passio Perpetuae* 2, ed and Eng trans [H.] Musurillo (Oxford 1972).
[46] *Ibid* 20.10.

differences in interpreting this aspect of the faith. Perpetua's stance would not have been praised universally. In Alexandria, her contemporary, Clement, compared voluntary martyrdom, such as hers had been, with the suicidal activities attributed to the devotees of Indian religion.[47] He accepted Christianity as the true philosophy, the climax of human endeavour, to which the individual attained gradually through study, ascetic practices, and subjugation of the passions leading to moral and spiritual perfection. This was to be the monastic ideal, and the Coptic monks were to accept this lead from the Christian intellectuals in Alexandria.

For Perpetua and her companions, however, the world, its philosophy and ways of life stood starkly contrasted with the church. The Holy Spirit who entered the prison with the confessor convicted the world of sin. Baptism was the sign of the convert's rejection of his pagan past and foreshadowed even his second baptism, that of martyrdom.[48] In this respect, the north African radical was to influence the attitudes of the rural Christian in the next century. Donatism was to be the religion of puritanical (as well as purely self-seeking) Carthaginian Christians as well as the Numidian villagers. In east and west, therefore, the interpretation given to the most drastic of all Christian witness, namely, martyrdom played its part in forming lasting relationships between urban and rural Christianities, and also the relationship between church and empire.

Meantime, however, common interests and common factors affecting their daily lives were tending to draw most urban Christians into relative harmony with their pagan neighbours. Between 250 and 300 the churches or Christian meeting places became part of the landscape of many of the larger cities, especially in the east. At Nicomedia, Diocletian's capital, the cathedral stood in full view of the palace[49]—anticipating the future relations between church and empire in the east. The church itself had become a property-holding corporation, with its buildings and movable assets.[50] Its members were an identifiable community, enjoying a sort of rudimentary *millet* status. Their leaders were respected by the authorities and, like Dionysius

---

[47] Clement, *Stromateis*, bk 4 cap 17 paras 1–4, ed O. Stählin and L. Früchtel, *GCS* (Berlin 1960) p 256.
[48] Thus, *Passio Perpetuae* 3.5 and Tertullian, *Apologia* 50.16.
[49] Lactantius, *De Morte Persecutorum* 13.3, ed J. Moreau, *SC* 39 (1954).
[50] A typical late third-century example is provided by the controversy over the ownership of the bishop's house at Antioch after Paul of Samosata had been deposed by a council in 268. See Eusebius *HE* bk 7 cap 30 para 19.

Town and countryside in early Christianity

of Alexandria (247–64), liable even to be used as intermediaries in important negotiations.[51] The urban Christian either in east or west was far from being a revolutionary. He was concerned with his own salvation, not in changing society according to the precepts of the gospel. Tobit, the example of the upright pharisee who was generous with his alms-giving and punctilious in charitable duties was also the Christian's ideal.[52] The lot of the Christian slave might be alleviated, but slavery itself was never challenged as an institution. Cruel punishments of slaves, and even their murder by their owners could be absolved by penance.[53] One of the features of the council of Elvira in south-eastern Spain, c300/10, is that adultery and sexual misdemeanours seem to take pride of place against other forms of wanton and unsocial behaviour.[54] The persecution of Diocletian and his colleagues 303–12, was an interruption, but no more than an interruption, in the process of growing together by church and secular authorities in the Mediterranean cities.

The last twenty years of the third century, however, saw the beginnings of the Christianisation of some important rural areas in the Roman empire. For reasons still obscure, the traditional deities that had watched over cultivators for centuries, even millenia, began to lose their hold, to be replaced by Christianity. In Numidia, the numbers of bishoprics in small centres increased considerably between 260 and 300.[55] The rural population around Cirta, the capital, in the time of Valerian (253–60) hostile to Christian confessors was in 300 enthusiastically Christian.[56] For Eusebius of Caesarea, north Africa was second only to Egypt in its toll of martyrs,[57] and not for nothing does the Coptic era open with the accession of Diocletian, the reign

---

[51] Recounted by Eusebius, *HE* bk 7 cap 21. Dionysius of Alexandria was a supporter of Gallienus against the rebel Macrianus. See C. Andresen, 'Der Erlass des Gallienus an die Bischöfe Aegyptens', *Studia Patristica* 12 (Berlin 1975) pp 385–98.
[52] Thus, Cyprian, *De Dominica oratione* 33, Hartel, p 290; and *De Mortalitate* 10, Hartel p 302.
[53] Thus, canon 5 of the council of Elvira. Seven years penance was decreed against a mistress who murdered her slave, five years for the equivalent of culpable homicide.
[54] See canons 7 (life excommunication for the repeated offence of adultery), 13, 14, 17, 35, 47, 63–5.
[55] See A. von Harnack, *The Mission and Expansion of Christianity in the First three Centuries*, Eng trans, *Theological Translation Library*, publ Williams and Norgate (London 1905) 2 pp 422–4.
[56] Contrast, *Passio Mariani et Jacobi* 2, ed Musurillo (Oxford 1972) p 195, with *Gesta apud Zenophilum* (= Optatus of Milevis, *De Schismate*, app 1, p 186).
[57] Eusebius, *HE* bk 8 cap 6 para 10.

that witnessed the triumph of the native Egyptian martyrs over the pagan empire.

The biblical ideal was being recovered. Antony's followers 'put on the whole armour of Christ', and like their Master before them, sought to destroy Satan's kingdom by combat with demons and powers of evil that had their abode in desert places. In North Africa, the communities in remoter parts of proconsular Africa were attracting young enthusiasts from Carthage, for that was where the true ideal of Christian brotherhood was to be found. 'These are my brethren who keep the commandments of God', were the words of the wealthy Carthaginian 'confessor', Victoria, regarding the martyrs of Abitina with whom she had been arrested at the end of 303.[58]

Yet there was a difference of emphasis between Egyptian monk and north African confessor. Antony did not seek martyrdom during the great persecution. He offered encouragement to those who did,[59] but clearly for him the ascetic ideal did not necessitate the martyr's witness. In north Africa on the other hand martyrdom was the ideal. One finds the same spirit of defiance among rural Christians as had existed among the Christians of Carthage at the beginning of the third century. Listen to this scrap of dialogue between Maximilian, brought to Theveste (Tebessa) probably from the surrounding Numidian countryside by his father as an army recruit, and the proconsul, Dion. He has refused to receive the military seal (*signaculum*) at the hands of Dion. The date is 295.

Dion: 'You must serve, and accept the seal—otherwise you will die miserably.'

Maximilian: 'I shall not perish. My name is already before my Lord. I may not serve.'

Dion: 'Have regard for your youth. Serve. That is what a young man should do.'

Maximilian: 'My service is for the Lord. I cannot serve the world. I have already told you. I am a Christian.'[60]

In vain, the proconsul told him that there were Christians serving in the imperial bodyguard. He would not be moved and went to his death.

---

[58] *Acta Saturnini* 5 and 14 – 'et illi sunt fratres qui Dei praecepta custodiant' – *PL* 8 (1844) cols 693, 698.
[59] *Antony* cap 46, col 909C. He was 'unwilling to give himself up, but aided the confessors in the mines and in prisons'.
[60] *Acta Maximiliani*, ed Musurillo, p 247.

Town and countryside in early Christianity

This was the spirit that survived among the rural Christians in north Africa and united them with many of their urban contemporaries in the Donatist movement. Between church and world and their respective institutions no dealings and no compromise was possible. The devil was always active. When persecution failed in its aim, he would use other means to destroy Christians and other agents to further his plans. From Satan in the imperial authorities to Satan in extortionate landowners as well, demanded no great imagination.[61] The circumcellion was the successor to the spirit of the martyrs of the great persecution. So, too, was the Egyptian monk, but in a different way. As heir to a tradition in which Christianity marked progress from superstition to illumination and truth, he would be a reluctant rebel, once the emperor had himself espoused the true religion. Constantine, by repudiating the pagan past of the empire, completely won the loyalty of both urban and rural Christian in the east.

A generation has passed. Our visitor has seen society in transformation. He would also have become wary of drawing too absolute distinctions. Gnostic sects and Marcionites, pre-eminently urban in the second century, included both town and country congregations in the fourth century. Sects in Syria and Egypt were tending to be village-based. The Nag-Hammadi gnostic library provides an obvious example. In the east, however, Christians whether heretical or orthodox were beginning to feel a common sense of identity, as belonging to 'the race of Christians', that marked them off from pagans and the Persian enemy. One Syrian Christian leader would have told our friend, 'Their[the Romans'] empire will never be conquered. Never fear, for the hero whose name is Jesus will come with power, and his might will sustain the army of the empire'.[62] Incidental defeats by the Persians were due to sin, punished by God accordingly, but final victory would be theirs. Ephrem Syrus and Aphraat spoke for the native provincials on the Persian frontier. Constantius II, even if of doubtful orthodoxy, was infinitely preferable to the Persians.

In the west, however, few would have displayed such a spirit of patriotism and unity. There were many cross currents. In north Africa,

---

[61] For the Roman authorities denounced as mouthpieces of Satan, see *Acta Saturnini* 6 – 'Quid agis hoc in loco, Diabole' – addressed by the confessor, Dativus, to the prosecuting advocate, *PL* 8 col 694A.

[62] Aphraates, *Demonstratio* bk 5 cap 24, ed G. Lafontaine, *CSCO, Scriptores Armenici* 7 (1977) p 59 of Latin translation.
For similar sentiments of jubilation at the defeat of the Persians in 350, see Ephrem Syrus, *Carmina Nisibena* 3, *CSCO, Scriptores Syria*, 92–3, ed E. Beck (1961) pp 11–15.

the Donatists, whether urban or rural, maintained the pre-Constantinian tradition of protest against idolatry in all its forms. Augustine, on the other hand, accepted a society still based on the superiority of town over countryside. He was aware of the inequalities of wealth between the inhabitants of the two, and knew of the rising tensions because of these, but he had no remedy.[63] Peasant risings, especially as part of the circumcellion movement he abominated, as contrary to apostolic precept.[64] As we know, between 427 and 439, African catholicism was shattered by a combination of revolt by African tribes and the Vandal invasion. Catholic clergy, admitted Augustine's biographer Possidius, were hated 'because of their lands'.[65] In the west as a whole, the contradictions between town and countryside, the ordered episcopal government and the sectarian, prophetic movement continued to exist into the middle ages. Indeed, the religious outlook of urban master and peasant servant are not to be reconciled easily through a common Christianity, even down to our own day.

University of Glasgow

[63] Augustine, *Enarratio in Ps* 39.7, *PL* 36 (1865) col 438; and *In Ps* 48.8, *ibid* cols 561–2.
[64] Augustine, *Ep* 108.5.18, ed A. Goldbacher, *CSEL* 34.2 (1895) p 632.
[65] Possidius, *Vita Sancti Augustini*, cap 28, *PL* 32 (1877) col 58.
I am grateful to Mr G. E. M. de Ste Croix, of New College, Oxford, for his help in checking this draft.

II

The Winning of the Countryside[1]

The Christian ministry of bishops, priests and deacons is essentially an urban one. It developed in the two generations after the fall of Jerusalem when the Church, though practically destroyed in Palestine, emerged as a religious and cultural force among the synagogues of the Dispersion. These were predominantly urban communities, and their organisation had developed accordingly. Except, however, for the final phase in Jerusalem, Jesus's message had been directed almost exclusively to the inhabitants of rural Palestine. The Greek cities he had passed by: he had preached in the territory of Caesarea Philippi, but not in Caesarea itself (cf. Mk. viii. 27) and the illustrations for his parables were drawn from the daily life of the Palestinian countryside. In this paper I propose to trace briefly how this message ultimately penetrated the countryside of the Graeco-Roman world and beyond, and to suggest how its inhabitants, finding the plain words of Jesus's teaching more intelligible than the philosophic commentaries of the urban Christians, may have played their part in shaping the development of thought and doctrine in the early Church.

The fall of Jerusalem in A.D. 70 had profound repercussions on the development of the Christian mission. Whereas the Essenes had fought to the last and a fragment of a Dead Sea scroll has been unearthed among the grisly relics of Masada,[2] the Christians, so far as we know, had stood aside from the conflict, and they paid the penalty of all 'moderates' in a nationalist rising. In the succeeding generation, whatever hold they had possessed in Jesus's homeland was almost entirely lost, and with that the chance of penetrating at this early stage the Syriac and Aramaic-speaking areas astride the Roman-Parthian frontier and the Jewish settlements in Parthia itself. Instead, Christianity became a 'western religion', and its language Greek, and as such it challenged the Hellenistic-Jewish hold on the semi-proselytes and inquirers who thronged the synagogues of Syria and Asia Minor.

Its mission, however, was urban. St. Paul and his fellow apostles had journeyed from city to city. We hear nothing of any mission in rural areas.

---

[1] This paper was read at the Summer Conference of the Ecclesiastical History Society at Oxford, July 1965.
[2] Reported in *Newsweek*, 10 February 1964, to be published fully by Y. Yadin.

II

The 'Seven Churches of Asia' are all in large centres of population—Ephesus, Smyrna, Thyateira, Pergamum and the like. Though in Pliny's time we are told of both town and countryside being affected by Christianity[1] in Bithynia, Pliny already foresaw that the combination of firmness and lenience would see the temples full again and beasts brought to be sacrificed at them.[2] He was right, for Bithynia has produced no less pagan inscriptions and no more Christian ones than anywhere else in the empire. Christianity was propagated by merchants, men like Marcion and immigrant traders like those from Phyrgia and Asia who settled in Lyons in the second half of the second century. Those who heard them were also in the main Greek-speaking artisans and traders like themselves, individuals such as the Asiatic immigrants who attended Justin Martyr's school in Rome.[3] At the end of the second century the Church was a federation of urban communities with a hierarchical organisation recognisably similar to those of its parent Hellenistic-Jewish body.

One can point, however, to one important exception—the population of Phrygia. This high inland plateau of Asia Minor resembled Numidia in North Africa geographically. Also, like their North African counterparts, the inhabitants adhered strongly to their own native language and traditional way of life.[4] This area, however, came under the influence of a dissenting Christian movement by about A.D. 175, viz., Montanism. Announcing the approaching descent of New Jerusalem near the Phrygian villages of Tymion and Pepuza, Montanus and his prophetesses attracted crowds of eager hearers imbued with the same apocalyptic expectancy as themselves. Moreover, when these events did not occur, and the prophets' message had been rejected decisively by nearly all the urban Christian communities in Phrygia and Asia, it took root in the Phrygian countryside, and was to retain its character there as a regional tradition of Christianity for the next seven centuries.[5] The cause of this upsurge of enthusiastic, Spirit-directed Christianity at this moment in Phrygia is obscure. In view of a recognisably Judaistic bias in their dating of Easter[6] and some other practices it might be connected with the presence of a comparatively large number of Jewish settlers in Phrygia originally brought in by Antiochus III of Syria c. 200 B.C., and possibly with the success of Christian missions in the Maeander and Lycus valleys which linked Phrygia to the coast. We know too, from Papias's surviving work that the Church's preaching in Phrygia owed much to Jewish apocalyptic models.[7]

Montanism is often regarded as a reaction against the growing organ-

---

[1] Pliny, *Ep.*, x. 96. 9 and 10.
[2] Ibid., 10.
[3] *Acta Justini* (ed. Knopf and Krüger, Tübingen 1929), iv. In general, see the author's article, 'A note on the influence of the Greek immigrants on the spread of Christianity in the West', *Mullus* (=Festschrift Th. Klauser, 1964), 125–9.
[4] For instance, Socrates, *Hist. Eccl.*, iv. 28.
[5] The best account of Montanism is still to be found in P. de Labriolle, *La crise montaniste*, Paris 1913.
[6] Epiphanius, *Panarion*, l.
[7] E.g. Papias cited in Irenaeus, *Adv. Haereses*, v. 33. 3–4; Eusebius, *H.E.*, iii. 39. 13.

II

THE WINNING OF THE COUNTRYSIDE

isation and power of episcopal government. This it certainly was, and bishops who attempted to intervene against the prophetesses received short shrift from the crowds that supported them.[1] But it was also quite a different expression of Christianity itself, as different as the Graeco-Pauline gospel was from the gospel of the New Testament, as different as the *Acta Carpi* are from the Acts of Polycarp. The strongly apocalyptic tendency of the Montanists was to be repeated elsewhere and at other times in rural Christian movements, whether we are considering the African Circumcellions, the preaching of John Ball and Wat Tyler or the German peasants' reaction to Lutheranism. Christianity really did mean the humbling of the mighty and the rich being sent empty away. Compromise with existing conventions was absent. Christianity was to be proclaimed from the housetops as the religion of the Last Age.

This was to be the permanent feature of the Phrygian movement. The important group of inscriptions found in the Tembris valley (northern Phrygia) and some found elsewhere in Phrygia dating from A.D. 249 to the end of the third century, contain open professions of the faith at a time when it was imprudent to declare it. The formula: 'From Christians to Christians' is accompanied by the exaltation of the virtues of asceticism and militancy. The worshippers decorated their gravestones with symbols of their calling, such as the plough, sickle or weaver's comb.[2]

For a century, however, rural Christianity in Phrygia seems to have remained an isolated phenomenon. The first decades of the third century saw the Roman Empire as strongly pagan as it had been at any time in its existence. 'The devotion of the masses was as unchanging as the depths of the sea', wrote Cumont of the situation in the East,[3] and the excavations at Dura Europos, a site sealed on its capture by the Persians in c. A.D. 256, confirm his statement. There, the century of Roman occupation had produced a multiplication of every sort of regional and local cult. Indeed, devotion to the gods seems even to have increased as time went on. Horoscopes worked out with considerable precision were one of the obvious preoccupations of the ordinary citizen.[4] Christianity and Judaism existed, but in no great prosperity.[5] The same picture could be painted in any other Roman province. Whether one is considering the distribution of cult-centres of Saturn in Roman North Africa, shrines of Serapis in Egypt, or Romano-British or Romano-Gallic cults, the early part of the third century seems to have witnessed a climax of popular devotion. Cocidius and the Dii Veteri on the Wall are examples in Britain. In East and West alike the Graeco-Roman world meant something to those who lived in it. The emperor, as the peasants of the African Saltus

---

[1] *Eusebius, H.E.*, v. 19. 3.
[2] W. M. Calder, 'Philadelphia and Montanism', *Bull. of John Rylands Library*, vii (1923), 309 ff., and for a defence of these inscriptions as Montanist, see 'Early Christian Epitaphs in Phrygia', *Anatolian Studies*, v (1955), 27–31.
[3] F. Cumont, *Les religions orientales dans le paganisme romain*, Paris 1908, Eng. trans., 201.
[4] *Dura, Preliminary Excavation Report*, Yale University 1933–52, iv. 105–19.
[5] Ibid., v. 238 ff. and vi. 309 ff.

Burunitanus show, was regarded as the source of divine munificence and compassion,[1] and the *'interpretatio romana'* exercised over the local cults in the provinces seems to have been accepted gladly enough. When, in 250, Decius demanded the support of the provincials, as the inscription of Aphrodisias states 'by just sacrifices and prayers', to avert impending disasters on the empire, he received full support.[2] The Christians, while gaining hearers as far afield as eastern Persia,[3] were still urbanised communities. At the moment of crisis they were overawed and apostasised in droves. Their leaders could easily be identified and either fled or were rounded up.[4] Had the empire possessed the means or the will to press home its advantage the progress of the Church might have been halted there and then.

However, in the decade before the Decian persecution there is one significant piece of evidence that the tide was beginning to turn in favour of Christianity. Origen's pupil Gregory the Wonderworker was from all accounts an exceptional man, but when he became bishop of Neo-Caesarea in 243 it was obvious that there were very few Christians either in the town or surrounding countryside. Allowing for legend-building and the exaggerations of his biographer, Gregory of Nyssa, writing more than a century later, there is no doubt that he was the cause of a considerable swing towards Christianity in the whole area of the lower Lycus valley on the borders of Pontus and Cappadocia.[5]

Gregory the Wonderworker's methods as a missionary were extremely intelligent. He combined public disputation, gifts of healing and sound commonsense with adaptability. Having shown up the cures and oracles of the local temples as swindles he began to replace traditional festivals with the celebration of the cult of the martyrs.[6] In the fifth century Theodoret of Cyrrhus shows us that the same method continued to be used to mop up the remains of paganism in eastern Syria. He writes, 'Instead of feasts in honour of Zeus, Thiasius, Dionysius and all the rest of the gods were ordered the celebration of Peter and Paul and Thomas and Sergius and Marcellus and Leontius and Panteleon and Antoninus and Maurice and other martyrs, and instead of the former disgraceful orgies there were decorous and orderly celebrations'.[7] Indeed, Theodoret gives many examples of the Syrian countryman's needs which had once

---

[1] *CIL.*, viii. 10570. See M. P. Charlesworth, *'Providentia and Aeternitas'*, *Harvard Theological Review*, xxix (1936), 119.

[2] *Monumenta Asiae Minoris Antiqua*, viii. 424.

[3] For the spread of Christianity in the third century eastwards beyond the Roman frontier, see the evidence collected by A. Mingana, 'The Early Spread of Christianity in Central Asia and the Far East', *Bull. of John Rylands Library*, ix (1925), 297–371 (especially 300 ff.).

[4] See Eusebius, *H.E.*, vi. 41. 9 ff. (Alexandria) and Cyprian, *De Lapsis*, vi ff. (Carthage).

[5] Gregory of Nyssa, *De Vita Gregorii Thaumaturgi*: P.G., xlvi. 909C and 954D (only 17 pagans on his death whereas there had been only 17 Christians on his arrival!).

[6] Ibid., 954C

[7] Theodoret, *Graecorum affectionum curatio*, viii: P.G., lxxxiii. 1033. For a similar retention of traditional rites by the Church, connected with rain-making, *Acta Archelai*, 2.

THE WINNING OF THE COUNTRYSIDE

been met by supplication to the gods being satisfied by prayers to the martyrs. But already in the mid-third century faith in the traditional gods of communities was becoming brittle. Perhaps not a few would echo the alleged words of Sharbil, high priest of the planetary gods of Edessa c. 250, that he had 'consumed all his days in sacrifices and libations of imposture'.[1]

In the period between the Decian and the Diocletianic persecutions changes like that brought about by Gregory the Wonderworker were taking place in other parts of the countryside in the Mediterranean world. Indeed, it seems increasingly clear that this half century was decisive for the fortunes of Christianity in the Mediterranean. Putting miscellaneous pieces of evidence from varied sources together one can see that in some provinces, notably Egypt, North Africa and perhaps in parts of Syria and Asia Minor also, there was a marked falling off in the worship of traditional cults coupled with a rapid expansion of Christianity into the rural areas. The facts regarding this movement have been given elsewhere[2] and I will be content with one example. Egyptians, as Eusebius of Caesarea points out, had been the most superstitious of people, but, as he saw the situation himself in 311, 'it was clear to the most unobservant that the Egyptians were deserting their hereditary superstition and were greeting every form of death for their duty to Christ'.[3] He provides abundant evidence for this in his *Ecclesiastical History* and his account of the *Martyrs of Palestine*. The era of Diocletian was to remain for the Copts the era of the martyrs. If one may add the statement of the deacon Habib, arrested in his village c. 310 near Edessa in Osrhoene, that there seemed to be more persecuted than persecutors,[4] one gets the impression of a pronounced movement towards Christianity in many parts of the eastern Mediterranean provinces in these years.

In this movement the most significant figure is St. Antony (250–356). He was the son of a Coptic farmer and throughout his long life never mastered Greek. The Christian monastic movement which may justly claim him as its founder was to express the religious ideals of the new generation of rural Christians which he represented. His interpretation of Christianity had little in common with that prevailing in the churches in the Graeco-Roman cities. His appeal was to a strongly Biblical form of religion. 'The Scriptures', he is reported to have said, 'are enough for instruction'.[5] Such ideas cut across the niceties of Trinitarian and Christological discussion in which the Greek-speaking and thinking clerics in Alexandria were engaged. The Egyptian monks thought in simple and

---

[1] *Acts of Sharbil* (printed in A.N.C.L. xx. ii, Syriac Documents, 56–60). See also, F. C. Burkitt's comments in *Cambridge Ancient History*, xii. 499–500.
[2] For instance in my 'The Failure of the Persecutions in the Roman Empire', *Past and Present*, xvi (1959), 10–30 and in ch. xiv of my *Martyrdom and Persecution in the Early Church*, Oxford, 1965.
[3] *The Proof of the Gospel* (ed. and tr. W. J. Ferrar), ix. 2. 4.
[4] *Acts of Habib* (printed in A.N.C.L. xx. ii, Syriac Documents, 91).
[5] Athanasius, *Vita Antonii*, 16.

violent terms. Doctrine was needed to enable the demons—the old gods of Egypt—with whom they were engaged in permanent and deadly conflict to be crushed. If it did not fulfil this purpose let it be anathema. Athanasius, Cyril and Dioscorus understood this, and became Coptic national heroes. Proterius did not, and in 457 he paid for his support of Chalcedon with his life.

In Coptic monasticism there was a strong streak of the apocalyptic, perhaps delving back into an early Judaeo-Christian trend of Egyptian Christianity, and this was fed by its rejection through despair and disillusionment of the former gods. How deeply this was felt by some of the converts of this period may be shown by an incident during the Great Persecution. In 308 some native Egyptians were brought before the governor of Palestine and charged with being avowed Christians. They refused to give their names saying that these recalled the names of idols which their fathers worshipped. Instead, to the amazement of the Jews who formed the population of Diocaesarea where the trial was being held, they assigned themselves names of Old Testament prophets such as Elijah, Isaiah, Jeremiah and Daniel, and, like many other Egyptians who had been transported for forced labour in Palestine, went cheerfully to their deaths.[1]

We find the same pattern repeated elsewhere, particularly in North Africa where the Donatists drew their strength from the countryside and inspired their followers with a will towards asceticism, militancy and martyrdom long after Christianity had become the religion of the empire.[2] In Asia Minor the Novatianists of the late third and early fourth centuries were also strong among the rural populations. Significantly, like the Montanists and the African Donatists, their bishops often represented villages and not towns.[3] In the person of Eutychian, described by the historian Socrates, one sees how among them, too, monasticism was finding a ready appeal among those whose leanings towards ascetic dissent had arisen from contempt for Christians who were prepared to compromise with the pagan world.[4]

If we may trust the emperor Julian, the causes of the popular movement can be sought primarily in the tradition of service and love towards one's neighbour for which the Christians had gained a well-deserved reputation in the calamities that beset the Roman world from the mid-third century onwards. 'Why', he wrote to Arsacius, the high-priest of Galatia, 'do we not observe that it is their benevolence to strangers, their care for the graves of the dead, and the pretended holiness of their lives that have done most to increase atheism?' (i.e. Christianity).[5] Christian inscriptions from rural

[1] Eusebius, *Martyrs of Palestine* (ed. Lawlor and Oulton), viii. 1; cf. xi. 7.
[2] Note *inter alia* the 'Donatus miles' inscription from Henchir Bou Said illustrated in *DACL.*, s.v. 'Circumcellions', and in general, my *The Donatist Church*, Oxford 1952, 171 ff.
[3] Sozomen, *Hist. Eccl.* (ed. Bidez-Hansen, Berlin 1960), vii. 19. 2.
[4] Socrates, *Hist. Eccl.*, i. 13.
[5] Julian, *Letter* (ed. Wright) 84; cf. Socrates, *H.E.*, iv. 27, pagans convinced by acts as much as words.

THE WINNING OF THE COUNTRYSIDE

Asia Minor tell the same story. A Christian presbyter was supposed to be an upright man, caring for the poor, the leader of his community. In Egypt, also, we see the same factors at work in the stories of individual conversions. In c. 314 Pachomius, for instance, found that the Christians were the only people who thought of bringing food to the draft of recruits to which he belonged when they had been shut up in a local prison for the night.[1] In Cirta in Numidia, *Acta* of the Great Persecution reveal that the church there was also a sort of social welfare and clothing centre.[2] This, together with a deadening formalism which was extending even to local cults seems to have lain behind the great rejection of the gods by the Mediterranean peoples in the half century either side of the Great Persecution. Constantine had the genius to take the tide in its flood.

In the fourth century the monks and holy men were the chief agents of the final rout of traditional paganism in the countryside. In the East, Sozomen for instance, narrates how in Palestine his grandfather and household were among the first Christian converts in the large and populous village of Bethelea near Gaza, where they were living c. 330. The village had a large temple sanctified by remote antiquity, but when his friend Alaphion became ill nothing that either pagans or Jews could do availed him. At this moment the monk Hilarion appeared and expelled the demon simply by calling on the name of Christ. The conversion of Alaphion and Sozomen's ancestor followed as a direct result.[3] Just as dramatic a story is told by Theodoret of events in a village in eastern Syria in the fifth century. The hermit Abram had settled near the village of Libanus with the object of converting it. He set up as a merchant in walnuts and by intervening successfully on behalf of the inhabitants in a dispute with tax-collectors won them over to Christianity. He was elected priest by the grateful people—another instance of local holy men wresting the leadership of communities from the traditional pagan priests.[4] Theodoret also tells of peasants converted by another hermit whose prayers had expelled the local god from his temple.[5] Indeed, while a few pagan centres continued to hold out, like Carrhae, by the end of the fourth century travellers recorded that the east Syrian countryside was peopled with monks and ascetics.[6]

The reverse side of this movement was the destruction of pagan shrines in the countryside by monks. Libanius, in his plea 'On behalf of the Temples' (c. 390) castigates 'the men dressed in black who eat more than elephants',[7] who committed such acts. This is confirmed by the action of

---

[1] *Vita Pachomii*, iv: P.L., lxxiii. 233.
[2] *Gesta apud Zenophilum* (ed. Ziwsa, *CSEL.*, xxvi), 187. Silvanus the sub-deacon who was elected bishop of Cirta in 305 was strongly supported by the country people round about Cirta (ibid., 196).
[3] Sozomen, *Hist. Eccl.*, v. 15. 14. Hilarion himself had been born in Thabatha, a village south of Gaza, of pagan parents, but converted in Egypt c. 310.
[4] Theodoret, *Historia religiosa*, xvii: P.G., lxxxii. 1421–3.
[5] Ibid., xxviii.
[6] *Pilgrimage of Etheria* (Eng. tr. McClure and Feltoe), 36–9.
[7] Libanius, *Pro Templis* (ed. R. van Loy, *Byzantion*, viii (1933), 7–39) 8.

II

John Chrysostom in selecting ascetics for destroying pagan temples in Phoenicia in 399.[1] Monks in Syria were responsible for part of the trouble at Callinicum which formed the background of the first of St. Ambrose's exchanges with the emperor Theodosius. The comment by the blunt and irritable soldier, Timasius, that 'the monks were constantly offending' in this manner was probably more than justified.[2] In Egypt, we hear that monks from Schenuti's White Monastery harried local pagans and destroyed their temples,[3] while in North Africa the overthrow of pagan shrines was one of the favourite means whereby the Circumcellions courted the martyr's crown.[4] In all these territories paganism had increasingly come to be associated with the polite but outworn Graeco-Roman society of the cities, against which the christianised peasants often felt they had old scores to repay.

Even so, there remained considerable pockets of paganism in the Byzantine empire as late as Justinian's reign. In 542, for instance, John of Ephesus, the historian of Monophysitism, was appointed official missionary to the pagans in the provinces of Asia, Caria, Lydia and Phrygia. This is a wide area about the size of the British Isles, but John found plenty to do. He records how with his priests and deacons he laboured for many years. At the end of it, he had baptised 80,000 persons, and built 99 churches and 12 monasteries.[5] This foray might resemble in some ways episcopal and archidiaconal visitations in rural areas of Europe during the Middle Ages. Paganism was not easily overcome once the immediate intensity of the apocalyptic message was past. There must have been many who, when pressed, would have echoed the reply a parishioner gave to St. Augustine, 'To be sure I visit the idols. I consult magicians and soothsayers, but I do not forsake the Church of God. I am a Catholic'.[6]

The winning of the countryside in the East had some interesting repercussions on the course of the great doctrinal controversies in the fourth and fifth centuries. The growth of the Church had led by 325 to the emergence of the great patriarchates of Rome, Alexandria and Antioch. By 381 these had been joined by Constantinople. They were not only the leading centres of great dependent territories, but were potentially capitals of great cultural and linguistic entities as well. As the fourth century wore on these factors assumed increasing importance in the debates over doctrine. Socrates states uncompromisingly, that when easterners and westerners parted at Sardica in 343, 'mount Soucis dividing the nation of the Thracians from that of the Illyrians' became the boundary between the

---

[1] Theodoret, *Hist. Eccl.*, v. 29: P.G., lxxxii., 1257.
[2] Ambrose, *Ep.*, xli. 27: P.L., xvi. 1120.
[3] J. Leipoldt, *Schenute von Atripe* (*Texte und Untersuchungen*, xxv, Leipzig 1904), 175–81.
[4] Augustine, *Contra Epistolam Parmeniani*, 1. ix. 15: P.L., xliii. 44 and *Contra Gaudentium* 1. 28. 32: ibid., 725: 'Vovebant autem Pagani iuvenes idolis suis quis quot occiderent'.
[5] John of Ephesus, *Vitae sanctorum*, *Orationes*, xl, xliii and xlvii and *Hist. Eccl.*, ii. 44. See A. H. M. Jones, *The Later Roman Empire*, Oxford 1964, 939.
[6] Augustine, *Enarratio* in Ps. 88, Sermo ii. 14: P.L., xxxvii. 1140.

II

THE WINNING OF THE COUNTRYSIDE

rival theologies of East and West.¹ A language boundary had become a theological one. A generation before this, we find the Meletians, whose strength lay among the Copts, bringing pressure on bishop Alexander of Alexandria to condemn Arius as a heretic.² Without this pressure Arius might have preached unscathed; but his doctrines, implying the inferiority of the Son to the Father, were anathema to those Copts who demanded that Christ should be fully God in order to save from sin and guarantee victory over demonic powers. Gradually, Antioch, Rome, Constantinople and Alexandria came to represent rival christologies backed by Syriac, Latin, Greek and Coptic-speaking Christians respectively. The conversion of the countryside had introduced into religious controversy social and regional passions. 'Christianity and nationalism'³ had become a fact by the decade which witnessed the 'Latrocinium' of Ephesus and the Council of Chalcedon.

Within this general framework, however, of regional religious allegiances one finds astonishing variations. The countryside in the eastern provinces during the fourth and fifth centuries was the refuge of many sects and heresies which reflected controversies of an earlier age. There they often took root and became the religion of an isolated community. Thus, one of the earliest dated Christian inscriptions from 'the village of the Lebaba' at Deir Ali, south of Damascus, dated 318, reveals the existence of a 'synagogue of the Marcionites' and its presbyter.⁴ There were Marcionite villages in the diocese of Ancyra in Galatia in 400.⁵ Half a century later we hear of Marcionite villages in eastern Syria and of a claim by Theodoret of Cyrrhus to have converted over a thousand inhabitants from eight of these.⁶ He also mentions, in the same breath, an Arian and an Eunomian village. Gnostic sects also seem to have continued to exist in the villages; that of the Sethites near Nag-Hammadi is now a well-known example and Bacatha in the province of Arabia boasted a Gnostic bishop.⁷ Manichaeism, too, flourished in the villages of Egypt.⁸ In Asia Minor Novatianists, like the Montanists, established themselves in strength in villages, and inscriptions illustrate the loyalty of many native Christians to their Church.⁹ If any conclusion may be drawn from this evidence, it would seem to be that rural Christianity in the East seldom fitted any accepted canon of orthodoxy. The bishops of the greater sees always seem to have

---

¹ Socrates, *Hist. Eccl.*, ii. 22.
² Ibid., i. 6, and Epiphanius. *Panarion*, lxviii. 4. 1. For the strength of the Meletian movement among the Copts, see E. R. Hardy, *Christian Egypt: Church and People*, Oxford 1952, 53.
³ The title of E. L. Woodward's work on the character of religious dissent in the fourth and fifth centuries (London 1916).
⁴ *Or. Graec. Insc. sel.*, 608. See A. Harnack, 'Die älteste Kircheninschrift', *Sitzungsberichte der Kgl. preussischen Akademie der Wissenschaften*, 28 Oct. 1915, 746–66.
⁵ Theodoret, *Hist. Eccl.*, v. 31.
⁶ Theodoret, *Epp.*, lxxxi, civ, cxiii: P.G., lxxxiii. 1259, 1261, 1298, 1316.
⁷ Epiphanius, *Panarion*, lviii. 1. 1.
⁸ As shown by the hoard of Manichaean documents found at Medinet Madi in 1931.
⁹ See the Novatianist inscriptions discussed by H. Leclercq, 'Novatiens' in *DACL*, xii. 2, 1758–9, as well as the Montanist inscriptions published by W. M. Calder, loc. cit.

had an uphill fight to spread their views among populations who more often than not spoke a different language from them and for generations had formed subject populations. They had developed their own traditions and defences against the foreign, urban culture of their one-time conquerors. These now expressed themselves through variant traditions of Christianity. The great dissenting movements, such as Novatianism, Nestorianism or Monophysitism drew their strength and power of survival from the support they gained from the rural populations of the East.

In considering the West, outside North Africa an entirely different set of circumstances has to be taken into account. At the time of the Great Persecution the Celtic West represented a solid block of territory whither Christianity had hardly penetrated. It would seem, where the evidence can be tested, that up to this time Christianity where it existed had been brought by scattered missionaries from the East. Lyons apart, the earliest bishops of Trier and Salona, both to develop as great Christian centres, seem to have been orientals. Even at Aquileia the earliest Christian inscriptions are in Greek and the Christian church was situated (as at Dura Europos) within a stone's throw of the Jewish synagogue.[1] Here social discontent did not take on Christian-apocalyptic forms—the Bagaudae were not Christians as were the Circumcellions—and the three bishops from Britain who made their way to Arles in 314 may be compared with the 270 Africans who hastened to Carthage in 336 at the behest of Donatus.[2] The persecuting emperors of 303-12 had nothing to fear in the Celtic provinces.

Nor did the situation change rapidly with the victory of Constantine. In the last thirty years a series of thorough and painstaking excavations has revealed that over the whole cultural province bounded by the Trent, the Rhine and the Loire, the Constantinian epoch was the period in which Romano-Celtic paganism seems to have reached its climax of prosperity. Temples, such as Woodeaton, Pagan's Hill in Somerset or Pesch near Coblenz were being rebuilt and re-furbished at this time, undisturbed by any Christian buildings.[3] In Britain there is even evidence for a pagan revival in the reigns of Valentinian and Valens, instanced by the elaborate temple in Lydney Park built in 364,[4] while the reign of Theodosius (of all people) saw the repair of a temple at Maiden Castle in full view of the town of Durnovaria (Dorchester).[5] When Gildas wrote a century and a half later that the Britons had given Christianity 'a tepid reception' he was not exaggerating.[6]

[1] I have summarised the evidence in my 'Influence of Greek Immigrants on the Spread of Christianity in the West', *Mullus*, 125-9.   [2] Augustine, *Ep.*, xciii, 43.
[3] See my 'Religion in Roman Britain during the Fourth Century', *Journal of the British Archaeological Association*, 3rd series, xviii (1955), 11.
[4] R. E. M. and M. V. Wheeler, *Lydney Park* (Reports of the Research Committee of the Society of Antiquaries, ix) Oxford 1932, 60 ff.
[5] R. E. M. Wheeler, *Maiden Castle* (Reports of the Research Committee of the Society of Antiquaries, xii) Oxford 1943, 75. The original temple dated to 367 or later.
[6] Gildas, *De Excidio* (ed. Th. Mommsen, *Chron. Minora*, iii), 9: 'licet ab incolis tepide suscepta sunt' (praecepta Christi).

II

THE WINNING OF THE COUNTRYSIDE

As in the East, however, the conversion of rural western and northern Europe was due very largely to intrepid individuals of monastic background and training. Episcopally inspired missions there were, for instance by Vigilius of Trent in the Alpine valleys, or Victricius of Rouen along the Channel coast, but the really effective work was done by monks who often settled among the people whom they aimed at converting. Northern Gaul in the fourth century, Celtic Britain in the fifth, Anglo-Saxon England in the seventh, and Holland and Germany in the eighth centuries tell the same story. Martin, Ninian, Columba, Cedd and Boniface all have in common the monastic vocation and the ascetic's zeal. Sulpicius Severus's 'Life' of Martin of Tours gives an almost eyewitness account of the destruction of paganism in north Gaul. Martin is described as working in a territory where 'few if any had previously received the name of Christ'.[1] His methods were simple and direct. At Levroux in Normandy he attempted to destroy a large and wealthy pagan sanctuary, but was sharply discouraged by the worshippers.[2] Nonetheless the sanctuary was eventually destroyed. The same thing happened in the country of the Aedui where he was threatened with being himself sacrificed.[3] Sulpicius Severus describes the processions going through field and pasture carrying the images of the gods.[4] But despite everything the mission succeeded. Paganism lacked staying power. Perhaps the Gauls felt, like Coifi the high priest of the Northumbrians two hundred and fifty years later, that the gods did little for those who served them and it was time to change.[5] At least, on some of the Gallic temple sites the coin series stops with Magnus Maximus (383–8), an unusual point in view of the immense output of small copper coins in the West in the early years of Arcadius and Honorius.[6] That Martin's influence may have reached Britain in this twilight of the western empire is suggested by the survival of a church dedicated to him in Kent in the next century[7] and by Bede's account of Ninian. He states that the Candida Casa at Whithorn 'was named after the holy bishop Martin',[8] whom Ninian is said by his biographer Aelred to have visited. Whatever the truth or otherwise of these traditions, it seems evident that monastic Christianity inspired from Gallic models was beginning to make an impression on Celtic Britain during the last generation of Roman rule.

---

[1] Sulpicius Severus, *Vita Sancti Martini* (ed. Halm, *CSEL.* i), 13. 9: 'immo paene nulli in illis regionibus Christi nomen receperant'. See H. Leclercq, 'Paganisme', *DACL*, xiii, 1, 329–34.
[2] Ibid., 14. 3.   [3] Ibid., 15.   [4] Ibid., 12. 2.
[5] Bede, *Hist. Eccl.*, ii. 13.
[6] See L. de Vesly, *Les Fana ou les petits temples gallo-romains de la région normande*, Rouen 1909, 78 and 113.
[7] Bede, *H.E.*, i. 26.
[8] Ibid., iii. 4. On the validity of the traditions preserved in Bede and Aelred concerning the life of Ninian, see N. K. Chadwick, 'St. Ninian: a Preliminary Study of Sources', *Trans. of the Dumfriesshire and Galloway Natural History and Antiquarian Society*, xxvii (1950); E. A. Thompson, *Scottish Historical Review*, 1958; M. Anderson, *St. Ninian*, London 1964 (somewhat uncritical).

It must, however, be admitted that we have little if any idea of how Celtic Britain was converted. The influence of the few urban bishoprics, of the sprinkling of Christian villa-owners or even of the fanatically orthodox Magnus Maximus, the Maxen Wledig of Welsh legend, all seem to have been small. For the mid-fifth century Vortigern is recorded by Nennius as being influenced by the counsel of 'magicians'[1]—perhaps druids, but hardly bishops. Yet, a century later, the British rulers and their peoples, so roundly abused by Gildas, were Christian. In the interval the work of monastic saints, such as Ninian and his successors in south-western Scotland and in the valley of the river Irthing, and Congar, Iltyd and Teilho in Wales and Cornwall, whose respective radiuses of action have been so laboriously mapped out by Canon Doble[2] and Professor Bowen,[3] must have borne fruit. We hear, for instance, of St. Sampson baptising pagans in Pagus Tricurius, somewhere in western Britain,[4] and in Brittany the province of Dol was pagan when he began to preach there.[5] Whatever the intervening stages, Celtic Christianity at the end of the sixth century was predominantly rural in character and based on monastic settlements such as Tintagel and Iona.

In other parts of the West, the struggle with rural paganism was only gradually won. In the high valleys of the Alps, for instance, we catch a glimpse of the dangers which missions ran when in 397 Alexander, Martyrius, and Sisinnius were martyred near Trent.[6] In Piedmont Maximus of Turin describes the countryside as still strongly pagan c. 460. 'If you go through the fields', he warns, 'you will see the wooden altars and stone images'. 'If you rise early you will espy the countryman drunk with wine, and if you ask the reason you will be told that he is a fortune-teller or an augur'.[7] Even in the time of St. Benedict a shrine of Apollo existed on Monte Cassino.[8] In northern Spain, too, Christianity advanced only slowly.

All over western Europe paganism took centuries to die out. The old gods went underground—sometimes quite literally as hoards of buried statues found on some Gallic sites show. In times of stress, however, theirs was the aid to be called upon. Gregory of Tours tells how Nicetius, bishop of Trier, was once making a journey to Italy and he found himself in company with a large group of country-folk who were pagans. A storm blew

---

[1] Nennius, *Historia Brittonum*, xli (ed. Th. Mommsen, *Chronica Minora*, iii, 129).
[2] G. H. Doble, 'Saint Congar', *Antiquity*, xix (1945), 32 ff., 85 ff.
[3] E. G. Bowen, 'The Settlements of the Celtic Saints in South Wales', *Antiquity*, xix (1945), 175. See also, the same author's 'The Travels of the Celtic Saints', ibid., xviii (1944), 16 ff.
[4] R. Fawtier, 'La Vie de Saint-Sampson', *Bibl. de l'École des Hautes Études*, cxcvii (1912), 60, and *Vita* (ed. Fawtier, ibid., cc. 48–9).
[5] He got a poor reception there, especially from the local king and his consort; *Vita*, 55–8.
[6] Letters of Vigilius, bishop of Trent, to Simplicianus of Milan: P.L., xiii. 549–58. Their mission was to a 'barbarian nation' where Christian peace was 'new'.
[7] Maximus of Turin, *Sermo*, ci: P.L., lvii. 734 A.
[8] H. Leclercq, 'Paganisme', in DACL., xiii. 1, 359.

THE WINNING OF THE COUNTRYSIDE

up. Nicetius called on the Lord and recommended prayers. The result must have surprised him for Jupiter, Mercury, Minerva and even Venus were the deities whose aid was implored. Needless to say, the story has a happy ending with everyone accepting 'the god of Nicetius', but the old gods still exercised their power.[1]

One comes finally to the problem of organisation. How did the Church organise its congregations in the countryside and consolidate its gains? The bias among the orthodox was almost always in favour of the extension of urban ecclesiastical authority. Villages would generally be placed under presbyters appointed by the bishop of the town on which they depended. Though the Donatists in Africa and the Novatianists in Asia Minor had rural bishoprics and bishops in charge of villages, or groups of villages, the Catholics were reluctant to follow their example. Thus, the Council of Serdica in 343, under the leadership of Hosius of Cordoba, laid down that 'it is not lawful to appoint a bishop in a village or a small city for which even one priest alone suffices, in order that the episcopal title and authority may not be cheapened'.[2] This canon was cited by pope Leo to the African bishops, who told them that in 'castella' presbyters would suffice,[3] and it expresses the general view in the western church. One finds, however, rural bishops in the western provinces, as in Africa in the fifth century and in the Italian peninsula, while the evangelisation of Holland and Saxony by Boniface and his fellow missionaries occasioned a reconsideration of the role of these *chorepiscopi* in the Frankish Church.[4] In the Celtic lands, whatever the formal designation of Church leaders, the monastery remained the central ecclesiastical unit. Abbots were sometimes consecrated bishops without being appointed to sees, and there were bishoprics in monasteries, such as St. David's, Bangor, St. Asaph and Llandaff in Wales. While deference might be paid to traditional ecclesiastical regularities, the abbot and his monks whether in priestly orders or not, governed the rural communities which comprised the Celtic Church in the post-Roman epoch.[5]

The East, always less legalistic and precise than the West in matters of organisation, allowed pragmatic considerations to prevail. Orthodox village bishoprics, we are told by Sozomen, were common in Cyprus,[6] and also in some of the villages in Cyrenaica in the fifth century.[7] Elsewhere, the *chorepiscopi* had a role outside the city boundaries, especially in Syria and also in Cappadocia where St. Basil ordained numbers of them.[8] It is true

---

[1] Gregory of Tours, *Liber Vitae Patrum* xvii (De Sancto Nicetio), *Mon. Germ. Hist. Scriptorum rerum Merovingicarum*, i. 732–33: 'solus eram inter illam rusticorum multitudinem christianus'.
[2] Council of Serdica, Canon 6. Discussed by H. Hess, *The Canons of the Council of Serdica*, Oxford 1958, 101 ff.
[3] Leo, *Ep.* xii. 10: P.L., liv. 654.
[4] W. Levison, *England and the Continent in the Eighth Century*, Oxford 1946, 66–8.
[5] C. J. Godfrey, *The Church in Anglo-Saxon England*, Cambridge 1962, 53–7.
[6] Sozomen, *Hist. Eccl.*, viii. 19. For eastern Syria, see Theodoret, *Ep.*, cxvi.
[7] Synesius, *Epp.*, lxvii and lxxvi. In general, A. H. M. Jones, *Later Roman Empire*, 877.
[8] See A. H. M. Jones, *The Cities of the Eastern Roman Provinces*, Oxford 1937, 184–6.

that their rights were viewed with a jealous eye by their urban colleagues. They were regarded as somewhat inferior beings, and compared to the Seventy whereas the bishops could trace their descent back to the Twelve,[1] and their prerogatives of ordaining clergy were circumscribed.[2] As in the West, however, they shared the administration of rural communities, which gradually, however, under the pressure of the Arab invasions came to look increasingly to the great monasteries for protection and inspiration.

The original teaching of Jesus was, as we have seen, directed to his own Aramaic-speaking people in the countryside of Palestine. It contained many absolute demands and much that was in line with contemporary Palestinian apocalyptic hopes. By the end of the second century, however, these aspects of His message were tending to be toned down and allegorised into innocuous sentiment by the dominant school of Alexandrian theologians. By contrast, in the countryside of Egypt and elsewhere they were heard as gladly as they had been in Palestine. Antony took the injunction 'sell all that thou hast' literally, and the movement that he started corresponded for centuries to the aspirations of the rural populations in the Mediterranean world and of Celtic and northern Europe. Monasticism played an extraordinary part in the conversion of these areas. The monks showed the practical value of Christianity both by their routine of prayer and work and by raising rural standards of life and education. This forms one part of the legacy of the winning of the countryside. The other part was the long survival of apocalyptic. The 'impatience populaire' of the Circumcellions and their imitators[3] rested on hopes for a reversal of personal fortunes and status through the promise of the Millennium, and was never far below the surface. Here too, the history of the Ancient World links up with the European Middle Ages. For more than a thousand years peasant movements tended to take on a religious form. The Peasants' Revolt of 1381, the Czech Adamites, the German Peasants' Revolt, or even the Cornish Rising of 1549 are only the more striking examples. Christianity provided both the evolutionary and the revolutionary elements in the countryman's creed.

[1] Canon 14 of the Council of Neocaesarea.
[2] Canon 13 of the Council of Ancyra (c. 314) and Canon 10 of the Council of Antioch (341).
[3] The phrase is J. P. Brisson's in *Autonomisme et Christianisme dans l'Afrique romaine*, Paris 1958, 325 ff.

III

THE GOSPEL OF THOMAS: IS REHABILITATION POSSIBLE?[1]

SINCE its discovery among the writings of the Gnostic Library at Chenoboskion in 1945, and more so since its translation from the Coptic, the *Gospel of Thomas* has been subjected to detailed and thoroughgoing criticism. Is it simply the compilation of a Gnostic group in Upper Egypt who drew upon the synoptic gospels and modified Jesus's sayings for their own purposes? Or, among its 114 *logia* does the gospel contain a substratum of tradition different from but related to that used by the Synoptists?[2] If so, does *Thomas* come in places nearer to the presumed authentic words of Jesus? Then, how did this non-canonical gospel based perhaps upon an independent Aramaic tradition find its way to the Coptic and Greek-speaking Christian communities of the Nile valley, and finally, what was its influence there?

The complexity of these questions has helped to divide critics. In 1957 and 1959 Gilles Quispel sought to demonstrate how the synoptic type sayings of Jesus in *Thomas* could indeed have come from an Aramaic gospel independent of synoptic traditions, and that it was the 'fifth source' from which Tatian in *circa* 180 drew when compiling the Diatessaron. Against Bultmann's disciples he urged that the existence of *Thomas* could vindicate the authority of the synoptic traditions. 'In this sense the Gospel of Thomas confirms the trustworthiness of the Bible.'[3] Subsequent criticism has, however, been on the whole unfavourable to Quispel's hypothesis. After all, *Thomas* was found in a library of Gnostic works, both pagan and Christian, and in the same codex as other Gnostic writings of the Sethite sect.[4] It must therefore have had significance for the Gnostics of the fourth and fifth centuries, if not earlier. Its tendency was less the glorification of Jesus than of 'Thomas the Twin', the ideal figure who could write for the Gnostic believer the 'secret words which the living Jesus spoke'.[5] It is not

[1] An expanded and corrected version of a paper read to Professor C. F. D. Moule's seminar in New Testament Studies at Cambridge in May 1966.
[2] I have used the text published by A. Guillaumont and collaborators, *The Gospel according to Thomas* (Leiden, 1959).
[3] G. Quispel, 'The Gospel of Thomas and the New Testament' (*Vigil. Christ.* xi (1957), pp. 189–207, at p. 207), and 'Some Remarks on the Gospel of Thomas' (*N.T.S.* v (1959), pp. 276–90).
[4] It was one of seven writings contained in the same codex which dates from the second half of the fourth century to the first half of the fifth (A. Guillaumont, op. cit., p. vi). For its place in the Codex, see Hennecke-Schneemelcher, *Neutestamentliche Apokryphen*, i, Evangelien (Tübingen, 1959), p. 230.
[5] *Gospel of Thomas*, Preamble.

surprising that Bertil Gärtner claimed that 'the gospel outwardly belongs in a Gnostic milieu where it also seems to have originated'.[1] This view is accepted by others, including Schrage whose painstaking analysis of the *logia* also emphasized their Gnostic character, and attempted to demonstrate how the compiler used his synoptic material to compose his own Gnostic gospel.[2] Grant and Freedman in their popular edition of *Thomas* concede that 'although the Gospel of Thomas is almost certainly based on our gospels, along with other materials chiefly Gnostic, it can provide us with a good deal of insight into the ways in which early Christians and Gnostics understood the teaching of Jesus'.[3] It cannot, however, be divorced from its Gnostic framework and its Aramaic background remained in doubt.

On the other hand, more favourable views have been expressed by R. McL. Wilson and H. W. Montefiore. To Wilson, the possibility of *Thomas* being 'early' is evident, and if that were so, he argues, it might be difficult for an editor to use all three synoptists simultaneously to build up his own composite work. The *logia* 'as a whole cannot be taken as mere extracts from our Gospels. They have been adapted, expanded, compressed, combined with material from other sources, into forms very different from anything we find in the canonical books.'[4] Montefiore goes further along the road of rehabilitation, comparing in detail the parables in *Thomas* with those in the canonical gospels.[5] While in many instances he considers that *Thomas*'s version was inferior to the synoptic tradition, due to *Thomas*'s gnosticizing tendency, it was also 'often the case that his divergencies from synoptic parallels can be most

[1] Bertil Gärtner, *The Theology of the Gospel of Thomas* (Eng. tr., E. J. Sharpe: London, 1961), p. 91.
[2] W. Schrage, *Das Verhältnis des Thomas-Evangeliums zur synoptischen Tradition und zu den koptischen Evangelienübersetzungen* (Berlin, 1964). See pp. 137–45, where the author discusses *Thomas*'s use of synoptic material in his Parable of the Wicked Husbandmen, but Schrage is obliged to admit (p. 143) the complete lack of allegorization in *Thomas*'s version, and in particular, the absence of any fore-shadowing of Jesus's death. It is difficult to deny the possibility that here *Thomas* was using an early tradition in which the Passion-narrative did not yet figure. See also H. W. Montefiore, *N.T.S.* vii (1961), p. 237 for *Thomas*'s independence.
[3] R. M. Grant and D. N. Freedman, *The Secret Sayings of Jesus, according to the Gospel of Thomas* (Fontana Books, 1960), p. 9.
[4] R. McL. Wilson, *Studies in the Gospel of Thomas* (London, 1960), p. 88. He cites on p. 111, logion 82, 'He who is near to Me is near the fire, and he who is far from Me is far from the kingdom', as a possible example of a genuine Saying of Jesus incorporated by *Thomas*. There is no exact parallel in the gospels, but the Saying is quoted by Origen, *In Jerem. Homil.* xx. 3 and by Didymus the Blind, *in Ps.* lxxxviii. 8 (*P.G.* xxxix. 1488 D).
[5] H. W. Montefiore, 'A Comparison of the Parables of the Gospel of Thomas and of the Synoptic Gospels' (*N.T.S.* vii (1961), pp. 220–48).

THE GOSPEL OF THOMAS

satisfactorily explained on the assumption that he was using a source distinct from the synoptic gospels'.[1] Sometimes this source seems to have been superior, he adds, inasmuch as it was free from apocalyptic imagery, allegorization, and generalizing conclusions. This source may have diverged from the synoptic tradition before the gospel material had been translated from Aramaic into Greek.[1] The *Gospel according to the Hebrews* cited by Clement of Alexandria *circa* 190 might also have been the source of many of the *Thomas* parables.[2]

Even this view demands an awkward transition between an Aramaic-speaking place of origin and later circulation in Egypt. How is this to be explained? The first thing that strikes even the casual reader of *Thomas* is the Jewish-Christian character of many of the *logia*, emphasized by a number of identifiable Aramaisms.[3] Its links with the Egyptian Gnostic writings of the second-century are less clear. Where comparable, for instance, these contain long revelations of the Pleroma, creation myths, accounts of the occult and mysterious, and far-fetched allegorizations and allusions to scripture. *Thomas*, however, is a gospel. There is a real contrast between it and works such as the *Gospel of Truth* and the Gnostic writings described by Irenaeus (*Adv. Haer.* I. xi). Gnostic terminology, such as references to aeons is avoided,[4] and some of the more gnosticizing elements such as the 'drunkenness' of the uninformed (*logion* 28) find parallels in non-Gnostic early Christian works.[5] But it is a gospel of asceticism. The virtues preached are childlikeness,[6] singleness and simplicity,[7] abstinence, and world-renunciation.[8] The aim is less the

---

[1] H W. Montefiore, op. cit., p. 248.

[2] One example of the equation *Thomas* = Oxyrhynchus *logia* = Clement of Alexandria citing the *Gospel according to the Hebrews* is *Thomas logion* 2 'Let him who searches not cease to search until he finds, and if he finds, he will be troubled, and when he has been troubled he will marvel and he will reign over all.' This = *Oxy. Pap.* 654, ll. 6–9, and *Stromateis*, II. ix. 45, 5 and v. xiv. 96, 3.

[3] G. Quispel, 'Some Remarks on the Gospel of Thomas', p. 282 and A. Guillaumont, 'Sémitismes dans les logia de Jésus, retrouvés à Nag-Hamadi' (*Journal asiatique*, 246 (1958), pp. 113 ff.), particularly concerning *logia* 30 and 80.

[4] This point was noted by Grenfell and Hunt in discussing the gnostic character of the Oxyrhynchus *logia* (*Oxyrhynchus Papyri*, iv, pp. 18–19).

[5] Compare *logion* 28 with the Syriac version of *Apology of Aristides* (ed. J. R. Harris, *Cambridge Texts and Studies*, i), 16. But the idea associated with πλάνη is prominent also in the Book of Wisdom.

[6] Especially *logion* 46: 'But I have said that whoever among you becomes as a child shall know the kingdom.' Also, *logia* 4, 21, 22, 37–39.

[7] *Logia* 4, 23, 39, 49, 106.

[8] *Logia* 6, 15, 27, 37, 79, 80, 81, 99, 101, 104, 105, 110, and 114. Fasting, however, alms-giving and prayer designed presumably to store up future merit are useless in the existing context of the *Gospel* (*logion* 14). For the emphasis on virginity among Jewish Christians in the fourth century see Epiphanius, *Panarion*, xxx. ii.

winning of salvation by sudden illumination than advance towards spiritual perfection through the practice of ascetic virtues and repentance, thereby gaining knowledge of the kingdom. In words that anticipate the spirit of the Syrian and Coptic monk we read, 'Blessed are the single ($\mu o \nu a \chi o i$) and the elect, for you will find the kingdom' (*logion* 49). By contrast there is no apocalypticism, though the compiler has no great liking for the 'great of this world',[1] the merchants,[2] and rulers 'clothed in soft garments'.[3] Such would not know the truth, but they are not threatened with doom, and the truth is to be preached and knowledge is to be earned by repentance. The kingdom indeed is present and 'within you',[4] not in some apocalyptic future. Only the 'three words' that Jesus says to Thomas (perhaps the Divine Name?) remain secret.[5] Otherwise, 'there is nothing that is hidden that shall not be revealed' (*logion* 7). Moreover, Jesus's ministry is accepted as real and not docetic. Jesus 'took his stand in the midst of the world and in flesh' ($\sigma \acute{a} \rho \xi$),[6] and he spoke as 'Jesus' and not as an otherworldly 'Saviour'. The tendency of the community that produced *Thomas* seems to be more towards Encratism than Gnosticism.

For the Jewish-Christian quality of the gospel one example out of many may be quoted. In *logion* 12: 'The disciples say to Jesus: we know that thou wilt go away from us. Who is it who shall be great over us? Jesus said to them: Wherever you have come you will go to James the righteous ($\delta \acute{\iota} \kappa a \iota o s$) for whose sake heaven and earth came into being.' The Jewish-Christian character of this saying needs no great emphasis. Even if the syncretistic Naassenes regarded James as the mediator of secret tradition from Jesus to Mariamme,[7] this *logion* deals with succession and the headship of a community, and the association of such claims on behalf of James with Jerusalem and the Jewish-Christian churches in Palestine and Syria is obvious. Moreover, the title 'Righteous' and the claim 'for whose sake heaven and earth came into being' echo similar statements made on behalf of both Judaism and the Church in the period A.D. 70–150. The writers of the *Apocalypse of Baruch*,[8]

---

[1] *Logion* 98.   [2] *Logion* 64; cf. Rev. xviii. 3.
[3] *Logion* 78.   [4] Notably *logion* 70.
[5] *Logion* 13; cf. Hermas, *Vis.* I. iii. 3, where Hermas in his vision of Rhoda hears 'great and wonderful things I cannot remember for all the words were frightful such as a man cannot bear'.
[6] *Logion* 28. Perhaps here as in Ps.-Clem. *Hom.* xvii. 14, the stamp of authenticity against others, such as Paul, who claimed to know Jesus through revelations. Indeed, the tenor of the Gospel is to represent Jesus as the giver of the keys to knowledge of the kingdom in contrast to the scribes and Pharisees who had hidden them (cf. *logion* 39).
[7] Hippolytus, *Refutatio* (ed. Wendland), v. vii. 1.
[8] *Apoc. of Baruch* (ed. R. H. Charles), xv. 7.

THE GOSPEL OF THOMAS

IV Ezra,[1] Hermas,[2] and the Jewish-Christians attacked by Celsus all use this terminology.[3] James is superior to the Twelve and his title is reminiscent of the 'Righteous Teacher' of the Qumrân sect.[4] It is found in Hegesippus' *Hypomnemata* (*circa* 170), which also attributes to James special connections with the Temple.[5] On the other hand, one finds criticism of Simon Peter for his lack of understanding and obtuseness in the final *logion* of *Thomas*.[6] It could perhaps be argued that one purpose of the gospel was to vindicate James's claims as leader of the Church against rivalry from those of Peter proclaimed in Matthew with which Gospel *Thomas* appears to have had some points of association.

The second characteristic of *Thomas* is its stress on the attainment of perfection through complete sexual abnegation. This could also indicate the tradition of a primitive Jewish-Christian community, for James was a Nazirite, and the example of the ascetic virtues of continuous prayer, fasting, and continence combined with the strictest orthodoxy.[7] It is noticeable too, that, whereas the Synoptists use Jesus's words to teach the need for preaching the message in anticipation of a rapidly approaching End, *Thomas* seems to use the same ideas to teach the need for abstinence. Thus in *logion* 75, which appears to be related to the theme of the Parable of the Virgins (Matt. xxv. 1–13), the 'many' who (like the foolish virgins) are left standing at the bridegroom's door are not reproached for inattention to their duties but merely that they were not single ($\mu o \nu a \chi o i$). These only would enter the bridal chamber. Other *logia* are designed to demonstrate an equation of perfection and asceticism that transcends differences of earthly descriptions, quality, and sex. Thus, in the jingle in *logion* 22, Jesus is quoted as replying to a question whether little ones would enter the kingdom by saying: 'When you make

[1] *IV Ezra* vi. 55 (ed. C. H. Box, p. 47), also vii. 11.
[2] *Vis.* I. i. 6. (ed. Whittaker, 1956, p. 2) ἕνεκεν τῆς ἁγίας ἐκκλησίας (God's creation).
[3] Origen, *Contra Celsum*, iv. 23, and cf. *Letter to Diognetus*, 10, and *Apology of Aristides*, 1 and 16.
[4] See also H. J. Schoeps, *Theologie und Geschichte des Juden-Christentums* (1949), p. 124, on the significance in Jewish Christianity of the title *Oblias* or 'Wall' and 'Righteous', as interpreted by Epiphanius, *Panarion*, LXXVIII. vii. 7. For James's role of guarantor of the truth of tradition and his superiority over the Twelve in pseudo-Clementine literature see O. Cullmann, *Le Problème du roman pseudo-clémentin* (Paris, 1930), p. 250.
[5] Hegesippus, cited by Eusebius, *Hist. Eccl.* II. xxiii. 6. James alone was allowed to enter into the sanctuary. For James being appointed 'bishop' by Jesus, see Ps.-Clem. *Recognitions*, i. 43; and see also Epiphanius, *Panarion*, LXXVIII. vii. 8. (ed. Holl. iii, p. 457).
[6] In *logion* 13 Peter can only tell Jesus that he is 'like a righteous angel'. There is no 'great confession' attributed to him.
[7] Hegesippus in Eusebius, *Hist. Eccl.* II. xxiii. 5. James's Church was 'rectissimis dispensationibus gubernata', Ps.-Clem. *Recog.* i. 43 (ed. Rehm).

the two one and when you make the inner as the outer and the outer as the inner and the above as the below, and when (or 'so that') you make the male and the female into a single one, so that the male will not be male and the female (not) be female . . . then you will go into the kingdom.'

Some have seen in this passage an exaggeration of the Pauline affirmation (Gal. iii. 28) that 'there is neither Jew nor Greek, bond nor free, neither male nor female, for ye are all one in Christ Jesus', and have pointed to the rejection of sexual intercourse by the Naassenes and other Gnostics.[1] This is true enough, but there may also be another explanation. First, part of the *logion* is preserved in *II Clement*[2] and is attributed to 'the Lord himself' as though the writer had before him a *logion* beginning 'Jesus said . . .'. Moreover, he also quotes other *logia*, which like those in *Thomas* resemble but are textually different from parallel sayings in the Synoptists.[3] *II Clement* is preaching the same message of self-denial and repentance as *Thomas*, but he combines this with a more sophisticated theology of salvation that suggests a later date. He is far from the spirit of the Gnostic leaders Basilides and Valentinus with whom he may have been contemporary. It would seem, however, that he was drawing for some of his scriptural quotations on a *logion*-source similar in content to that used by *Thomas*.

Thomas's final *logion* also puts clearly the compiler's interest in the transcendence of sexual differences among the perfected. Simon Peter is rebuked for wishing to send Mariham away, 'for women are not worthy of life'. Jesus answers that he will make her a man so that 'she too may become a living spirit'.[4] The elect were complete beings, whether they were male or female.

Such ideas can of course be found among the Egyptian Gnostic sects, and among the Pythagoreans where they may be illustrated by the Urbanilla funerary mosaic from Lambiridi in southern Numidia.[5] A more straightforward approach to their emphasis in *Thomas*, however, might be to look for the existence of attested early Christian communities in the East where one might expect to find a pronounced Jewish-Christian outlook allied to a rigorist interpretation of the Christian message. Syria appears to have been the home of such groups.

---

[1] Grant and Freedman, op. cit., pp. 136–7, citing Hippolytus, *Refutatio*, v. vii. 14 (Primal Man as bisexual), and v. vii. 39.   [2] *II Clement* xii. 2.

[3] For instance, *II Clement* xiii. 4 conflates vi. 32–35 into a single injunction, and turns the Lucan question $\pi o \iota a \ \dot{\upsilon} \mu \hat{\iota} \nu \ \chi \acute{\alpha} \rho \iota s \ \dot{\epsilon} \sigma \tau \acute{\iota}$; into a statement $o\dot{\upsilon} \ \chi \acute{\alpha} \rho \iota s \ \dot{\upsilon} \mu \hat{\iota} \nu$. See Justin, *I Apol.* xv. 9 for similar textual conflations of parts of Matt. v and vi and Luke. vi. 28–36. Note also the existence of *agrapha* such as 'Woe unto him on whose account my name is blasphemed', (ibid. xiii. 2) which appear neither in the synoptics nor *Thomas*, but are recorded by *Clement* as $\tau \grave{\alpha} \ \lambda \acute{o} \gamma \iota \alpha \ \tau o \hat{\upsilon} \ \Theta \epsilon o \hat{\upsilon}$.   [4] *Logion* 114.

[5] J. Carcopino, *Aspects mystiques de la Rome païenne* (Paris, 1942), pp. 208 ff., and Pl. iv.

THE GOSPEL OF THOMAS

The Syriac writing known as the *Doctrine of Addai* relates how an emissary from the Christians in Palestine named Tobia contacted the Jewish community in Edessa and established the first Christian community there.[1] The researches of A. Vööbus into the primitive Syrian Church have shown both that complete abstinence was for long regarded as a condition for receiving baptism, and also the likelihood that the origin of the Christian message there 'must have been related to Aramaean Christianity in Palestine'.[2] The baptized Christian was an ascetic. Legends reflecting popular Syrian Christianity tell of the separation of spouses after conversion[3] and in the mid-fourth century even Aphraates wrote against the marriage of baptised Christians.[4] Women were the instrument by which Satan fought the believer and self-renunciation was necessary for winning the contest.[5] But in these east Syrian communities male and female were equally saints once the pledge of abstinence had been given. One can see how this ideal would fit precisely the *Thomas logia* we have quoted. Illumination depended primarily, as in *Thomas*, on the acceptance of stringent ascetic practices. As Vööbus points out, it is not surprising that in the second and third centuries the Marcionites, who considered marriage as $\phi\theta o\rho\acute{a}$ and $\pi o\rho\nu\epsilon\acute{\iota}a$ and regarded difference of sex among the redeemed as abolished, were the most powerful Christian community in eastern Syria.[6] Apparently, even in the fifth century they were 'the Christians' while others were known by the names of their leaders.[7] Not surprisingly too, Tatian's *Diatessaron* with its injunction (as in *logion* 101 of *Thomas*) that 'he who does not

[1] *Doctrine of Addai* (ed. G. Philips, *A.N.C.L.* (1876), 5 ff.). The details of the story are legendary, but for proselytism by Jewish merchants in the same part of the world, in first century A.D., see Josephus, *Antiquities*, xx. 3–4 (concerning Helena and Izates, the rulers of Adiabene).
[2] A. Vööbus, *Celibacy in the Early Syrian Church* (Papers of the Estonian Theological Society in Exile: Stockholm, 1951), p. 10.
[3] See A. Mingana, 'Some early Judaeo-Christian Documents in the John Rylands Library: Syriac Texts' (*Bull. of John Rylands Library*, iv (1917), pp. 66 ff.).
[4] In the *Seventh Homily* he writes, for 'solitaries the struggle is suitable'. But anyone betrothed or married 'let him retreat and rejoice with his wife'. See A. Vööbus, op. cit., p. 50, and also F. C. Burkitt's view, 'In Aphraates baptism is not the common seal of every Christian's faith, but a privilege for celibates, or at least those who intend to live a celibate life for the future' (*C.A.H.* xii, p. 499). Vööbus suggests (p. 48), however, that these stringent requirements were becoming obsolete, though they reflected accurately the teaching of the Syrian Church in the second and third centuries.
[5] One might also point to the opening passage in the Clementine *Recognitions* (Syria, third century) where Clement introduces himself: 'Ego Clemens in urbe Roma natus, ex prima aetate pudicitiae studium gessi.'
[6] A. Vööbus, op. cit., pp. 14–16.
[7] Cited from *Histoire de Mar-Jabalaha, de trois autres patriarches, d'un prêtre et de deux laïques nestoriens* (ed. P. Bedjan, Paris, 1895, p. 213)—though this is a late source.

abandon father and mother, wife and children is not worthy to become my disciple' was in use in eastern Syria down to the middle of the fifth century.

If the hypothesis were acceptable that the compilation of *Thomas* could be set within a framework of primitive Syrian Christianity,[1] where Aramaic and Syriac were the spoken languages of the countryside, many problems connected with it might be advanced towards solution. First, there are the undeniable parallels between *Thomas* and the *Diatessaron* and other works such as the *Acts of Archelaus* which were current in Syria, but had little circulation elsewhere. Some of the points of contact between *Thomas* and these writings which have been worked out by Quispel[2] and Baker[3] would be more intelligible. In addition, an explanation might be offered for the apparent close relationship between the *Gospel* and the *Acts of Thomas* whose origin is attributed to Edessa.[4] Finally, one might find a clue towards solving the problem of the juxtaposition of *Thomas* and Matthew in pseudo-Clementine literature, where Matthew provides a very high proportion of the New Testament quotations, but one can also find others which seem to derive from *Thomas*.[5] If both stem from a Syrian/Palestinian environment and *Thomas* like Matthew 'collected *logia* in the Hebrew tongue',[6] their common usage by Jewish Christians in Syria for whom the pseudo-Clementines were probably written, would be accounted for. The common fund of *logia*, especially those lying behind the Parables of the Kingdom in *Thomas* and Matthew would also be explained,[7]

---

[1] Van Unnik also places the origins of *Thomas* in Syria, pointing to a Syrian tradition that Judas–Thomas was the twin brother of Jesus, and therefore fellow-initiate in the hidden words of the Messiah (*Newly Discovered Gnostic Writings* (London, 1960), p. 49).

[2] G. Quispel, 'L'Évangile selon Thomas et le Diatessaron' (*Vigil. Christ.* xiii (1959), pp. 87 ff.).

[3] A. Baker, 'The Gospel of Thomas and the Diatessaron' (*J.T.S.* N.S. xvi (1965), pp. 449–54).

[4] Hennecke-Schneemelcher, op. cit., i, pp. 206–7. Since *Thomas* appears to be cited in second-century documents such as the *Gospel according to the Hebrews*, there is no call to accept the editors' view that the Gospel and the Acts emerged contemporaneously in the third century.

[5] G. Quispel, 'L'Évangile selon Thomas et les Clémentines' (*Vigil. Christ.* xii (1958), pp. 181 ff.). Compare Origen, *I Homil. in Lucam* (ed. Rauer, 1959, p. 5). 'Scio quoddam evangelium, quod appellatur secundum Thomam et iuxta Matthiam.' At Oxyrhynchus, third-century fragments of Matthew (= *Oxy. Pap.* 2) were found near the *logia* published as *Oxy. Pap.* 1 during the excavations. (*Oxyrhynchus Papyri*, i, p. 4).

[6] *Eusebius, H. E.* III. xxxix. 16.

[7] On this problem, see Wilson, op. cit., pp. 53–54, and Montefiore, op. cit., p. 239, for the possibility of *Thomas* having drawn on an independent source for his version of the Parables of the Treasure and the Pearl.

THE GOSPEL OF THOMAS

as well as what critics have rightly singled out as the vivid Palestinian background of some of *Thomas*'s parables.[1]

Finally, much of the light symbolism and moral dualism that has provided evidence for the Gnosticism of *Thomas* perhaps might as easily be accounted for by parallels in the writings of the Covenanters of Qumrân and the Fourth Gospel. For instance, in *logion* 50 Jesus tells his disciples to answer questioners that 'we have come from the light, the place where the light has come into existence through itself'. In John xii. 36 the disciples are told that 'while ye have the light believe in the light that ye may be the children of light'. In the War Scroll these 'sons of light' fight and overcome the 'sons of darkness'. One does not have to stray far beyond the borders of first-century Palestine to find the origins of these ideas.

Indeed, the crucial question in any claim to *Thomas* preserving an independent tradition whether Aramaic or not is that of date. The Oxyrhynchus *logia* which appear to be a slightly variant version of the Gospel[2] can hardly date earlier than the middle of the second century.[3] This is also true of *II Clement*, and the Gospels *according to the Hebrews*, and *according to the Egyptians*, where other fragments of *Thomas* material have been preserved. That, however, would leave half a century at least between the generally assumed dates for the compilation of the canonical Gospels and the earliest traces of *Thomas*, time enough for a compiler to weave his own tapestry of Sayings from synoptic material and ascribe it to 'Thomas'. One has to be able to point at least to the existence of earlier *logia* traditions similar to *Thomas* in order to maintain the possibility of the independence of *Thomas*.

Apart from the Pauline *agrapha*, there is one important source of which critics do not appear to have made full use. The writer of *I Clement* seems to have had *logia* rather than a gospel before him, and *logia* which, like those in *Thomas*, do not appear to have included a Passion narrative.[4] One finds a similar mosaic of Matthaean words from the Sermon on the Mount with textual variants, such as one encounters

---

[1] R. P. C. Hanson, *Vindications* (ed. A. Hanson: London, 1966), pp. 52–53.
[2] Hennecke-Schneemelcher, op. cit., p. 214.
[3] Grenfell and Hunt opted for 'earlier than 140' for *logion* 1 (*Oxy. Pap.* 1), (*Oxyrhynchus Papyri* i, p. 2) but suggested a later date, namely third century, for *Oxy. Pap.* 654. Schneemelcher, op. cit., p. 61, accepts 'late second century/ early third century' for this.
[4] Arguments *ex silentio* can be snares, but it is fair perhaps to point out that when in *I Clem.* xvi Clement wants to refer to Jesus's humility, he does not mention his trial, but harks back to the Suffering Servant of Isaiah liii. Pilate and the Sanhedrin are not mentioned. One notes also that in *I Clem.* xiii. 1, the writer reminds his listeners of τῶν λόγων τοῦ κυρίου 'Ιησοῦ, and similarly in xlvi. 8.

in *Thomas*.[1] In the one parable which *I Clement* quotes, namely the Sower,[2] there appear also to be some points of contact between *I Clement* and *Thomas*.

Matthew xiii. 3–9 text begins: 'Behold the sower went forth to sow and as he sowed some seeds fell by the wayside. . . .' *Thomas* (*logion* 9), however, reads: 'The sower went out. He filled his hand; he threw. Some fell on the road. The birds came, they gathered them. Others fell upon the rock and did not strike root down in the earth and did not produce ears. . . .' At the end of the parable, Matthew tells us that the good seed yielded fruit 'some a hundredfold, some sixty and some thirty. He that hath ears to hear let him hear'. *Thomas*, however, gives the multiplication as 'sixty and at times as one hundred and twenty', and he does not conclude with the exhortation found in Matthew, though he uses it on six other occasions.

These differences may just possibly indicate a desire to elaborate a given text, or to give a Gnostic twist to the story, by indicating that the good seed, or perfected soul, ascended to heaven.[3] This view would be acceptable if it were not for the existence of *I Clem.* xxiv. 4–5. His version leads up to the story: 'Let us take the crops. How and in what way does sowing take place? The sower went forth and he threw each of the seeds into the ground, and they fall on the ground, parched and bare, and suffer decay; then from their decay the greatness of the providence of the Master raises them up and from one grain more grow and bring forth fruit.' One can detect one important similarity between *Thomas* and *I Clement*, namely their inclusion of the act of throwing the seed,[4] which is absent in Matthew, and both seem to be simpler versions of the synoptic story. *I Clement* omits details about birds pecking up the seed, saying merely that 'it decayed'. But he telescopes the end of the parable in order to illustrate that God's providence was responsible for the growth of crops and the natural order. This procedure is what one would expect of an author using the *logion* of the parable to illustrate his own teaching. *Thomas*'s approach is different. There is no attempt at explanation and no moralizing lecture. He tells the parable in a straightforward way, but with obvious differences from Matthew.

[1] *I Clem.* xiii. 2 = Matt. v. 7, vi. 14, vii. 1, 2, 12.
[2] *I Clem.* xxiv. 5 = Matt. xiii. 3 = *Thomas logion* 9.
[3] Grant and Freedman, op. cit., p. 122.
[4] *Thomas* has his seeds falling 'on the rock', *I Clement* on 'bare hard ground' and Matthew on 'stony ground'. Neither *I Clement* nor *Thomas* refer to the shallowness of the soil and its lack of moisture. As an additional reason against *Thomas* (and *I Clement*) simply miscopying Matthew, one finds in the pseudo-Clementines the 'seeds' falling 'on the road' and 'in stony places': cf. *Recog.* iii. 14. 7, and Quispel, 'L'Évangile selon Thomas et les Clémentines', pp. 183–4.

III

THE GOSPEL OF THOMAS

In particular, the highest yield of the good seed 120 times might suggest Aramaic influence, 12 being, as Montefiore points out, the Hebrew number of completion.[1]

The conclusion one might reach is that if by 140 *Thomas* was in its final state and was circulating in the Nile valley,[2] a generation or so earlier, at the time *I Clement* was written, *logia*-traditions similar to those found in *Thomas* were circulating independently of the Synoptists in widely separated Christian communities. *I Clement* and *Thomas* seem to have been drawing on a similar source, Jewish-Christian in character and parallel to Matthew.[3]

If one concedes then that *Thomas* may have come into being early, and from an independent Aramaic source, how does one explain its popularity in Egypt? Palestine and Syria are one thing, the Nile valley is another; yet *Thomas*, or a version of him, has turned up on different parts and contexts of the Oxyrhynchus site and much further south, at Chenoboskion. The question becomes less extraordinary, however, when one remembers that early Christianity in Egypt presents two quite different faces. First, there is the school of Alexandria, dominated by Clement, Origen, Dionysius the Great, and their successors, whose theology derives ultimately perhaps via Valentinus and Heracleon, back to Philo. On the other hand, there was the Christianity of the smaller towns and later of the Egyptian countryside, the Christianity preserved on the papyri and represented by Nepos of Arsinoe, Hieracas, Anthony, and Pachomius. It was a literalist Christianity that had little place for the allegorization of scripture, but much for non-canonical gospels, for prophecy and late-Jewish prophetic works,[4] even where 'the Bible was sufficient for instruction',[5] as Anthony told his followers.

In the formation of this Christianity Jewish-Christian models played a large part. The survival in Egypt of fragments of the *Gospel according to the Hebrews* and *according to the Egyptians*, the *Preaching of Peter* and the *Epistle of Barnabas* are all examples of these. A recent critic of the *Epistula Apostolorum* has concluded that its author belonged to a Jewish-

---

[1] H. W. Montefiore, op. cit., p. 225. H. W. Bartsch, however, suggests that whereas the synoptic account needs knowledge of the Aramaic sources, that of Thomas is intelligible as it stands, and he concludes that Thomas is therefore a correction of the synoptic text; cf. 'Das Thomas-Evangelium und die synoptischen Evangelien', *N.T.S.* vi (1960), pp. 249-61, at pp. 250-1.

[2] Hennecke-Schneemelcher's dating, op. cit. i, p. 222.

[3] The question naturally arises why these traditions should be at home in Rome. One explanation might be the Jewish-Christian character of the Roman community at this period, which was soon to produce the prophet Hermas.

[4] Prophetic works *Oxy. Pap.* 403—fragments of *Baruch* and *VI Ezra* = *Oxy. Pap.* 1010: Jewish-Christian works such as the *Acts of Peter* = *Oxy. Pap.* 849.

[5] Athanasius, *Vita Antonii*, 16.

Christian community in Egypt in the first half of the second century and instances parallels with the sectarian writings of Qumrân.¹ Even Egyptian Gnostic documents such as *Apocryphon Joannis* set their scene by the Jerusalem Temple² and introduce their readers to carping Pharisees and Levites, while the writer of the fragment preserved on *Oxy. Pap.* 840 tells of a dramatic encounter between Jesus and a chief priest in the Temple. He knew something about its ritual and he dramatizes his story with the details of 'pigs and dogs' washing in the Temple pool where the priest had claimed to purify himself daily.³ Clearly Jerusalem and the Temple enjoyed prestige, perhaps the prestige of distant, half-forgotten splendour. Among these Christians *Thomas* with its Palestinian background and its ascetic teaching would gain a ready audience.

If one needs an explanation of this affinity between the non-Alexandrian Christians in Egypt and the Christianity of Palestine and Syria, one can point first to the age-old connexions between these areas. Egypt had been the centre of Jeroboam's opposition party against the house of Solomon (1 Kings xii. 2). Egypt had had its garrison of Aramaic-speaking troops in the fifth century B.C.⁴ Then it shared with Babylon the role of the biggest recipient of Jewish immigrants in the Seleucid period and these were settled all over the country from Edfu in the south to the coasts of Cyrenaica. There were comings and goings in plenty, and not all of them harmless to the authorities.⁵ Political and religious currents ran strongly between the two areas, and the Egyptian Jews were not behind the Palestinians in acceptance of the Temple mystique.⁶ Perhaps one of the main links was the group of colonies of Essenes which existed near the Dead Sea and also on the edge of the Egyptian desert in Philo's day. There were also the Therapeutae and the even more radical connexion with Palestine through the Zealots, who after the fall of Masada were able to raise support for rebellion against Rome in Egypt. It is not perhaps surprising then that outside Alexandria

¹ Manfred Hornschuh, *Studien zur Epistola Apostolorum* (Berlin, 1965). One might also add that what is still the most complete text of the *Zadokite Work*, now proved to have been part of the Qumrân library by the discovery of fragments of it in Caves IV and VI, was found in a Qaraite *geniza* in Cairo.

² *Secret Book of John* (ed. W. Till, *Texte u. Untersuchungen*, lx), p. 78.

³ See E. Riggenbach's note in the *Z.N.T.W.* xxv (1926), pp. 140–4 and J. Jeremias's brief discussion, *N. T. Apokryphen*, i, pp. 57–58.

⁴ A. van Hoonacker, *Une communauté judéo-araméenne à Éléphantine* (Schweich Lectures for 1914).

⁵ Note, for instance, Claudius' threat to the Alexandrian Jews against 'those Jews who sail down from Syria' to cause trouble in Alexandria (H. I. Bell, *Jews and Christians in Alexandria* (Oxford, 1924), pp. 21 ff.), and Paul's arrest in Jerusalem as an Egyptian trouble-maker, Acts xxi. 38.

⁶ The Temple at Leontopolis was closed in 73, Josephus, *Wars*, VII. x. 4.

Christianity also took on a radical tinge. Even without the hypothesis of Egypt being a refuge for Jewish-Christians after 70, the riddle of Jewish-Christian documents turning up among both Gnostic and non-Gnostic communities of Christians in the Nile valley from the early second century onwards might be approached on these lines.

If *Thomas* belongs originally to Aramaic Christianity and is 'early', then rehabilitation in some form or another is assured. But what fragments can eventually be added to our stock of primitive tradition of Jesus's teaching will always tend to be subjective. It will be difficult, however, to dispute Montefiore's view that some of *Thomas*'s material used in the parables reposes on sound tradition, superior even to that contained in the canonical Gospels.[1] We may perhaps return to the position taken up by Grenfell and Hunt at the conclusion of their careful study of the Oxyrhynchus *logia*; these finds 'had an obvious bearing on the question of the sources of the Synoptic Gospels'.[2] So does *Thomas*.

However, *Thomas*'s rehabilitation goes further than that. He is more important than a series of texts 'illustrating the relationship between Gnostic and Christian literature in the second century A.D. . . .'.[3] Indeed, except where that literature was already heavily permeated by Jewish-Christian influences his significance in that field may be less than many commentators have thought. His value lies rather in the light he sheds on development of an ascetic interpretation of Jesus's teaching among the rural and semi-rural Christians in the great band of territory that extended south of Edessa to Palestine and from Palestine to the Nile valley. This was the area that was to reject both the Greek idiom and the Greek philosophical interpretation of the faith that underlay Chalcedon. It was to form part of the monastic empire of the Monophysites. But four centuries previously Christians were already listening to the absolute commands contained in *Thomas* of abandonment of parents and kin in order to undertake the solitary life of the perfected. Μοναχοί and elect coincided even then. In this context the *Gospel of Thomas* becomes one of the main channels by which the ascetic cultus of the Nazirites and Essenes of first-century Judaism became transformed into an equally ascetic interpretation of Christianity, which appealed strongly to the native populations of the East. By the middle of the second century at least, Jesus's words preserved in *Thomas* were preparing the ground for the ready acceptance of the monastic movement among the Coptic and Syriac-speaking Christians. No

---
[1] H. W. Montefiore, op. cit., p. 248.
[2] Grenfell and Hunt, *Oxyrhynchus Papyri*, iv, p. 22.
[3] Bartsch's view, op. cit., p. 258.

wonder that the same injunctions found their way into Manichaean works, for throughout this whole area Christians and Manichees were presenting rival systems of asceticism to the rural populations, often based on the same writings. The Christians won, Alexander of Lycopolis claims, because their teachings were 'simple'.[1] As a contribution to the formation of a distinctive ascetic outlook among the native Christians of the East, *Thomas* emerges as one of the key documents of the early Church.

[1] *De Placitis Manichaeorum*, 1 (*P.G.* xviii. 412).

IV

THE ECOLOGY OF
THE EARLY CHRISTIANITIES

WHAT significance should one give to the so-called non-theological factors in the formation of the early Christian Churches? The question is relevant to any student of Church history, and to an understanding of the problems of Christian unity to-day. For, if we believe that there is one truth represented by one communion, however sympathetic we may be towards other communions, it is towards organic unity with that one communion that our efforts must be directed. We could not stop short at a fellowship of different Churches. If we reject this idea, can we assert the reality of a number of different Christian traditions, representing insights born of economic, social, and national situations that have given them cohesion and power of survival? Can questions, for instance of episcopacy versus presbyterian government, be brought down to questions of right and wrong thinking, or do these mark deeper differences in the lives of those concerned, which it is the duty of the historian to discover? In this case the way to Christian unity must be sought through the coming together of different traditions, each of which embodies particular aspects of the truth which are uniquely their own.

The history of the Church in general supports the second thesis against the first. If organic unity has been the goal of Christians, the story of the Church is the story of successively more futile efforts to attain it. The Councils of Nicaea, Ephesus, and Chalcedon, the *Henotikon* of Zeno, the *Ecthesis* of Heraclius, the Papal Councils of the Lateran of 1215, and Florence/Ferrara, 1435, all these strove manfully but hopelessly to find common ground on which all Christians might unite. Reformation and Counter-Reformation showed that the price of unity was loss of human life and idealism out of any proportion to the success achieved, and has resulted in an enduring bitterness against the Christian faith itself. At the end of his survey, the historian can point perhaps to the decade 170-80 when the Church might be said to have been united from one end of the Mediterranean to the other. But even then, the age of Irenaeus had its fill of tensions. Montanists, Marcionites, Gnostics, and Ebionites, to mention only a few, had their rival interpretations of orthodoxy. The great Church, however, spoke one language, Greek, accepted one liturgy, one canon of Scripture, and, with small variations, one Rule of Faith. From "Gaul to Osrhoene"[1] there was a norm of Church government through the bishops who themselves looked back to apostolic foundations.

Why did this situation fail to continue? The aim of this chapter is to look briefly at the material background of the division between Eastern and Western Christianity and of the subsequent divisions within these great Communions. What effect had geography and history on their emergence, and if they did, has that any message for us to-day?

Jesus' gospel of love, freedom, repentance, and of the approaching Kingdom, was preached to the people of rural Palestine, using an imagery familiar to them. The task of Paul and his immediate following was to translate that message into the idiom of the Greek-speaking inhabitants of the cities of the eastern Mediterrenean who, whether Jews or Greeks, tended to regard religion as a "mystery" and a system of salvation from demonic powers. It is evident that by 58 when Paul returned to Jerusalem tensions were already arising between his interpretation of the message of the risen Christ, and that represented by James, Jesus' brother, who presided over the Church in Jerusalem.[2] Was the Greek or the Aramaic interpretation the true one? The development of this controversy was cut short by the martyrdom of James in 62 and the fall of Jerusalem in 70. The effect of this latter event was that in the next generation or so the Christians gradually lost their hold

[1] Eusebius, *Hist. Eccl*, V 23. 4, referring to the conferences of bishops that met to discuss the dating of Easter, 190.
[2] Suggested for instance in Acts 21. 21-6 and in Gal. 2. 4 and Phil. 3. 2.

The Ecology of the Early Christianities

on the Aramaic-speaking population of Jesus' homeland, and even in Palestine, as Matthew's Gospel shows, Christianity became Greek-speaking. In return, however, it began to win its way among the proselytes and God-fearers who formed the outer ring of the synagogue population in the cities of Syria, Asia Minor, and Greece. One detects in the early chapters of the Book of Revelation echoes of the bitter struggle between the orthodox Jews and the Christians for predominance in the province of Asia. Which was the synagogue of Christ, and which the synagogue of Satan?[3]

By the middle of the second century this battle had largely been won for the Christians. The story of the martyrdom of Polycarp of Smyrna[4] shows how the Jews were now siding with the pagans in a vain hope of stemming the advance of their rivals. This victory, however, resulted in the Church becoming almost an entirely Greek-speaking organization, centred in the larger towns, particularly where these already had colonies of Jews. This was the environment which led to the flourishing Christian communities of the second century of which Eusebius writes,[5] and to those whose strength and relative harmony Irenaeus' work *Against the Heresies*, c. 185, bears witness. It was the age too, of the Greek Apologists, stressing the loyalty of Christians to the Empire and claiming toleration from the State on the grounds that ultimately the destiny of Church and Empire was one.[6]

The success of the Christian missions ended this situation. In the last quarter of the second century the message was beginning to spread, perhaps by the intermediacy of Jewish-Christians, among the Aramaic-speaking populations of eastern Syria.[7] We know little about this movement, but the evidence as it stands suggests that in this environment Christianity was far from regarding itself as a partner to the Empire. The influence of Tatian, the one truly anti-Imperial Apologist, was strong; the new faith took on an emphatically ascetic tinge which in the more organized Churches in the

[3] See Rev. 3. 9.
[4] Eusebius, *Hist. Eccl.*, IV 15, 26, and 41.
[5] *Hist. Eccl.*, IV 7, 1, "Like brilliant lamps the churches were now shining throughout the world."
[6] Cf. Melito of Sardis, writing c. 175 cited by Eusebius, *Hist Eccl*, IV. 26. 7, Christianity appearing in the reign of Augustus, as an "omen of good" to the Roman Empire.
[7] See F. C. Burkitt's account, *Early Christianity outside the Roman Empire*, Cambridge, 1899. 12ff.

towns was denounced as Encratism. In East Syria, however, Tatian's *Diatessaron* (Gospel Harmony) compiled *c*. 180 which stressed the absolute commands of self-renunciation contained in the Synoptic Gospels, and the equally ascetic *Gospel of Thomas* enjoyed great popularity.[8] It seems also, that the Marcionites, who made sexual abnegation a condition of baptism, became the predominant group among the Christians. More than two centuries before the Council of Chalcedon in 451 urban and rural Christianity in Syria had begun to part company.

The real division, however, that appeared in these years was that between the Greek and Latin interpretations of the faith. The details of this division have been described elsewhere.[9] It suffices to say that it covered a wide field of doctrine and discipline and that every attempt to harmonize the Eastern and Western views ended in failure. Basically, at the beginning of the third century Greek-speaking Christians under the leadership of the Alexandrians, Clement (d. *c*. 213) and Origen (d. *c*. 254), were leading towards a theology of the Trinity that blended the Logos teaching of the Fourth Gospel with that of current Platonic and Stoic philosophy. The Divine Word incarnate in Jesus Christ was also God's agent of creation and through the Incarnation the saviour of the human race. His function was to guide, instruct, cure, and heal so that mankind might rise gradually toward the fulfilment of its destiny to be "like God", and this salvation would be for all, so that God might truly be all in all. The West, on the other hand, following Irenaeus and Tertullian, while not rejecting all aspects of the Logos-theology, laid equal stress on the work of the Holy Spirit vivifying the Church and "reproving the world of sin, and of righteousness, and of judgement" (John 16.8), "testifying of Jesus" (John 15.26). Whereas the Greek Apologists were looking forward to the harmonization of Church and Empire, the Westerners, influenced by a latent apocalypticism and a corresponding doctrine of the Spirit, emphasized the division between "Jerusalem" and "Babylon" representing the Church and the Empire respectively. Tertullian, in particular,

[8] W. C. van Unnik, *Newly Discovered Gnostic Writings*, S.C.M. Press, 1958, p. 49, places the composition of *Thomas* in Syria. Also, G. Quispel, "L'Evangile selon Thomas et les Clémentines", *Vigiliae Christianae*, 12, 1958, pp. 181ff.

[9] See, for instance, my *Martyrdom and Persecution in the Early Church*, Blackwell, 1965, Ch. XII, "The Great Divide".

The Ecology of the Early Christianities

viewed without dismay the ultimate destruction of the society represented by the latter in a Great Assize which would take place on the Last Day.[10]

In fact, the Eastern teaching tended towards a Binitarian view of the Godhead. To Origen, the Holy Spirit was a creature, the highest of the angels indeed, in whose name the Christian was baptized, but otherwise of importance more to angels than to men. A century later, one line in the Creed of Nicaea (A.D. 325) sufficed to acknowledge the mystery of his being. If all moved forward under the influence of the Divine Word, what place exactly had the Spirit in the economy of the Trinity? Eastern theologians were to grapple with this problem for centuries. In the generation after Nicaea the definition of the Dedication Council of Antioch in 341 placed on the Son the work of reflecting the image of God for the salvation of mankind. The Word of God was "the exact image of the Godhead, substance, will, power, and glory of the Father, the first-begotten of all creation, who was in the beginning with God".[11] This brilliant intermingling of Plato and Scripture summed up the beliefs of the Easterners in the year of the first great crisis between them and their Western colleagues.

This was also an optimistic view of man embracing the whole experience of the human race both secular and religious. The world was God's world and therefore good. At the Fall man had indeed lost his birthright, the image of God, but by exercise of his free will he had power to follow the example of Christ and to grope his way upward towards recovering that goal. No damnation was final;[12] the fires of hell were cleansing, not consuming fires. The apostate, even Satan himself, could ultimately be saved.

To this majestic doctrine of hope, the West was to reply with an anthropology equally dependent on its view of the Godhead. If the ultimate end of man was to be decided at Divine Judgement, as foretold in Scripture, could anything useful be learnt from the secular philosophies of the day? Western theologians, from the time of Tertullian to Paulus Orosius, denied the possibility. Lactantius, for

---

[10] *De Spectaculis* 30.
[11] See J. N. D. Kelly, *Early Christian Creeds*, Longmans, 1950, pp. 268-9.
[12] Though among less sophisticated Christians in the East, Judgement still had its terrors. See, for instance, Mark the Deacon, *Life of Porphyry, Bishop of Gaza* (ed. G. F. Hill), p. 67.

all his Ciceronian style, and his sense of Christian virtue perfecting pagan *humanitas*, regarded the world as the devil's domain, and the wrath of God as the inevitable lot of the unconverted.[13] The awesome dream related by Jerome, when Christ the Judge faced him with the issue, "Thou art a Ciceronian, not a Christian"[14] summed up what many Western Christians thought. While the Alexandrians and the Cappadocian Fathers who followed them emphasized the essential harmony of much of Greek philosophy with Christianity, particularly as a preparation towards the ascetic life, the Westerners took a less constructive view. "It is philosophy which is the subject-matter of this world's wisdom", wrote Tertullian, "that rash interpreter of the divine nature and order. In fact, heresies themselves are prompted by philosophy ... for heretics and philosophers handle the same subjects. Whence came evil, and why? Whence came man, and how? ... What is there in common between heretics and Christians? Away with all projects for a Stoic or a Platonic or a 'dialectic' Christianity. After Jesus Christ, we desire no subtle theories, no acute enquiries after the Gospel . . . ."[15]

There was to be no contamination with the world. The Holy Spirit received by the convert in the water of baptism and inspiring every word of Scripture, guided Christians along a predestined road of faith and suffering. The Western doctrine of the Trinity led to the Augustinian doctrine of Grace. Man was destined, perhaps predestined, not to the likeness of God but to Heaven or to Hell.

The wonder, perhaps, is not that East and West separated finally during the Crusades, but that they did not separate many centuries before. With hindsight, it is easy to see how the scene at the Council of Serdica in 342-3 when the Easterners "walked out" on the West, or the Acacian Schism of 482-518, the conflicts over the Three Chapters in the reign of Justinian, and the Monothelete issue in the 640s were all demonstrations of the incompatibility between Eastern and Western interpretations of the faith. The mutual anathemas of 1054 were another but rather more serious incident.

One must, however, ask a further question, whether or not this tradition of diagreement arose from factors other than personal

---

[13] See E. A. Isichei's interesting essay on Lactantius in her *Political Thinking and Social Experience*, Christchurch, 1964, pp. 58-71.
[14] *Ep.* XXII 30.
[15] *De Praescriptione* 7.

IV

misunderstandings and mistakes. These there were in plenty, but did not perhaps the actors in these dramas represent other powerful forces which were making for the disruption of Christendom?

Of these, language was the first. In the period c. 50-200 one can properly talk of a common Graeco-Roman civilization in the Mediterranean. Merchants, officials, representatives of their cities, and men of letters travelled widely from one part to another, and though Latin was the official language of the Empire, knowledge of both Greek and Latin seems to have been regarded as part of the equipment of the ruling classes. By the fourth century, however, the situation had changed and a language frontier divided the Empire. West of a line which ran through Thrace just north of the Macedonian frontier and through Albania, then crossing the Mediterranean to the Altars of Philene on the Tripolitanian-Cyrenaican frontier, Latin was the universally understood language. East of that line Greek was the lingua franca, though its predominance in Syria and Egypt was being increasingly challenged by Coptic and Syriac. The division left some Latin-speaking areas in what, since the division of the Roman world between Diocletian and Maximian in 286, had become the Eastern half of the Empire, while the West could claim influence in Macedonia. Where they predominated, however, these languages marked a real cultural barrier, a barrier which has not ceased to have its effects down to our day. In Latin territory, Greek was a foreign tongue, and not much liked. "Why did I hate the Greek classics?"[16] asks Augustine of himself in boyhood. Nor were traders from the East popular in the West. "Is the life of the Syrian merchants who have seized the greater part of all our towns—is their life anything else but plotting, treachery and falsehood?"[17] So, Salvian of Marseille writing in about 439. Similarly, as Augustine also points out, Latin was not understood in the Greek world. "You would no more hear a crow in Africa than Cicero in Greece", he proclaimed.[18] Perhaps this was an exaggeration. After all, there was a school of Roman Law at Berytus, and the African professor Lactantius had found no difficulty in fulfilling his appointment as Professor of Latin at Nicomedia at the turn of the fourth century, but even so, there was some truth in his remark.

[16] *Confessions*, I 11. 19.
[17] *De Gubernatione Dei*, IV 14.
[18] *Ep.* CXVIII 9 (ed. A. Goldbacher, p. 674).

This division of language between East and West not only made theological discussions between Latins and Greeks in the fourth and fifth centuries extremely difficult, but even exacerbated their differences. Throughout a great deal of the Monarchian and Arian controversies Latins and Greeks were speaking at cross-purposes, simply because they did not understand each other's terminology. Thus, in the well-known controversy between Dionysius of Alexandria and Dionysius of Rome in the 260s, the existence of only one Latin term *substantia* to translate the two Greek words *ousia* and *hypostasis* caused the Latins to believe that the Greeks were asserting that God existed in three different natures *(ousiai)* whereas three different individualities *(hypostaseis)* were intended. This wretched misunderstanding was to hamper all efforts of mutual comprehension between Latins and Greeks in the succeeding century, and as St Basil ruefully informed Count Terentius, "the West was aware of the poverty of its own languages" [19] and could not grasp the idea of the subsistence of three Persons in the Godhead. Apart from metaphysical problems, language difficulties led to disputes on other matters of doctrine and discipline which need not have occurred at all. At the Council of Diospolis in December 415, the Pelagian issue became hopelessly confused by the fact that Augustine's emissary against Pelagius, Paulus Orosius, knew no Greek and Bishop John of Jerusalem no Latin. That the proceedings broke up in confusion, and that Pelagius found himself cleared of charges of heresy brought against him by Orosius is not surprising. Nor is the ineffectiveness of the Roman intervention against Dioscoros at the second Council of Ephesus in 449 to be wondered at when the contributions of the legates were confined to the single word "contradicitur" and even that had to be translated.

However, behind the language barrier between East and West was the more serious one of civilization. Theological strife was not occasioned simply because the West produced no interpreter of Plato until Marius Victor in 360, or because the actual decrees of the Council of Nicea were not circulating in Gaul when Constantius was attempting to enforce semi-Arianism there after his victory over Magnentius. The fact was that in the Greek-speaking provinces, the Roman Empire had proved to be a direct continuation of Hellenistic civilization. There was continuity of religious and

[19] *Ep.* CCXIV.

secular tradition. The same cities which had flourished in the great days of Athens and of Alexander the Great and his successors, flourished in the Roman period, and on the land even, institutions such as systems of post and public conveyance, the *angareia*, can be traced through 1500 years of Persian, Greek, Roman, and Byzantine history. The history of the Hellenistic world was a continuous one from the conquests of Alexander down to the Arab invasions. Contantine, "equal of the Apostles" followed the tradition of the divinized Hellenistic monarch.

When one turns to the West, the contrast is striking. Rome was everywhere an imposed culture, imposed either on a defeated people such as the Carthaginians, or implanted amidst a culture like that of the Celtic peoples of Gaul, Britain, or Spain where towns, stone-built country-houses, and the apparatus of commerce and administration had previously been almost unknown. It was in fact a civilization of conquest. One can think of the Graeco-Roman world of the eastern Mediterranean in which Greece and Rome contributed equally. It is difficult to think in the same terms of the Latin West. In Christian terms, there was one patriarchate claiming supremacy over the whole of the West, while in the East three cities of nearly equal standing divided the leadership of Greek Christendom between them.

There is another point. Outside of Palestine the very numerous Jewish communities in the Mediterranean world had tended ever since the last two centuries B.C. to think and write in Greek. However deep the ill-feeling between Jew and Greek in the cities of the Hellenistic world, the Jew realized that to some extent his fate was bound up with that of his Greek neighbours. The barbarian world beyond the city walls was unfriendly to both. The Greek was not destined to perish in a fiery conflagration. His philosophy might be incomplete and reflect "an imperfect knowledge of the true nature of God", but some perception there was.[20] All wisdom was the product of the Divine Wisdom that permeated nature. Where the Torah represented the complete reflection of reason, philosophy contained within itself the means of completion if it accepted the guidance of the Jewish Law. It was an optimistic view of mankind, the opposite

---

[20] Josephus, *Contra Apionem*, II 36. Note Philo's belief that "ignorance" was the greatest evil of all (*Legatio ad Caium*, I 3).

to the vengeful apocalypticism that prevailed among the Jewish sects in Palestine. Strangely enough this apocalypticism seems to have taken root in the West and contributed to the formation of Western principally North African theology.

From this one can appreciate that behind what appear to be pettifogging arguments lay deep divisions of language, religious tradition, and history. Contemporaries were quick to recognize the power of these non-theological aspects of the disagreements between the Eastern and Western bishops. As the fifth-century historian, Socrates, wrote concerning the breakdown of relations of the Council of Serdica, "From that time, therefore, the Western Church was severed from the Eastern, and the boundary of communion between them was the mountain called Sukis which divides the Illyrians from the Thracians."[21] A geographical division corresponded to a theological one.

So much for the major division in Christendom between East and West. When one looks closely, however, at the schisms within the Eastern and Western Churches, one is conscious of similar forces of history and geography at work. The story of the African Donatists has often been told,[22] but it is relevant to this study, for behind obvious points of Church discipline which divided Catholics from Donatists in Roman North Africa lay cultural and geographical conditions which made Numidia and the proconsular province around Carthage completely distinct territories. In the time of Tertullian and Cyprian, divisions between the puritan and moderate wings of the Christian Church in Africa were always simmering, but they were controllable so long as a powerful enough figure remained at the centre of affairs in Carthage. By the end of the third century this was no longer the case. No amount of diplomacy on the part of Mensurius (d. 311) and his successors succeeded in bringing the Donatists back into the Catholic fold. In the end, such success as the Catholics achieved was the product of force, backed by an alliance between the Catholic hierarchy and Catholic and ex-pagan landowners in the decade that followed the sack of Rome in 410. Donatism was driven underground just as Protestantism was to be

---

[21] *Hist. Eccl.* II 22.
[22] See the author's *The Donatist Church*, Oxford, 1952, J. P. Brisson's *Autonomisme et Christianisme dans l'Afrique romaine*, Paris, 1958, and E. Tengström, *Donatisten und Katholiken*, Gothenburg, 1964.

The Ecology of the Early Christianities

in Styria and Carinthia during the Counter-Reformation. Unlike Austrian Protestantism, however, it re-emerged once more as an active force on the landed estates of the Roman see in Numidia at the end of the sixth century.

The event that caused the aftermath of the great persecution of 303-5 in North Africa to be so much more serious than that of the Decian persecution of 249-51, was the conversion of a large proportion of the rural population of Numidia to Christianity.[23] In the 250s, there were scattered Christian bishoprics in this area, in 300 there was an aggressively anti-pagan population determined to mete out justice on any who had shown the slightest willingness to co-operate with the authorities against the Church. Moreover, archaeological evidence has been accumulated by Berthier and his associates from a detailed investigation of large samples of the Romano-Berber villages that occupied central Numidia between the Aures and coastal ranges.[24] This shows that while in the second and third centuries many of these villages had shrines dedicated to a native god romanized as Saturn, in the fourth and later centuries these same villages were Christian. Sometimes the same village was served by as many as half-a-dozen churches, built in precisely the same way with a dedication to a martyr or to a martyr's reliquary below the altar. There is no reason to doubt the evidence of the anti-Donatist Optatus of Milevis (itself in Numidia) and of Augustine that Donatism both started and drew its strength from Numidia.[25]

Moreover, the Donatist religion, based on a Biblical literalism and apocalyptic fervour, had its background in the social discontents which prevailed among the rural population. The exact causes of these are perhaps obscure, but we know that chronic indebtedness, overtaxation, and what appears to have been a simple dislike of the rich and of officials as such were among them.[26] The struggle of the martyr against the Devil, represented by the Imperial authorities

[23] *The Donatist Church*, pp. 84 ff.
[24] A. Berthier and colleagues, *Les Vestiges du Christianisme antique dans la Numidie centrale*, Algiers, 1942.
[25] Optatus, *De Schismate Donatistarum* II 1; Augustine, *Ep.* CXXIX 6, and *Ad Catholicos contra Donatistas Epistula* 19. 51. Also Praedestinatus, *De Haeresibus* 61—Donatist Circumcellions localized in Numidia Superior, i.e. in the country north of the Aures mountains where the great majority of the Roman-Berber chapels investigated by Berthier have been found.
[26] Evident from Optatus, op. cit., III 3 and 4. See also Zosimus, *Historia Nova* IV 16 for overtaxation as a cause of revolt in North Africa.

during the era of persecutions, was now extended to cover a similarly directed struggle against the rich and powerful of the day.

Of the Donatists extremists, or Circumcellions, named because of their tendency to dwell round the shrines of the martyrs *(circum cellas)* Augustine leaves the following description, written to a Roman official in 409.

> Among the Donatists [he says], herds of abandoned men are disturbing the peace of the innocent for one reason or another in the spirit of the most reckless madness. What master was there who was not compelled to live in dread of his servants if he had put himself under the guardianship of the Donatists, who dared even threaten one with punishment who sought his ruin, who dared exact payment of a debt to one who had consumed his store, or from any debtor whatever who sought their assistance and protection? Under the threat of beating and burning and immediate death, all documents comprising the worst of the slaves were destroyed, that they might depart in freedom. Notes-of-hand which had been extracted from debtors were returned to them. Anyone who had shown contempt for their hard words was compelled by harder blows to do what they desired. The houses of innocent persons were razed to the ground or burnt. Certain heads of families of honourable parentage, brought up with good education, were carried away half dead by their deeds of violence, or bound to the mill, or compelled by blows to turn it round after the fashion of the meanest beast of burden. And what assistance from the laws rendered by the civil powers was ever of any avail to them? What agents ever exacted payment of a debt which they were unwilling to discharge? What official even dared to breathe in their presence?[27]

As one reads that letter, perhaps reminiscent of an account of some socio-nationalist inspired terrorism to-day, it is hard to resist the conclusion that religious, social, and economic factors all combined to promote the Donatist cause. One can dispute whether the Numidian countryside was in fact Berber-speaking, or whether this or that identification of a Donatist see is justified, or the amount which religious oppression by the Catholic bishops in Numidia

[27] *Ep.* CLXXXV 15 (tr. M. Dods).
[28] E. Tengström, op. cit., pp. 121 ff and 164 ff.

The Ecology of the Early Christianities

contributed to the movement,[28] but the heart of the matter lay in the Donatist's apocalyptic view of the relation of Church to world, and that was deeply influenced by the hard facts of his daily life. Given the martyr-inspired theology of North Africa as a background, the Donatist movement was something of an inevitability.

In the West, eccleciastical protest made itself felt in schisms, in the East in heresy. As one looks at the geographical distribution of Monophysitism in the sixth century,[29] one is struck by the similarities it shares with Donatism. In Egypt the Orthodox were able to survive in Alexandria and in some of the larger centres and among the Hellenized landowners, but by 550 the Nile valley was as Monophysite as it was Coptic. The One-Nature doctrine guaranteed the Coptic peasant full participation in the nature of Christ-in-God which was necessary for victory over the demonic powers. The desert monastery was the arsenal against the demons, the old gods of Egypt who had failed. They must now be driven into outer darkness and rendered harmless, and this the monk and the solitary set out to do, as the martyr had done in the previous era. In addition, the monastery was an economic unit replacing the village whence most of its inmates had fled, giving them immunity from the tax-collector with food, shelter, and work. In the Nile valley as in Numidia, economic and religious needs coincided and were expressed in a movement of religion.

In Syria also, the Monophysite areas in the east of the province contrasted with Antioch and the Greek cities of the western and central parts of the province. As in Egypt, the prevalent interpretation of Christianity had always been that of the ascetic. In the sixth century the Monophysite theology of the ascetic and contemplative was accepted readily in the desert areas where the great monastries were growing up. James Bardai (d. c. 580) only gave expression to a movement already long in being.[30]

In the Ancient World, as in our own day, one must therefore look behind the differences over formulas which plagued the theologians. A single letter or a single preposition sometimes expressed distinc-

---

[29] The reader's attention is drawn to E. L. Woodward's *Christianity and Nationalism in the Later Roman Empire*, Longmans, 1916.

[30] On the conversion of Eastern Syria to monophysitism see L. Duchesne, *L'Eglise au Vie. siècle*, Paris, 1925, Ch. X.

tions covering an entire way of life. Copts and Orthodox could never be reconciled however finely the definitions of the *Henotikon* were drawn, and the same would apply with even greater force to the divergencies between Eastern and Western Christendom.

What the study of religious sociology teaches is that no formulas can really suffice to bring the major Christian communions together. The fiasco of the short-lived reunion of the Eastern and Western Churches at Florence/Ferrara is a lesson to be pondered.[31] Ultimately, Rome's Eastern policy only succeeded in leaving six Churches where there had previously been three. Though the fluidity of modern society and the shrinkage of the world in terms of time and distance has broken the ancient moulds in which religious differences were cast, the social and economic factors which underlay those divisions have survived. Today, it is still necessary to accept our differences as the outcome of the conditions under which we live on earth. By realizing this, we may appreciate that the views of our fellow men may be as valuable before God as our own, and join with them to build bravely God's kingdom here and now.

---

[31] On the popular rejection of the formulas of reunion after these had been agreed by the theologians, see J. Gill, *The Council of Florence*, Cambridge, 1959, Ch. X.

V

The Archaeologist and Church History

IN more than one way the publication of the *Atlas of the Early Christian World* in 1958 was a significant event. Here for the first time was brought together in a single volume the enormous additions which archaeology had brought to our knowledge of the history of the early Church. The publishers were not putting their claims too high when they spoke of the ' 620 gravure plates ' being ' unrivalled as a collection, illustrating all facets of early Christianity '. They did. There were the great churches of Ravenna, Istanbul, St Peter's and Sabratha, side by side with cemeteries, sarcophagi, mosaics, papyri, lamps and a host of other objects which tell us something of the life and thought of Christians in the first seven centuries. And though, here and there, emphases and omissions betrayed the hand of orthodoxy, it was also a work of ecumenical scholarship, a monument to the efforts of all Christian traditions.

Archaeology, as Professor Josi pointed out in a lecture to the Pontifical Gregorian Academy,[1] has touched nearly all aspects of the study of Church history, including the development of its mission, the background to its doctrines, and the growth of its liturgy. The implications of this are worth considering, for it may well be that the archaeologist will eventually face the theologian with greater problems than those raised by Biblical criticism in the last century. To some extent, the mantle of the Higher Critic has now descended on the archaeologist.

In this paper we shall first be discussing briefly some of these new archaeological discoveries and then considering their significance for the future study of Church history. During the last thirty years the harvest has been immense. The accidental discovery of more than 1000 leaves of papyrus codex, comprising forty-nine Gnostic works in a library of the Sethite sect at Nag-Hammadi near Luxor in 1946 has not only put into our possession works which may include those of Valentinus himself, but has thrown an entirely new light on the nature of Gnosticism.[2] It may be necessary to abandon Harnack's dictum of ' extreme Hellenization '[3] in favour of an appreciation of the part played by Jewish mysticism in the development of these sects. In any event, the heretics now speak for themselves without the often distorting mirror of the works of their orthodox opponents. A similar

---

[1] Enrico Josi, ' Il Contributo dell' Archaeologia cristiana alla Storia della Chiesa antica ', *Analecta Gregoriana*, LXX, 1954, 3–17.

[2] Extracts of one codex of these documents have been studied by Professors H. C. Puech, G. Quispel and W. C. van Unnik and the results of their work presented to English readers by Professor F. L. Cross in *The Jung Codex*, Mowbrays, 1954. H. C. Puech's ' Les nouveaux Ecrits gnostiques découverts en Haute-Egypte ', in *Coptic Studies Presented in Honour of Walter Ewing Crum*, Boston, 1950, 91–154, is still the most useful work on the collection as a whole.

[3] A. Harnack, *Lehrbuch der Dogmengeschichte*, 1, 236 (E.T. 1, 229).

find in 1931 at Medinêt Madi in the Fayum has resulted in knowledge of the original works of the arch-heretic Mani (A.D. 216–277) and of the liturgy of the Manichaean communities in 4th-century Egypt. Another accidental discovery, this time while digging a gun-pit south of Cairo in 1941 brought to light some lost works of Origen, and even more fascinating, of his disciple Didymus the Blind (flor. c. A.D. 380). Here, in hitherto lost commentaries on the Psalms, was revealed part of the intellectual background to the Alexandrian position in the great Christological controversies of the fifth century.[4] Then, finally, to crown everything, the Dead Sea Scrolls and the Essene (?) monastery at Q'mran, are epoch-making discoveries which will influence permanently Biblical studies. These are the sensational chance finds, but of equally lasting value have been the results of systematic campaigns in the field such as those carried out by French archaeologists in Algeria and British and Turkish scholars in Anatolia. These have added greatly to our knowledge of the spread of Christianity and of its impact on the rural populations of the Roman provinces.

Some of the discoveries belong almost to the realm of science fiction. Take, for instance, the discovery of the Manichaean documents from Medinet Madi.[5] In 1930 the German historian and papyrologist, Professor Carl Schmidt was on a visit to Cairo. The trip was a normal one, entailing a round of calls on local dealers from whom he hoped to buy papyri for the Kaiser Friedrich Museum in Berlin. Schmidt was a busy man and had brought with him the proofs of a new edition of Epiphanios' great dossier of early heresies (the *Panarion*) which a friend was engaged in editing.

The night before a visit to a life-long acquaintance he happened to be working over his author's account of the Manichaeans. Apart from some texts found in Central Asia the literary remains of these heretics, who for ten years had numbered St Augustine among their adherents, had utterly perished. Nothing was known about their writings except from the descriptions of their enemies. But Epiphanios had mentioned a work he called the *Kephalaia* or Principles as one of the chief Manichaean books. Schmidt had just reached this place in the text and meant to carry on the next evening.[6]

After the usual black coffee the dealer brought out for inspection what looked like a wad of thick, dry felt and put it on the counter. It seemed pretty hopeless, when Schmidt noticed that at any rate the Coptic lettering on the first sheet was remarkably well set out. He looked at the papyrus more closely, and then in the top right hand corner his eye lit on the word *Kephalaion* and a little lower down the page the words ' And then the Illuminator said '. He had found an original Manichaean manuscript, the first ever discovered within the boundaries of the Roman Empire.

Eventually, seven complete works were recovered, which a native had originally found in a waterlogged chest in the rubble of a Roman house in a village in the Fayum, and brought with him into Cairo. Here were not only some translations of the works of Mani himself, but more interesting, the hymns and psalms sung by his humble followers in Egypt. For the first time the impact of this sad dualistic religion of resignation and fatalism on the ordinary people of the Roman Empire was revealed. The mutual reproaches of ' Manichaeism ' bandied between Athanasius and his opponents were more than mere ecclesiastical abuse. Manichaeism was the underlying peril to the position of the Church in both the Eastern and Western halves of the Empire in the fourth century. Its existence forces doctrinal disputes into certain set channels in order to avoid the stigma of this heresy. The

---

[4] A. Gesché, ' L'âme humaine de Jésus, dans La Christologie du IVe. s.', in *Revue d'Histoire Ecclésiastique*, LIV, (1959) 385 f.
[5] Schmidt's description of the event is given in his paper, *Neue Originalquellen des Manichaismus aus Aegypten*, Stuttgart, 1933.
[6] Epiphanios, *Panarion* (ed. Holl), 68.

THE ARCHAEOLOGIST AND CHURCH HISTORY

importance of the discovery for the study of the early history of the Church, not least for the background of the doctrine of St Augustine, was immense.

Of the systematic campaigns with a specific object in view two may be quoted, the excavations beneath St Peter's from 1940-9 and continued since, and the intensive work by French scholars in Algeria extending back to the 1890s, which resulted in a great increase in our knowledge of the native African civilization associated with the Donatist schism. The Vatican excavations were surely one of the boldest efforts ever undertaken to solve a problem of Church history through archaeology.[7] Could St Peter's resting place be determined or not? If it could, and if the bones of the Apostle could be proved to have been buried beneath the spot now marked by the high altar in St Peter's, then part of the Petrine tradition would have been vindicated. The last wish of Pope Pius XI in 1939 to be buried as near as possible to the Confessio in St Peter's led to excavations being begun under the Church immediately after his death.

His successor had listened with enthusiasm to Monsignor Duchesne's lectures on Christian archaeology when a young man, and with great courage and scholarly zeal authorized the work in the area beneath the high altar. In July and August 1944, my own duties with the Foreign Office brought me into contact with the Vatican authorities, and I was privileged to see the work in progress on more than one occasion and spend some hours in the excavations.

Conditions were extremely difficult. The foundations of the basilica built in honour of St Peter by the Emperor Constantine impeded the alignment of trenches. Much had been destroyed in the Renaissance by the foundations of the walls of the crypt under Bernini's Church. So cramped was the excavation that the proper disposal of soil which had been examined seemed to be an insoluble problem. This meant that the purely technical but vital task of establishing sections for dating was almost impossible.[8] The result was an untidy dig and the consequent difficulty in assessing its results. The presence, however, of an imposing pagan cemetery which dominates the site, the lack (with a possible single exception) both of graffiti invoking the Apostle, and of datable Christian material before the 3rd century A.D.[9] suggests that the place of St Peter's burial has not been found. On the other hand, this spot may have been where Christians in the mid-2nd century A.D. themselves located it.[10]

In Africa also, the problem was one of testing the truth of an existing literary tradition. A great deal was already known about the history of the North African Church from the writings of the African Fathers, Tertullian, Cyprian, Optatus of Milevis and Augustine. From the works of the two latter authors it was clear that the last century of Roman rule in North Africa had been one of religious stress and turmoil, that the vast majority of the

---

[7] The most useful estimates of the results of the excavations are: J. M. C. Toynbee, 'The Shrine of St Peter in its Historical Setting', *Journal of Roman Studies*, XLIII, 1953, 1–26; J. Carcopino, *Etudes d'Histoire chrétienne*, 1953, 99 f.; O. Cullmann, *Petrus*, 1952, 73–169 (E.T. 1953, pp. 132 ff.); and J. M. C. Toynbee and J. Ward-Perkins, *The Shrine of St Peter and the Vatican Excavations*, Longmans, 1956.

[8] No stratigraphical sections were published in the official *Report*. Cf. the author in *Journal of Theological Studies*, N.S. VIII, 1957, 159–62.

[9] This lack is in marked contrast to the great number of third century invocations to SS Peter and Paul which adorn the walls of the *Memoria* of the Apostles beneath the present church of San Sebastiano. See H. Chadwick, 'St Peter and Paul in Rome', *Journal of Theological Studies*, N.S. VIII, 1957, 31 ff.

[10] The opinion of Toynbee and Ward-Perkins, *op. cit.* 159, is worth quoting. 'That the Christian community of the mid-second century did in fact believe St Peter to be buried in approximately this spot, and that the builders of the Red Wall in trenching for their foundations, did hit upon one end of a deeply buried grave, which was promptly identified as that of St Peter, is a hypothesis that would explain a great deal that is otherwise puzzling in the archaeological record.' The work by E. Kirschbaum, S. J. *The Tombs of St Peter and St Paul* (E.T. London, 1959) does not advance the argument.

natives rejected orthodox Catholicism, which they associated with economic oppression. They turned instead to a stern puritanical schism, which took its name from its first great leader, Donatus of Carthage. Here was the chance of finding out how the ' Donatists ' lived, and perhaps why St Augustine found them such intractable opponents.

This work was laborious. It involved a detailed survey of more than one hundred sites of Romano-Berber villages in an area 60 miles by 25 miles in Central Algeria, sometimes approachable only by mule, followed by trial excavations.[11] On one occasion, I was told to go round a large group of ruins counting up the remains of olive presses which littered the ground. There was some method in this particular madness, as olives and barley were the principal crops grown by the natives in Roman times, and these presses provided a clue to the density of the population and to its social structure.

On the whole, the work was surprisingly well rewarded. We found that in the 4th and 5th centuries Christianity had been the universal religion of these Africans. In some sites of villages remains of no less than six churches were found. There were seldom less than two. All these contained the typical characteristics of the Donatist cult, such as the fervent veneration of ' martyrs ' (mostly completely spurious), devotion to the triumphant psalmody of the Old Testament (shown by texts cut on the lintels of the doors), and sometimes even the watch-word *Deo Laudes*, dreaded by the opponents of the sect more than the lion's roar.[12] Gradually a pattern emerged.

We were able to see how Donatism had swept through the native villages like a forest fire and why Augustine and his friends were unable to suppress it. It was a real, popular movement, with its own art as well as its own services. The scores of little chapels which we found bore witness to its enduring strength. There had been nothing left for the Imperial government but to use force against it. The arguments in favour of persecution with which Augustine supplied the authorities[13] have left an evil legacy from his day to our own.

Where they have been published, the contents of some of the newly-discovered documents are as interesting as their discovery. The informality of Church Councils in the 3rd century A.D. is strikingly revealed by a papyrus containing a lost work of Origen, which was found during the construction of defence works against Rommel's advance near Cairo in 1941.[14] Origen himself is introduced at one point with the words: ' This is Brother Origen, who teaches that the soul is immortal ',[15] and Origen stands out, not as a misty theologian, but as a fighter for the faith, and a man who believed in the spiritual powers and dignity of his fellow men.[16]

Another document provides a striking criticism of Christianity in the 3rd century A.D., written by a great religious leader who saw the new religion from the outside, from the neighbouring country of Persia.[17] Mani criticizes Jesus of Nazareth severely for not having put His ideas into writing and for having left them to chance interpretations by ignorant disciples. Christianity, he complains, was a local religion, confined to the ' West ', that is,

---

[11] Described by André Berthier, *Les Vestiges du Christianisme antique dans la Numidie centrale*, Algiers, 1942.

[12] Augustine, *Enarratio in Psalmum*, 132, 6. A. Berthier, *op. cit.*, 205 ff.; W. H. C. Frend, *The Donatist Church*, Oxford, 1952, Ch. IV.

[13] See Augustine, *Letters* 93 and 185.

[14] J. Scherer, ' Entretien d'Origène avec Héraclide et les Evêques ses collègues sur le Père, le Fils et l'Ame ' (Publications de la Société Fouadi de Papyrologie, Textes et Documents, IX) Cairo, 1949, p. 1.

[15] *Ibid.*, Ch. 24 (Scherer, p. 166).

[16] *Ibid.*, Chs. 24–27.

[17] C. Schmidt and H. J. Polotsky, ' Ein Mani-Fund in Aegypten ', *Sitzungsberichte der Berliner Akademie der Wissenschaften*, 1933, Phil. Hist. Klasse, 4–89, at pp. 41–42 (Mani, *Kephalaion*, 154).

THE ARCHAEOLOGIST AND CHURCH HISTORY

to the Roman Empire, just as Buddhism, which he knew from a visit to India in A.D. 240, was confined to the East.[18]

Mani aspired to take what he believed to be the best from both these religions and preach a universal faith, and he saw to it that his ideas were written on the finest papyrus, and translated into a large number of different languages. In vain, for his religion perished almost without trace. It has been left to the present century to re-establish its tenets and appreciate its threat to Christianity.

An unexpected result of the discoveries of Gnostic documents at Nag Hammadi was the recovery of the *Gospel of Thomas*. This is an extraordinarily interesting document, consisting of a collection of 114 logia or sayings attributed to Jesus, and dating to about A.D. 140. It is remarkable, in that while many of the sayings narrate the same incidents that are found in the Bible, such as the Parable of the Vineyard, and the Sower, or Jesus' saying about the New Wine in the Old Wineskins, none of these sayings agrees word for word with the text of the canonical Gospels. Often too, the writer has given the saying or parable quite a different meaning. For instance, there is notably less criticism of Pharisees in the Parable of the Husbandmen and less interest in the Gentile mission than one finds in the Gospels. One would agree with Quispel[19] that the *Gospel of Thomas* was neither compiled from the books of the New Testament, nor, in all probability, constitutes one of the sources of those books. We are confronted by an independent tradition but an ancient one, with a markedly Aramaic background. This fact leads on to a second point of interest. If the *Gospel of Thomas* did not influence directly our own Bible, there is some reason for believing that it influenced the *Diatessaron* of Tatian, a harmony of the gospels written in *c*. 170, and used for a long time by the Syriac-speaking Church. We find that Tatian has used word for word the *Gospel of Thomas* in some places and not the canonical Gospels. This same text too, may have influenced the Western Text of the New Testament on which the Bible as used in North Africa from the 2nd to the 4th century A.D. was based. Again, we find variations from the canonical Gospels in the latter, reproduced in the *Gospel of Thomas*. Thirdly, this document fits into place besides other collections of *logia* which were circulating in Christian communities in the 1st and 2nd centuries. It is very similar (especially in the text of the Parable of the Sower), to a collection used by the writer of 1 *Clement* in Rome, *c*. A.D. 100. We are confronted by new perspectives in New Testament criticism. If we have not found ' Q ' itself, we have now at least a strong idea of what ' Q ' looked like.

In England we can hardly hope to match these discoveries which will influence permanently the study of the history of the Early Church. Some interesting additions, however, have been made to our knowledge of the Church in Roman Britain. The Roman villa at Lullingstone, in Kent, has yielded priceless evidence for the existence of a House-church in one of its upper rooms during the late 4th century.[20]

The plaster which had decorated the walls of this room had fallen into a cellar below and was preserved practically intact. Many fragments were recovered, and slowly a representation of a church and figures standing praying emerged to the astonishment of the discoverer. The result was entirely unexpected. In other parts of the country the existence of a Christian community of this period is attested by objects marked by Christian symbols, including what appear to be large leaden fonts.[21] There seems to be no doubt that the Church in

---

[18] *Ibid.*, pp. 42–46 (Mani, *Kephalaion*, 154).
[19] See G. Quispel, ' The Gospel of Thomas in the New Testament ', *Vigiliae Christianae*, XI, 1957, 187–201, and the author's talk on the BBC, published by the *Listener*, 3 March, 1960, p. 389–90.
[20] Lt.-Col. A. W. Meates, *The Roman Villa at Lullingstone, Kent*, 1955, Chs. XII–XIV.
[21] J. M. C. Toynbee, ' Christianity in Roman Britain ', *Journal of the British Archaeological Association*, XVI, 1953, 15.

Roman Britain shared to the full the rites and creed of the Church throughout the rest of Latin Christendom.

What of the future? From now on the archaeologist will probably be the principal source of new evidence on the early history of the Church. Occasionally, monastic libraries may reveal a lost text like the famous discoveries made in 1875 and 1907 of the *Didache* and *Epideixis* of Irenaeus, but this source, valuable though it is, cannot be relied upon permanently. Many of the lost Christian writings originated as letters or tracts written to individuals, or were controversial works composed for a particular occasion. Unless they were copied quickly and preserved in a library (like that of Pamphilus of Caesarea) they would almost certainly be lost. The social standing of many of the writers also would militate against the literary survival of their works. In addition, heretical works such as those of the Manichaeans were systematically destroyed. But factors which would prevent survival of books in a library would not prevent their discovery on an ancient site. Papyrus was valuable, and it has happened that a tract dealing with a half-forgotten controversy was used on the back for a more utilitarian purpose, such as making a tax receipt, and so found its way into the office of the village secretary.[22] Moreover, the archaeologist generally directs his efforts towards investigating the culture of people whose sole records are their utensils and graves. This has led to the excavation of great Christian cemeteries such as Timgad, and the exploration of artisan quarters in Roman cities where Christianity flourished at an early date. The cemetery at Timgad produced some interesting evidence of the literal manner in which these African Christians regarded bodily resurrection. Many of the bodies had been laid in plaster which preserved exactly the features of the dead.

Thus, a whole new field of study inaccessible to previous generations of scholars and theologians is opening up. There is no possibility now of Church history stagnating through lack of fresh material. Indeed, through archaeology, the student has been brought into closer contact with both the environment and the ideas which characterize the Age of the Fathers. Knowledge of both Tradition and Heresy are expanding as never before. At a critical moment in the Church's long history we are able once more to recapture something of the period in which the great traditional doctrines were formulated. This is all to the good, for thus Christianity will never lose contact with history.

In the Mediterranean provinces of the Empire, the Church is revealed from the rudely carved inscriptions, and the rustic buildings and native artistic traditions of its adherents, to have been part of a great popular movement. The statements which we read in the Fathers merely put into articulate form ideas bandied about in the baths or marketplace.[23] This is in itself interesting, because it sheds light on influences at work during the formative period of Church doctrine. Moreover, many problems which have been the sport of literary critics for decades are now liable to rapid solution. Few, for instance, would continue to assert a mid-2nd-century date for St John's Gospel when fragments have been found copied on papyrus in handwriting datable to approximately A.D. 150.[24] Similarly, the use of Tatian's *Diatessaron* among the Syrian Christian communities in the early 3rd century can be proved by the discovery of a fragment at Doura-Europos which fell to the Persians in 256 and was

---

[22] For instance, fragments of Bk. 18 of the Κέστοι of Julius Africanus written not later than 235 were preserved on the back of a tax register dated to the reign of Tacitus (275–6). See W. Bauer, *Rechtgläubigkeit und Ketzerei*, Tübingen, 1934, 162.

[23] For the intense interest taken in theological problems by the populace in Constantinople in the 4th century, see Gregory of Nazianze, *De Deitate Filii, Patrologia Graeco-Latina*, 46, 557B.

[24] Pap. Rylands Greek, 457, containing parts of John 18. 31–33 and 18. 37–38. Published by C. H. Roberts, *An Unpublished Fragment of the Fourth Gospel*, Manchester, 1935.

THE ARCHAEOLOGIST AND CHURCH HISTORY

not reoccupied.[25] The archaeologist can be relatively accurate where the Higher Critic could only weigh up probabilities. Definite answers can replace speculation.

One final point. How far are we in this country participating in this movement? It must be admitted that the answer is less encouraging than it should be. The publication of the *Atlas of the Early Christian World* is a challenge to scholarship in Britain. Despite the work of Ramsay and Calder in Asia Minor, and more recently of Ward Perkins and Goodchild in Tripolitania, the period A.D. 150–350, which saw the great expansion of Christianity, is among those least studied here. Partly due to the poverty of our own annals, partly perhaps, to insular conservatism and inertia, the 3rd century A.D. has been written down as 'anarchy', and left as a sort of wilderness of scholarship spurned by Classicist and Mediaevalist alike. Moreover, the Church historian, traditionally literary in his approach and inexperienced in practical archaeology, has tended to study his subject in isolation from its environment. We have not developed an *Antike und Christentum* school in Britain. There is not, to the writer's knowledge, a single post in any British University in Christian Archaeology. Hence, we start with a handicap, for the application of archaeology to the study of the early history of the Church demands just such an approach. One cannot understand, for instance, the significance of the Return of Ulysses fresco in the catacomb of the Aurelii in Rome without having absorbed something of the religious life of the late 2nd century.[26] This brings the problem home to us. Rightly the Anglican Communion has always been noted for its scholarship. The names of Lightfoot, Burkitt, Gore, Kidd and Sanday are only few of the great scholars who have served the Church. But reputations do not stand still. The new techniques of study must be learnt laboriously and employed to advantage if the Church in this country is to keep abreast in this field. Here is a challenge worth accepting. For we have the chance as never before of making the past history of the Church intelligible to our contemporaries, and that chance must not be lost.

[25] C. H. Kraeling, 'A Greek Fragment of Tatian's Diatessaron from Doura', *Studies and Documents*, III, 1935.
[26] Published by Carlo Cechelli, *Monumenti cristiano-eretici di Roma*, Rome, 1944, at p. 100.

VI

Ecclesiastical History: Its Growth and Relevance

Whither Ecclesiastical History? At some time in their careers all scholars should face the ordeal of attempting to explain their subjects in general terms to an audience not necessarily acquainted with them. To do so offers a chance of surveying where one's subject stands in relation to its past and what new areas of research are opening up, and for the individual, whether what he is doing is relevant and whether he has any message to offer to his contemporaries. I am greatly honoured by the Society's invitation to speak this afternoon.

The story of the Christian Church lends itself to precisely this challenge. My predecessor, Professor John Foster, has told me that a Church that is not on the move is not a Church, and his great contribution to his subject was in the field of Christian mission from the time of Paul to our own day. Ecclesiastical history demands that width of interest, for it covers nearly 2000 years of human experience. Since the time when the Emperor Constantine accepted Christianity as the faith of the Roman Empire its history has been bound up intimately with the development of the general history of mankind, first in the Mediterranean lands, then in Europe, and, in the last four centuries, in the world. If it is an exaggeration to believe with Bishop Westcott that 'all history from the Day of Pentecost is a sacred history',[1] it is true that for the period 300-1300 from Diocletian to Boniface VIII it is no more possible to study the history of Europe without reference to the history and doctrine of the Christian Church and its offshoots, than one can understand our own day without an acquaintance with economics and the political and social implications of the ideas of Darwin and Marx. Today even, no grasp of European values is possible without an understanding of Christianity.

Moreover, the Church as a continuing institution proclaiming a way of salvation through the life, teaching and death of Jesus Christ, has inspired its defenders and critics from the earliest period. These have been well aware that the events they were discussing were historical events taking place at a well-established point in historical time, namely the

Ecclesiastical History: Its Growth and Relevance

middle of the reign of Tiberius during the long governorship of Pontius Pilate in Palestine. The Church's origins, like its claim to be a divine society among men, have been the matter for historians and apologists from the outset. The writer of St Luke's Gospel and the Acts of the Apostles set out to narrate the events as he understood them following the Crucifixion to St Paul's arrival in Rome. Like other contemporary historians he used a variety of sources, including what may perhaps be accepted as eyewitness accounts of events, and with the aim of commending Christianity to the authorities. Towards the end of the second century, a converted Palestinian Jew, Hegesippus (*circa* 120-180) wrote a series of memoranda preserving an account of events in the life of the Church that he considered memorable, and these included the death of James, the Lord's brother and head of the Church in Jerusalem in 62. The greatest of all these early historians was, of course, Eusebius of Caesarea (*circa* 270-339), whose ten books of Ecclesiastical History tell the story of the Church from the Crucifixion to the moment immediately preceding the Council of Nicaea in 325. This remains the primary source of all ecclesiastical history in the first three centuries.

Eusebius himself had witnessed the final effort of the emperors to crush the Church, followed by its triumph in the reign of Constantine. He was an eyewitness of the last, bloody phase of the Great Persecution, when the excesses of the emperor Maximin in Upper Egypt assured that for the Coptic peasant the era of Diocletian should henceforth be known as the Era of the Martyrs. He regarded the victory of the Church under Constantine as providential, and he felt it his duty, as he says himself, to record the history of 'the race of Christians', 'and the number of those who were distinguished in her (the Church's) government and leadership in the provinces of greatest fame', as well as 'those who were ambassadors of the Word of God either by speech or pen', and, he adds, 'the evil works of its enemies'.[2] Eusebius was one of those rare writers who had seen the hopes of a lifetime fulfilled, and his history resounds with optimism for the future of mankind in the Christian empire of Constantine.

The school of Greek ecclesiastical historians who in the fifth and sixth centuries continued his work shared his respect for detail within the bounds of an orthodox framework for truth, though they criticised Eusebius' devotion to the theology of Origen and his opposition to Anathasius. Socrates and Sozomen (both *circa* 370-440) were laymen lawyers in Constantinople, prepared to tell the history of the Church from Nicaea to their own day (438) in a critical spirit, not hesitating to give the Emperor Julian his due or to point to the garrulous folly of Nestorius and the wickedness of his opponent Cyril. The Syrians Evagrius and John of Ephesus, despite taking opposite sides in the Monophysite issue, nonetheless provide dependable witness for the events in the history of the Church between the Council of Chalcedon in 451 and the reign of Justin II, 565-578.

These historians are, however, all in the tradition of the contemporary document. They were not critics. Deeper causes of events are not probed, the writer being content to follow the narrative, pausing only to point out when 'the enemy of truth' stirs up a riot or persecution. They are in the Thucydides succession a thousand years later than Thucydides and, like him, seeking to 'report accurately' what they had either seen themselves or 'tried by the most severe and detailed tests possible'[3] with the object that the events recorded should not be lost to memory. The story, too, is told in providential terms, as the story of man's progress towards recapturing what he had lost at the Fall, namely the image of God.

Byzantine historiography failed to develop as a science. In the fourteenth century we find Nicephorus Callistus using his scissors and paste to construct a mosaic out of the literary remains of authors hundreds of years before, but never thinking for a moment to assess their stories or survey the age in which they were writing from the perspective of his own time. In the West, the Latin Fathers, Augustine and Paulus Orosius, used history to attempt to interpret the nature of man's continuing relationship to God. The story of the *Civitas Dei* was not 'the history of the Church'. In the Middle Ages, Matthew Paris and Froissart though well-informed and entertaining are still essentially chroniclers. Ecclesiastical history as a critical study of the teaching, spread and organisation of the Church is a child of the Renaissance and Reformation.[4] The one brought within the inquirer's grasp texts, particularly of the Greek Fathers, that had hitherto been known in the West only in translation; the other a more critical approach to the history of the Church, indeed hostile to the traditional Western and Papal standpoint. The printing-press enabled the production of the works of the Greek Fathers in considerable numbers and their study by scholars all over Europe. Between 1559 and 1574 one group centred in Basle, known as the Centuriators of Magdeburg, produced the first continuous critical history of the Church, from the Crucifixion to A.D. 1400. Unfortunately, it was not only biased strongly against Rome and in favour of Lutheranism, but it was also inaccurate, and this encouraged a challenge from the Counter Reformation. Baronius' huge twelve folio volumes of Church history, the *Annales Ecclesiastici*, took twenty years between 1588 and 1607 to complete, but in these books he mobilised the whole of the Latin tradition in the service of the Roman Catholic Church, but typically failed to understand and do justice to the Greek Patristic tradition.

Though we may plead guilty to prejudice on behalf of our own scholars, it may be said of Hooker that his *Ecclesiastical Polity*, Book Five, contains some shrewd assessments of events in early Church history, based on a thorough acquaintance with Greek and Latin texts. In considering Cyprian and the Donatists, for instance, he provides a succinct analysis of how the schism arose and the factors that favoured its survival. He does not spare the unworthy conduct of the Christian leaders in Carthage at the time of the Great Persecution, and though he condemns the schismatics for rashness and perversity he is critical of the severity of the penal laws imposed by the imperial government against them. He was shrewd enough to compare the Donatists with the Anabaptists of his own day. Hooker was writing in the reign of Elizabeth, in the era that on the Continent saw the massacre of St Bartholomew and the Netherlands revolt. In comparison with the fanatical attitudes that prevailed on the Continent, his work offers an astounding example of the Elizabethan settlement in the sphere of scholarship.

Hooker had no immediate successors of note, and the seventeenth century belongs almost entirely to the great Roman Catholic compilers, the Bollandists and the Benedictines of St Maur. The Bollandists were a society of Jesuits in Brussels who conceived the idea of publishing in a scholarly manner the original manuscripts of the lives and legends of saints and martyrs. Theirs, as Professor Knowles has pointed out,[5] was a work of real importance as the first great enterprise of co-operative scholarship in the modern world, and through all the vicissitudes of wars and the abolition and restoration of the Jesuit Order, it has continued to the present day. The first two volumes of the *Acta Sanctorum* were published in 1643, and by 1658 the two editors Jean de Bolland and Godefroy Henshens had reached the end of the saints of February. Monastic and cathedral librarians all over Europe were being made aware of the historical as well as the devotional and liturgical value of some of the priceless manuscripts in their possession. Today one may criticise the Bollandists for their method in arranging their study in strictly calendrical order. The labour has mounted like the weight of Sisyphus' stone, and it is not altogether surprising that after three centuries the month of November has not yet been exhausted.

The Maurists were more practical. In Jean Mabillon (1632-1707), Baluze (1630-1718) and Ruinart (1657-1709) they produced scholars of the highest order, the real polymaths whose range of knowledge and sheer industry amazes us today. Mabillon, apart from editing the entire surviving work of St Bernard, produced six vast volumes of *Acta Sanctorum* between 1668 and 1680 giving an account of the life and work of monastic saints to A.D. 900, and in appendices dealing fully and often magisterially with historical problems such as the spread of the Rule of St Benedict or the practice of Communion in both kinds. In addition he began the scientific study of chartularies with his *De Re Diplomatica*, constructing a new discipline of paleography essential for advanced work in medieval history.[6] These men and their like, such as Le Nain de Tillemont (1637-1698), established a tradition of French Catholic encyclopaedic scholarship which continues until today. In our own Dom Henri Leclercq, completing almost single-handed the final volumes of the massive *Dictionnaire d'archéologie Chrétienne et de liturgie*, was their direct heir.

VI

The polymaths were the children of French culture at the height of its achievement in the reign of Louis XIV. To some extent, with all their probity as historians, they were bound by the discipline of their Church. Mabillon himself was unable to print Abbot Peter's denunciation of the evils of his time, the late twelfth century, for fear of causing scandal.

Objective writing such as we may attempt it today had to wait until the Enlightenment. The first man who attempted to encompass the whole of Church history down to his own day in an objective and scientific spirit was Johann Lorentz von Mosheim (1694-1755), who took a leading part in founding the university of Göttingen and held a Chair there. Von Mosheim felt no doubt as to the providential nature of Christianity – its spread by ignorant and unlettered disciples was nothing short of miraculous, but he took a severely pragmatic view of the nature of the historian's duty towards it. 'Ecclesiastical history', he says, 'is a clear and faithful narration of the transactions, revolutions, and events, that relate to that large community which bears the name of Jesus Christ and which is vulgarly known under the denomination of the Church.'[7] The study was simply divided into 'Internal' and 'External' history of the Church. It approached the subject by way of the Jewish background and pointed to such facts as the 'variety in the ritual and discipline of the primitive churches' and analysed with an eye to the detail of the evidence the reasons for the persecutions. This was a Church history in the modern sense of the term a generation before Gibbon's *Decline and Fall*. Moreover, it reflected something of the spirit of the age. Mosheim's translator, Rev. Archibald Maclaine, Minister of the English Church at The Hague, felt no illusions about the character of the history of the Church. In his Preface he tells his patron Prince William V of Orange-Nassau, 'You will see on the one hand, the religion of Jesus rising upon a benighted world striking conviction into the hearts of mortals by the irresistible lustre of its divine truths, conquering the passions and prejudices of men and confounding the opposition of Nations and Empires . . . but you will also observe the lamentable changes that have been introduced in consequence of the corruption of men, the ambition of a licentious and despotic priesthood and the bigotry and tyranny of wicked sovereigns.'[8]

Gibbon's concern was less with the Church as such, than as the leading element in the famous 'Christianity and barbarism' on whom could be laid the blame for the fall of the Empire. Yet the XVIth chapter devoted to the emergence and development of Christianity is hardly surpassed in its depth of judgment today. Mosheim's work had been translated in 1767 and was therefore available to Gibbon who wrote a decade later and sometimes Gibbon seems to follow Mosheim's approach closely. Both men asked the same basic question concerning Rome's dealings with the Christians, namely how was it the Romans allowed the Jews to live under their own religion and law, while the Christians were treated with such severity. Both historians pointed to the obvious paradox of the purity of the Christian religion and the barbarous manner in which the emperor persecuted it. To Mosheim, 'this important question seems more difficult to be solved, when we consider that the excellent nature of the Christian religion and its admirable tendency to promote the public welfare of the state and private felicity of the individual . . .'.[9] Gibbon must have had this paragraph in mind when he wrote, 'If we seriously consider the purity of the Christian religion and its moral precepts and the innocent as well as the austere lives of the greater number of those who during the first ages embraced the faith of the Gospel, we should naturally suppose that so benevolent a doctrine would be received with due reverence even by the unbelieving world . . . that the magistrates instead of persecuting would have protected an order of men who yielded the most passive obedience to the laws, though they declined the active care of war and government . . .'.[9a] Interestingly enough, both men gave practically the same answer why this did not come about. Mosheim considered that 'atheism' was the Christians' main offence: 'they were looked upon', he says, as 'a sort of atheists, and by the Roman laws those who were chargeable with atheism were declared the pests of human society'.[10] Gibbon echoes this with a famous dictum: 'The Jews were a nation, the Christians were a sect', and when they rejected the gods of the Empire, city, and family, they were regarded as impious.[11]

With slight modifications these judgments hold good today. 'Atheism' certainly was the main accusation against the Christians. 'Away with the atheists' as the crowd at Smyrna shouted against Polycarp in *circa* 165 remains the monument to these sentiments of the provincials of this period towards the Christians. It is only in the spheres of the legal situation of the Christians and the proceedings against them and the outlook of the Christians themselves, that two centuries of scholarly study has brought advances from Gibbon. Gibbon himself had no successor in Britain. In the reaction to the French Revolution there was no room for the calm sceptical stare of the man who had passed from Toryism to Catholicism, back to Protestantism and then to a hostility towards all forms of Christianity. His regret at the triumph of Christianity 'which erected the triumphant banner of the Cross on the ruins of the Capitol' was not a popular sentiment in the age that produced the Methodists and Evangelists. It has been pointed out how Robespierre failed to replace Catholicism in France by the Religion of Reason because he was unable to provide this with a Biblical justification.[12] With Gibbon it was the same. Deism and Olympian indifference were not enough for the England at the end of the struggle with France of the Revolution and Napoleon. The next advance was to come from men who felt a greater allegiance to traditional theological disciplines.

Credit for the final winning of Ecclesiastical history as a subject for scientific research belongs mainly to German Protestant scholarship in the mid 19th century.[13] It develops as part of the great advance of classical and historical scholarship that one associates with the names of Mommsen and Ranke. In this brief survey two names only can be mentioned, but each began a development whose results have not been exhausted today. F. C. Baur (1792-1860) was appointed to the Chair of Historical Theology at Tübingen in 1826 and held it until his death in 1860. He was primarily a New Testament scholar and he influenced the whole school of German scholarship that has treated Church history as a continuation of New Testament studies. It was Baur who saw the key to much of both in the opposition between Peter and Paul, of Judaistic legalism and the free Spirit religion implanted in Greek Christianity by Paul; to an astonishing degree he was right, and discoveries in the field today have tended to emphasise the differences between the Jerusalem (Peter and James) tradition of Christianity and that of the Pauline Churches, though Paul himself was far more indebted to Jewish influences than Baur would have allowed. The other scholar was Neander, a Jew who had become a Christian who became Professor of Church History at Berlin University in 1812 at the age of 24, after writing a brilliant study on the Emperor Julian. Church history meant for Neander the study of the development of doctrine and institutions and religion itself as an expression of feeling and that Christianity was the divine leaven working in the history of mankind. It is interesting to point out how ideas of development which so influenced Newman were being represented in the German universities a generation before, but entirely different conclusions were being drawn from there. Chairs of Ecclesiastical History were unfortunately rarities in the British Isles in the first half of the nineteenth century.

German scholarship had benefited from its university system. For the rulers of the thirty-nine principalities into which Germany found itself divided in 1815 a university was as much a necessity as a court. This gave an impetus to scholarly study over a wide area and in some fields of history such as the study of Late Antiquity, a lead which Germany has never lost. In England on the other hand, learning was concentrated in Oxford and Cambridge, and these universities in the period before the passing of the Universities Act of 1871 deserved at least to an extent their reputation for 'port and prejudice'. As a result, the Anglican episcopal bench included few scholars, while the strife between the different parties within the Church, of High Anglicans, Evangelicals, Rationalists, Enthusiasts, and reformers of every hue prevented the emergence of wide-ranging and impartial scholarship in ecclesiastical history. It was sometimes more than one's career was worth to hold theological views which could be regarded as unorthodox. The Tractarians moved heaven and earth to prevent the appointment of the vague and unconventional Dr Hampden to the Regius Chair of Divinity at Oxford, and Hampden replied in kind by failing B.D. candidates who held Tractarian views. The fate of Bishop Colenso,[14] in trying to adapt Genesis to the outlook of his Zulu converts, and the writers of *Essays and Reviews* in trying to make the Bible understood of men of science showed what scholarship might expect. One notable achievement can, however, be credited to this period, namely the Library of the Fathers compiled by the Tractarians from 1838 onwards. Though these volumes of translation from the Early Fathers formed part of the Tractarian campaign to prove the 'antiquity' of the positions they adopted, they provided a basis for renewed scholarly interest in the Patristic period. With Newman's *History of the Arians* we still feel ourselves in the pre-history of historical scholarship, where the proving of dogma from history was the main concern of the writer. It took another generation before J. B. Lightfoot's great essay on origins of the Ministry, published in 1869, demonstrated how New Testament and Patristic study could combine an acceptance of an orthodox position with the keen criticism of an historian.

The 1860's and 1870's are a watershed for many forms of intellectual life in Western Europe. The old conflicts arising from the Revolutionary and Napoleonic wars have been replaced by the intellectual challenges of the Industrial Revolution and resultant expansion of Europe in every field. In historical writing it is the age that produced Waitz, Hefele and Bishop Stubbs, the last-named the true founder of the study of British medieval constitutional and ecclesiastical history.[15] For the ecclesiastical historian the product of the fifty years of peace in Western Europe that followed the Franco-Prussian war have been immense. It suffices to mention only the production of the great series of texts of the Patristic, Medieval and Reformation periods that the scholar today owes to that period. In Paris the Benedictine *Patrologia Latina* begun in 1844 had already resulted in 221 volumes by 1864, and these were being succeeded by the *Patrologia Greco-Latina* with 157 volumes from 1857 to 1886, and this in turn by the *Patrologia Orientalis*, 1901 and still continuing. Today one stands amazed at the labour and devoted scholarship of the men who compiled these works with the faultless Latin translation from the Greek and the learned notes and cross-references. The Vienna Corpus of critical texts of the Latin Fathers began in 1866 and continues today, as does the Berlin Corpus of the Greek Fathers (*Die griechischen Schriftsteller der ersten drei Jahrhunderte*). Over all this great period presided the genius of Adolf von Harnack.

Harnack was a Baltic German from Dorpat in Estonia. At the early age of 28 he became Professor of Church History in the university of Giessen – an excellent example of how the smaller German universities could provide a niche for a promising scholar at the outset of his career. Three years later he started the publication of the *Texte und Untersuchungen zur altchristlichen Literatur* which became and has continued to be the means by which critical studies of major documents of early Church history have been published. Harnack himself contributed at the rate of a learned monograph a year, and he also wrote the vast surveys of

Christian Literature until Eusebius and *History of Dogma*. His *Mission and Expansion of Christianity in the first three centuries* published in 1902 remains indispensable today despite all that has been discovered since. When he died in 1930 he had done more for the advancement of the study of the New Testament and early Christianity than any other single scholar before or since.

In these years the contribution of the United Kingdom and indeed of the English-speaking world generally to the study of Church history was less in every way than that of the Continentals. The four volume *Dictionary of Christian Biography* remains a valuable work, and the publication of chronicles in the Rolls Series, and the volumes published by the Canterbury and York Society, the Camden Series of the Royal Historical Society and of the Parker Society have contributed richly to the provision of material for the study of Christianity in England. But giants of the character of Harnack or Duchesne, Leclercq and Batiffol have not been forthcoming; William Bright and Mandel Creighton are perhaps the exceptions that prove the rule. This has been partly due to the too close association of a university with a normal clerical career with its host of administrative and pastoral duties on the one hand, and, on the other, to the simple belief that ecclesiastical history was either a preserve for clerics or 'foreign history' which had little relevance to the development of Britain. In either case it was not the concern of professional historians.

In the last years of the nineteenth century new developments were beginning which were to give greater scope for British scholars. To the detailed literary criticism of existing texts was now added the discovery of entirely new evidence from archaeological expeditions. In these we have been among the pioneers. Sir William Ramsay's successive journeys through Asia Minor and above all in Phrygia in the 1880s opened up a completely new perspective of early Christian studies to the historian. It was possible now to begin to study the growth of Christianity within the social and political context of Greco-Roman provincial life supported by the evidence of buildings, inscriptions and objects as well as by texts. Up to now, ecclesiastical history had been confined to the library where the essential qualities had been linguistic knowledge and the skills of a philologist and literary critic. Now it came within the scope of the field archaeologist whose approach was that of a social historian and researcher.

As early as 1865, Lightfoot had predicted, 'If only we could recover letters that ordinary people wrote to each other without any thought of being literary, we should have the greatest possible help in understanding the language of the New Testament generally.'[16] He was not to be disappointed. In 1897 British excavations in Egypt led to the discovery at Oxyrhynchus of a number of papyri containing hitherto unknown Sayings of Jesus. These Logia were found near a copy of Matthew's Gospel to some parts of which they bear a strong resemblance. Dismissed by so accomplished a New Testament scholar as Charles Guignebert as 'disappointing'[17] they have proved to be incomplete copies of the *Gospel of Thomas*, a work probably going back to an Aramaic original and emphasising the virtue of the ascetic life as the true means of gaining knowledge of and entrance to Christ's Kingdom. It was a work that in Syria had been used by Christians alongside the four canonical gospels and may be one of the main literary influences on the development of what became the monastic tradition there and in Egypt.

These discoveries were already giving the ecclesiastical historian a wider view of his subject even before the sensational finds were made in the Judaean desert and in Egypt since the war. The Dead Sea Scrolls discovered between 1947 and 1956 throw light both on the ideas that inspired a Jewish sect contemporary with the formation of the Christian community in Jerusalem and some light on the latter's organisation and writings. For the historian it provides a means of comparison between Jesus' ideas and those of another Jewish religious sect who also awaited the coming of a messiah. In Egypt the Gnostic texts in Coptic discovered at Nag-Hammadi in Upper Egypt in 1945 enable the historian to read the ideas of these non-orthodox Christians without the often distorting intermediacy of orthodox writers. Even more important than these sensational finds has been the steady accumulation of churches, catacombs, monastic buildings, inscriptions and small objects which show how the Christians of the early centuries lived and thought.

The study of Church history, then, now includes the entire range of historical evidence, literary and archaeological. It is an advancing and expanding subject and one which in the past has been served by some of the greatest scholars in Europe. One may ask fairly, however, what good is it all? If we admit, as we must, that deep matters of human faith lie beyond its scope, what is left?[18] Is there still what one may call a Christian interpretation of history in the way in which Eusebius and Augustine believed there was? If not, why should we bother today about the ideas of obscure and generally quarrelsome people in periods so different from our own? The answer is straightforward. Churches are institutions run by people. Their life and thought is as much the concern of historians as any other institution. Many of the issues which have divided Christendom, and still defy the efforts of those who strive to bring the Churches together at least in fellowship, turn on questions of historical fact. Other differences also can best be understood in the context of their historical origins. Today, when all Christian traditions aim at closer mutual understanding, the historian may be able to throw light where the theologian has hitherto failed. To give an example: ever since the Reformation, Churches have been divided on the question of the significance of the Christian ministry. Are Church orders to be regarded as valid only when they have been conferred by a bishop representing episcopal descent from the Apostles? Some Churches, including the Roman

Catholic and Anglican, insist on this condition, others do not. Yet until this hurdle is crossed progress toward the reunion of the Churches will be slow.

To the historian, however, the claims of both episcopalian and non-episcopalian are, within limits, valid. Those limits, however, are imposed by what we now know of the early history of the Christian community. Jesus did not set out to 'found a Church'. What He did was to build on the existing prophetic tradition in Israel and saw His followers as the 'holy remnant', the Saints, and the new Israel. After the Crucifixion one finds two traditions developing among His followers. At Jerusalem, whatever one is to make of Mt. 16.18 and 18.16 in which Jesus is recorded as naming Peter as His earthly successor, the leadership of the Christian community devolved on James, Jesus' brother. The latter governed first with two 'pillars', John and Peter, reminiscent of the triumvirate that ruled over the Covenanters at Q'mran, but by the time of the Apostolic Council in 49, it was he alone who made the decisions in the name of the Church. 'Therefore I judge' (διὸ ἐγὼ κρίνω), a strong term, denoting judicial authority, is that used by James in pronouncing decision regarding the obligations of converted Gentiles to the Christian community (Acts 15.19). James was indeed a High Priest in the Jewish sense of the term; according to tradition arrayed with the high-priestly *petalon* and known like Zadok in Maccabaean times as 'the Wall of Righteousness'. It was to him that Paul came to Jerusalem and made his report on his mission and submitted to a test of his Jewry at James' orders by taking a Nazarite vow by shaving his head. James was the supreme ruler of the Church and Jerusalem, with the Temple was his centre. Here surely is one of the most important sources of the tradition of monepiscopacy and apostolic succession. It was a tradition, however, applicable only so long as the Temple and High-priesthood lasted, and of interest only so long as the Church was based on Jerusalem and its appeal primarily to 'the cities of Judah' and to 'the lost sheep of the house of Israel'. By A.D. 70 James had been murdered and Jerusalem had fallen. Christianity in the ensuing years was to lose its appeal in Jesus' homeland.

With this in mind, one turns to the Churches as established by Paul among the Hellenistic Jewish and Gentile populations of the Greek-speaking eastern Mediterranean. Here the Temple, its organisation and its ceremonial, was less significant to the Jew, and the Christian communities that Paul and his helpers founded tended to resemble outwardly Hellenistic synagogues with a wide variety of organisation: prophets and teachers in Acts 13.1, presbyters 'in every church' in Acts 14.23, 'bishops and deacons' in Philippi (Phil. 1.1), while at Ephesus the leaders of the Church are called in the same speech by Paul first 'presbyters' and then 'bishops' (Acts 20.17 and 20.28). It is evident that in the 'interim' before the expected Coming of Christ, the actual organisation of the Church was not regarded as something that needed a standard pattern,

Ecclesiastical History: Its Growth and Relevance

and in fact tended to follow the local usage of the Jewish community on whose periphery it was established. So it is that both traditions, episcopal and non-episcopal, have their justification reaching back to Apostolic times, but each corresponded to particular environments. Monepiscopacy and apostolic succession belong to the Jerusalem Church and mainly Aramaic community. Presbyter-bishops, leaders, prophets, 'mercy helps' and the rest of that colourful band catalogued by Paul as in some way connected with the running of a Church in I Cor. 12.28 and Eph. 4.11, belong to the Greek-speaking mission. Both are equally valid and today those who appeal to one or other tradition should not deny fellowship to the other.

The validity of Ministry and Sacraments is a matter of Church order on which the historian may have an opinion to give. On the wider issues also of why divisions have taken place, his advice has a claim to be heard. The immense accumulation of evidence regarding the crises of Church history, Chalcedon in 451, the formal schism between East and West in 1054, the German Reformation in 1517, have allowed every aspect of each situation to be examined. 'Were the Ancient Heresies nationalist or social movements in disguise?' has been asked pertinently. Though the answer probably is, more so in the West than in the East, i.e. Donatism was more of a social movement than Monophysitism, it is clear that Church divisions have not been the result of the rejection by misguided or wicked men of a central truth represented by the ruling hierarchy. Intellectual dissent takes its place as one only among a whole range of causes including national and social issues which lead to the formation of long-standing religious divisions. The abolition, then, of the term 'heresy' and all that it implies, and the substitution of that of differing religious traditions expressed through different Christian communities may also be set at the door of the scholar in ecclesiastical history.

Finally, I would claim the sense of perspective as the greatest of the historian's contributions to the understanding of Church history. His knowledge must not only cover 2000 years of time, but he must be able also to interpet each major development in Christian history against the background of the events of the period. He can unfold and explain the revelation of Providence. There are few inevitabilities in history, even in the history of war, but it would be, if one may put it like that, for each generation, a bold man who did not sense that some cataclysm in Western Christendom would accompany the rise of the middle classes to learning and power once the Conciliar movement had failed to reform the administrative and financial abuses in the Papacy. Similarly in the eighteenth century some movement such as that of Wesley could hardly have been avoided to respond to the needs of mission and the new industrial society which the Church of England had failed to meet. The historian's role is to narrate the facts, explain the causes and assess the results. Perhaps in so doing he may prevent similar mistakes happening in his own day.

What, then, of the future? It is no part of the historian's task to play the prophet, yet at the same time no scholar today can remain purely a man of the study, however dedicated he may be. Events press in upon him and he cannot avoid taking part. Moreover, his historical judgments must be coloured by his own experiences and his knowledge of people and events in the contemporary world. One may look forward then with some certainty to an increasing degree of integration between ecclesiastical history and the other branches of the historical sciences. The *Acts of the Apostles* do not stand, for instance, on the margin of first-century history. They provide priceless evidence not only for the growth of Christianity but also for the way in which a writer in the eastern provinces regarded his surroundings. They cannot be ignored by anyone who wishes to understand Roman provincial government in the first century. This process of comprehension will continue. It will, I believe, affect other more practical issues. The more 'ecclesiastical history' is brought out of isolation – and in Scotland there is an urgent need for the revival of the Ecclesiastical History Society – the more likely the existing barriers between Church and people will be able to be broken down, and finally between the Churches themselves. It is salutary to remember the warning about the 'room swept and garnished'. It was not a happy place. The same would apply to any centralised, logical and monolithic structure, however well kept and administered. 'In my Father's house are many abiding-places', differing but complementary. Bishop and presbyter should co-exist in harmony. There is no place for FIDESCO. It is the historian's task to tell his contemporaries how these have come into being, and if by so doing he may persuade the inhabitants to live in fellowship with each other then he has served his trade and his time as he ought.

REFERENCES

1. *The Gospel of Life*, London, 1892, p. 279.
2. EUSEBIUS, *Ecclesiastical History*, I.1.
3. THUCYDIDES I. 22.
4. See C. W. DUGMORE, *Ecclesiastical History. No Soft Option*. Inaugural Lecture, London, 1959.
5. *Great Historical Enterprises*, Cambridge, 1963, pp. 3–4.
6. See Professor KNOWLES' Essay, 'Jean Mabillon' in *The Historian and Character*, Cambridge, 1963, pp. 213–240.
7. MOSHEIM, *Ecclesiastical History* (English Translation A. Maclaine, Dublin, 1767), p. xxiii.
8. Ibid., p. vii.
9. MOSHEIM, op. cit., p. 48.
9a. GIBBON, ch. xvi, opening paragraph.
10. MOSHEIM, op. cit., p. 49.
11. GIBBON, ch. xvi, p. 5 in Everyman's Edition.

12. See JOHN MACMANNERS, *The French Revolution and the Church*, London, 1969, p. 105.
13. See G. P. GOOCH, Chapter on 'The Jews and the Christian Church' in *History and Historians of the Nineteenth Century*, London, 1923, pp. 521-549.
14. For Colenso's troubles see P. B. HINCHLIFF, *John William Colenso*, London, 1964.
15. For the story of *Monumenta Germaniae Historica* during these years see KNOWLES, *Great Historical Enterprises*, pp. 64 ff.
16. Quoted in G. MILLIGAN, *Selections from Greek Papyri*, XX.
17. CH. GUIGNEBERT, *Jesus*, Paris, 1933, p. 55.
18. Compare P. B. HINCHLIFF, *Ecclesiastical History, its Nature and Purpose*, Rhodes University, 1960, p. 19.

Henri Leclercq 1869-1945: vom Autodidakten zum Kompilator Grossen Stils. By T. Klauser Pp. 165, 6 plates. (Jahrbuch für Antike und Christentum, Ergänzungsband 5. Münster: Aschendorff, 1977. D.M. 48

WHEN, in 1903, Dom Fernand Cabrol began the publication of the *Dictionnaire d'archéologie chrétienne et de liturgie,* he had a relatively small work in mind, perhaps four volumes in all. Exactly forty years later the last page of a massive fifteen-volume (or thirty half volumes) work had been written and awaited the end of the Second World War for publication. The transformation in size and scope was due to the almost single-handed work of Cabrol's assistant and successor, Dom Henri Leclercq. Farnborough Abbey, where Cabrol was Prior, was an off-shoot of the French Benedictine monastery of Solesmes. It had been built by the empress Eugénie in memory of her husband Napoleon III and their only son, Louis Napoleon killed in a skirmish in the Zulu war in 1879. Set up in the middle of Hampshire it had no advantages as a centre of learning that could rival Solesmes. Cabrol, however, chose his colleagues carefully. They included Férotin, an acknowledged authority on the early Church in Spain, Wilmart, and the Celticist, Gougaud. In addition, he had insisted on bringing with him two novices, Pierre de Puniet, a liturgiologist, and the naturalized Belgian, Henri Leclercq d'Orlancourt.

At this time, in 1896, there was nothing to show that Leclercq would prove to be other than the competent research assistant that Cabrol needed. Indeed, how between 1896 and 1901 Leclercq mastered the techniques of scholarship, let alone gained the fantastic range of knowledge and powers of assimilation that was to characterize his work, remains a mystery. Already in 1897, he was assisting Cabrol to assemble every conceivable patristic text relating to the early liturgies for a sourcebook for the study of liturgy to A.D. 1000. There was no time for any other careful scholarly preparation. He had shown no particular promise at school; in fact, he left before his final year. His greatest success in his early career had been promotion up the ranks as a volunteer in the French army, to end his three-year engagement in 1892 as a junior officer on the reserve. Early discipline, however, sound health, an unbounded admiration for the work of the great Benedictine scholar, Jean Mabillon, and an uncanny ability to apply himself totally to the task in hand, had evidently overcome earlier shortcomings. Cabrol could not have chosen a better aide.

Theodor Klauser has now assembled all the information available to date about Leclercq. He was inspired to do so, through the reliance which his own mentor F. J. Dölger had placed on Leclercq's work. Was this reliance justified? To answer this he felt the need to write an objective study of this enigmatic and controversial figure, whose acknowledged achievement was never recognized by any university in his lifetime.

That much of the text is occupied by fairly detailed accounts of Leclercq's contributions to the *Dictionnaire* is not surprising. Leclercq seems to have kept no diary; he was an archetypal loner, even his acquaintances were few, as are outstanding events in his life. He seems to have been almost wholly self-taught, but once learnt, the information was stored and never forgotten. He was a prodigious worker, calculating on doing six hours concentrated work each day, with an iron self-discipline, and he became the greatest compiler of historical material of all time.

Klauser's story reveals what one would expect. For more than a quarter of a century, 1896–1924, Leclercq was in good standing as a Benedictine monk. He rose early for the morning offices, catching the 7 a.m. train from Farnborough to Waterloo, arriving at 9 a.m. punctually at the British Museum and returning to the monastery in time for the evening meal at 7.30 p.m. Like some other famous characters, he made the Reading Room of the British Museum his real home. At this stage, however, he was not the only Farnborough monk engaged in intensive scholarship. Apart from Cabrol himself, Puniet, Férotin, Wilmart, and Gougaud, were all contributing major scholarly work. After 1908, he was allowed to spend an increasing part of his life in London. It was only after the end of the First World War that strains appeared that resulted in 1924 in Leclercq's secularization. Even so, he may have contributed to the ending of his career at Farnborough. A monk who can greet the news in 1911 that his name would appear henceforth on the title-page of the *Dictionnaire* with that of Cabrol with a laconic telegram to his publisher beginning, 'Cabrol capitule', would seem to lack the humility necessary for his calling. Thenceforth, until his death in March 1945, Leclercq acted as chaplain to a convent of the Sisters of Sion in Bayswater. He retained, however, his monastic habit, and his title of Dom, and just occasionally, as for the funeral of Cabrol in June 1937, he returned to visit Farnborough.

By the time he broke with his community he already had enough scholarly acievement for a single lifetime. Five volumes of the *Dictionnaire* had appeared, eight volumes of his revision of Hefele's *Konziliengeschichte*, a manual of 681 pages on Christian archaeology, considerable works on early Christianity in Spain, and in North Africa (two volumes); there was the *Monumenta ecclesiae liturgica* published with Cabrol, a study of the Fall of the French Monarchy and learned articles on topics such as the *libelli* in the Decian persecution, and a prayer to the Virgin Mary on an ostrakon found at Luxor. And all the time, he was preparing another magnum opus, a three-volume study of Mabillon (eventually published in two volumes in 1953 and 1957).

Klauser traces the last twenty years of Leclercq's life and work rapidly and most expressively through his contributions to the *Dictionnaire*. Each half volume included 1,400 columns of closely packed print replete with maps, illustrations, and above all, Leclercq's compendious bibliographies. To take volume 13 as an example (published in 1938), Leclercq wrote 134 columns on Paganisme, 155 on Palestine, 150 on Papyrus, 120 on Pasteur (Bon), 454 on Paris, including a survey of the early manuscripts in the Bibliothèque nationale, 234 on Pape (list of Popes and the archaeology to date of their tombs), 131 columns on Paul, and much else. When at last, sometime in 1943, he considered his work complete and ceremoniously handed in his Readers' card for the British Museum Reading Room, he found he had nothing more to do, and died within eighteen months.

Behind this massive work of compilation, the selection was not always entirely scholarly. Klauser rightly points to the streak of French chauvinism in Leclercq's outlook, akin to Action française of the 1930s. He hated anything Germanic, whether it was the Vandals and Visigoths or German scholars of his day. He blamed his contemporaries for 'making a fetish out of Mommsen', and for years he passed over the work of von Harnack in silence. He carried his prejudices to the length of never attempting to master English, though he stayed forty years in England. He had little use for American contributions to scholarship. He set out to build a monument to French achievement in the Maurist tradition, and his work shows both the grandeur and the sectarian narrowness of that scholarship.

Some of Leclercq's work can be criticized in detail. He never visited, so far as is known, either the Roman catacombs or the North African early Christian sites on which he wrote, and archaeologists such as Antonio Ferrua were quick to point out his shortcomings. He was not an original scholar. His programme left him little time for advanced research. He wrote much too much with little critical power. Many of his later contributions to the *Dictionnaire* are little more than verbatim extracts from the reports of others.

Klauser, however, is right to sum up positively. The *Dictionnaire* is not only a monument to the scholarship (mainly French) of the period 1890-1930, with many clerical prejudices of the time embalmed in the process, but retains its use today. Very many of the sites in North Africa on which Leclercq concentrated have disappeared under the plough, and accounts of their survey in the early years of the century are lost among rare and scarcely accessible periodicals. The long extracts reproduced by Leclercq for the *Dictionnaire* are now an invaluable source and provide a basis for further research.

We may thank his friend and admirer, H. I. Marrou (d. April 1977), for seeing the final volumes of the *Dictionnaire* through the press, and for inspiring the establishment of the present Centre de Recherche Le

Nain de Tillemont at the Sorbonne. To Klauser himself, scholars will be in debt for providing some insights into the character and motivation of one of the most remarkable scholars of the present century.

THE CHURCH AND THE ROMAN EMPIRE

VIII

THE CHURCH OF THE ROMAN EMPIRE
313–600

I · *The Situation in 313*

THE triumph of Christianity during the last quarter of the third century had brought its own problems in its wake. In the field of doctrine, Eusebius (*H.E.* VIII.1, 7) describes the mounting tensions between rival groups of Christians that characterized the period immediately before the Great Persecution. In the field of church order, equally grave problems were arising, and these were to have their effect on the relationship between the clergy and the laity in the succeeding age. The Church in the first two centuries had been a small and closely-knit body scattered through the cities of the Roman Empire. So long as it remained such, the laity retained an important role in its organization and liturgy. When, in 197, Tertullian described the Church in Roman Africa, he calls it 'a society with a common religious feeling, a unity of discipline and a bond of hope' (*Apology*, ed. Glover, 39.1). 'Where three are together,' he says elsewhere, 'there is the Church, even if they are laymen.'[1] The Holy Spirit imposed an equality on priests and laymen alike: the services which Tertullian describes were evidently not yet standardized. The congregation met 'to read the books of God' (*Apology* 39.3), and then 'each from what he knows of the Holy Scripture or from his own heart is called upon before the rest to sing to God' (*ibid*. 39.8).

As we have seen in the previous chapter, the laity took a leading part in this liturgy, and behind these practices lay a theory of the Church, which regarded Christianity less as an organization than as a way of life under the continuous guidance of the Holy Spirit. The return of the Lord was expected as an event which Christians would witness, and therefore the 'spiritual man', and above all the martyr, was looked upon as the perfected Christian.[2] Confessors and martyrs were taken from laity and clergy alike, and theirs was the right of 'binding and loosing',[3] and of receiving commands from the Lord. The clergy administered discipline among the congregation, but Paradise was for the martyr and the martyr alone.[4]

The third century was to see some radical changes in this point of view, changes which affected adversely the position of the laity within the Church. The dual influence of the failure of the Second Coming to take place in a temporal form, and the influx of a large number of nominal Christians in the years of peace between 212–249, altered men's views about the nature of the Church. Patently, it had become a mixed body, containing sinners as well as the elect, and the bond of unity was to be found in the sacraments administered by the clergy. In both East and West the transformation can be studied in the bitter comments of Hippolytus[5] at Rome, and the nostalgia of Origen for the 'golden age' of the Severan persecution (202–203).[6]

By the middle of the century, the monarchical episcopate had become the universally recognized system of church government. Ordination was a permanent step, setting the cleric rigidly apart from the world he had renounced.[7] In 251, confessors in Carthage who aspired to forgive the sin of apostasy after the Decian persecution (249–251) were firmly rebuked by Cyprian,[8] and some, at Cyprian's discretion, were promoted to the ranks of the clergy.[9] At the same time, significant changes were going on among the clergy themselves which increased the distance between them and the mass of the faithful. 'Minor orders', of sub-deacons, acolytes, doorkeepers, exorcists and readers were being built up into a regular hierarchy of ecclesiastical grades.[10] The deacon was tending to become more pronouncedly an administrator, and thus encroaching on functions which laymen were performing in the service of the Church. In Carthage, the deacons are mentioned as supervisors of funds belonging to the Church in 251.[11] Fifty years later, the senior deacon there, the 'archidiaconus', had become the heir presumptive to his bishop's see.[12] The Holy Spirit was being firmly guided into ecclesiastical channels. Thus, at the time of the Great Persecution in 303, doubts were being cast in Carthage on the value of unregulated martyrdom as a means of obtaining divine mercy. Vigils outside prisons in which lay confessors were housed were sharply discouraged by Caecilian, the archdeacon of Carthage.[13] Martyrs and their relics were held to have no merit until duly approved by ecclesiastical authority.[14]

The Church of the Roman Empire

The Great Persecution brought the implicit conflict of authority between cleric and inspired layman into the open. In Africa this conflict formed the background to the Donatist controversy. In Egypt, a similar development set in motion the Melitian schism. Just at the very moment when more and more of the provincials were turning to an intense and eschatological form of Christianity, the government of the Church was becoming solidified on a formal, hierarchical basis. Moreover, after the Edict of Milan in February 313, the avenue of martyrdom became closed. Lay Christianity had to find new outlets. It is no accident that in the fourth and fifth centuries monasticism and various forms of ascetic life were, in the main, movements among the laity. In the East, these were regarded as deliberate substitutions for martyrdom.[15] But they were supplemented by a general and intense interest in theological problems among the Christian provincials as a whole. The fact that laymen could still influence the outlook and practice of the Church rendered their subordinate position in its organization and liturgy tolerable.

II · *The Layman in the Worship and Organization of the Church*[16]

'The layman should honour the good shepherd [the bishop], respect him like a father, lord and master, as the high priest of God as guide in piety.' 'He who hears the bishop hears Christ.' Thus, the *Apostolic Constitutions*, probably in the earlier part of the fourth century,[17] defined the role of the layman. In the plan of the churches which were being built all over the Mediterranean provinces of the Roman Empire, a substantial screen of stone or marble divided the nave, or *quadratum populi*, from the altar and apse whither only the clergy might approach.[18] No layman might participate in the administration of the sacraments.[19] No psalms written by individual Christians were to be sung in church.[20] Laymen were to sit 'quietly and seemly' in their places.[21]

Such were the rules, but even so, there were occasions when necessity knew no law, as when perhaps in a time of local persecution by the pro-Arian emperor, Valens (d. 378), Basil of Caesarea authorized laity to keep the communion at home and partake of it themselves (*Letter* 93).[22] There is also some evidence to show that the practice of lay preaching, exemplified by Origen during the third century, did not die out at once. Asterius the Sophist, unordained because of lapse during the Great Persecution, was apparently permitted to preach his semi-Arian doctrines in Syrian churches between 331–335, and to attend synods of bishops.²³ In the West, Pope Leo had to remind correspondents in the mid-fifth century that laymen were not to preach.²⁴ In Africa a layman might still teach in the presence of clergy if invited to do so,²⁵ and he retained the right exercised by all laymen of all ages to grumble at the services. The retired tribune, Hilarius, complained bitterly to the clergy of Hippo against a new-fangled practice introduced there from Carthage of singing parts of the Psalms before the offertory at the Eucharist. Augustine apparently gave him short shrift.²⁶ In both East and West, however, congregational singing was becoming established. We hear how *c.* 375 the two Antiochene ascetics Flavian, later to be Bishop of Antioch, and Diodore, later Bishop of Tarsus, had the congregation at Antioch divided into two choirs to sing the responses antiphonally.²⁷ Their plan was not accepted at once without opposition, but gradually it became the rule in the East. In the West, we find Ambrose of Milan instituting a similar practice. The people sang psalms and hymns in alternate choirs and their responses echoed 'like the roar of waves on the seashore'.²⁸ To him this was the most effective service the laity could perform in the liturgy.²⁹ Nearly a century later we find the same practice in Gaul.³⁰ 'We had assembled', writes Apollinaris Sidonius, *c.* 465, 'at the tomb of St Justus. The annual procession before daylight was over, attended by a vast crowd of both sexes which even that great church could not hold with all its cincture of galleries. After Vigils were ended, chanted alternately by the monks and the clerics, the congregation separated; we could not go far off, as we had to be at hand for the next service at Tierce, when the priests were to celebrate the Mass.'³¹ It is a scene which says much. The laity have their function, to support the intercessions of the clergy, to escort them during the great processions on feast days, and on these occasions to assemble in their thousands and do them honour.

Organizationally, the West provides examples of a tendency to extend the principle of hierarchy to the laity themselves. Thus, Victricius of Rouen (*c.* 390) indicates the order in which the laity may approach holy relics in the course of a procession.³² After the priests, deacons and clergy in minor orders, come the monks, the children, the widows, the *continentes* (laics who, while remaining in the world, had voluntarily accepted certain ascetic practices), the old men, the mothers, and finally the mass of the people. A serious effort seems to have been made to give the widows, at least, a fixed status among the laity. This was due partly to a traditional dislike of second marriages as something akin to adultery,³³ partly to the honour in which widows were held in the

The Church of the Roman Empire

Early Church.[34] The Fathers insist on the merits of the widows and attempt to define their duties. We learn from the Council of Orange in 441 that there was a formal profession of widowhood before the bishop and that those professed wore special vestments.[35] At the Council of Elvira,[36] and at Carthage in 348, regulations were laid down for the conduct of widows.[37] In Africa, we learn that at the end of the fourth century one of the tasks allotted to them was the preparation of catechumens for baptism, especially in country districts (*Statuta eccl. antiqua* 12).

Even so, the clergy seem to have been constantly on the look-out for possible encroachments on their privileges. The widows, even if learned, were not to baptize nor to teach men, we are told.[38] At the end of the fifth century Pope Gelasius forbade their veiling and benediction.[39] In the last resort, the Church was not prepared to leave them very much more than constant prayer and continuous charity on her behalf in return for a small stipend.[40] The layman of mature years who sought ordination faced an almost interminable *cursus honorum* of ecclesiastical offices before he attained the presbyterate.[41]

Even the rather mundane work of administering church finances and property was tending to become, outside of Africa, the preserve of clerics. In the mid-fourth century, the Council of Antioch (Canon 25) had advised bishops not to use their clergy for such purposes, but to employ their lay friends and relatives. In 451, however, the Council of Chalcedon decided that the office of examiner of church accounts should be held by a cleric,[42] and three years later, Pope Leo saw reason for requesting the Emperor Marcian not to allow civil judges 'in a manner without precedent' to audit the accounts of 'the oeconomos of the church of Constantinople'. He claimed that these should be examined by the bishop alone.[43] In the sixth century, it seems to have been the usual practice for the landed property of the great sees to be administered by the deacons as well as by lay officials.[44] A Roman council held in July 595 laid down that the Bishop of Rome should have no lay servants to wait on him and Pope Gregory replaced his lay attendants by clergy and monks.[45]

Some shreds of active lay participation in the internal life of the Church, however, persisted. The laity, in dire need, might still baptize.[46] They never lost the right of electing their bishop, and of approving, at least in theory, his clergy. The election of Caecilian at Carthage in 312, for instance, was said to have been by 'the voting of the entire populace', and the new bishop appealed to the 'whole body of the citizens' for their support against the charges brought against him by the Donatists.[47] Socrates's account of the synodical letter of Nicaea included the proviso that the people (subject to ratification by the Bishop of Alexandria) should elect successors to any Catholic or Melitian cleric who should die.[48] In November 374, on a celebrated occasion, Ambrose was acclaimed bishop by the thronging crowd in the cathedral of Milan, and though he was a layman at the time, this example of *vox populi, vox Dei* was adjudged binding. Both he and the cathedral clergy accepted it. On a lower plane, Jerome records that when he was ordained priest at Antioch by Bishop Vitalis, the congregation called out three times, 'He is worthy'.[49] By the same token, the Canons of the African Church laid down the need for the assent of the laity before a bishop proceeded to ordain a priest.[50] They could also object to the transfer of their bishop to another see,[51] and bring pressure on individuals such as Augustine[52] himself, or his rich friend Pinianus, to accept ordination in a particular church.[53] We hear, too, of laymen being present at church councils. At the beginning of the fourth century, the Council of Elvira was held in the presence of laymen as well as clergy,[54] and at that of Tarraco in 516[55] it was laid down that letters of summons to Councils should be sent to some laymen as well as clergy. At Riez in Gaul in 469, the Council met 'in the presence of judges and councillors and private citizens',[56] while even at Rome, Gelasius's council of 495 specifically records that members of the lay nobility were there also.[57] But, even so, the Church has moved a long way since the time when Cyprian could assert as a matter of principle that important issues, such as whether the lapsed during persecution should be readmitted to the Church, must be decided only 'with the consent of the whole people'.[58]

There was, however, one important exception to the progressive decline in the status of the laity in the Church, namely the *seniores* in North Africa. Deservedly, they have attracted the attention of scholars.[59] First, these lay representatives of the Christian congregation formed an integral part of the organization of both the Donatist and Catholic churches in North Africa in the fourth and early fifth centuries. Secondly, they are clearly a survival of lay control derived from a much earlier period. There is plenty of evidence for their existence from both texts and inscriptions. They are the *fideles seniores* (faithful elders) of Optatus, *De Schismate* 1.17, the *seniores plebis* (elders of the common people) of the *Gesta apud Zenophilum* (AD 320), the *seniores christiani populi* (elders of the Christian people) of the *Acta Purgationis Felicis*

(AD 314–315), and the *seniores laicorum* (elders of the lay folk) of the *Codex canonum Africae ecclesiae* (Canon 91). From the last mentioned, we learn that in Catholic churches, they took precedence over the *clerici*, coming immediately after the deacons. Augustine mentions their existence at Hippo (*Letter* 78), and an inscription (*CIL* VIII.17414) records a Christian 'senator' who seems to have functioned twice as a representative of the people. In the Donatist Church, the crisis involving the Primate, Primian of Carthage, in 392–393 was directly due to the complaints made against him by the *seniores* of the Donatist congregation.

Their functions were both administrative and disciplinary. Among the former duties, they co-operated with the bishop in administering and safeguarding church property. For instance, when in 311 Mensurius, Primate of Carthage, departed from his see to justify the conduct of a member of his clergy to Maxentius in Rome, the movable wealth of the Church was left under the guardianship of the *seniores* (who promptly abused Mensurius's trust!).[60] In the same period, the *seniores* of Cirta in Numidia and Apthunga in Byzacena seem to have formed an administrative council for their churches. In 320, Purpurius of Limata addresses a letter to the '*clericis et senioribus*' of Cirta.[61] Apart from these duties were others of a judicial and disciplinary character, which allowed the *seniores* a check even on the conduct of their bishop. In the inquiry concerning the alleged *traditio* (surrender of sacred books and vessels) of Felix of Apthunga the *seniores* of 'the Christian people' engage an advocate to open their case against Felix.[62] In 392 Primian, the Donatist Primate, restored a group of local schismatics and some notorious evil-doers to communion. The *seniores* at once protested, and failing to persuade Primian they went on to hold a council and decided to support the claims of a rival candidate for the see. They then drew up a document which they circulated to the Donatist episcopate as a whole, outlining their bishop's misdeeds, and demanding the summoning of a formal council to investigate their charges.[63] We also hear of the *seniores* of Musti associated with a presbyter accusing their bishop before the Proconsul in 395.[64] A few years later, a similar affair, though on a lesser scale, involved the Catholic church at Nova Germanica in Numidia. Here, too, the *seniores* brought a complaint against their bishop, which was examined by a council presided over by the Bishop of Carthage. In this case, the Council decided that episcopal arbitrators should be appointed to hear both sides and that the (Catholic) Primate of Numidia should be informed of the results.[65]

These were interesting cases, because they show that the element of lay control in the Church in Africa was still remarkably strong. It was a vigorous survival long after it had ceased in other parts of the West. Ambrose, for instance, refers to a time in the distant past when *seniores* had existed in the Church in Italy,[66] and there is no evidence for *seniores* in other provinces at this period. At the same time, the office in Africa is evidently a traditional one connected with church discipline, as Tertullian refers to *seniores*, who do not seem to be presbyters, empowered to excommunicate unworthy members of the Christian community (*Apology* 39.4).

No entirely satisfactory explanation has been given either for the origins or the survival of this office. The analogy of the local headmen, the *seniores* who ruled African native villages, has been mentioned,[67] but direct influence of this institution on that of the Church would be surprising, in view of the purely urban origins of the latter. Caron, the most recent critic, has seen the *seniores* as the lineal descendants of the plenary assemblies of members of the Church, such as met in Apostolic times (cf. Acts 1.15). When such assemblies became unwieldy, the *seniores* would naturally emerge as representatives of the people as a whole. There is something to be said for this view, in particular as Cyprian stated on several occasions that there were matters in the Church which must be discussed by the whole people, *apud plebem universam* (*Letter* 16.4). The phrase used to describe the *seniores* as '*seniores ex plebe*' (elders chosen from among the common people) is a further reason for accepting the representative character of the office. Caron also takes its origin back to the very beginnings of Christianity. This, too, is useful, for it seems evident that many of the peculiar features of the organization of the African Church may be explicable by reference to primitive Christian, or perhaps Judaeo-Christian, influences.

Various facts point in this direction. For instance, the 'sacerdotalism' of the African bishop has long been attributed to an Old Testament attitude towards priesthood, which would account for the bishop (or priest) being regarded as subject to the same taboos of purity as the Levite.[68] It has also been recognized that the ethical code imposed by the rigorist element in the African Church, bore a striking resemblance to the Jewish *halaka* of the day. Detailed comparisons can be made between Tertullian's prescriptions for avoiding contact with pagan society, contained in the *De Idololatria*, and those to be found in the Jewish *Aboda Zara* of the same date.[69] Christians and Jews were apparently buried side by side in the cemetery of Q'mart at Carthage,[70] and now it has been pointed out that the Western text of the Bible, in use in North Africa, may have been influenced by the Judaeo-Christian *Gospel of Thomas*.[71] Thus, it is reasonable to look for parallels to the *seniores* further afield than Africa, perhaps in the organization of the most primitive Church in Palestine. It may be worth recalling that at Qumran the highest direction of the Sect of the Dead Sea Scrolls lay in the hands of a council of three priests and twelve laymen. These decided administrative and disciplinary matters.[72] If we are confronted by a similar oligarchy of lay and priestly officers in the churches in North Africa, it may be that the explanation must be sought in a Jewish or Judaeo-Christian environment out of which the North African Church developed.

Another lay office which appears to have been purely Western is that of defender of the Church (*defensor ecclesiae*). In the African Church these *defensores* are mentioned twice in the *Codex canonum*. The Emperors are requested by African Catholics c. 400 to order their establishment. They were to be lawyers (*scholastici*) and their duties were to be first, to act with the bishops to prevent oppression of the poor by the rich,[73] and secondly, to act as advocates for the Church in lawsuits in which the interests of the Church were involved.[74] We do not know how effective they were, and they do not seem to have survived the Vandal conquest.

In the Roman Church, however, the *defensor* was to have a long career as lay supervisor of the enormous patrimony of St Peter. By the end of the fifth century this included not only land in Italy, but great estates in Sicily, North Africa, Dalmatia, Corsica and Sardinia.[75] Thus in the pontificate of Gelasius (492–496) we find the *defensor* Faustinus associated with the archdeacon Justinus in the management of church property.[76] Their duties included the supervision of the settlers on the land (*coloni*), acting as assessors in the bishops' courts, and above all, administering the poor relief provided by the papal bounty.[77] Lay *defensores* continued to be employed in the sixth century until Gregory the Great replaced them by ecclesiastics as part of his general policy of clericalization.[78]

It seems, therefore, evident that a real change, to the detriment of the laity, came over the organization of the Church after the conversion of Constantine. Not very much remained of the 'royal priesthood' shared by all members of the People of God of the first three centuries. Only among the Donatists of North Africa do we find explicit solidarity between the clergy and people. There, the people 'shared in battle against the Devil', participating in the suffering of the righteous which was the mark of the true Church from eternity to eternity.[79] But this was a theology of a bygone age. Elsewhere, unity of Church and world emphasized the Sacraments and their impersonal dispensers as the guarantors of salvation.[80] The elevation of the priesthood to the status it was to hold throughout the Middle Ages was the natural consequence.

III · The Layman in the Life and Thought of the Church

To consider the layman, however, in terms of church worship and organization alone would give a false impression of his influence in the life of the Church during the Patristic period. The fourth and fifth centuries saw the completion of the Christianization of the Mediterranean, and its spread beyond the bounds of the Roman Empire. From now on, except for the interlude under Julian 361–363, the Emperor was a Christian, and Christianity was the religion of the Roman Empire. The Church received valuable tax remissions and other privileges,[81] Christians were often favoured in the Imperial service, and the inhabitants of townships could sometimes invoke their devotion to Christianity as a means of winning Imperial favour.[82] The Emperors believed, like their pagan predecessors, that material prosperity depended on the observance of right religion, and that right religion was practised by the orthodox representatives of the Church.

In this new situation, the laity, though deprived of their former powers in the inner life of the Church, found scope as its advocates and benefactors. The closeness of the relationship between Church and State required the skilled diplomacy of Christian administrators, and the influence of these powerful lay officials on church affairs could be very great. The Church Council was modelled on the Senate, and its president was the Emperor (as at Antioch in 341 or Milan in 355), or his delegate who would be a senior official. At the same time, the persistence of the classical tradition in education had the effect of training Christian laymen to think in the philosophical terms in which the doctrine of the Church was being expressed. So long as that tradition survived the laity produced theologians every whit as instructed as the clergy themselves. And always present were the traditions associated with eschatology and martyrdom which formed the background to the monastic and other movements of lay asceticism.

The Church of the Roman Empire

Let us first take some examples of the influence exercised by the educated laity in important ecclesiastical issues. Senior officials had become notorious for their intervention in church affairs by the reign of Constantius II,[83] and they played a large part in the perennial struggle for power between the three great sees of the East, Constantinople, Antioch and Alexandria, from 381–451.[84] Thus, the eunuch Eutropius was among those responsible for the choice of John Chrysostom as Patriarch of Constantinople in 398. In the next generation, Counts Candidian, John and Irenaeus were active behind the scenes at the Council of Ephesus in 431. For his part, Cyril of Alexandria spent enormous sums in bribing important officials, such as the Chamberlain Chrysoretus,[85] whose support against Nestorius he considered essential. Another Chamberlain, Chrysaphius, was patron of Eutyches in 449. In the West, we find Count Marcellinus, a friend of St Augustine, presiding over the conference at Carthage in May 411, to decide whether the Donatists or Catholics constituted the 'Catholic Church' in Africa. These men acted as representatives of the Emperor, a reminder that the guiding hand in church affairs was his.

More beneficial, but less widely known, was the missionary influence exercised by Christian merchants trading beyond the frontiers of the Empire, or by Christian captives in barbarian hands. The story of the conversion of the kingdom of Axum in northern Ethiopia is an astounding one. We are told, admittedly a century after the event,[86] how Frumentius and his brother Edesius were captured by the 'Indians' on the Red Sea coast, and that having risen high in the service of their king, began their work of evangelization about the year 320 (or even earlier). They were then helped by Christian merchants trading in Ethiopia; they set up churches, and finally returned to Alexandria with the story of their doings. At this point Frumentius was ordained by Athanasius and appointed bishop, but all the spadework had been done by him and his helpers as laymen. Much the same chain of events was taking place at this time in the Black Sea kingdom of Iberia. Here, too, the chosen instrument was originally a Christian captive called Nina, who herself preached the gospel, and caused churches to be built before the arrival of a bishop and consecrated clergy.[87] A century later, the same combination of a Christian captive from a Roman province and Roman merchants was to bring about the conversion of Ireland by St Patrick. In Justinian's reign Longinus and his companions travelled far up the Nile to plant Christianity in the hitherto pagan kingdom of Merowe. They even got as far as the neighbourhood of Khartoum.

Within the Empire itself, lay influence and example had an enormous effect in promoting a real Christianization of values among the population as a whole. Imperial policy sought to secure religious uniformity as needful for the survival of the Empire, without, however, showing overmuch concern for the application of Christian standards of conduct. If Constantine facilitated the emancipation of slaves,[88] prohibited gladiatorial shows[89] and the infliction of branding in the face,[90] other equally cruel punishments were retained by him and his successors.[91] Even regarding so vital a subject as marriage, the Church was unable to enforce its views on the Emperor and his advisers. Marriage was and remained a civil contract, dissoluble by either party on certain accepted grounds, throughout the period covered by this chapter.[92] In these circumstances, Christianity in its deeper meaning was largely a matter of home influence. This is confirmed by an interesting remark made by the pagan philosopher, Libanius, *c.* 390, probably concerning Antioch. He is speaking of efforts being made by a friend to win back support for the traditional rites of paganism. 'When men are out of doors, they listen to your plea for the only right course, and they come to the altars. But when a man gets home, his wife and her tears and the night plead otherwise, and draw him away from the altars.'[93] This statement rings true, and is borne out by what we know of the part played by the Christian womenfolk in the early lives of Ambrose, Augustine, John Chrysostom and Basil of Caesarea. Each of these owed much to a sincerely Christian mother or sister.

It was in the example of ordinary daily life that the Christian layman showed himself to such advantage over his pagan contemporary. The Emperor Julian (d. 363), one of the best observers of social conditions of his time, contrasted the apathy of the pagan priesthood in Asia Minor and their lack of interest in the religious education of their families, with the devotion of the Christians to works of charity. 'The Hellenic religion', he wrote to the high-priest of Galatia in 362, 'does not prosper as I desire.... Why do we not observe that it is their benevolence towards strangers, their care of the graves of the dead, and the pretended holiness of their lives, that have done most to increase atheism (Christianity)?'[94] There were no pagan Fabiolas,[95] founders of hospitals for the sick in Rome. It is not surprising, perhaps, that when in 365 a great earthquake struck Cyrene, the capital of the province of the same name, the pagan shrines were not rebuilt. The churches were.[96] By the end of the century 'even the Egyptian Serapis' had become a Christian.[97]

Christian example extended to Christian giving. Here, the Church benefited from the example of Constantine. In the very year of the Edict of Milan, the Emperor had handed over the Lateran Palace, which belonged to his wife Fausta, to the Bishop of Rome, together with a wealth of gold and silver.[98] From then on, his gifts to that see were on a magnificent scale. They included two great new basilicas, those of St Peter and St Paul, with extensive endowments which brought in respectively 3,710 and 4,070 *solidi* a year.[99] In the East he rebuilt the cathedral of Nicomedia, destroyed during the Great Persecution in 303; he built the Golden Church at Antioch, and a vast new basilica on the supposed site of the Holy Sepulchre at Jerusalem.[100] His example was widely followed. The prefect Rufinus, whose reputation Claudian has blackened for posterity, had an enormous church built in his villa at Drus (The Oak) near Chalcedon, *c.* 395.[101] The pilgrim Etheria records having seen a church near Jerusalem which had been built by a tribune.[102] In North Africa, the chapel in honour of St Salsa at Tipasa (west of Algiers) was embellished during the fifth century by a layman named Potentius,[103] and in Donatist Numidia three tribes are recorded as having combined to build a church in the village of Henchir Zerdan.[104] Very rich and very poor united in these services to the Church.

All this time legacies and gifts were flowing in. Since 321 it had been legal to bequeath property to the Church,[105] and advantage was freely taken of this. In addition, the Church transformed the pagan custom of leaving money for sacrifices for the dead into a demand on the laity to bequeath a certain part of their incomes to the Church.[106] This sum was regarded both as an insurance against the flames of hell,[107] and more constructively as a contribution towards the relief of the poor. It is interesting that St Basil, who was the first churchman to link the monastic vocation to a system of ordered social reform, should have been the first to define the scope of this Christian duty among the laity. He urged that a fixed sum, amounting even to as much as half the value of an estate, should be set aside for the benefit of the soul, before the remainder of the estate was divided among its heirs.[108] His friend, Gregory of Nazianze,[109] was equally emphatic. 'We must share our wealth with Christ, so that it may be sanctified, and shared with the poor.' One finds the same advice to rich laity in Ambrose,[110] Augustine,[111] and Salvian of Marseille[112] (*c.* 440). Though the Roman bishops of the late fourth century were stigmatized for their active legacy-hunting,[113] it was sometimes a question of clergy dissuading pious laity from impoverishing their children by over-generous gifts to the Church. Augustine records a case in which a rich lady in a fit of pique had given a whole fortune away to two monks.[114] Almost invariably Catholic families left money or property to the Church.[115] Even the Donatist Church in Africa, which drew its support for the most part from the poor, shared in legacies,[116] while the Catholics were enriched by the proceeds of the enormous estates of Melania and Pinianus. Other rich Christians, like Paulinus of Nola, did likewise for their own churches. The foundations of the immense wealth of the medieval Church were laid in the century after the conversion of Constantine.

These are not isolated instances of Christian piety. In this Indian summer of the Ancient World,[117] when standards of education still remained high and the framework of the city-state held together, theology was the ruling passion of the Christian provincial. It was not only in Constantinople, the capital of the Empire, that abstruse points of doctrine were argued in bazaars and market-places. There, to be sure, the laity seem to have thought of little else. 'If in this city', states Gregory of Nazianze in 379, 'you ask anyone for change, he will discuss with you whether the Son is begotten or unbegotten. If you ask about the quality of the bread, you will receive the answer that the "Father is greater, the Son less". If you suggest that a bath is desirable, you will be told that "there was nothing before the Son was created".'[118] What Arianism was to the inhabitants of Constantinople, Modalism was to the people of Ephesus. In 431 this helped Cyril of Alexandria on the way to his victory over Nestorius. A true politician, Cyril knew the value of public relations, and on the morrow of the Council he wrote a long letter to his friends in Alexandria describing how 'from morning until nightfall' crowds demonstrated in the streets of Ephesus in favour of his doctrine. The town was illumined and Cyril's supporters were fêted.[119] Here, too, the abstruse formula worked out by the professionals merely put into the language of Platonist theology the aspirations of the mass of the laity of Egypt and Asia Minor.

In the West, at Rome, we find Roman ladies petitioning Constantius for the restoration of Pope Liberius in 357,[120] and Roman mobs engaged in bitter struggle over his succession.[121] A generation later, in Africa and later in Italy, the early career of Augustine gives ample evidence for the passionate interest in theology which existed among his intellectual contemporaries. We can see him at the age of 18 or 19 discussing with his friends at the university of Carthage the merits of Manichaeism as a more rational and authentic form of Christianity.[122]

We see him fourteen years later, in 387, still a layman, urging the case for Catholic Christianity with his friends and pupils in the villa at Cassiciacum.[123] Four or five years later, crowds gather in the baths of Sossius at Hippo to hear him debate in public against the local Manichaean champion Fortunatus.[124] In his later years Augustine used the appeal of direct propaganda to the Donatist laity in his efforts to overthrow their Church. We hear, even, that the questions of free-will and grace mooted in Pelagianism were debated 'in synagogues and marketplaces' in Italy and Africa.[125] It is the same story of popular religious activity and enthusiasm in the Greek and Latin worlds of this period.

In North Africa the bitterness of the religious conflict throws some unexpected light on the part the laity was playing in the daily life of their churches. We have mentioned St Augustine, but we find that Donatist lay discussion groups existed in rivalry to him at Hippo[126] and in other North African towns. These laymen knew the story of their Church and could answer their great antagonist when it came to debate.[127] One of these laymen, Cresconius the grammarian from somewhere in Proconsular Africa, has left a record of his views, which Augustine was obliged to answer in four longish books written in 405–406.[128] Cresconius was an ordinary well-read layman who aspired no higher in his profession than primary schoolteacher. He was not a rhetorician, and he was not a philosopher. Nor had he any formal training in theology. Yet when Augustine's first book against Petilian of Constantine came into his hands about the year 405 he had no qualms about setting to and answering it. He performed commendably enough. He knows that his Church is the heir to that of Cyprian in its views on baptism and the relationship between Church and society (*Contra Cresconium* II.31, 39). He can defend the legitimacy of schism; he can appeal to the right of religious toleration for minorities on the legitimate ground that truth develops from minority opinion,[129] and he can drive his argument home with an apt text from Scripture. He makes a classic definition of schism as opposed to heresy.[130] At the same time, his work is a curious mixture of biblical fundamentalism and conventional rhetorical quibble. On the one hand, he takes his opponents to task for calling the Donatists 'Donatistae' instead of 'Donatianae';[131] on the other, he defends Petilian's failure (temporary, as it proved) to reply directly to Augustine's work by citing the example of Ezekiel who declared that Israelites should speak only to Israelites,[132] and he upbraids Augustine for using pagan metaphors in Christian religious writing.[133]

This latter point illustrates the ever-present tension between the traditional pagan-inspired education and the new Christian knowledge and values. Cresconius evidently had immersed himself in the latter without ridding himself of the influence of the former. Indeed, in the African Church neither Cyprian nor his Donatist successors ever quoted pagan works, even if they wrote in faultless Latin. This African layman was also well informed about other events in the Christian world. It is he who quotes the Council of Serdica against Augustine to show that the Donatists were in fact in communion with Churches outside Africa (*Contra Cresconium* III.34, 38), and he indicates that Augustine's Manichaean background, embroidered with some additional details, was common knowledge among the Donatist laity.[134] Altogether, Cresconius testifies to the existence of a remarkably high standard of instruction and alertness among the Donatists at the turn of the fifth century.

Cresconius is represented as an ordinary, instructed layman.[135] If one accepts this description, it is not difficult to understand how it was possible for laymen to gain a degree of theological knowledge which enabled some to make significant and far-reaching contributions to Christian thought. In this connection the all-important factor was the Christian attitude towards classical education. The division between the predominant, orthodox Greco-Latin Christians who, with some heart-searchings and reservations, favoured its retention, and the native, provincial Christians in Egypt and Syria, and the heirs to the Judaeo-Christian tradition in North Africa, who opposed it, was of vital significance. The former accepted the relevance of the present world and sought to Christianize the classical tradition; the latter, their eyes fixed firmly on the Day of Judgment and the expectations of Christ's Church at that time, rejected both the world and its learning. Thus the third-century *Didascalia Apostolorum* which for a long time enjoyed considerable influence in the Syriac-speaking Church states bluntly, 'Have nothing to do with pagan books.'[136] The Bible provided both for supernatural and cultural needs. The rest came from the devil. The result of this outlook was schools, like that of Nisibis, on the Persian side of the Romano-Persian frontier, whose curriculum was founded entirely on the Christian sacred writings, and whose aim was the propagation of the Christian ascetic ideal unalloyed by classical influences.

The ascetic tradition was destined to triumph within the Roman frontiers as well. But, up to the fall of Rome in 410, loyalty to the classical cultural tradition was just strong enough to provide a medium through which men educated in it could contribute to Christian thought

The Church of the Roman Empire

without a sense of incongruity. After that, consciousness of a real decline from the standards of the past induced a fatalistic acceptance of the view that the end of the world was approaching, and that the world therefore should be renounced. In this atmosphere both classical culture and a spirit of inquiry into the secrets of the universe were regarded as irrelevant.

But until the catastrophes of the early fifth century a different spirit, more hospitable to educated lay participation in theological questions, prevailed. Attempts made to adapt the old wine of the classics directly to the new bottles of the Christian Scriptures were indeed short-lived failures. The two Apollinarii, father and son (*flor.* 350-370), for instance, do not appear to have progressed very far in their effort to turn the Pentateuch into heroic verse, when in 362 Julian forbade Christians to teach the pagan classics.[137] The pious Paula, Jerome's friend, found few followers to chant the psalms in Hebrew;[138] but, in contrast, Prudentius (348-410) realized that Christian ideas could easily be expressed in classical metres, and the former governor of the province of Tarragona, a layman, became the first great poet of the Christian Church. He demonstrated the feasibility of using the classical heritage as a vehicle for conveying the ennobling truths of Christianity.

Thus, the last part of the fourth century became the great age of the lay theologian in the early Church. Synesius, before he was induced to become Bishop of Ptolemais in 409, and Marius Victorinus are examples of laymen whose background of Neo-Platonism was of vital importance. Both men underwent a long period of hesitancy and sympathetic inquiry before accepting Christianity. Synesius had prayed in the churches of Constantinople and married a Christian,[139] while still nominally a pagan. Victorinus had had a long friendship with the Christian priest Simplicianus.[140] Both seem to have regarded Christianity as a fulfilment of Platonism, assuring to the believer, however, a salvation from sin which Plato could not give. Victorinus was the founder of the tradition of Christian Platonism in the West, and his influence on Augustine was of prime importance. The application of Neo-Platonist categories to the interpretation of Scripture in the West enabled the Church to win back the allegiance of intellectuals, such as Augustine, who otherwise would have preferred Manichaeism.[141]

Another layman who made an important, but quite different, contribution to scriptural exegesis in the West was Tyconius (*flor.* 380). Tyconius was not a Platonist; indeed, he was a Donatist from Proconsular Africa, and Greek influence was entirely absent from his work.[142] He seems to have set to work with the characteristic African concern for the doctrine of the Church and little else in mind. Granted the truth of the prophecy of Isa. 53.10–12, that Christ and his Church formed one whole, how could the 'immense forest of prophecy' which occupied most of the Old Testament be interpreted to demonstrate this? Tyconius's answer was his *Liber Septem Regularum*, the Seven Rules of Interpretation, by which all prophecies could be referred in some way to Christ or his Church. He used immense ingenuity to arrive at his results, including a fantastic numerology, by which almost any number mentioned in Scripture could mean any other, but his work (thanks to Augustine's recommendation) remained a textbook of exegesis in the Western Church throughout the early Middle Ages.[143]

Important, too, was his contribution to the philosophy of history accepted in the Western Church. This was the direct result of his study of Scripture and of his preoccupation with the doctrine of the Church. Tyconius had taught in three of his Rules that humanity was organized under two great institutions, the institution of Christ which was the Church, and the institution of the world which was ruled by the devil. Like the Jewish writers of three centuries before,[144] and like his younger contemporary Petilian of Constantine,[145] Tyconius demonstrated how the Bible told the story of two societies, that of Cain and that of Abel, the lust for power contrasted with righteous suffering. These societies were eternal and for ever in conflict. They were worldwide and not local, membership of each being determined by the will of the individual. 'One aimed at serving Christ, the other at serving the world. The one desires to dominate in this world, the other flees from this world. Each labours in common, the one towards its own damnation, the other towards salvation.'[146] The two societies were two Churches. In Tyconius's mind, the righteous would include the African Donatists, but more besides. Though his more strait-laced colleagues were shocked at the idea of the existence of righteousness among those who were not in communion with them, and he was censured,[147] he did not leave the Donatist communion; in spite of this Augustine valued his work greatly.[148] He became one of the major formative influences in Augustine's doctrine of grace; and his concept of the Two Cities, and hence his thought, that of a layman inspired by the African Bible, contributed to the development both of Western theology and Western medieval political ideas.

Two other lay theologians, both Westerners, should be noted here, namely Ambrosiaster and Pelagius.

Of the former very little is known, though much has been speculated. That he was a layman seems certain, and the most convincing evidence points to his identification with the Roman official of consular rank Hilarius Hilarianus (*flor.* 370–410).[149] In any event, he was a widely read and widely travelled individual, one who has a hearty contempt for 'the boastfulness of the Roman deacons', as he put it,[150] and whose attitude towards the internal organization of the Church was that of a candid critic and observer. However, his surviving works, the *Commentaries* on the Pauline Epistles and the *One Hundred and Twenty-seven Questions on the Old and New Testaments*, tell a story of profound meditation on Scripture. Like Tyconius, he was a biblicist, but unlike him was not the slave to one aspect of Christian doctrine alone. His service was to set the foundations for a study of St Paul which did not run counter to human justice and reason. Utterly opposed both to Manichaeism and to Judaism, he emphasized personal responsibility and freedom from legalistic interpretations of Christianity. One recognizes a kindred spirit in another layman, Helvidius (*flor.* 380–390), who laughed at the idea of the superiority of the celibate over the married man, and had modern views about the reality of Jesus' home circle.[151] It is not surprising that one of those whom Ambrosiaster influenced was a younger contemporary named Pelagius.[152]

It would be out of place to discuss Pelagius's theology in any detail.[153] From the point of view of the laity in the Church his importance is twofold. First, his career demonstrates the vital part which the lay teacher was still playing in spreading the Christian message in the West at this time. Secondly, the advice which he gave to his hearers appealed to that sense of individual responsibility and self-reliance on which civilized society must ultimately be built. Pelagius regarded Christianity as his profession in the world and not as an escape from the world. 'I want you to be a Christian, not to be called monk, and that you possess yourself of virtue for its own worth, rather than a foreign name', he writes to one correspondent.[154] His closest friends, such as Celestius, his disciples, like James and Timasius,[155] were laymen, and his correspondents, like Celantia, Demetrias, Marcella and Claudia, lay aristocrats of the type who sat at the feet of his rival and opponent, Jerome.[156] At times, he places special emphasis on a text because he sees it has particular application to the laity. His appeal was directed above all to the younger members of the noble Roman houses who might be expected to become the Empire's leaders in the early years of the fifth century.[157]

His message was well adjusted to his hearers. Like Ambrosiaster, he saw that reason and equity lay at the core of the Divine Providence, that God was no respecter of persons, and that he did not ask the impossible of any man.[158] The same Providence, he pointed out, enforced constraints on man and nature alike, and these were constraints intelligible to the human mind. His view of human knowledge was the opposite therefore of that of the Christian ascetic who denounced the search after the secrets of nature as irrelevant to salvation. On the contrary, faith, taught Pelagius, was not enough to save a man.[159] It must be reinforced by active good works and good conduct. A man's will-power, aided by grace, which, however, could be won by good inclinations and supported by an active charity, would secure him a pure life, free not from temptation, but ultimately from sin.

It was an optimistic theology, blending a theory of Christian morality with active social reform directed against the excessive riches of the Roman senatorial class.[160] It would have been well-fitted to a vigorous society willing and capable of setting its house in order. But this was not the society of the last century of the Western Empire.

Ambrosiaster and Pelagius each had his devoted following among the Roman laity. From Pelagius's opponents, Augustine and Jerome, we catch sight of other aristocratic laymen more world-renouncing perhaps, but equally at home with theological issues. It was in answer to questions put to him by Flavius Marcellinus, the high official who presided over the conference between the Donatists and Catholics at Carthage in May 411, that Augustine started to write the *De Civitate Dei* ('The City of God'),[161] and his first two books on the subject of Sin and Free-will[162] in 412. From Jerome's circle we have a letter from a Roman noble named Oceanus, who had interested himself both in the problem of Origenism[163] and later in the Pelagian controversy.[164] Pammachius, a mutual friend of Augustine and Jerome, forwarded to the latter Jovinian's criticism of the grosser aspects of the ascetic's life,[165] which called forth the most scurrilous of all Jerome's tracts, the *Adversus Jovinianum*. At the same time, he so impressed the old man that he was described as 'thoroughly learned in the law of the Lord' and capable of instructing others[166]—no mean compliment from one so jealous of his scholarship as Jerome.

Thus, the turn of the fifth century sees some extraordinarily fruitful work in the Church carried out by educated Christian laymen. The Church was enriched intellectually and materially by their efforts, and the clergy were forced to define their terms in response to the pressure of their interest and arguments. Why did this movement fail to last? Why had Europe to wait for a thousand years before the lay theologian reappeared? No single answer can be given. A number of factors combined to prevent the continuation of intelligent lay interest in theology. It depended, as we have seen, on the existence of a comparatively large and ultimately optimistic educated class of provincials. This in turn depended on the continuance of security and stability in the Roman Empire in which classical education might flourish. In the West this did not happen. The massive invasion of Gaul in 406-407 by Franks, Vandals, Alamans and Goths, followed by the sack of Rome by Alaric in 410, destroyed for ever the confidence of the Romanized middle classes in the Western Empire. As Marrou points out,[167] the invasions resulted in a complete breakdown of Roman life, and the disappearance of the old schools where the classical traditions had been preserved. It seems fairly certain that in Gaul, for instance, the generation that came after Ausonius, the Christian Gallic poet who had been tutor to the Emperor Gratian (375-383), was the last to be familiar with the normal system of classical education. For about seventy years after this, until about 470, the torch is kept alive by individual tutors attached to noble Gallo-Roman families, like that of Sidonius Apollinaris (*flor.* 460), and an active interest in theology is maintained among the laity.[168] After that, the old culture fades out. In the sixth century the only education was the ascetic religious education given by the Church. 'Alas, for our age,' writes Gregory of Tours, in 576, 'the study of literature has perished among us, and the man is no longer to be found who can commit to writing the events of the time.'[169]

In Africa and Italy, the process was more drawn out. The Italian kingdom of Theodoric the Ostrogoth produced lay Christian philosophers, such as Boethius (executed 523) and Cassiodorus (d. 584), but there, too, the days of the secular school, and with it of the lay theologian, were numbered. In Africa the classics scarcely survived the 'Vandal peace'.

Material calamities brought their psychological repercussions. The humane, balanced approach to theology was the product of a classical background, but it had little attraction to men and women who believed that the Last Days were at hand. With each successive crisis the certainty of this dread event took deeper hold. From Salvian (*flor.* 430-440) onwards, the West has its fill of prophets of doom. At such a time, 'the same mouth', said Pope Gregory, 'could not sing the praises of Jupiter and praises of Jesus Christ.'[170] It was a grave scandal for bishops to engage in human sciences, he tells Desiderius of Vienne, who was lecturing in literature.[171] To the Christian layman little now remained but the alternatives of ordination or the ascetic life of the monastery.

This was already taking place during the latter half of the fourth century. The laymen who have left their mark on the correspondence of Jerome and Augustine were nearly all ascetics at heart. Increasing distaste for the formal, bourgeois Christianity represented by Jerome's parents or the poet Ausonius was combined with deepening pessimism over the future of the world in which they were living. Christian as well as pagan society in Rome was empty and uninspiring. Jerome could write to Eustochium, c. 382, 'I would not have you consort with matrons. I would not have you approach the houses of nobles. I would not have you see what in contempt you have renounced in order to remain a virgin.'[172] Ammianus Marcellinus, a pagan critic, was equally strong in his denunciation of the lives of the Senatorial nobility: 'the few houses', he says, 'that were formerly famed for devotion to serious disputes now teem with the sports of sluggish indolence, re-echoing to the sound of singing and tinkling of flutes and lyres.'[173]

In these circumstances the reactions of the serious-minded laity tended towards other-worldly asceticism. As early as 355, we hear of Ambrose's sister, Marcellina, solemnly taking the veil at the hands of Pope Liberius.[174] From Augustine[175] we learn of the enthusiasm which the story of Antony and his companions aroused among the more idealist of the Roman nobility. Among these was Marcella, at whose house on the Aventine Jerome and his pupils used to meet to study Hebrew and join in prayer. Her influence, backed by a remarkable knowledge of theological literature, contributed largely to the condemnation of Origenism by Pope Anastasius in 401.[176] It was from her circle that Jerome recruited his companions Paula and Eustochium to share in his self-imposed exile at Bethlehem in 385.

Aristocratic lay ascetism was not confined to Rome and Italy. In Spain, about 375, a rich nobleman, Priscillian, was converted by an Egyptian holy man to an extreme form of the ascetic life.[177] His following included the Christian poet Latronianus, clergy and wealthy women. Whatever strange practices, inherited from a surviving Gnostic legacy, they may have indulged in, this too was partly at least a revolt against the worldliness of an established ecclesiastical order. In 385 Priscillian and his companions paid for their views with their lives; but in the next century Priscillianism was a clandestine religious movement

The Church of the Roman Empire

which dominated Galicia in north-west Spain.[178] In Africa, too, the success of Manichaeism, with its demands for a world-renouncing life, on young intellectuals of Augustine's generation, and Augustine's own preference for monasticism until he was persuaded to accept ordination,[179] are further examples of the tendency of laymen in the West to neglect their responsibilities to society, and ultimately the culture to which they owed their intellectual being, for the benefit of their own souls. 'Après moi le déluge' could have been said by Paulinus of Nola or Priscillian as well as by Louis XV.

In the West, asceticism was a symptom of a declining culture. In the East it was part of a mass movement. In both, it was a protest against Greco-Roman society and some aspects of the Greco-Roman Church. In Egypt and Syria also it was the concern of laymen, closely allied to the rising regional and native cultures that had been emerging into new life towards the end of the third century. Antony, Hierakas, Pâkhom and Amoun were Copts. They thought in Coptic, and if they wrote, they wrote in Coptic.[180] Their flight to the deserts bordering the Nile valley may be interpreted as a revolt both against the still-predominant pagan Hellenistic culture and against social and economic injustice. Their religious outlook, however, contrasted with the progressive standardization of church services and orders which we have noted in the early part of this chapter. The monks of Egypt and Syria were reviving a much earlier tradition of Christianity, that of the prophet, wonder-worker and martyr. Their enemies were demonic powers both here and hereafter, and these they fought through the Holy Spirit. The Bible and the Holy Spirit replaced dogmatic Creed and Logos. The layman's church of the martyrs which had been the main victim of the alliance between Church and State in the East, returns in the form of the monk's cell. 'The monks', as Leclercq so justly writes, 'were the successors of the martyrs.'[181]

Contemporary accounts leave no doubt as to the enormous influence of biblical study on the lives and views of the monks. Antony, for instance, is reported to have told his monks that the Bible was enough for instruction, and that through its power they could overthrow the demon.[182] Hierakas, his contemporary, was said to know the whole Bible by heart in Coptic.[183] In 431 Schenute of Atripe could equate 'proclaiming the gospel' with 'becoming a monk'.[184] As a result, metaphysical speculation concerning the Divine Logos or the Person of Christ was entirely alien to their outlook. Christ was Saviour, or, more potently, Judge. Heretics were names of curse-laden individuals, whose doctrines, like those of Nestorius, were denounced but not understood.[185] Like the confessors of the previous era, the monk believed himself to be in direct contact with the Lord and received visions and revelations from him. The martyrs were his supreme object of veneration.

The monk was not anti-ecclesiastical, especially after Antony's friend Athanasius became patriarch. He was simply non-ecclesiastical, regarding orders as on a different footing from his own vocation. Monks such as Ammonius would mutilate themselves rather than accept ordination.[186] Others adopted passive resistance. The priesthood was either something too holy to be aspired to, or was not strictly relevant to monastic life. As Duchesne points out,[187] Antony could hardly have received communion from clergy during the twenty years he was in seclusion. Basil of Caesarea, indeed, confirms (*Letter* 93) the fact that the hermits in the Egyptian desert partook of the communion sacrament at their own hands. One feels that the local bishop and his eight priests who ministered to the 5,000 or so monks at Nitria every Saturday and Sunday must have been somewhat exotic.[188] Progress towards sanctity was a matter of individual progress under the direction of master ascetics who also were laymen.

This tradition of individual lay asceticism may be traced back to the prophetic, Spirit-guided movements which opposed the Great Church in the second and third centuries. In Asia Minor it is possible to establish a personal link in Eutychian, a Novatianist layman of Bithynia who was also a monk.[189] Here, one can see the process at work, whereby a lay monastic movement grew out of the individualistic religion of the puritan sect. Among the equally puritanical Egyptian Melitians monasticism was also characteristic.[190] In Africa, one may point to the Donatist Circumcellions who, though not monks in any orthodox sense, combined lives of the wandering ascetic with a fierce lust for martyrdom and hatred of social injustice.[191] In this, too, they shared the outlook of Schenute's followers in the White Monastery. In the same non-ecclesiastical, individualistic context we may place the numerous ascetic sects, such as Messalians, Adamites, Pastores, Gyrovagi, Stylitesi, etc., which infested Asia Minor and Syria in the fourth and fifth centuries.[192] These are the forerunners of the ascetic lay heresies of Europe in the Middle Ages.

The austerities of the Egyptian and Syrian monks resulted in one final contribution to lay religious practice from the West, that of the pilgrimage to the Holy Land and to the great monastic settlements in

The Church of the Roman Empire 81

Palestine and Egypt.[193] By 350 there was a regular pilgrims' route from Gaul to Palestine. Towards the end of the century one lady named Etheria travelled from Galicia in north-western Spain to Mount Sinai, Jerusalem, Antioch, and, 'having satisfied my curiosity', Constantinople. She has left us a careful account of her travels, and of the services and ceremonies in which she had taken part. One such, the description of the service at daybreak on Good Friday, may be quoted. 'And when they arrive before the Cross the daylight is already growing bright. There the passage from the Gospel is read where the Lord is brought before Pilate, with everything that is written concerning that which Pilate spake to the Lord or to the Jews.' Then after an address by the bishop, still before sunrise, 'they all go at once with fervour to Sion to pray at the column at which the Lord was scourged'. Later, 'a chair is placed for the bishop in Golgotha behind the Cross which is now standing: the bishop duly takes his seat, and a table covered with a linen cloth is placed before him. The deacons stand round the table and a silver casket is brought in which is the holy wood of the Cross.' The Cross is touched with the eyes and foreheads of the people passing by in procession (ed. McClure and Feltoe, pp. 73-4). We are here coming very near to the Middle Ages, and the popular piety of later times.

We conclude, therefore, on the note of subordination. The Roman Empire is Christian. The clergy are the chosen servants of God, the laity his people. Even so, not all laymen could be fitted into this logical pattern. What of the Emperor himself? In the East, Eusebius of Caesarea regarded Constantine as the representative of the Divine Logos on earth,[194] whose authority extended therefore to religion as well as to secular affairs. Throughout the period covered by this chapter, the patriarchs of the great sees in the East were in practice though not in theory dismissible by the Emperor and appointed by him. No Council would decree contrary to the Emperor's known will, though the Emperor did not himself presume to determine the formularies of the faith.[195] In the West, however, non-Platonic and more deeply influenced by Judaeo-Christian ideas, Church and State were always separate. 'The Emperor is within the Church, not above it' of Ambrose[196] repeated only a little more violently Donatus of Carthage's question, 'What has the Emperor to do with the Church?'[197] Behind these differences of outlook lay basic doctrinal differences between East and West which eventually would rend Christendom in twain.

The Emperor's position, however, safeguarded that of the laity as a whole. The Emperor was a layman himself, yet no one denied his sacred character, nor his right to legislate on ecclesiastical matters. In his person the 'royal priesthood' of the whole people of God had its representative, and thus the layman could never be completely ignored. In this period, as the Ancient World melts into the Middle Ages, the laity played an astonishingly active part in the intellectual and moral life of the Church. The succeeding age was to be less fruitful, but once the pessimism that had descended on the Western world in the fifth century had lifted, the way was open again to full lay discipleship. The Later Roman Empire provides an example of this for our own day.

NOTES

1. Tertullian, *De Exhortatione Castitatis* 7 (ed. Oehler, p. 744), and see also *De Baptismo* 6 (ed. Reifferscheid, *CSEL* XX, p. 206).
2. See Tertullian, *De Pudicitia* 22; *Apol.* 50.16.
3. Eusebius, *H.E.* (ed. Kirsopp Lake) V.2, 5, regarding the martyrs of Lyons.
4. Tertullian, *De Anima* 55 (*CSEL* XX, p. 389).
5. Hippolytus, *Elenchos* 9.12 (ed. Wendland). See G. L. Prestige, *Fathers and Heretics* (London, 1954), pp. 33 ff.
6. Origen, *Homil. in Jeremiah* 4.3 (ed. Klostermann, p. 25).
7. Cyprian, *Letter* 1.1 (ed. Hartel, *CSEL* III.2, p. 466).
8. Cyprian, *Letter* 27 (ed. Hartel). See also, *The Apostolic Constitutions* (ed. Robertson and Donaldson, 1870) VIII.23.
9. Cyprian, *Letters* 39.1 and 40.
10. For the situation in Rome *c.* 250, see Cornelius's letter to Fabius of Antioch, cited by Eusebius, *H.E.* VI.43, 11.
11. Cyprian, *Letter* 52.1.
12. Optatus of Milevis, *De Schismate Donatistarum* 1.16 (ed. Ziwsa, *CSEL* XXVI, p. 18).
13. *Acta Saturnini* 17 (*PL* 8, 701 A).
14. Optatus, *De Schismate* 1.16. Lucilla's martyr was not yet formally accepted as such by the Church.
15. Note, for instance, the interesting statement preserved in the seventh-century romance, *Barlaam and Joasaph* (ed. Woodward and Mattingly) 12.103: Monasticism arose 'from men's desire to become martyrs in will, that they might not miss the glory of them that were made perfect by blood'.
16. See J. Gaudemet, *L'Église dans l'Empire romain* (Paris, 1958), pp. 185-91. H. Leclercq, art. 'Laïques', in *Dict. d'archéologie chrétienne et de liturgie* VIII, 1063-4, and J. R. Palanque, G. Bardy and P. de Labriolle, *De la Paix Constantinienne à la Mort de Théodose* (vol. III, in *Histoire de l'Église depuis les origines jusqu'à nos jours*, ed. A. Fliche and V. Martin, 1947), pp. 398 ff. For Roman Africa, P. Monceaux, *Histoire littéraire de l'Afrique chrétienne* III (Paris, 1905), ch. 4.
17. *Apostolic Constitutions* II.16 and 21.

Notes: *The Church of the Roman Empire* 83

18. For examples, see H. Leclercq, art. 'Basilique' in *Dict. arch. chrét. et de liturgie* II. 1, 540. Also, *Council of Laodicea* (ed. Bruns, *Canones Apostolorum et Conciliorum*, Berlin, 1893, I, p. 75), Canon 19.
19. *Apost. Canons*, Canon 40.
20. *Council of Laodicea*, Canon 59 (Bruns, *Canones* I, p. 79).
21. *Apost. Canons*, Canon 57.
22. This is an important letter, because Basil adds that 'long custom had sanctioned the practice from very force of circumstances' (ed. De Ferrari, p. 146).
23. Athanasius, *De Synodis* 18 (*PG* 26, 713 B–C); Socrates, *H.E.* 1.36.
24. Leo, *Letters* 119.6 and 120.6 (*PL* 54, 1045 and 1054).
25. *Statuta ecclesiastica antiqua* (= *Statuta*; ed. Bruns, *Canones* I, p. 140) 98.
26. Augustine, *Retractationes* (ed. Bardy) II.11.
27. Socrates, *H.E.* 6.8. Cf. Basil, *Letter* 207.2–4.
28. Ambrose, *Hexaemeron* III.5.23 (*PL* 14, 165 D).
29. Ambrose, *Sermo contra Auxentium* 34 (*PL* 16, 1017).
30. Apollinaris Sidonius, *Letters* V.17.3 (ed. C. M. Dalton, *Letters of Sidonius* II, pp. 71–2).
31. Note, in this connection, the pilgrim Etheria's description of the laity at Jerusalem, c. 390. (*Pilgrimage of Etheria*, ed. McClure and Feltoe, pp. 45, 52 and 96.)
32. *De Laude sanctorum* 3 (*PL* 20, 445).
33. Athenagoras, *Supplicatio* 33, *Canones Apostolorum* (ed. Bruns, *Canones* I, pp. 1 ff.) 16 and 17; Gregory Nazianze, *Oratio* 37; Canon 19 of Council of Ancyra (Bruns, I, p. 70); Canon 7 of Council of Neo-Caesarea (Bruns, I, p. 71).
34. Polycarp, *Philippians* 4, Tertullian, *De Jejunio* 8, Augustine, *De Bono Viduitatis* 12, 15, Ambrose, *In Ep. Tim.* 1.5 (*PL* 17, 476 B and C).
35. Canon 27 (Bruns, *Canones* II, p. 126).
36. Canon 72 (Bruns, II, p. 11). 37. Canon 4 (Bruns, I, p. 113).
38. *Statuta*, c. 99 and 100 (Bruns, I, p. 150).
39. Gelasius, *Letter* 9.21 (*PL* 59, 54 C). Also, 9.13. In the sixth century Rome is consistently hierarchically-minded. Thus, Pope Sylvester is reputed to have forbidden laymen to bring a suit against a priest!—*Liber Pontificalis* (Loomis, p. 45).
40. *Statuta*, c. 103. See J. Gaudemet, *L'Église dans l'Empire romain* III, p. 189.
41. Canon 13 of Council of Serdica (Bruns, I, p. 99). Gelasius, *Letter* 9.2 and 3 (*PL* 59, 49).
42. Canon 26. See W. Bright, *Notes on the Canons of the First Four General Councils* (1882), p. 191. 43. *Letter* 137.2 (*PL* 54, 1101).
44. For instance, Peter the Sub-deacon, who administered the Papal estates in Sicily, in the pontificate of Gregory the Great, and to whom many of Gregory's letters are addressed.
45. Gregory, *Decreta* 5.2 (*PL* 77, 1335 B). Cf. F. Homes Dudden, *Gregory the Great* (London, 1905), p. 262.
46. Council of Elvira, Canon 38. Augustine, *Contra Epistolam Parmeniani* II.13, 29 (*PL* 43, 71).
47. Optatus, *De Schismate Donatistarum* 1.18 (Ziwsa, p. 20).
48. Socrates, *H.E.* 1.9.
49. Cited from J. Steinmann, *Saint Jérome* (Paris, 1958), p. 83.
50. *Statuta* 22. 51. *Ibid.* 26.
52. Possidius, *Vita Augustini* 5 (*PL* 32, 37–8).
53. Augustine, *Letter* 126.3.

54. *Council of Elvira*, Preface (Bruns, *Canones* II, p. 2).
55. Canon 13.   56. Canon 10 (Bruns, *Canones* II, p. 121).
57. Gelasius, Concilium Romanum II (*PL* 59, 183 B).
58. Cyprian, *Letters* 14.4 and 16.4 (Hartel, pp. 512 and 519).
59. See P. Monceaux, *Histoire littéraire de l'Afrique chrétienne* III, pp. 83-4; P. Caron, 'Les *Seniores laici* de l'Église africaine', *Revue internationale des Droits de l'Antiquité* VI (1951), pp. 7-22; W. H. C. Frend, *Journal Theol. Stud.* N.S. XII (1961), pp. 280-4.
60. Optatus, *De Schismate* 1.17 and 18 (Ziwsa, pp. 19 and 20).
61. *Gesta apud Zenophilum* (Ziwsa, p. 189).
62. *Acta Purgationis Felicis* (Ziwsa, p. 198). Also, *ibid.*, p. 201.
63. Augustine, *Enarratio in Ps.* 36.20 (*PL* 34-5, 377-9).
64. Augustine, *Contra Cresconium* III.56, 62 (*PL* 43, 529).
65. *Codex canonum Eccl. Afr.* 100 (Bruns, *Canones* I, pp. 185-6).
66. Ambrose, *Comment. in I Ep. ad Timoth.* 5.1 (*PL* 17, 475 D): 'I do not know what neglect caused this custom to fall into disuse.'
67. P. Monceaux, *op. cit.*, p. 83, n. 10. P. G. Caron, *art. cit.*, pp. 20-1.
68. Tertullian, *De Baptismo* 17 (*CSEL* XX, p. 214). Cf. J. B. Lightfoot, 'Essay on the Christian Ministry' (pp. 179-267 in his commentary on *Philippians*, 1869), pp. 243 ff.
69. W. A. L. Elmslie, 'The Mishna on Idolatry, Aboda Zara', *Cambridge Texts and Studies* VIII.2 (1911), p. xxiv.
70. P. Monceaux, *Rev. des Études Juives* (1902), p. 12, and *Histoire littéraire* I, pp. 8-12. Here, too, strict adherence to Talmudic funerary prescriptions is evident.
71. G. Quispel, 'The Gospel of Thomas and the New Testament', *Vigiliae Christianae* XI (1957), p. 199.
72. *The Manual of Discipline* VIII.1. Discussed by B. Reicke, 'The Constitution of the Church', in *The Scrolls and the New Testament*, ed. K. Stendahl (New York and London, 1957/8), p. 151.
73. *Codex canonum eccl. Afric.* 75.   74. *Ibid.* 97.
75. F. Homes Dudden, *Gregory the Great* (London, 1905), Bk II, ch. 3, and E. Spearing, *The Patrimony of the Roman Church in the time of Gregory the Great* (Cambridge, 1918), pp. 6 ff.
76. Gelasius, *Letter* addressed to Justin and Faustinus (*PL* 59, 149 C).
77. E. Spearing, *op. cit.*, pp. 33 ff.
78. John the Deacon, *Vita Gregorii* 2.15. Cf. F. Homes Dudden, *Gregory the Great*, p. 300.
79. Cited from an anonymous fourth-century Donatist sermon, published by A. Pincherle, *Bilychnis* XXII (1923), pp. 134-48.   80. Cf. Optatus, *De Schismate* 2.1.
81. See, for instance, Sozomen, *H.E.* V.5; Ammianus Marcellinus XXI.16; and *Cod. Theod.* XVI:2:8, 9 and 15.
82. For instance, in about 325, the people of Orcistus in Phrygia petition Constantine for the rank of *civitas* on the grounds *inter alia* that they are all Christians. Published by W. M. Calder, *Monumenta Asiae Minoris antiqua* VII, No. 305.
83. See, for instance, Hosius to Constantius in 355, 'Do not use force, write no letters, send no Counts . . .': Athanasius, *Historia Arianorum* 44.
84. See N. H. Baynes, 'Alexandria and Constantinople: A Study in Ecclesiastical Diplomacy', *Byzantine Studies and Other Essays* (London, 1955), pp. 97 ff.
85. Figures in J. B. Bury, *History of the later Roman Empire* (reprinted 1958) I, p. 354.
86. Socrates, *H.E.* (written *c.* 440) I.19. Sozomen, *H.E.* II.24.

Notes: *The Church of the Roman Empire* VIII 85

87. Socrates, *H.E.* I.20. See P. Peeters, 'Les Débuts du Christianisme en Géorgie', *Analecta Bollandiana* 50 (1932), pp. 5–58.
88. *Codex Theodosianus* (ed. Mommsen and Meyer) IV:7:1.
89. Socrates, *H.E.* I.8. See also, *Cod. Theod.* IX:40:8 of Valentinian I.
90. *Cod. Theod.* IX:40:2.
91. Such as swallowing molten lead or being eaten by bears (Ammianus Marcellinus, *Rerum gest.* XXIX.3, 9, on Valentinian I). On the tendencies in Constantine's legislation, see A. Alföldi, *The Conversion of Constantine and Pagan Rome* (ET by H. Mattingly, Oxford, 1948), p. 128.
92. Note the complaint by Ambrosiaster, *c.* 380, *Quaestiones in Vet. et Nov. Testamentum* 114: 'Here, in the city of Rome, which is called the most holy city, women are permitted to dismiss their husbands.'
93. Libanius, *Letter* 1057 (cited from B. J. Kidd, *Documents Illustrative of the History of the Church* II, p. 131).
94. Julian, *Letter* 22 (ed. W. C. Wright). 95. Jerome, *Letter* 77.4 (ed. F. A. Wright).
96. See R. G. Goodchild, *Cyrene* (1958), p. 23. 97. Jerome, *Letter* 107.2.
98. *Liber Pontificalis* (ed. Mommsen), pp. 52 ff. Cf. A. Alföldi, *The Conversion of Constantine and Pagan Rome*, pp. 51–2.
99. Cited from A. H. M. Jones, *Constantine and the Conversion of Europe* (London, 1948), p. 215. For the vast extent of the patrimonies of the Western churches, especially Rome in the sixth century, see F. Homes Dudden, *Gregory the Great*, Bk II, ch. 3; L. R. Loomis, *The Book of the Popes* (1916), p. 43.
100. Eusebius, *De Vita Constantini* 4.58–60; Socrates, *H.E.* I.16.
101. See L. Duchesne, *The Early History of the Church* II (ET, London, 1931), p. 495.
102. *The Pilgrimage of Etheria* (ed. McClure and Feltoe), p. 30.
103. *CIL* VIII.20914 (after AD 442).
104. S. Gsell, *Monuments antiques de l'Algérie* (Algiers, 1901) II, p. 341.
105. *Cod. Theod.* XVI:2:4.
106. E. F. Bruck, *Kirchenväter und soziales Erbrecht* (Göttingen, 1956), p. 36.
107. See Gregory of Nazianze, *De Pauperum Amore* 22 (*PG* 35, 885).
108. Basil, *In Divites* 7.39 (*PG* 31, 299).
109. Gregory of Nazianze, *De Pauperum Amore* 18 (*PG* 35, 880).
110. Ambrose, *In evang. S. Lucae* 8.79 (*CSEL* XXXII.4, p. 432).
111. Possidius, *Vita Augustini* 24 (*PL* 32, 53).
112. Salvian, *Ad Ecclesiam* (ed. Pauly), II.12, 13.
113. *Cod Theod.* XVI:2:20 (July 370), and Jerome, *Letter* 52.6 (*PL* 22, 532).
114. Augustine, *Letter* 262.5 (ed. Baxter, p. 507).
115. Augustine, *Comment. in Ps.* 103.16 (*PL* 36, 1371).
116. Augustine, *Comment. in Joh. Ev.* 6.25 (*PL* 34–5, 1436).
117. The spirit of the fourth century is nowhere better described than by T. R. Glover, *Life and Letters in the Fourth Century* (Cambridge, 1901).
118. Gregory of Nazianze, *Sermon concerning the Deity of the Son*: *PG* 46, 557.
119. *Letter* 24 (*PG* 77, 137). Cf. L. Duchesne, *The Early History of the Church* (ET by Claude Jenkins, London, 1948) III, pp. 244–6.
120. Theodoret, *H.E.* II.17 (ed. Parmentier, p. 137).
121. Ammianus Marcellinus (ed. Rolfe), XXVII.3, 11–13.
122. *Confessions* III.10 and 11. Cf. J. O'Meara, *The Young Augustine* (London, 1954), pp. 64 and 81 ff.

123. In *De Beata Vita, De Vera Religione* and *De Ordine*. See Ch. Boyer, *Christianisme et Néo-Platonique dans la Formation de Saint Augustine* (Paris, 1918), ch. 4.
124. Possidius, *Vita Augustini* 6 (*PL* 32, 38). For popular participation in this debate, Augustine, *Contra Fortunatum* X.19 (*PL* 42, 121).
125. Julian of Eclanum, cited by Augustine in *Contra Julianum opus Imperfectum* IV.37 (*PL* 44-5, 1356-7).
126. That of Centurius, Augustine, *Retractationes* II.19, 46.
127. Augustine, *Letters* 43 and 44.
128. See P. Monceaux's full account of Cresconius in *Histoire littéraire de l'Afrique chrétienne* VI, pp. 87 ff. On other Donatist lay writers and chroniclers, *ibid.*, pp. 233-58.
129. Augustine, *Contra Cresconium* III.66, 75 (ed. Petschenig, *CSEL* LII, p. 480).
130. *Ibid.* II.3, 4: 'Heresy is division between those who follow diverse principles; schism is separation between those who follow the same principle' (Petschenig, p. 363).
131. *Ibid.* II.1, 2.   132. *Ibid.* I.10, 13.   133. *Ibid.* IV.65, 81.
134. *Contra Cresconium* IV.64, 79.
135. P. Monceaux, *Histoire littéraire* VI, pp. 86 ff.
136. *Didascalia Apostolorum* 3 (ed. Connolly, 1929, p. 13). For this attitude in North Africa, see *Passio Marculi*, *PL* 8, 760 (*c.* AD 350).   137. Socrates, *H.E.* III.16.
138. Jerome, *Letter* 108.27.   139. T. R. Glover, *op. cit.*, pp. 337 and 347.
140. Augustine, *Confessions* VIII.2, 14. See P. Henry, *Plotin et l'Occident* (Louvain, 1934).
141. See P. Courcelle, *Recherches sur les Confessions de Saint-Augustin* (Paris, 1950), p. 137.
142. See P. Monceaux's essay on Tyconius in vol. VI of the *Histoire littéraire de l'Afrique chrétienne*, pp. 165-219; E. Buonaiuti, *Il Cristianesimo nell' Africa romana* (Bari, 1928), pp. 335 ff.; and F. C. Burkitt, 'The Rules of Tyconius', *Cambridge Texts and Studies* III.1, Cambridge, 1894.
143. Burkitt, *op. cit.*, p. xxiv.   144. Cf. *4 Maccabees* 17.21.
145. Petilian of Constantine, a lawyer before being elected Donatist bishop of Constantine *c.* 395, cited in *Contra Litteras Petiliani* II.92, 202 (*CSEL* LII, pp. 123 ff.).
146. Tyconius, *Comment. in Apocalypsim* (*apud* Beatus of Libana, Madrid, 1772, p. 507). See T. Hahn, *Tyconius-Studien* (Leipzig, 1900), p. 29.
147. Augustine, *Contra Epist. Parmeniani* I.1.
148. Augustine, *De Doctrina christiana* III.41, 46.
149. See A. Souter, 'A Study of Ambrosiaster', *Cambridge Texts and Studies* VII.4, pp. 183-5, and Dom G. Morin, *Revue Benedictine* XX (1903), pp. 113-24.
150. *Quaestiones in Vet. et Nov. Testamentum* 101 (*PL* 35, 2301).
151. Jerome, *Adversus Helvidium* (*PL* 23, 183 ff.).
152. For Ambrosiaster's influence on Pelagius, G. de Plinval, *Pélage, ses écrits, sa vie et sa réforme* (Lausanne, 1943), pp. 86 ff.
153. See Plinval, *op. cit.*; J. Ferguson, *Pelagius* (Cambridge, 1956); and particularly, J. Tixeront, *Histoire des Dogmes* II, ch. 11.
154. Pelagius, *De Divina Lege* 9 (*PL* 30, 115 D); Plinval, *op. cit.*, p. 103.
155. Augustine, *De Gestis Pelagii* 23.47 (*PL* 44, 347).
156. On Jerome's lasting hostility towards Pelagius, Plinval, *op. cit.*, p. 53.
157. Plinval, *op. cit.*, pp. 211-16.   158. Pelagius, *De Vera Circumcisione* 2.
159. Pelagius, *Vita* 13: 'man is not justified by faith alone'.
160. Cf. Augustine, *Letter* 156 (Hilarius of Syracuse to Augustine): *PL* 33, 674; Pelagius, *De Divitiis* 9 and 10; Plinval, *op. cit.*, p. 221.
161. Augustine, *De Civitate Dei* I.1.

Notes: *The Church of the Roman Empire* 87

162. The *De Spiritu et Littera*, and the *De Peccatorum Meritis et Remissione*. See *Retract.* II.33 and 37. Marcellinus was also a friend of Jerome. He and his wife wrote to the latter asking for information about the origins of the soul (Jerome, *Letter* 126, ed. Wright).
163. Jerome, *Letter* 8.3 (*PL* 22, 743).   164. Jerome, *Letter* 126 (*PL* 22, 1085).
165. Jerome, *Letter* 48 (*PL* 22, 493).
166. Jerome, *Letter* 126 to Marcellinus and his wife Anapsychia. For an account of Jerome's circle of lay acquaintants, F. A. Wright, Appendix I to *St Jerome Select Letters* (Loeb ed., 1954).
167. H. I. Marrou, *A History of Education in Antiquity* (ET, 1956), p. 343
168. Sidonius Apollinaris, *Letters* II.9.5 (ed. Dalton, I, p. 49).
169. Gregory of Tours (ed. Dalton): Preface to *Historia Francorum*.
170. Gregory, *Letter* 11.34. Verses of the poets were 'unfit to be recited even by a religious layman'. In general, G. Bardy, 'L'enseignement au Ve. siècle', *Mélanges F. Cavallera*, pp. 191 f.
171. Gregory, *ibid*. Cf. Homes Dudden, *op. cit.*, p. 286.
172. Jerome, *Letter* 22.16 (ed. Wright).
173. Ammianus Marcellinus, X.V.6, 18 (ed. Rolfe).
174. Ambrose, *De Virginibus* III.1 (*PL* 16, 219–20).
175. *Confessions* VIII.15.   176. Jerome, *Letter* 127.6 (ed. Wright).
177. Sulpicius Severus, *Chronicon* (ed. Hahn, *CSEL* I) II.45–8. Cf. A. d'Alès, *Priscillien et l'Espagne chrétienne* (Paris, 1936), and art. 'Priscillianus' in *DCB* IV, pp. 470 ff.
178. See Council of Braga I, of 448; seventeen canons directed against Priscillianism, and Council of Braga II, of 563, Canon 10 (ed. Bruns, *Canones* II, pp. 30 and 42).
179. Possidius, *Vita Augustini* 5 (*PL* 32, 37).
180. Cf. Epiphanius, *Panarion* 67.2 and 6 (ed. Holl, p. 133); Athanasius, *Life of Antony* 1 (*PG* 26, 840 B) and 77 (Antony spoke Greek through an interpreter); K. Heussi, *Der Ursprung des Mönchtums* (Tübingen, 1936), pp. 58 ff.
181. H. Leclercq, art. 'Monachisme', *DACL* XI.2, 1848.
182. Athanasius, *Life of Antony* 16.
183. Epiphanius, *Panarion* 67. See Heussi, *op. cit.*, p. 59.
184. Cited from Leipoldt, *Schenute von Atripe* (Texte und Untersuchungen, XXV, 1904), p. 42.   185. *Ibid.*, p. 88.
186. Palladius, *Lausiac History* (ed. Lowther Clarke), p. 64. Socrates, *H.E.* 4.23.
187. L. Duchesne, *Early History of the Church* II, p. 390.
188. Palladius, *Lausiac History* VII (Lowther Clarke, p. 58).
189. Socrates, *H.E.* 1.13. From Phrygia comes another Montanist inscription, set up by Aurelius Kyriakos, dated to the late third or early fourth century, commemorating an 'ascetic', now in the Museum of Afyon.
190. H. I. Bell, *Jews and Christians in Egypt* (Oxford, 1924), pp. 48–9. Cf. Epiphanius, *Panarion* 68.1, for monastic support of Meletius against Peter when both were in prison in Alexandria in 305.
191. See W. H. C. Frend, *The Donatist Church* (Oxford, 1952), pp. 171–5.
192. Listed by H. Leclercq, art. 'Monachisme', *DACL* XI.2, 1829–31.
193. See ch. on 'Women Pilgrims', in T. R. Glover's *Life and Letters in the Fourth Century*, ch. 6.
194. *De Laudibus Constantini* 1.6 (ed. Heikel, p. 198).
195. L. Duchesne, *op. cit.* II, p. 522.
196. Ambrose, *Contra Auxentium* 36 (*PL* 16, 1018). Cf. *Letter* 20.23.
197. Optatus, *De Schismate* 3.3.

IX

A SEVERAN PERSECUTION?
EVIDENCE OF THE «HISTORIA AUGUSTA»

Anyone who has tried to understand the history of the Church in the third century knows the problem of unsatisfactory material. Eusebius even, was largely ignorant of events in the west. His western contemporaries, Lactantius and Arnobius, do not figure in his *Ecclesiastical History*; there is a single reference to Cyprian's correspondence in a letter written by Dionysius, Bishop of Alexandria [1]. Tertullian's *Apologeticum* he knew from a Greek translation [2], and he himself is often inaccurate in his account of events, foreshortening the record perhaps for the sake of dramatic effect. Even so, his account of the situation of the Church's relations with the empire as these unfolded through the third century is straightforward and coherent compared with other sources of information. The object of this note in honour of the work of Professor Michele Pellegrino is to examine one of the more notorious texts regarding these relations, namely Spartian's statement that the Emperor Septimius Severus prohibited under severe penalty conversion to Judaism and to Christianity. «In itinere Palestinis plurima iura fundavit (Severus). Iudaeos fieri sub gravi poena vetuit. Idem etiam de Christianis sanxit» (Spartian, *Severus* 17.1).

Is the reference to the Christians an interpolation [3] or is the text as a whole a fabrication by an author of a subtly designed anti-Christian tract written at the end of the fourth century [4], or has it after all a ring of truth, representing perhaps what may have happened?

---

1. EUSEBIUS, *Historia Ecclesiastica* (ed. KIRSOPP LAKE and OULTON) vi.43.3 and compare viii.3. Both passages suggest that Eusebius knew of Cyprian's writings and views only through Dionysius of Alexandria's correspondence. In the sixth century, however, documents relating to the Rebaptism controversy were available to Severus of Antioch at Antioch (see SEVERUS of ANTIOCH, *Sixth Book of Select Letters*, ed. E. W. BROOKS, London 1902-04, pp. 212, 279 and 296).

2. EUSEBIUS, *Hist. Eccl.*, ii.2.4 and iii.33.3.

3. As suggested by A. A. T. EHRHARDT, *Politische Metaphysik von Solon bis Augustin*, ii, Tübingen 1959, p. 154.

4. The problem, whether the *Historia Augusta* has an anti-Christian design or

A SEVERAN PERSECUTION? EVIDENCE OF THE «HISTORIA AUGUSTA» 471

There are two ways in which we shall be looking at the text. First, we shall take it in its context with other references to Christianity found scattered through the pages of the *Historia Augusta*. We shall enquire briefly whether collectively they make sense for the period of the Tetrarchy and Constantine in which they are supposed to have been written, or do they, like the Gnostic Apocryphal Gospels of the late second century bear obvious marks of the fabricator's art?[5] Secondly, if we decide that *prima facie* they do not contradict what is known from other sources about the relationships between Judaism and Christianity, and both religions with the policy of the imperial government, we shall return to Spartian and attempt to fit his information about Severus' attitude towards the Christians with other evidence for the same period.

The remaining eight texts relating to Christianity in the *Historia* are listed for convenience below. (Ed. E. Hohl, *Scriptores Historiae Augustae*, 2 vols., Teubner, Leipzig 1927, reprinted 1955).

    a. « Dicebat (Heliogabalus) praeterea Iudaeorum et Samaritanorum religiones et Christianam devotionem illuc transferendam, ut omnium culturarum secretum Heliogabali sacerdotium teneret » (Lampridius, *Antonius Heliogabalus* 3.5).

    b. « Iudaeis privilegia reservavit. Christianos esse passus est » (Lampridius, *Alexander Severus* 22.4).

    c. « ... in quo (larario suo) et divos principes sed optimos electos et animas sanctiores, in quis Apollonium et, quantum scriptor suorum temporum dicit, Christum, Abraham et Orfeum et huiusmodi ceteros habebat

---

is aimed perhaps at promoting toleration for paganism in the reign of Theodosius, or has no recognisable bias at all, has exercised scholars ever since H. DESSAU's masterly article in «Hermes» of 1889 *Über Zeit und Persönlichkeit der «Scriptores Historiae Augustae»* («Hermes», XXIV (1889), pp. 332-392). That the *H. A.* was a «pamphlet against Christianity» is represented by A. ALFÖLDI in the *Cambridge Ancient History*, XII, pp. 222-23; J. GEFFCKEN, *Religionsgeschichtliches in der «Historia Augusta»*, «Hermes», LV (1920), pp. 279 ff., and J. STRAUB, *Heidnische Geschichtsapologetik in der christlichen Spätantike. Untersuchungen über Zeit und Tendenz der Historia Augusta* (Antiquitas, Bd. 1, 1963). As a pagan plea for toleration, K. H. SCHWARTE, *Das angebliche Christengesetz des Septimius Severus*, «Historia», XII (1963), pp. 200-207. No recognisable bias, see A. D. MOMIGLIANO, *An Unsolved Problem of Historical Forgery: The «Scriptores Historiae Augustae»*, «Journal of the Warburg and Courtauld Institutes», XVII (1954), pp. 22-46, reprinted with emendations and additional notes in *Studies in Historiography*, London 1966, pp. 143-180 (quoted in this article). All the important literature on the *H. A.* before 1965 is noted in this article.

    5. See Momigliano's cautious argument in this direction, *art. cit.*: «The religious, dynastic and economic problems of the Constantinian period are somehow present» (p. 162).

ac maiorum effigies, rem divinam faciebat (Alexander Severus) » (Lampridius, *Alexander Severus* 29.2).

d. « Christo templum facere voluit eumque inter deos recipere (Alexander Severus). Quod et Hadrianus cogitasse fertur, qui templa in omnibus civitatibus sine simulacris iusserat fieri, quae hodieque idcirco quia non habent numina, dicuntur Hadriani, quae ille ad hoc parasse dicebatur; sed prohibitus est ab his, qui consulentes sacra reppererant omnes Christianos futuros, si id fecisset, et templa reliqua deserenda » (Lampridius, *Alexander Severus* 43.6-7).

e. « Cum Christianis quendam locum, qui publicus fuerat, occupassent, (Severus) contra popinarii dicerent sibi eum deberi, rescripsit melius esse, ut quemammodumcumque illihic deus colatur, quam popinariis dedatur » (Lampridius, *Alexander Severus* 49.6).

f. « Clamabatque saepius (Severus), quod a quibusdam sive Iudaeis sive Christianis audierat et tenebat, idque per praeconem, cum aliquem emendaret, dici iubebat: ' quod tibi fieri non vis, alteri ne faceris ' » (Lampridius, *Alexander Severus* 51.7).

g. « Epistula Aureliani de libris Sibyllinis. Nam ipsam quoque indidi ad fidem rerum. ' Miror vos, patres sancti, tamdiu de aperiendis Sibyllinis dubitasse libris, proinde quasi in Christianorum ecclesia, non in templo deorum omnium tractaretis ' » (Flavius Vopiscus, *Aurelianus* 20.4).

h. « Nam in eis (Aegyptii) Christiani, Samaritae et quibus praesentia semper tempora cum enormi libertate displiceant » (Flavius Vopiscus, *Quadrigae Tyrannorum* 7.5).

i. « Hadrianus Augustus Serviano consuli salutem. Aegyptum, quam mihi laudabas, Serviane carissime, totam didici levem, pendulam et ad omnia famae momenta volitantem. Illic (Aegyptum) qui Serapem colunt, Christiani sunt et devoti sunt Serapi, qui se Christi episcopos dicunt, nemo illic archisynagogus Iudaeorum, nemo Samarites, nemo Christianorum presbyter non mathematicus, non haruspex, non aliptes. Ipse ille patriarcha cum Aegyptum venerit, ab aliis Serapidem adorare, ab aliis cogitur Christum... Unus illis deus nummus est. Hunc Christiani, hunc Iudaei, hunc omnes venerantur et gentes » (Flavius Vopiscus, *Quadrigae Tyrannorum* 8.1-7).

From these texts it is not easy to discover a consistent attitude by the authors (or author) [6] towards Christianity. They were obviously not over-concerned by the issue as only nine comparatively short passages

---

6. The view that the *H. A.* was the work of a single fabricator writing *circa* 395 has been stated with learning, wit and ingenuity by R. SYME, *Ammianus Marcellinus and the « Historia Augusta »*, Oxford 1968, criticised by A. D. E. CAMERON, « Journal of Roman Studies » (= JRS), LXI (1971), pp. 255-265 with Syme's rejoinder *The Composition of the « Historia Augusta », Recent Theories*, JRS, LXII (1972), pp. 123-233. For N. H. Baynes' view that it derives from the reign of Julian, *The Historia Augusta. Its date and purpose*, Oxford 1926.

are devoted to it and these are scattered through some five hundred
pages of text. This in itself should rule out the suggestion that the
Historia was intended to be an anti-Christian tract. It is noticeable too,
that Christianity even where disapproved as in Vopiscus, is never called
a *superstitio* or *prava religio*, terms usually employed to denote noxious
forms of religious practice throughout the whole period of the empire.
When he puts into Aurelian's mouth the sarcastic comment that the
Senate's doubts about inspecting the Sibylline Books suggested that they
might be transacting their business « in a Christian church » rather than
a temple of the gods, he uses the term *ecclesia* and not some derogatory
word like *spelunca* (cave), found in ecclesiastical rhetoric towards the
end of the fourth century [7]. There is also, as Momigliano points out,
an outburst of what may be termed petulance in the minor *Life* of
Firmus and Saturninus in which among other Egyptian misdemeanours,
the « Christians and Samaritans enjoy excessive licence »; but in Egypt
whatever religion they subscribed to, everyone worshipped money [8].

On the other hand, the five passages in Lampridius, including the
famous statement that the emperor had his own sanctuary with effigies
of Apollonius of Tyana, Christ, Abraham and Orpheus (*Alexander Severus* 29.2) are all mildly favourable towards Christianity. As one could
expect from a senatorial writer, they tend to be patronising and detached, but the citation of the « golden rule » observed by Jews and
Christians (« what you do not wish to happen to yourself, do not do
to others ») (*Alexander Severus* 51.7) suggests some admiration for the
Christian and Jewish ethical code. It may not be accidental that the
more favourable references to Christianity occur in two of the *Lives*
supposedly presented to Constantine, namely *Antoninus Heliogabalus*
and *Alexander Severus*, whereas the less favourable are contained in
Vopiscus and Spartian which seem to relate either to the period of
the First Tetrarchy or the reign of Constantius I [9]. The difference in

---

7. Aurelian is alleged to show great interest in the words of the Sibyllines,
and urged on to the Senate the proper performance of traditional sacred rites as
the best means of aiding the empereor, VOPISCUS, *Aurelianus* 20.7. Maxentius did
consult the Sibyllines before the Milvian Bridge in 312 with fatal results to himself.

8. VOPISCUS, *Quadrigae Tyrannorum* 7.5. See Momigliano's comment, art. cit.,
p. 163.

9. See the chronological references assembled by MOMIGLIANO, art. cit., pp.
168-170. I would, however, suggest the possibility that Lampridius' *Ant. Heliogabalus*
may have been compiled after Constantine's first victory over Licinius in 315, rather
than after Chrysopolis. The list of the various unsuccessful commanders including
(Domitius) Alexander whom Maxentius defeated in 311, and the criticism of Maximian
(for whose death Constantine was responsible in 310) would be apposite in the

474

tone fits the change in the climate of official opinion towards the Christians in the west spanning the period preceding the Great Persecution, the seven years of tolerance from 305-312 under Constantius I and Maxentius following the abdication of Diocletian and Maximian, to the years of increasing favour under Constantine after the Milvian Bridge and Constantine's successful campaign against Licinius in the war of 314-315 [10]. In the period of the Tetrarchy, to give one example of verisimilitude, the steady advance of Christianity was causing, as Arnobius indicated, fears for the neglect of the gods, desertion of the temples, the derision and abandonment of long revered rites [11]. The suggestion found in Lampridius' *Alexander Severus*, placed albeit in the time of Hadrian, that toleration of Christianity would lead to the desertion of the temples had a ring of truth in the last decade of the third century [12]. Moreover, when before 320 the Christian artist who composed the funerary mosaic in the cemetery beneath the Vatican, portrayed Christ as the Sun-god driving the chariot of the Sun [13], the association of Christ with Orpheus, Abraham and Apollonius at this period need not be far-fetched [14].

The one consistent thread running through the references to Christianity is the association of Christianity with Judaism, and to a lesser degree with the Samaritans. Both religions are contrasted with the gods of Rome. Thus, perhaps as a sort of foil to Spartian, *Severus* 17.1. Lampridius declares that Alexander Severus « preserved the privileges of the Jews, and permitted the Christians to exist » (*Alexander*

---

period 315-324 when Constantine was still ruler of the west. After Nicaea some of these names would hardly be remembered. Vopiscus seems to fit the period 306-312 with Diocletian in retirement (*Aurel.* 43.2) and Constantius I as emperor *Aurel.* 44.5. I cannot see the *Quadrigae Tyrannorum* any later than this.

10. An interesting example of the change of official attitude towards the Christians in the west between 305 and 315 is revealed in the interrogation of Ingentius by the Proconsul Aelian at Carthage in February 315. Aelian says: « [Constantinus] Maximus semper Augustus et Licinius Caesares ita pietatem christianis exhibere dignantur ut disciplinam corrumpi nolint sed potius observari religionem istam et coli velint », i.e. Christianity was favoured and associated with *discipline* beneficial to the empire. (= C. ZIWSA, Optatus, *De Schismate Donatistarum*, App. ii, p. 208, CSEL XXVI, Vienna 1895).

11. ARNOBIUS, *Contra Gentes* 1.24 « Neglegentur dii clamitant (pagani) atque in templis iam raritas summa est, iacent antiquae derisui caerimoniae et sacrorum quondam veterrimi ritus religionum novarum superstitionibus occiderunt ».

12. LAMPRIDIUS, *Alexander Severus* 43.7.

13. See J. M. C. TOYNBEE and J. WARD PERKINS, *The Shrine of St. Peter*, London 1956, Pl. 32 and pp. 116-17.

14. LAMPRIDIUS, *Alexander Severus* 29.2.

Severus 22.4.). The same emperor, as already noted, allegedly included both Jews and Christians in his commendation of the «golden rule» to the attention of wrongdoers (*ibid.* 51.7). Christ and Abraham were allegedly associated in the emperor's *lararium* with Apollonius and Orpheus. Vopiscus differentiates Christians and Jews from «all the nations» in his diatribe against the irresponsibilities of life in Egypt [15]. He mentions Jewish *archisynagogi* along with Christian bishops and presbyters as people who one might expect equally to be worshippers of Serapis or dabbling in magic. It was all very clever and confusing, but the basic association between Judaism and Christianity was clearly intended to stick in the reader's mind [16]. At the same time, both religions vere differentiated strongly from the Roman religion. Lampridius does this on a neutral basis, contrasting *omnia Romanis veneranda* which were rightly resident on the Capitol, with the Jewish, Christian and Samaritan cults which Elagabalus planned to introduce there [17]. Vopiscus is more hostile, as we have seen, setting the *ecclesia Christianorum* against the *templum deorum* and indicating that the church was not a suitable place for consulting the sacred Sibylline Books [18].

The association of Judaism with Christianity would be incongruous after Christianity became the official religion of the Empire after the Council of Nicaea, but was not necessarily so in the decades before this. Many pagans, Eusebius of Caesarea said, regarded conversion to Christianity as zealous acceptance of the mythology of the Jews [19]. His two great apologetic works, the *Demonstratio* and *Praeparatio evangelica*, completed probably shortly after Constantine's victory over Maxentius, attempt in reply to prove that though the race of Christian extends back through the Old Testament to the creation of the world, it could claim descent from the pure race of *Hebrews* from whom the patriarchs took their rise. Except for physical ancestry, the *Hebrews* had nothing to do with the *Jews* who were subjected to the law of Moses and had

---

15. Vopiscus, *Quadr. Tyr.* 8.7.
16. Vopiscus, *Quadrigae Tyrannorum*, 8. The problem of the Jewish patriarch visiting Egypt raised by Momigliano, *art. cit.*, p. 179, is surely resolved if one accepts the evidence of Origen (*Ep. ad Africanum* 14) that the Jewish patriarch whom he encountered in Palestine in the 230s was an extremely powerful individual («power not less than royalty») and might be expected to visit Jewish communities, including those in neighbouring Egypt as Vopiscus indicates. There is no need to see *patriarcha* as a veiled allusion to Athanasius as suggested by N. H. Baynes, *The Historia Augusta*, i, p. 66.
17. Lampridius, *Ant. Heliogab.* 3.5.
18. Vopiscus, *Aurelianus* 20.4.
19. Eusebius, *Praeparatio Evangelica* 1.2.

gone to their ruin [20]. Nonetheless, to the outside world the Old Testament was a Jewish book. Constantine himself seems to have been scandalised that up to Nicaea some Churches (principally Antioch) accepted their compilation of the Easter cycle from the dating of the Jewish Passover [21].

One can only deal with a balance of probabilities, but the texts in the *Historia* appear to have relevance for the period in which they were supposed to be written. As Momigliano points out, the alleged late fourth century forger was uncommonly able in his avoidance of hundreds of pitfalls [22]. With this in mind we go back to Spartian. The *Life* on which he based his compilation is according to one recent scholarly critic, « (basically) reliable » [23]. Spartian is supposed to have written in the reign of Diocletian, and understandably therefore, the reference to Christianity is unfavourable. There is, however, the same association between Christianity and Judaism that we have noted elsewhere in the *Historia*, and the context does not suggest interpolation. The narrative, purporting to record events that took place between the end of Severus' Parthian campaign in 199 and his departure to Rome in the summer of 202 is condensed and confused. These have been put in the wrong order. The progress through Palestine has been set in 201 instead of late 199, and Severus' journey from Alexandria to Antioch where he invested his elder son Caracalla with the Consulship and younger son Geta with the *toga virilis* in 201/02 was almost certainly by sea [24]. The actual events, however, took place. There are mistakes in correct chronological sequence just as serious in other historians of the time including Eusebius of Caesarea [25]. They are evidence for care-

---

20. Principally in *Praeparatio*, Bk. VII. For a concise summary of Eusebius' argument, see J. PARKES, *Jews and Christians in the Constantinian Empire*, Studies in Church History, Vol. I (ed. C. W. DUGMORE and C. DUGGAN, London 1964), pp. 69-79.

21. See SOCRATES, *Hist. Eccl.* 1.9.

22. A. MOMIGLIANO, *art. cit.*, p. 162. I find it very difficult to believe that an author (or group of authors) who was so well informed about so wide a range of subjects, like the reasons for the building of Hadrian's wall (*Hadr.* 11.2), the Blemmye incursions into Egypt in the late-third century (*Probus* 17), and the employment of Germanic generals by Valerian (*Aurelianus* 11.4), should be written off as a late fourth-century fabricator. The argument *cui bono* in favour of a Theodosian or even Julianic date still has to be answered. This " fabricator " had an uncommon touch for what happened in the third century!

23. Thus T. D. BARNES, *The family and career of Septimius Severus*, « Historia », XVI (1967), pp. 87-107 at p. 91.

24. See T. D. BARNES, *Legislation against the Christians*, « Journal of Roman Studies », LVIII (1968), p. 41.

25. Eusebius, for instance, makes no mention of Claudius Julianus being Prefect

lessness and perhaps striving for rhetorical effect, but do not necessarily point to romance.

The real problem concerns the terms of Severus' alleged rescript. There are parallel orders against Jews and Christians designed to prevent the expansion of both. Is such a rescript against the Christians likely at this period? It is generally admitted that the alleged order against Jewish proselytism is quite credible. From the reign of Antoninus Pius the policy of successive emperors had been to accept Judaism as *religio licita* but to confine it within the strictest possible limits [26]. Only born Jews were permitted to observe the law of Moses. The circumcision of non-Jews, particularly the Gentile slaves of Jews, was prohibited under severe penalties, and Roman citizens who underwent circumcision or allowed their slaves to do so were banished to an island in perpetuity and the doctors who performed the operation, liable to execution [27]. This policy was maintained by Constantine [28]. Conversion to Judaism was punishable while conversion from Judaism to Christianity was to be encouraged. Thus, the alleged rescript of Severus fits into a general policy towards the Jews extending from the mid-second to the fourth century and merely reaffirms existing practice. The pretext may have been ill behaviour by the Jews in Syria during Severus' campaign against Hatra. Jewish sympathy with the Parthian cause against Rome was long-standing. We are told that Severus allowed his son Caracalla a « Jewish triumph » [29] when he came to Syria, which suggests the possibility of military operations against Jewish insurgents.

The addition of the Christians presents fewer difficulties than appear at first sight. As we have seen, even in the early years of the fourth century the association of Christianity with Judaism as kindred religions was not incongruous. It was much less so a century before. Christianity and Judaism stood out as monotheistic religions relying on their own sacred Scriptures, antipathetic to pagan society, with analogous rites of initiation and burial [30], and even the same misdemeanours (apostasy,

---

of Egypt between Maecius Laetus (201-203) and Subatianus Aquila (206-210), and suggests (*Hist. Eccl.* vi. 3) that persecution under Aquila followed on that of Laetus.

26. Thus, *Digest.* 48.8.11 « Circumcidere Iudaeis filios suos tantum rescripto divi Pii permittitur: in non eiusdem religionis qui hoc fecerit castrantis poena irrogatur ».

27. Pseudo-Paulus, *Sententiae*, 5.22.3 ff. See K. H. Schwarte, *art. cit.*, p. 188.

28. *Codex Theodosianus* 16.8.1 (18 Oct. 315). Compare *ibid.* 16.8.3, 2 and 4 of 321, 330 and 331. See J. Parkes, *Jews and Christians in the Roman Empire*, p. 77.

29. Spartian, *Severus* 16.7.

30. The points of contact between Judaism and Christianity in the early third century are discussed by Y. Baer, *Israel, the Christian Church and the Roman Empire*, *Scripta Hierosolymitana*, VII, 1961, p. 79 ff.

adultery and bloodshed) to be regarded as « deadly sins ». « Jews and Christians » were also freely associated in the minds of educated contemporaries as people who demanded unquestioning faith among their adherents [31]. Where there was conflict between the two as in Carthage and Rome, it was fratricidal conflict [32]. In Carthage the Jews regarded the Christians not as *Christiani* but *Nazareni*, i.e. heretical sectaries [33]. Many pagans would have agreed with Celsus (*circa* 178) that there was not so much as « the shadow of a donkey » between the two religions [34]. The Christians were simply Jews who had abandoned the statutes of their fathers [35]. This impression could only have been enhanced by the concern shown at this time by the Christian leaders for *minutiae* of calendrical detail regarding the relationship of their Easter festival to the Jewish Passover. Official attitudes towards the Jews might be expected to extend to the Christians. Restriction of proselytism to Jews whose religion was *religio licita* might logically be extended to Christianity which had no such claim to consideration.

Christian proselytism was a real problem at this time. The decade 190-200 saw in two major cities in the empire, Carthage and Alexandria, what can only be described as purposive missionary advance by the Christians. In Carthage we have the well-known evidence of Tertullian that Christianity was making striking progress and that this was becoming deeply resented by the masses of the pagan provincials. Every day, he says, « you (the pagans) groan over the ever increasing number of Christians. Your constant cry is that the state is beset by us, that the Christians are in your fields, your camps and in your blocks of houses (*insulas*). You grieve over it as a calamity, that every age, in short every rank is passing over from you to us » (*Ad Nationes* 1.14). *Fiunt non nascuntur Christiani* [36], which is what Severus' alleged rescript

---

31. Thus Galen cited by R. WALZER, *Galen on Jews and Christians*, Oxford 1949, p. 14 from *De Pulsuum Differentiis* iii.3. Note also, how the Ship remains the symbol of both Old Israel and New Israel. Compare *Test. of Napthali*, 6, and HIPPOLYTUS, *De Antechristo*, 59, and in Roman catacomb paintings and early Christian epitaphs from Carthage.

32. On the enmity between Jews and Christians in some of the large cities of the empire at this period, see the writer *A note on Jews and Christians in third century North Africa*, « Journal of Theological Studies », N. S., XXI (1970), pp. 92-96.

33. TERTULLIAN, *Adv. Marcionem* iii.8.

34. ORIGEN, *Contra Celsum* iii.1.

Note how Dio Cassius writing *circa* 220, indicates that Roman citizens becoming converts to Judaism could be regarded as *atheists*, and in connection with Domitin's « persecution » blurs the distinction between Jews and Christians (*Epitome*, 67.14).

35. ORIGEN, *Contra Celsum* ii.4.

was designed to prevent. In Alexandria, Clement, the head of the Christian catechetical school, was conducting a similar missionary campaign among educated Greeks in the city. The school itself and Clement's *Protrepticus* were avowedly missionary in their aims [37], both concerned to persuade educated provincials to abandon the traditions of pagan custom and embrace Christianity.

In both cities the reaction of the populace was hostile. Tertullian himself bears witness to the anger of the mob and that the sure road to popularity for magistrates was to pander to it [38]. Clement speaks of « roastings and burnings » of Christians in Alexandria [39], and in Rome Hippolytus has left a vivid picture of Christians being haled out of their churches to face the magistrates' tribunal accused of defying « the decree of Caesar » [40]. There is indeed evidence for persecutions of the Christians in the first decade of the third century on a scale far wider than ever before. Apart from Alexandria, Carthage and Rome [41], Corinth and Antioch [42] saw persecution and even in the vast province of Cappadocia [43] Christians were menaced. Moreover, in contrast to outbreaks later in the third century, the weight of persecution fell on Christian converts and laymen, whereas most of the leaders apparently remained unmolested. The evidence of Eusebius for Alexandria and for Carthage in the *Acts of Perpetua and Felicitas* is clear on the subject. While Perpetua and her friends were not accused by the Procurator of being « converts to Christianity » the writer of the *Acts* emphasises that this was their status [44], and that the only cleric involved in their trial and punishment was the presbyter Saturus who gave himself up voluntarily. Eusebius paints a similar picture at Alexandria. Whether Origen's father who was executed in 202 was a convert is not stated explicitly, but the second wave of persecution under the Prefect Subatianus Aquila (206-210) struck converts and catechumens. Many of Origen's friends

---

36. TERTULLIAN, *Apol.* 18.4.
37. Thus CLEMENT, *Protrepticus* x.83 and xi.90. Also in *Stromateis* i.1.12 (ed. STÄHLIN/FRUCHTEL, GCS, Berlin 1960), « Wisdom must be passed on », and vi.80 where Clement stresses the value of philosophy in the task of convincing Greeks of the truth of Christianity.
38. TERTULLIAN, *Apol.* 37 and 50.12.
39. CLEMENT, *Stromateis* ii.20.125 (ed. STÄHLIN/FRUCHTEL, pp. 180-1).
40. HIPPOLYTUS, *In Danielem* (ed. N. BONWETSCH, GCS, Leipzig 1897) 1.20.
41. Hippolytus cited in the *Lausiac History* of PALLADIUS, ch. 61.
42. EUSEBIUS, *Hist. Eccl.* vi.11.4 and 12.1.
43. *Ibid.* vi.11.5. That ALEXANDER was imprisoned while in Cappadocia is clear from *ibid.* 11.2 and 8.7.
44. *Passio Perpetuae* (ed. KNOPF/KRUEGER) 2 and 3.

were martyred [45] and he himself looked back on those days as the heroic period for the Church [46]. On the other hand, neither Demetrius, who had been bishop since 189 and was presumably relatively wellknown in the city, nor any of his clergy are reported to have been arrested. Eusebius, using what must have been a third century Greek source independent of the Latin biography used by Spartian, believed that the initiative for the events came from Severus himself [47].

Widespread persecution directed largely against laymen and converts, popular resentment abetted by compliant magistrates and provincial governors, what does it add up to? If we follow Hans Lietzmann, Schwarte and Barnes, we would accept the fact of persecutions in the reign of Severus, but deny that emperor's hostility towards the Christians, and his intervention in the situation. The outbreaks were due to local happenings and the outlook of individual governors [48]. This may be true for the initial events, as it was in the case of the persecution at Lyons in 177 [49]. There, however, the governor after attempting to act within the existing code of practice towards the Christians had to report the matter to the emperor and await a rescript from him before proceeding [50]. Did a similar train of events in the major cities of the empire around the year 200 result in an approach to Severus and the rescript recorded briefly by Spartian? Existing evidence falls short of proof, but in balancing probabilities the totality of the evidence, of which *Quellenforschung* is only one aspect, must be taken into account. On the whole, it would seem that Spartian was a relatively truthful if a confused witness. The view of many Christians of the time recorded by Eusebius coincides with the information he provides. All in all, the weight of circumstantial evidence still points in the direction of an initiative by Severus in the persecutions against the Christians during the middle part of his reign.

GLASGOW

---

45. *Hist. Eccl.* vi.3 and 4.
46. ORIGEN iv *Homil. in Jeremiah*, 3 (ed. E. KLOSTERMANN, GCS, ORIGENES, 3, pp. 25-26).
47. EUSEBIUS, *Hist. Eccl.* vi.1.
48. H. LIETZMANN, *Geschichte der alten Kirche*, Berlin 1936, ii, p. 164. Also K. H. SCHWARTE, *art. cit.*, and T. D. BARNES, *Legislation against the Christians*, p. 41.
49. EUSEBIUS, *Hist. Eccl.* v.1.8 and 14. The governor had held preliminary hearings before deciding to refer the issue to the emperor.
50. *Ibid.* v.1.47.

X

THE FAILURE OF THE PERSECUTIONS IN THE ROMAN EMPIRE*

The Great Persecution of 303–312 has been often discussed.† The purpose of the present article is to ask contemporary writers what kind of men, in what parts of the Roman Empire, championed the new religion, or looked kindly upon it, and why the government attacked it, both then and in the previous half-century. This was the period that had witnessed the disasters of barbarian invasions, defeat by the Persians, civil war, and economic collapse. But for the innate soundness of the central and provincial administration the Roman Empire might well have been wholly destroyed there and then. The years of restoration, however, culminating in the twenty years' rule of Diocletian, witnessed profound changes in men's traditional opinions. The old gods had not brought the aid expected of them, and men were turning to the new, Christian faith. By 300, Christian and non-Christian were hardening into fixed, opposing loyalties. But within the Christian camp, contemporaries were already noting the presence of deep rifts (Eusebius, *Ecclesiastical History*, VIII. i. 9). And these, in the very hour of the Church's triumph, were to break out in the Donatist and

---

* From no. 16 (1959).
† See in particular, N. H. Baynes, Ch. xix in *CAH*, XII, A. Manaresi, *L'Impero romano e il Cristianesimo* (Turin, 1914), Ch. x, Henri Grégoire, *Les Persécutions dans l'Empire romain* (Mémoires de l'Académie royale de Belgique, tome XLVI. i, 1951), G. E. M. de Ste Croix, 'Aspects of the "great persecution",' *HTR*, xlvii, 2, 1954, 75–113, and J. Moreau, ed., Lact., *De Mort. Pers.*, Sources chrétiennes 39, Paris, 1958, W. Eltester, 'Die Krisis der Alten Welt und das Christentum', *Zeitschrift für die neutestamentliche Wissenschaft*, xiii (1949), 1–19.

Arian controversies which were to dominate its life for the next century.

It was about the year 248 that Origen wrote his famous challenge to the Empire in the *Contra Celsum*. Christ was stronger than Caesar. The Church had survived despite all that its enemies could do against it. 'The Roman Senate, the contemporary emperors, the army, the people and the relatives of believers fought against the Gospel and would have hindered it; and it would have been defeated by the combined force of so many, unless it had overcome and risen above the opposition by divine power, so that it has conquered the whole world that was conspiring against it' (*C. Cels.*, 1. 3, tr. Chadwick).[1] Origen believed in ultimate Christian victory (*ibid.* viii. 70), and his assurance was not disturbed by the onset of the Decian persecution in the following year. More prescient than most, he had come to the conclusion that the era of partial and local pogroms against the Christians was over, and that the next conflict would be on a world scale.[2] So, he was prepared for what happened, and his comment, preserved in the Latin text of his commentary on the *Book of Joshua*, is eloquent. 'Israel's enemies had attacked Joshua. Now Christ's enemies attacked the Church. The prophecy had been fulfilled in his own time. It was in vain that the Emperor and Senate forbade the name of Christ "(ut non sint Christiani)". Every city had condemned the Christians; in vain! Not only would the Christian name spread more widely and swiftly, but the Lord Jesus would crush his enemies beneath the feet of his servants'.[3]

Origen's confidence was well justified. The great efforts made by Decius, Valerian, and, a generation later, the Tetrarchy failed to defeat the Church. The Roman Empire did not possess the means of overthrowing an organisation whose ramifications extended from 'Gaul to Osrhoene' even in the time of Pope Victor (189-198),[4] and whose adherents in 250 already numbered a sizeable proportion of the population in the provinces bordering

[1] See also Orig., *c. Cels.* (ed. and tr. H. Chadwick), ii. 79 and viii. 44.
[2] Orig., *Comm. in Matt.*, 24. 9, Sermo 39 (ed. Klostermann, *Griec. Christ. Schriftsteller*, p. 75). I accept the view that Origen was thinking of his own day as well in terms of eschatology.
[3] Orig., *Homil. in Jesu Nave*, 9. 10 (ed. Baehrens, *Griec. Christ. Schriftsteller*, p. 356-57).
[4] Euseb., *Eccl. Hist.* (ed. Lawlor and Oulton), v. 23. 4.

X

FAILURE OF PERSECUTIONS IN THE ROMAN EMPIRE

the Mediterranean. The exile of Christian leaders to remote parts was an unwitting means of spreading the Word. Thus, the natives of the oasis of Kufra were converted by Dionysius of Alexandria and his clergy who had been exiled thither by the Prefect of Egypt, Aemilianus, in 257. As Dionysius wrote, 'Then for the first time was the word sown through our agency among those who had not received it'.[5] Much the same happened a century later when Valens exiled monks to a still-heathen island in the Nile Delta. They cured the local priestess of a malady and converted the inhabitants![6] Christian missionary zeal was one of the obvious reasons why the Persecutions eventually failed. The conversion of Constantine comes as the climax of a long historical process. Origen himself had looked forward to a Christian Empire, and the unification of mankind under the Christian law.[7] To his disciple Eusebius of Caesarea (died 339) this happy state of affairs had come about under the Constantinian monarchy.[8]

Origen's own career is itself a landmark. His personal contribution to the final victory of the Church was no mean one. Although his outlook combined what appear to be two conflicting principles, namely a philosophical approach to religion and life, and zeal for a martyr's death, he was able to make both serve the cause of the Church. As a Christian philosopher he sought to wed the current interpretation of Plato to the traditional teaching of the Church. He could speak with the philosophic aristocracy of the early third century on level terms, and he lifted the Church out of the rut of Judaistic sectarianism in which it had threatened to founder in the second century. His influence among educated Greek-speaking provincials with whom he came into contact in Alexandria and Caesarea was immense. During his exile at Caesarea

[5] *Ibid.*, vii. 11. 13.
[6] Socrates, *Hist. Eccl.*, iv. 24.
[7] Orig., *c. Cels.*, viii. 72.
[8] Euseb., *Tricennial Oration*, 3 (ed. Heikel, p. 201). Compare Constantine's view of his role as minister of a divine order for the human race, Euseb., *Vita Constant.*, ii. 28. The Almighty 'starting from the British sea and the lands where the sun is ordained to set, He repulsed and scattered by His divine might the encompassing powers of evil, to the end that the human race might be recalled to the worship of the supreme law, schooled by my helping hand, and that the most blessed faith might be increased with the Almighty as guide' (Text from A. H. M. Jones, *JEH*, v. 2, 196–200, and Ernest Barker *From Alexander to Constantine* (Oxford 1956), 478–480).

in Palestine, from 232, he met and converted a young Cappadocian lawyer named Gregory. The latter has left a remarkable account of his influence on him.

> Like some spark kindled within my soul, there was kindled and blazed forth my love towards Him, most desirable of all for His beauty unspeakable, the Holy Word, and towards this man, His friend and prophet. I was led to neglect all that had seemed to concern me, business, study, even my favourite law, my home and my kin, no less than those with whom I was staying. One thing only was dear to me, philosophy and its teacher, this divine man.
> (*Address to Origen*, ed. Metcalfe, Ch. 6.)

In the event, Gregory returned to his native Caesarea in Cappadocia in 243. He allowed himself to be consecrated bishop and remained there till his death in about 272. If it is not strictly true, as his biographer, Gregory of Nyssa,[9] claimed a century later, that when he arrived there were 17 Christians and when he died there were 17 pagans, there is no doubt that he was responsible for a perceptible movement towards Christianity in Cappadocia. His missionary methods were as intelligent as anything recorded about Christian proselytism in the Ancient World. He broke the power of the traditional local priests by revealing their oracles and cures as swindles, but he replaced the local festivals with those of the martyrs, celebrated also with a good deal of jollification.[10] We thus have an interesting example of the actual transition from the pagan cult of local divinities to the Christian cult of saints and martyrs accompanying the conversion of the inhabitants.

In linking Platonism and Christianity, Origen had built on an Alexandrine tradition whose origins extended beyond the arrival of Christianity, back to Philo and even to the Jewish apologetic enshrined in *The Letter of Aristeas*. But in Asia Minor it was to prove extraordinarily fruitful for the Church. Gradually, Platonism became for the upper classes the bridge between the conflicting philosophies of Hellenism and Christianity. The process begun by Origen leads directly to the ideas and influence of Basil (his

---

[9] Gregory of Nyssa, *De Vita Gregorii Thaumaturgi*; ed. Migne, *Pat. Graec.* 46, col. 909 C and 954 D.

[10] *Ibid.*, col. 954 B and C. See A. Harnack, *Die Mission und Ausbreitung des Christentums* (Leipzig, 1902), p. 476.

FAILURE OF PERSECUTIONS IN THE ROMAN EMPIRE

grandmother herself a convert of Gregory) and the great Cappadocians a century later.

The significance of Origen's success may be judged in the light of other possibilities. In the 240s it was not at all sure that the heir to the Platonic tradition would eventually be Greek Christianity rather than pagan neo-Platonism. As against Origen, Gregory, and Eusebius of Caesarea one can set Plotinus, Longinus, Porphyry, Iamblichos and Hierocles; and if Origen made Christianity acceptable to the court of the Severi,[11] it was Plotinus and his disciples who influenced the ideas of the rulers of the Roman world in the period from 253–300, from Gallienus to the Tetrarchy. Only gradually did these two systems of thought, similar both in ultimate aim and method but at variance regarding the Incarnation, emerge as rivals. Yet by 275 this development had taken place, and neo-Platonist leaders such as Porphyry and Hierocles, who was successively governor of Bithynia and prefect of Egypt (303–305 and 305–308), were among the most determined of the enemies of Christianity at the time of the Great Persecution.[12]

That victory ultimately went to the Church may be due in part to the other side of Origen's Christianity. Logically, Platonic contemplation of the divine and martyrdom are irreconcilable as ends. Union with God through gradual self-purification is a ladder of ascent. It demands long life, not sudden death. The next century accepted the taming of the human passions through asceticism as a substitute for martyrdom. Even Antony, though he encouraged the Egyptian confessors, did not become one himself. Yet Origen realised truly enough that what had given the Christian Church its power of survival had been its followers' readiness to die for it.

The youth who had to be forcibly restrained from following his father, Leonidas, to execution in 202 was to exhort hearers in season and out of season to activities, including actual defiance of authority, which would lead to martyrdom.[13] He who sought the

---

[11] Eusb., *Eccl. Hist.*, vi. 21. 3.
[12] Lact., *Div. Inst.* (ed. Brandt), v. 2, and 11. 15. For the view that Hierocles was the author of the heathen objections in the *Apocriticus* of Macarius Magnes, see T. W. Crafer's ed. of Macarius (Translations of Christian Literature, S.P.C.K., 1920) XV. H. Delehaye, 'Hierocles in Egypt', *Analecta Bollandiana*, 40 (1922), p. 28.
[13] *C. Cels.*, I. I.

spiritual truths hidden beneath the bare words of the Scriptural texts, applied the literal text to himself when he read Matt. 19:12.[14] An intense idealism was never far below the surface. Christianity, he reminded his friend Ambrosios, was a religion of martyrdom, and that singled it out as unique among the religions of mankind. 'But the only people who fight for religion are "the elect race, the royal priesthood, the holy nation, a people for God's possession". (1 Peter 2:9). The rest of mankind do not even try to make it appear that if there is persecution of religious people they intend to die for religion and to prefer death rather than deny their religion and live'.[15]

He would not have disagreed with Tertullian that 'the blood of Christians is seed' (*Apol.*, 50), but he also said that 'true religion was utterly impossible to one who was not a philosopher' (Gregory Thaumaturgus, *Address to Origen*, 6). It was this combination of philosophy and zeal that gave the Church its invincibility in the final conflict with the Empire.

Even so, the Decian persecution (249–251) came near to success. The main weakness of the Church in the first half of the third century was that, except perhaps in parts of Asia Minor, it was almost entirely an urban organisation. In the previous century it had been both the heir and the rival of the Jewish synagogues which were to be found in nearly every centre of any size near the coasts of the Mediterranean. Though the Church had increased its members considerably[16] during the period of practical toleration under Alexander Severus (222–235), Gordian (238–244) and Philip (244–249), the pattern of development had not changed. Penetration of the countryside had been slow. The Church was based on an urban episcopate. The persecutions it had suffered had been urban pogroms, the result of riots, as at Lyons in 177[17] or Alexandria in 248.[18] Its leaders seem to have been drawn mainly from middle-class urban provincial life. Justin, the wandering philosopher from Neapolis (Nablus) in Palestine, Marcion the ship-owner

[14] Euseb., *Eccl. Hist.*, vi. 8. 2.
[15] *Exhortation to Martyrdom* (ed. Oulton and Chadwick), 5. Compare Josephus' assertion of the superiority of Judaism over Hellenism on the same grounds, *Contra Apionem* (ed. Niese) 1. 8. 42.
[16] Euseb., *Eccl. Hist.*, vi. 36. 1, Orig., *Comm. in Matt.*, 15. 26 (Klostermann, p. 426).
[17] Euseb., *Eccl. Hist.*, v. 1. 7.
[18] *Ibid.*, vi. 41. 1 ff.

FAILURE OF PERSECUTIONS IN THE ROMAN EMPIRE

from Sinope, Theodotus the money-changer in Rome, his namesake the tanner from Byzantium, Florinus, a member of the governor's staff in the province of Asia, or Tertullian, son of a centurion in the Proconsul's guard at Carthage, these men seem to have been representative of Church or sect life in the period 150–220.

Concentration in the cities had brought stability and sound organisation. By 250 the priesthood was an attractive profession commanding a regular monthly stipend.[19] But it also rendered the Church more vulnerable to attack. When the blow fell about the end of 249, the leaders were marked men[20] who faced the alternatives of flight or arrest and execution; and their flocks, swelled by too many nominal adherents, fell away in droves.

At this stage, the authorities still had the initiative, and acts directed against the Church commanded a large measure of public support. Confessors in Carthage were mishandled by an enraged crowd (*ferociens populus*, Cyprian, *Letter*, 6. 4). Trials were conducted there and in Smyrna to the accompaniment of the shouts of the mob.[21] Loyalty to the Roman Empire, expressed by an outward cult act, had become accepted as a matter of course in the provinces. Tribal and municipal centres had their *fora*, and these were often dominated by a Capitol dedicated to the Roman gods. Such temples had continued to be built in the first decades of the third century. To this was added the view that on the safety and prosperity of the Emperor (the *Salus Augusti*) depended that of his subjects, and this in turn hung on the good-will of the gods.[22] Thus Celsus had told the Christians in 178 'even if someone tells you to take an oath by the emperor among men, that also is nothing dreadful. For earthly things have been given to him, and

---

[19] Cypr., *Letter* (ed. Hartel), 34. 4. See Euseb., *Eccl. Hist.*, v. 28. 10, for the payment of 150 denarii a month to Natalius, schismatic bishop of Rome in 200, by his adherents.

[20] For instance, Dionysius of Alexandria says of himself, 'when the persecution under Decius was publicly proclaimed, that selfsame hour Sabinus sent a *frumentarius* to seek me out'. Euseb., *Eccl. Hist.*, vi. 40. 2. Fabian of Rome was seized and executed on 20 January 250, see Cypr., *Letter* (ed. Hartel), 55. 9.

[21] Cypr., *Letter* 40, and 56. 1–2, *Acta Sancti Pionii* (ed. Krüger and Knopf), 7, 10, 11.

[22] See A. Alföldi's important study of the Decian persecution, 'Zu den Christenverfolgungen in der Mitte des 3. Jahrhunderts', *Klio*, 31 (1938), pp. 323–47.

whatever you receive in this world you receive from him'.²³ The coins in common use, exalting the 'providentia' and 'pax' of the emperor and his titles of 'pius felix', emphasised the point.

Therefore, when in the spring of 250 Decius ordered as a 'dies Imperii', that is a sort of general supplication to the gods for the safety and victory of the emperor and his house in the face of mounting threats to the State, the idea was not unfamiliar. Indeed, something similar may have taken place in 212 on the promulgation of the *Constitutio Antoniniana*.²⁴ It was complied with by the vast majority of the inhabitants of the Roman world, including the Christians. Their acquiescence may have been made the easier by the arguments used by the authorities both then and in the persecution of Valerian (257–259). The Christians were told that they were not being asked to give up their own religion, but simply to pay respect to the gods on whom the welfare of the Empire depended.²⁵ Thus, the deputy prefect of Egypt, Aemilianus, told Bishop Dionysius of Alexandria at a hearing in 257. 'And,' he continued, 'who prevents you from worshipping this god (the Christian God) also, if he be a god, along with the natural gods? For ye were bidden to worship gods, and gods whom we all know' (Euseb., *Eccl. Hist.*, vii. 11. 9). In Carthage, numerous Christians sacrificed cheerfully, and then proceeded to offer themselves for the Sacrament.²⁶

Contemporaries emphasise the vast numbers of the lapsed. The Church was saved from utter ruin by a few noble examples. In Alexandria, Dionysius has left a vivid description of events (Euseb., *Eccl. Hist.*, vi. 41, 11–13, ed. and tr. Oulton):

> On the arrival of the edict all cowered with fear. And of many of the more eminent persons, some came forward immediately through fear, others in public positions were compelled to do so by their business, and others were dragged by those around them. Called by name they approached the impure and unholy sacrifices, some pale and trembling, as if they were not for sacrificing but rather to be themselves the sacrifices and victims to the idols, so that the large crowd that stood around heaped mockery upon them,

²³ Orig., *c. Cels.*, viii. 67.
²⁴ A. Alföldi, *op. cit.*, p. 333.
²⁵ Euseb., *Eccl. Hist.*, vii. 11. 7.
²⁶ Cypr., *De Lapsis*, 15.

and it was evident that they were by nature cowards in everything, cowards both to die and to sacrifice. But others ran eagerly towards the altars, affirming by their forwardness that they had not been Christians even formerly; concerning whom the Lord very truly predicted that they shall hardly be saved. Of the rest, some followed one or other of these, others fled; some were captured, and of these some went as far as bonds and imprisonment, and certain, when they had been shut up for many days, then forswore themselves even before coming into court, while others, who remained firm for a certain time under tortures, subsequently gave in.

The effective staff of this already important see was reduced to four priests who were in hiding and 'secretly visited the brethren'. Two others, Faustinus and Aquila, 'who are better known in the world, are wandering about in Egypt' (Euseb., *Eccl. Hist.*, vii. 11. 24).

In Africa, matters were, if anything, worse. Cyprian admits (*Letter*, 11. 1) that the great majority of his flock had lapsed; few of his clergy stayed at their posts. The treatise *On the Lapsed*, written in 251, recounts in awe-inspiring terms the extent of the disaster. The magistrates at Carthage were so busy that they begged would-be sacrificers to return the next day (*De Lapsis*, 8). In the provincial towns whole congregations apostatised, in one case led by the bishop himself (*Letter*, 59. 10). Nor are we dependent on the word of a single bishop whose own role had not been a heroic one. The whole problem of the *libelli pacis*, that is the pardons given out in quantities by surviving confessors to their friends and relatives at the end of the persecution, arose only because of the enormous numbers of those concerned. Cyprian indeed says that they were given out 'by the thousand' (*Letter*, 20. 3).

In Asia Minor, the hitherto triumphant mission of Gregory in Cappadocia came to an abrupt halt. Gregory himself seems to have accepted the fact that most of his new converts would give way under the threat of persecution, and he himself fled.[27] In Smyrna, bishop Euctemon and other leading Christians sacrificed.[28] Here, perhaps for the last time, the pagan magistrates felt really confident of their superiority. They know that the Christians

---

[27] Gregory of Nyssa, *Life*, Migne, *Pat. Graec.* col. 46, 945 D.
[28] *Acta Sancti Pionii* (ed. Knopf and Krüger, 1929), 15. 2 and 16. 1.

'worship the crucified one', and openly laugh at the idea.[29] They also know that the Church was riddled with sects. Pionius was asked at his trial to which one he belonged.[30]

Half a century later the atmosphere has changed. Once more one looks at the contemporary accounts, this time of the Great Persecution (303–312), and the contrast is evident.

The Imperial directives indeed were carried out in the provinces without hesitation. In Africa the magistrates were kindly and fair-minded. Sometimes even, they were friends of the bishop, as is shown by evidence given by Alfius Caecilianus, Duumvir of Aptunga, at the inquiry into the conduct of Bishop Felix in 315.[31] But they were prepared to do what was asked of them. Munatius Felix, the Curator of Cirta, refused to close his enquiry until Bishop Paul and his clergy had surrendered all the Scriptures they possessed.[32] Churches were burnt down, and the general order to sacrifice contained in the Fourth Edict in the spring of 304 was carried out.[33] Panic and apostasy in the ranks of the Christians there was too. Optatus of Milevis records two generations later how 'the devil triumphed in the temples', that grey-beards, infants in arms, and indeed everyone, hastened to sacrifice.[34] An eye-witness of the events of Cirta in 303, Victor the Grammarian, tells how the first reaction of the Christians there to the Imperial edict was flight.[35] In Palestine, Eusebius describes in contrast to the heroes, that many others 'gave way at the first assault',[36] and sacrificed; and at Antioch 'numbers of men, women and children crowded up to the idols and sacrificed'.[37] In Rome, Bishop Marcellinus may have apostatised.[38]

This tale of weakness is not, however, the dominant feature.

[29] *Acta Sancti Pionii*, 16. 5.
[30] *Ibid.*, 9. 2, 19. 4, and 21. 4.
[31] *Acta Purgationis Felicis* (ed. Ziwsa, *C.S.E.L.* XXVI).
[32] *Gesta apud Zenophilum* (ed. Ziwsa), pp. 187–8.
[33] The question whether or not the Fourth Edict was applied in Africa has been ably discussed by G. E. M. de Ste Croix, 'Aspects of the "Great" persecution', *HTR*, lvii. 2, p.
[34] Optatus of Milevis, *De Schismate Donatistarum* (ed. Ziwsa) iii. 8.
[35] *Gesta apud Zenophilum*, p. 186.
[36] Eusebius, *Mart. Pal.*, 1. 3 (Lawlor and Oulton, p. 333).
[37] *Ibid.*, 2. 2, pp. 336–7.
[38] Indicated by mutually independent sources; August., *Contra Litteras Petiliani*. ii. 92. 202 (Migne, *Pat. Lat.* 43), col. 323, and *Acta Synod. Sinuessae*, Mansi, *Concilia*, i. 1250.

FAILURE OF PERSECUTIONS IN THE ROMAN EMPIRE

Rather, examples of apostasy are used to set off what was the real character of the Christians at that time, namely their constancy and their defiance of the persecuting magistracy. Thus, the passage we have just quoted from the *Palestinian Martyrs* is followed by a description of the confessor Romanus, 'who mingled with the multitude' and appeared on his own initiative before the magistrate to preach Christianity at him.[39] In Egypt defiance was carried to extraordinary lengths. Eusebius was an eyewitness of some of the events of Maximin's reign (306–313) and records as follows (*Eccl. Hist.*, trans. Oulton, viii. 9. 2):

> And we ourselves also beheld, when we were at these places, many all at once in a single day, some of whom suffered decapitation, others the punishment of fire; so that the murderous axe was dulled and, worn out, was broken in pieces, while the executioners themselves grew utterly weary and took it in turns to succeed one another. It was then that we observed a most marvellous eagerness and a truly divine power and zeal in those who had placed their faith in the Christ of God. Thus, as soon as sentence was given against the first, some from one quarter and others from another would leap up to the tribunal before the judge and confess themselves Christians; paying no heed when faced with terrors and the varied forms of tortures, but undismayedly and boldly speaking of the piety towards the God of the universe, and with joy and laughter and gladness receiving the final sentence of death; so that they sung and sent up hymns and thanksgivings to the God of the universe even to the very last breath.

The authorities worked with energy born of desperation. Lactantius alludes to the 'blind and irrational fury' of the persecutors.[40] In the East there was the feeling that this was not persecution but 'war', in which one side or the other would emerge finally victorious.[41]

Once again, the pattern is repeated in North Africa. In Numidia, pagan shrines and even Imperial property were looted by Chris-

---
[39] *Mart. Pal.*, 2. 2 (Lawlor and Oulton, p. 337).
[40] Lact., *Div. Inst.* (ed. Brandt), v. 21. 2, 'caeco et irrationabili furore'.
[41] Euseb., *Eccl. Hist.*, viii, 13. 10.

tians, and those who took part were regarded as popular heroes.[42] Their failings, even their acts of apostasy and simony, were pardoned. The spirit too, of those in prison was that this was either the gateway to Paradise or merely a temporary phase of demonic oppression before victory. Their discussions ran on what would happen after the Persecution and how the lapsed should be treated.[43] Any idea that the Emperors might be successful was evidently far from their thoughts. Their optimism and idealism reflected the spirit of many. Services went on despite the lapse of a bishop. We hear of young Christians in the African cities leaving their houses to 'go and join', as they said, 'the brethren who obeyed the precepts of God'.[44]

Quite clearly, the intervening years had seen a change of public opinion towards the Church. There is some contemporary evidence. Cirta, the capital of Numidia, for instance, had been violently hostile towards the Christians during the persecution under Valerian. The mob hounded the two confessors Marianus and Jacobus before the magistrates.[45] In 305 the same city was the scene of a formidable Christian demonstration, ending in the election of the sub-deacon Silvanus as bishop. His most fervent supporters were described fifteen years later as the lower orders and country folk.[46] Indeed, there is no evidence in 303, except perhaps at Gaza, of people welcoming the persecuting edicts as many of the inhabitants of the Roman world had done in 250.[47] In the largely Jewish city of Dio-Caesarea in Palestine the sympathies of the inhabitants turned in favour of the Christians when the latter were put to torture.[48] Even in Diocletian's and Galerius' capital, Nicomedia, wholehearted support seems to have been

[42] *Gesta apud Zenophilum* (Ziwsa, p. 193) 'Nundinarius dixit, "de cupis fisci, quis illas tulit"?' These had been housed in a temple of Serapis.
[43] For instance, in the prisons of Alexandria (Epiphanius, *Panarion*, 68. 3 (ed. Holl. p. 142), and Carthage, *Acta Saturnini*, 18. (Migne, *Pat. Lat.* viii, col. 701.)
[44] *Acta Saturnini* 5 and 14, concerning Victoria. (*Pat. Lat.*, viii, cols 693C and 698D.)
[45] *Acta Mariani et Jacobi*, ii. 2 (ed. Knopf and Krüger) 'in qua tunc maxime civitate (i.e. Cirta) gentilium caeco furore et officiis militaribus persecutionis impetus quasi fluctus saeculi tumescebant...' Cf. N. H. Baynes, *CAH*, xii, p. 658.
[46] *Gesta apud Zenophilum* (ed. Ziwsa), p. 194.
[47] *Mart. Pal.*, 3. 1.
[48] Euseb., *Mart. Pal.*, 8. 1.

FAILURE OF PERSECUTIONS IN THE ROMAN EMPIRE

lacking. Lactantius could write that God had allowed the persecution in order to bring the pagans within the community of the Church.[49]

A number of factors have long been recognised as contributing to this situation. Since 260, the date of Gallienus' restoration of Church property,[50] Christianity had been a *religio licita*. Though little has come down in the way of literature for the next forty years, it is evident that the Church had been gaining vastly in power and authority. The pagans themselves admitted that the Gospel had been preached in every corner of the inhabited world.[51] In Africa alone, the number of bishoprics seems to have doubled in the period 260–300, to a total of about 250.[52] In fact, we know that the Church made a remarkably rapid recovery from the effects of the Decian persecution. Cyprian's letters covering the period 251–258 give an unmistakable picture of vitality and assurance. New converts there were in plenty.[53] Indeed, the question of re-baptising those who had been baptised in the first place by the Novatianists would never have arisen unless this had been the case. The finances of the Church of Carthage were flourishing and were used to ransom prisoners on the outbreak of the Kabyle revolt of 253, while the behaviour of its ministers during the plague of 252–253 gained it lasting respect.[54] The comings and goings of clergy from Carthage to Rome and distant Cappadocia, and the assembly of frequent episcopal councils, culminating in the meeting of no less than 87 African bishops on 1 Sept., 256, leaves no doubt as to the resilience of the Christians, and the strength of their organisation in Africa. Nor does Africa stand alone. It was in these years that Bishop Dionysius of Rome (259–268) sent gifts to the church of Caesarea in Asia Minor, whose munificence was remembered a century later, and was recorded by Basil.[55] What is more, he sent a private embassy to

---

[49] Lact., *Div. Inst.*, v. 21. Other examples are cited by N. H. Baynes in his chapter on the Great Persecution in the *CAH*, xii. pp. 676–7.
[50] Dating, see R. Marichal, 'La date des graffiti de la basilique de Saint-Sébastien à Rome', *La Nouvelle Clio*, v (1958), p. 119.
[51] Macarius Magnes, *Apocritus* (ed. Crafer), iv. iii (Crafer, 124).
[52] A. Harnack, *Mission*, 520.
[53] Cypr., *Letter*, 66. 5 (Hartel, 730) 'Novus credentium populus'.
[54] Cypr., *Letter*, 62. 4. (Hartel, 700) 'Misimus autem sestertia centium milia nummorum'. Cf. N. H. Baynes, *CAH*, xii, p. 658.
[55] Basil, *Letter* 70 (ed. Courtonne, 166.).

negotiate the ransom of prisoners taken by the Gothic invaders.[56] In Neo-Caesarea, Bishop Gregory's mission was resumed with even greater success, and in Alexandria, Dionysius restored the church to its former prosperity despite civil war and plague.

Then, during the period 260–300 all the evidence points to the growing together of Church and Roman society. Paul of Samosata (*flor.* 260–270) was only the first of the clerical politicians of the late Roman Empire. In 303, in Diocletian's court, Eusebius mentions Dorotheus, Peter and Gorgonas as high officials who were active Christians.[57] There were Christians or their supporters among the families of the emperors.[58] Christianity was no bar to advancement; indeed, at times the opposite may have been true.[59] There were distinguished converts like the Africans, Arnobius and Lactantius, and the former is probably quite justified in his assertion that members of the liberal professions could be numbered among those who having once despised the Word now believed.[60] The Council of Elvira in southern Spain shows that Christianity had penetrated so deeply there, that the problem was arising of Christians who held nominal pagan priesthoods, as part of their recognised obligations as members of the ruling body of their city.[61]

Lactantius, however, warns us against placing too much emphasis on the influence of prominent individual Christians. Tertullian, he says roundly, 'found little popularity', and Cyprian was understood 'by the faithful only'. 'By the learned of this world, to whom his writings have by chance become known, he is commonly ridiculed'. He was dubbed 'Koprian' ('dung-head') and that, so far as his influence went, implies Lactantius, was that.[62]

The Great Persecution might still have succeeded but for one important development which took place during these years. In

[56] Basil, *Letter* 70.
[57] Euseb., *Eccl. Hist.*, viii. 1. 4 and 6. 5; cf. B. de Gaiffier, 'Palatins et Eunuques dans quelques documents hagiographiques', *Analecta Bollandiana*, 75 (1957), pp. 17 ff.
[58] Lact., *De Mort. Persec.*, 15.
[59] Euseb., *Eccl. Hist.*, viii. 1. 4; ct. *ibid.*, vii. 32. 3.
[60] Arnob., *Adv. Nationes* (ed. Reifferscheid), ii. 5.
[61] Canons 2 and 3 (ed. Hefele-Leclercq, *Histoire des Conciles*, 1907, I. 1 pp. 231–64).
[62] Lact., *Div. Inst.*, v. 1, 22–27.

FAILURE OF PERSECUTIONS IN THE ROMAN EMPIRE

three great territories of the Empire, Anatolia, Egypt and North Africa, the second half of the third century sees the conversion of large numbers of the country populations to Christianity. From a mainly urban movement, Christianity becomes a universal and popular one, and this decisively altered the balance between Church and paganism. Moreover, Egypt and Africa were the sources of grain and other supplies for the eastern and western halves of the Empire, and in Africa the native population was large.[63] Here, certainly, there was no depopulation in the later Empire. The Roman Empire could not survive the loss of large provinces by invasion or successful agrarian revolt which would cut off supplies from the towns and cities. Constantine faced the spectre of famine in Rome in the first winter after the Milvian Bridge, just as Maxentius had done in 310 during the temporary loss of the African provinces to a usurper.[64] The unexpected surrender of North Africa without a blow was of immense value to his cause, and he realised it.[65]

What evidence is there for these religious changes? The course of events in all three areas is often obscure and difficult to establish, but on the whole, the story is intelligible. One finds, for instance, in each case, evidence for a decline in the popularity of the hitherto all-powerful native cults, coupled with positive indications for the extension of Christianity. For Egypt, Idris Bell has remarked that, 'as we advance into the Roman period, we get the impression that even the traditional temple worship of Egypt was losing some of its vitality'. Outwardly, all was the same. Sacrifices were still offered with due formality. The festivals were observed, the animal deities, such as Petsouchos the Crocodile-god still recruited their priests. But a certain formality and lifelessness was becoming apparent. Mummies were often embalmed in a perfunctory fashion, the symbolism on the mummy-cases shows that the original religious meaning of the signs was becoming lost. Hieroglyphic inscriptions degenerated, until after about 250 no more are to be found.[66] It is not perhaps surprising that one reads

[63] Herodian (ed. Stavenhagen), vii. 9. Euseb., *Eccl. Hist.*, x. 5. 18. Cf. the author's *The Donatist Church* (Oxford, 1952), p. 67.
[64] *Chronica minora* (ed. Mommsen, *Mon. Germ. Hist.*, 1. 148). 'Maxentius Imp. ann vi ... fames magna fuit'.
[65] Euseb., *Eccl. Hist.*, x. v. 18. (letter to Miltiades) on the spontaneous character of the surrender of North Africa
[66] H. I. Bell, *Cults and Creeds in Greco-Roman Egypt* (1956), p. 64.

of deserted temples of Serapis affording shelter to monastic saints in the late third and early fourth centuries.

In Asia Minor too, the third century sees a decline in the popular religion of the countryside. Ramsay indeed believed that the old Phrygian religion had degenerated into a superstition before the century was out, and that educated men and women were therefore prepared to listen to the new Christian preaching.[67] However, cult organisations such as the Tekmoreian brotherhood flourished on the Imperial estates around Pisidian Antioch in the late third century,[68] and one shrine at least, that of Mén at Colonia Caesarea near the same city retained its worshippers until early in the next century.[69] Indeed, the more obvious signs of collapse, such as the wholesale abandonment of temples, neglect of cults, the transfer of temple lands to the Church, and the absorption of priestly families into Christianity, did not come about until the second quarter of the fourth century.[70] Julian watched the process as a despairing eye-witness (*Letter* 89, ed. Bidez). In Africa, however, the erstwhile national deity of both Carthaginians and Berbers, Saturn (Baal-Hammon), seems to have forfeited his popularity some time before the more Romanised cults which flourished in the cities lost theirs. No dedication to him has been found dated later than A.D. 272, and though in itself this might not be very significant, the next dated religious inscriptions in the same area (A.D. 299 and 324) are Christian.[71] There was no revival of interest in the Tetrarchy, such as the Roman gods experienced in some of the towns. At Cuicul in Mauretania, dedications in Saturn's honour were even being used as paving stones in the fourth century.[72] The cult had died out. When Constantine wrote to Miltiades of Rome in 314 concerning the Donatist schism, he

---

[67] W. M. Ramsay, *Cities and Bishoprics in Phrygia* (London, 1883), p. 137.
[68] W. M. Ramsay, 'The Tekmoreian guest-friends, an anti-Christian society on the imperial estates at Pisidian Antioch', *Studies in the East Roman Provinces* (1923), pp. 305–77.
[69] W. M. Ramsay, 'Studies in the Roman province of Galatia', *JRS*, viii (1918), pp. 107–45.
[70] Julian (ed. Bidez), *Letter* 84 to Arsacius, High-Priest of Galatia.
[71] P. Massiera, 'Inscriptions chrétiennes de Maurétanie Sitifienne', *Revue Africaine*, c (1956), p. 325. See W. H. C. Frend, *The Donatist Church*, pp. 84 ff. Since I wrote this, a dedication of A.D. 323 to Saturn was found in Western Tunisia.
[72] M. Leglay, 'Les stèles à Saturne de Djemila-Cuicul', *Libyca*, i (1953), p. 36.

appears to treat Africa as Christian, but divided between the Catholics and their opponents.[73] Paganism became increasingly isolated as the cult of the traditional ruling groups in some of the African cities, such as Timgad and Calama.[74] It had lost contact with the people.

At the same time, the last half of the third century was not one of universal decay and despair for the native populations of the Empire as it was for the old urban middle-class.[75] In all of these three areas, for instance, new art forms based on traditional pre-Roman motives were beginning to supersede the stereotyped provincial art of the previous two centuries.[76] In Egypt, Coptic was emerging from being an important adjunct for the magician and was becoming a national Egyptian literary language.[77] None of these literary and artistic movements were connected with Christianity initially, indeed, the first example of the elaborate geometric designs typical of Berber art in the fourth century comes from a temple frieze at Timgad,[78] but Christianity provided each with a vigorous means of expression which evidently could not be found in the traditional cults. As the art historian, Gauckler, has stated, 'in the domain of art as well as that of politics the triumph of the Church assures the victory of the native over the foreign'.[79]

Quite apart from the evidence for the decline in the popularity of the main pagan cults, there are certain facts pointing to the actual conversion of the rural areas to Christianity. For Egypt the testimony of Eusebius is impressive. He was, as we have seen, an eyewitness of the final ferocious stages of Maximin's persecution in 311–312. He stresses that Christians formed the majority of the population, and that while the evil spirit of idolatry was striving to keep the Egyptians in a ferment, 'thousands' were deserting

[73] Euseb., *Eccl. Hist.*, x. 6.
[74] *CIL*, viii, 2403; Augustine, *Letter* 90, cf. L. Leschi, *REA*, L., 1948, 71 ff.
[75] For a good example of despair, Cypr., *Ad Demetrian.* (ed. Hartel), 4 and 5.
[76] W. H. C. Frend, 'The revival of Berber art', *Antiquity* (1942), pp. 342–52. On a similar movement in Asia Minor, Miss Ramsay, in *Studies in the East Roman Provinces*, pp. 3–92.
[77] For the part played by magic in the evolution of Coptic, W. E. Crum, *PBA* (1931), pp. 235–87.
[78] Frend, *art. cit.*, Pl. ii.
[79] P. Gauckler, 'Mosaiques tombales d'une chapelle des martyrs à Thabraca', *Monuments Piot*, xiii (1906), p. 225.

paganism—'and anyone who is not wholly lacking in vision can see this'.[80] Fifty years before, Dionysius of Alexandria had stated that though Christianity had made some progress in the countryside there were still places near Alexandria which had not heard of the name of Christ,[81] but now 'His altars were now in every town and village.'[82] We know from another source that at Oxyrhynchos there were two churches in the town about the year 300 and that many of the inhabitants were Christians.[83] But it was from the villages that most resistance to the persecution came. In the Thebaid for a period extending over years, as Eusebius says, 'sometimes more than ten, at other times above twenty persons were put to death: and at others not less than thirty, now nearer sixty, and again at other times a hundred men would be slain in a single day along with quite young children and women, being condemned to manifold punishments which followed one on the other'.[84] That there really were numerous Egyptian confessors is shown by the fact that in 308 parties of more than 100 each were being sent up north to work in the mines of Palestine and Cilicia, as though there were sufficient in those of the Thebaid.[85] All efforts to crush the Church proved vain, but in the mind of the Copt, the 'era of the martyrs' replaced the official 'era of Diocletian'.

In all this ferment of religious change, the beginnings of the monastic movement were being born; in its first stages it was entirely Coptic and rural in inspiration.[86] Antony's flight from even the primitive surroundings of his village took place about the year 270. There were monks in the prison at Alexandria when Bishop Peter quarrelled with Meletios in 307–308, and they took the latter's side.[87] As a perceptive Egyptian Neo-Platonist, Alexander of Lycopolis, remarked, round about A.D. 300, Chris-

---

[80] Euseb., *Demonstratio Evangelica*, ix. 2. 4; see also, vi. 20. 9.
[81] Euseb., *Eccl. Hist.*, vii. 11. 15.
[82] Euseb., *Demonstr. Evangelica*, viii. 5. Cf. N. H. Baynes, *CAH*, xii, p. 675.
[83] C. Schmidt. 'Fragmente einer schrift des Märtyrerbischofs des Petrus von Alexandrien', *Texte und Untersuchungen, Neue Folge*, v. 4.
[84] Euseb., *Eccl. Hist.*, viii. 9. 3. Schmidt, *op. cit.* 23.
[85] Euseb., *Mar. Pal.*, 8. 13. cf. H. Delehaye, 'Les martyrs d'Egypte', *Analecta Bollandiana* 40 (1922), pp. 5–154.
[86] Athanasius, *Vita Antonii*, i. cf. Epiphanius, *Panarion*, 67. 1. 3. and 6 (Hieracas and his followers).
[87] Epiphanius, *Panarion*, 67. 3. 4.

FAILURE OF PERSECUTIONS IN THE ROMAN EMPIRE

tianity had become the religion of the populace, attracted to it by its simplicity and high ethics (in contrast to the complicated dualism of the Manichees).[88] In another part of the Roman East, Edessa, the writer of the *Acta Sancti Habibi*, remarks that under Licinius there were more persecuted than persecutors![89]

For Africa, there seems to be little doubt about the rapid extension of the Church in the rural area in the latter part of the third century. Recorded dated Christian inscriptions begin in 266.[90] The huge popularity of the cult of the martyrs in the next century, and the evil reputation achieved by the 'persecutor', the *Praeses* Florus, who was governor of Numidia Militana 303–304 are relevant facts and there is evidence for the establishment of new bishoprics in the Numidian countryside, such as Tigisis, between 256 and 300. The enthusiasm aroused by Christianity among the common people was real enough. In the next century no village yet investigated has failed to yield one or more churches.[91] In Numidia too, the presbyterate was a post worth having. Victor the fuller was prepared to pay 20 folles (i.e. 20,000 nummi) for his election at Cirta in 305.[92]

Similar events were taking place in Asia Minor in the same period. Here the literary evidence has been supplemented by the archaeological. Both Eusebius and Lactantius mention the total destruction of a small unnamed Phrygian town (perhaps Eumeneia) in which all the inhabitants, including the city magistrates, were Christians.[93] In the same province, the village of Orcistus was able to gain the rank of *civitas* from Constantine about A.D. 325, among other reasons because, as it claimed 'everyone was Christian'.[94] Indeed, a close study of Phrygian religious inscriptions during the third century shows a steady movement towards Christianity in

---

[88] Alexander of Lycopolis, *De Placitis Manichaeorum*, *Pat. Graec.* 18, col., 411.
[89] Published in *Ante-Nicene Fathers*, XX, f. 91.
[90] *CIL*, viii. 8430. cf. P. Massiera, 'Inscriptions chrétiennes de Maurétanie Sitifienne', 329.
[91] Frend, *The Donatist Church*, p. 84.
[92] *Gesta apud Zenophilum*, p. 194 (top).
[93] Euseb., *Eccl. Hist.*, viii. 11. 1. Lact., *Div. Inst.*, v. 11. 10, cf. W. M. Ramsay, *Cities and Bishoprics*, pp. 505–8.
[94] Re-published with amendments by W. M. Calder, *Monumenta Asiae Minoris Antiqua*, vii, no. 305, with Calder's comments that 'the situation it discloses did not come about in a day', p. xxxviii.

some of the towns, and a more violent one in the countryside. In the northern part of the province, near Dorylaeum (Eski-Sehir) a group of inscriptions dated between 249–279 leaves no doubt about the religion of those whom they commemorated.[95] They contain a ringing message 'from Christians to Christians'. On two, the Cross has been included in the design, and the qualities of the deceased as an ascetic and 'a soldier' of Christ have been recorded.[96]

The term 'soldier' brings us to the problem of theology. The rural Christianity of all three areas had much in common. It was first and foremost a religion of the martyrs and the elect, inspired by the Holy Spirit and the Word of God contained in the Bible. Thus, Athanasius wrote of Antony that he considered 'the Scriptures were enough for instruction' (*Life*, c. 16). They alone sufficed to rout the power of the demons. Antony scorned both pagan philosophers who visited him and urban theologians. To these simple minds acceptance of the Bible implied complete rejection alike of the native pagan past and the classical literary heritage.[97] So far did some of the Egyptian confessors who were converts carry this, that when they were asked their names by the governor of Palestine at Caesarea while en route to the mines of Cilicia, they refused to give them since they recalled the names of idols. Instead, they called themselves Elijah, Jeremiah, Isaiah, Samuel and Daniel (Euseb., *Mart. Pal.*, 8. 1).

A similar outlook may be found in both Africa and Asia Minor. Part of the anger felt against the Betrayers (i.e. the *traditores*) was due to the fact that the Bible itself was the object of their defection. As the martyrs of Abitina asserted in 304, even to alter a single letter of Scripture was a crime, but contemptuously to throw the whole Bible into the flames at the command of heathen magistrates was an act of apostasy which merited eternal punishment. Persecution was the work of anti-Christ, and this itself was a sign that the last days were at hand, when the martyrs would enjoy their reward in Paradise and sit in judgment on their enemies.[98]

In Asia Minor the strength of the Montanist and Novatianist

---

[95] J. G. C. Anderson, 'Paganism and Christianity in the Upper Tembris valley', *Studies in the East Roman Provinces*, pp. 186 ff.
[96] W. M. Calder, 'Philadelphia and Montanism', *Bulletin of John Rylands Library*, 7 (1923), p. 35 and figs 2 and 3.
[97] For Africa, see *Passio Marculi*, 1, *Pat. Lat.*, viii, 760C.
[98] *Acta Saturnini*, 18. (*Pat. Lat.*, viii, 701C.)

FAILURE OF PERSECUTIONS IN THE ROMAN EMPIRE

movements in the countryside testifies to the existence of the same puritanical view of Christianity at this period.

But theologically all this was a century out of date. In the East, the failure of the prophetic Succession and the discrediting of Montanism had opened the way for the more liberal Alexandrian tradition, the Logos theology, to become the predominant Christian idea. The conservatives protested from time to time, such as in the *Refutation of the Allegorists* by Bishop Nepos of Arsinoe (circa 260), but in vain.[99] Now however, the Church was confronted, as a result of the conversion of the countryside with a revival of the old Biblical and Millenarist Christianity in a militant and uncompromising form. While in the towns the gulf between Church and Roman society was diminishing, that between Christian and Christian was widening. The Great Persecution was to be the signal not only for conflict over Trinitarian doctrine, but between the representatives of two forms of ecclesiastical order. On the one hand, there were those who thought in terms of a universal Church with its elaborate hierarchy and strict division between layman and cleric; on the other, those who believed that the Church was the Church of the martyrs and the elect, and who regarded the safe-keeping of the sacraments, regardless of geography, as its essential duty. Meletianism in Egypt, Donatism in Africa and Novatianism in Asia Minor, all showed the latter outlook, and all represent the same primarily rural Christianity.

Why were the new Christians inspired by this puritan and apocalyptic form of Christianity?

A clue may be found in the strongly social basis of the new religion's appeal in all three parts of the Roman world. From the outset, monasticism in Egypt had a bias towards righting acknowledged social wrongs. Flight from the world, as Athanasius pointed out, included flight from the tax collector (*Life*, 44). The same term 'anachoresis' was used to describe withdrawal in the face of secular debt and withdrawal to satisfy religious vocation. The great monasteries of the Pachomian rule that grew up in the first half of the fourth century were economic units as well as centres of prayer and ascetic practices. We may perhaps agree with K. Heussi that their very success denoted widespread misery in the countryside whence their recruits were drawn.[100]

[99] Euseb., *Eccl. Hist.*, vii. 24. 3.
[100] K. Heussi, *Der Ursprung des Mönchtums* (Tübingen, 1936), p. 118.

In Africa also, it was a well-attested fact that the ranks of the would-be martyrs included those who found their debts to the Treasury too burdensome.[101] In the next generation the depredations of the 'leaders of the saints' (*duces sanctorum*) who commanded the Circumcellion bands, demonstrated the connections between the social and religious discontents of rural Numidia.[102] The martyr's 'agon' against the persecuting authorities in the first three centuries had by this time become extended to a defence against injustice in the present world.

The question may well be asked, whether the conversion of the countryfolk in the areas of which we have been speaking was in itself influenced by changing conditions in the third century. Grégoire, in his study of the persecutions, has assembled evidence to show the extent of the rise of prices during this period and the repercussions on the life of the provincials as a whole.[103] The harassed town-dwellers, unable to support traditional fixed obligations, attempted to push them on to the countryfolk. A papyrus dated to 251 records an inquiry held by the prefect of Egypt into a complaint by peasants, that they were being forced to undertake forced labour from which an edict of Septimius Severus had exempted them. The lawyer representing the citizens replied, 'Yes, that is true, but the towns were prosperous then'.[104] Half a century later, Lactantius paints a grim, if biased, picture of the effects on the inhabitants of Diocletian's Edict of the Maximum, following the reorganisation of the Roman provinces.[105]

A remark by the emperor Julian suggests that increase in economic hardship and the desertion of the traditional deities was more than a coincidence. Writing to Theodorus, high priest of Asia in 362 he observes that 'It was the sight of their undeserved misery that led the people to despise the gods'. It was not, however, 'the gods who were responsible for their poverty, but rather our own insatiable greed. It was that which gave men a false idea of the gods, and in addition, was an unjust reproach against

---

[101] Augustine, *Breviculus Collationis cum Donatistis*, iii. 13. 25. *Pat. Lat.* 43, 637.
[102] Optatus, *De Schismate Donatistarum* (ed. Ziwsa), iii. 4, p. 82.
[103] H. Grégoire, *Les Persécutions dans l'Empire romain* (Académie Royale de Belgique, Classe des Lettres, xlvi. 1. 1951), pp. 75 ff.
[104] Cited from Grégoire, *op. cit.*, p. 75.
[105] *De Mort. Pers.*, 7 and 23.

X

FAILURE OF PERSECUTIONS IN THE ROMAN EMPIRE

them'.[106] In contrast, he points out to Arsacius, Theodorus' colleague in Galatia, how Christian social and ascetic ideals had attracted the mass of the provincials to the faith. 'Why do we not observe', he says, 'that it is their benevolence to strangers, the care for the graves of the dead, and the pretended holiness of their lives that have done most to increase atheism (Christianity) ?'[107] The fact was that the Anatolians failed to secure earthly 'σωτήρια' from the traditional gods, and turned to Christianity instead. The same may have been true in Africa and Egypt as well.

Eschatological hopes of the Second Coming heralded by the final destructive efforts of Anti-Christ, bringing to the martyrs the joys of Paradise and a happy release from physical sufferings on earth, provided an inspiration to many. Sanctity, martyrdom and poverty are associated themes which recur in the puritan school of Western theologians from Tertullian to Petilian of Constantine and Commodian. Riches and sin were identified. To preserve one's wealth was to prefer Mammon to Christ. Possession of goods, indeed, implied contempt for the poor.[108] Commodian, whether he wrote in the late third or early fifth century, seems to have been an exact interpreter of a mood of popular desperation which found an outlet in Christianity. In the late third century, economic and social conditions would seem to have justified the acceptance of this theology.[109] And this movement ultimately proved too strong for the emperors.

Such are some of the underlying causes of the failure of the persecutions. Given the limited means available for repression— even in the Decian persecution there was not the prison accommodation to house the recalcitrants[110]—and the dependence of the authorities on the good-will of the peasants for the defence and victualling of the Empire, as well as for the maintenance of communications and other services, it was impossible to destroy the Church when it had ceased to be a purely urban movement. Once the villages had been won over, final victory could not be far away. The spread of Christianity beyond the boundaries of the

[106] Julian, *Letter* 89b (ed. Bidez, p. 157).
[107] *Ibid.*, 84 (ed. Bidez, p. 144).
[108] See J. P. Brisson, *Autonomisme et Christianisme dans l'Afrique romaine* (Paris, 1958), pp. 370-1 (texts from Tertullian and Cyprian).
[109] J. P. Brisson, *op. cit.*, pp. 394 ff.
[110] Gregory of Nyssa, *Life of Gregory Thaumaturgus*, Pat. Graec. 46, col. 945 C.

Empire to Armenia, moreover, made persecution absurd from the higher political and military viewpoints. This Maximin found during the winter of 311–312.

By the end of the third century, educated provincials, particularly in the East, had had long contact with Christianity. Many, as the personal stories of Gregory Thaumaturgus and others show, had been attracted to it. The Church combined monotheism, a high ethical ideal and a philosophy of history, which enabled individuals to see their own lives within the setting of God's providence. The cults of paganism could provide some of these elements but not all together. One has only to turn to Eusebius' *Demonstratio Evangelica* or the first chapters of the Ecclesiastical History to sense the force that the Christian philosophy of history exercised on his mind. All the time, too, the cults were moving in the direction of monotheism. Towards the end of paganism all the various gods were represented as powers of the Sun-God. And from the Sun-God to Logos, expressing the creative power of God in the universe, was no great step. Constantine took it. So had others before him. The Christos-Helios mosaic in the vault of Tomb M in the cemetery beneath the Vatican, is visible evidence of the fact.[111]

Among the countryfolk the Church represented two ideas which the old religion had lacked, social justice and freedom from an oppressive world. Christianity gave direction to an otherwise confused mass of economic, social and religious discontents, which had previously found vent in works, such as the Egyptian Apocalypse of the Potter[112] which was circulating in the third century, and other magical and oracle literature. The influence of Antony and his disciples ensured that the movement of protest represented by monasticism in Egypt should have a Christian form. In North Africa the puritan tradition emerges as the Donatist Church, all powerful among the densely peopled villages of Numidia and Mauretania. The successive edicts of toleration issued by Maxentius in Rome, by Galerius, Constantine and Licinius, and finally even by Maximin, set the seal on a process which had already run its course.[113]

[111] J. M. Toynbee and J. Ward-Perkins, *The Shrine of St. Peter and the Vatican Excavations* (Longmans, 1956), Pl. 32.
[112] W. Wilcken, *Hermes*, xc (1905), pp. 544 ff. and *Pap. Oxy.* 2332.
[113] The more important recent publications (in addition to de Ste Croix's

article reprinted in this volume) include: T. D. Barnes, 'Legislation against the Christians', *JRS*, lviii (1968), pp. 32–50; Daniel De Decker, 'La politique religieuse de Maxence', *Byzantion* xxxviii, 1968 (1969), pp. 472–562; W. H. C. Frend, *Martyrdom and Persecution in the Early Church* (Oxford, 1965), ch. xiv, xv; J. Moreau, *Die Christenverfolgungen im römischen Reich* (Berlin, 1961); Lactantius, *De la mort des persécuteurs*, ed. J. Moreau, 2 vols (Paris, 1954); J. Molthagen, *Der römishe Staat und die Christen im zweiten und dritten Jahrhundert* (Göttingen, 1970); G. S. R. Thomas, 'Maximin Daia's policy and the edicts of Toleration', *L'Antiquité classique*, xxxvii (1968), pp. 172–85; J. Vogt, *Zur Religiosität der Christenverfolger im römischen Reich* (*Sitz. d. Heidelberger Acad. d. Wiss.*, 1962, no. 1); A. Wlosok, *Rom und die Christen* (Stuttgart, 1970); J. Ziegler, *Zur religiösen Haltung der Gegenkaiser im 4 Jh. n. Chr.* (*FAS Frankfurter Althistorische Studien*, iv, 1970).

XI

EASTERN ATTITUDES TO ROME DURING THE ACACIAN SCHISM

THE Acacian schism which lasted from 484 to 519 has been regarded as a bitter affair, characterised by intransigence on both sides and ending in an unqualified disaster for the Byzantine church.[1] A closer look at the evidence suggests that the rigid attitudes of popes Gelasius (494–8) and Hormisdas (514–23) were far from being reproduced on the Byzantine side even at moments of provocation, and among the populace as a whole its existence was for most of the time a matter of indifference. The eventual ending of the schism through the initiative of the emperor Justin I was not regarded in the east as involving a derogation of the rights of the eastern patriarchates and of the church at Constantinople in particular.[2]

Though differences of interpretation of the status of the council of Chalcedon and its definition of the doctrine of the Person of Christ were always in the background, the schism was caused largely by a clash of jurisdictions between Old and New Rome, and a clash of personalities between pope Simplicius and the patriarch Acacius. The quarrel was made the more intractable because neither side could envisage a permanent breach with the other. Yet if final rupture between Old and New Rome was unthinkable, the issues that divided the two were scarcely soluble. Moreover, almost equally difficult problems bedevilled the relations between Constantinople and Alexandria, and between the pro and anti-Chalcedonians within the east Roman provinces. The emperors Zeno (474–91) and Anastasius (491–518) had to weigh up their priorities. Given existing circumstances, was harmony between Constantinople and Alexandria more

[1] The element of triumph from the Roman point of view is indicated by L. Duchesne, *L'Eglise au vie siècle* (Paris 1925) p 51—'Un succès plus complet ne se peut imaginer'— and in sorrow by V. Bolotov, *Lectures in the History of the Early Church* 3, Christianskoe Chtenie (Petrograd 1915) pp 362–3 (cited from A. A. Vasiliev, *Justin the First*, pp 165–8).

[2] A. A. Vasiliev, *Justin the First*, Dumbarton Oaks Studies 1 (Cambridge, Mass., 1950) pp 161 seq. I am inclined to believe that there was a temporary collapse of the Byzantine position due perhaps to the personal weakness of the patriarch John, but that the situation was rapidly restored by the actions of Justin and his nephew Justinian. See [W. H. C.] Frend, [*The Rise of the Monophysite Movement*] (Cambridge 1972) pp 237–9.

important than harmony with Rome? After the revolt of Vitalian in 513, the question became broader. How far could the diplomatic contest with pope Hormisdas be continued without risking the loyalty of the western and Latin-speaking provinces of the empire on the one hand, and alienating the Syrian and Egyptian populations on the other? That eventually Justinian managed to retain the loyalty of both, together with the restoration of communion between Rome and the eastern patriarchates[3] represents a very considerable achievement.

The issues that resulted in the outbreak of the Acacian schism went back to the council of Chalcedon in 451 and beyond. While Rome and Constantinople had accepted the doctrinal definition of the Person of Christ subsisting in two natures inseparably united, Rome had never agreed to the twenty-eighth canon that confirmed the primatial standing of the see of Constantinople saving only the primacy of honour to Rome as 'Old Rome', contrasted with the empire's capital, 'New Rome'. Yet so long as there remained emperors in the west, Rome's main concern was with them and with the diminishing empire they controlled. Between 460 and 477 ecclesiastical diplomacy between east and west was evidently at a low ebb and no papal correspondence between Rome and Constantinople has survived. In 476, however, the situation changed. In August the emperor Zeno was restored to his throne after the eighteen month usurpation by Basiliscus, and in the same month the last of the emperors in the west, Romulus Augustulus was removed by the Herul chieftain Odoacar. The latter's followers proclaimed him king and in 477 Odoacar's envoys returned the imperial insignia to Zeno. Thenceforth, Odoacar was nominally the emperor's vice-gerent in Italy with the title of patricius. The pope like the patriarch at Constantinople therefore became a subject of the same emperor and was brought willy-nilly into the day-to-day religious politics of the empire. One of the aims, however, of Basiliscus had been the renunciation of the two-nature Christology agreed at Chalcedon. The support of the anti-Chalcedonians at Ephesus, Antioch and Alexandria had led him to neglect the interests of Acacius, the patriarch of Constantinople, against the violent and eventually successful opposition of its citizens. Once restored, Zeno had no wish to go on his travels again. On 17 December 476 the privileges of the see of Constantinople were solemnly reaffirmed.[4] It was to be regarded as 'the mother of our Piety and of all Christians of

---

[3] Though in Alexandria only with the restored melkite patriarchs after 537.
[4] *Cod Just* 1.2.16.

Eastern attitudes to Rome during the Acacian schism

the orthodox religion'. The pope regarded this as a further unwarranted challenge to the see of Peter.

Zeno's immediate task, however, was to restore harmony between the four eastern patriarchates and dampen the fires of urban faction that threatened the security of some of the larger eastern cities. The anti-Chalcedonian leaders in Ephesus, and Antioch, were exiled, and the same fate was being prepared for Timothy the Cat at Alexandria when he died on 31 July 477. There, however, the clergy, monks and people refused to accept his Chalcedonian rival, also named Timothy and immediately consecrated another long-standing anti-Chalcedonian, Peter Mongus, in his stead. Acacius at once appealed to his colleague in Rome, pope Simplicius (468-83) for support. Peter Mongus he denounced as a 'friend of darkness' and subverter of the canons of the fathers.[5] Simplicius needed no prompting. Peter was unfit even to be a deacon. For a moment Old and New Rome were acting as one.

This was not to last. Gradually Acacius came round to the view that some accommodation must be made with the monophysite opinion in Alexandria including Peter Mongus, if another revolution was to be avoided. He found the germs of compromise in a formula proposed by the new patriarch of Jerusalem, Martyrius in 478, whereby the true faith was to be found in the decisions of the first three ecumenical councils (Nicaea, Constantinople and Ephesus I), and anyone who accepted different doctrines whether pronounced at 'Ariminum, Serdica, Chalcedon or elsewhere' was anathema.[6]

During the next three years Acacius succeeded in holding the ring between Chalcedonian and anti-Chalcedonian in the east Roman provinces without upsetting his relations with Rome. After the patriarch Stephen had been murdered in Antioch by an anti-Chalcedonian mob in 479, Acacius himself consecrated his successor, Calendio, a firm Chalcedonian, in the capital. He informed Simplicius, and promised that the election would be confirmed by a provincial synod at Antioch, (that is, he did not intend establishing a precedent in favour of his see).[7] This undertaking was not kept. Meantime,

---

[5] *Acacii Epistula ad Simplicium*, ed E. Schwartz, C[ollectio] V[eronensis] 4, publ in P[ublizistische] S[ammlungen zum acacianischen Schisma], *ABAW* PhK, NS 10.4 (1934) no 4 pp 4-5.

[6] Text given in Zacharias Rhetor, *HE* V. 6, ed E. W. Brooks, *CSCO, Scriptores Syri*, 3, 5 (Louvain 1919) pp 153-4, the association of Chalcedon with the semi-Arian council of Ariminum is interesting.

[7] Referred to in Simplicius' letters to Zeno and Acacius in June 479, C[ollectio] A[vellana] 66 and 67, ed O. Guenther, *CSEL* 35, 1 and 2 (1895).

Acacius may have opened a correspondence with Peter Mongus. In the winter of 481-2 events played into his hands. Peter's ageing rival Timothy sent a delegation to the capital asking for his successor to be appointed. His choice, the monk John Talaia, however, became involved in political intrigues threatening the position of Zeno, and before he returned to Alexandria he was obliged to swear that he would not accept the patriarchate. However, when Timothy died in February 482, John was prevented by his supporters from keeping his promise. Acacius saw himself free to abandon the Chalcedonian minority in Alexandria and stated his terms for recognising Peter Mongus as patriarch. His rival, John Talaia, betook himself to Rome and eventually became bishop of Nola in south Italy.

The terms for the restoration of communion between Acacius and Peter Mongus were contained in a skilfully drafted letter addressed to the bishops, monks and laymen of Alexandria, Egypt and Cyrenaica. This document dated 28 July 482 and known to history as the *Henotikon* of Zeno, aimed at the complete reconciliation of the sees of Constantinople and Alexandria which had been at loggerheads almost continuously since the second council of Constantinople in 381. The only right and true faith was that pronounced by the three hundred and eighteen fathers at Nicaea and confirmed at Constantinople and Ephesus. It asserted the canonicity of Cyril's *Anathemas* (not accepted at Chalcedon). It proclaimed that Christ was 'one and not two', and concluded that 'every person who has thought or thinks anything else either now or at any time either in Chalcedon or in any other synod whatever, we anathematise'. Chalcedon was effectively dethroned as a dogmatic synod, though retained as a disciplinary body that condemned Nestorius and Eutyches; however its canons, including the famous canon 28, remained valid.[8]

This fine piece of caesaro-papism, however, was not the cause of the Acacian schism. This had already become inevitable a fortnight earlier. On 15 July, pope Simplicius sent two angry letters to Acacius accusing him of double-dealing and perfidy in recognizing Peter Mongus. 'Even if Peter were now orthodox, he should be admitted to lay communion only.'[9] He was aghast at the reports reaching him concerning the situation in Alexandria. Acacius now took care not to keep Simplicius informed of events.

[8] Zacharias Rhetor, *HE* V.8. See Frend pp 177-80 (further references).
[9] Simplicius to Acacius. *CA* 68 and 69: Miramur pariter.

Eastern attitudes to Rome during the Acacian schism

Another letter from the pope dated 6 November 482,[10] complaining of events in Alexandria (but still not of the *Henotikon*), and of Acacius's silence about them, went unanswered. Events meantime consolidated Acacius's position. The *Henotikon* and Peter Mongus were immediately accepted by Martyrius of Jerusalem and unity was restored throughout the east Roman dominions. Simplicius became ill, to die in March 483. His successor Felix (483–92) seemed in no hurry to push matters to extremes. At length, he was stirred into action by Acacius's opponents in the capital. The Sleepless Monks were strongly pro-Chalcedonian and hated the *Henotikon*. Roused by their report Felix summoned Acacius to Rome to answer for having restored Peter without his permission and accused him of claiming that he was 'head of the whole church'.[11] The wound administered by Zeno's edict six years before had not healed. A papal delegation sent to Constantinople during the summer of 483 found itself participating in a eucharist attended by Peter Mongus's representatives and at which the name of Peter Mongus was commemorated on the diptychs. At last Felix acted. On 28 July 484, just two years after the *Henotikon* a synod of twenty-seven bishops met at Rome and solemnly excommunicated Acacius 'for his many transgressions'. He was a double-dealer (*hypocrita*), had promoted known heretics, and insulted the pope's legates.[12] A Sleepless Monk from the monastery of Dius pinned the sentence to the patriarch's pallium while he was celebrating the eucharist. On 1 August 484, Felix wrote to the emperor Zeno telling him he must choose between the apostle Peter and Peter Mongus.[13]

Part of the difficulty had been caused by a simple lack of communications. Rome had not learnt from the experience of popes Celestine and Leo and had no officially accredited agent in the capital. Apart from the timelag of months for correspondence imposed by distance, the need to rely on the casual reports from groups who may have had their own reasons to oppose the patriarch, deprived the pope of regular and unbiased information about the situation in the capital and the problems that confronted its leaders. Not until the reign of Justinian was the pope to have a permanent *apocrisiarius* at court. Now, lack of accurate information exacerbated feelings in Rome and was one of the factors leading to the schism.

[10] *CV* 3, p 3–4.
[11] Felix to Acacius, Mihi crede nescio quemadmodum te ecclesiae totius asseras esse principem. Schwartz, *PS*, p 73=C[ollectio] B[erolinensis] 21.
[12] Felix to Acacius, Multarum transgressionum. *CV* 5, pp 6–7.
[13] Felix, *Ep* 8. Schwartz, *PS*, p 81=CB 33.

Personal rancour and frustration at their relative impotence also contributed to the angry and arrogant tone adopted by the popes, with the exception of Anastasius, to the emperor and his representatives. The doctrine established in the west of the contagion of evil was invoked by Felix and his successor Gelasius (492-6) to brand Acacius as guilty of heresy 'by association' with Peter Mongus, who was the successor of Timothy the Cat and of Dioscorus who had been condemned at Chalcedon. In this context also the *Henotikon* was not explicitly an issue, only the 'tendency of the Greeks towards heresy'—and here one discerns the contempt now being felt in Rome for the Byzantines, though the final rejection of Byzantium in favour of a Frankish empire was still over two centuries away. Above all, the popes aimed at humiliating the see of Constantinople so that never again could its patriarch claim ecumenical status, and hence, the inclusion of Acacius's successors as worthy of condemnation, and, finally, the emperors Zeno and Anastasius themselves.[14]

In face of the unrelenting hostility of the popes, the east, from the emperor and patriarch to the anti-Chalcedonian populace in Syria and Egypt reacted coolly. There was no anti-papal outburst in the provinces. Acacius, if he felt any discomfiture did not show it. He dropped Felix's name from the diptychs, but that was all. His aim as that of Zeno and his successor Anastasius (491-518) was to secure religious peace in the empire on the basis of the *Henotikon*. Relations with Rome were not neglected, but until the revolt of Vitalian in 513 showed the latent power of the Latin-speaking and pro-Chalcedonian provinces, Rome was allowed to express its anger in a void. To Zacharias Rhetor, John Talaia was a 'liar' and by implication Simplicius was foolish to write to the emperor on his behalf.[14a] Acacius died in November 488. His two successors, Fravitta (d. 489) and Euphemius (489-95) both sent letters to Rome announcing their election, only to be caustically rebuffed.[15] Macedonius (495-11) wished to include Rome among the recipients of his synodical letter, but this time the emperor vetoed the move. Chances of the restoration of union, however, were not neglected on the Byzantine side. In the short but significant reign of pope Anastasius (496-8), a great effort

---

[14] For an account of the attitude of the popes towards the emperor and the Byzantine church at this period, see F. Caspar, *Geschichte des Papstums*, 2 vols (Tübingen 1930-3) 2, pp 35 seq.
[14a] *HE VI* 7.
[15] Gelasius told Euphemius that he belonged to 'an alien body'. *Epp* 2 and 3. See Frend pp 192-4.

Eastern attitudes to Rome during the Acacian schism

was made not only to restore harmony between Old and New Rome, but also between the former and Alexandria. Anastasius was the opposite in temperament and inclination to Gelasius. He was a Roman by birth and the son of a presbyter, very much a Christian aristocrat who looked instinctively to the emperor at Constantinople as his earthly sovereign. The reaction of the patriarch Athanasius, Peter Mongus's successor, to the chance of negotiation was surprising. In tones flattering to the pope, he emphasised the links of orthodoxy and fellowship that united the sees of Peter and of 'Mark, his imitator', and their joint guardianship of the faith. The existing sorry division had been caused by the devil. In particular, he had caused Leo's letter when translated into Greek to be susceptible to Nestorian interpretations. The dissension was unjustified and if the pope would accept the Alexandrian confession of faith, unity could be restored. This confession, of course, included the *Henotikon*, which the Alexandrians cite almost verbatim, Cyril's *Anathemas*, and acceptance of Dioscorus, Timothy the Cat and Peter Mongus as guardians of that faith. If the pope had aught against them, let him prove his case or restore them to the diptychs. For their part the Alexandrians were prepared to send a delegation to Rome to discuss the unity of the churches.[16]

This was not intended as sarcasm. The tone of the letter was firm and sincere. In the capital the pope's ambassador, the Roman senator Festus intimated that Anastasius might be prepared to sign the *Henotikon* if the hostile reference to Chalcedon was omitted and Acacius were dropped from the diptychs. Cyril's *Anathemas* had never been condemned, and it was left to the initiative of the pope to prove charges against Dioscorus and his successors as, one hundred and fifty years before, pope Julius had demanded of the eastern bishops to prove their case against Athanasius. After the Acacian schism had ended in 519, Justin and Justinian returned to the record of the negotiations with Anastasius to impress on pope Hormisdas their view of the settlement,[17] that is, no one was to be condemned except Acacius.

The negotiations in the capital in 497 between the representatives of Rome, Constantinople and Alexandria indicate a desire on all sides to reach agreement, and the absence of ill-feeling towards Rome on the

---

[16] Cited by pope Anastasius *Ep* 5=*CA* 102, (The *Libellus* of the Alexandrian church).
[17] Justin to Hormisdas, 9 Sept 520: Anastasius palam aperteque constituerit, cum ob hoc idem scriberet negotium decessori nostro, satis esse pacem affectantibus, si nomen tantum reticeatur Acacii=*CA* 232, p 702.

part of the two major eastern patriarchates. As time went on the schism hardened. Anastasius, however, was prepared to ask for pope Hormisdas's mediation in 515 when Vitalian seemed to be in a position to overthrow him, but all the time he stuck to two principles: he would not impose the creed of a Latin-speaking minority on the empire as a whole and he would not make the living pay for the errors of the dead. Only in 517, when the negotiations with pope Hormisdas had dragged out to an inordinate length, did the aged emperor Anastasius lose patience, and tell the pope that he was not prepared to be insulted by him.[18] Normally, the exchanges if uncompromising in substance, were courteous in tone. On the Byzantine side the schism was a matter of regret, and in this the court and patriarchate reflected opinion outside the capital.

For the monks of Egypt Rome was venerable and far away, a place where there were aristocratic ascetics and a martyr chapel in honour of Peter.[18a] For those subjects of the emperor who supported the doctrinal definition of Chalcedon, it was also the touchstone of orthodoxy and a protection against the increasingly pro-monophysite policy of the emperor Anastasius. In the end, such real success as the pope could claim at the ending of the schism was due to the massive support his cause received from the monks in the province of Syria Secunda and the churches in the Latin-speaking provinces of the Balkans.

At the same time, opposition to Chalcedon did not imply opposition to the papacy. This can be seen on the popular level, in the *Plerophoriae* (*Witnesses*) of John of Beit Rufin. Set down about 512, there is much horrific denunciation of pope Leo and his *Tome*, 'a treasure house of all blasphemy and impiety', and an abomination.[19] There is no criticism against the see of Rome, as such. Nor is there a tendency to invoke the doctrine of the contagion of evil, popular in the west, which would have involved Leo's successors in the heresy perpetrated in the *Tome*. This, by combining doctrinal with emotional antagonism would have rendered the schism irreconcilable. The *Plerophoriae* carry no attacks on Leo's successors and, so far as they may be understood, contain no reference at all to the existence of the Acacian schism. Pope Gelasius was not answered in his own theological language. A possible explanation of this may be that western concepts of papal primacy were

---

[18] *CA* 138, p 565.
[18a] Palladius, *Lausiac History*, ed and tr W. K. Lowther Clarke (London 1918) caps 41, 45, 4 and 46.
[19] *Plerophoria* 89, *PO* 8.1 (Paris 1912) p 151.

Eastern attitudes to Rome during the Acacian schism

of little interest to the mass of eastern Christians. It has been pointed out for instance that leaders of the early Syriac tradition, such as Aphrahat (c 340) and Ephrem Syrus (d. 374) had a high sense of episcopal office and its continuity from apostolic times but, within that college they had nothing to say about a Petrine primacy. Ephrem comments on Matt. 16.18 without referring to Christ founding his church on Peter. Hence the impact of Acacius's quarrel with Simplicius was muted. Individual popes might be praised or blamed, but questions relating to the status of the see of Rome had not yet impinged fully on popular consciousness.[19a]

More urbane and less strident, the writings of Severus of Antioch, the monophysite patriarch of that city between 512–18 point in the same direction. Severus was a hellenist of hellenists, a Christian philosopher in the tradition of the Cappadocian fathers, but his writings lack any systematic treatment of the papacy in the light of the Acacian schism. This applies to those written in Constantinople in 509–11, such as the *Philalethes*. Leo's disgraceful utterances in the *Tome* which appeared to vindicate Nestorius affected only himself, though he had brought discredit on his see. 'Would that he had never been bishop', is Severus's verdict.[20] For Severus, Rome was a holy see whose bishops were ordinarily worthy of respect: 'those who preside over the holy church of the city of the Romans'.[21] They are placed, however, on exactly the same footing as other leaders of major churches, such as 'the great Dionysius', of Alexandria (247–64)[22] or his own predecessors 'of this Christ-loving city of Antiochus'. Their authority is quoted as of equal weight with that of these orthodox leaders, no more and no less. When Severus cites the text Mt 16.18. it is to the church and its faith, and not to Peter personally or to his descendants, that he refers the Lord's words.[23] Allegorical interpretation applied as much to this text as to others.

One example of Severus's attitude to the bishops of Rome may be given. The touchstone of Severus's religious outlook was 'accuracy' of doctrine, which involved the acceptance, as he says of every word of Cyril of Alexandria as canonical, and the toleration of the *Henotikon* only in the sense that it annulled the definition of Chalcedon. In this

---

[19a] Thus, Robert Murray, *Symbols of Church and Kingdom* (Cambridge 1975) pp 236–8.
[20] Thus, the sixth book of the *Select Letters [of Severus Patriarch of Antioch]*, ed E. W. Brooks (London 1904) IV 3, p 258.
[21] *Ibid* bk V 6, p 296 (referring to pope Stephen and similarly bk V 3, p 284, referring to pope Julius).
[22] *Ibid* p 297.   [23] *Ibid* p 295.

respect he was almost as much opposed to his contemporary, the patriarch Macedonius, as he was to pope Leo himself. Much of his time when he was patriarch was taken up in examining and if possible reconciling the numerous waverers among his clergy who placed less emphasis on doctrinal accuracy than he. Should clergy previously pro-Chalcedonian who renounced Chalcedon be rebaptised or not? Severus who lived in the bible and the fathers at once went back to the documents relating to the rebaptism controversy in north Africa in Cyprian's time. Cyprian he regarded as over-scrupulous, preserved from dogmatism only by his conciliatory letter to the Mauretanian bishop Quintus. The proper solutions were arrived at by pope Xystus and Dionysius of Alexandria who agreed that heretics who had been baptised in the name of the Trinity should not be rebaptised on conversion to orthodox communion. Pope Xystus was cited as an 'orthodox opinion'.[24] However, the complete validity of his views could be questioned, for those heretics who were astray on doctrinal grounds, particularly as regards the Person of Christ, should be rebaptised. Here Severus cited canon 19 of the council of Nicaea, which singled out the Paulianists (followers of Paul of Samosata) as requiring re-baptism.[25] The decree of Nicaea was all important. The pope's opinion was valuable corroboration when it was needed.

Severus was glad to have the support of the pope against anything that smacked of two-nature Christology; and to his correspondents in the monastery of Tagais in Isauria who had raised the problem of re-baptism he cited the letter of pope Julius to an alleged presbyter Dionysius in which the adherents of Paul of Samosata are called *Paulianisti*.[26] This letter is a forgery, as is another alleged letter of pope Julius, addressed to Prosdocius also condemning the two-nature Christology as 'blasphemy', and glorifying the Virgin from whom Christ took flesh and reigns for ever 'in mortal form'. This letter provided Severus with some of his favourite proof texts in support of the one nature of the incarnate Christ.[26a]

By no means all of the questions concerning these 'papal letters' have been cleared up.[27] Examination indicates a passable imitation of the

---

[24] *Ibid* bk V 1, p 279.   [25] *Ibid* bk V 6, p 298.
[26] *Ibid* bk V 3, p 285. It seems that Severus mistakenly thought Dionysius was bishop. See the note in Migne *PL* 8, col 928.
[26a] Text in Migne, *PL* 8, cols 953–9.
[27] Briefly recorded in B. Altaner/A. Stuiber, *Patrologie, Leben, Schriften und Lehre der Kirchenväter* (Freiburg 1966) p 314. It seems that no one since the editors of Migne *PL* 8 has given any exhaustive study to these documents, which would repay consideration.

Eastern attitudes to Rome during the Acacian schism

indignant style of Julius' surviving letters ('I am amazed', etc.),[28] and his recourse to 'apostolic tradition' to support his authoritative utterances.[29] The writer knew what he was about and was clever enough to direct their attack against Arianism and Paul of Samosata and to avoid obvious Apollinarianisms. The Virgin is not referred to as '*Theotokos*'. The letters can hardly date later than the last quarter of the fourth century when Arianism was still a living issue and 'Theotokos' not yet a badge of Alexandrian orthodoxy. These letters were accepted as genuine throughout the east from the council of Ephesus I until they were denounced as forgeries by the monks of Syria Secunda in 514,[30] and as such they provided a point in favour of Rome. Julius was described by the Armenians at the council of Duin in 506 as 'the guide of the way of life for the westerns', and his outstanding orthodoxy could be set off against Leo.[31] The bishops of Rome might be guilty of misunderstanding the difference between the theological terms of *ousia* and *hypostasis*,[32] but there was no tradition of heresy to which the popes were victims. Severus had no rancour against Rome, but only against Leo as purveyor of false and indeed nonsensical doctrine, and in this he was supported by a large proportion of eastern Christians.

In all his long and varied correspondence, Severus makes no reference to Acacius or to the schism caused by his actions. Events at Constantinople or Rome were judged against the touchstone of doctrinal accuracy. When in April/May 518, with the end of Anastasius's reign in sight, a new patriarch, John, was consecrated in the capital, Severus wrote, 'As to the man who has just been instituted and holds the prelacy of the royal city, we have learnt that he is John . . . who is thought to be inclined to the right opinions and holds out some pleasing hope to the orthodox, but is more desirous of adopting a deceitful middle course'.[33] Rome is not mentioned. It was John's 'orthodoxy' in relation to Chalcedon that mattered.

Ultimately, this unremitting zeal brought its inevitable reward. There was a storm of protest in Severus's patriarchate led by the monks of Syria Secunda. Late in 517 they appealed to pope Hormisdas,

---

[28] Compare the style of Julius's genuine letter to the Eusebians preserved in Athanasius *Apologia Contra Arianos*, cap 35, especially in the final paragraph, with the first paragraph of his letter to Dionysius, *Miramur cum nonnullos* . . . (*PL* 8 col 930).
[29] *Ad Prosdocium* 1, ibid col 953.
[30] Evagrius, *HE* bk 3, 31.
[31] Letter from the Armenians to the orthodox in Persia, cited from K. Sarkissian, *The Council of Chalcedon and the Armenian Church* (London 1965) p 204.
[32] *Ep* 22, written *c* 520, ed E. W. Brooks, *PO* 12.2 (1916).
[33] *Select Letters* VI.1, pp 260–1.

denouncing Severus as a heretic, and declaring that 'Nestorius, Eutyches, Dioscorus, the two Peters and Acacius, and all those who defended so much as one of those heretics' should be excommunicated. The language in which they wrote to the pope was flattering in the extreme (Hormisdas was addressed as 'patriarch of the whole world'), but we should be wary of accepting this as proof that papal jurisdiction was acknowledged by the petitioners. The letter reads as though written by people at the end of their tether. Everything else had failed, including a petition at Constantinople. Now they turned to Hormisdas as 'a haven from storm and tempest' but the emphasis remained on the validity of Chalcedon. Leo was praised as a vindicator of the council and Acacius was condemned because, like Severus, he was associated in their minds with those who rejected it.[34] 'Four Councils' like 'Four Gospels' had become a slogan, and those who proclaimed them were as ready to appeal to the emperor as to the pope against Severus. In the new emperor, Justin they found a ruler who would restore the true faith, and there were no further appeals to Rome. The revolution succeeded. Severus ended his days an exile.

If for the west, the Acacian schism concerned the vindication of papal discipline and jurisdiction against the eastern patriarchates, for the east the issue was always seen against the background of the controversy over Chalcedon. In this, of course, the popes could never be left out of account permanently. The *Tome* of Leo was crucial to the credibility of the papacy as a source of authority, but even here, Leo was only one pope who could be regarded as unorthodox and against many illustrious predecessors who were models of rectitude. The two sides, however, were thinking in different terms, Rome in those of discipline and the Roman primacy, the easterners in terms of doctrine and also consensus among the 'college' of patriarchs. Mutual understanding was as far off under Justin and Justinian as it had been under Zeno and Anastasius. The ultimate power, too, remained with New Rome. The schism ended through the initiative of the Latin-speaking emperor, Justin, and not through any action by pope Hormisdas. After preliminary negotiations he was instructed by Justinian 'to hasten to the capital' so that communion could be restored between the two Romes according to the emperor's will.[35]

---

[34] *CA* 139. The western chronicler, Victor of Tunnuna, (*Chronicon* ad ann 516) records that the monks in Palestine and Transjordan sent a similar letter to the emperor Anastasius. *MGH, AA Chronica Minora* 2, ed T. Mommsen (Berlin 1894) p 195.

[35] *CA* 147: 'We expect your arrival without delay'. In case of some obstacle, the pope should send plenipotentiaries, but in any event speed was of the essence.

Eastern attitudes to Rome during the Acacian schism

The events of 28–31 March 519 were regarded by contemporaries as the ceremonial enactment of this restoration, based on the mutual acceptance of Chalcedon and agreement that Rome was an orthodox and apostolic see. Acacius could be dropped from the diptychs together with 'his associates'—variously defined—but not canon 28 of Chalcedon. The patriarch John, whatever his momentary weakness in accepting the papal *libellus* as it stood, was the first openly to use the title of ecumenical patriarch.[36] Justin and his all-powerful nephew Justinian were soon at pains to show that relations between Old and New Rome would remain precisely as they had been under their predecessors.

University of Glasgow

[36] Mansi 8, col 1038.

THE WEST

XII

Ecclesia Britannica · *Prelude or Dead End?*

When Augustine and his monks landed at Thanet in 597, they were confronted with a situation rare even in the *Völkerwanderung*. What was to become the church of the English people had to be built up from scratch. In his despatches to Pope Gregory during the first years of his mission, Augustine gives no hint of an existing native Christian population, survivors of Roman Britain under Jutish rule, who might form the nucleus of a Church.[1] There was Ethelbert's Frankish Queen Bertha and her retainers for whose use a church dedicated to St Martin outside the royal city of Canterbury, had been restored, and Bede mentions that this had been 'built of old while the Romans yet inhabited Britain'.[2] But despite Canterbury providing evidence for Christianity in the late fourth century[3] and being relatively near sites such as Lullingstone, Richborough and Faversham, where there had been Christian worship in Roman times, Augustine's problems were concerned entirely with how to deal with Germanic paganism. What had happened? How was it that the *ecclesia Britannorum* failed to provide foundations for the *ecclesia Anglicana* even in Kent?

The answer to that question has challenged generations of scholars. Of itself, the literary evidence for Roman-British Christianity is meagre and tantalising. All records of its councils and even its controversies have perished. Its major figures, Ninian and Patrick, stood too far on the periphery to provide leadership for the Church as a whole. After the Council of Arles in 314 no name of a British bishop in the fourth century has survived. Archaeological evidence is now beginning to fill in some of the gaps, though because of the chance character of many of the finds the results are uneven. A combination, however, of both types of evidence is making it possible to place Christianity in Roman Britain in the context of

---

[1] Bede, H[istoria] E[cclesiastica], ed. B. Colgrave and R. A. B. Mynors, Oxford 1969, i. 27, citing Gregory *Ep.* xi. 56 (in the Ewald and Hartmann ed. *MGH*). See R. A. Markus, 'Gregory the Great and a Papal Missionary Strategy' in *Studies in Church History* VI, ed. G. J. Cuming, Cambridge 1970, 29–38.

[2] Bede, *HE*, i. 26: 'dum adhuc Romani Britanniam incolerent in qua regina, quam Christianam fuisse praediximus, orare consuerat'.

[3] K. S. Painter, 'A Roman silver treasure from Canterbury', J[ournal of the] B[ritish] A[rchaeological] A[ssoc.], xxviii (1965), 1–15.

its development throughout the Gallic Prefecture of which it formed part. Comparisons and contrasts, particularly with Gaul, may throw further light on why Augustine faced so difficult a task.

As elsewhere in the west, literary sources show that Christianity was beginning to penetrate Britain during the first half of the third century. Leaving on one side the rhetorical references to British Christians in Tertullian (c. 200)[4] and Origen (c. 240),[5] one finds early traces of Christianity associated with military centres, such as Caerleon, while the name Aaron of an early confessor (c. 250–60), martyred there (or at Chester), suggests a Jewish background.[6] In the Romano-British towns, Verulamium has always been associated with Alban's death,[7] but the date of that event, whether under the Caesar Geta in 209 or in the Decian or Valerianic persecutions half a century later, remains uncertain. Levison's '*Ignoramus* and *ignorabimus*', still holds the field.[8] However, by the beginning of the fifth century there was a shrine in his honour at the scene of his death that had become a centre of pilgrimage[9] (probably on the hill east of Verulamium, where the cathedral now stands), and this was surviving when Bede wrote c. 731.

By the time of Constantine's victory over Maxentius in 312, Christianity in Britain was organised on an urban and episcopal basis. There were bishoprics at York, London, and perhaps Colchester (or Lincoln) of which the last named, whose bishop was accompanied to the Council of Arles by a priest and a deacon, would seem to have been the senior. It looks as though there was a bishopric in each of the four provinces into which Britain was divided.[10] The next reference to Britain was in 342/3

[4] Tertullian, *Adv. Iudaeos* vii.

[5] Origen, *Homil. iv in Ezekiel*, Hieron. interp. i (W. A. Baehrens, *Die Griechischen Christlichen Schriftsteller*, Origenes 8, Leipzig 1925, p. 362). The best short study of Christianity in Roman Britain remains J. M. C. Toynbee, 'Christianity in Roman Britain', *JBAA*, 3rd ser, xvi (1953), 1–24. See also, K. S. Painter, 'Villas and Christianity in Roman Britain', *B[ritish] M[useum] Q[uarterly]*, xxxv (1971), 156–75 (good bibliography) and J. H. Chandler, *The Bibliography of Christianity in Roman Britain*, Aberystwyth 1976.

[6] Bede, *HE*, i. 7, and Gildas, *De Excidio*, 10 (*MGH*, Chron. min. iii. 31). Caerleon seems the more likely site. See Toynbee, op. cit., 2.

[7] Bede *HE*, i. 7, 'usque ad hanc diem curatio infirmorum et frequentior operatio virtutum celebrari non desint'. See the discussion by W. Levison, 'St Alban and St Albans', *Antiquity* xv (1941), 337–59; John Morris, 'The date of St Alban', *Hertfordshire Archaeology* (1969), 1–8; and W. H. C. Frend, 'The Christianisation of Roman Britain' in *Christianity in Britain 300–700*, ed. M. Barley and R. P. C. Hanson, Leicester 1968, 37–49 at p. 38.

[8] Levison, op. cit., 350.

[9] Constantius of Lyon, *Vita S. Germani* 16, (*Acta Sanctorum*, ed. Bollandiana, July, vii, 200 ff), repeated by Bede, *HE*, i. 7.

[10] See J. G. Mann's note. 'The Administration of Roman Britain', *Antiquity*, xxxv (1961), 316–20. At Cirencester (Corinium) which may have been the capital of Britannia Prima and in the civilian settlement attached to the fort at Manchester (Mancunium) SATOR AREPO word squares dating probably to the late second century have been found. (For Manchester, see J. Perrott, *Observer*, July 1978, and forthcoming.) These squares, however, may be Jewish (see J. Meyring, *Rev. des sciences religieuses* xl, (1966), 321–52), and in the first two centuries AD this seems likely.

when at the Council of Serdica its Churches were included among those that accepted the creed of Nicaea and urged the return of Athanasius to Alexandria.[11] In 359, at the Council of Ariminum, the Britons were still pro-Nicene and resisted the attempt by the emperor Constantius II to impose a compromise though basically Arian creed on the West. Three British bishops, however, accepted the emperor's offer to pay their return journey from the imperial treasury. Their action, though resented by some western bishops, was defended by others on the ground that the poverty they pleaded was real.[12]

For another quarter of a century, literary records are silent about the British Churches. The administration of the island, however, took on the same Christian colouring as over the remainder of the west. The commander of the forces on Hadrian's Wall, Magnus Maximus, who usurped power in the west in 383 was a strong, even fanatical Nicene Christian. Sometime, also, about 380 Pelagius was born, perhaps the son of a Roman official, and a decade or so later saw the birth of Patrick, the son of Calpurnius, a town councillor (*decurion*) and a deacon, and the grandson of a Christian *presbyter*, Potitus. This urban middle class family had been Christian for three generations.[13] We know also that the Church in Britain had its internal problems during the 390s and that some of its leaders prevailed on Victricius, bishop of Rouen and friend of Paulinus of Nola to come to Britain and attempt to solve them.[14] He came, c. 396, but what exactly were 'the precepts of the martyrs' that he took with him is uncertain. Links between Gallic and British Christianity may also be indicated by the mission of Ninian, based perhaps on a bishopric at Carlisle (Luguvallum). Ninian aimed to extend Christianity across the Roman frontier to the Pictish *foederati* settled on the north side of the Solway Firth. The association between Ninian and Martin of Tours seems to rest on long-standing tradition,[15] and the episcopal but at the same time ascetic Christianity associated with his work could well owe something to Martin's influence.[16]

The impression left by the literary evidence down to the end of the fourth century is of a Church that conformed to the western pattern in doctrine and discipline. It was in contact with the Gallic Churches, but it

---

[11] Athanasius, *Apol. ad Constantium imperatorem*, 15 (P.G., xxv, 613).

[12] Sulpicius Severus, *Chronicon* (ed. Halm, *CSEL*, i) ii. 41.

[13] Patrick, *Confessio* 1 (ed. L. Bieler, Dublin 1952).

[14] Victricius, *De Laude Sanctorum* (P.L., xx, 443-4). He evidently went to carry out some work on behalf of the Gallic Churches. 'Nam quod ad Britannias profectus sum, quod ibi moratus sum, vestrorum fecit exsecutio praeceptorum.'

[15] On Ninian, see A. C. Thomas, 'The Evidence from Northern Britain,' in Barley and Hanson (above note 7), 93-117, especially notes 11 and 12. My view remains that Ninian was a late Romano-Briton, that he did work with Martin and returned to his native land to preach at first to an existing nucleus of Pictish Christians, a monastic type of Christianity within an episcopal framework, just as Martin himself had done.

[16] Bede, *HE*, iii. 4. Of the considerable discussion, see particularly E. A. Thompson, 'The Origin of Christianity in Scotland' *Scottish Hist. Review*, xxxvii (1958), 17 ff, and other literature cited by Thomas, art. cit.

did not represent a popular movement in the sense that Christianity represented one in North Africa and Egypt. While Britain was reckoned a wealthy island, and worth defending to the very end of the century, the Church remained in a somewhat depressed and impoverished condition. This impression is both confirmed and belied by archaeological evidence. As one would expect, there are still two main zones of Christian activity, just as the present writer mapped them more than twenty years ago.[17] The first comprises the romanised and urbanised south and south-east from the Wash to Exeter, the second from York north-west to include Carlisle and the Cumbrian coast, the military zone, especially the western end of it. A new map would include more find-spots, particularly in Dorset where the Christian cemetery of Poundbury outside Dorchester (Durnovaria) and the Christ-mosaic in the villa of Hinton St Mary have been outstanding discoveries, while previous finds at Brougham, Maryport and Carlisle itself just about support the claim made out for a late-Roman bishopric based on the large *vicus* of Carlisle (Luguvallum).[18] The gaps, however, also gain significance, because research into early Christianity in these islands has been intensive during the interval. To date no Christian building has been found on a village site (though Christian remains have been found in a building on the villa estate at Gatcombe in Somerset[19]), and in towns where one might have expected the detailed work of archaeologists to produce some evidences of Christianity, such as at Wroxeter, this has so far not done so.

For urban Christianity, one must therefore attach a good deal of weight to the one indisputable basilican church in Britain, that found at Silchester in 1892, and exhaustively re-excavated and discussed by the late I. A. Richmond and Sheppard Frere.[20] It was prominently sited near the town's forum but was a relatively small building. It included some unusual features in a western church. The 'altar enclosure' marked by a black and white chequer-board mosaic stood nearer the apse than is usual and resembled the eastern more than the western arrangement.[21] At the north end of the narthex were found traces of a circular foundation which 'strongly suggests the presence of an offering table on the foundation; here in the narthex it would be accessible to the unbaptised members of the congregation'. Richmond pointed out that these arrangements resembled those of fourth- and fifth-century Syria,[22] while another

---

[17] See W. H. C. Frend, 'Religion in Roman Britain in the Fourth Century AD', *JBAA*, 3rd ser., xviii (1955), 1–18, at pl. i, and Thomas's comments filling out the picture to 1967, art. cit, 97.

[18] Thomas, art. cit, 99 ff., and idem, *The Early Christian Archaeology of North Britain*, Glasgow/Oxford 1971, 12–13.

[19] *Britannia*, viii (1977) 444, Building 19.

[20] S. S. Frere, 'The Silchester Church: the excavation by Sir Ian Richmond in 1961', *Archaeologia*, cv (1976), 277–302. The church was 42 ft (12·80 m) in overall length and 24 ft 3 ins (7·39 m) wide. The side aisles were narrow, no more than 5 ft (1·52 m) wide.

[21] Ibid., 293.

[22] Ibid., 294.

XII

ECCLESIA BRITANNICA: PRELUDE OR DEAD END?

curious feature was the existence of what appears to be a rectangular piscina in an open forecourt that lay outside the atrium. The latter feature is as yet unknown in Gaul, but a fine example exists in the great Damous el Karita church at Carthage,[23] and parallels are found in connection with synagogues where ablution was required before entering the building.[24] The problems are puzzling, but not inexplicable. If Christianity was spread to Britain through merchants from the Mediterranean, as it was spread to other parts of the west, the survival of Mediterranean features among some of the communities is not unexpected.[25] The church, however, erected 'a decade either side of 350', was eventually abandoned and occupied by squatters.[26] Its history may underline some features of the Church in Britain, its immigrant origins, its period of prosperity in the reign of Constantius and Valentinian and its gradual decline later, leading to its abandonment as a church and use by squatters. It is this final phase, the result of neglect, and not of destruction by invaders, that raises questions for the historian.

In recent years some large urban cemeteries have been identified as Christian. York, with its bishopric, could be expected to have a Christian cemetery. One probably existed in the Castle Yard, for a burial was recorded as being furnished with a bone plaque inscribed 'Domine Victor Vincas Felix': the combination of invocation of the Lord, and a blessed conquest (of death) must indicate Christianity. Of greater interest is the isolated burial consisting of a coffin in which was the skeleton of a woman with glass vessels and jewellery and a delicately carved bracelet in bone, an open-work inscription reading 'S[or]or Ave Vivas in Deo'.[27] This has the authentic ring of fourth-century Christianity, still a closely knit religion of the brethren, placing their hope in heavenly resurrection. The array of grave goods testifies to the social level of the deceased, whose family seem to have regarded Christianity as a valuable personal adjunct to traditional rites. A less expected discovery has been the cemetery at Poundbury. Evidence for Christianity in the town of Durnovaria had been confined to a hoard of late Roman silver spoons marked with a fish and

---

[23] The writer's observation on the ground in 1976. See also H. Leclercq, art. 'Carthage', D[ictionnaire d'] A[rchéologie] C[hrétienne et de] L[iturgie], ed. F. Cabrol, H. Leclercq, 11. 2, 2252–8, and fig. 2129.

[24] The Jewish evidence is cited by Frere, op. cit., 295–6.

[25] On the immigrant contribution to the Christian mission in the west, see Frend, 'A note on the influence of Greek Immigrants on the spread of Christianity in the West', Mullus (Festschrift Th. Klauser = Jahrbuch für Antike und Christentum, Ergänzungsband 1964), 125–30.

[26] This important feature is discussed by Frere (above note 20), 287 ff.

[27] See H. G. Ramm, 'The end of Roman York' in Soldier and Civilian in Roman Yorkshire (Essays to commemorate the nineteenth centenary of the foundation of York), ed. R. M. Butler, Leicester 1971, 179–99; Royal Commission on Historical Monuments; an inventory of Historical monuments in the City of York i, Eburacum, London 1962, 135; and G. Home, Roman York, London 1924, 190 (illustration).

symbol,[28] but Poundbury cemetery contains upwards of 4,000 burials extending over a period of about two hundred years, of which 1,070 have been excavated. Gradually it has become clear that many of these graves must be Christian and that the users were relatively wealthy. In one mausoleum was a coin of Magnentius with prominent Chi-Rho reverse which had been used as an amulet. A lead coffin found below another bore the inscription on the underside of the lid, IN DNE (In n[omine] D[omin]ne), and in this there was evidence of embalming. Most interesting was a group of plaster-lined coffins,[29] and while these bore no Christian symbol, the purpose to preserve the outline of the body may be paralleled by tombs in Christian cemeteries in North Africa, notably at Timgad.[30] At the Last Day the body would be given back to the Christian for Judgment.

Where did this large and relatively wealthy Christian community come from? Though no certainty is possible, it can be said that by 350 a number of the landowning familes who lived in the Roman villas in what may be presumed to be the cantonal territory of Durnovaria were Christian. To the villa at Frampton north-west of the town with its fine mosaic on which both Neptune and a Chi-Rho are represented and the silver ring and spoons at Fifehead Neville,[31] one may add the villa at Hinton St Mary excavated in 1963. Here forming part of a mosaic that carpeted a large room (28 × 29 square feet), was a roundel containing the bust of a youthful, beardless figure with a Chi-Rho monogram behind the head and flanked by pomegranates. This can hardly be other than Christ. Four half circles surrounded the central feature, one containing a tree while on the other three a hound chases or confronts a stag. In each corner there was a male bust, two flanked by rosettes and two by pomegranates. In an adjacent portion of the same mosaic there is a representation of Bellerophon seated on Pegasus slaying the Chimaera, and in

---

[28] See O. M. Dalton, 'Roman spoons from Dorchester', *Antiquaries Journal*, ii (1922), 89 ff: associated with 50 *siliquae* dating from Julian (361-3) to Honorius (395-423).

[29] C. J. S. Green, 'The Significance of Plaster Burials for the recognition of Christian cemeteries' in *Burial in the Roman World*, CBA Research Report 22, ed. R. Reece, 1977, 46-53, and the same author's Interim Report on his excavations at Poundbury in *Proc. Dorset Nat. Hist. and Arch. Soc.*, xci (1969), 125-8. In a letter of 27 October 1978, Mr Green writes, 'So, I see in fourth-century Dorchester, a small but active and well organized church with one or two rich and/or influential families supporting them as patrons, this group having a distinct burial site and a separate, private cemetery perhaps organized by the church, and hence the regularity and standardisation of burial, contrasting with the chaos in the normal cemeteries, of which one, Poundbury ii abutting cemetery iii, was contemporary with, and was respected by it'. Green estimates the Christian population at between two and four hundred, or about 5%-10% of the population of Durnovaria as a whole. Other Christian burials may be suspected in Romano-British cemeteries at Winchester, Ancaster and Southwark.

[30] For the Timgad example, see Frend, 'Der Donatismus und die afrikanische Kirche' (=*Wissenschaftliche Arbeit der Martin Luther Universität*, x/i (1961), 53-62, at p. 60, pl. 3.

[31] Frend (above note 17), 7, and J. M. C. Toynbee, 'Pagan Motifs and Practices in Christian Art and Ritual in Roman Britain', in Barley and Hanson (above note 7), 177-92.

ECCLESIA BRITANNICA: PRELUDE OR DEAD END?

lateral panels, hunting scenes rather more elaborate than those on the Christ mosaic.[32]

Dr Smith may well be right in thinking that the Frampton and Hinton St Mary mosaics were made by the same school of craftsmen, c. 325–50.[33] Of interest is the association of pagan imagery with Christianity in the setting of the home of a wealthy fourth-century landowner. At Lullingstone[34] one may point to the same phenomenon. The house-church, consisting of three rooms was indeed self-contained, a corridor leading to the apsed *triclinium* of the villa being blocked, but the conversion of these rooms for purely Christian devotional purposes seems to have taken place not much later than 350, at a time when the rest of the villa was in full domestic use. The mosaic of the floor of the *triclinium* was also a representation of Bellerophon slaying the Chimaera and in each corner were portraits of the Four Seasons.[35] In none of these instances, do we get the impression that adoption of Christianity involved any violent change from the past. Christ was being added to an already well peopled pantheon of protecting deities. Like Bellerophon, He would lend His strength to ward off evil from the household.

The long, slow transition that seems to have been going on among the upper strata of Romano-British society in the middle of the fourth century, may also be illustrated by the superb collection of Roman Christian silver found at Water Newton (Hunts.) in 1975. The find was made by a perceptive amateur on the site of what may turn out to be a small Romano-British town.[36] The *pièce de resistance* is a beautiful plain, two-handled silver goblet, surely a Eucharistic chalice and the first ever found in the western provinces of the empire. A bowl had been given by 'Viventia and Innocentia'. Other objects, cups, a silver strainer, and a flagon are almost equally striking. The translation of one dedication reads, 'Lord we humbly honour thy sacred altar'.[37] The community to which they belonged were not impoverished. But, most interesting from our point of view, are a series of silver foil triangular plaques, their outer faces shaped and ornamented like a feather and at the base of the triangle a roundel containing a Chi-Rho flanked by α/ω. These plaques made of

---

[32] J. M. C. Toynbee, 'A new Roman mosaic pavement found in Dorset', *J[ournal] of R[oman] S[tudies]*, liv (1964), 7–14.

[33] D. J. Smith, 'Three fourth-century Schools of Mosaic in Roman Britain' (in *La mosaïque gréco-romaine*, Paris 1965), and 'The Mosaic pavements' in *The Roman Villa in Britain*, ed. A. L. F. Rivet, London 1969, 71–125, at 109–13, discussing the existence of a 'Durnovaria school' of mosaicists in the fourth century.

[34] G. W. Meates, *Lullingstone Roman Villa*, London 1955, chs xii–xiv. Dating post-354. (See B. W. Pearce, 'The Coins' = App. iv to G. W. Meates *et al.*, 'The Lullingstone Roman Villa, Second Interim Report, *Arch. Cantiana*, lxv (1952), 68.)

[35] For the Christian interpretation of the Bellerophon myth, see Toynbee (above note 32), 14, and M. Simon, 'Bellérophon chrétien', *Mélanges Carcopino*, Paris 1966, 899–904. Also Toynbee, 'Mosäiques à Bellérophon', *Gallia*, xiii (1955), 91–7.

[36] K. S. Painter, *The Water Newton Early Christian Silver*, London 1977.

[37] Ibid., pls. 6, 8 and 9.

silver or bronze are fairly frequent finds on Romano-Celtic temple sites.[38] They were used as votive offerings and hung by a nail to the walls of the shrine, and the name of the god, or a symbol, engraved in the roundel. At Water Newton, however, this same space has been occupied by a Christian symbol and a hole in the apex of the triangle and through the haft of the Chi-Rho symbol on one such plaque shows that the votive purpose remained in the Christian as in the pagan setting.[39]

One other series of finds is also relevant, namely, the lead water-tanks, some marked with Christian symbols, of which a dozen have now been discovered.[40] These are large and expensive objects, capable of holding up to sixty-five gallons of water. They have been found in a variety of settings, from near a Roman villa such as at Icklingham in Suffolk, Bourton-on-the-Water in Gloucestershire, 'Roman buildings' at Wiggonholt in Sussex, or simply dredged up from the River Ouse near Huntingdon, or from the bottom of a Roman well at Ashton in Northants.[41] Not all are definitely Christian, but the Chi-Rho symbol stamped on the sides of some show that these served a Christian purpose. This could have been baptism. An inscribed fourth/fifth-century marble funerary slab from Aquileia shows a neophyte standing in a large bowl while water flows over him/her from above while the officiant places a hand on his/her head.[42] On another engraving from Aquileia the neophyte is also shown standing in a basin while water flows from the beak of a dove into a bowl held ready by the officiant to pour over her head.[43] No explanation can be offered for these baptismal rites, so different from their normal association with a baptistery attached to the church. The hexagonal baptismal font at Richborough shows that this form existed also in Roman Britain and that baptism by immersion was practised.[44]

Christianity in fourth-century Britain presents a series of disjointed cameos. The literary evidence suggests a poor and rather undeveloped Church, following the lead of more experienced continental Churches but contributing little itself. The Church may still have included a

[38] The silver crowns and feathers from Cavenham in Suffolk (N. F. Layard *Ant. Journ.*, vi (1925), 258–65, and figs 4 and 5), are a fine example of a pagan parallel to those in Water Newton Treasure. See also, R. E. M. and T. V. Wheeler, *Lydney Park* (Report of the Research Committee of the Society of Antiquaries, ix, 1932), 90, and pl. xxvi–xxix, especially object no. 137.

[39] Painter, op. cit., pls. 11, 12, 13 and 14.

[40] Discussed by Toynbee (above note 5), 15–16, and by Painter in *BMQ*, xxxv (1971), 163.

[41] Reported in *Britannia*, viii (1977), 399, and 443–4, in a well associated with late-fourth-century material. A second similar lead tank from Icklingham in Suffolk is reported in ibid., 444–5.

[42] G. Brusin, 'Il R. Museo archeologico di Aquileia' (Itinerari dei Musei e Monumenti d'Italia, no. 48), 1936, 12, 45 and fig 26.

[43] F. Cabrol, *Aquilée, DACL*, i. 2, 1907, fig 877, 2 and 871.

[44] See P. D. C. Brown, 'The Church at Richborough', *Britannia*, ii (1971), 225–31 and plates. The date could be c. 350.

ECCLESIA BRITANNICA: PRELUDE OR DEAD END?

considerable number of immigrants. The Silchester community did not survive the end of the town and the site of their church retained no special sanctity to be remembered by later generations. Other archaeological evidence, however, presents a different picture, of the progressive Christianisation from c. 330 onwards, of an educated and landed class who would have dominated life in the province, people who could afford fine mosaics, and pewter dinner services.[45] The wall paintings at Lullingstone show also that these Christians were in no way behind the Continent in their power of artistic expression and that Christian art in Roman Britain was following the same patterns as elsewhere. The representation of the *Orante*, the Christian monogram set within a wreath with birds—Christian souls—pecking at fruit and flowers, and the painting of the church(?) would have done credit to a Christian artist in a fully christianised area in the west.[46] They demonstrate that Christianity in Roman Britain cannot be understood in isolation.

What then can one learn from the progress of Christianity across the Channel? In Gaul, the records reach back much further than in Britain. The Rhône valley had its Christian communities by 175, and the story of the Martyrs of Lyon reveals Christians as largely members of a trading and immigrant community from Asia Minor.[47] In the third century, however, Christianity expanded only slowly. We know that there was a bishopric of Arles in 254 as well as at Lyon, because Marcianus of Arles was delated as a Novatianist to Cyprian of Carthage by the bishop of Lyon and other unnamed colleagues.[48] The story of Christianity, however, as a widespread movement outside the main trading areas begins, as it does in Britain, with the Council of Arles. Northern Gaul was represented by the solitary bishop of Rouen who was accompanied by a deacon. As has been pointed out, his and other Gallic bishoprics resembled islands in a 'sea of paganism at this time.[49]

The transformation comes, again as in Britain towards the middle years of the fourth century, and it affects the urban and literate part of the population rather than the countryside. In general terms, Hilary of Poitiers writing c. 365, describes how people were now streaming into the churches. 'Every day, the believing people increases, and professions of faith are multiplied. Pagan superstitions are abandoned together with the

---

[45] As for instance from the villas at Welney and Appleshaw near Andover.

[46] Described by Meates (above note 34), 137. See J. M. C. Toynbee, *Art in Britain under the Romans*, Oxford 1964, 225–6, and Painter (above note 5), 167 and n 76.

[47] See the papers presented to mark the 1600th anniversary of the Martyrs of Lyon = Colloques Internationaux du centre national de la Recherche scientifique, no. 575, Paris 1978; and Eusebius's account of the martyrdoms in *HE*, v. 1 and 2.

[48] Cyprian, *Ep.* 68 (ed. Hartel, *CSEL*, iii. ii), Cyprian speaks of 'coepiscopos nostros in Gallia constitutos', but mentions only Faustinus of Lyon.

[49] See Aline Rousselle, 'Aspects sociaux du recrutement ecclésiastique du ive siècle, *Mélanges de l'Ecole française à Rome: Antiquité*, lxxxix, (1977. i), 333–76, at 335–6: 'Reims, Rouen, Autun, Cologne, Trèves, Bordeaux, toutes épiscopales, quelques points dans un désert païen.'

impious fables of mythology, and the altars of demons and the vanity of idols. Everyone is moving along the road to salvation'.[50] This was optimistic at the time, but events were to justify it. Thirteen years before, the usurper, Magnentius (350–3), though by birth a Germanic pagan soldier, had thought it worthwhile, during his final stand against Constantius II in Gaul, to mint a series of large bronze coins from Amiens (Ambianum) whose reverses were dominated by a Chi-Rho.[51] The appeal was to the Christian sentiment of their users, to demonstrate that he and not his rival was the true Christian emperor.

Gallic Christianity in the mid-fourth century, however, was not a popular religion confronting paganism as was its counterpart in North Africa. It built on traditional pagan values, especially Gallic pagan, and transformed them to its own model. It would be tempting to quote the Mildenhall treasure, with its synthesis of pagan and Christian motifs as an example, but its attribution to the Caesar Julian's Christian general, Lupicinus, sent to Britain from Gaul in 360, is unproved, and so too, the Gallic origin of the magnificent silver.[52] One may, however, point to the life of the poet and politician, Ausonius (c. 310–c. 390) as an instance of how a figure firmly immersed in the patriotic Roman tradition of the Gallic nobility had adopted the new religion.[53] Ausonius was a Christian, but not outspokenly so. He occasionally attended Easter celebrations at Bordeaux, but otherwise his poems give few hints as to his religious allegiance. He evidently believed that the same tongue could sing praises of Jupiter as well as to Christ. How his family became Christian is unknown, though one may suspect maternal rather than paternal influence.[54] Apart from his formal adherence to the Church, Ausonius is entirely absorbed in the pagan past, in Roman history and literature, and by no means least in the claims of friends to trace their ancestry to Druid priests.[55] He shows us a society in the process of slow christianisation in which pagan values and traditions were being gradually absorbed and

---

[50] *Tract. in Ps*, 67. 20 (*CSEL* 22, ed. Zingerle/Feder). No bishop of Poitiers is known before Hilary. Tours had no bishop before c. 337 when Litorius was consecrated (Gregory of Tours, *Hist. Francorum*, i. 48), but no church until c. 350.

[51] On the significance, see J. Ziegler, *Zur religiösen Haltung der Gegenkaiser in 4 Jh. n. Chr*, = F[rankfurter] A[lthistorische] S[tudien], 1970, 57–64.

[52] Lupicinus had an estate in Gaul (Sulpicius Severus, *Vita S. Martini*, 8). See K. S. Painter's discussion of the treasure, 'The Mildenhall Treasure': a reconsideration, *BMQ*, xxxvii (1973), 154–80.

[53] For Ausonius's background, see H. Isbell, 'Decimus Magnus Ausonius: the poet and his world' (=22–57 in *Latin Literature of the Fourth Century*, ed. J. W. Binns, London 1974).

[54] Women did exercise a considerable influence on their menfolk in south Gaulish and Spanish families. Paulinus of Nola goes to live on his wife's estates after their marriage. Ausonius has the highest regard for his mother's probity and chastity, though he does not say she was a Christian.

[55] Thus, *Commemoratio Professorum* (ed. H. G. Evelyn White, Loeb Class. Lib., Harvard/London 1951), iv. 7–10 and x. 22–30.

replaced. Bellerophon retained his place in his scale of moral values as he did in those of the villa owners of Hinton St Mary and Lullingstone.

There were, however, two developments in Gaul after 370 that did not take place in Britain. First, there was the career and missionary zeal of Martin of Tours (d. 397) and, secondly, Christian practices took an ever deepening hold on popular religion, replacing similar pagan rites. Down to 370 Gallic Christianity remained largely urban and aristocratic. Sulpicius Severus, Martin's biographer, notes the presence of many young nobles among Martin's early followers,[56] and perhaps more significant, when, c. 368, Martin was put forward for the vacant bishopric of Tours, there was strong opposition from his future episcopal colleagues on the grounds of Martin's plebeian background and unconventional appearance.[57] There was nothing democratic about the leadership of the Churches in either Gaul or Britain.

Martin, however, had other ideas. He combined an episcopal see and acceptance of the ascetic life with missionary zeal. Sulpicius Severus writes as though paganism was still flourishing in northern Gaul in the 370s. In some areas 'few if any had previously received the name of Christ'[58]—a commentary on the missionary aims of the bishops of Rouen—and Martin went about the work of destroying temples and sacred groves by characteristically simple, direct and often violent means. Sometimes miraculous cures succeeded in converting pagan worshippers now convinced that Martin's God was all powerful. In another instance, Martin caused a sacred pine tree adjacent to a 'most ancient' temple to fall in an unexpected direction, whereupon a 'great crowd' of pagan rustics believed in Christ.[59] At other times, however, more forceful methods were used. Once he had the temple burnt down and on another occasion he scarcely avoided being sacrificed himself by an infuriated crowd.[60] The impact of his mission was considerable. Some pagan statues were thrown into marshes.[61] It has been observed from early days that of the very many Romano-Celtic shrines situated in Normandy, some were burnt, while in others the coin series ends abruptly with Magnus Maximus (383–388).[62] Moreover, Martin found imitators. Sulpicius Severus himself established a church for his retainers on his estate at Primulacium, and may have hoped to continue Martin's work until the barbarian invasions overwhelmed him (c. 410).[63]

[56] *Vita S. Martini*, x. 8, 'multi inter eos nobiles habebantur'.
[57] Ibid., x. 3. Martin's own supporters were townsmen from Tours and other neighbouring centres.
[58] Ibid., xiii. 9.
[59] Ibid., xiii. 1–8.
[60] Ibid., xiv–xv.
[61] See Olwen Brogan, *Roman Gaul*, London 1953, 209.
[62] L. de Vesly, *Les Fana ou les petits temples gallo-romains de la région normande*, Paris 1909, 78 and 113.
[63] Paulinus, *Epp.* 31 and 32. For Sulpicius Severus's death possibly at the hands of Germanic invaders, see N. K. Chadwick, *Poetry and Letters in early Christian Gaul*, Cambridge 1955, 94.

XII

The God of Martin was worshipped, if the idols were not entirely neglected. Even in the time of Gregory of Tours, their aid would be invoked in times of peril.[64] However, on the eve of the great barbarian invasion across the Rhine in 406/7, we can see how Christian ritual and liturgical practices had replaced pagan in popular esteem. The presbyter, Vigilantius, was probably a freedman of Paulinus of Nola and had been employed by him to take some of the proceeds of the sale of his master's estate to Jerome and his companions at Bethlehem. Evidently he formed a poor opinion of the latter and c. 403 not only wondered whether their upkeep was the right use of charitable funds, but also questioned the monastic vocation itself and a number of popular religious practices he associated with it. These included the burning of tapers and candles, vigils by the tombs of saints and martyrs, and the veneration of relics ('bits of powder wrapped up in a costly cloth in a tiny vessel'). Such activities, which he deplored as superstitious and yet recognised, had become part and parcel of the popular expression of Christianity in Gaul.[65]

In Britain, in contrast, there was no Martin, no evidence for so much as a parochial system, and few indications that Christianity was becoming the religion of the mass of the Romano-Britons, even in the 'Saxon-Roman' period.[66] In this case, the negative evidence is supplemented by pointers towards a survival of paganism.

The 'pagan revival' of the late-fourth century may be exaggerated but cannot be gainsaid. As Painter has pointed out, there are fourteen temples at each of which more than 150 coins have been found (at Lydney there were over 6,000 and at Woodeaton 2,750), and all of these with the exception of Verulamium are in the countryside. The coins, and other small finds, are overwhelmingly fourth-century, and date from Constantine onwards.[67] Some temples were actually built after Constantine and restored at later periods. Thus, the temple and guest-house attached to the precinct in honour of Nodens in the hill-fort at Lydney dated originally to post-AD 364, and when part of it collapsed because a wall had been built over an Iron Age pit, it was restored (post-367) and improved. It continued in use into the fifth century before falling gradually into decay.[68] Among the offerings found on the site were 270 or so bronze bracelets, with some justification claimed as 'the votive

---

[64] Gregory of Tours, *De Sancto Nicetio*, 5 (*MGH*, SS. Rer. Merovingicarum, i. 732).

[65] Jerome, *Contra Vigilantium*, 5 and 9. Such practices may have been beginning in Roman Britain but failed to survive the Anglo-Saxon invasions. (See Bede *HE*, i. 18, Germanus's use of relics of apostles and martyrs in connection with his devotion at the shrine of St Alban.)

[66] See, however, Philip A. Rahtz's short article 'Sub-Roman cemeteries in Somer⁻ ' ῐn Barley and Hanson (above note 7), 193–5. For the survival of romanised names among users of 'Saxon-Roman' pots, see *Ant. Journ.*, 1 (1970), 265 ('Diseta').

[67] K. S. Painter (above note 5), 157–8.

[68] R. E. M. and T. V. Wheeler (above note 38), 63. 'We are virtually compelled to carry the last phase, at least, well into the fifth century'.

offerings of the poor'.⁶⁹ The builders of the Lydney temple evidently took advantage of the toleration to all cults, except Manichaeism, that prevailed under Valentinian I (364–75), and 'the officer in charge of the supply depot of the fleet' (presumably in the Severn estuary) laid a mosaic pavement out of offerings to the god while an interpreter on the governor's staff supervised the work.⁷⁰

No exact parallel to what happened at Lydney has been found, but the construction of so large a pagan temple a generation after the empire adopted Christianity as its official religion and a decade after Constantius banned the offer of sacrifices to the gods,⁷¹ can be seen against the continuing prosperity of the Romano-Celtic temples throughout the Constantinian era. Some, such as Woodeaton seem to decline after Valentinian-Valens (364–78),⁷² but others such as at Maiden Castle (not built before Gratian, 367, and repaired after 379),⁷³ Jordan Hill, also in Dorset, Frilford near Oxford, and Pagan's Hill in Somerset provide evidence for continued use into the fifth century.⁷⁴ The fate of the rural temples was in nearly all cases gradual decline, including conversion to domestic purposes, rather than violent destruction as happened elsewhere in the empire.⁷⁵

Christianity in Britain in the early part of the fifth century continues the same pattern as before. Its clergy put a high premium on literacy, to judge from Patrick's ideas.⁷⁶ In some towns it was a vigorous movement, capable of sustaining a defence of Pelagianism and bishops of the calibre of Fastidius, whose works, c. 420, *On the Christian Life* and *On Preserving Widowhood*, were addressed to Fatalis, a British woman, and were regarded by the pro-Pelagian Gennadius of Marseille (c. 490) as 'sound and godly teaching'.⁷⁷ Pelagianism itself was a vigorous intellectual movement which fits well with the determination of the Romano-British *civitates* to defend themselves regardless of and, indeed, despite Honorius's orders from Ravenna. Direct connection between the mood of defiance that inspired the British rejection of Roman laws and adminis-

---

⁶⁹ Ibid., 82.

⁷⁰ Ibid., 102–4.

⁷¹ *Codex Theodosianus*, xvi, x. 6.

⁷² R. G. Goodchild and J. Kirk, 'The Romano-Celtic Temple at Woodeaton', *Oxoniensia*, xix (1954), 15–36, at 36.

⁷³ R. E. M. Wheeler, 'The excavation of Maiden Castle, Dorset. First Interim Report', *Ant. Journ.*, xv. 3 (1935), 271.

⁷⁴ See Frend (above note 17), 10 (references); M. J. T. Lewis, *Temples in Roman Britain*, Cambridge 1966, 140–6.

⁷⁵ As in Phoenicia by monks, see Libanius, *Pro Templis*, 8.

⁷⁶ *Life*, ii. 326, line 29 (tr. Stokes) and compare H.-I. Marrou, *Histoire de l'éducation dans l'Antiquité*, Paris 1949, 476.

⁷⁷ Gennadius of Marseille says. Fastidius 'Britannorum episcopus scripsit ad Fatalem quendam de Vita Christiana librum et alium de Viduitate servanda sana et Deo digna doctrina'—*De Script. Ecclesiast.*, 57 (P.L., lviii. 1091). See J. R. Morris, 'Pelagian Literature', *J[ournal of] T[heological] S[tudies]*, n.s., xvi (1965), 33–5 ff.

trators and the reforming, self-reliant teaching of Pelagius and his colleagues, may be suggested rather than proved.[78] The contrast, however, between the self-reliance of the Romano-British and the passivity of some of their north Italian counterparts, is evident at this time. These latter were influenced by fatalistic teaching of bishops concerning the inescapability of the approaching Judgment.[79]

For more than a decade, from 420–30, Britain shared with south Italy and Sicily the distinction of being the territories most open to Pelagian teaching. Prosper of Aquitaine records *sub anno* 429. 'The Pelagian Agricola, son of the Pelagian bishop, Severianus, corrupts the churches of Britain by introducing his doctrine; but at the suggestion of the deacon, Palladius, Pope Celestine sends Germanus, bishop of Auxerre as his own representative and after the overthrow of the heretics, guides the Britons to the Catholic faith'.[80] As far as Prosper was concerned, the story ended happily. Germanus refuted the heretics he encountered and defeated the Picts and Saxons. Two years later, Palladius was consecrated bishop and sent to Ireland to root out heresy there.[81]

The Romano-British leaders who met Germanus were Christian, but many of the troops he mustered to fight the invaders were not. A mass baptism had to be held before the 'Hallelujah' victory on Easter Sunday 429.[82] As direct Gallic and Roman influence waned so did Christianity in Britain. The respite from the invaders secured by Germanus's victory was not followed by a Christian upsurge such as took place in Provence under the inspiration of the monastic bishops of Lérins, when that area reverted to the empire after the Visigoths had failed to take Arles in 427. There is no evidence for the establishment of monasteries or of episcopal schools in Britain as in Gaul, nor do the bishops take a lead in the affairs of the province as their colleagues in Gaul were doing at this time. Instead, Celtic chiefs replaced Roman civil administrators and the most prominent of these, Vortigern, Christian though he may have been, consulted 'magi' and not bishops and clergy.[83]

The failure of Christianity to emerge as the predominant religion in Britain in the first half of the fifth century was to have far-reaching results. By and large, Roman Britain did not collapse amid fire and sword.[84]

---

[78] See J. N. L. Myres's stimulating if also speculative article, 'Pelagius and the end of Roman rule in Britain. *JRS*, l (1960), 21–36. Note however, E. A. Thompson, 'Britain A.D. 408–410', *Britannia*, viii (1977), 303–18 at p. 314.

[79] Thus, Maximus, bishop of Turin, discouraged the citizens from attempting to put their city in a state of defence, on the grounds that 'it would be better if they put their souls in readiness for the approaching Last Day', *Sermo* lxxxv. 2 (ed. A. Mutzenbacher, p. 348).

[80] *Chron. ad ann. 429* (P.L., li. 594–5).

[81] Ibid., ad. ann. 431, col. 595.

[82] Constantius, *Vita S. Germani*, 16. Repeated by Bede, *HE*, i. 20, 'Madidus baptismate procedit exercitus'.

[83] *Historia Brittonum*, 40 (*MGH*, Chron. min. iii. 180).

[84] See S. S. Frere's view in *Britannia*, 360 ff.

XII

ECCLESIA BRITANNICA: PRELUDE OR DEAD END?

Deeds of destruction and violence by marauding Picts, Scots and Saxons, or rebellious Germanic *foederati* there were, and Gildas preserves the folk-memory of those times.[85] If however, we had only the accounts by Quodvultdeus and Possidius of the Vandal invasion of North Africa in 429, we should gain equally the impression that that province dissolved in catastrophe[86]—which, of course, it did not. In sub-Roman Britain the squatters' fires on the *opus signinum* pavement of Ditchley Park villa, or roof tiles lying on the mosaics of disused rooms at Bignor are more typical of the close of the Roman era,[87] than 'the crackling flames' that marked the end of the villa and chapel at Lullingstone.[88]

The historian is left with the problem of what happened between the end of the 'Pelagian' period in Britain, say c. 440, and the implanting of the first Celtic monastic settlements in the far west of the island c. 480.[89] These latter represent a distinctive Mediterranean type of monastic Christianity different from the episcopal tradition hitherto predominant in Britain. A complete blank is not conceivable, and gradually some features linking Romano-British and Anglo-Saxon Christianity are beginning to emerge. Bede provides evidence for the continuity of the cult of St Alban at Verulamium, of the sick visiting the shrine and cures being performed.[90] Elsewhere, evidence is beginning to accumulate that some Anglo-Saxon chapels may have been built on or near the remains of Christian buildings. Faversham may provide one such example where a fourth-century structure (a mausoleum?) was incorporated as the chancel of a Christian church.[91] Brixworth in Northants may provide another, for Roman remains can be discerned in a field some one hundred and fifty yards from the fine seventh-century church.[92] Press reports have indicated finds of the same type, a suspected Romano-British church under a modern church at Gloucester.[93]

These are the tenuous links to be expected with a Church, which though rich in personalities and ideas, lacked the popular support that

[85] *De Excidio*, 24–25.
[86] *De Tempore barbarico* ii, written c. 437 (P.L., xl. 700–1), and Possidius, *Vita S. Augustini*, 28, (P.L., xxxii. 57).
[87] Cited from Frere, *Britannia*, 373–4.
[88] Meates (above note 34), 166. The coin series extends down to Honorius. (See B. W. Pearce's report in Meates *et al.*, 'Second Interim report on Lullingstone Roman Villa', *Arch. Cantiana*, lxv (1952), 67.) The final destruction is therefore fifth-century. For violence and disease as influences in the collapse of the Romano-British towns, see J. S. Wacher, *The Towns of Roman Britain*, London 1974, 414–22.
[89] A. C. Thomas (above note 18), 25–7, and C. A. R. Radford, 'Tintagel: the castle and Celtic monastery', *Ant. Journ.*, xv (1935), 401–19 (Interim report).
[90] Bede, *HE*, i. 7. See above, note 6.
[91] See, Lord Fletcher and Col. G. W. Meates, 'The ruined church of Stone-by-Faversham. First report', *Ant. Journ.*, xlix (1969), 273–94, and Second report, ibid., lvii (1977), 67–72.
[92] Personal observation, summer 1967.
[93] Brief report in *The Times*, 18 August 1978. A similar report of the discovery of a large church at Lincoln is made by Norman Hammond: *The Times*, 24 July 1978.

ensured its survival elsewhere in the west. After c. 450, in the north and west beyond the limits of Anglo-Saxon advance, some Christian communities may also have survived.[94] Generally, however, as the Roman towns and villas were abandoned, only sites of special holiness continued as centres of Christianity. Bede indicates there were degrees of reminiscence of the Christian faith when Augustine landed. Churches could be identified as such and repaired, as well as new buildings constructed for worship.[95] But his own records as well as his historical instinct led him to the view that Augustine's mission opened a new chapter in the christianisation of the British Isles. Augustine found no congregation and no organisation on which to build, and the British bishops he met at Aust were unwelcoming.[96] To Bede, these belonged to the same people who under Cadwallah wrought havoc on the land of his hero, Edwin of Northumbria in 633–4.[97] Continuity with Romano-British Christianity had been lost. The *Ecclesia Anglicana* was a new foundation. Will further research prove Bede wrong?

This brief survey of evidence is dedicated to the Reverend Professor Clifford Dugmore, whose studies in early Christian liturgy and the *Ecclesia Anglicana* have inspired colleagues and enhanced the study of ecclesiastical history as 'no soft option' among the historical disciplines.

---

[94] Sites such as Llantwit Major where Christian (?) burials have been laid in graves cut into the floor of a villa, and similarly at Barnwell in Somerset, or the cemetery at Ancaster (reported by D. R. Wilson, in Barley and Hanson (above note 7), 197–9) may be examples of the continuity of Christianity into sub-Roman times.

[95] Bede, *HE*, i. 26.

[96] Bede, *HE*, ii. 2. He notes how Augustine foretold the destruction of the British monks at Bangor, which duly took place shortly after.

[97] Bede, *HE*, ii. 20, and ibid., iii. 1: 'rex Brettonum Caedvalla, impia manu ...'.

XIII

A NOTE ON THE INFLUENCE OF GREEK IMMIGRANTS ON THE SPREAD OF CHRISTIANITY IN THE WEST

The discovery of an inscription composed in honour of Flavius Antigonus Papias, described as a *civis Grecus*, at Carlisle on the extreme north-western frontier of the Roman Empire would arouse interest in any circumstances [1]. What had brought this foreigner, presumably a merchant, to so remote a part of the world, where he had married a native woman, had settled and died? The phrasing of the text, however, using the intentionally vague »vixit annos plus minus LX«, suggests that he may have been a Christian, while the spidery lettering enclosed in badly cut parallel lines reminds one of some similar inscriptions from North Africa and elsewhere of the fourth and early fifth centuries.

If one is correct in assuming that Antigonus Papias was a Christian, then the Carlisle inscription takes its place among the considerable group of memorials to Greek-speaking Christians which have been found in the Western provinces of the Empire, notably at Concordia in North Italy, Aquileia, Trier and Salona [2]. They are mainly those of merchants from Asia Minor and Syria, the latter punctiliously recording the names of their native villages which they had left behind [3]. They appear to date from the mid-3rd to the first quarter of the 5th century, and there is no doubt that some of the merchants who have been commemorated played a prominent part in the Christian communities where they had settled. Can one say more than this? Are these inscriptions merely curiosities, or can they be combined with literary evidence to shed some light on the way Christianity spread in Western Europe? The problem is a complex one governed by many contradictory factors. It is clear, however, that compared with the Western provinces of the Empire the Celtic and Germanic lands away from the Mediterranean seaboard were remarkably slow to accept the new religion. By the eve of the Great Persecution, the Church had won its battle wherever the influence of the Jewish Dispersion had been strong, such as in Asia Minor, Syria and Alexandria, or where the predominant native religion had a Semitic basis, as in North Africa. In these areas the Church had also been able to associate itself with radical movements of protest among the rural populations angered at worsening economic conditions arising from currency inflation, barbarian inroads and above all, the growth of a ruthless bureaucracy following the administrative reforms of the Tetrarchy [4]. No salvation could be expected from the old gods. Let us turn therefore to the Christians. No such movement, however, took place in the Celtic provinces of the Empire despite an equal deterioration of social and economic conditions. The Bagaudae were not Christians. Egyptian monks and African Circumcellions were.

---

[1] E. Diehl, *ILCV*, 3308A. The doubt as to the deceased's religion arises from the fact that the text continues »quemadmodum accommodatam fatis animam revocavit«, but a reference to the fates has been found on Christian inscriptions, such as *ILCV*, 3308.
[2] For an example from Trier, note the Agricius insc. probably 4th century, (E. Gose, *Katalog der frühchristlichen Inschriften in Trier*, Berlin, 1958, 2).
[3] See J. B. Keune's art. »καπροζαβασαίων«, *P. W.* 10.2, 1918—20, for a useful survey of the inscriptions recording Syrians in Western Europe in the fourth and early fifth centuries.
[4] See the evidence I have given in some detail in my »Failure of the Persecutions in the Roman Empire«, *Past and Present*, 16, Nov. 1959, at pp. 19—26.

The slowness of the Christian advance in the West was not without its effect on the religious history of the Roman world. The Illyrian emperors came from an area where Christianity had hardly penetrated by the end of the third century; and if the 33 bishops who met at Arles on 1 August 314 represented about the whole strength of the Church in the Gallic prefecture a similar state of affairs seems to have prevailed there. Yet the martyrs of Lyons had perished nearly a century and a half before. There the blood of martyrs might have produced some head-shakings, but it was not seed[5].

One explanation is that the majority of Christians in the Celtic West before Constantine were either people whose contact with the Church came through Judaism, or were members of Greek-speaking immigrant communities. In either case Christianity would represent to the provincials what the people of Lyons in 177 called a »strange and new worship«[6] hostile to the Classical culture which they had accepted with enthusiasm. It was a foreign sect, and not a popular one.

Of the Jewish influence there is no doubt. The vegetarianism of the confessors of Lyons and their probable use of the kosher market for their meat[7], the presence of a large synagogue within a stone's throw of the early Christian building complex at Aquileia[8], the existence of lay administrators (*seniores*) alike in synagogue and church in Italy[9], names such as Aaron among reputed British martyrs all point in this direction, quite apart from any rules of catechumenate and baptism derived ultimately from the Synagogue.

On the other hand, when one looks for direct evidence for the Greek immigrant character of Christianity in the West one is not disappointed. It is worth remembering perhaps that the Church in Rome was Greek-speaking as late as 230/240. To a large extent it was the religion of immigrants from Asia such as those who attended Justin's school[10], or freedmen like those who had gradually been possessing themselves of catecombs on land originally granted to them for burials by their patrician masters. The Church there was a wealthy and powerful outpost of the Hellenistic Church, just as in an earlier period its Jewry had been an equally wealthy outpost of the Hellenistic synagogue. There is little evidence that either exercised wide influence on the surrounding Latin-speaking populace[11]. Rome unlike the Christan communities in Asia was not a missionary centre in the first three centuries A. D.

With this in mind, we turn to the next earliest Christian community in the West, that in the Rhone valley, known from the account of the martyrdoms at Lyons in 177 (Eusebius, *H. E.* v. 1—3) and from the career of Irenaeus. Here Christianity was following one of the main trade routes linking Gaul with the Eastern Mediterranean.

---

[5] Eusebius, *Hist. Eccl.* (ed. Kirsopp Lake) v. 1.60.
[6] Ibid. v. 1.63.
[7] Ibid. v. 1.26. See the interesting and amusing note by A. A. T. Ehrhardt, »Der Sonntagsbraten der christlichen Hausfrau« from *Existenz und Ordnung* (*Festschrift für Erik Wolf zum 60. Geburtstag*, Frankfurt, 1962) pp. 156—167.
[8] Described by P. L. Zovatto, »Le antiche Sinagoghe di Aquileia e di Ostia«, *Memorie storiche forogiuliesi*, 44, 1960—61, 53—63. Note also how at Salona the identity of the Christian cemetery is emphasised as »coemeterium legis sanctae christianae«, as if to differentiate it from a rival »coemeterium legis iudaicae«, *CIL.* iii. 9508; and see for further evidence of this, B. Gabričevič, »Una nuova iscrizione Salonitana«, *Atti dell' iii Congresso Internaz. di Epig. Greca e Latina*, Roma, 1959, 79.
[9] Ambrosiaster, *Comment. in 1 Ep. ad Timoth.* v. 1 (*P. L.* xvii, 475 D): »Unde et Synagoga et postea Ecclesia seniores habuit quorum sine consilio nihil agebatur in Ecclesia. Quod qua negligentia obsoleverit nescio«.
[10] *Acta Sancta Justini* (ed. Knopf-Krüger, 1929) iv.
[11] See R. la Piana's survey in »The Roman Church in the End of the Second Century«, *Harvard Theological Review*, 18, 1923, 201—277, especially 250 ff.

A note on the influence of the Greek immigrants

Marseilles not far from the mouth of the river, Arles, Vienne and Lyons, were all early centres of Christianity and were all connected with this trade. Both Lyons and Vienne were relatively speaking thriving industrial centres, with iron-foundries, glass factories, pottery and dye works, and markets for the sale of flax, linen, wool and clothing[12]. Thither came merchants and settlers from the eastern Mediterranean, such as Epagathus and his children Onesimus and Onesiphorus[13], the families of Julia Artemesia from Asia[14], Julius Pusinius »natione Graeca«[15], and many others. They settled down and some had picked up enough Latin for their families to use it on their funerary memorials.

This is precisely the impression one gains from a study of the Christian communities in these towns preserved in Eusebius, *Hist. Eccl.* v. 1. Their immigrant character need not be laboured[16]. Not only had the Christians there the strongest links with the churches of Asia and Phrygia to whom they wrote their account of their sufferings[17], and from whom they received an account of the Montanist movement, but their language was Greek, any Latin spoken by their members being specially noted[18], and the leaders together with about half of whose names have survived among the 48 martyrs indicate Greek, probably Asiatic, origins[19]. The brethren of men such as Attalus the Pergamene, or Alexander the Phrygian physician, or Irenaeus himself, those who »had the same faith and hope of redemption« were a thousand miles away in Asia Minor[20].

One other piece of corroborative evidence provided by Irenaeus has often been neglected. Irenaeus did not write his *Adversus Haereses* in *circa* 185 without reference to his own surroundings. From his description of the Gnostic Marcus, it is clear that this heretic and his followers were active both in the Rhone valley and in the province of Asia: »Such are the words and deeds by which in our own district of the Rhone they have deluded many women who have their consciences seared as with hot iron«[21], while his detailed description of the fall of the wife of a deacon in Asia suggests that he spoke from personal knowledge[22]. These adherents of Marcus are described by Irenaeus as wealthy, and this corresponds with other information about the Lyons Christians. Far from being »dregs of the population« and illiterates, they had their own slaves[23], numbered members of the liberal professions among them[24], and in every way corresponded to what one would expect of an immigrant group who had brought their religion with them, prospered, — and become exceedingly unpopular with the Romanised natives.

The foreign character of the Church in Gaul in its early stages of development is further indicated by various chance finds made fairly recently in the Rhone valley. At St. Remy de Provence, near Marseilles, for instance, two Christian inscriptions

---

[12] See M. P. Charlesworth, *Trade Routes and Commerce of the Roman Empire*, Cambridge, 1926, 196—205.
[13] *CIL*, xii, 2007 (Vienne).
[14] *CIL*, xiii, 2004 (Lyons).
[15] *CIL*, xiii, 2005 (Lyons).
[16] See the evidence assembled by A. Fliche, »A propos les origines chrétiennes de la Gaule«, *Rev. des Sciences réligieuses*, XL, 1951—2 (= *Mélanges Lebreton*), p. 166. In opposition to H. Leclercq's arguments against the immigrant origins of the Church in Gaul, art. Lyon, *DACL*. X. 1,77.
[17] Eusebius, *H. E.* v. 1. 2.
[17a] Ibid. v. 3. 4.
[18] Ibid., v. 1. 20 (Sanctus of Vienne), cf. v. 1. 44 and 52.
[19] See H. Quentin, »La Liste des Martyrs de Lyon de l' an 177«, *Analecta Bollandiana*, 39, 1921, 113—138.
[20] Eusebius, *H. E.* v. 1. 3.
[21] *Adv. Haer.* 1. 13. 7.
[22] Ibid. 1. 13. 5.
[23] Eusebius, *H. E.* v. 1. 14.
[24] Ibid. v. 1. 49 (Alexander) and 1. 47 (Roman citizens among the Christians).

written in Greek, one an ἰχθύς graffito and the other a greeting to a person called Gorgoné, may be dated to the third century[25]. At Marseilles itself the celebrated Volusianus inscription, though in Latin, records the name of the martyr's(?) father as Eutyches[26]. Greek survived on funerary inscriptions in that area into the fifth century[27], and perhaps it is significant that the earliest reference to the celebration of the Epiphany in the West comes from Vienne on 6 Jan. 361, the last recorded occasion when the emperor Julian attended a Christian service[28].

The effect of the specialised nature of the Church in South Gaul was twofold. On the one hand, the Asiatic settlers planted the Christian religion in a new area, but on the other hand, the fact that it was their religion did not help it to spread. Irenaeus himself was certainly inspired with missionary zeal, and in three places in the *Adversus Haereses* speaks of using Celtic to spread the Gospel[29]. But evidently he did not think it worthwhile to have the Scriptures translated into that language, or even into Latin, the language of educated Gauls. This was the only means of spreading the Gospel beyond a narrow circle of foreigners and their converts. His own works were written exclusively for a Greek-reading audience, and he was worried about the effect of Celtic on his own Greek style! To the Christian community as a whole the Gauls were »wild and barbarous tribes« among whom they were obliged to dwell[30]. No wonder perhaps that these returned the compliment and regarded these self-satisfied immigrants with their secret cult as fitting substitutes for expensive gladiators hired for the annual games at the Feast of the Three Gauls[31]. It is interesting that only 3rd-century Christian inscription from Lyons was also in Greek and probably that of an immigrant[32]. Indeed, it was not until a generation after Constantine that a native Latin Christianity owing, as Hilary of Poitiers suggests, little to the East[33], began to make its presence felt in southern Gaul. It took another half century before the pagan cults of the northern part of the country succumbed to the preaching of Martin of Tours.

The situation in southern Gaul was not unique in the West. At Salona, Rudolf Egger has established with a considerable degree of certainty that Christianity also was brought in the last part of the third century by immigrant traders from Asia and Syria moving along the Via Egnatia. As at Lyons, there was a large foreign trading community in the town, and it was among its members that Christianity seems first to have developed. The outlandish element which Bishop Domnio and his immediate successors in the early fourth century represented was strikingly illustrated by the massive funerary monument which was erected in the Christian cemetery. No parallel to this strange building could be found in Europe or even in Asia Minor, but Egger eventually traced prototypes in Mesopotamia[34]. Domnio and his friends appear to have come from Nisibis[34a].

---

[25] The handiest description is in *DACL*, XV. 1, 511—512. The discoveries were made in 1945.
[26] See art. »Marseille« in *DACL*, X 2. 2247—2251.
[27] E. Leblant, *Inscriptions chrétiennes de la Gaule*, ii. 303, n. 547 (Callinikos), and *Nouveau Receuil*, p. 211 (Castor).
[28] Ammianus Marcellinus (ed. Rolfe), XXI. 2.5.
[29] *Adv. Haer.*, Proemium 3, iii. 4. 2 and iv. 24. 2.
[30] Eusebius, *H. E.* v. 1. 57.
[31] See the excellent article by J. H. Oliver and R. E. A. Palmer, »Minutes of an Act of the Roman Senate«, *Hesperia*, xxiv, 1955, p. 325, touching on the probable origins of the *pogrom* of 177.
[32] *CIL*. xiii, 2267. Significant also because of the rarity of Greek inscriptions at Lyons.
[33] Hilary, for instance, did not know the actual text of the creed of Nicaea until he was sent into exile in Phrygia in 356. It does not seem that Lyons was the missionary centre whence other cities in Gaul were evangelized (See W. Telfer, The Office of a Bishop, London 1962, 99).
[34] R. Egger, *Römische Antike und frühes Christentum* (*Festschr. zum 80. Geburtstag*) Klagenfurt, 1962, 186—188. [34a] Ibid.

A note on the influence of the Greek immigrants

At the same time, Salona provides an example of how, once established, the religion of the immigrants gradually extended its hold until it became the religion of the majority of the population. So thorough was the conquest that the centre of urban life in the fifth and sixth centuries gradually shifted to what had originally been the Syrian quarter in the N. W. of the city, but which now had become the focus of its Christian life [35].

At Aquileia also, Christian origins seem to have owed much to similar groups of eastern immigrants. One of the most touching of early Christian inscriptions in Greek was dedicated there probably in the second half of the third century by Aurelia Maximina for her child Asclepiodotes »who believed in God«. One of the early benefactors of the church of St. Euphemia left her memorial in mosaic in Greek; another immigrant rather pathetically records his homeland as Taychira, somewhere in Syria, »but now Aquileia« [36].

This last inscription is post-Constantinian and belongs to the same class as that of Azizos, son of Agrippa, who came to Trier from near Apamea in Syria, and died perhaps in the reign of Valentinian I [37]. At Trier also, Christianity seems to have been influenced in its origins by immigrants. The first recorded bishop, Agroecius, who participated at the Council of Arles, seems to have been one, to judge from his name [38], and in 409 another Syrian, Cassianos, from the village of Addana, was buried in the Christian cemetery [39]. These Syrians, however unpopular they may have been as merchants [40], contributed with their wares and their firm Christianity to maintain the links between the crumbling Western provinces of the Empire and the Mediterranean world. Even in Britain similar factors of mutual trade and adherence to Christianity enabled some contact to be maintained between the Celtic west of the country and the civilisation of Byzantium. Like the merchants of Alexandria who traded with the kingdom of Dumnonia in the sixth and even seventh centuries [41], Flavius Antigonus may have been an earlier representative of those links. What is clear, however, is that research into the origins of the Church in the Celtic provinces cannot afford to ignore the traces of immigrant eastern merchant communities whether in the form of inscriptions or even coins. The distribution map of these may well provide evidence for the distribution of the primitive Church in the Celtic lands of the Roman Empire.

Meantime, it is in honour of the methods of research pursued by the *Antike und Christentum* school that this paper is offered to the greatest living exponent of this tradition, Professor Th. Klauser.

CAMBRIDGE

---

[35] H. Leclercq, art. »Salona«, *DACL*, XV. 603—605.
[36] H. Leclercq, art. »Aquileia«, *DACL*, 1. 2, 2677—2680.
[37] H. Gose, *Katalog der frühchristlichen Inschriften in Trier*, i.
[38] Mansi, *Concilia*, ii. 476. For the name Agroecius, Gose, op. cit., 2. So also his colleague from London, Adelphius.
[39] Cited from Rau, art. »Treveri«, *P. W.* Suppl. vi. 2350.
[40] Salvian, *De Gubernatione Dei*, iv. 14.
[41] See C. A. R. Radford, »Imported Pottery found at Tintagel, Cornwall: an aspect of British Trade with the Mediterranean in the Early Christian Period«, *Dark Age Britain* (Essays presented to E. T. Leeds), London, 1956, 59 ff.

XIV

PAULINUS OF NOLA AND THE LAST CENTURY OF THE WESTERN EMPIRE

The part played by Christianity in the downfall of the Roman empire in the west has fascinated historians for more than two centuries. The Encyclopaedists in the person of Montesquieu opened the debate, but the latter's subtle anti-Christianity in his *Considérations sur la Grandeur et la Décadence des Romains* (published 1734) was succeeded by the thorough-going attack of Gibbon who singled out Christianity as the main cause for the change and decadence in the empire's structure. Since then the debate has continued. New factors have been brought into play, such as the annihilating effect of the barbarian attacks or the sense of social injustice so graphically described by Salvian in Gaul and Spain that drove many provincials to welcome the rebel Bagaudae and the Germanic invaders as liberators from Roman tyranny. Salvian, however, was not unpatriotic. He was a far greater *laudator temporis acti* than Augustine and Orosius, and unlike them found positive merit in the poverty and virtue of the Old Romans.[1] What he criticized was the heartless wealth, luxury and oppression of his own day and the failure of the Catholic clergy to do anything about it.[2] Indeed a case may be made out that some of the Western Christian traditions, notably Pelagianism, far from undermining morale, aimed at instilling a sense of purpose into otherwise indifferent and wealthy Christians, and that if these traditions had been allowed to develop new patterns of society could have emerged in the successor states of the Roman empire in the West. The association of Pelagianism among the local urban aristocracies in southern Britain and the uprisings that accompanied the formal ending of Roman rule on the island has been remarked upon with justice.[3] No other province produced a ' municeps '[4] as pretender to the Imperial throne.

Despite all that has been said, however, about the superiority of Christianity over paganism as a dynamic and integrating force in the life of the later empire, the charge levelled by the pagans at the time of Alaric's capture of Rome still stands. ' When we used to sacrifice to our gods,' Augustine reported African pagans as saying, ' Rome was flourishing, but now when one sacrifices to your God everywhere, and our sacrifices are forbidden, see what is happening to Rome.' (*Sermo* 296, 7). There were plenty of martyrs' bones in Rome, including Peter's and Paul's, but that did not avert capture and pestilence from the city (ibid. 296, 6). Christianity did not encourage virtue, it was alleged. It merely gave impunity to vice. Instinctively men felt that the new victorious religion was not compatible with the commonweal—' utilitati non convenire reipublicae '.[5] Was this the case ? In his essay on ' Christianity and the Decline of the Roman Empire ' our past President (Arnaldo Momigliano) has reasserted the view ' that there is a direct relation between the triumph of Christianity and the decline of the Roman Empire '.[6] How far does the life and thought of the Gallic aristocrat Paulinus of Nola bear this out ? For instance, was Paulinus' ascetic and world-renouncing interpretation of Christianity at variance with the needs of an effective government confronted by the massive barbarian attacks and social unrest in the provinces ? There were ascetics enough in the East, and there the Goths were supported by the prestige of their great victory over Valens at Adrianople in 378. Yet not only did their leaders fail to emulate Alaric and seize control of Constantinople, but the anti-Gothic party was led by Christian aristocrats such as Synesius of Cyrene. The Gothic forces were routed as the result of a popular uprising among the inhabitants of the capital a decade before Alaric sacked Rome. The Germanic threat was laid. The Eastern empire survived the fifth century ; the Western did not. Do divergent religious patterns, centred round the part played by asceticism in the thought of individuals in the two halves of the Empire, provide any clue ?

---

* The text of an address given to the Annual General Meeting of the Roman Society on 18th June, 1968.
[1] *De Gubernatione Dei* i, 2, 10.
[2] Ibid. v, 5, 20: ' nam aut tacent plurimi (sacerdotes) eorum aut similes sunt tacentibus.'
[3] J. N. L. Myres, ' Pelagius and the end of Roman Rule in Britain ', *JRS* L, 1960, 21–36.
[4] Paulus Orosius, *Historia Adversus Paganos* VII, 40, 4.
[5] Augustine, *Ep.* 137, 20.
[6] *The Conflict between Paganism and Christianity in the Fourth Century*, ed. A. Momigliano (Oxford, 1963), 1–16.

Paulinus' life spans the age of the barbarian invasions in the West.[7] He was born in Aquitaine in 354/5, a year that witnessed the great invasion of the Franks and Alemanni across the Rhine. He was at Nola in Campania when Stilicho battled with Radagaisus for control of Italy, and in 410 the Goths were at Nola itself. He died in June, 431, the year Hippo Regius fell to Gaiseric. He was thus almost an exact contemporary of Augustine's, whose firm friend he was for over a quarter of a century. His parentage, however, that of a Gallic senatorial family, was very different and he carried the ease and self-assurance of his class to the end. He did not have to work hard for his position, and his conversion to the ascetic way of life would have been a famous event whatever the reason. His retirement in 395 to the shrine of St. Felix at Nola, where he was to remain in pious leisure 'away from the tumult of the world'[8] for more than thirty years, also fits the pattern of an aristocratic ideal of the times. For Augustine, however, a pushing middle-class Numidian who nearly ruined his health by the age of thirty-three in the pursuit of a political career at the Court of Valentinian II, retreat to the 'otium liberale' of Cassiciacum could only be an interlude. He was destined willy-nilly for the episcopate and an active life in the service of the Church. Of Paulinus as bishop we hear little, and he never finished his one recorded polemical work, the *Adversos Paganos*.

Both Paulinus and Augustine were recognizable provincial types in the West in the late-fourth century, but while it would be hard to imagine Augustine settling down to the *curia* of Thagaste, Paulinus embarked on a predictable administrative career. His education, one may assume from his later writing, was in the traditional mould of grammar and rhetoric, and his promise was brilliant. In all probability during his stay at the university of Bordeaux Ausonius had been his mentor. In 378, however, the year before Ausonius became consul, he left Bordeaux for Rome, probably to take over his father's role as a senator or to fill a magistracy.[9] Thence he went to Campania as *consularis*, an appointment which could be reckoned as a good starting-point for a career in government.[10] Sometime between 379 and 383 he was *consul suffectus*, for Ausonius refers to his consulship as well as his own.[11] A combination of family reasons[12] with the sudden end of Gratian's rule in Gaul on 25th August, 383, and perhaps also changes imposed in the administration of Italy by Valentinian II and Justina's arrival in Milan early in 384, resulted in his return to Aquitaine that year. A few months later he visited north-eastern Spain and married a rich heiress named Therasia.

Paulinus had been born a Christian[13] and this early period of his life is interesting because it typifies the non-assertive though instinctively Nicene Christianity that had come to prevail among a large section of the aristocracy in the Prefecture of the Gauls. In Britain it is the Christianity of the Hinton St. Mary and Frampton mosaics, which show Christ and the *Chi-Rho* symbol in the ascendant but traditional pagan mythology by no means excluded.[14] In Gaul it was the Christianity of Ausonius, whose religious allegiance would be in doubt if he had not once told his correspondent Axius Paulus that he had to be in Bordeaux for the rites of Easter.[15] For him the Roman gods might be literary figments but he still retained a strong underlying respect for Druids and the priests of the gods of Gaul

---

[7] The standard works on Paulinus remain Pierre Fabre's *Saint Paulin de Nole et l'Amitié chrétienne* (Bibliothèque des écoles françaises d'Athènes et de Rome, fasc. 167, 1949) and *Essai sur la chronologie de l'œuvre de saint Paulin de Nole* (Publication de la Faculté des Lettres de l'Université de Strasbourg, fasc. 109, Paris, 1948). See also P. G. Walsh, *Letters of Paulinus of Nola* (Ancient Christian Writers 35 (publ. 1967) and 36 (forthcoming)), and C. H. Coster, ' Paulinus of Nola ', *Late Roman Studies* (Harvard, 1968), 183-204. The text of Paulinus' *Epistulae* and *Carmina* are published by G. von Hartel in *CSEL* XXIX and XXX.

[8] Ambrose, *Ep.* 58, 1, and what Augustine describes as ' Christianae vitae otium ', *Retract.* I, I, I.

[9] Ausonius, *Ep.* 24, 2-3. Fabre, *Saint Paulin* 22.

[10] Two individuals in this period who were to rise high in the administration held the governorship of Campania among their first steps to promotion: Q. Clodius Hermogenianus Olybrius who was successively *praefectus urbi*, *praefectus praetorio* of Illyricum and then of the Orient before being consul in 379 (*CIL* VI, 1714); and Julius Festus Hymetius, *vicarius urbi* and later proconsul of Africa (*CIL* VI, 1736). Fabre, op. cit. 25, n. 2.

[11] Ausonius, *Ep.* 27, lines 64-5 : 'Paulinum Ausoniumque, viros, quos sacra Quirini/purpura et auratus trabeae velavit amictus.' See also *Ep.* 29, lines 60-1.

[12] Paulinus, *Carmen* XXI, 398-9 :

'sollicitae matri sum redditus : inde propinquos trans iuga Pyrenes adii peregrinus Hiberos.'

[13] Evident from Paulinus, *Ep.* 12, 12, when he refers to a chapel dedicated to his parents' memory ' ad parentum nostrorum memoriam obsequiis '.

[14] See J. M. C. Toynbee, ' A New Roman mosaic pavement found in Dorset ', *JRS* LIV, 1964, 7-14.

[15] Ausonius, *Ep.* 4, lines 9-10 : ' instantis revocant quia nos sollemnia Paschae/libera nec nobis est mora desidiae.'

as social leaders and for their powers of prophecy and divination.[16] At this stage Romano-Gallic paganism was as much a living force as was Romano-British paganism.

In Gaul and Britain Christianity was still mainly an urban and aristocratic religion. Down to the end of the reign of Gratian it looked as though outside Africa the West might produce the same blend of the Christianity and the Classical that had so lasting an effect on the development of theology in the East. The great victories of Julian over the Germanic tribes ushered in a sort of Indian summer of security and prosperity in the western Roman world, though broken temporarily by the 'coniuratio' of the barbarians in Britain in 367–369. Though the Codex Theodosianus tells its sombre tale of administrative abuses, and Ammianus Marcellinus impresses the reader with the wasted lives of a wealthy and idle senatorial aristocracy,[17] a combination of the literary with archaeological evidence shows that the situation in many areas of the Gallic prefecture was not one of unrelieved gloom. In Britain it was the age of the great manor houses, of North Leigh and Chedworth, Bignor, Lullingstone and Otford whose mosaics or frescoes show survival of interest in a classical heritage even if of a school variety.[18] In Aquitaine, Paulinus owned a 'regnum' of private estates,[19] and though Ausonius' picture of the 'rich glebe with its blithe peasantry' on his estates near Bordeaux is obviously idealized,[20] it is interesting that throughout his correspondence with Paulinus he complains of nothing worse than occasional local shortages.[21] Raiders and Bagaudae have no place. In this relatively wealthy society there had evidently been little discontinuity between the pagan past and Christianity. How families such as those of Paulinus or Ausonius had come to accept the new religion is not known, but there is no hint of crisis and we should be surprised if it had been brought about by anything as sensational as that through which the forebears of the historian Sozomen had been converted by the monk Hilarion in Palestine in the 330's.[22] Apart from Martin of Tours and Priscillian, the Gallic prefecture boasted of few monks and little serious religion in the reigns of Valentinian I and Gratian. Ausonius' sketches of his fellow professors at Bordeaux resemble Spy cartoons rather than forerunners of the *Confessions*.

On his return from Campania Paulinus felt himself fully at home in this secure and easy-going society. His earliest surviving letters, those to his fellow landowner, Gestidius, concern the quiet life of the countryside and follow the pattern of Ausonius' own. He sends a gift of wildfowl in return for the fish and oysters he has received.[23] What changed all this? It would be tempting to point to the impact of some disaster like Adrianople that so impressed Ambrose and Jerome, though both had accepted the ascetic life beforehand. This was clearly not the case with Paulinus. Generally speaking Magnus Maximus did not behave like a tyrant in Gaul. So far as can be seen, there was no widespread purge even of his predecessor's administration. Ausonius, supporter of both Gratian and Theodosius I though he was, thought it safe to remain in Trier,[24] and there is nothing to suggest that Paulinus, despite similar sympathies, might not have been able to continue his career. There was order and security on the western frontiers. We are still a generation away from Jerome's despairing letter concerning the young Pacatula—'She will know of tears before laughter, feel sorrow sooner than joy. Scarcely has she trod the stage when the curtain falls...'[25] This was far from the situation in southern Gaul under Magnus Maximus.

Even so, one may detect the hint of a changing atmosphere. In Spain, Priscillian, like Paulinus, a wealthy landowner, had renounced his possessions for extremities of asceticism

---

[16] Ausonius, *Professores* IV, compliments Attius Patera for being able to trace his descent from Druids of Bayeux, and hence his name 'Patera' derived from their worship, and that his brother was named after Phoebus Apollo, and his son had received a name connected with prophecy—Delphidius.
[17] Ammianus Marcellinus, XIV, 8, 7 ff. See A. H. M. Jones' assessment of the position occupied by the senatorial aristocracy in both parts of the empire, *Later Roman Empire* (1964), ch. xv.
[18] Sheppard Frere, *Britannia* (London, 1967), 313–314. Most of the villa mosaics in Britain date between A.D. 300 and 370, ibid. 321.
[19] Ausonius, *Ep.* 27, line 116 'veteris Paulini regna'.
[20] *Ep.* 27, lines 90–5.
[21] *Ep.* 26, lines 43–4. For southern Gaul at this period, C. Jullian, *Histoire de la Gaule* VIII, 130 ff.
[22] Sozomen, *Hist. Eccl.* (ed. Bidez/Hansen) v, 15, 14.
[23] *Carmina* 1 and 2.
[24] *Ep.* 20. Ausonius had been *praefectus praetorio Galliarum* in 378. St. Martin too was on friendly terms with the usurper until Priscillian was executed.
[25] Jerome, *Ep.* 128, 3, dating to *circa* 413. P. R. L. Brown, *Augustine of Hippo* 27, is surely mistaken in quoting this letter as evidence for prevalent pessimism in western society at the time of Augustine's conversion.

that were to bring him to excommunication and finally execution at Trier in 384 for witchcraft.[26] Others were beginning to follow the same road though more temperately. In Gaul, the aristocrat Sulpicius Severus was one. At Milan, Augustine and Alypius renounced the world in 386 in favour of a life dedicated to philosophy in the service of Christ. Divine Judgment was becoming a pressing reality. Jerome's celebrated dream (*Letter* 22, 30) points to dilemmas that neither his parents nor Ausonius had faced, and in his case too, the decision was in favour of abandonment of the world for the ascetic life. Paulinus was to solve his dilemma similarly. In his long apologia to Ausonius explaining his conversion he leads up to the issue of the Judgment. 'This is my fear, that the Last Day overtake me not asleep in the black darkness of profitless pursuits and spending wasted time amid empty cares.'[27] He goes on to speak of 'the general doom of things for ages yet to come'. The harsh contrasts long current in North African theology between Athens and Jerusalem and Caesar and Christ were becoming more generally accepted in the West; the tradition of public service and social responsibility among the aristocracy, whether nominally Christian or not, was to be the loser.

Even so, Paulinus' conversion was not marked like Augustine's by any single acute crisis of belief. It was induced apparently by a series of comparatively trivial events. Step by step he was led to abandon the ideals he had shared hitherto with Ausonius. Classics gave way to Christianity, and service to the community to service to Christ performed in a monastic habit at the shrine of Felix of Nola. For Paulinus, as for Augustine at this stage, full acceptance of the Christian ideal entailed rejection of secular values. Those contemplating God, he tells Ausonius, 'love to repose void of empty cares and shun the din of public life (a phrase he will use again), the bustle of affairs and all concerns hostile to the gifts of heaven'.[28] Unlike contemporary religious leaders in the East Paulinus saw no possibility of combining monastic idealism with the intensely busy life in public and ecclesiastical affairs that absorbed Basil of Caesarea, nor could he regard pagan literature and philosophy as the first constructive stage towards the Christian's goal of communion with God. In the West it was increasingly a question of Either-Or, for Athens or for Jerusalem, and Paulinus opted for Jerusalem.

During his governorship of Campania, Paulinus had come into contact with the cult of St. Felix. This saint had allegedly been martyred in the Decian persecution and, more authentically perhaps, was said to be the son of a Syrian, another example of eastern immigrants bringing Christianity to the west. Paulinus had had the road to his shrine from Nola repaired and a hospice for pilgrims begun.[29] Now the saint began to summon his benefactor.

Even so, the first years after his marriage were spent perambulating his various residences in Aquitaine.[30] If anything, his friendship with Ausonius grew firmer. He writes, for instance, a long poem on the Kings of Rome for Ausonius' comment. The latter is highly complimentary. He commends this 'longe iucundissimum poema' and the author's ability to condense three books of Suetonius into a single poem. 'I can absolutely take my oath that for fluency in verse none of our Roman youths is your equal.'[31] High praise indeed.

Meantime, two obscure incidents had drawn Paulinus back to thoughts of Nola. First, probably an eye affliction was healed by St. Martin, the now aged bishop of Tours and the doyen of the missionary and ascetic ideal in Gaul;[32] secondly, there occurred a family tragedy centred round the murder of his brother.[33] Some critics have seen Paulinus among the instigators and pointed to the coincidence of his departure for Spain shortly afterwards, but there is no evidence for this. Paulinus' letters (ed. Hartel, *Epp.* 35 and 36) at the time show himself broken[34] and he receives the condolences of the Bishop of Bordeaux,

---

[26] See Sulpicius Severus, *Chronica* II, 50, 8 and *Vita Sancti Martini* 20, 3.
[27] Paulinus, *Carmen* x, lines 316 ff.
[28] Paulinus to Ausonius, *Carmen* x, lines 166-8: 'otia amant strepitumque fori rerumque tumultus cunctaque divinis inimica negotia donis ab Christi imperiis et amore salutis abhorrent.'
[29] *Carmen* XXI, 381-394.
[30] *Carmen* XXI, lines 404-7. These included considerable property on the coast, 'qua maris Oceani circumsona tunditur aestu/Gallia'.

[31] Ausonius, *Ep.* 23.
[32] Sulpicius Severus, *Vita Martini* 19. He met Martin at Vienne, *Ep.* 18, 9
[33] Paulinus, *Carmen* XXI, lines 416 ff. See P. Fabre, op. cit. 33-4.
[34] *Ep.* 35, 'obruamur pudore redeundi et in longinqua regione commorati ut in custodiam escamque porcorum indignam . . .' Was this self-reproach justified? His friends in Bordeaux apparently did not think so.

PAULINUS OF NOLA AND THE LAST CENTURY OF THE WESTERN EMPIRE

Delphinus, and the priest Amandus, both of whom remained warm friends. That they would have done so had Paulinus been even so much as suspected of fratricide seems unlikely. But perhaps as an upshot Paulinus was baptized at Bordeaux by Delphinus in 389 and left with his wife for her native Spain the same year with the crime much on his mind. He had said farewell to Aquitaine, to an official career and even literary and leisured ease of a Christian Gallic aristocrat. From now on, the two abiding influences in his life were to be his wife and the memory of Felix of Nola.

Therasia was a strong-minded and pious woman of a type which played an immense part in the conversion of the Roman world on an individual basis to Christianity. One has only to think of the influence of Macrina on Basil of Caesarea [35] or of Marcellina on Ambrose, or in the next generation of the female members of the old pagan aristocracy in Rome in converting their husbands, to appreciate the pressure used by these highly educated women in favour of Christianity in the last half of the fourth century.[36] It was a phenomenon of the Later Roman Empire, and another example of the effect of the combination of Christianity as the religion of the state with a widely diffused classical culture when education was still regarded as an ally of religion. On a lower level the words of Libanius are interesting. He says explicitly ' when men are out of doors they listen to your plea for the only right course and they come to the altars. But when a man gets home, his wife and her tears and the night plead otherwise, and draw him away from the altars '.[37] The women of the Mediterranean world were among the most powerful allies of Hellenistic Judaism in the first century A.D., and of Christianity in the fourth.

Therasia did not have to drag her husband from pagan altars, but there is little reason to doubt Ausonius that this ' Tanaquil ', as he calls her, gradually drew him away both from his former love of the Classics and his friendship with himself. One can see in Ausonius' letters to Paulinus the developing rift. Banter about his former bailiff using one of Paulinus' villas as a storehouse for goods he had bought up on various estates (*Ep.* 26) gradually changes first to grumbles at his friend's neglect and then to suspicion and outright attack on his wife. He complains bitterly that Paulinus had ' shaken off the yoke wherewith I was joined to thee in the pursuit of letters '.[38] ' Let thy Tanaquil know naught of this,' [39] he writes elsewhere. Finally Paulinus replied, denying that he suffered from Bellerophon's gloomy delusions, defending Therasia as ' not a Tanaquil but a Lucretia ' (*Carmen* x, 191–2) and admitting that he regretted not ' his perversion ', as Ausonius had called it. From now on he was ' to live for Christ as Christ appointed '.[40]

A few years later, *circa* 395/396, writing from Nola to Sulpicius Severus, Martin's biographer, he was more explicit ; and his exposure of his motives then and at other times and his zeal to hear the similar experiences of Alypius and Augustine may have been one of the factors behind Augustine's resolve to write the *Confessions*.[41] His own letters, like the *Confessions*, contain long passages of prayer to Christ, where his recollection of past misdeeds recalls powerfully Augustine's similar autobiographical reminiscences in the first Book of the *Confessions*. Paulinus tells Sulpicius how ' physical frailty had taken the edge from enjoyment of pleasures, his secular life was full of troubles and toils '. These taught him to ' hate what perturbed me and increased my practice of religion through my need for hope and my fear of doubt. Finally, when I seemed to obtain rest from lying scandal and from wanderings unbusied by public affairs and far from the din of the forum, I enjoyed the leisure of country life and my religious duties, surrounded by pleasant peace in my withdrawn household '.[42] Augustine might have written the same from Cassiciacum, but for Paulinus, on whom the burden of yet another tragedy through the death of his infant son Celsus had been added, there was no desire at all to resume active life. ' Respuens

---

[35] See Gregory of Nyssa, *Vita Sanctae Macrinae*, *PG* 46, 965.
[36] P. R. L. Brown, ' Aspects of the Christianisation of the Roman Nobility ', *JRS* LI, 1961, 1–11. For the influence of the Christian *matronae* at Rome in Constantius II's reign, see Theodoret, II, 17.
[37] Libanius, *Ep.* 1057 (cited from B. J. Kidd, *Documents Illustrative of the History of the Church* II, 131).
[38] Paulinus to Ausonius, *Carmen* XI, lines 30–1.
[39] *Ep.* 28, line 31, ' Tanaquil tua nesciat istud.'
[40] Paulinus to Ausonius, *Carmen* X, lines 284–5.
[41] On Paulinus' possible influence on Augustine's *Confessions*, see P. Courcelle, *Les Confessions de Saint Augustine dans la tradition littéraire* (Paris, 1963), Appendix III.
[42] *Ep.* 5, 4.

patrimoniorum onera ceu stercorum ' remained his outlook.[43] Even enrolment as presbyter at Milan under Ambrose was rejected.[44]

For nearly six years, 389-394, Paulinus remained on his wife's estate near Barcelona. Then one day, probably Christmas Day 394, the local congregation demonstrated, demanding his ordination as presbyter,[45] hoping perhaps, as in the case of Pinian at Hippo in 411, that they would reap a substantial harvest from the sale of Paulinus' estates that would follow on his ordination.[46] If so, they were disappointed. Within a few months, Therasia and Paulinus had left Spain and by slow stages journeyed to Nola. Well received at Milan by Ambrose, they were, however, rebuffed by Pope Siricius at Rome,[47] who disliked both officials turned clerics and eminent ascetics (perhaps he had seen enough of Jerome). They arrived in Nola late in 395. There they were to settle for the rest of their lives, Paulinus becoming bishop after the death of Therasia *circa* 408.

What in fact had Paulinus done? What significance can the historian attach to his ideals and actions? To contemporaries his main offence was that he had deserted his responsibilities as a landowner [48] and allowed by choice his house to become extinct.[49] He had indeed abandoned his career, some of his former friendships including Ausonius and his ties with Aquitaine. Birth in Christ he interpreted strictly as a life of poverty and simplicity (vegetarian dishes and meagre cups [50]), centred on a devotion to the service of Felix in whose honour each 14th January he wrote a yearly song of praise in memory of his martyrdom (*natalicia*). On the other hand, he did not renounce completely his Classical heritage. His letters and poems abound in classical allusions. He was no Biblicist like many of his African counterparts. He might be said to be carrying out his advice to his pagan friend, Jovius, to be a 'Peripatetic for God and a Pythagorean as regards this world ',[51] i.e. to travel to preach the Word in the guise of an ascetic. He made yearly visits to Rome to celebrate the feast of the Apostles. His love of friendship shown in his relations with Ausonius became with his devotion to the saint at Nola a ruling passion. This involved him in intense literary exchanges with old friends such as Sulpicius Severus, Delphinus and Amandus of Bordeaux and Victricius of Rouen, and newer acquaintances, particularly with the African 'servants of God', Augustine and Alypius.[52] At the same time, he remained on the best of terms with members of the Roman senatorial aristocracy such as Melania the Younger and Pammachius, as well as Siricius' successor as bishop of Rome, Anastasius, and with the Campanian bishops.[53] All this consumed his energies, but it also involved the maintenance of a staff and the retention of a certain style of life. More than once he refers to his servants and couriers, such as 'my man Julianus' whom he sent to visit Bishop Aurelius at Carthage.[54]

Paulinus, as his long correspondence with Augustine shows, was immensely influential despite his retiring ways. He acted as a sort of clearing house for the religious ideas of the time. He was the only notable ecclesiastic who managed to keep on terms with both Jerome and Rufinus [55] and to number both Pelagius and Augustine among his friends.[56] His qualities as an aristocrat enabled him to stand above the purely personal rancours that beset Jerome and his adversaries, and his theological outlook, evolved like Augustine's from his experiences, kept him with a foot in both the Pelagian and Augustinian camps.

---

[43] *Ep.* 5, 6.
[44] *Ep.* 3, 4.
[45] Ibid.
[46] Augustine, *Ep.* 126 on this affair.
[47] *Ep.* 5, 13-14. Antipathy amounting to virtual excommunication does, however, point to more than personal causes. It is impossible, however, to follow Babut (' Paulin de Nole et Priscillien ', *Rev. d'Histoire et de littérature religieuses*, N.S. 1, 1910, 97-130 and 252-275) and suggest that Paulinus had been involved in Priscillianism in Aquitaine. The scandals around Priscillian's arrival there date to 382-383. Ausonius who despised Priscillianism heartily (*Professores* v, 37 ff.) would hardly have refrained from reminding Paulinus of this particular folly had he been implicated. Delphinus who excommunicated Priscillian and his followers also would scarcely have baptized Paulinus in the circumstances.

[48] Ausonius, *Ep.* 26, lines 115-16.
[49] Ambrose, *Ep.* 58, 3.
[50] Paulinus, *Ep.* 19, 4; compare *Ep.* 11, 13 to Sulpicius Severus.
[51] *Ep.* 16, 7.
[52] On Paulinus' ideals of Christian friendship see P. Fabre, op. cit., ch. III.
[53] *Ep.* 20, 2.
[54] *Ep.* 3, 1.
[55] On his relations with Jerome see P. Courcelle, ' Paulin de Nole et Saint Jérôme ', *Revue des études latines* 25, 1947, 250-280.
[56] Augustine, *Ep.* 186, 1 written in 417 indicates that Paulinus was still on friendly terms with Pelagius. Pelagius had also sent him some of his works.

Paulinus at Nola is as much representative of the intellectual outlook of the period as he had been while in Gaul. Poet of distinction he remained, but he was also now a holy man who believed (like some of Honorius' generals) that the bones of saints and supplications to St. Felix were the best protection against Radagaisus and Alaric.[57] His was the world of miracles, of immediate answers to prayers and invocations, and of divine intervention even in the most trivial events in life, the popular counterpart to the Providence-centred philosophy behind the *De Civitate Dei*. He represents the dramatic shift that seems to have taken place in the west after the death of Theodosius I in January, 395, from the predominance in public affairs of literary men like Symmachus and Ausonius, moulded in the classics, to men of the intense and sombre religiosity that characterized a Count Marcellinus or Augustine himself. Religious orthodoxy, not literary success, now opened the way to high office. The old conventions of polite correspondence between friends in the Classical tradition remained, but the content was now entirely religious, and discussion revolved round the inner lives of committed Christians awaiting the Day of Judgment. Until the barbarians beat on the gates they seemed a long way off.

Paulinus' long and active friendship with Augustine extending from 395 until it passes out of history in 421 typifies this shift of interest. Indeed, there could be no greater contrast between the Ausonian and the Augustinian phases of his career, between the mandarin and the monk. Though the details of a correspondence begun through Paulinus' contact with Augustine's friend Alypius do not concern us here, the broad outlines throw considerable light on Paulinus' views and influence.

Paulinus recognized Augustine at once as a kindred spirit, a Christian thinker ' who dispersed the murk of heresy and by the impact of his word made the truth shine through the darkness '.[58] In fact, he was particularly grateful for Augustine's anti-Manichaean works, perhaps because, after all, his own religion concealed a latent dualism.[59] At the same time he shows how his interests remained well rooted in the present world. At one point Augustine asked his opinion about what the situation of the blessed was after the resurrection.[60] Paulinus replied politely that his concern was his ' situation in the present life ' and what he wanted to learn from Augustine was how to do God's will here and now. He was beginning also to cultivate the friendship and respect of the practical-minded clergy of southern Italy to whom Pope Anastasius had commended him. These men, like Bishop Memor of Beneventum, represented the Christian counterpart of the pagan *patronus* and *pontifex* of their cities a generation before.[61] Christianity had indeed triumphed, but theirs was not a Christianity that involved renunciation of civic duties. Instead, it emphasized the positive virtues of wisdom, fair judgment and hospitality. Estates might be sold to raise money in time of famine, but not for the sake of an ascetic ideal. The clergy married, and one of these unions, that between Bishop Memor's son Julian, Bishop of Eclanum, and a local heiress named Titiana, Paulinus himself blessed with a poem.[62]

Among these intelligent and public-spirited clergy, Pelagianism had already taken a firm hold by 411. What was the use, it could be asked, of practising Christian virtues, if through Adam's sin the mass of humanity was irretrievably doomed ? No irreversible fall of man, but only a thin wall of corrupt manners stood between the Christian and his recapture of man's original innocence.[63] Paulinus sympathized. Had he not deserted the comforts and opportunities of his life in Aquitaine in order to follow step by step Christ's example ? How could this avail him if God did not will the salvation of all men ?[64] Not wealth in itself, but its misuse by man was the crime in the eyes of God,[65] and misuse involved active free will. Was not grace in this context to be regarded as an ' adjutorium ', an extra aid to virtue rather

---

[57] Compare *Carmen* XXVI, 425–7 :
' Sic modo bellisono venientes flumine pugnas
De nostris averte (Felix) locis. Manus impia sacris
Finibus absistat, quibus tua gratia vallum .'
See also C. H. Coster, op. cit. 197. Paulinus himself tells us nothing of the siege of Nola by Alaric in 410.
[58] *Ep.* 45, 1.
[59] The power of God and his angels is frequently contrasted with that of Satan, and Paulinus' gloomy view of Judgment indicates strong dualist tendencies, as does his horror at the possibility that the blessed bread which Augustine sent him (*Ep.* 31) might be of Manichaean origin ! (See P. Courcelle, *La Confessions de Saint Augustin* 567.)
[60] Paulinus, *Ep.* 45, 4.
[61] See P. R. L. Brown's fine description in *Augustine of Hippo* 381 ff.
[62] *Carmen* xxv.
[63] P. R. L. Brown, *Augustine of Hippo* 382.
[64] *Epp.* 18, 6 ; 24, 9 ; 49, 4 ; 50, 11. This salvation was a manifestation of *gratia*.
[65] *Ep.* 13, 20 to Pammachius, ' Denique ut scias non divitias sed homines pro earum usibus esse culpabiles vel acceptos deo . . . '

than some inbred quality present in a few foreknown to God ?[66] Yet his experiences also made him aware of the all-embracing character of Adam's fall and Augustine did not hesitate to remind him of these views.[67] The grace bestowed by Felix had preserved him from harm. Was this merely incidental ? Clearly, though he liked both Pelagius[68] and Julian of Eclanum, he respected Augustine as the master-mind whose grasp of the truths of God was unsurpassed. His own sense of justice was acknowledged by Honorius when in 419 he invited him to participate in the council summoned to Ravenna to settle the disputed succession to the Papacy following the death of Zosimus, and this quality prevented him becoming a partisan. Had he been more of an exegete and a speculative thinker, he might also have contributed towards the formulation of a more even balance between Grace and Free-will in the West and thereby preserved more of the optimistic heritage of the Classics for mediaeval Europe.

On Paulinus' old age texts are practically silent. After his final exchange with Augustine in 421 there is a brief letter which he wrote to Eucherius and Galla dated either to 423 or 426, in which he praises the incipient monastic settlements at Lerins,[69] but the rest is silence. There is no long and busy final phase such as occupied Augustine after he had seen his successor Heraclius consecrated as his co-adjutor in 426. No Vandals disturbed the quiet of Nola.

The significance of Paulinus' conversion and his retirement to Nola lies in two different directions. On the more positive side, his unending quest of friendship furthered the growth of close ties between the leading western ecclesiastics, whether their sees or monasteries were situated in northern Gaul, Italy, Africa or Bethlehem. These intellectual links were valuable in an age of increasing theological debate, and their existence also encouraged the development of a close episcopal network throughout the West at the very moment when the western provinces of the empire were being overrun by the barbarians. A common organization and outlook among the western bishops was maintained in face of Germanic Arianism and rural paganism. In the fifth century the Church rather than the State recruited men of outstanding administrative ability like Sidonius or Leo. Part of Paulinus' contribution was to provide this movement with an intellectual background which was still in touch with the modes of thought that belonged to the Classical past. In addition, Paulinus had the shrewd sense to see that Christianization could also involve pacification, and barbarians and local brigands once converted could become allies of law and order. His letter to Victricius of Rouen (*Ep.* 18) and his poem in honour of Nicetas of Remesiana (*Carmen* xvii) both equate missionary enterprise with peacemaking and concord. The Channel coast had been rendered safe by Victricius[70] and the barbarous Bessi round Nish ' harsher than their winter snow were now led as sheep into the hall of peace ' by Nicetas.[71] In addition, the example of his way of life, ascetic yet not extreme,[72] combined with a theology of Grace that accepted the form of Augustinianism while rejecting much of its content contributed to the formation of the western monastic ideal as it emerged with Benedict in the next century in much the same part of south Italy.

There is, however, a debit balance. Conversion to asceticism as interpreted by Paulinus was a negative act. To be ' ab istius mundi strepitu profugam ',[73] as he writes in his final surviving letter, implied alienation from society and its responsibilities. Moreover, Paulinus offered his correspondents no choice. The young Licentius accompanying his father Romanianus to Rome was gravely counselled to ' avoid the slippery dangers of exacting state service ' where, like other Africans before him, he had hoped no doubt to make his career. Position had an inviting title but it condemned its holder ' to slavery and a wretched end '.[74] His advice to Victor, a soldier whom he had never seen, was ' to break your chains

---

[66] Augustine, *Ep.* 186, 34, tries to persuade Paulinus that, if one thought, there was no place reserved for any form of grace that could be regarded as merely ' assisting ' intermittently.
[67] Ibid. 40. Paulinus had written ' Durat enim mihi illud per Adam virus paternum, quo universitatem generis sui pater praevaricatus infecit '.
[68] Evident from Augustine *Ep.* 186, 1. ' Pelagium . . . quod ut servum Dei dilexeris .'
[69] *Ep.* 51, 2.
[70] *Ep.* 18, 4.

[71] *Carmen* xvii, lines 206–8 :
  ' Et sua Bessi nive duriores
  Nunc oves facti duce te gregantur
  Pacis in aulam.'
[72] He did not regard asceticism by itself as an end in life. It was one of the means by which the soul gained salvation and could even be fallible. ' Per ipsas virtutum vias in vitia delabi possumus ', he warns, *Ep.* 40, 3. Fabre, op. cit. 113 (n. 9).
[73] *Ep.* 51, 2.
[74] *Ep.* 8, 3.

and whatever retains you bound in the present age ', and exchange earthly service for service to God.[75] His friend Victricius was praised for having publicly renounced his profession of arms.[76] He has no word of encouragement for those responsible for administering and defending the tottering structure of society. His departure from Aquitaine, his ' bonorum relictio ' implied a complete break with the past. He never displays any hint of the provincial patriotism or historical vision that makes the final chapters of Paulus Orosius' *Historia adversus Paganos* so interesting a contemporary document.

Moreover, Paulinus represented the views of a whole sector of the former ruling class in the West in the crisis years of the early fifth century. Few of the dedicated Christians who formed his circle of correspondents attempted, like Pammachius, to be Christian senators equally devoted to practical affairs and religion. When one adds the fact that the western emperors depended on the active support of the great landowners for the execution of policies, for instance against the Donatists, the political effect of the world-renouncing attitude of some of the richest of their number was obviously great. So too were the social effects of unloading onto the market of great blocks of estates on which hundreds, if not thousands, of people were employed.[77] Ausonius pointed to the lamentable situation that would arise from the splitting up of Paulinus' estates among a mass of lesser men.[78] There would be no one to check the depredations of bailiffs or the impact of local famine. With the exit of the traditional leaders of society the way was left open for oppression by meaner individuals who felt none of the ties that bound the Gallic senator to his estates. The natural responses in the West to this situation were Bagaudae, Circumcellions and the new barbarian possessors.

The vital factor was, however, a theological one. The significance of the Western view of the ascetic's role which Paulinus, Melania and Pinian exemplify, can be understood by reference to the contrasting mood in the East. There, too, from the middle of the fourth century onwards a considerable number of members of the landowning aristocracy, particularly in Asia Minor, chose the monastic vocation. This, however, though entailing renunciations and abstinences, did not involve forsaking the world. Basil's monasteries, for instance, were often placed in populated areas and served as schools, orphanages and hospitals for the local community. In the fifth and sixth centuries the monastic leaders of both the Chalcedonian and Monophysite parties in the Church were often as not the bishops of great dioceses. The lives of Severus of Antioch or John of Amida, the missionary bishop of Asia Minor under Justinian, provide examples.

One should beware, too, of overemphasizing the impractical individualism and anti-worldly attitude of the mass of the Egyptian and Syrian monks. These attitudes existed, but in many ways the Pachomian settlements in Egypt were themselves productive and self-supporting units which merely substituted the villages whence their recruits were drawn.[79] The great Pillar-Saints such as Simon and Daniel Stylites combined awesome feats of ascetic endurance with profound practical wisdom placed at the service of the community and even of the state. Daniel was consulted by the emperor Leo I after the fiasco of his attack on the Vandals in 468 and assured him that Gaiseric would not be marching on Alexandria.[80] Simon also was a man of business as well as of prayer, who manumitted slaves and made bonfires out of debtors' bonds. The eastern monks did not in general qualify for the gibe of Rutilius Namatianus about the monks of Capri, that ' they feared evil and refused all good '.[81] The historian Theodoret has many tales of Syrian monks actively engaged in bettering the lot of the local inhabitants among whom they settled. Converting pagans and heretics was accompanied by actions such as curing the sick and redressing fiscal wrongs.[82] From the early fifth century onwards the eastern monks had become the representatives of the religious and social life of the populace at large. In this, they sought to reform abuses, not to overturn the structure of society. The emperors, whatever their failings by modern

---

[75] *Ep.* 25.
[76] *Ep.* 18, 7.
[77] See A. H. M. Jones, op. cit. 559 ff. on the family wealth of the senatorial aristocracy at this time.
[78] Ausonius, *Ep.* 27, lines 115–16 : ' ne sparsam raptamque domum lacerataque centum/per dominos veteris Paulini regna fleamus .'
[79] ' The Pachomian monasteries were highly organized industrial and agricultural concerns '— A. H. M. Jones, op. cit. 931.
[80] *Vita S. Danielis Stylitae* (publ. *Analecta Bollandiana* 32, 1913, 121–216) ch. 56.
[81] *De Reditu suo* 1, 443, ' Munera fortunae metuunt, dum damna verentur .'
[82] Theodoret, *Historia religiosa* XVII, compare XXVIII.

western standards, had the good sense to consult the monastic leaders and use them as channels of public opinion. Religion as expressed through the monks provided a safety valve for discontent and welded the diverse populations of the Byzantine empire together in the face of external threats. Eastern monasticism, begun as a popular movement, never degenerated into the vogue of an escapist aristocracy.

The secret of the differing attitudes of the eastern and western ascetics towards the Roman empire lies in two centuries of diverging interpretations of Christian teaching regarding man's relations with God and his ultimate destiny. Whereas the western Christian tended to believe that human history and human salvation depended exclusively on acts of God, the easterner, taking his cue from Clement and Origen, accepted that man through his free-will was responsible at least for the intermediate stages that separated life on earth from the ultimate ideal of communion with God. The world and the created order were the work of the Divine Word. They could not therefore be shunned. Christianity, leading to the monk's vocation as its climax, was seen as a 'philosophy', the highest form of philosophy achieved as the result of 'the perpetual exercise of the intellect' in 'following out the commands of the Saviour in every act'.[83] The Christian purified the world from the forces of unreason, but he did not necessarily turn his back on it. For Paulinus, however, and other western ascetics of his day, alienation from society also resulted from theological assumptions which had become traditional. If the tradition of the Hellenistic Church tended towards universalism, that of the Latins looked towards the doctrine of the Remnant. Christians were the elect few, pre-destined to salvation, safe in the Noah's ark, while the world was represented by the drowning multitude without.[84] This gathered community was under the inspiration of the Spirit who would come 'reproving the world of sin, and of righteousness and of judgment' (Jn. 16 8), inspiring its adherents to martyrdom and consequent release from sin and vindication at the Last Day. The secular belonged to the Devil and separation from it was a matter of course.[85]

There were also social and political implications in this theology. If the Alexandrians, from Philo onwards, stressed the individual's way of communion with the divine through the progressive estrangement of soul from body, the parallel concept in the West of *alienatio* had a more practical application.[86] On earth one was alienated from one's true *patria* (for Augustine, the heavenly city), which one could serve only by renouncing service to all that belonged to its secular counterpart. In this context the Roman Empire was no reflection of divine polity, however distorted, as it was in the East, but 'the earthly city'. It was Babylon, in standing contrast to the heavenly Jerusalem, whose service must be abandoned if salvation was to be won. By accepting baptism the individual indicated his recognition of this. Paulinus' rejection of the 'tumult of the forum' is reflected by Tertullian's utterance of two centuries before, 'Nothing is more foreign to us than the state'.[87] Civil responsibilities and the army also represented the power of Satan, witness Lactantius' denunciation of the duties of a soldier or a magistrate.[88] Fifty years after Constantine's conversion, Pope Damasus still praised soldier confessors who threw away their weapons thus courting martyrdom.[89] Siricius and Pope Innocent declared that no former magistrate could be ordained,[90] thus emphasizing the clear-cut division between the ecclesiastical and civil powers. Paulinus himself emphasized that as a magistrate he had shed no blood.[91]

These were essential differences of theological emphasis, and they go far to explain why asceticism in the West was so negative a factor. Some of the old harshness of the antithesis between Church and Empire might disappear under the influence of philosophy and the pressure of events,[92] but underlying contrasts remained. Their persistence and the beliefs

---

[83] Clement, *Stromata* IV, 7, 43–4. Compare II, 97, 1 and II, 20, 104–5. For Eastern monasticism as a 'philosophy', see Sozomen I, 14, 11; VI, 28, 1, and 34, 6.
[84] Cyprian, *Ep.* 74, 11; compare Tertullian, *De Baptismo* 12.
[85] Compare Tertullian, *De Spectaculis* 15, 'Sed tamen in saecularibus separamur, quia saeculum dei est, saecularia autem diaboli'.
[86] See R. A. Markus, '*Alienatio*, Philosophy and Eschatology in the Development of an Augustinian Idea', *Studia Patristica* IX (= *Texte und Untersuchungen*, Bd. 94): Berlin, 1966, 431–450.
[87] *Apol.* 38, 3.
[88] *Institutes* VI, 20, 14 ff., 'ita neque militare iusto licebit'.
[89] *ILCV* 1981 (*Nereus et Achilleus martyres*).
[90] Siricius, *Ep.* 6, 1; Innocent, *Ep.* 2, 2.
[91] *Carmen* XXI, line 395–6: 'nulla maculatam caede securim' and ibid., line 376.
[92] Note for instance Paulinus, *Ep.* 29, 13 'iam et ipsa urbs (Roma) in pluribus filia Sion est quam filia Babylonis'.

associated with them may help, perhaps, to answer the question we posed at the outset. Christianity itself was not the cause of the downfall of the empire. Indeed its consolidating influence in the East was a considerable factor in the survival of the Byzantine empire from the crises of the fifth and seventh centuries. The predominance, however, in the West of doctrines developed in the age of persecution, when the Church was an embattled minority in a world believed to be doomed to an early destruction, had the reverse effect. By the end of the fourth century ideas previously characteristic of an anti-imperial provincial middle-class and lower-class, such as the African Donatists, were becoming accepted by way of monasticism by 'the Romans of Rome'. This movement, combined with increasing barbarian pressure on the frontiers, social unrest in the provinces, and economic decline, contributed to the collapse of the Roman administration of the western provinces during the first half of the fifth century. There was a failure of nerve sanctified by traditional western interpretations of Christianity. In this development Paulinus of Nola, Gallic aristocrat turned ascetic, was truly representative of the deeper psychological causes that led to the fall of the Roman Empire in the West.

Gonville and Caius College, Cambridge

XV

BLANDINA AND PERPETUA:
TWO EARLY CHRISTIAN HEROINES

Twenty five years separate the martyrdom of Blandina at Lyon and Perpetua in the amphitheatre at Carthage, probably on 7 March 203. To most people living at the time, the actions of both in defying the authorities and placing themselves in the situation where torture and condemnation to the beasts awaited them, were indefensible folly. At Lyon the crowds, at times prepared to show a modicum of mercy were finally enraged beyond control by Blandina's persistence and contempt for her pagan opponents, while at Carthage Perpetua, having once been respited and allowed through the Gate of Life from the amphitheatre, was in the end returned for public execution on the demand of the spectators. The execration felt by the latter for those who appeared to have insulted the gods was intense. The best that people at Lyon could say for Blandina and her companions was the incredulous, "Where is their God, and what good was their religion to them, which they preferred even to their lives?"[1]. Most were happy to see their corpses dismembered so that their claim to rise from the dead would be frustrated. They were relieved that the gods had triumphed[2]. In Carthage, the confessors were regarded as perpetrators of black magic who would be able to use their arts to escape justice[3]. Fear and hatred were the dominant emotions of the crowds whether at Lyon or Carthage at this time.

---

1. EUSEBIUS, *Hist. Eccl.* V.1.60. Both *Acta* have been edited and translated into English by H. Musurillo, *Acts of the Christian Martyrs* (Oxford Early Christian Texts, ed. H. Chadwick, Oxford 1972).
2. EUSEBIUS, *H.E.*, V.1.63.
3. *Passio Perpetuae* 16.2.

168

Few doubted that the gods both existed and would be vindicated. The last quarter of the second century AD saw the high watermark in the growth and prosperity of the Greco-Roman cities around the Mediterranean. Population was visibly increasing[1]. There was relative security, an element of social mobility, lip-service at least to marital fidelity[2] and above all, confidence in the justice and permanence of the system represented by the emperor and his officials[3]. The Antonines and their Severan successors had some right to proclaim to their subjects the Happiness of the Times under the providential care of the emperor.

Yet, there was opposition. In Palestine and Syria many Jews still hoped for the coming of the messiah[4], and their risings under Marcus Aurelius[5] and Severus[6] demonstrated their continuing discontent. They were the only group actually to take up arms against the empire, but the Cynics maintained a barrage of criticism against authority, wealth and power, and the Christians, sometimes identified with the Cynics[7], added their own rejection of the religion of Rome and the Roman way of life.

Of these three opposition groups, some observers believed the Christians were potentially the most dangerous. Celsus, circa 178, an educated provincial probably resident in Syria or Palestine, was prepared to concede the right of the Jews to their religion on the grounds of its antiquity[8], but was not prepared to see the Christians tolerated similarly. To him, they were renegades and apostates from Judaism, whose differences with the Jews were so minimal as to amount to no more "than a fight about the shadow of an ass"[9]. They shared the same wrong-headed ideas of God and of man, but they were also subversive attempting all the time to

---

1. TERTULLIAN, *De Anima* 30. See FREND, *The Donatist Church*, Oxf 1971, p. 42-3.
2. For instance, an inscription from Zriba near Segermes (publ. in *Bull-Arch du Comité* of 1934, p. 322) "... Furio Donato coniux/[in]comparabili benigno adfectu ac mente bona..."
3. Note, for instance, the confident appeal by the *coloni* on the Imperial estate around Henchir Mettich to the emperor Commodus in 183, *CIL* VIII 10570 ("ut beneficio maiestatis tuae rustici tui vernulae et alumni saltum tuorum non ultra a conductoribus agrorum fiscalium in quiete manere...").
4. Celsus, cited by Origen, *Contra Celsum* II.29 (ed. and tr, H. Chadwick, Cambridge 1953).
5. AMMIANUS MARCELLINUS, *Historia* XXII.5.5, "malodorous and rebellious Jews".
6. AELIUS SPARTIANUS, *Severus* 16.7, "Iudaicum triumphum", *Scriptores Hist. Aug.*, ed. Hohl, I, p. 149.
7. See FREND, *Martyrdom and Persecution in the Early Church* (Blackwell, Oxford, 1965), p. 273-6.
8. *Contra Celsum*, V.41.
9. *Ibid.* III.1.

influence the "ignorant and uneducated", and destroy the traditional authority of the pater-familias over his dependants. It was in private houses that "they get hold of children in private and some stupid women with them, and they let out some astounding statements, as for example, that they must not pay any attention to their father or school teacher but must obey them"[1]. Moreover, what they taught must be accepted without argument.

This is an important passage. It certainly relates to what may have happened in Vibia Perpetua's household, and it may concern Blandina also. We learn that her mistress (but not her master) was a Christian and herself a confessor, who feared simply that her favourite slave, small and delicate in physique as she was, would not stand up to the ordeals that she might have to face[2].

Of the heroism and dedication of both martyrs there can be no question. At Lyon Blandina emerges as the leader and inspiration of the confessors after the death of Bishop Pothinus. The survivor of the massacre who wrote the account of events to the Churches of Asia and Phrygia tells how popular hatred fastened on her, of her first encounter in the amphitheatre after torture "so that her entire body was broken and torn"[3]. She was hung on a post and exposed to the beasts, but she "seemed to hang in the form of a cross", and none of the beasts would touch her. There, she inspired her fellow confessors and won the crown of immortality for herself[4]. From then on the authorities realized that she was the leader. She was kept back until the final day of the games, and with a youth named Ponticus, faced the full fury of the crowd. On this occasion also she inspired others "like a noble mother encouraging her children" and finally went triumphantly to her death. Even those who wished her end conceded "that no woman had suffered so much in their experience"[5].

Vibia Perpetua showed exactly the same qualities. A member of the urban upper middle classes, whose family may have held an estate near Carthage[6] as well as property at Thuburbo some 40 miles

---

1. *Ibid.* III.55.
2. EUSEBIUS, *H.E.*, V.1.18.
3. *Ibid.*, I, 16 and 18.
4. *Ibid.*, 1.41-2.
5. *Ibid.*, 1.56.
6. See H. LECLERCQ's discussion of A. L. DELATTRE's discoveries in the Basilica Majorum at Carthage (*Dict. d'Arch. chrétienne et de Liturgie (= DACL)*, IV.1, art "Carthage", col. 2248). While much must remain speculation, the names "Vibia" and "Perpetua" occur on early levels on the site. The inscriptions, left in a disordered state after the excavation, are now being researched and catalogued by Mme Liliane Ennabli for the "Institut national d'Archéologie et d'Art de Tunisie".

away, she was also the acknowledged leader of the group of Christians arrested probably early in 203. She knew Greek and much of the material (Chs 3-14) comes from the diary which she kept in prison. This must be an authentic narrative. This is not only a matter of the direct and conversational style suggestive of what an educated Roman-African would write. One can surely catch the ring of actuality in her remark after her arrest and baptism. "A few days later we were lodged in the prison; and I was terrified, as I had never before been in such a dark hole. What an awful time it was. With the crowd the heat was terrible and there was the extortion of the soldiers, and to crown all, I was tortured with worry for my baby there"[1]. It is surely the experience of the stark reality of prison now that the heroics before the procurator and her father were past. She was happy to be transferred to a more salubrious part of the dungeon. She discusses reasonably about the future of her baby with her (pagan?) brother and her mother. She describes her hesitations whether to give it up or not, and perhaps not until she decides to do so does she finally steel herself to become a martyr. Her diary shows a glimpse of her struggle between her duty to her infant and her duty to her faith[2]. There is little doubt that the barest acknowledgment the emperor's genius would have been greeted with sighs of relief. In being required to sacrifice "for the welfare of the emperors" she was asked to do no more than Jews had done willingly in the years before the revolt of 66. Christians were more extreme in their attitude, and this could fairly enough be regarded as a treasonable outlook by the procurator before whom she appeared[3]. To "blaspheme the times and the emperors and speak ill of the idols" was costing a Christian at Corinth her life at the same time[4].

But if Perpetua was embarrased at first, she proceeded to show herself completely divorced from her family and utterly ready for death. "Perpetua", the continuator of the narrative and editor of her diary wrote, "went along (to the amphitheatre) with shining countenance and calm step as the beloved of God, as a wife of Christ, overthrowing the (hostile) stares of all by her intense

---

1. *Passio Perpetuae*, 3.6.
2. For example *ibid.* 3.6 and 3.8, and Ch 6.8.
3. By the third century treason ("maiestas") as well as belonging to an illegal associltion had become grounds for prosecuting Christians. See, for instance, TERTULLIAN, *Apol.* X.1, "You Christians do not worship the gods; you do not sacrifice for the emperors" and the Acta Proconsularia relating to Cyprian's condemnation in 258 (ed W. HARTEL, *CSEL* III.3, Vienna, 1871, p. CXII-CXIII).
4. Hippolytus (d 235) cited in Palladius *Lausiac History* 65 (ed W. H. Lowther Clarke, London, 1919, p. 171-2), and see Frend, *Martyrdom and Persecution*, p. 323.

gaze"[1]. She was by now a fanatic, and even after being tossed by a maddened cow found strength to address her other brother (a catechumen as she had been) and catechumens. "You must all stand firm in the faith and love one another, and do not be weakened by what we have gone through"[2]. These could be the words of a modern extremist leader. They are almost incredible in the mouth of a young woman amid the peace and apparent prosperity of the Severan age.

What lay behind this attitude? The first thing that strikes the reader of both *Acta Martyrum* is the strength of conviction that the Last Times were at hand. At Lyon, the Christians regarded the sudden persecution as "the Adversary swooping down with full force", in this way anticipating his final coming which "is sure to come"[3]. He is directly opposed by the Spirit working within the confessors, inspiring their example to would-be backsliders, and their bearing in the arena. The confessors themselves "boil with the Spirit"[4] and "overwhelm the Adversary", and they are rewarded with insensitivity to pain and in Blandina's case, also "converse with the Lord"[5]. What at Q'mran[6] is portrayed as the struggle between the two spirits in each human being was translated by the Christians to the cosmological plane of a combat between the Adversary and his allies, the pagans, informers, backsliders, etc. and the Spirit, represented by the Confessors and none more than Blandina.

In the *Passio Perpetuae* the eschatological theme is even more prominent. In his introduction, the editor reminds his readers with reference to Joel 2[7] that these were the last times, that the Spirit would be poured out on all flesh, that their sons and daughters would prophecy and that these extraordinary graces had been promised for the last stage of time[7]. Perpetua like Blandina believes that she is engaged in a personal combat with the Devil (in the guise of an Egyptian)[8]. There is, however, a more developed theology of the Spirit than is discernible in the Acta of

---

1. *Passio*, 18.2.
2. *Ibid.*, 20.10.
3. EUSEBIUS, *H.E.*, V.1.5.
4. *Ibid.*, 1.9 (Vettius Epagathus of whom the writer ways "Called the Christian's advocate he possessed the Advocate within him, the Spirit that filled Zacharias...").
5. *Ibid.*, 19 and 56.
6. On the rival spirits striving to dominate the world and each individual featuring among the beliefs of the sectaries, see IQ S3 : 17-23. Cited from F. M. CROSS, *The Ancient Library of Q'mran*, London, 1957, p. 156-158.
7. *Passio*, 1.3-5.
8. *Ibid.*, 10.14.

the Lyon martyrs. The Spirit urges the confessors to martyrdom. Water-baptism precedes the baptism of blood[1]. Where converse with Christ *(Homilia)* is merely mentioned with reference to Blandina, this is transformed in the *Passio Perpetuae* into a vivid series of visions that the heroine could expect as a matter of course. "For I knew", she writes, "I could speak with the Lord whose blessings I had come to experience. And so I said (addressing her catechumen brother), I will tell you to-morrow, and this is the vision that I had"[2]. There follows the vision of the ladder reaching to heaven guarded by a dragon and her own entry into Paradise. At the end, the confessors tell the mocking bystanders to remember their faces so that "they would recognize us on the day"[3]. In the amphitheatre itself, the male confessors threatened the procurator Hilarianus. "You (have condemned) us; but God (will condemn) you"[4]. The sentiments and ideals are those reflected in Tertullian's panorama of the Day of Judgment in *De Spectaculis* 30.

With conviction that Judgment was approaching, is associated an interpretation of Christianity that owed little to the synoptic Gospels and Epistles. It appears to be based on the Pentateuch and late-Jewish and Jewish-Christian writings. Links with the Montanists of Carthage also must have been close. Perpetua was a catechumen at the time of her arrest, and her visions and those of her companions, provide some insight into how they had been instructed. Perpetua's vision of the ladder must surely be a reminiscence of Jacob's ladder (*Gen* 28^{12}) while the Egyptian wrestler against whom she is pitted (Ch. 10) could be a "Pharaoh" figure. The rest of her material would seem to be derived from late-Jewish and New Testament apocalyptic. Paradise is imagined as a park in terms of the Book of Enoch (32.3) and perhaps the *Apocalypse of Peter*. While the angels chanting endlessly, "Holy, holy, holy" come from Rev 4^8, the white garments of the righteous and the fragrance of Paradise may be from the *Apocalypse of Peter* describing how the perfume (of the flowers and fruits of Paradise) "was so great that it was borne thence even to us"[5]. The "aged man with youthful face and white hair" (*Passio* 12.3) is surely the Ancient of Days of Dan 7^9, and the dragon could be the Leviathan of Hermas' Vision (*Vis* IV). In the *Passio* the "leaders" and "righteous men in Paradise" (Rev 20) are martyrs,

1. *Ibid.*, 3.5.
2. *Ibid.*, 4.2.
3. *Ibid.*, 17.2.
4. *Ibid.*, 18.8.
5. *Apoc of Peter*, 16 (ed M. R. JAMES, Oxford, 1926). In Saturus' vision (*Passio* 11-13), the ideas seem very close to this Apocalypse.

the true leaders of the Church. Clergy (unless they are martyrs) are kept outside (*Passio* 13)[1]. The curious detail in Perpetua's dream of her fight with the Egyptian that "she became male", might be Pythagorean,[2] but could also be a reminiscence from the Logion of the *Gospel of Thomas* that refers to "the inside becoming the outside" and the ending of all sexual differences at the end of the world (*Logion* 23), while in a second *Logion* (*Logion* 112), Jesus states, "for every woman who makes herself a man shall enter the Kingdom of Heaven". This is precisely what Perpetua dreamt had happened to her before her combat with the Devil in the form of an Egyptian. It was the climax of *Thomas'* eschatology.

At Lyon, there is also late-Jewish inspiration but of a different sort. The survivors' record of the events must have the story of the heroic Maccabaean mother and her sons defying Antiochus IV, as he wrote about Blandina[3]. She is "the noble mother", who like her Maccabaean predecessor, "encouraged her children, sent them forth triumphant to the King and then, duplicating in her own body all her children's sufferings, she hastened to rejoin them"[4]. As the mother of the Maccabees, she dies last encouraging the youngest of the confessors to be steadfast. One can point to other resemblances to II Maccabees which the author may have had in mind, when he wrote of Vettius Epagathus who came forward to plead for the Christians after their arrest. He may be perhaps compared with Razis of II *Macc* 14[37] the one "advocate of the Christians", the other "the father of the Jews"[5], both ready to give their lives in defiance of an idolatrous tyrant. The restoration to the confessors of their vigour after torture, their resistance to suffering, insensibility to pain, the defeat of the desperate strength of the executioners are all features in the story that point to the Maccabees as recorded in II and IV *Macc* as sources of their ready acceptance of martyrdom[6].

In both *Acta*, therefore, one may point to a late-Jewish legacy, and it is within that framework that the question of Montanist

---

1. *Passio*, 13: See also, TERTULLIAN, *De Anima* 55.
2. Thus, Urbanilla on the third century sepulchral mosaic from Lambiridi in Numidia, see J. CARCOPINO, *Aspects mystiques de la Rome païenne*, Paris, 1941, pp. 281-4. The texts from the *Gospel of Thomas* are taken from the Grant and Freedman ed, Fontana, London 1960.
3. See FREND, *Martyrdom and Persecution*, pp. 19-20 (with references on p. 29).
4. EUSEBIUS, *H.E.*, V.1.55. Compare *II Macc* 7[22-3].
5. *Ibid.*, 1.10. Compare II *Macc* 14[37].
6. See the discussion by O. PERLER, Das vierte Makkabaerbuch, Ignatius von Antiochien und die ältesten Martyrerberichte, *Rivista di archeologia cristiana* 25, 1949, 47-72.

influence should be viewed[1]. While this is undeniable in the *Passio Perpetuae*, it would seem more relevant to suggest that Montanism itself, and the *Acta Martyrum* from Lyon and Carthage all point to a movement within Christianity in the last quarter of the second century based on a profound conviction of the approaching end of the existing age and the glorification of the role of the confessor and martyr as vehicles of the Holy Spirit in bringing that about. The Roman authorities were cast in the role of the Seleucid kings, as servants of the Devil and oppressive idolators.

Within this general framework there are, however, significant differences between the two *Acta* and their heroines. At Lyon, the confessors are defiant to the end and reject in the amphitheatre charges of cannibalism against them[2], but they die without visions of Paradise and hopes of vengeance. The emphasis throughout lies on positive imitation of Christ, the one true perfected martyr, and in his and the protomartyr Stephen's example of loving and forgiving their enemies[3]. Among themselves, it is said "peace they had always loved and it was peace they commended to us for ever"[4]. They "bound none and loosed all"[5], while it is assumed that they possessed these powers as confessors. Apostates only, they regarded as "sons of perdition"[6]. Theirs was certainly a religion of protest, for they had little use for the "wild and barbarous people" among whom they lived[7]. They felt superior to them, but they were not active opponents, asking only to be allowed to worship God in truth. Blandina suffers, but does not threaten her torturers with punishment hereafter. Her reward is her opportunity of complete imitation of Christ and identification with His own perfect martyrdom.

Perpetua shows us a different side of this same sectarian Christianity. Hers is a situation more like that described by Celsus, of profound rejection of the values of the pagan and of her family's religious tradition. What led to the family crisis we shall never know, but there is a real poignancy in her father's continuous efforts to save her from humiliating death as a result of which the family itself would hardly recover. "Give up your pride. You

---

1. On Montanism in these *Acta*, see the old but excellent discussion in P. DE LABRIOLLE, *La Crise Montaniste*, Paris, 1913, p. 220 ff, and J. Armitage ROBINSON, The Passion of St Perpetua, in *Cambridge Texts and Studies*, 1, 1891, pp. 50-2.
2. EUSEBIUS, *H.E.*, V.1.52.
3. *Ibid.*, 2.5.
4. *Ibid.*, 2.7.
5. *Ibid.*, 2.5.
6. *Ibid.*, 1.48.
7. *Ibid.*, 1.57.

will destroy us all.   None of us will be able to speak freely again if anything happens to you"[1].   Perpetua was obviously an adored only daughter who grew up into a spoilt and wilful young woman, but in her case, her frustrations drove her into fanatical adherence to an apocalyptic form of Christianity and hostility to the society in which she had been reared.   Though she is fighting the powers of Satan rather than imperial Rome, there is a contempt and sarcasm for the empire and its rulers in her remark to the military tribune.   "Why can't you allow us to refresh ourselves at all? We are the most distinguished criminals (noxiis nobilissimis). We are Caesar's and we are due to fight on his very birthday. Would it not be to your credit if we were produced on the day in a fatter condition (pinguiores)[2]?"   She shared with her confessor, Saturus, open rejection of the "golden age" of the Severi.

Her story and that of Blandina tell us much about the spirit of Christianity in the last quarter of the second century.   They bear out Celsus' attack on the Christians as subversives who deserved the persecutions that befell them.   They show, too, a Christianity still drawing much of its inspiration from late-Jewish apocalyptic and Maccabaean defiance of the idolatrous rulers of this world.   It is a Christianity whose adherents awaited eagerly the Judgment and the end of the Age.   At the same time, for reasons which are still obscure this outlook reflected a deep dissatisfaction with the apparent prosperity of the period.   The new religion was not confined to slaves and freedmen.   Those who joined found themselves in a close-knit society without social or sex distinction.   Blandina and her mistress are both confessors and die in the same persecution.   Perpetua and her slave Felicitas also perish together.   Christianity provided scope for the human need of achievement and daring for a cause.   In the equality practised by the Christians many women found their chance of self-fulfilment. Isis-worship could sustain the mother but not the intellectual and would-be leader.   Flora, the correspondent of the Gnostic, Ptolemaeus, probing into the true worth of the Old Testament, Marcellina a Gnostic leader at Rome, Blandina and Perpetua all found scope for leadership and a cause to fight for, which pagan society could not provide.   Amid the light and shade of second century Christianity, its mixture of idealism, search for truth, self delusion and angry protest, Blandina and Perpetua stand out as examples of the spirit that resulted in the ultimate triumph of the faith.

1. *Passio*, 3.3, 5.1-4, 6.5.
2. *Ibid.*, 16.3.

NORTH AFRICA

XVI

THE EARLY CHRISTIAN CHURCH IN CARTHAGE

Byzantine Carthage was a city dominated by its churches, monasteries and government buildings. It was perhaps no accident that the University of Michigan's excavation area in the Save Carthage Project should have included a large late Roman church, much enlarged in the Byzantine period. It had been cleared partially by a Tunisian team directed by M. A. Ennabli in 1970-71, but examination awaits completion. It had been an imposing building, divided into five aisles in its Byzantine form, its floors paved with mosaic, and, including its adjacent ecclesiastical complex, perhaps covered half an insula. There was also a baptistery on the south side. It is tempting to think of this church as one of the regionary churches of the city, and a stylistic dating of the first church on the basis of the mosaics makes it likely that it was first constructed shortly before or after the conference of 411 as a Catholic church. It may have gone out of use for much if not all of the Vandal period, but was rebuilt on a much enlarged scale in the Byzantine period, when again it seems to have been one of the more important churches within the city walls. According to the evidence from the 1976 excavations along its south side, it is likely to have gone out of use not long after the middle of the 7th c. (see p. 43 below). About 300 m. to the northwest, another well preserved baptistery (two periods) and church (Byzantine mosaics) has been uncovered on the rise along which the TGM railway runs and awaits excavation. The baptistery was a substantial building with a hexagonal basin in period I, into which a smaller circular basin had been inserted in period II. These two Christian monuments so close to each other symbolise the Christian character of the later centuries of Roman and Byzantine Carthage, and will help to fill the lacuna for such monuments in the center of the city lamented by Duval.[1]

Christianity had a history in the city lasting more than 500 years, from the second half of the 2nd c. to some time in the 8th, though remnants of a Christian community survived for as much as another three hundred years. Christians emerge suddenly out of obscurity. In July 180, twelve Christians from the small town of Scilli were brought before the proconsul, Vigellius Saturninus, and, after interrogation in the Proconsul's *secretarium* in Carthage, were condemned to death.[2] In March 203 another group of Christians, including the youthful matrona, Vibia Perpetua, and her slave, Felicitas, were martyred in the amphitheatre at Carthage.[3] How Christianity had gained its first converts is unknown, but the likelihood is that the large Jewish community, whose presence is attested by the cemetery at Gamart and other discoveries, may have contributed. In the first decade of the 3rd c., Christians in Carthage were still known as "Nazarenes" (Tertullian, *Against Marcion* iv. 8) and a Jewish inscription of the 2nd or early 3rd c. has been found in a cemetery bordering the great Christian church of Damous el Karita.[4]

Carthaginian Christianity was an exacting and puritanical religion. From the outset, martyrs and martyrdom were held in special honour. Baptism, too, was regarded as an act symbolising total rejection of the values of the pagan world and entry into an exclusively Christian society. In the last

---

[1] N. Duval, "Etudes d'architecture chrétienne nord-africaine," *MEFR* 84 (1972) 1077-78.
[2] See Acts of the Scillitan martyrs (ed. and tr. H. Musurillo) in *The Acts of the Christian Martyrs*, Oxford 1972, 86-89.
[3] Also, ed. and tr. Musurillo (supra n. 2) 106-31.
[4] J. Ferron, "Inscriptions juives de Carthage," *Cahiers de Byrsa* 1 (1951) 184-87.

years of the 2nd c., Christians were proud of being a sect. "We are a society with a common religious feeling, unity of discipline, a common bond of hope."[5] Thus, Tertullian (ca. 160-ca. 240) defined the ideal of the Church; he was the first of the western Fathers, a Carthaginian who typified the unbending attitudes of the Church there.

Tertullian did not die a martyr, unlike the next Carthaginian Christian leader of whom we know anything, Cyprian, who was bishop between 248 and 258. Cyprian's church experienced the Decian (250) and Valerianic (257-260) persecutions, and he himself was martyred on 14 September 258. His 82 letters, 15 treatises, as well as the *Acta* of the Council of bishops in September 256, over which he presided, tell us much about the life of the Church in Carthage at this time. Cyprian's church was still "Noah's Ark," an exclusive, authoritarian and episcopally-led body, promising salvation to those within, but damnation to all without, whether schismatics, heretics, Jews or pagans. "He can no longer have God for his father who has not the church for his mother" (*On the Unity of the Catholic Church,* ch. 6). There was "no salvation outside the church" (*Letter* 73.21). Priests must be spotless vessels of the Lord, dispensing pure sacrifices. No priest in a state of sin, nor a heretic, nor schismatic, could provide the means of salvation (*Letter* 67). It was the duty of a congregation, as the "people of God" to separate themselves from such a cleric. Cyprian went to his death without hesitation, condemned as the "ringleader of an unlawful association"[6] disloyal to Rome.

The test for his ideas came in the Great Persecution of 303-304. Great bitterness was engendered between those who on the whole had been prepared to collaborate with the authorities and hand over Scriptures to be burnt as demanded, and those who had been ready to confess their faith and risk a martyr's death. The issue came to a head in Carthage in 311 when the archdeacon, Caecilian, was elected bishop. He was, however, identified with those who regarded confessors, particularly volunteers, as fanatics, and was also suspected of having been consecrated by a *"traditor"* (i.e. someone who had handed over the Scriptures). Opposition coalesced round a certain Donatus of Casae Nigrae, a Numidian town on the edge of the Sahara. Donatus was consecrated as rival bishop, practically ousted his rival, and the resulting schism lasted in one form or another as long as Christianity survived in North Africa.[7]

Until ca. 400, the Donatists, as they were called, were the predominant party throughout North Africa, including Carthage. Thus, churches identifiably built before 400 in Carthage are likely to have started as Donatist churches. They continued the ecclesiastical tradition of Cyprian. Theirs was a religion of the Bible and martyrdom, of evangelical praise, and of inspiration by the Holy Spirit. As one of their writers defined it, "In our Church, the virtues of the people are multiplied by the presence of the Spirit. The joy of the Spirit is to conquer in the martyrs and triumph in the confessors."[8] The tombs of the martyrs could be expected to form the centres of Donatist worship.

However, after 400, there was a resurgence of the Catholic opposition led by Aurelius, Bishop of Carthage, and St. Augustine of Hippo. Aided by the imperial authorities, the Catholics were able to bring their opponents to a conference held in the Baths of Gargilianus in Carthage in May 411. This meeting lasted through three long sessions and was presided over by an imperial official, the Tribune and Notary, Marcellinus.[9] Not surprisingly, the Donatists were defeated, and as a result,

---

[5] Tertullian, *Apologeticum* 39.1.
[6] *Acta Proconsularia* (ed. W. Hartel, *CSEL* iii.3, Vienna 1871) pp. CX-CXIV.
[7] On the origins of Donatism, see Frend, *The Donatist Church,* Oxford 1971, ch. 1.
[8] *Acta Saturnini,* 20 (Migne *Pl.* viii, col. 703). See Frend (supra n. 7) 318.
[9] The proceedings of the conference of Carthage have been ed. and tr. by S. Lancel, *Les Actes de la Conférence de Carthage* (Sources Chrétiennes 195), Paris 1972-76.

THE EARLY CHRISTIAN CHURCH IN CARTHAGE

their cult was proscribed by imperial decree on January 30, 412 (*Codex Theodosianus* XVI 5.52). For the next seventeen years the Catholics enjoyed triumphant prosperity broken only by the arrival of the Vandals on African soil in 429 and in Carthage in 439. If an accurate dating of churches were possible, evidence for these years of ascendancy might be traceable in the excavation of some of the Carthaginian basilicas (e.g. perhaps in the radical alterations to the Damous el Karita complex). We know, however, from the Catholic writer Victor of Vita (who died after ca. 490) of some of the churches in Catholic hands at the time of the Vandal capture of Carthage in 439. He mentions the Basilica Majorum,[10] the Basilica Restituta perpetua,[11] the Basilica Novarum,[12] two churches built in honour of Cyprian,[13] churches commemorating the martyrs Celerina and the Scillitans,[14] and the Basilica Fausti[15] named perhaps after a pious donor or the proprietor of an *area* that became a Christian centre.

In 439, Carthage fell to the Vandals. Victor indicates that the Vandals seized all the Catholic churches located within the walls of Carthage, including the cathedral, the Basilica Restituta, but left the Catholics with most of their churches outside the walls, with the striking exception of the two churches associated with Cyprian.[16] Gaiseric and his people were Arians, and the Vandal rulers were hostile to the Catholics and the Afro-Roman nobility whom they regarded as their natural opponents. For long intervals (i.e. between 439-54, 457-80, 505-23) the Church in Carthage had no bishop, and the Catholic congregations were harrassed. After nearly 90 years, however, the wheel turned once more. The Vandal ruler, Hilderic (523-30), who had been brought up at the Byzantine court, restored toleration to the Catholics, and a Catholic council met in Carthage under Bishop Bonifatius in 525. A reaction followed under Gelimer who supplanted Hilderic in 530. Within a few years, however, the Vandals had been defeated by the Byzantines under Belisarius, and in August 535 Catholicism was restored by the emperor Justinian in all its former privileges.[17] Next year, Bishop Reparatus held a Council of 227 bishops at Carthage symbolising the restoration and renewal of the Church.

Catholicism now enjoyed an Indian summer of prosperity. Carthage became the seat of an archbishopric occupied by a succession of independent-minded and able prelates that continued to the end of the century. The canons of the pre-Vandal era were codified and updated to form the basis for the Canon law of the Church.[18] The author was the Carthaginian deacon, Ferrandus. There was a great amount of building activity. It is interesting that all the churches excavated by modern methods within the city walls were either built in Byzantine times or show signs of embellishment in that period. This applied particularly to the large Christian complex near the Antonine baths (Duval's "Dermech I"). This complex, consisting of a church with five naves, a large baptistery attached to a chapel, all paved with mosaic, seems clearly to date to the period of Justinian, and may have been the seat of the archbishopric.[19] Other churches in the vicinity, such as the "Chapel of Marina" (Dermech III) and the elaborate tombs of Redemtus and Asterius are also Byzantine.[20]

---

[10] Victor Vitensis, *Historia Persecutionis Africanae Provinciae* (ed. M. Petschenig, *CSEL* vii, Vienna 1881) 1.9.
[11] Ibid. 1.15.
[12] Ibid. 1.25.
[13] Ibid. 1.16.
[14] Victor says "Celerinae vel Scillitanorum," *Historia* 1.9. He could, therefore, be referring to one church only, but one can see no connection between the Scillitans and Celerina. Referring to the monastery of Bigua, he speaks of Celerina only (*Passio Septem Monachorum* 16).
[15] *Historia* 1.25.
[16] *Historia* 1.15-16. See Ch. Courtois, *Les Vandales et l'Afrique,* Alger 1955, p. 284.
[17] Justinian, *Novella* XXXVII 5 and 8, 1 Aug. 535.
[18] Ferrandi, "Brevatio canonum," ed. C. Munier in *Concilia Africae* (= vol. CXLIX of *Corpus Christianorum,* Turnhout 1974) pp. 284-311.
[19] Duval (supra n. 1) 1081-1092.
[20] Ibid. 1094-96 and 1100-02.

Monasteries, too, were built. Procopius mentions in particular the great monastery built by the military commander, Solomon, near the port area *(Mandracium).*[21]

Despite these favours, relations between the churches of Carthage and Constantinople were not always harmonious. The Byzantines brought their own ideas and forms of worship with them, and these had evolved considerably since the Vandals took Carthage. Place had to be found in the traditional Christianity of Carthage for the religion of the Christ-God, of the Virgin *Theotokos* and eastern saints and martyrs. The chapel built in honour of the *Theotokos* in the governor's palace characterized the new regime.[22] The cult of the *Theotokos* and the eastern saints took root, as shown by the many lead seals found in Carthage dating to the 7th c.,[23] but in other ways Byzantine forms were resisted. At the time of the Fifth General Council (553) the North Africans, led by Archbishop Reparatus, and the Archdeacon Liberatus, opposed the emperor, and Reparatus was deposed and exiled the year before the Council opened. The prosperity, too, of the early years of the Byzantine occupation proved brittle. The pontificate of Pope Gregory I (590-604) saw a lively exchange of letters between him and Archbishop Dominicus of Carthage, but the seventh century was one of decline for Christianity. It is probably not accidental that the large church in the American sector of "Save Carthage" was already in ruins well before the fall of the city to the Arabs (see p. 45). The presence of burials of Byzantine date in the port area suggests a contraction of this part of the city.[24]

There was a brief flurry of activity in the 640's when refugees poured into North Africa from Syria and Egypt. The North African Church became caught up in the debate over Monothelitism (i.e. that there was one Will only in Christ, namely, a divine Will). In 645 there was a debate between the exiled patriarch of Constantinople, Pyrrhus, and the monk Maximus, and in the following year a Council was held at which Monothelitism was solemnly condemned.[25] Four years later, Archbishop Victor who presided was referred to at the Lateran Council of October of that year. One African bishop, Victorianus of Uzalis, attended.[26] After that date no archbishop of Carthage can be identified with certainty. When Carthage was eventually captured by the Arabs in 698, little of the Church may have been surviving. The remnants were organized during the 8th c. under the Patriarchate of Alexandria.[27] The rest is ruins and little to break the silence of obscurity.

The development of the Church in Carthage may be pieced together from archaeological and literary sources. The earliest centres of Christian worship were the cemeteries, the *areae* as they were called, located beyond the city walls. As early as 212, Tertullian, protesting to the Proconsul Scapula against persecution, shows that these were arousing popular anger. "Down with the cemeteries," the pagans were shouting.[28] Throughout the 3rd c., *areae* and *cymeteria* characterized the Carthaginian Church. The names of some of these have survived, such as the *areae* Macrobii where Cyprian was buried, the *areae* Fausti, Tertulli and the Novae *areae,* all of which were in use by ca. 300.[29]

---

[21] Procopius, *De Aedificiis,* B 339.
[22] Procopius, ibid. Identified tentatively by A. Lézine with the church found on the Byrsa: see A. Lézine, *Carthage. Utique. Etudes d'architecture et d'urbanisme,* (Paris 1968) 177-180.
[23] See H. Leclercq, "Carthage," in *DACL* ii.2, col. 2303 (plates 2152-55).
[24] R. Lantier, *CRAI* 1922, p. 27.
[25] See L. Bréhier and R. Aigran, *Grégoire le Grand, les Etats Barbares et la Conquête Arabe,* (= Vol. v of Fliche and Martin, *Histoire de l'Eglise,* Paris 1947, 163-65).
[26] See J. L. Maier, *L'Episcopat d'Afrique Romaine, Vandale et Byzantine,* Institut Suisse de Rome, 1973, p. 84.
[27] H. Gelzer, "Ungedrückte und wenig bekannte Bistümsverzeichnisse der orient. Kirche," *BZ* 2 (1893) 22ff.
[28] *Ad Scapulam* (ed. V. Buhlart, *CSEL* LXXVI, Vienna 1957) 3.1.
[29] Augustine, *Brevic. Collationis cum Donatistis* iii.13.25. Mentions also a *"domus episcopi."* See P. Monceaux, *Histoire littéraire de l'Afrique Chrétienne,* Paris 1902-23, vol. iii, p. 15 (references).

Among the burial places, those connected with martyrs acquired special sanctity. In 203 Vibia Perpetua had in all probability been buried in a plot on the family estate of her parents near the city.[30] Cyprian, we know from his biographer, the deacon Pontius, was buried in the "areas . . . quae sunt in Via Mappalensi juxta piscinas,"[31] a site which may now with some degree of probability be identified with that of the "Basilique Sainte Monique" just north of the city boundary.[32] Basilicas associated with the Scillitian martyrs and with the martyr, Celerina (who died, probably ca. 240), mentioned by Victor of Vita, have not yet been identified. These sites became particularly sacred. Where they have been excavated, it is clear that they became the centres of great cemetery basilicas, as Christians ardently desired to be buried in the closest association with the martyrs of the faith.

The *Basilica Majorum,* situated outside the city walls on a rise about half-way between Sainte Monique and La Marsa, is the principal example of a cemetery/martyrological basilica.[33] When it was excavated by Père Delattre in 1906-08, it was found to have been very robbed, but even with the excavation methods of the day, it was possible to establish that it had been a vast building, 61 x 45 m. excluding the apse, consisting eventually of nine naves with a small central chapel square in shape with an apse and mosaic pavement (3.6 x 3.7 m.) set in the middle of the central nave. Below this was a crypt approached by steps on either side. It may have been a "confessio" built over what was believed to be the tomb of martyrs for special veneration. Delattre believed these were no other than Perpetua and her companions. There is, however, the reservation to be made, that the inscription which Delattre reconstructed is clearly Byzantine in date, and two other dedications to these famous martyrs have been found elsewhere in Carthage.[34] However, the evidence in this case points cumulatively to close association with Perpetua and her companions. The church had been built over a pagan burial ground, and some Christian inscriptions were cut on the back of pagan memorials. Amphorae found on the site date back to the 2nd c. A.D., and one inscription was marked VIBIA, the praenomen of Perpetua.[35] While the evidence is circumstantial, Christians almost certainly believed that the bodies of Perpetua, Felicitas, and their friends were buried there, and Delattre was justified in drawing attention to the finely cut marble inscription in honour of the martyrs, though he dated it too early:

+ [Hic] sunt Marty[res
+ Saturus Saturn[inus
+ Rebocatus Secu[ndulus
+ Felicit Per[pe]t Pas[non Mart

(Here are the martyrs, Saturus, Saturninus, Revocatus, Secundulus, Felicitas, Perpetua, who suffered on the nones of March.)[36]

The whole area of the basilica, both inside and around the walls, was occupied by tombs, representing every section of the population, from those who could afford graves decked with mosaic to humble tile-covered graves. Nearly 4,000 epigraphic fragments were found. In one great pit near the centre of the church several hundred skeletons were found, and among the inscriptions found among them was one reading, "Perpetue Filie Dulcissimae" (*CIL* VIII, 25272). The lettering

---

[30] I accept H. Leclercq's view (following Père Delattre) in "Carthage" *DACL* ii.2, col. 2247-48.
[31] Pontius, *Vita Sancti Cypriani* (ed. Hartel, *CSEL* iii.3) ch. 5, p. cxiii.
[32] See Liliane Ennabli, *Les Inscriptions Funéraires Chrétiennes de la Basilique dite de Sainte-Monique à Carthage* (Institut National d'Archéologie et d'Arts de Tunis, 1975) pp. 15-16, although Duval (supra n. 1) 1075 says "not proven."
[33] I have followed Leclercq's description (still the best), cols. 2223 ff. See also Duval (supra n. 1) 1116-19.
[34] *CIL* VIII.25037 ("St. Stephen's Convent") and in a room in the underground baptistery found beneath the Lycée on Sayda hill to the north of the city. See N. Duval and A. Lézine, *CahArch* 10-11 (1959-60) 120-21.
[35] Reported by Delattre; see Leclercq (supra n. 23) col. 2248.
[36] Illustrated in Leclercq (supra n. 23) figs. 2123 and 2124. Also *CIL* VIII.25038.

is third century. While any identification is speculation, one is tempted to think (with Leclercq) of the last affectionate memory of Perpetua from her parents from whom she had so violently estranged herself.

No baptistery was found; the *Basilica Majorum* was a huge commemorative monument, remembered even in Vandal times as "ubi corpora sanctarum martyrum Perpetuae et Felicitatis sepulta sunt"[37] (the resting-place of the bodies of Perpetua and Felicitas). Victor says the Vandals took it over for their own worship, together with the *Basilica Celerinae* and *Basilica Scilitanorum* and "others that they did not destroy" (*Historia Persecutionis* 1.3). The Catholics may perhaps have protested too loudly, for the cemetery-basilica was primarily a Donatist innovation, even frowned upon at first by some of the Donatist bishops (Optatus of Milevis, *De Schismate Donatistarum* iii.4). The climate of opinion changed, however, and pilgrimages to the martyrs' tombs and burial around them developed as characteristic Donatist practices through the 4th c. By the 6th c., as the tombs around the basilica of St. Salsa at Tipasa show, the practice was general in North Africa.

The second major cemetery basilica outside the Theodosian walls is the *Damous el Karita.*[38] It occupies a large area in a valley just beyond the north line of the city wall, some 200 m. by 60 m., and the various constructions connected with it extend from the 4th to the 7th centuries. It is also an extremely complicated site, and the complications seem to have defeated Père Delattre and other early researchers. At the height of its development, probably early in the 5th c., the church was set in a square 65 x 45 m. oriented NE-SW and was approached by way of a large semicircular courtyard with a nymphaeum set in the middle. It formed the centre of what can best be described as an ecclesiastical quarter. Its nine aisles were divided from each other by eleven ranges of columns giving the impression today of a veritable forest of stone.[39] The central nave was 12.8 m. wide and in the middle had been built a small square shrine or ciborium. (This seems to belong to this phase of building rather than the Byzantine period.[40]) At the northeast end, at the central point of the courtyard, was a small trefoil shaped chapel containing a single well-made stone sarcophagus (probably not later than the 4th c.).[41] A Byzantine-type trefoil baptistery was built on the south wall of the church near the southeast corner.

Beyond the apse at the southwest of the church were ranges of buildings including a square baptistery with a hexagonal piscina preceded by a small vestibule. Beyond this, in turn, were small square stone buildings that could be monastic cells. To the west extended a cemetery containing stone sarcophagi. One of the tombs, a subterranean rotunda (9.15 m. in diameter), had a long history. It was filled with niches alternating with marble columns and the walls still show traces of pink plaster. In the centre was a round piscina 2 m. in diameter surrounded by small columns. This building has often been discussed.[42] It must have started as a tomb; the piscina seems to be later and indicates possible use as a subterranean baptistery. The discovery of capitals ornamented with eagles and rams' heads suggests embellishment in the first decades of the 5th c. even if it had been built many years before.[43] It looks as though at one stage it formed part of a large ecclesiastical complex which

---

[37] Victor Vitensis 1.3.
[38] With variations based on my observations of the site during June 1976, I have followed Leclercq (supra n. 23) col. 2252 ff. See also Duval (supra n. 1) 1107-13.
[39] For illustrations taken in 1925, see vol. II, pls. to chapter 7.
[40] For the Byzantine date, see Duval (supra n. 1) 1112.
[41] One is reminded of the use at Tipasa by Christians in the 4th c. of a sarcophagus belonging to a *matrona* Fabia Salsa, who had died in the previous century, as the *memoria* of St. Salsa. See H. Grégoire, "Sainte Salsa," *Byzantion* 12 (1937) 213-24.
[42] A. Lézine, *Architecture romaine d'Afrique* (Tunis 1963) 80-86, and Duval (supra n. 1) 1113-15.
[43] See M. Pinard, "Les chapiteaux à Beliers et à Aigles de Damous el Karita," *Cahiers de Byrsa* 9 (1960-61), 37-48: "nous proposons donc de dater ces chapiteaux à zones entre 408 et 439" (p. 47).

THE EARLY CHRISTIAN CHURCH IN CARTHAGE

extends northwards across the existing road—perhaps a pilgrim church with the tomb as the point of attraction.

As usual, Delattre took his excavations down to natural soil, but failed to record his stratigraphy. This omission is hardly repaired by the discovery of 20,000 epigraphic fragments on the site. The reconstruction of the dating of the Damous is accordingly very difficult. It covered an extensive burial ground, containing pagan and some Jewish tombs. One of the latter bilingual, Greek and Hebrew, found beyond the west end of the church, belonged to Annianus, the son of Annianus, and dates to the end of the 2nd or early 3rd c.[44] In the same area a small catacomb containing two stages of *loculi* had been constructed within a cistern. This catacomb bore a family resemblance to some of the richer Jewish burials at Gamart. The significance of the catacomb seems to have been missed by scholars to date, but observation on the ground indicates that the earliest church, consisting probably of three naves, one ending with the apse two-thirds of the way towards the south wall of the church, was aligned on it. This was a small *area* church perhaps also including the burial over which the *ciborium* was erected later. There are some very early Christian funerary inscriptions from the site. A second stage involved raising the floor level and considerable enlargement on the same alignment; a new apse was built using the top of the cistern as the raised *bema*. The third stage was the radical re-orientation of the church to face northeast-southwest as already described. There was a final phase reverting to the original orientation in which it can be seen that the apse of the earliest church was used as a foundation for a successor. The whole history of Christianity in Carthage from *area* church to great ecclesiastical complex and then in Byzantine times to a small, rather neglected suburban church, can be traced by careful observation of the remains.

What was the Damous? Its size indicates its importance. Inscriptions found on the site refer to a "bishop," presbyters, deacons and lectors;[44a] but it is impossible to equate it with the Basilica Restituta that served the Catholics as their cathedral, for this is stated by Victor to have been *intra muros* (1.15). Perhaps further examination of the inscriptions from the site may provide a clue. The solitary tomb in the *trichorium* at the northeast end of the complex points to the memory of a martyr. Could it have been Celerina? If so, the adjoining buildings could be the Monastery of Bigua referred to by Victor Vitensis (*Passio Septem Monachorum* 16). Though this is speculative, funerary inscriptions of sacred virgins have been found nearby in the cemetery south of the basilica (*CIL* VIII. 25056-60).

More likely is the identification of the *memoria Cypriani* with the "Basilique Sainte Monique," situated on high ground overlooking the sea, just beyond the line of the north wall of the city.[45] It was another large (seven naves) cemetery-church (71.34 x 35.55 m. internal), oriented southeast-northwest partly over a pagan building (perhaps a temple to Securitas), whose traces can still be seen along the foundations of the northeast wall of the church. There was also an early Christian cemetery where Cyprian himself was reputed to have been buried. The actual site has been described recently by Mme. Liliane Ennabli, but many clues as to the history of the site had previously been lost. (It is clear, for instance, that the cistern which occupies part of the narthex of the church belongs to an earlier, domestic occupation of the site.) This church also attracted numerous burials, and sarcophagi can still be seen alongside and inserted into the northeast wall. Several thousand fragments of inscriptions were found by Delattre during his excavations between 1915-20 and a considerable proportion of them has now been reassembled and restored by Mme. Ennabli after a decade of patient work. The publication of 402 of them shows that nearly all are burial inscriptions recording the name of the deceased, his/her age, and the description *"fidelis in pace."* Only one is

---

[44] J. Ferron, *Cahiers de Byrsa* (supra n. 43) 184.
[44a] *CIL* VIII. 25040-55.
[45] L. Ennabli (supra n. 32), supplemented by my observations.

dated, namely to 439 (Ennabli, No. 46), but the character of the writing and formulae indicate Christian usage from the late 4th or early 5th c. to the late 6th c., including the Vandal period. No baptistery has yet been found.[46]

The second church dedicated to Cyprian which Victor mentions was erected in the Ager Sextii on his place of execution. A *church at Bir Ftouha* northwest of the Basilica Majorum was suspected by Delattre as corresponding to this. It was also a cemetery church which had some of the same features as the Damous el Karita. In particular, a small funerary chapel or martyrial triconch was found, containing ten large sarcophagi.[47] In nine there was a body laid in white plaster without grave goods. In the tenth, there was a single skull around which had been grouped pottery fragments, and human hand and foot bones. One female skeleton measured 1.61 m. and a male 1.74 m. (It is a great pity that more attention was not paid in these massive excavations to skeletal remains.) Only part of the basilica was excavated by Delattre in 1928, a property boundary preventing further work. This church had also been built over an existing cemetery whose use went back to Punic times. No clear evidence, however, links it as yet with Cyprian.[48]

Another church, known as *Bir Knissia* (the "Spring of the Church") just beyond the south front of the Theodosian wall between Douar Chott and Salammbo (west of the railway) proved to be of the same general type as the Basilica Majorum. It was found in 1913 and excavated by Delattre in 1922-23. It was a rich cemetery church, built over existing pagan and Jewish (?) graves and was used probably in Vandal as well as Byzantine times. A small hoard of 92 Vandal coins found with pottery and lamps suggests this, although it may also have been buried for safety in a derelict building. The several phases of use have, however, not been well defined by the excavators, but in Byzantine times it measured 46.6 x 25.6 m. with a central nave 12 m. across and was oriented northwest-southeast. Delattre noted that the bases of columns had been chosen as points around which tombs were grouped.[49]

Churches within the walls differ in several ways from those outside. Unless there are further Christian buildings to be found in the Dermech area, it does not seem as though Carthage possessed any single exclusively Christian quarter, such as existed in other towns such as Hippo Regius and Djemila (Cuicul).[50] It had, however, the cathedral churches of the Catholics and Donatists and also churches belonging to minor sects such as the Tertullianists and perhaps an Arian cathedral. All these have yet to be identified on the ground. There would also be regional and parish churches. They were community centres, and though burials sometimes occur within and near them[51] within the city bounds, the primary function of such churches would be worship and instruction. The baptistery, with its round, square or trefoil piscina, into which steps descended, would always be prominent (though apparently it had no fixed position vis à vis the church) and the chapel attached to that at Dermech I may be connected with the baptismal ritual. The churches are usually large buildings, paved with mosaic floors, with marble fittings, testifying to relatively wealthy congregations.

Two other Christian monuments, exceptional because they may lie just within the Theodosian wall, deserve mention here. First, there are the two elaborate underground tombs, found in the

---

[46] L. Ennabli (supra n. 32) 16-20 for description of the church and its inscriptions.
[47] P. Lapeyre, *Atti IV Congresso di arch. cristiana 1938*, i, p. 184, 206, 230-31.
[48] A. L. Delattre, *CRAI* 1929, 23-29.
[49] A. L. Delattre, *CRAI* 1922, 302-307 and 1923, 449-51. A broken inscription beginning with the Jewish formula ἐυὸ αδ ε[κειται was found on the site. Also J. Vaultrin, "Les Basiliques chrétiennes de Carthage," *RAfr* 1932, 309-12.
[50] See J. Lassus, "Edifices de culte autour de la basilique," *Atti VI Congresso di arch. cristiana (Ravenna)* Rome 1965, 581-610, and *CRAI* 1922, 380-407.
[51] For example, at Dermech I (Duval 1082) and in the basilica in the American sector where funerary inscriptions have been found (see chapter 6 below).

Sayda area near the Sainte Monique (while digging the foundations of the present Lycée), in honour of the Archdeacon Redemtus and Asterius. Both tombs were shaped like miniature basilicas.[52] In Asterius' tomb, there was an altar and reliquary in the apse which was approached by steps.[53] In Redemtus' tomb the altar and relics were in a similar position but nearer the centre of the church. The tombs were in the "nave." Both were Byzantine, and in the case of Asterius' tomb, later than the reign of Maurice Tiberius (578-582) whose coins were found below the mosaic pavement. Redemtus was described as "archdeacon of the fifth region," but Asterius though clearly an important personality was not identified. He may have been a layman. In the same area a large subterranean baptistery was discovered in 1955-56, in use in Byzantine and probably Vandal times also.[54] The excavators believe (obviously rightly) that it belonged to another large Christian complex. It is evident that the Sayda area was covered with Christian buildings in Byzantine times.

Christian Carthage was divided into ecclesiastical regions *(regiones)*. They existed at least since the end of the 4th c. and probably much earlier.[55] They continued into the 7th c., for the lead seal of Bishop Fortunius who was bishop ca. 640 is engraved $\frac{RG}{VI}$, i.e. regio sexta.[56] Another similar lead bull associates this Bishop with the first region also.[57] Inscriptions provide evidence for the second, fourth and fifth regions. They were supervised by an archdeacon, of whom we know of Liberatus the archdeacon of regio VI in 566[58] and Redemtus archdeacon of regio V in the Byzantine period, which could have included the present Lycée area where it was found.[59] Inscriptions show how other clergy including deacons and lectors were directly associated with regional churches.[59a]

The regions were probably subdivided into parishes in charge of presbyters. Some of them, such as the Byrsa parish, had existed since Cyprian's time.[60] In those days the presbyters were the most powerful clergy after the bishops. Five dissident presbyters challenged Cyprian's authority. By 300, however, they were tending to be displaced in the order of precedence by the archdeacon, the earliest mention of whom is the ill-fated Caecilian whose unpopularity precipitated the Donatist schism.[61]

From the 4th c., the Church in Carthage was organized under its bishop who was also primate of Africa: below him would be the archdeacon (archdeacons took over the ecclesiastical regions of the city): then the presbyters, the parish ministers, then the deacons and lectors. The latter would be children who usually ceased to officiate in that order after reaching puberty.[62] Below them were minor orders, the sub-deacons, important in church administration, the janitors *(janitores)*, gravediggers *(fossores)*, and acolytes *(acolouthi)*. Those who had taken religious vows were denoted as such *(religiosus* or *virgo sacra* or *puella sacra)* on their tombs (e.g. *CIL* VIII, 25051, 25059, 25251). Even when the Vandal occupation was at its most settled, in the 480s, the Church in Carthage numbered "more than 500 clergy."[63] In Byzantine times, the Archbishop would have a senior

---

[52] Duval and Lézine, "Necropole chrétienne et baptistère souterrain à Carthage," *CahArch* 10-11 (1959-60) 78-82 and 95-99.
[53] Idem, "La Chapelle funéraire souterraine d'Astérius à Carthage," *MEFR* 71 (1959) 346.
[54] Duval and Lézine, *CahArch* 1959-60, 107-147.
[55] See P. Monceaux (supra n. 29) 66.
[56] See H. Leclercq (supra n. 23) col. 2271.
[57] Ibid.
[58] Author of *Breviarium causae nestorianorum et eutychianorum*, = *Pl* 68, col. 969.
[59] N. Duval, "Notes d'epigraphie chrétienne africaine," *Karthago* 7 (1956) 191-95 (quotes references to *regiones*).
[59a] E.g. *CIL* VIII 13423 (Menas, lector of the fourth region) and Duval op. cit. 192-93.
[60] See P. Hinchliffe, *Cyprian of Carthage*, London 1974, p. 39.
[61] Optatus of Milevis, *De Schismate Donatistarum* (ed. C. Ziwsa, *CSEL* 26, Vienna 1895) i.
[62] *Breviarium Hipponense*, ed. C. Munier, in *Concilia Africae*, Canon 18, p. 38, but Menas the lector (*CIL* VIII.13423) died at the age of 37.
[63] Victor Vitensis, iii.9.34 (p. 89).

member of the diaconate as his representative or *apocrisarius,* who could be expected to succeed him in office, as Primosus succeeded Reparatus on the latter's exile in 552.[64]

A peculiarity in North African ecclesiastical government was the existence of a powerful body of "lay elders" *(seniores laici).*[65] They can be traced back in Carthage to at least 300 A.D., and continued to exist into the 5th c. They were lay officials charged with the oversight of the Church's property whether estates or movable goods. When members of their order disclosed in 311 that the Carthaginian presbyters had tried to embezzle the movable property of the Church, this group had obviously been in existence for a long time. The question arises whether the *seniores* continued a similar office known to have existed in Jewish synagogues in the west. They existed also in other churches outside Carthage, and in some seem even to have had the power to arraign clergy suspected of malversations. It is difficult not to see in them the extension of some existing tradition and Jewish seems the most likely.

With this organization, one would expect to find the cathedral church, one large basilica in each *regio* of the city, and a number of smaller parish churches. The Catholic cathedral at the end of the 4th c. was the Basilica perpetua Restituta, in whose *secretarium* the great quasi-annual councils of the Church were held, and where Augustine often preached on his visits to Carthage.[66] Some of the regional churches were also large enough for councils to be held in them. Other literary evidence records a church of St. Peter in the Third Region[67] and perhaps one dedicated to St. Paul in the Sixth Region.[68] On the restoration of toleration by Hilderic in 523, the Catholics used the church of the martyr Agileus as their cathedral,[69] which had been given back to them by Gunthamund ca. 487, probably because the Basilica Restituta remained in Vandal possession.

The plan of the churches served the needs of organization and liturgy. As those in Syria, the North African churches are basilican in layout and usually oriented east-west. In Carthage, however, a number are oriented northwest-southeast. Dermech I has its apse at the east end, but most of the churches outside the walls of the city had their apses at the west end; the reasons for these variations are not known at present. The body of the church would be divided into naves, separated by ranges of columns. This rectangular area was the *quadratum populi* where the congregation would stand, men and women separately.[70] Behind would be a broad rectangular entrance hall, the *narthex* where the penitents and catechumens stood for the "Mass of the Catechumens" but would be excluded from the celebration of the Eucharist. The altar would stand within a railed enclosure, at Dermech I about three-quarters of the way down the aisle and approached by a rectangular enclosed passage, but tending in later Byzantine times to be nearer the apse. Under the altar would usually be relics, and it would be covered by a *ciborium,* a sort of square pavilion set on small columns, a feature of Byzantine churches, but originating probably earlier. The apse was the semicircular area reserved for the clergy who would sit either side of the presiding bishop or priest whose *thronos* (seat) would be at its point. On either side of the apse would be annexes, the *diaconicum* for storing the movable property of the church, including stores and clothing for charitable distribution, and the *prothesis* where the eucharistic offerings were taken. Some larger churches could be expected to have other suites of rooms, such as a *secretarium* for administrative services and assemblies, adjoining these annexes.[71] There is an element of doubt as to the position

---

[64] Victor of Tunnuna, *Chron* ad ann. 552, ed. Mommsen, *MGH Script. Ant.* xi.1, p. 202.
[65] See Frend, "The Seniores laici and the origins of the Church in North Africa," *JThS* NS 12 (1961) 280-84 (references).
[66] Augustine, *Sermo,* 19, 29, 90, 112, 277.
[67] P. Monceaux (supra n. 29) 66.
[68] Ibid.
[69] Bonifatius was consecrated in 523 and held his Council in 525 (*Concilia Africae,* p. 255). For its return to the Catholics by Gunthamund, see *Laterculus* ed. *MGH* A.A. XIII, p. 459.
[70] Augustine, *De Civitate Dei* ii.28, "Churches . . . . where a seemly separation of the sexes is observed."
[71] For example, see J. Lassus, (supra n. 50), p. 588. (fig. 4) Hippo.

of the celebrant of the Eucharist. At Dermech I, he could only have faced the apse, as Duval points out,[72] but a mosaic from Tabarka in the Bardo shows the priest apparently facing the congregation and in some Tunisian churches (Duval cites Haidra I) this seems also to have been the case. In the Basilica Majorum, as already noted, the central feature was the "confessio" built over the tombs of martyrs set in the centre of the church. In the *quadratum populi* there would usually be a pulpit from which the lector would read from Scripture, and the bishop would preach, if he did not, like Augustine, address the congregation from his episcopal chair. As illustrated by Dermech I, the baptistery adjoining the church would often be a fair-sized building, large enough to be used to instruct catechumens as well as to baptise. The plan of the church and its dependencies emphasised the role of the bishop and his clergy, intermediaries between God and His people.

Scholars have pointed to the enlargement of many churches in the Byzantine period and the addition of new features such as a second apse and further chapels on the sides of the church. These features have been connected with the elaboration of the liturgy in the Byzantine period and indicate perhaps attempts to amalgamate the traditional North African cult of martyrs and relics with the needs of Byzantine ritual.[73]

The floors of the basilicas would usually be paved with mosaics, sometimes contributed by the faithful: the walls would be covered with white stucco, but sometimes also decorated with mosaics or even with square tiles depicting Biblical scenes, or animals with a Christian significance, such as the stag or lion.[74] Fragments of such tiles have also been found on the south side of the basilica in the University of Michigan field and will be published by J. A. Riley in a later volume. Altogether the Byzantine basilicas in Carthage reflect a wealthy, influential and self-reliant Church.

Monasticism was late taking root in North Africa. Augustine's foundation at Thagaste on his return from Italy in 387 may have been the first monastery on North African soil. The Donatists would have nothing to do with monks.[75] In the west in general, they were associated with Manichaeism. Bishop Aurelius, however, was receptive to his friend's zeal for monasticism, but even so he did not find it an easy plant to cultivate. Circa 400, people were commenting on individuals who found monastic life too much and moved into the priesthood. "Bad monks make good clerics," the saying went.[76] Augustine was more optimistic. In his *Retractations* he spoke of the period ca. 400-405 as the time when "there began to be monasteries in Carthage,"[77] but problems remained. The first monks were undisciplined and inexperienced. Aurelius asked Augustine a series of questions about their conduct. Were monks to earn their keep by toiling with their hands, or were they to rely on alms? (*De Opere Monachorum* 1).[78] He refers him to advice given by Paul to the Corinthians; apparently with success, for towards the end of Augustine's life, monasticism had become more of a feature of Catholic Carthage. In Vandal times, Victor refers to a monastery of Bigua adjoining the Basilica of Celerina (*Passio Septem Monachorum* 16). The cell-like buildings adjoining the Damous el Karita might correspond to this description.

Under the Byzantines, monasticism flourished. Monasteries are referred to in the Council of Carthage in 536 as enjoying certain "liberties" from episcopal oversight.[79] Procopius records

---

[72] Duval (supra n. 1) 1088. The aim may have been always to have the celebrant and people facing east.
[73] P. Garrigue, "Une basilique byzantine à Junca en Byzacena," *MEFR* 65 (1953) 173-96.
[74] See J. Ferron and M. Pinard, "Plaques de terre cuite d'époque byzantine découvertes à Carthage," *Cahiers de Byrsa* 2 (1952) 97-112.
[75] Augustine, *Letters* 22 and 60. For Donatist opposition to monasticism, Augustine *Enarratio in Ps.* 132.6.
[76] Augustine, *Letter 60*.
[77] Augustine, *Retract*. ii.21 (*Pl.* 32, col. 638). The *De Opere Monachorum* was written to Aurelius and referred to Carthage.
[78] *De Opere Monachorum* 1, and "long-haired monks" ibid. 31-32.
[79] *Concilia Africae*, p. 283, "monasteria etiam ipsam libertatem plenissimam perfruantur." The "liberty" is not closely defined. Note the complaint by Abbot Peter against episcopal interference at the Council of 525 (p. 273ff).

Solomon the military commander building a fortified monastery "on the shore" in the port area of the city (the *Mandracium*), circa 546.[80] This could lie below a large mound situated behind the military harbour area to be excavated by the British team led by Mr. Henry Hurst. To the north of the city a convent perhaps dedicated to St. Stephen was occupied in Byzantine times.[80a]

The life of the North African Church revolved round the bishop of each see, and there were a great many of these. At the height of its prosperity in the early years of the fifth century there must have been more than 700 bishops, both Catholic and Donatist, in North Africa, and even some villages and landed estates could claim bishops. Numbers did not lessen their power and authority of their office. Since Cyprian's time the tendency of the Church had been strongly episcopal, the authority of the bishop being regarded as absolute in his community, unless he was found guilty of grave sin, in which case he was liable to deposition by a council of his colleagues. For Cyprian no crime was worse than disobedience to a bishop.[81] Defiance of his judgment could bring condign punishment. The fate of Dathan, Kore and Abiram were held up as awful warning to dissenters. The North African Church (and particularly the Donatist) was a Church of the Pure, an exclusive body for whom the Bible was the sole source of knowledge and inspiration and the bishops were the guardians of that integrity. This tradition, characteristic of a small community battling against the surrounding world, continued when Christianity became the religion of the majority of the North African Christians, and in Carthage showed every sign of wealth and prosperity. The favourite symbols on Carthaginian Christian tombs include the dove, the ark, the anchor, and the Good Shepherd as well as the Constantinian monogram. On the lamps used in churches the Three Holy Children or Daniel in the Lions Den were popular. The firmly held doctrines of pre-destination and grace, of original sin and its results, of separation from the world and of Judgment hereafter, are those of a gathered community and were accepted by Donatist and Catholic alike. Supreme episcopal authority was acknowledged by individuals far outside the Church. Thus Felix the Manichee ruefully admitted in 405, when confronted by Augustine seated on his episcopal throne in his cathedral at Hippo, "The bishop's position is wonderfully powerful."[82] Augustine confirms this by his description of himself preaching to his congregation standing patiently in the nave and aisles of the church, while he sat in state in the raised apse behind the altar. "I do not want married women to lie down under this," he asserted, when examples of marital infidelity had come to his notice. "I solemnly warn you, I lay down this rule. I command you as your bishop: and it is Christ that commands in me...."[83] Augustine was comparatively moderate in his denunciations. Once he wrote some fatherly advice to a young bishop, who in his enthusiasm had excommunicated an entire household for the sin of one of its members.[84]

The authority of the Bishop of Carthage was, if anything, even more absolute. He was officially *primus inter pares* among his colleagues, and Donatist and Catholic alike exercised their prerogatives over their colleagues. Aurelius, Bishop of Carthage 392-426, and a firm friend of Augustine exclaimed at a council, "As for me, by the will of God, as you know, my brethren, I sustain the burden of all the churches."[85] No wonder, his colleagues knew him as "the chief of the priests" *(princeps sacerdotum)*, a term to which Aurelius objected.[86] Even so, he presided over the yearly councils of the African Catholic Church, guided their deliberations, and summed up their conclusions. He fixed the date of Easter, he confirmed episcopal elections, and authorized the primates of

---

[80] Procopius, *De Bello Vandalico* iv.26.17. See Vaultrin, *RAfr* 1933, 145, and under "Monasteries El" below, appendix.
[80a] See below "Monasteries E3," appendix.
[81] Cyprian, *Letter* 59.5.
[82] *Gesta cum Felice* 1.12.
[83] *Sermo* 359 and 392.4 and 6: cited from P. R. L. Brown, *Augustine of Hippo* (London 1967) 248.
[84] *Letter* 250.
[85] *Codex Canonum Ecclesiae Africae* 55.
[86] *Breviarium Hipponense* 25 (Munier, p. 40); Aurelius preferred the title "primae sedis episcopus."

the African provinces to hold elections. He received appeals against decisions by the provincial primates and submitted matters of importance to general councils; and he acted as intermediary between the African Church and those overseas, including Rome.[87] His power over his colleagues was, practically speaking, unchallengeable.

Aurelius was a vigorous man and an active reformer. He worked in close contact with Augustine, four of whose extant letters are addressed to him (*Letters* 22, 60 and 174, with 41 written jointly with Alypius) and the treatise *De Opere Monachorum*. Unfortunately, Aurelius' replies have not survived, nor indeed any other writing of his, except the canons of the Councils in which he played so great a part. These canons, while dealing principally with the internal government of the Church, occasionally shed light on the authority exercized by clergy in the community at large. Thus, one canon in the collection refers to judges appointed in each province by the primate of that province, and the need of obeying them on pain of excommunication. Clergy were themselves involved in trying cases.[88] A canon lays down that a judgment given by a cleric in a complaint brought by his parishioners was not subject to appeal in the secular courts if one of the parties disagreed with it.[89] Giving judgments seems to have taken up much of Augustine's time. Brothers rarely agreed about property. The bishop had to arbitrate.[90] Since Cyprian's day, the Church had acted as trustee for widows' incomes.[91] The bishop was also the legal guardian of minors.[92] Much wrangling and litigation could arise out of disputes over property belonging to the latter. The manumission of slaves also took place in church.[93] The Church was involved in an active championship of the poor against powerful oppressors and the emperors were petitioned by a Council of Carthage in 401 to appoint special officers, called *"defensores ecclesiarum"* to aid the bishops in their defense.[94] Intercessions on behalf of those who fell foul of the law, yet seemed worthy of leniency, would seldom go unheard. On the other hand, the Church's views were to be enforced by law.[95] Emperors were also petitioned by the Catholic Councils to complete the destruction of paganism and suppress the Donatists. The bishops and clergy of Carthage (whether Donatist or Catholic) stood out as civic leaders in the community, loved, feared, or respected as the case might be; and this must be true of their colleagues throughout North Africa in the fourth and early fifth centuries.

In the Byzantine period, the powers of bishops in civil affairs were greatly increased. The bishop's concern was not merely the dispensation of charitable funds and gifts in kind,[96] but the financial administration of the cities, including their provisionary and public works,[97] and even the supervision of the actions of the civil governor.[98] In cases where a governor's verdict was disputed, the bishop was empowered to rehear the case sitting jointly with the governor.[99] The civil authority of the Archbishop of Carthage was comparable to that of the governor himself.

What property the Church had in order to maintain the status of the bishop and pay his 500 or more clergy is also unknown. It must have been very considerable. In the third century, Cyprian

---

[87] Thus, P. Monceaux (supra n. 29), 89.
[88] *Codex Canonum* 122 (Munier p. 226).
[89] *Codex Canonum* 59 (Munier p. 196).
[90] Augustine, *Sermo* 359. See P. R. L. Brown (supra n. 83) p. 226.
[91] Cyprian *Ep.* 52.1.
[92] In Cyprian's time, Cyprian *Ep.* 52.1 and 2; for the Byzantine period, *Cod. Just.* 1.4.24.27.
[93] *Codex Canonum* 64.
[94] *Codex Canonum* 75.
[95] See P. R. L. Brown, "St. Augustine's attitude to religious coercion," *JRS* 54 (1964) 107-116.
[96] As suggested by basilicas furnished with store-troughs and silos in which grain could be stored before distribution. See N. and Y. Duval, "Fausses Basiliques (et faux martyrs)" *MEFR* 84 (1972) 708-10.
[97] *Cod. Just.* 1.4.26 (June 24, 530).
[98] Ibid. 1.4.33.
[99] *Novel* 86.2. See E. Stein, *Histoire du Bas Empire*, Brussels 1949, 2, p. 400.

never seems to have lacked funds to support the widows and needy, to send his clergy on distant voyages to Cappadocia, and to ransom with 100,000 sesterces Christians captured by Kabylie raiders in 253 (*Letter* 62.4). We know that in the early fourth century the wealth of the Church in Carthage included gold and silver movable chattels and that in the Vandal period these were used to ransom captives taken by Gaiseric when he sacked Rome in 455;[100] but of the extent of its landed wealth and whether it included estates outwith North Africa is not known, though it seems likely from the analogy of estates belonging to the Church of Milan in North Africa.

The main outlines of the story of the Church in Carthage may be reconstructed from a variety of literary and archaeological evidence. Its growing impact on the life of the population can be studied in the writings of Tertullian and Cyprian. The dramatic events leading to the outbreak of the Donatist schism in 311-12 are recorded by Optatus of Milevis and the passion of politics and religion in those days can be appreciated by reading the Donatist *Acta Martyrum*. Carthage was the scene of the great confrontation between the two parties in 411, and the proscription of the Donatists by the imperial government. It was the centre of the power and influence of the African Catholic Church in the two decades that followed. So much is well documented.

The historian's problems are concentrated in the latter centuries of Carthaginian Christianity. There are major gaps in the story. Ignorance about the sources of the Church's wealth is one. Another is the reason for its decline after the end of the sixth century. Whereas the Copts and Nubians put up a vigorous resistance to Islam in the seventh and eighth centuries, the Church in Carthage crumbled. Even before the arrival of the Arabs the churches in Carthage were becoming dilapidated. Questions relating to the decline of Christianity in Carthage are relevant to the history of the Mediterranean area as a whole. The present excavations of ASOR around the Byzantine church in their area may help to shed some light on these problems, as well as continuing the work of Delattre, Lézine and Duval and their Tunisian colleagues in filling in the map of Christian Carthage.

---

[100] Victor Vitensis, *Historia* 1.25.

BIBLIOGRAPHY

The best recent bibliography is contained in N. Duval's article on the churches of Carthage, *MEFR* 84 (1972) 1072-74 *et passim.*

Among other recent publications, note:

P. R. L. Brown, *Augustine of Hippo,* London 1967.

L. Ennabli, *Les Inscriptions Funéraires Chrétiennes de la Basilique dite de Sainte-Monique à Carthage* (Institut National d'Archéologie et d'Arts de Tunis, École Française à Rome, 1975); includes bibliography to 1974.

N. Duval and A. Lézine, "La chapelle funéraire souterraine dite d'Astérius à Carthage," *MEFR* 71 (1959), 339-357.

N. Duval and A. Lézine, "Nécropole Chrétienne et Baptistère souterrain à Carthage," *CahArch* 10 (1959) 71-147.

André Mandouze, *Saint Augustin* (Etudes Augustiniennes), Paris 1968.

C. Munier (ed.), *Concilia Africae* 345-525 = *Corpus Christianorum,* Ser. Lat. CXLIX, Turnhout 1974.

S. Lancel, *Les Actes de la Conférence de Carthage,* 4 vols. (Sources Chrétiennes 195) Paris 1972-76.

J. Lassus, "Les Edifices du culte autour de la Basilique," *Atti del VI Congresso Internazionale di archeologia cristiana (Ravenna 1962)* Rome 1965, 581-610.

For older summaries, see A. L. Delattre, articles on excavations reproduced in H. Leclercq "Carthage" *DACL,* and notes in *CRAI* 1922, 1923, 1928, 1929. Also. J. Vaultrin, "Les Basiliques chrétiennes de Carthage," *RAfr* 1932, 182-318, and 1933, 118-135.

XVI

APPENDIX

In all, twenty two churches are known from literary evidence, to which archaeologists have added another half dozen which cannot be identified from literary sources. This appendix draws heavily on earlier published syntheses (Vaultrin, Lapeyre and Pellegrin, etc.).

A. BASILICAS OUTSIDE THE WALLS

Name	Literary Evidence	Archaeological Evidence
1. Basilica Majorum (i.e. "Basilica of the ancients" probably the earliest Christians known to 4th c. tradition)	Augustine, *Sermo*, 258 (*Pl.* XXXVIII, col. 1194). Victor Vitensis, *Hist. Persecutionis* 1.3. (Known therefore from ca. 400, but area was sacred to Christians from the 3rd c.)	Information about Père Delattre's excavations consolidated by H. Leclercq, "Carthage," *DACL* ii cols. 2223-51.
2. Basilica Celerinae	Victor Vitensis, 1.9. *Passio Septem Monachorum* 16.	Not yet identified.
3. Basilica Scillitanorum	Augustine, *Sermo* 155 (*Pl.* XXXVIII, col. 840). Victor Vitensis 1.9.	Not yet identified. (Hardly the Basilica Majorum as Ch. Courtois suggests, *Victor de Vita et son oeuvre*, Alger 1954, p. 43).
4. Basilica Fausti (*Area* Fausti)	*Concilia* of 418 and 536. Victor Vitensis 1.25, ii.18.48 and iii.34. See also *Sententiae episcoporum* 30-31 (ed. Hartel *CSEL* iii.1, p. 448, n. 8). Augustine, *Sermo* 235 and 261.	Not yet identified.
5. Basilica Novarum (Name suggests a later foundation than the Basilica Majorum)	*Sententiae episcoporum* 30 (ibid. ed. Hartel p. 448, n. 3). Augustine, *Sermo* 14 (*Pl.* XXXVIII, col. 111) and *Breviculus Collationis cum Donatistis* iii.13.25 (*Pl.* XLIII, 638). Compare P. Monceaux, op cit, p. 13. Probably the cathedral ca. 300.	Not yet identified.

Name	Literary Evidence	Archaeological Evidence
6. Damous el Karita	Not yet identified.	Père Delattre's excavations consolidated in *DACL*, "Carthage" cols. 2252-2261.
7. Memoria Cypriani (*ad areas* Macrobii)	(a) *Acta Proconsularia* (ed. Hartel, *CSEL* iii.3, CXIII) (A.D. 258) (b) *Acta Sancti Maximiliani* (ed. H. Musurillo, *Acts of the Christian Martyrs*, Oxford 1972, p. 248) (4th c., referring to events in 295) Augustine, *Conf.*, V.8.15. Fulgentius of Ruspe, *Sermo* 6 (*Pl.* 65, col. 740). Procopius, *De Bello Vandalico* 1.21.17.	L. Ennabli, *Les Inscriptions Funéraires Chrétiennes de la Basilique dite de Sainte Monique à Carthage*, Rome 1975.
8. Mensa Cypriani	Augustine, *Enarratio in Ps.* 80.23 (*Pl.* XXXVII, col. 1046) and *Sermo* 310.2 (*Pl.* XXXVIII, col. 1443). Victor Vitensis 1.16.	
9. Bir el Knissia (Douar Chott)		Delattre, *CRAI* 1922, 302-307 1923, 449-451
10. Bir Ftouha church, martyrium and baptistery		Delattre, *CRAI* 1928, 252-55 and 1929, 23-29. Vaultrin, *RAfr* 1933, 254-58.
11. West of Damous el Karita, associated with the rotunda		Excavations by a Bulgarian team in the Save Carthage campaign.

38

B. BASILICAS WITHIN THE WALLS:

I. *Literary evidence*

1. Basilica perpetua Restituta (Catholic cathedral, first mentioned as such in 390).
   Concilia of 390, 397, 399, 401, 408, 419 (ed. Munier).
   Augustine, *Sermo* 19, 29, 90, 112 and 277.
   Victor Vitensis 1.15.

2. Basilica of the Second region
   Concilia of 403, 404, 405, 407, 409, 410 (ed. Munier).

3. Basilica Sancti Petri (Third region)
   Augustine, *Sermo* 15 (*Pl.* XXXVIII, col. 116).

4. Basilica Sancti Pauli (Sixth region)
   Perhaps the basilica of the archdeacon Liberatus, see Liberatus, *Breviarium*, *Pl.* 68, col. 969 (but no identification here with St. Paul). See P. Monceaux, p. 66.

5. Basilica Sanctae Primae
   Procopius, *De Aedificiis* VI.5.9. (= B. 339).

6. Basilica Sancti Agilei
   Concilium of 525 (Munier, p. 254) and Laterculus (*MGH* A.A. vol. XIII, p. 459).

7. Basilica of the *Theotokos*
   Procopius, *De Aedificiis* VI.5.9 (= B. 339).
   Compare the "Great Sanctuary" in the *Palatium, De Bello Vand.* IV, 14, 37.

8. Basilica Honoriana (former temple of Caelestis)
   Augustine, *Sermo* 163 (*Pl.* XXXVIII, col. 889) and Quodvultdeus, *Liber de Promissionibus et Praedictionibus Dei.* 3.44-45 (Sources Chrétiennes 101).

9. Basilica Gratiani
   Augustine, *Sermo* 156 (*Pl.* XXXVIII, col. 849).

10. The Theoprepeia, the Donatist cathedral
    Existence not known before 411 and as yet unidentified. (In view of the reference to a "meeting of patriarchs" concerned with "Second Marriages" from a site in the Douar Chott area, one suspects this area as a possible Donatist centre (*CIL* VIII, 25045).
    Gesta Collationis Carthag. iii.5 (*Pl.* XI.1364D) and Augustine, *Ep.* 139.

11. Church "near the forum"
    Procopius, *De Bello Vand.* iv.14.27.

II. *Archaeological Researches*

Up to now, with the possible exception of the church on the Byrsa, it has been impossible to identify churches found within the city walls with those mentioned in literary sources.

1. The most important complex is that consisting of three churches in the area north of the Antonine Baths, Dermech I, II and III. They have been re-examined and exhaustively described by Duval (*MEFR* 1972, 1078-96). Dermech I could be the archiepiscopal church, and must at least have been a Regional basilica.

2. On the Byrsa, a large church and baptistery with traces of mosaics, oriented almost north-south. Plan in Lézine, *Carthage. Utique,* p. 177. Perhaps the church dedicated to the Theotokos (see n. 22 above).

3. Basilica in the field allotted to ASOR (University of Michigan), exposed by the Institut in 1971. Byzantine. Baptistery excavated in 1979.

4. Baptistery and probable basilica in the field north of the supermarché, partially exposed by the Institut in 1971.

5. On the lower slopes on the east side of the Byrsa hill. Delattre reports finding a square *subterranean chapel* associated with a cistern. This building attracted pilgrims. A fresco (now lost) possibly showed Cyprian in episcopal robes flanked by Perpetua and Felicitas. The suggestion that it could have been a prison, in which Christians were kept after condemnation by the Proconsul and prior to execution, cannot be dismissed (recorded by H. Leclercq, *DACL* "Carthage," 2275-77, and Duval *MEFR* 1972, 1122).

6. The "Circular Monument," the massive foundation of a rotunda situated just west of the Roman theatre and inside the line of the Theodosian wall. The foundation, misnamed by G. C. Picard the "Mausoleum of St. Cyprian" (*BAC* 1948, 507-11 and 1951-2, 191-95, pl. xviii) dates possibly to the 4th c. and Duval suspected that there might be an adjoining Christian building (*MEFR* 1972, 1115). Now within the concession of the Canadian team, it is discussed by P. Sénay, *Cahier des Études Anciennes* VI (1976) *passim,* although no identification is proposed, but the existence of a basilica (late 4th c?) seems confirmed (Sénay, p. 81). This is now confirmed. A large Christian area has been discovered by M.Senay in 1979 (information Professor J.Humphreys).

C. OTHER BASILICAS

1. The basilica used by the Christian community ca. 300 (possibly the Basilica Novarum referred to by Augustine, *Brev. Coll. cum Donatistis* iii.13.25), Optatus, *De Schismate Donatistarum* 1.19.

2. The church of the Tertullianists, Augustine, *De Haeresibus* 86 (*Pl.* 42, col. 46 D).

3. Church of the Martyr Julianus, *Vita Gregorii Agrigentini* 10, *PG* 98, col. 563.

D. OTHER CEMETERIES

1. Bir ez Zitoun. See H. Leclercq, *DACL* ii.2 col. 2268 and A. Audollent, *Carthage Romaine* p. 189.

2. Bir el Djebbana, ibid. 2268-59 and Audollent 190.

3. Koudiet Zateur (very wealthy graves). Delattre *CRAI* 1916, 14-16, and R. Lantier, *CRAI* 1922, 22-28.

4. *Area* Tertulli, possibly to be identified with the *area Novarum* and basilica built over this before 300.

5. Bou Khris, Delattre, *BAC* 1903, p. cxciv-cxcviii.

6. Burials of Byzantine date in the port area within the probable line of the Theodosian wall, R. Lantier, *CRAI* 1922, p. 27. (There may also be a church nearby in the area of the French Tophet excavations.)

E. MONASTERIES

1. Fortified monastery at the Mandrakion (port), Procopius, *De Bello Vandalico* IV, 26.17 and *De. Aedif.* B. 339, and Victor of Tunnuna *Chron.* ad ann. 555 (ed. Mommsen, *MGH Script. Antiq.* XI.1).

2. Monastery of Bigua, Victor Vitensis (?), *Passio Septem Monachorum*, 16.

3. Nunnery of St. Stephen, mentioned by Quodvultdeus, *Dimidium Temporis, Liber de Promissionibus et praedictionibus Dei* 9 (ed. Braun, Sources Chrétiennes 102 and vol. 2, p. 607). Perhaps that found by P. Gauckler near the Odeon. It was occupied in Byzantine times. See Vaultrin, *RAfr* 1932, 316-18 and Duval *MEFR* 1972, 1078 (bibliography) and 1096-98 (description).

XVII

JEWS AND CHRISTIANS IN THIRD CENTURY CARTHAGE

The question how far Jews or Jewish Christians played a part in the origins of the Church in Carthage has attracted the attention of scholars for many years. In 1901 Paul Monceaux expressed his belief that at Carthage as elsewhere in the Roman empire Christian preaching and mission had originated from the Jewish community. Christian burials, he pointed out, had been found among those of the Jews in the ancient Jewish cemetery at Gamart, just north of the city, and that in Tertullian's time circa 200 Jews and Christians regarded each other "en frères ennemis".[1]

Though the evidence for Christian burials at Gamart seems less watertight today than it did when Monceaux wrote[2], his view has held the field until recently, and meantime further evidence has been put forward to support it. In 1946 Marcel Simon published his important study on native African Judaism in ancient North Africa («Le judaïsme berbère dans l'Afrique ancienne»). He pointed to the links that in the first Christian centuries bound African Jewry to Palestine.[3] Rabbi Akiba (martyred in 135) came traditionally from North Africa. Three rabbis quoted in the Talmud were designated as "from Carthage," and that Tertullian was a witness for the persistence of Hebrew among the Jews in Carthage.[4] He also discussed some curious semi-Christian sects and

---

(1) P. Monceaux, *Histoire littéraire de l'Afrique chrétienne* 1, Paris 1901, pp. 8-9.

(2) Indicated by J. Ferron, "Épigraphie juive", *Cahiers de Byrsa* VI 1956, p. 105ff., and T. D. Barnes, *Tertullian, a historical and literary study*, Oxford 1971, p. 274. There are, however, examples of Christians buried in Jewish cemeteries before Constantine, eg at Bologna. See Ambrose, *Exhort. Virginitatis* 1.7 (*PL* 16 col. 338). Delattre claimed that *CIL* VIII 25347 ("fideles in pace") came from Gamart and that he saw a graffito, "Stefani martyr filius" in one hypogeum there.

(3) M. Simon, "Le judaisme berbère dans l'Afrique ancienne"— pp. 30-87 in Recherches d'Histoire judéo-chrétienne (Mouton, Paris 1962). First published in 1946 in the *Revue d'Histoire et de Philosophie religieuses*, pp. 1-31 and 105-145.

(4) Tertullian, *Apol.* 18, "Hebraei retro qui sunt Iudaei; igitur et litterae hebraeae et eloquium, ie. "Those who are called Jews today were formerly Hebrews, so their

traditions, such as the Caelicoli and Abelonii that survived into the fifth century in parts of rural North Africa which seemed to be inspired by Judaism.[1] Twenty years later, Gilles Quispel approached the problem from another angle. In a short but very valuable discussion in *Vigiliae Christianae* he pointed to previous research showing that the Old and New Testament used by the North African Christian in the third century might have been influenced respectively by the Hebrew text rather than the Septuagint and by the Jewish-Christian *Gospel of Thomas*.[2] In addition, the North African Christians of this period appeared to adhere to the ritualistic Jewish-Christian understanding of the Decree of the Apostolic Council of 48/49. African Christians in the time of Minucius Felix (circa 230) "would have to go to the Jewish butcher if they wanted to eat some meat." African Christianity probably owed this interpretation to Jewish Christians.[3]

The smooth progress towards solving one of the most intractable problems of early Christianity received a severe blow at the hands of Professor T. D. Barnes of Toronto University. In an article in the *Journal of Theological Studies* in 1969 on Tertullian's *Scorpiace* and in his work on Tertullian, Barnes engaged in a thoroughgoing criticism of prevailing theories of the origins of North African Christianity and in particular that of its possible Jewish background.[4] Far from being ancient, "the Jewish community may-not have existed in Carthage before the second century AD," and outside Carthage "none of the available evidence (for Jewish communities) appears to antedate the fourth century".[5] Christians were not buried alongside Jews at Gamart. Epigraphic evidence to that effect was unreliable or had been misinterpreted. Tertullian could not be cited as evidence for Jewish hostility towards the Christians in Carthage, for Tertullian was talking about the Jews in Apostolic times and not in his own day. Tertullian's "references to contemporary Jews betray a lack of real contact".[6]

alphabet and language is still called Hebrew." Tertullian seems, therefore, to have known that some Carthaginian Jews spoke Hebrew.

(1) Simon, *op. cit.*, rabbis (p. 48), p. 55 (Abelonii) and p. 57 (Caelicoli).
(2) G. Quispel, "The Discussion of Judaic Christianity, Additional Note," *Vigiliae Christianae* 22, 1968, p. 81-93 at p. 93.
(3) Minucius Felix, *Octavius* 38.1 and Tertullian, *Apol* 9.13, and *De Monogamia* (ed. V. Buhlart, *CSEL* LXXVI) 5.4, "et libertas ciborum et sanguinis solius abstinentia". See Quispel, *loc. cit.*, p. 93.
(4) T. D. Barnes, "Tertullian's *Scorpiace*,", *JTS* N.S. XX, 1969, p. 105 ff. and especially p. 132, and *Tertullian, a Historical and Literary Survey*, Oxford 1971, especially pp. 64-8, 90-3, 273-6, 283-5.
(5) Barnes, *Tertullian*, p. 284.
(6) *Ibid.*, p. 92.

For him, "Judaism was an unchanging, fossilised faith, not to be taken seriously or deserving proper attention."[1] "Nothing," Barnes claimed, "supports the prevailing theory that the Carthaginian Church grew out of the Jewish community around 150. If reliable evidence is wanted the enquiry cannot penetrate beyond the nature of the African Church in the days of Tertullian and the beliefs concerning its origin which are reflected in the *De Praescriptione Haereticorum*".[2] An eastern origin for Christianity in Carthage, perhaps, through the immigration of Greek-speaking Christians was as far as one could reliably go.[3]

This was indeed Spartan fare. Destructive criticism of prevailing theories based on an acute interrogation of the texts such as Barnes undertook can be extremely valuable. Too many theories about the life and thought of the early Christians have been built up on insecure foundations in studies remote from the scene of events, or have been conditioned by confessional considerations. In this case, however, the pendulum has swung too far. Scholars are left with a vacuum which the widely based research into different aspects of Jewish influence on Carthaginian Christianity does not deserve. A placid acceptance of a verdict of *Ignoramus* to one of the key questions relating to Mediterranean civilisation in the ancient world is not possible. How does the evidence stand?

First, the Jewish community in Carthage was a relatively large one. Even though it was in use for several centuries, the cemetery at Gamart alone covers the whole of that hill, completely enveloping the French War Cemetery that stands on the crest. Many of those buried there were comparatively wealthy, as witnessed by the well-constructed family catacombs whose remains may still be seen on the north slope of the hill. There was also a wide variety of cultural background represented. Of the 29 inscriptions from Gamart published by J. Ferron in 1951, three were in Greek, two in Hebrew, one bilingual Greek and Hebrew and the remainder were in Latin.[4] All three languages were in use therefore in the community. Some individuals may perhaps have come from an elevated social position, such as P. Annius Fuscius Masurius commemorated on an inscription dating to the second century.[5]

---

(1) *Ibid.*
(2) *Ibid.*, p. 64.
(3) *Ibid.*, p. 68 and 276.
(4) J. Ferron, "Inscriptions juives de Carthage," *Cahiers de Byrsa* 1, 1951, p. 175-206.
(5) *Ibid.* Also Leclercq (*DACL* VI. 1 "Gamart") indicates that about 200 individual hypogea existed and some were richly decorated with painted designs.

In addition, literary evidence shows that in Tertullian's time there were some signs of intellectual life, represented by proselytes who had long and vigorous arguments with local Christians.[1] This community was well equipped to provide the background in which learning and cultural life could flourish. Tyre and Carthage are bracketed together as in the Mis'hna as points beyond which "Israel was not known, nor his Father who is in the heavens".[2] Untrue, of course, but Carthage was clearly recognised as an important outpost in the west.

Nor is it correct to suggest that Jewish communities did not exist beyond Carthage before the fourth century. Archaeology may be a wayward provider of evidence, but when it does provide, that evidence is usually irrefutable. An inscription dating to the third century (before Diocletian) from Volubilis proves the existence of a synagogue there governed by a certain Caecilianus who was designated *protopolités* and "father of the synagogue".[3] Volubilis was the furthest removed of Roman cities from Carthage. Is it to be contended that no Jewish communities existed in between?[4]

On the basis that Jews formed a noticeable part of the population in Carthage and in some other North African towns in the third century, we can turn to the second issue. How far did they influence Christianity at that period? One interesting fact is that while we hear practically nothing about Christians before Tertullian's time, they seem to have been equipped with a standard Latin text of both Testaments when they emerge on the scene in the last two decades of the second century. Tertullian assumes knowledge of the Latin version of the Scriptures in his writings. How did this come into existence? Quispel has pointed out hat apart from a number of key words which the Christians must have taken from the Jews, the influence of the Hebrew text on the *Afra* of the Old Testament can be recognised. This may be due to its being read aloud during the synagogue service and translated *ex tempore*. Christians who at one time formed part of the synagogue

---

(1) Tertullian, *Adv Iudaeos* 1 (*CSEL* LXX, p. 251). "Disputatio habita est Christiano et proselyto Iudaeo. Alterius vicibus contentioso fune uterque diem in vesperam traxerunt."

(2) M. Simon, *op. cit.*, p. 49.

(3) See E. Frézouls, "Une synagogue juive attestée à Volubilis." *Acta* of the Fifth International Conference of Greek and Latin Epigraphy (Cambridge 1971), p. 287-293.

(4) The synagogue at Setif where M. Avilius Januarius is also called "pater synagogua" might be earlier than the fourth century, to judge from Januarius' use of the *tria nomina*, See *CIL* VIII 8499.

may have inherited the local Latin translation of the Hebrew text.[1] The custom of reading a Hebrew text of scripture seems to have been retained in some churches in the province of Asia where Jewish influence was strong, notably at Sardis, in the middle of the second century.[2] The same might have applied at Carthage. The African New Testament also reveals in its vocabulary the influence both of Jewish Christians who knew Hebrew and the Jewish-Christian *Gospel of Thomas*.[3] A number of variants from that gospel can be pointed out, that do not occur in other representatives of the Western text. *Thomas* is notable for its elevation of James of Jerusalem to the role of successor to Jesus and undisputed head of the Church. Monarchical episcopacy with the bishop of Carthage occupying a position of unchallenged eminence is characteristic of the North African Church from the time of Agrippinus (circa 220) and of the Donatists in the fourth century. The apparent use of *Thomas* strengthens the case for seeing Jewish or Jewish-Christian influences behind other peculiarities in the North African Church. While pagans called the Christians in Carthage "Chrestiani", the Jews stuck to the name "Nazoreni," i.e. schismatic sectaries denounced in the *Shemoneh Ezra*.[4] Christians as already mentioned seem to have observed the ritual food laws imposed on Gentile converts at the Council of Jerusalem in 48/49. In the 250s Cyprian's congregation still called the collecting-box in the church by the Jewish name of "corban".[5] In Augustine's time, as in Tertullian's some African Christians kept the Jewish Sabbath.[6]

These deductions have now been reinforced by an interesting piece of archaeological evidence. The Damous el Karita situated in a valley a few hundred metres outside the city wall on the north

---

(1) G. Quispel, *loc. cit.*

(2) See Melito of Sardis, *Peri Pascha* (ed. O. Perler, Sources chrétiennes 105), lines 1 and 2. Perler considers that the reading of "books of the exodus of the Hebrews" might refer simply to the books without any reference to the language of the text, but see also G. Zuntz, "On the opening sentence of Melito's Paschal Homily," *Harvard Theological Review*, XXXVI 4, 1943, p. 299-316, who gives examples of Hebrew readings being retained by some churches.

(3) G. Quispel, "The Gospel of Thomas and the New Testament," *Vigiliae Christianae* XI 1957, p. 189-207, at p. 197 ff.

(4) Tertullian, *Apol.* 3.5 "Sed et cum perperam Chrestianos pronuntiatur a vobis (pagans); and *Adv Marcionem* IV.8 "unde et ipso nomine nos Iudaei Nazarenos appellant per eum." For Jewish Christians (Nazarenes) reading the Law and Prophets in Hebrew, see Epiphanius *Panarion* XXIX.7.4 (Holl, p. 329).

(5) Cyprian, *De Operibus et Eleemosynis* 15.

(6) Tertullian, *De Ieunio adv. Psychicos* 14 (*CSEL* XX, p. 293); Augustine, *Ep* 54.2.3. (*CSEL* XXXIV.2, p. 160). For Sabbath observance imposed in Jewish-Christian circles, see *Gospel of Thomas*, Logion 28.

side of Carthage, is by far the most elaborate Christian complex yet found in the Carthage area.[1] It consisted of a church, originally oriented north-south, but later greatly enlarged and re-oriented east-west probably in the early fifth century. Adjoining was a baptistery and a suite of cell-like buildings extending to the west. It was known that it stood over a cemetery, but obscurely published and apparently unheeded by scholars, one of the memorial stones was Jewish. Written in Greek and Hebrew it commemorated "Anianos, son of Anianos in peace," the words "Anianos in peace" being repeated in Hebrew and flanked by lulabs and a dove. The date suggested is late second or early third century, i.e. contemporary with Tertullian.[2] At the north west corner of the complex was also a family catacomb with eight *loculi* in two stages. To judge from the careful workmanship and ornamentation, it belonged to a wealthy family, and its plan which set the *loculi* round a central space was identical with those at Gamart.[3] The Damous inscription, apart from proving the existence of a second Jewish cemetery in second/third century Carthage, shows that this burial area and the catacomb on which the first Christian church on the site was oriented, provided a location for a major Christian complex.

Acceptance of the "Jewish factor" would throw light on some institutional features of the Church in Carthage which are otherwise hard to explain. Thus, it is noticeable that on some more important occasions the number of bishops assembled to take a decision was 70. In circa 220 Agrippinus summoned that number from Proconsular Africa and Numidia to decree that those baptised by a cleric not in communion with the Church should be rebaptised on conversion to orthodoxy.[4] Cyprian's first council in 256 on the same subject consisted of 71 bishops (i.e. 70 plus himself) also from these two areas and they sent a formal letter to Pope Stephen setting out their collective view[5] (*Ep* 72). In 311 Secunus of Tigisis, Primate of Numidia, brought 70 bishops with him to Carthage to strengthen his cause in the crucial election of a Bishop of Carthage after Mensurius' death.[6] These bishops

---

(1) Best described in *DACL*. II. 2 under "Carthage," cols 2252-61. The Jewish area evidently lay immediately west of the pagan cemetery (indicated in ibid., Plate. 2131).

(2) J. Ferron, art. cit., *Cahiers de Byrsa* 1, 1951, p. 184-187.

(3) Observed by the writer while working for the Michigan University "Save Carthage" project, June 1976.

(4) Cyprian, *Ep.* 71.4 and 73.3. Augustine, *De Unico Baptismo* 13.22.

(5) Cyprian, *Ep.* 72 and 73.1. The importance of this council is rightly stressed by M. M. Sage, *Cyprian* (Patristic Monographs Series No 1, Philadelphia 1975), p. 318-9.

(6) Augustine, *Ad Catholicos, Epistola* 18.46.

formed a Council that condemned Caecilian and thus opened the Donatist controversy. Why this particular number? Was it accidental? It could be, until one remembers that 70 plus the High Priest was the number of the Sanhedrin both in Jerusalem and Alexandria and that this looked back to the passage in Numbers 11[16], where Moses is described as "gathering seventy men of the elders of Israel whom you know to be elders of the people." Much of the ethos of the North African Church as well as Cyprian's justification for the strict hierarchical organisation and monarchical episcopacy, seems to be derived from Numbers and Leviticus.

Was it purely a matter of Christians looking to these books for guidance, or did they inherit these attitudes from the Jewish community from which many of them may have seceded?

In this connection, one may look again at the North African institution of the *seniores*,[1] lay-elders charged with administrative functions in the church, e.g. supervision of property, such as was carried out elsewhere by deacons. The clue provided by Ambrosiaster that such officials were to be found in Jewish synagogues in Italy whence they were adopted by the Church, should not be ignored.[2] It would be surprising if these were not already traditional in Africa when they are mentioned first in connection with the disputed election in church in Carthage in 311. The *seniores* referred to by Tertullian (*Apol* 39.4) do not seem to be presbyters.

One comes finally to Tertullian himself. Do his utterances betray a lack of real contact with contemporary Judaism? Certainly, he does not give any credit to the Jews of Carthage as allies in their common struggle against idolatry. He praises their fidelity to ancestral tradition once[3], but whatever sympathy he may have felt on occasions was outweighed by profound hostility that bracketed them with the pagans whom he hoped to see condemned to destruction on the Last Day. In his anger, however, against "them who vented their rage and fury on the Lord"[4] (i.e. the Jews), he indicated that his information about them was not confined to the Scriptures. The reference to Jesus as the "son of a harlot" (*De Spect.* 30.5), already identified by T. R. Glover as "a piece of

---

(1) Discussed by the writer in "*The Seniores laici and the origins of the Church in North Africa*," *JTS* NS XII, 1961, pp. 280-284. Against; T D Barnes, *Tertullian*, p. 273-4.

(2) The information is specific: "Unde et synagoga, et postea Ecclesia seniores habuit quorum sine consilio nihil agebatur in Ecclesia. Quod qua negligentia obsolevint nescio." *Comment. in 1 Ep. ad Timotheum* s.i (*PL* 17, col. 475D).

(3) *De ieiunio* XIII.6.

(4) *De Spectaculis* XXX.

Jewish polemic..,[1] is combined with a reference to "the gardener" *(hortulanus)* removing the body of Jesus, (with a typical Tertullianic sarcasm "lest his lettuces should be trampled by the throng of visitors"). Dr W. Horbury has pointed out hat the earliest attestation of the story is from *Toledoth Jeshu*,[2] but that it was current in the form of an accusation that the Christian disposed of the body at the time when Commodian was writing (late third century?), and he rebuts it.[3] The combination of two items known from post-Biblical Jewish sources suggests that Tertullian was citing contemporary Jewish polemic, concentrated in this case on the credibility of Jesus as Messiah and Saviour.[4] The source must have been the Jews of Carthage.

Other references to the Jews in Tertullian's writings indicate accurate knowledge of the local community. Thus, in *De ieunio* he describes the Jews on Fast days celebrating their services in the open air by the seashore.[5] This would probably be in obedience to the rule laid down in the Mishna that on fast days the Holy Ark was to be moved outside the synagogue and prayer made in the open.[6] Tertullian was concerned also, that in all ethical matters, especially abstinences and even apparently unimportant religious practices such as veiling virgins, Christians should outstrip the Jews. "Our righteousness," he writes, "should exceed the righteousness of the Scribes and Pharisees. If righteousness, then also modesty".[7] The result was, as has been stated, that in Tertullian's hands Christianity became a "baptised Judaism",[8] an attitude which fits a situation in which Christianity was something of an upstart, thrusting rival confronted by a long established Jewish community. Tertullian admitted that the Christians so far as age was concerned were "minor" *(Adv. Iudaeos 1)*. The

---

(1) Ed. T. R. Glover (with G H Rendall) *Tertullian: Apologia, De Spectaculis: Minucius Felix*, Loeb ed. 1931, p. 298. For the Jewish accusation in the second century see Origen, *Contra Celsum* 1.32 and H Chadwick's note *Contra Celsum* (Cambridge 1953), p. 31.

(2) W. Horbury, "Tertullian on the Jews in the light of *De Spectaculis* XXX 5-6," *JTS* NS XXIII 2, pp. 455-459.

(3) Commodian, *Carmen Apologeticum* (*CSEL*. XV ed. B. Dombart) line 440, where the Christians were accused by putting Christ's body down a well, "infamant: in puteum misimus."

(4) Horbury, *loc. cit.*, p. 458-9.

(5) *De Ieiunio* XVI.

(6) *Mishna Taan* II.1. See Simon, *op. cit.*, p. 48-49.

(7) *De Monogamia* 7.1. (Buhlart, p. 56).

(8) Thus R. P. C. Hanson, "Notes on Tertullian's interpretation of Scripture," *JTS* NS XII.1, p. 273-279 at p. 279. Tertullian's concern whether Christian virgins should be veiled, see *De Oratione* XXII.6. For him this was a serious business.

Jews regarded Christians as schismatics from Judaism to be barred from the synagogue. In these circumstances, the rivalry and enmity between the two communities that existed even in Cyprian's time can well be understood. The "frères ennemis" aspect of the Jewish-Christian relationship discussed by the writer elsewhere needs no further justification.[1] *Aemulatio* existed on both sides and the Carthaginian lamp depicting Christ treading on an upturned *menorah* indicates what Christians thought about their Jewish neighbours during the third century.[2]

Judaism and Jewish-Christianity may therefore be restored as factors in the origin of the North African Church especially at Carthage. But they were not the only factors. Outside Carthage especially in the rural areas of Numidia and Mauretania Sitifensis it has long been evident that in the background of many aspects of native Christianity, especially Donatism, stood another age old Semitic oriented religion namely that of Saturn-Caelestis.[3] This contributed to the emphatically sacrificial element in native Christianity, while the Christian nomenclature of North Africa, with the frequency of theophoric names such as Fortunatus, Praedestinatus, Donatus, Rogatus, Servus Dei, etc. show the same innate tendency towards fatalism and utter subservience to the decrees of an inscrutable God that is discernible in the Punic names that they translate.[4] Basic attitudes to Christianity as well as some religious formulae such as "Bonis bene", found on dedications looked back to Carthaginian religion.

Much research still needs to be done before problems relating to the origins of North African Christianity can be solved. Monceaux' view that the origins of the North African churches was not single or even double but multiple, holds the field.[5] Yet how these multiple origins produced a Church so single-minded in its rigorism and acceptance of monarchical episcopacy is uncertain. More than any other community the North African Church was the "Church of the Martyrs," the most complete example of the

---

(1) Thus, "A note on Tertullian and the Jews," *Studia Patristica* X (ed. F. L. Cross Berlin, 1970), p. 291-296, and "A Note on Jews and Christians in Third Century North Africa," *JTS*. NS XXI 1970, pp. 92-96.

(2) M. Simon, "Le Chandelier à Sept Branches symbole chrétien?, *Recherches d'Histoire judéo-chrétienne*, p. 181-187 at p. 187. For Jewish "aemulatio" against the Christians, Tertullian, *Apol.* 7.2.

(3) See Frend, *Donatist Church*, Ch. VI, and M. M. Sage, *Cyprian*, p. 24, "Rather than in rigorism the influence of the Punic cult of Saturn may be traced in the concept of sacrifice which strongly flavours African Christianity."

(4) Frend, *Donatist Church*, p. 79.

(5) P. Monceaux, *op. cit.*, p. 7.

"Gathered Church" in early Christianity. How did diverse origins produce this result? Solutions, however, require constructive rather than destructive criticism. It is to the lasting credit of Professor Marcel Simon that the first established in detail the probable links between Judaism and Christianity in Carthage. It is a privilege as well as a pleasure to dedicate this short memoir in his honour.

XVIII

THE *MEMORIAE APOSTOLORUM* IN ROMAN NORTH AFRICA[1]

A certain number of extant inscriptions and oral traditions which still linger in remote places, as in the Djebel Nefouça,[2] to the south of Leptis Magna and Oea, indicate that there was a time when the cult of the Apostles SS. Peter and Paul existed in Roman Africa; but the distribution of evidence, which is largely derived from the fringes of the Roman province, in Mauretania and in southern Numidia, invites the question why places so far removed from the Latin influence of the proconsular province should show such interest in the see of Rome and its founders.

The relevant texts are as follows :—

IN MAURETANIA CAESARIENSIS

1. From Kherba, 12 km. from Oppidum Novum and Tigava: *CIL* viii, 21496; *ILCV* 2064; Monceaux, 'Enquête' 326.
   Postulantibus a creatore Deo et (chrismon) me|moria sanctorum Petri et Pauli deside|rante Onesta matre cum Gratia (sorore?) | Petronianus, Cassius et Patricius cum suis | in hoc tabernaculo pro sua prece posuerunt.

2. From Castellum Tingitanum[3] (Orléansville): *CIL* viii, 9714; *ILCV* 2063a; Monceaux, 'Enquête' 329. Scratched on a tile in two pieces. (chrismon with A and Ω in a circle) | [me]moria | [sanc]ti mart[yris] | [...]iesi pas[si...] *b* [... u?]irco i [...] | [...]issimo aet [...] | [...] pium dixit c[...] | [... memo]ria apostolorum | [... Pet]ri et Pauli passa | [...]I non. Mai ann. | [pr... iu]bente deo et Χρο | [eius...] ctsoiu.
   P. Monceaux, 'Enquête' 329, conjectures as an emendation for 1 *b*. [s]anc(t)o e[t bea]|[t]issimo Ae[...] | [marty]rium dixit [...]. This reading seems the more probable.

3. From Castellum Tingitanum:[4] *CIL* viii, 9715; Monceaux, 'Enquête' 332. [Me] (chrismon with A and Ω in a circle) moriae | [N... in]nocentis. | [precessi]t [nos] in pace | [Domini, o]ctobr[i]s die sex|[ta, anno] pr(ovinciae) CCCLXVII. Fu|[scius] tribunus pater et | [...]e mater eius aput | [sancto]s apostolos Petru(m) et | [Paulu(m) i]n nom[i]ne Dei et Cri|[sti m]emor[iam fece]runt.
   Date: Sept.–Oct. A.D. 406.

[1] *Cf.* P. Monceaux, 'Enquête sur l'épigraphie chrétienne d'Afrique' iv, in *Mémoires présentés par divers savants à l'Académie des Inscriptions et Belles-Lettres*, xii, 1908, 161–339; *Académie des Inscriptions et Belles-Lettres. Comptes Rendus* (= *CRAI*) 1920, 74–83; 1924, 78–85. H. Jaubert, 'Anciens Evêchés et Ruines chrétiennes de la Numidie et de la Sitifienne,' in *Recueil des notices et mémoires de la Société archéologique du Département de Constantine*, xlvi, 1912, 1–218. Aug. Audollent et J. Letaille in *Mélanges d'Archéologie et d'Histoire* (= *Mélanges*) x, 1890, 441 ff. *Acta Saturnini*, *Passio SS. Donati et Advocati*, *Passio Isaaci*, all in Migne *Patrologia Latina* (= *PL*) viii.

[2] Siar of Chemmakhi, for instance, mentions the existence of a 'great apostolic mosque', at Temezda (quoted by Père J. Mesnage *Le Christianisme en Afrique. Les origines* (Alger, 1914), 32).

[3] For the name see *CIL* viii, p. 829.

[4] I have not included the suspect inscription *CIL* viii, 9716, *b*.

4. From Castellum Tingitanum: *CIL* viii, 9716; *ILCV* 2066; Monceaux, ' Enquête ' 330. Scratched on a tile.
[mem(oria)] martyiru | [Pa]ulus, Petru(s) | [Mar]cia, Ceselia. | [hic S]ecundilla | [in] pace se[pulta . . .].

IN MAURETANIA SITIFENSIS.[5]

5. From Kherbet Oum el-Adham,[6] near the modern Tixter: *CIL* viii, 20600; *ILCV* 2068; Audollent et Letaille in *Mélanges* x, 1890, 441 ff.; Monceaux, ' Enquête ' 317.
   a. Victorinus septimu id|us sept(e)m(b)r(es). | Miggin (i)du(s) (septembres).
   b. *in corona* (with chrismon): memori|a sacta.
   c. *inter lineas*: et dabula it de lignu crucis, | de ter(r)[a] promisonis, ube natus est Cristus, | apostoli Petri et Pauli, nomi|na marturu(m) Datiani, Dona|tiani, Cipriani, Nemesani, [C]itini et Victo|[r]ia[i]s ano proui(nciae) | [t]recenti uiges(imo). *in parte antica*: posuit Bene|natus et Pequaria.
   A.D. 359. An Agape *mensa*.

IN BYZACENA.

From Uppenna. *CIL* viii, 23040-23041.

6. *CIL* viii, 23041; Monceaux, ' Enquête ' 238; *Nouvelles Archives des Missions scientifiques et historiques* xv, 1907, 415-19.
Hec sunt nomina martirum: Petrus, | Paulus, Saturninus presbyter. | idem Saturninus, Bindemius, Saturnin|us, Donatus, Saturninus, Gududa, | Paula, Clara, Lucilla, Kortun, | Iader, Cecilius, Emilius. passi die | nonas a(u)gustas: depositi IIII idu|s nobembres. gloria in escel|sis Deo et in tera pacs omnibus.
Mosaic found in the apse of a basilica of early Byzantine date.

7. *CIL* viii, 23040a. Mosaic in the apse of an earlier basilica on the same site, destroyed during the Vandal period, and covered by the ruins of the later church. The same list of martyrs appears on this mosaic, with the addition of the exact date of the Passio—IIII nonas a(u)gustas, and the omission of ' Gloria in excelsis Deo. in terra pax omnibus '.
This group of martyrs appears in no martyrology.

8. At Thelepte the basilica wherein the Council of Byzacena was held in 418 was dedicated to the Apostles, Peter and Paul. Père J. Mesnage, *L'Afrique chrétienne* (Paris, 1912), 111.

9. At Ruspe, Bishop Fulgentius was buried in a basilica in which he had deposited relics of the Apostles, Peter and Paul which he had brought back from Rome. *Vita S. Fulgentii* 73, *Acta Sanctorum* i, 44.

IN NUMIDIA.

10. From Hr. el Hassi (Ain Berrich), 15 km. from Ain Beida. *CIL* viii, 18656; Monceaux, ' Enquête ' 288.

---

[5] I have not included in this list a lead plaque found with a reliquary at Biar Haddada, W. of Sétif, which Monceaux, ' Enquête ' 312, reads (Mig)ginis, Don|[at]i, Paul[i], P[e]t[ri], cal(endas) [fe]br[uarias]. This reading is highly conjectural, as the metal plate on which it was scratched is very much oxidised. A glance at the inscription in *CIL* viii, 8731, and the ' Enquête ' does not altogether confirm M. Monceaux's conclusions.

[6] The lines of this inscription ' Victorinus septimu idu septembres | Miggin idus septembres | memoria sacta | et dabula it de lignu crucis ' are in a rougher script than the rest of the inscription, and are almost certainly later. The *corona* in this case is simply the usual round depression one finds in Berber funerary tables of the Pagan Christian and Moslem periods. An examination of the stone in Algiers Museum leads me to believe that the cross in the middle of the depression is contemporary with the *later* inscription.

H(i)c memorie sancto|ru(m) Pauli, Petri, Donati, Mig|ginis, Baricis.
Probably sixth century.

11. Hr. Deheb, SW of Theveste: *ILCV* 2065; H. Jaubert, *Recueil de Constantine* 1912, 156 f.
[Memoria sa]nctorum (chrismon) Petri et Pauli.
Fourth century.

12. Djebel Djaffa, 8 km. S of Mascula (Khenchela): *CIL* viii, 17715; H. Jaubert, *Recueil de Constantine* 1912, 158.
Mem|oria | apostolo|ru(m).
Fourth century, from a rural chapel.[7]

13. Hr. Magroun, S of Vegesela, N of the Aurès mountains: *CIL* viii, 10693; *ILCV* 2065; Monceaux, ' Enquête ' 266.
Memoria domni Petri et Pauli.
Fourth century, probably from a lintel over the doorway of the chapel.

14. Ksar Ouled Zid, S of Theveste: Monceaux, ' Enquête ' 336; H. Jaubert, *Recueil de Constantine* 1912, 212.
[Memoria s]anctorum a[postolorum ?] [8] | . . . Donatiani hic confe[ssorum].[9]
Fourth–fifth century.

15. Hr. Taghfaght, 5 km. W of Mascula: *CIL* viii, 17714; Monceaux, ' Enquête ' 272.
Hic e[st dom]|us [Dei, hic] | memo[riae] | apostol[or(um) et] | beati Emeri|ti gloriosi | consulti.
Fourth–fifth century.

16. Ain Ghorab, on the Nemencha Plateau, SW of Theveste, S of Mascula: *CIL* viii, 10707, 10708, 17615; H. Jaubert, *Recueil de Constantine*, 1912, 164 f. *Cf.* De Rossi, *Bulletino di arch. crist.* ser. 3, iii (1878), 14.
Cede prius nomen [no]uitati cede uetustas :
Regia letan[t]er uota dicare [l]i[b]et.
Haec Petri Paulique sedes Cristo [i]ubente resurgit.
Vnu[m q]ues[o par]es, unum duo [sumit]e munus + Aeclesia
Vnus [hon]or celebre[t quos h]abet una fides + Dom
[Pre]s[byteri ta]men [h]ic o[pus est] et cura Probanti + tist
The inscription has been reconstructed from several fragments. De Rossi proved that the dedication was modelled on that in the basilica of St. Peter-ad-Vincula at Rome set up under Sixtus III, 432–440 (*cf.* De Rossi, *Inscriptiones Christianae Urbis Romae* ii, 1 (Rome, 1888)). It probably belongs to the beginning of the sixth century, the priest Probantius being an exile returned from Rome. The Roman inscription on which it is modelled is referred to in *CIL* viii, p. 948, and in the *Bulletino*, 15.

17. Timgad, from a chapel to the N of the Arch of Trajan: Monceaux in *CRAI* 1920, 75–83, and *ibid.* 1924, 78–83; *cf.* S. Gsell, in *Revue africaine* lxix, 1928, 20–22.
B(onis) b(ene). | et gaudet Pe|trus et Laza|rus. | rogo te, | Domine, | su(b)ueni, | Criste, tu | solus me|dicus, sanctis et | peniten|tibus amare manib[us] | [e]t pedibus Dei.
Alternatively, . . . penitentibus ma[t]re(m) manib[us] et pedibus de[fendentibus] | —Monceaux *CRAI* 1924, 80.
Fourth-fifth century, cut on the re-used foot of an ornamented stone table.

---

[7] This is H. Jaubert's explanation, *l.c.* I think it more probable than the suggestion made in *CIL* viii, p. 1680, that the stone was brought from Hr. Taghfaght, 7 km. away.

[8] I have filled in ' a[postolorum] ' after seeing the copy of the stone published in Monceaux, *l.c.* The only alternative would seem to be ' a[ngelorum] ' and that is unparalleled, while ' [sancto]s apostolos ' is to be found on the inscription from Castellum Tingitanum, *CIL* viii, 9715.

[9] Monceaux gives as an alternative conjecture ' hic conf[essi sunt] ' *l.c.*

35

18. Mzara Sidi Youssef between Batna, and Bordj-bou-Arreridj: Monceaux, ' Enquête ' 314.
Micael | Paulus | .. al.
Cut on a semi-oval frame between the flutings of the capital of a pillar. The opening formula ' Hic memoria sanctorum ', or ' Nomina marturum ' was probably cut on another column.

19. In a sanctuary some 3 km. NW of Calama: H. Jaubert, *Recueil de Constantine*, 1912, 22.
+ Hic reliquie | beati Petri apost[o]li | et s(an)c(t)orum Felicis | et Vincenti martyri.
Byzantine period.

20. Ain Regada, near Thagaste (Souk Ahras): *CIL* viii, 5666.
Bfm | ofm | Petrus | Florus | et Susanna | . . . . .
Fourth century. Cut on a rounded stele. Found with two other similar stones referring to martyrs.

21. Ain Zirara, E of Macomades: *CIL* viii, 17746; Monceaux, ' Enquête' 274; H. Jaubert, *Recueil de Constantine*, 1912, 213.
a. Monceaux's version.
Hic [e]st ex[auditio s(an)c(t)orum] | [Pe]tri, Pa[uli, apostolorum,] | [Stefan]i, Laur[entii, Xysti,] | [Hippo]liti, Me[nae, marti]|[rum S]cil[litanorum,] Le[ontii.] | [dedic]at[io ec]cl(esiae) s(ub) [d(ie k]a[lendas] | [. . . De]o laus et g[l]or[ia] | [et in terra pax hominibus ?].
b. De Rossi's reconstruction, cited by H. Jaubert, *l.c.*, 213.
Hic [domus Dei . . . hic e]st ex[auditio precum.] | [hic memoriae Pe]tri Pa[uli] . . . Laur[entii . . . Hippo]liti Me[nae ? Dedicatio Ec]cle(siae) s(anctae) . . . [oct]ob(res). [semper De]o laus et g[loria].
The writer does not pretend to judge between the merits of these two interpretations except on the following points. (1) ' Deo laus et gloria ' is certain, and appears on both. (2) There is no evidence at all from the stone as published in the text of Monceaux, *l.c.*, for the inclusion of Xystus, and only the final ' i ' to justify ' Stefani '. (3) There does appear to be a ' cil ' and a ' Le ', which might suggest the possibility of the Scillitans, and the martyr bishop of Hippo, Leontius.
The fragments of the inscription were found in association with the ' capsella argentea ' reliquary published by De Rossi in *Bulletino arch. crist.*, 1887, 118–129.
Probably it dates to about the end of the fifth century.

In discussing these inscriptions, there is no need to enter into an argument about the alleged ' apostolicity ' of the See of Carthage and the African Church in general.[10] A moment's thought on their distribution will show how futile any attempt to connect them with an apostolic visit to Africa would be. There is no evidence that SS. Peter and Paul knew, for instance, the Libyan language, or that they ever spent time wandering about the Aurès and Kabyle mountains. The solution must be sought along different lines. Christianity in North Africa reached the deepest intensity of its development

---

[10] The view of Professor H. Lietzmann seems to be the most reasonable. ' Wir haben keine Kunde über das Eindringen der neuen Religion in Afrika. Dass sie von Rom aus dorthin gekommen ist, darf man als wahrscheinlich annehmen.' *Geschichte der alten Kirche* ii (Berlin-Leipzig, 1936), 220.

in two great regions. The first spread from Carthage up the Romanized area of the cities clustered on each side of the fertile banks of the Bagradas and Meliana rivers : the second ran in a wide belt of hill country from the district east of Theveste, through the high plateaus, north of the Aurès Mountains, and thence northwards to the highlands of Mauretania Sitifensis, west of Sitifis (fig. 4). The two areas are radically different in character. The Bagradas valley is comparatively flat and cultivable, with a steady rainfall enabling a good wheat-crop to be raised, and was inhabited to a large extent by town-dwellers speaking Punic or Latin. Numidia and Sitifis have, on the other hand, a dry and salty soil,[11] more suited to olives than to wheat-crops, and hence tending to be divided into great estates with a population of *coloni*. These latter were for the most part Libyan by race and speech.

From the fourth to the seventh century these regions formed the rival camps of two different conceptions of Christianity, the Donatist and the official Catholic. In the early stages the struggle in Africa between these two beliefs became identified with a conflict between a Church of the Holy Spirit, and a hierarchical Church, as in Gaul, Rome, and Asia Minor. The latter form involved an acquiescence in the City-State, which alone could give reasonable security to the lands and goods necessary for the upkeep of an institution and the discharge of charitable works : the former, a complete denial of clerical sovranty and humanist culture alike—the point of view expressed by Philadelphia as opposed to that of Laodicea.[12] The fight for mastery between these two points of view can be traced with varying degrees of clarity from the publication of the *Passio Perpetuae* about A.D. 206 [13] almost to the time of the Arab invasions.[14] If the official Church could claim Cyprian and Augustine as its protagonists, that of the Spirit could boast Tertullian, Donatus and Petilian. To Tertullian, except perhaps in his earliest works, as to the Donatists later, clerical office is secondary. He never dwells on his own : to him the effective Church, that body which represented the Lord on earth and could forgive the worst of sins, was ' ecclesia spiritus per spiritalem hominem, non ecclesia numerus episcoporum ' (*De Pudicitia* 21). The Prophet and, above all, the martyr who literally ' dwelt with Christ ' [15] and through whom Christ spoke, were the ' spiritual men '. The hierarchy was only the administrative office

---

[11] With the exception of the valley of the Seybouse, and an area west and south of Sitifis.
[12] *Revelation* iii, 11 and 14.
[13] Published by J. A. Robinson *Texts and Studies* (1891) i, no. 2.
[14] The last letter of Pope Gregory dealing with Donatism is dated to 598 (*Ep.* viii, 13 and 15).
[15] Tertullian in *De Anima*, 55, emphasises that Perpetua in the vision of Saturus saw only martyrs in Paradise ' solos commartyres ' : *cf. Passio Perpetuae* (Robinson, *o.c.*) 11.

charged with putting into practice such discipline as the ' new prophets '. instructed them.[16]

One of Tertullian's chief arguments against the Catholic bishop in the *De Pudicitia* was that Christ had given power of binding and loosing to St. Peter as a ' spiritual man ', *spiritu instinctus*, and as a martyr. This gift did not necessarily descend to his successors, so that, to prove his own divine powers, the bishop must bring forward his own ' examples of prophecy '. ' Exhibe igitur nunc mihi prophetica exempla, ut agnoscam diuinitatem, et uindica tibi delictorum eiusmodi (adultery, etc) remittendorum potestatem.'[17] It is, further, largely on the works of St. Paul that Tertullian relies to prove the rigorist tendencies of Montanism, and it is perhaps significant that St. Paul's *Epistles* seem to have been the source of inspiration to the intractable Scillitans.[18]

The commercial relations between Rome and Carthage, together with a very large African colony in Rome, would explain an interchange of ideas taking place between the two parts of the Empire, leading to the early spread of Christianity to the African coast towns.[19] The parallel development of the new religion in Africa and Rome would be accompanied by a regard for the Apostles as propagators of the faith. But, as in the eyes of a large number of African Christians the cleric does not claim so much reverence as the ' saint ', we need not be surprised that the Apostles should have been honoured as spiritual men, martyrs, rather than as ecclesiastics or founders of an authoritarian Church. Tertullian himself in his *De Exhortatione Castitatis* declares, ' For the Apostles have the spirit properly, who have Him fully, in the operations of prophecy, and the efficacy of (healing) virtues, and the evidences of tongues ; not partially as all others have.'[20] The emphasis is on ' spiritual virtues ', in contrast with Cyprian's point of view, whereby the Apostles are bishops chosen by God.[21]

That Tertullian's attitude was by no means extinct by the fourth century is suggested by the inscription of that date from Henchir Magroun,[22] a settlement south of Vegesela, north of the Aurès range. Here, the Apostles are called ' Domini ', a title often applied to specially revered martyrs. For instance, the confessor Celerinus, writing from Rome to his colleague Lucian, refers to the martyrs of the Decian persecution as ' eos dominos

[16] Tertullian, *De Pudicitia* 21.
[17] *Ibid*.
[18] *Acta Scillitanorum*, ed. J. Armitage Robinson in *Texts and Studies* i, 2 (1891), 106–121. ' Saturninus proconsul dixit : Quae sunt res in capsa uestra ? Speratus dixit : Libri et epistulae Pauli uiri justi.'
[19] At Hadrumetum, and probably at Tacape and Sullectum also, catacombs,

dating from the early second century A.D. have been discovered. See J. Mesnage, *Le christianisme en Afrique*. 57.
[20] *De Exhortatione Castitatis*, iv (ed. A. Roberts and J. Donaldson, Edinburgh, 1870, 8).
[21] Cyprian, *Ep*. iii, 3 (*CSEL* 471).
[22] *Supra*, p. 34, no. 13 : *CIL* viii. 10693.

meos qui coronati fuerint ',[23] while the Donatist martyr Marculus is honoured as ' Dominus ' in the church built to his memory at Vegesela (Ksar el-Kelb) itself.[24] More significant are perhaps the first two lines of the Uppenna inscriptions [25] quoted above (p. 33) : ' Hec sunt nomina marturum, Petrus, Paulus, Saturninus presbiter,' etc. In this case even the usual distinction between Apostles and martyrs, preserved at Oum el-Adham, is dropped, and the Apostles are not only regarded as martyrs without any qualifications at all,[26] but put on the same level as the leader of the Abitinians, Saturninus.[27]

The distribution of these *memoriae* points to the same conclusion. Save for a dedication of a basilica to St. Peter in the Third Region of Carthage, wherein Augustine preached a sermon on one occasion,[28] and a dedication to St. Paul in the Sixth Region,[29] no trace of the cult of the Apostles has yet been found in Proconsular Africa. This fact is significant, as it was there that Roman Catholicism in Africa was strongest, the Proconsular being the only province in which the Catholics outnumbered the Donatists in 411.[30] At the Council of Carthage in 419 it alone produced 217 bishops.[31] Elsewhere, in the cities where there were undisputed Catholic sees, no dedication has yet come to light. Only [32] at Thamugadi (Timgad) and Thelepte, the one the Donatist capital and the other a place where in 411 the Donatists had two bishops to their opponents' one,[33] is there evidence in the larger African cities for the cult.

On the other hand, inscriptions or mosaics referring to this cult of the Apostles have been found in Uppenna, a small Libyco-Roman town [34] which possessed no recorded bishop till 484,[35] in native *castella*, as Castellum Tingitanum (in 411 an unchallenged Donatist see),[36] agricultural settlements as Ain Ghorab,[37] south-

---

[23] Cyprian, *Ep.* xxi, 3 ; *CSEL* 531. Cf. *Collatio Carthaginensis* i, 187, ' Domnus Marculus ' (*PL* xi, 1329).

[24] P. Cayrel, ' Une basilique donatiste de Numidie,' *Mélanges* li, 1934, 133.

[25] *Supra*, p. 33, nos. 6 and 7.

[26] Cf. *CIL* viii, 9716, from Castellum Tingitanum.

[27] ' Presbyter Saturninus,' in the *Acta Saturnini* 2, 6, 8, etc. (*PL* viii, 689–703).

[28] *PL* xxxviii, 116. no. 15.

[29] ' Codex canonum Eccl. Africana,' in Hardouin, *Concilia*, 1, b. 388.

[30] The Catholics held at that date 62 identifiable sees in this province to their opponents' 34, with 61 divided between rival claimants.

[31] H. T. Bruns, *Canones apostolorum et conciliorum, saeculorum* iv–vii (Berlin, 1839), 156.

[32] Said with reserve on a probable ' Petrus ' dedication seen in the vaulting of a Byzantine basilica at Sicca Veneria (Kef) *CIL* viii, 27690 ; cf. R. Gauckler, *Bulletin archéologique du comité des travaux historiques*, 1897, 413.

[33] *Coll. Carth.* (in o.c., n. 23) 121, 198, 208. The Catholic bishop might be from Thelepte in he proconsular province.

[34] R. Hamy in *Bulletin de géographie historique*, 1904, 33–61, cited by S. Gsell, *Histoire ancienne de l'Afrique du Nord* vi (Paris, 1927), 178. Uppenna is not a Punic name and dolmens are found in the neighbourhood.

[35] *Notitia Byzacensis* 82, in Victor Vitensis vii, 126.

[36] *Coll. Carth.* i, 180.

[37] *Supra*, p. 34, no. 16 : *CIL* viii, 10707, 10708.

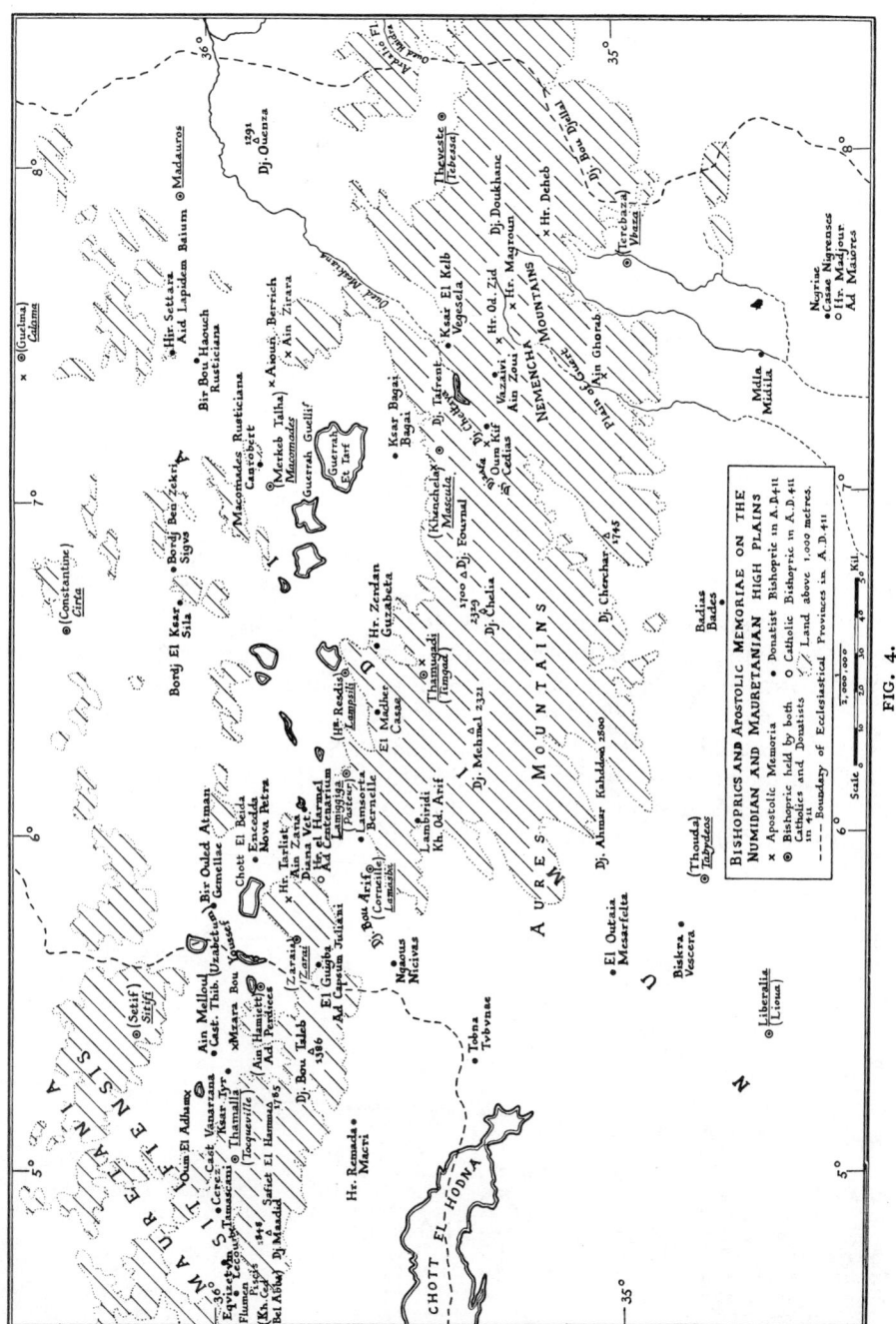

FIG. 4.

west of Theveste on the Nemencha plateau, and in remote places like Oum-el-Adham, in Sitifensis.[38] The *memoriae* occur particularly in the area south-west of Theveste, and on the High Plains between, and north of Timgad and Bagai, north of the Aurès, regions where a hierarchical form of Christianity was unlikely to be popular. It was, however, precisely in this district that Montanist [39] and Donatist tendencies were most powerful. Out of the fifty sees marked on the map of bishoprics (fig. 4) on the High Plains in Central Numidia and Mauretania thirty-two were held in 411 by Donatists without Catholic rival, and only three by Catholics in like position [40] : only in the larger towns, where some energetic prelate such as Aurelius of Macomades could keep a congregation together, or in isolated centres such as Ad Centenarium (Hr. el-Hamel ?), was Catholicism to be found.[41]

In contrast, the existence of the Donatist holy cities of Timgad and Bagai,[42] the great size of such basilicas as the cathedral at Theveste, Timgad,[43] and the large number of sites yielding Donatist inscriptions,[44] should leave little doubt as to the views of the majority of the population. The Mancian colonate was a living institution even in A.D. 500,[45] and much of Donatism was the expression in terms of religion of a struggle against the oppression of the great landowners, not the least of whom was the Catholic Church.[46] The scene of the battles of these villagers, Octava [47] and Bagai,[48] of Bishop Marculus's death at Nova Petra,[49] of Optatus of Thamugadi's and Gildo's kingdom, of the latter's defeat on the Ardalio River,[50] all lie within the area containing the bulk of the inscriptions, which are, moreover, for the most part contemporary with the events just mentioned.

The distribution of these Apostolic *memoriae* follows closely that of the rest of the chapels to the martyrs, of which more are to be found in Numidia than in the rest of the provinces of Africa

[38] *Supra*, p. 33, no 5 : *CIL* viii, 20600.
[39] A Montanist inscription of late fourth-early fifth-century date was found at Mascula ; *CIL* viii, 2274.
[40] As one can see, neither Ad Maiores nor Ad Turres on the edge of the Sahara are strictly speaking on the High Plains.
[41] *Coll. Carth.* i, 133.
[42] Augustine, *Enarratio in Psalmum* 21, ii, 26 (*PL* xxxvi, 177) ; cf. E. Albertini, *CRAI*, 1939, 100.
[43] It measures 46 m. by 22 m., excluding the *atrium* in front. The Donatists held a council at Theveste in 363 (Optatus, *De schismate Donatistarum* ii, 18, i, ed. Ziwsa *CSEL* (1893), 52).
[44] See P. Monceaux 'L'épigraphie donatiste,' *Revue de Philologie* xxxiii (Avril-Juillet, 1909), 112–161.

[45] E. Albertini in *Journal des Savants*, 1930 (Jan.), 23–30.
[46] For land-grabbing on behalf of, and by members of this organisation, *cf.* for Africa, Cyprian, *De lapsis*, 6 (*CSEL* iii, 240) ; *Passio Donati* 2 (*PL* viii, 754) ; Augustine, *Tractatus* vi, in *Johann* 25 (*PL* xxxv, 1436) ; 'Codex Canonum Af. eccles,' in Bruns, *Canones selectae conciliorum* 192 (no. cxxi), 114 (canon viii, First Council of Carthage), 397 (Third Council of Carthage), 134 (Canon xlix).
[47] Optatus iii, 4 (*CSEL* 82).
[48] *Ibid.* iii, 4, p. 81.
[49] *Cf. Coll. Carth.* (o.c.) 1, 187.
[50] Orosius vii, 36 ; *cf.* Augustine, *Contra litteras Petiliani* ii, 184 ; 209 (*PL* xliii, 316, 330).

put together. The Donatist Church was above all the Church of the Martyrs,[51] whereas the Catholics (except in places such as Hippo, where polemical reasons advised the prominent observance of martyrs' anniversaries), were tending to lay less and less emphasis on both martyrs and martyrdom in proportion as they relied more and more for their success on non-African forces—the Imperial Court and the Papacy. The statement of Petilian,[52] that the Catholics did not reverence the cult of martyrs, is explicitly confirmed by Prudentius.[53] He has no knowledge, for instance, of Pontius's account of Cyprian's death; and of the lesser folk ' even their memory is extinct, their fame itself has perished '. It is, on the other hand, precisely in the period in which he wrote that most of the southern Numidian *memoriae martyrum* were built.[54]

On the majority of the inscriptions found in the *memoriae* we are considering, the Apostles are associated with local martyrs, and above all with the martyrs of Abitina who, by their solemn repudiation of all who should communicate with ' traditores ', gave in 304 the signal for revolt against the Church of the Capitol at Carthage.[55] Hence, at Hr. Taghfaght the Apostles are associated with Emeritus,[56] at Uppenna with the presbyter Saturninus and his family (the leaders of the Abitinian congregation)[57] and at Oum el-Adham with Victoria[58]; and finally a shrine some 3 km. outside the city of Constantine is connected with Felix and Vincentius,[59] the latter the patron of Calama in Byzantine times.[60] The phrasing, as well as the situation, of these inscriptions, and of others as at Ain Berrich,[61] at Castellum Tingitanum,[62] and Ain Zirara,[63] further sheds doubt on their strict orthodoxy. In these last mentioned cases, Miggin, Marcia and Ceselia, and Mennas—all, so far as is known, African saints— are placed on the same plane as the Apostles.

It has indeed been urged by H. Jaubert[64] that the martyrs mentioned on the Ain Berrich stone may be namesakes of the Apostles. In the Martyrology of Jerome, under the date of

---

[51] *Acta Saturnini* 18, 19; *Collat. Carth.* iii, 258; *Passio Donati*, 13-14 (*PL* viii, 757-758), *cf.* Augustine, *Contra Epistolam Parmeniani* ii, 3, 6 (*PL* xliii, 53); *Contra Gaud.* i, 27, 31 (*PL* xliii, 724, etc.).
[52] Augustine, *Contra litteras Petiliani* ii, 159 (*PL* xliii, 308): ' uos ergo non colitis. . . .'
[53] Prudentius, *Peristephanon* i, 74, and xiii, especially lines 60-70.
[54] As those of Calendio at Aquac Caesaris (Youks), Hr. el-Hamascha and Ksar Tibinet. Jaubert *l.c.*, 18, 173, 207.
[55] *Acta Saturnini* 19.
[56] *Supra*, p. 34, no. 15 : *CIL* viii, 17714.
[57] *Supra*, p. 33, no. 7 : *CIL* viii, 23040*a* ; *cf. Acta Saturnini* 2-4. Saturninus also

appears on a stone recently found by M. André Berthier in a cemetery basilica at Hr. R'Zel some 30 km. N of Timgad. ' Lucilla ' on the Uppenna stone may or may not be the same person as the founder of the Donatist party: Optatus i, 20, p. 22.
[58] *Supra*, p. 33, no. 5 : *CIL* viii, 20600 ; *cf. Acta Saturnini* 5 (*PL* viii, 693).
[59] H. Jaubert, *Recueil de Constantine* 1912, 22.
[60] *Supra*, p. 35, no. 19 : *CIL* viii, 5352.
[61] *Supra*, p. 33, no. 10 : *CIL* viii, 18656.
[62] *Supra*, p. 32 f., nos. 2-4 : *CIL* viii, 9714-6.
[63] *Supra*, p. 35, no. 21 : *CIL* viii, 17746.
[64] *l.c.* 153.

12th April, one finds mention of ' Paulus, Petrus, Donatus, Miggin, Baric '. Both ' Petrus ', and ' Paulus ' have been found as names on African inscriptions.[65] But the order ' Paulus Petrus ', offensive to a Catholic, occurs on an inscription from Castellum Tingitanum together with ' Marcia ' and ' Ceselia '.[66] This pair find no place in any official martyrology, but are in turn associated with Tipasius at Oppidum Novum.[67] At Castellum Tingitanum, again, a local martyr takes precedence over the Apostles.[68] If the latter were regarded as messengers of Christ inspired by the Spirit, not as the founders of the centre of the hated ' Catholic unity ',[69] then the order in which they were placed would be of little moment. In 411 Castellum Tingitanum possessed no Catholic bishop, though the Donatists had one. In all probability at the time when the dedications to the Apostles found there were set up (end of fourth century, beginning of fifth ; one is actually dated to A.D. 406) the bulk of the Christian inhabitants, and hence the dedicators, were Donatist. Further, Baric, Miggin and Donatus are found together at Hr. el-Hamascha near Ain Beida, between Constantine and Theveste, without the Apostles. They are far more likely to be the martyrs of Guruzi, who were honoured in an inscription in the Donatist see of Castellum Thibuzabetum [70] in Mauretania Sitifensis, just as Emeritus or Saturninus are associated with the same Apostles. The exaggerated reverence paid, for instance, to Miggin in Numidia at the end of the fourth century would make such association perfectly intelligible.[71]

There is a certain emphasis on the designations of the Abitinian martyrs in these inscriptions which make them suspect from an orthodox point of view. Emeritus was lector to the congregation,[72] and hence, by reading God's word, he would become a transmitter of the Holy Spirit.[73] He is therefore styled ' gloriosus consultus '—

[65] E.g. at Theveste on a third century inscription, CIL viii, 16589 ; at Calama, CIL viii, 5492 ; and at Sitifis, CIL viii, 8645.
[66] Supra, p. 33, no. 4 : CIL viii, 9716.
[67] And two other unknown martyrs ' Fioras ', and ' Vitalis ' ; cf. S. Gsell in Bulletin du comité des travaux historiques, 1897, 573 ; Monceaux, ' Enquête ' 325.
[68] CIL viii, 9714 ' sancto et beatissimo Ae . . . martyrium dixit ' (Monceaux's reading of the inscription ; ' Enquête ' 329). The phrase ' martyrium dixit ' probably means ' he confessed '. It occurs both in the Passio Montani, and the Donatist Passio Donati 2 (cited from Monceaux, l.c.).
[69] Cf. Passio Donati (o.c.) 3 ; Optatus o.c. iii, 1, p. 67.
[70] Monceaux Enquête, 311 ; Recueil de Constantine, 1912, 133. Donatus, Miggin and Baric are also mentioned along with other native martyrs as Methun and Stiddin at Hr. el-Hamascha (CIL viii, 10686).
[71] Cf. the letter of Maximus, a grammarian of Madaurus, to Augustine, about 386 (Aug. Ep. 16, 2 ; CSEL xxxiv, 37), and CIL viii, 16660 from Theveste—' Meggini sanctissime '. Miggin both in this inscription and in that at Kherbet Oum el-Adham may be a Circumcellion. In that case the Donatism of both could hardly be in doubt. See J.H. Baxter, JTS 1925, 21-37.
[72] Acta Saturnini, 9.
[73] It may have been for this reason that lectors were often boys : cf. CIL viii, 453, from Ammaedara ; Victor Vitensis, De Persecutione Vandalica iii, 34, p. 89. The bishop preaching a sermon was merely the mouthpiece of the Holy Spirit. Cf. decision of Donatist Council at Zertei, 414, reproduced in Augustine, Contra Gaud. 1 37, 48 (PL xliii, 736).

God's pleader against the ' powers of darkness ', represented by
' idolatry ' and the ' traditores '—everything that favoured Roman
civilisation. In much the same way Maximian, a ' miles Christi ',
and Isaac, heroes of the Donatist *Passio Isaaci*, are called ' doctores ',
even though they were only laymen (after their confession[74] in
A.D. 347). The view of the Church held by the writer of this
Passio, and the dedicator of the Hr. Taghfaght inscription is
spiritual and prophetic, emphasising martyrdom, very different
from that put forward by Catholics like Pontius in his *Vita Cypriani*,
written about A.D. 260–280. The latter is disgusted with the
praise given to the martyrdom of ' plebs ', and ' catechumens '
(*i.e.* Perpetua and Saturus), while bishops, as his hero Cyprian,
are passed over. Even had he not suffered martyrdom, the Bishop
of Carthage would have been a worthy example through his ' good
works ', and ' merits ', as well as his teaching ability.[75] Saturninus,
the presbyter on the Uppenna inscription was, on the other hand,
an example of what the Donatists expected of a priest. ' O martyrem
primatum omnibus dantem. non enim presbyterum fratribus
praetulit, sed presbytero fratres confessionis consortione
copulauit.'[76] He is a martyr and confessor first, a leader of his
people to that goal.

At Ain Ghorab, Emeritus is again associated with a *memoria
apostolorum* in terms which leave little doubt as to his own
connection, and it would seem that of the Apostles with the
Donatist cause.

a. The Hr. Taghfaght inscription: *CIL* viii, 17714.
Hic e[st dom]]us [Dei hic] | memo[riae] | apostol[or(um) et] | *Beati
Emeri|ti gloriosi | consulti.*

b. Ain Ghorab: *CIL* viii, 2220, corrected in *CIL* viii, p. 948. *Cf.* De Rossi,
Bull. crist. 1878, 8.
H(i)c domus D(e)i nos[tri . . . .] h(i)c auitatio Sp(iritus) S(an)c(ti) P[aracleti].
H(i)c memoria *beati martiris Dei consulti* [*E*]*mer*[*iti*].
H(i)c exaudietur omnis q(u)i inuocat nomen D(o)m(i)ni D(e)i omnipot[entis].
(c)ur homo miraris D(e)o iubante meliora uideuis a[nno regis N.] XI.

Apart from the scandal of putting a mere lector on the same
terms as the Apostles, and glorifying him with the title of ' consultus
Dei ', the emphasis on the Paraclete, perhaps even against Christ
Himself, is in keeping with the doctrine of the Donatist Church.[77]
Not only Emeritus, but leaders like Donatus and Petilian, spoke

---

[74] *Passio Isaaci* 8 (*PL* viii, 771) ' ambos uoluit Dominus sibimetipsos esse doctores '.

[75] Pontius, *Vita Cypriani* i (*CSEL* iii, xci): *cf.* the mosaic from the funeral chapel of Alexander, Bishop of the Catholic town of Tipasa, ' Clausula iustitiae est | martyrium uotis optare. | habes et aliam similem ae|li-mosinam viribus facere ' | (*CIL* viii, 20906).

[76] *Acta Saturnini* (*o.c.*) 4.

[77] *Cf.* an inscription found at Berrouaghia near Zabi, dated to A.D. 474 and dedicated in the name of God and the Holy Spirit only: E. Albertini in *CRAI* 1925, 261.

as incarnations of the Holy Spirit.[78] It is the Spirit who guides the faithful in their acts and speech, whether it be the collecting of the dead after the massacres attendant on the carrying out of Constantine's decree of unity (12th March, 317),[79] or in inspiring the defiance of Isaac against the Catholics at Carthage in the persecution of 347.[80] The final words of the Donatist version of the *Acta Crispinae* are ' in unitate Spiritus ', a formula which the Catholics changed to a more orthodox one.[81] The legal shade of meaning implied in the phrase ' consultus Dei ', is more in keeping with the Donatist than with the Catholic outlook : in the Appendix to the *Acta Saturnini*, the Donatist continuator refers to any member of the ' ecclesia martyrum ', as ' quisnam est diuini iuris peritia pollens '.[82] The argument in so far as Ain Ghorab is concerned is further strengthened by the discovery of a ' Deo laudes '[83] inscription from a basilica, which Professor L. Leschi suggests is the one whence the dedication to Emeritus was robbed for the building of the early Byzantine fort.[84] The Vandal date of this dedication is of special interest.[85]

That this same basilica, or one in the immediate neighbourhood, was dedicated to the Apostles is indicated by the inscription set up under Hilderic, or in Byzantine times, by the priest Probantius, on the occasion of a reconsecration.[86] It is written in terms which, though closely paralleled by an inscription placed in St. Peter-ad-Vincula, Rome, under Sixtus III, can leave little doubt as to its former denomination. The first line, ' Cede prius nomen nouitati, cede uetustas,' would have been pointless had the basilica ever been anything other than orthodox. The same applies to ' Unus honor celebret quos habet una fides '—surely this, and the harping on ' unus ' in ' unum quaeso pares, unum duo sumite munus ', is a suggestion of the happy results that follow from the restoration of unity, with both ex-Donatists and Catholics now holding one faith and engaged in a single task.

---

[78] Augustine, *Contra Cresconium* ii, 1, 2 (*PL* xliii, 468) ' quia Donatum habent pro Euangelio ' ; *Contra litteras Petiliani* iii, 16, 19 (*ibid.* 356–7), ' Paracleti nomen imponat. . . .'
[79] *Passio Donati* 13 (*PL* viii, 757).
[80] *Passio Isaaci* (*PL* viii, 769).
[81] *Acta Crispinae* (Th. Ruinart, *Acta Martyrum*, Ratisbon, 1859, 477–9, at p. 479). Ruinart, p. 479, footnote 10, ' . . . Iesum Christum, cui est laus, uirtus, honor et imperium cum Patre et Spiritu Sancto per infinita saecula.'
[82] *Acta Saturnini*, Appendix, 19.
[83] That ' Deo laudes ' was the Donatist war-cry is shown by Augustine *Contra litteras Petiliani* ii, 65, 146 (*PL* xliii, col. 306) *Enarratio in Ps.* 132, 6 (*PL* xxxvi, xxxvii, col. 1732).

[84] L. Leschi ' Basilique et cimitière donatistes de Numidie (Ain Ghorab) ', *Revue africaine* lxviii, 1936, 35.
[85] This is suggested by the method of dating ' a(nno regis N.) XI ', differing from the Byzantine ' indictiones ', and the Roman ' anno provinciae . . . ', and also by the type of cross on the inscription. The stone from Hr. Taghfaght is probably fourth-early fifth-century. The matter would be clinched if *CIL* viii, 17716 ' . . . is ep . . . ' from the same basilica could be reconstructed, as H. Jaubert suggests, ' [Vital]is ep[iscopus].' Vitalis was Donatist bishop of Mascula in 411, but the reconstruction seems to be too hazardous to serve as foundation for an argument : *cf.* H. Jaubert, *o.c.* 203.
[86] *Supra*, p. 34, no. 16 : *CIL* viii, 10707, 10708.

45

Two more inscriptions in the series give positive indications that they were erected by Donatists. At Ain Zirara the dedication of a *memoria* to saints whose relics were contained in a silver casket did not take place till towards the end of the fifth century, at a time, therefore, when Donatism was proscribed.[87] We have noticed, though, that, apart from mention of the Apostles, the only fragment whose reading is certain is ' [De]o laus et gloria.' [88] However conciliatory the Catholics may have been in this period, they would hardly have tolerated the inclusion of their opponents' watchword in the dedication of hallowed relics. At Ain Ghorab they did their best to remove by the chisel the offending phrase.[89] In addition, we know of no large-scale conversions in this district, which contained Donatist bishops and churches at Macomades,[90] Rusticiana,[91] Foum el-Amba [92] and probably Lamiggiga [93] and Idassa.[94] The Catholics were in a minority even in Macomades, where they were forced to live, it would seem, a subterranean existence.[95]

The ' Petrus et Lazarus ' inscription at Timgad was probably Donatist also. ' B(onis) B(ene) ' has never yet been found on an unquestionably Catholic dedication, whereas it does appear on the same stone with ' Deo laudes ' at Hr. Bou Said,[96] and in the same basilica as another, already mentioned, at Ain Ghorab.[97] It is to be found also on inscriptions coming from such Donatist strongholds and centres of rebellion against the official Church as Nova Licinia [98] and Lambaesis.[99] Lazarus, as S. Gsell points out,[100] is here not the friend of Jesus but the beggar covered with sores, the symbol of poverty and oppression which has its reward in Heaven. Moreover, in the early Church, and among the Donatists, all Christians were *sancti*, except the penitents.[101] The mention of these two classes on the inscription is emphatic. Christ, the one true physician, is called on to aid ' the saints and the bitterly penitent ' (' sanctis et penitentibus amare ') in terms which recall

[87] *Supra*, p. 35, no. 21 : *CIL* viii, 17746 ; Monceaux, ' Enquête ' 237 ; Jaubert *o.c.* 212. The Ain Ghorab inscription *CIL* viii, 2220, of Vandal date, shows that Donatism was still a force in this period.
[88] *Supra*, p. 35, no. 21 b.
[89] L. Leschi, *Basilique et cimetière* 32.
[90] *Coll. Carth.* (*o.c.*) i, 116.
[91] *Ibid.* i, 197.
[92] M. André Berthier has recently found a ' Deo laudes ' inscription here, now in Constantine Museum.
[93] *Collat. Carth.* i, 187.
[94] *Ibid.* i, 182.
[95] H. Jaubert, *Recueil de Constantine* xlvii, 1913, 789–791. The mention of the monarchist anti-pope St. Hippolytus on this inscription is not surprising. In the Donatist hierarchy the Bishop of Rome yielded precedence only to the Primate of Numidia and the Bishop of Carthage. Hippolytus was himself a martyr.
[96] P. Monceaux, *Rev. phil.*, 1909, 116, 132 ; H. Jaubert, *o.c.* 198.
[97] L. Leschi, *o.c.* 31.
[98] *Cf. CIL* viii, 20482 ; Monceaux, ' Enquête ' 310.
[99] The see of Bishop Privatus, excommunicated for ' indiscipline ' about 243 (Cyprian, *Ep.* 59, 10 ; *CSEL* iii, 677).
[100] *Revue africaine*, 1928, 21.
[101] *Cf.* 1 *Corinthians* i, 1 ; 1 *Thessal.* iii, 15.

the cry of the Abitinian martyrs at their trial before Anulinus [102] or the *Instructiones* of Commodian.[103] Rigorous penitential practice, and a claim to be themselves the 'just',[104] and 'the saints',[105] were natural consequences of the Donatist contention that even on earth the Church of Christ must be pure, ' without spot or wrinkle,' and that they were the only representatives of it.[106] The Timgad inscription does not stand as the sole expression of this idea. It is found on inscriptions, for instance, at Cedias,[107] Hr. el-Ogla,[108] and from the Vallée des Roumies in Tripolitana,[109] the same district where oral tradition of a cult of the Apostles is preserved. The leaders of the Circumcellions, Fasir and Axido, in A.D. 340 were, further, styled ' duces sanctorum.'.[110] The Timgad inscription dates from the period of Augustine, a time when the Christian community there was ruled by such commanding personalities as the Donatist bishops, Optatus and Gaudentius, and the town was a citadel of Donatism.

There is no evidence as to the religion of the dedicators of the inscriptions from Kherba,[111] or Ain Regada [112]; indeed, the ' Petrus ' on the latter stone might well be just a local martyr and not the Apostle. There is, on the other hand, possible ground for ascribing the dedications from Djebel Djaffa,[113] Hr. Deheb,[114] Ksar Ouled Zid[115] and Mzara Sidi Youssef [116] to Donatists. The geographical position of these chapels in the countryside north of the Aurès or on the Mauretanian High Plains, the home and centre of Donatism, together with the association of the Apostles as at Ksar Ouled Zid with ' spiritual powers ', confessors and angels, suggests this conclusion. In the case of the *memoria* on the Djebel Djaafa, south of Mascula, the inscription was cut on an oblong stone panel beautifully decorated with Berber designs.[117] At Ain Tazougart, just over a mile away, a series of panels of similar size and ornamentation were found. On two of these, ' Deo laudes ' was inscribed.[118]

One would be tempted to apply the same arguments to determine the religion of the dedicators of the ' agape mensa ' at Oum el-Adham. The site is on the Mauretanian High Plains and

---

[102] *E.g. Acta Saturnini (o.c.)* 8, 9, 12.
[103] *Instructiones* ii, 8.
[104] Augustine, *Psalmus contra Partem Donati* l. 16 (*PL* xliii, 25).
[105] Augustine, *Contra litteras Petiliani* ii, 20, 44 (*PL* xliii, 273).
[106] Augustine, *Ad catholicos ep.* 15–37, 16–40 (*PL* xliii, 419 and 421); *Coll. Carth.* iii, 258 (*PL* xi, 1409).
[107] Le Commandant Bigeard in *Recueil de Constantine*, 1907, 19.
[108] H. Jaubert, *o.c.* 189.
[109] *CIL* viii, 10969.
[110] Optatus *o.c.* iii, 4.

[111] *Supra*, p. 32, no. 1 : *CIL* viii, 21496.
[112] *Supra*, p. 35, no. 20 : *CIL* viii, 5666.
[113] *Supra*, p. 34, no. 12 : *CIL* viii, 17715.
[114] *Supra*, p. 34, no. 11 : *ILCV* 2065.
[115] *Supra*, p. 34, no. 14 : Monceaux, Enquête ' 336.
[116] *Supra*, p. 35, no. 18 : Monceaux, 'Enquête' 314.
[117] The stone in question is now in the church of the Sacré Coeur, at Constantine.
[118] S. Gsell and H. Graillot, ' Les ruines romains au nord de l'Aurès,' *Mélanges* 1893, 498–502.

near the unchallenged Donatist sees of Castellum Thibuzabatum [119] and Tamascani (Cerez) [120]. Yet the date of the dedication, A.D. 359, shows that the *memoria* in which it stood was built during a period in which the Donatists were proscribed. This evidence is not, however, absolutely conclusive. It seems that the basilica in honour of Marculus at Vegesela was first built in the same period,[121] while it was in this part of Mauretania, from Flumen Piscis (Kherbet Ced el-Abbas ?) to Zabi, that the revolt which led to the overthrow of Catholicism in 362 originated.[122] The revolutionary bishops appear to have had the whole-hearted support of the country people, such as Pequaria and Benenatus.[123]

One notices, too, the same association of the Apostles with a medley of African martyrs, including an Abitinian Victoria and an 'uncanonical' martyr, Cittin. Cyprian again, Catholic Bishop of Carthage though he was, was also the formulator of what later became the Donatist doctrine of rebaptism, and as such was held in immense respect by the dissidents.[124]

There is a small additional point. The most sacred relic, to which the Apostles themselves give precedence, is the earth of the Holy Land. This cult does not seem to have been prominent in Catholic circles till about 425, when the Catholic landowner Hesperius brought it to the fore.[125] Previously Augustine had made bitter gibes at the practice of a similar cult on the part of his adversaries. If anyone were to bring them some earth from the East, they would worship it, he writes to his Donatist cousin, Severinus, towards A.D. 400.[126] The evidence is by no means watertight, but it should be borne in mind before rejecting it as inadequate, that the inscription quoted above (p. 33, no. 5) which is probably not later than the turn of the fifth century,[127] was found worthy to bear the name of Miggin and his companion Victorinus.

In North Africa, then, it would appear that the cult of the Apostles SS. Peter and Paul tended to be divorced from any regard for the Papacy as such, and was inspired rather by that tradition of African thought most opposed to Catholic ideas of ecclesiastical discipline. As regards the association of the Apostles with local martyrs, it is possible in this case to rule out the plea

[119] *Coll. Carth.* i, 187.
[120] *Ibid.* i, 198.
[121] P. Courcelle, 'Une seconde campagne de fouilles à Ksar-el-Kelb,' *Mélanges* 1936, 183.
[122] Optatus *o.c.* ii, 18 (Ziwsa ed. 51).
[123] Their native language seems to have been Libyan. The use of the form 'Victoriais' suggests this. See Schmidt's comment under *CIL* viii, 15791.

[124] Augustine, *De baptismo contra Donatistas* i, 1; *Contra Cresconium* ii, 31, 39, iii, 1, 2, and iv, 17, 20 (*PL* xliii, 109, 489, 497 and 559).
[125] *De Civitate Dei* xxii, 8; *CSEL* xl, 602.
[126] *Ep.* 52, 2; *CSEL* xxxiv, 2, 150.
[127] On the dating of the chrismon, see S. Gsell, *Monuments antiques de l'Algérie* ii (1901), 115 n.

of 'simple faith', on which the orthodoxy of the dedicators might be upheld.[128] It has been shown that there were reasons why from the first the Apostles should have been reverenced by the rigorist school of thought in the African Church, as examples of martyrs and men endowed to the highest degree with spiritual gifts. When the rigorists finally renounced association with the official Catholic Church, to become 'Donatists' in 311, the attitude towards the Apostles underwent no change. It was natural for men 'with the Gospel ever on their lips and thoughts of martyrdom in their heart',[129] determined to maintain to the uttermost the discipline of the Early Church, to regard the Apostles as the source of their inspiration and associate them with their greatest heroes. It may be for reasons such as these that the *memoriae* or other forms of dedication to the Apostles are to be found in Donatist sees, or where Donatist influence was overwhelmingly strong. The texts of such of these inscriptions as are legible, or give any clue to the beliefs of the dedicators, point to the same conclusion. There is, on the other hand, no evidence for any widespread Catholic cult of the Apostles centred in the Catholic cities, whence it might spread to country districts and there become mixed up with former popular beliefs. One can differentiate very clearly between a rather exotic veneration of relics brought over from Rome in Vandal times, by exiles like Fulgentius of Ruspe or Probantius, who were able to return to their own country, and the African cult of the Apostles and martyrs and the Apostles as martyrs. This cult was most popular, as has been shown, in the mountainous country on the fringes of the Roman province, where Latin influence was least likely to penetrate, where Libyan culture persisted, and Donatism was strongest. Significantly enough, it was strong in Byzantine times, as the inscriptions from Ain Berrich [130] and from the district NW of Calama, and the later mosaic at Uppenna [131] show. It was, then, particularly a cult of the countryside; for the great cities on whose survival the official Church depended for its strength had perished,[132] or else, after a century of desertion been 'restored' as agricultural settlements [133] or clumps of squalid *gourbis*.[134] A large number of inscriptions referring to African Christianity in Byzantine times relate to martyrs. The old devotion to the memory of martyrs and of holy men outlasted the religion of Augustine and his friends. The Berbers rejected what military force had thrust

---

[128] As might be suggested from Irish evidence where St. Bridget was sometimes associated with St. Mary. Cited from A. J. Toynbee, *Study of History* ii, 326.
[129] *Passio Marculi* (PL viii, 762).
[130] *Supra*, p. 33 f., no. 10 : *CIL* viii, 18656.
[131] *Supra*, p. 33, no. 6 : *CIL* viii, 23041.
[132] As Leptis Magna : cf. Procopius, *De aedificiis*, vi, 4.
[133] As Thuburbo Maius.
[134] As Thamugadi.

upon them. No *memoria* was put up in Africa to the Catholic leaders : Augustine's own see at Hippo was forsaken half a century after his death,[135] while Donatism steadily gained ground as the years wore on. In this milieu the cult of the Apostles enjoyed a fleeting hour of prosperity, before being lost in the turmoil of the seventh century, absorbed possibly among the djinns and marabouts of the Moslem cult of saints.

Addendum

Since this article was written M. M. Labrousse has published a new inscription from a church at Hr. Tarlist (Gsell, *Atlas archéologique*, Feuille 26, Bou Thaleb, no. 71). The text is as follows :

[Hic reliquiae] . . . .
| [beati aposto]li Iohan[nis], ..., s(an)c(t)i . . . . ., | [s(an)c(t)i] Cristofor[i], s(an)c(t)i . . . ., s(an)c(t)i Iu[liani ? | s(an)c(t)i] Luciani, s(an)c(t)i Rest[ituti], s(an)[c(t)i . . . . , | s(an)c(ta)e . . . . .]t(ae), s(an)c(t)i
Teodo[ri], s(an)c(t)i D . . . . , s(an)c(t)i . . . . . | . . . .
    [s(an)c(ta)e . . . . ,]
[an?]no d(o)m(i)n(i) . . . . . | . . . . . condit(ae) s(unt ?) A chrismon.
    Mélanges, 1938, 224–258.

The inscription contains nothing opposed to the conclusions arrived at in this article.

1. The inscription is late Byzantine, dating from the same time and coming from the same place as the renewed outburst of Donatist activity at the end of the sixth century. Gregory, *Ep.* ii, 48, and iv, 35 (*PL* lxxvii, 588 and 710).

2. There is the same association of other martyrs with St. John as we have noted in the case of SS. Peter and Paul. The church in question was a cemetery basilica : while as a rule the Catholics hesitated to bury even their bishops inside their churches (Ferrandus, *Vita Fulgentii* 150, 165 (*PL* lxv)), the Donatists had no such prejudices, as in the case of Cedias, Oum Kif (*Recueil de Constantine*, 1907, 15 ff.).

The incineration found at Hr. Tarlist would seem more likely to be a Circumcellion suicide than an orthodox burial. Augustine, *Contra Gaud.* 1, 27, 30 (*PL* xliii, 724).

[135] Hippo does not appear on the episcopal list of 484 ; see *CSEL* vii, 119-123.

XIX

CIRCUMCELLIONS AND MONKS

IN a brief study published in the *J.T.S.* of 1952, I suggested that the *cellae rusticanae* round which Augustine stated that the African Circumcellions dwelt for the sake of their sustenance (*victus sui causa*)[1] were probably the martyrs' shrines to be found in the villages that dotted the plains of Numidia and Mauretania Sitifensis in the fourth and fifth centuries.[2] Since then much has been written about the Donatists and in particular about the Circumcellions,[3] but on the whole, the 'martyrs' shrines' hypothesis has not won favour. 'Tuttavia Frend non convince' is the verdict of the most recent critic.[4] Scholars have preferred the more traditional interpretation of *cella* = barn, particularly in view of the renewed interest in the economic role and legal status of the Circumcellions.[5] Were the latter members of a clearly designated *ordo*, the lowest group of free men in Roman African society, but superior to the *coloni* and slaves? Was their role primarily economic, as free workers employed particularly at harvest time on the great olive plantations of central and southern Numidia, and only incidentally religious activism on the side of the Donatists? Is one justified in believing with Brisson that the information to be gleaned about the Circumcellions from Honorius' anti-Donatist edict of 30 January 412 (*Cod. Theod.* xvi. 5. 52) is 'peut-être [le renseignement] le plus précieux' concerning them?[6]

[1] Augustine, *Contra Gaudentium* (*C.S.E.L.* 53. 231), i. 28. 32. Compare *Enarr. in Ps.* 132.3 'Circumcelliones dicti sunt quia circum cellas vagantur' (*P.L.* 36–7, 1730).
[2] 'The Cellae of the African Circumcellions', *J.T.S.*, N.S. iii (1952), pp. 87–90.
[3] See the Bibliography to 1964 in Emin Tengström's *Donatisten und Katholiken* (Studia graeca et latina Gothoburgensia xviii, Göteborg, 1964), pp. 195–200, and the careful study by P.-A. Février, 'Toujours le Donatisme, à quand l'Afrique', *Rivista di storia e letteratura religiosa*, ii (1966), pp. 228–40.
[4] S. Calderone, 'Circumcelliones', *La Parola del Passato*, fasc. cxiii (1967), pp. 94–109 at p. 102.
[5] For instance, J.-P. Brisson, *Autonomisme et christianisme dans l'Afrique romaine* (Paris, 1958), p. 332 n. 4.
[6] J.-P. Brisson, op. cit., p. 334.

The attempt to solve the problem of the Circumcellions by beginning with their legal *condicio* has produced some interesting results. Following Brisson, H. J. Diesner has seen the Circumcellions as an Ordo consisting of juridically free workers who were able to use their standing to provide a sort of *patrocinium* to the multitude of ruined *coloni* and runaway slaves referred to by Augustine as forming the mobs who sacked Catholic churches and terrorized agrarian society.[1] Diesner's detailed survey of Augustine's references to Circumcellions in the diocese of Hippo[2] has led him to believe that one could divide the movement into the solid core of Circumcellions who formed the Ordo, and the wide fringe of labourers who from time to time 'went over to the Circumcellions'[3] and participated in violent actions against the authorities and the Catholics.

Diesner's emphasis however, on the social revolutionary role of the Circumcellions has been challenged by Emin Tengström. The latter's thorough examination of the relevant texts of Optatus and Augustine brings him to the conclusion that the primary role of the Circumcellions was that of seasonal workers,[4] though they incidentally formed a special group within the Donatist Church. Even the famous clubs they carried, the 'Israels', were perhaps simply staves used to knock down the olives off trees during the harvest.[5] Their main offence in the eyes of the authorities and Augustine was that by violent and illegal acts they prevented their co-religionaries being forced to go over to the Catholics.[6] In this situation the *cellae rusticanae* were most likely to be *cellae oleariae*, the storage-houses where the oil from the Numidian olive harvest was garnered.[7]

Recently, Professor Salvatore Calderone has examined Tengström's thesis and insisted once more on the religious role of the Circumcellions as providing the real clue towards understanding them.[8] He has taken the argument further by pointing to the slightly embarrassed

---

[1] Augustine, *Epp.* 108.6.18–19, 111 and 185.4.15. See H. J. Diesner, 'Methodisches und Sachliches zum Circumcellionentum' = *Kirche und Staat im spätrömischen Reich* (Berlin, 1963), pp. 53–77.

[2] 'Die Circumcellionen von Hippo Regius', ibid., pp. 78–90.

[3] Augustine, *Ep.* 35.2, (*C.S.E.L.* 34.28) describing how a subdeacon and two Catholic *sanctimoniales*, all of whom were *coloni* on a Catholic estate in the diocese of Hippo, had now joined the Circumcellions.

[4] E. Tengström, op. cit., pp. 44 ff. and 64.

[5] Ibid., pp. 51–2.

[6] Tengström, op. cit., p. 69: 'Die Circumcellionen versuchten also durch ungesetzliche Aktionen vor allem zu verhindern dass die donatistischen *coloni* und *servi* genötigt wurden, zur katholischen Kirche überzugehen.'

[7] Ibid., p. 56.

[8] S. Calderone, op. cit.

comparisons made by Augustine[1] and by later writers, such as Praedestinatus (c. 440) between the Circumcellions and monks.[2] In so doing he draws attention to the strange term *Cotopitae* used by Isidore of Seville and following him by Beatus of Liebana to describe them. 'Circumcelliones dicti, eo quod agrestes sint, quos Cotopitas vocant.'[3] Beatus (or Tyconius) believed that the word Cotopitae came from the Greek,[4] but Calderone has suggested with a good deal of plausibility that in reality it was formed from two Coptic words, Kōté / ket- meaning 'to move around' or 'wander', and 'aouet', a cenobitical monastic settlement.[5] The word as pronounced 'ketaubit' would be transliterated into Latin Cotopita, and the Coptic characters could easily be mistaken for Greek where Greek was not widely learnt. That Isidore intended to compare the Circumcellions with monks is evident from another passage in which he lists the Circumcellions as 'the fifth category of monk'.[6] Moreover, their wandering from place to place that has caused some recent critics so much trouble is precisely the activity, apart from their violence and revolutionary outlook, that most impressed contemporaries.[7]

Even without Isidore's suspect etymology one would be led to associate the wandering about of the Circumcellions less with seasonal labour than with martyrs' shrines. Tyconius, quoted by Beatus, says that the Circumcellions were superstitious folk and that they spent their time visiting the tombs of martyrs, as they believed, for the salvation of their souls.[8] Augustine moreover, though he hated them for

---

[1] Augustine, *Enarr. in Ps.* 132. 3 (*P.L.* 36–7. 1730); *De opere monachorum*, 28. 36 (*C.S.E.L.* 41. 585) and *Epistola ad Cathol. contra Don.* 19. 50 (*C.S.E.L.* 52. 297). [2] Praedestinatus, *De Haeresibus*, 69 (*P.L.* 53. 611B).

[3] Isidore, *Etymologiarum Libri* (*P.L.* 82. 302) viii. 5. 53.

[4] Beatus, *in Apocalyps.* Praefatio 5. 53. T. Hahn, *Tyconius-Studien* (Leipzig, 1900), p. 68 n. i, attributes this passage to Tyconius. Augustine, *Ep.* 53.2 and *Ad Cathol. Ep.* 3. 6, says that the Roman Donatists were called Cutzupitae, and so the term may have been in use at the end of the fourth century. On the other hand, Beatus apart from drawing on Tyconius may have also been conflating a number of passages concerning the Circumcellions from Augustine and Isidore (his phrase referring to the Circumcellions as 'circumeunt provincias' occurs in *De opere monachorum*, 28. 36, and in Isidore, *De offic. eccl.* ii. 16. 7). Cotopita is not known to have been used by the Donatists as a description of the Circumcellions in their controversy with Augustine.

[5] Calderone, op. cit., p. 102. References in n. 22.

[6] *De offic. eccl.* ii. 16: 'Quintum genus (monachorum) est Circumcellionum qui sub habitu monachorum usquequaque vagantur' (*P.L.* 83. 796–7).

[7] Augustine, *Enarr. in Ps.* 132. 3; cf. *De opere monachorum*, ii. 28. 36.

[8] 'Sed ut diximus, diversas terras circuire et sanctorum sepulchra pervidere quasi pro salute animae suae'. Tyconius, ap. Beatum. Cited from Hahn, op. cit., p. 68. Compare also Augustine, *Ep. ad Cath.* 19. 50, 'ad eorum sepulchra (i.e. of Circumcellion 'martyrs') ebriosi greges vagorum et vagarum ...'.

their violence and treated them as a menace to established agrarian order, did not deny that there was a religious aspect to their activities, namely imitation of and service to martyrs.[1] He accepts that the women ascetics who accompanied them shared the name of *sanctimoniales* with their Catholic counterparts however grossly they abused it.[2] Moreover, the Circumcellions were 'idle' so far as honest work was concerned.[3] Never once does he imply that their peregrinations had anything to do with the needs of the Numidian olive-harvest. Rather they were aimed at selling martyrs' relics.[4]

It is easy to point to Egyptian ascetics in the late fourth and fifth century who shared to some extent the outlook and activities of the Circumcellions. In general, wandering monks were regarded as a pest by those who drew up monastic Rules and by the authorities. If found in the cities they were sent back to the desert.[5] There some of their leaders made little attempt to disguise their antagonism for oppressive landowners, especially if they were pagans. At Schenuti's behest island vineyards belonging to proprietors in the town of Ashmin were sunk beneath the waters of the Nile when local farmers complained that unfair rents were being extorted from them.[6] In Syria the destruction of debtors' bonds by Simon Stylites provides an exact parallel to the activities of the Circumcellions,[7] and it is undeniable that the Syrian monks owed much of their popularity to their ability to protect villagers among whom they settled from oppression.[8] Thus in East and West we find ascetic religious groups dominated by passions for egalitarian justice coming into being in response to the social and economic conditions of the day. In the East, however, the activities of the monks were tolerated, partly because monasticism was the most highly regarded means of salvation, and perhaps also because monks were concerned

---

[1] For instance, *Contra epist. Parmeniani*, iii. 6. 29 (*C.S.E.L.* 51. 138), 'ad suum nomen convertere cupientes interim temporalia supplicia schismatis sui conferre audent passionibus martyrum, ut eis poenarum suarum natalicia celebrentur magno conventu hominum furiosorum . . .'. Compare *Ep.* 108. 6. 18, 'agonistici confessores vestri'.

[2] *Contra Gaudentium*, i. 36. 46 (*C.S.E.L.* 53. 246). For Catholic *sanctimoniales*, see *Contra litteras Petiliani*, iii. 17. 20 (*C.S.E.L.* 52. 177) and *Ep.* 35. 2.

[3] *Contra Gaudentium*, i. 28. 32, 'ab utilibus operibus otiosum'.

[4] *De opere monachorum*, 28. 36: 'Alii membra martyrum, si tamen martyrum, venditant.'

[5] *Codex Theodosianus*, xvi. 3. 1 and 2; compare xii. 1. 63.

[6] Bohairic *Life of Schenuti* by Besa (eds. H. Wiesmann and R. Draguet), *C.S.C.O.* 129, Script. Coptici 16 (Louvain, 1951), cc. 85–6.

[7] See A. Vööbus, *History of Asceticism in the Syrian Orient* (*C.S.C.O.*, Subsidia 17, Louvain, 1960), p. 376, citing the Syriac *Vita Symeonis*.

[8] See, for instance, the exploits of the monks Maisumas and Abraames as narrated by Theodoret, *Hist. relig.* xiv and xvii.

to right individual wrongs and were not considered enemies of the existing system of economic and social relationships. The Circumcellions on the other hand were so regarded. It was not only their Donatism but their liberation of slaves, reversal of the established social order, and in general their encouragement of 'audacia rusticana' that made them so feared and hated.[1] Their courtship of the martyr's death at the hands of the authority was a direct continuation of the theology of suffering and martyrdom that had dominated African theology in the previous century. In the East, however, the monk had effectively replaced the confessor.

The Circumcellions were not, however, monks, and the Donatists repudiated the term.[2] One cannot therefore go the whole way with Calderone and see in their *cellae* colonies of monastic cells, whose presence in North Africa is marked by place names such as Chellenses Numidae or Cellae Vatari.[3] Fortunately evidence has now come to light which does away with this need. In 1964, P.-A. Février published the following inscription from Koudiat Adjala in Mauretania Sitifensis:

C(aius) J(ulius) Castus grado sacerdotali legis / sacrae secundus C(aius) Jul(ius) Honori filius / iam LXVIIII annos agens hoc sibi in animum / deliberavit ut incolumis et in rebus huma/nis agens hanc suae memoriae sedem perpetuam constituere a(nno) p(rovinciae) CCCXXII cel/lam martyrum vocavit Luciani et Lucillae. Dep(ositus?) vi. K. sep.[4]

The inscription, dated to 361, is interesting for many reasons, not least that in this elaborate memorial Christianity is described as a 'law', 'lex sacra'. Lucianus and Lucilla are not known elsewhere as a pair of martyrs, though there was a Donatist bishop named Lucianus who signed the original appeal to Constantine against Caecilian in 313[5] and Lucilla was the wealthy sponsor of the original anti-Caecilianist bishop Majorinus. Whatever the identification of the two martyrs may be at whose shrine Caius Julius Castus was buried, it seems quite clear that the building erected in their honour was called a 'cella martyrum' (*cel/lam martyrum vocavit Luciani et Lucillae*). As Circumcellions also were characterized as spending their time on a constant round of visits to the tombs of martyrs, the derivation of their name from 'circum cellas' from 'around the tombs of martyrs' becomes arguable once more.

---

[1] See Augustine, *Epp.* 108. 6. 18 and 185. 4. 15—the classic statements of Circumcellions as revolutionaries. Compare Optatus of Milev, iii. 4, dealing with the situation seventy years before.

[2] Augustine, *Enarr. in Ps.* 132. 3, and *Contra litteras Petiliani*, iii. 40. 48.

[3] Calderone, op. cit., p. 104 n. 31.

[4] P.-A. Février, 'Inscriptions funéraires de Maurétanie', *Mélanges de l'École française de Rome*, lxxvi (1964), p. 158. Cf. also ibid., p. 127.

[5] Optatus, *De schismate*, 1. 22.

In this situation one may also look again at the archaeological evidence. Archaeologists have been puzzled by the existence of a number of elaborate but apparently wholly domestic structures associated with churches in rural Numidia and Mauretania. At the little Numidian chapel of Azrou Zaouia on the plains south-west of Constantine the sacristy on the north side behind the altar contained two deep silos for storing grain, and there was a range of rooms leading off it whose extent, however, remains to be determined (see Plate 1). Here, at any rate, the Circumcellions visiting the chapel and its relics could have received sustenance.[1] Other more elaborate Christian buildings in the same areas whose function has never been adequately explained begin to fit the Circumcellion–Cotopitae picture. In 1933, for instance, W. Seston published the description of a building at Ain Tamda in Mauretania which he believed to have been a monastery.[2] This massive complex of buildings consisted of a church 25 m. long on to which had been built a series of rooms set round a rectangular court 20 m. × 18 m. so that the church formed the west side. The area was entered by a door on the east side of the court. Seston was puzzled because these buildings did not fit into any known monastic plan, and in particular, the buildings set round the court did not suggest monks' cells. Moreover, the erection of a monastery up country and far from civilized centres seemed to conflict with the specific advice given by Fulgentius of Ruspe, c. 500, that monasteries should be built on fertile land near a villa well provided with gardens.[3]

Ain Tamda does not, however, stand alone. At the central Numidian site at Bir Djedid, the main church in the village was separated by a narrow corridor from an extensive complex of roughly constructed buildings set round a courtyard.[4] The rooms included a number obviously used for storing grain and olives. At Kherbet Bahrarou, northwest of Timgad, the writer of this article partially excavated another similar complex, the church occupying the east end of a courtyard, and again, numerous fragments of storage jars in some of the rooms left little doubt as to their purpose. The building was only a few yards away from an olive press of the same period.

[1] Two silos were found also in a room adjoining the south-west angle of a church at Mechta el Tein north of Batna, in one of which a Christian lamp was found: A. Berthier and colleagues, *Les Vestiges du christianisme antique dans la Numidie centrale* (Algiers, 1942), p. 147. For Azrou Zaouia see ibid., p. 139.

[2] W. Seston, 'Le monastère d'Ain Tamda et les origines d'architecture monastique en Afrique du Nord', *Mélanges de l'École française de Rome*, li (1934), pp. 74–113.

[3] Ferrandus, *Vita Sancti Fulgentii*, 10 (ed. Lapeyre, 1931).

[4] Briefly described by A. Berthier, op. cit., p. 129. Silos were found in the floors of some of these rooms.

At the time, the parallel of the modern Moorish *tighremt* suggested itself, which is a courtyard building one side of which is occupied by a mosque but the remainder used for domestic purposes. It is difficult to see the origins and use of these buildings outside rural North African religious life, and this involves in the fourth and fifth centuries some purpose within the context of Donatism. The comparison between Circumcellions and monks becomes more interesting as these buildings had both a religious and an economic purpose. The churches housed relics of martyrs and the surrounding rooms provided ample means of sustenance for temporary or semi-permanent inmates. The famous *turmae* or 'bands' of Circumcellions could have found them convenient centres, and their use as habitations could have brought to mind a comparison with the host of small monasteries that were springing up at this period in the Egyptian countryside, and hence the application of the term 'Cotopitae' to them.

One final point concerns the term 'ordo' as applied to the Circumcellions. Saumagne,[1] Brisson,[2] and many others have justifiably drawn attention to this description used in 412 by imperial civil servants at Ravenna, and at first sight their identification with seasonal workers on the lines suggested by the famous third-century inscription (*C.I.L.* viii. 11824) is attractive. As we have seen, however, there is no evidence for this, and one suspects that too much weight may have been placed on the appearance of the term in the single edict of Honorius. *Ordo* can be used more simply as a 'guild';[3] and perhaps more significantly, the monks in Egypt and elsewhere sometimes referred to in the fifth century as forming part of a *taxis* (τάξις) or *tagma* (τάγμα),[4] a term that has the same meaning as Ordo. On papyri it denotes an organized and recognizable body of individuals, such as the monks were, as well as an official grade or rank, such as the *tagma* of gymnasiarchs from Oxyrhynchus.[5] For instance, at the second session of the Second Council of Ephesus on 22 August 449, what is described as 'the entire laity and the τάγμα of the monks' swore that they would not remain in communion with Sophronius, Bishop of Tella who was accused of

---

[1] C. Saumagne, 'Ouvriers agricoles ou rôdeurs de celliers? Les Circumcellions d'Afrique', *Annales d'Histoire économique et sociale*, vi (1934), pp. 351–64, especially pp. 355–6.

[2] J.-B. Brisson, op. cit., p. 338.

[3] *C.I.L.* vi. 33885 (2nd cent.) and xiv. 250 (A.D. 152). I owe these references to Mr. H. G. Lee.

[4] For instance, *Vita Danielis Stylitae* (ed. H. Delehaye, *Les Saints Stylites* (Paris, 1923), 86), ταῖς ἁγιωτάταις ἐκκλησίαις καὶ τῷ μοναστικῷ τάγματι εἰρήνην καὶ παρρησίαν . . . δωρούμενος.

[5] See F. Preisigke's *Wörterbuch der griechischen Papyrusurkunden* (Berlin, 1927), ii. 573 and 575–7.

practising magic.¹ One might argue that with his rough monk-like appearance,² his club, and his dwelling round the shrines of martyrs in the villages on the great landed estates of Numidia, the Circumcellion could well be classed for the purpose of punishment as an Ordo. He was a member of a distinctive group and could, if identified, be mulcted 10 lb. of silver. Since the term is not applied to him subsequently nothing more technical may have been implied.³

Most of the questions relating to the pattern of rural society in late-Roman North Africa must await renewed work by archaeologists. From time to time a chance find like the inscription from Koudiat Adjala sheds light on a problem which has hitherto defied solution. If the *cella* of the Circumcellion can now be said with more confidence than previously to have been a chapel where martyrs' relics were housed, then a reconsideration of the texts of Optatus, Tyconius, and Augustine may lead once more to the Circumcellions being studied primarily within the context of Donatism. To their supporters they were the *agonistici*, continuing by their way of life traditional aspirations to martyrdom in the African Church, while their resistance to every form of persecution maintained the struggle of the Christians against 'the world and its rulers' of pre-Constantinian times.⁴ In the framework of apocalyptic and martyr-dominated Donatist theology their role as agrarian revolutionaries becomes easy to understand. The combination of both activities is attested by an abundance of surviving texts; and this was how their African contemporaries saw them.

---

¹ *Akten der ephesinischen Synode vom Jahre 449* (ed. J. Flemming, Abhandlungen König. Gesell. Göttingen, N. F. Band 15, 1914–17, l. 82).

² Isidore's description of Circumcellions (*De offic. eccl.* ii. 16. 7) 'qui sub habitu monachorum usquequaque vagantur', and Praedestinatus' of them 'veluti monachos' (*De Haeres.* 69).

³ Is there any need for instance to accept with Diesner ('Methodisches und Sachliches', p. 75) that as part of the government's anti-Donatist measures between 412 and 414 the Ordo of the Circumcellions was dissolved? For discussion of the problem, see E. Tengström, op. cit., pp. 27 ff.

⁴ Augustine, *Enarr. in Ps.* 132. 6: 'Agonisticos eos vocant.' Compare Optatus, iii. 4, 'circumcelliones—agonisticos nuncupans' (*C.S.E.L.* 26. 81). In particular, Augustine, *Ep.* 108. 6. 18 (*C.S.E.L.* 34. 632) where the connection between *agonistici* and *rusticana audacia contra possessores* is plainly set out.

XIX

Fig. 1.

Fig. 2.

Fig. 3.

(Photo: M. Martin)

Plate 1.

XX

The Revival of Berber Art

MUCH has been written about the revival of Celtic art in Britain during the last century of the Roman occupation, but so far evidence for similar movements in other parts of the Roman Empire has received but little attention from British archaeologists. Yet it is now nearly half a century since M. P. Gavault, a French architect, excavated a 4th–5th century Christian church at Tigzirt on the Mediterranean coast west of Port Gueydon, and drew attention to the unclassical character of the ornamentation of the supports to the clerestory arches in the church. His suggestion was that the ornamentation was inspired by pre-Roman, Carthaginian originals, and implied a popular movement away from classical design.[1]

That was in 1895. In 1898 Gsell published the result of his work on the Bled-Guitoun, a 4th-century Christian royal tomb situated near Ménerville, 35 miles southeast of Algiers, and some 50 miles southwest of Tigzirt. Gsell pointed out that the elaborate geometric designs which had been chipped out on the flat surface of a false doorway to the tomb owed nothing to Rome, but in fact represented a renaissance of native art inspired to a large extent by the triumph of Christianity.[2] As emphasizing the native element in this revival, Gsell showed that the tomb was constructed on much the same plan as the Kbor Roumi, the mausoleum of king Juba II, built about 100 miles westward along the coast four centuries previously.[3] The tumulus was probably the prototype of both.

Gsell's later researches[4] suggested that the Bled-Guitoun might with some probability be attributed to Firmus, the ruler of a confederation of tribes in that part of the Kabylie about A.D. 370, and leader of

---

[1] P. Gavault, *Etude sur les Ruines romaines de Tigzirt*. Paris, 1897, p. 22. 'Au déclin de l'Empire l'art chrétien, essentiellement populaire, revint aux thèmes anciens, en croyant peut-être faire du nouveau. Nous dirions qu'il eût alors une sorte de renaissance punique, si le terme n'était pas trop fort'.

[2] S. Gsell, ' Comptes-Rendues de l'Académie des Inscriptions et Belles Lettres ', (=*CRAI*) 1898, p. 481–99. 'On surprend là les symptomes d'une renaissance determinée sans doute en grande partie par le triomphe de chrétienté', p. 496.

[3] S. Gsell, op. cit. p. 495.

[4] S. Gsell, *Recueil de Constantine*, 1902, XXXVI, p. 27 ff.

THE REVIVAL OF BERBER ART

the Berber rising of 371–75 against the fiscal oppression of the Imperial officials. The allusion to the influence of Christianity in stimulating the revival of native art deserves notice in this connexion, for Firmus, if not a Donatist Christian himself, was supported by the Donatist Church in his revolt, as was his brother Gildo in a similar uprising twenty-five years later.[5] In both cases, the Imperialists were supported by the African Catholics.

Possibly, influenced by the statements of Augustine that the native population in North Africa spoke Punic at this period,[6] both Gsell and Gavault were inclined to associate any revival of native art to underlying Punic rather than Libyan or Berber influences. But up to now, evidences for the spread of Punic language and art in Algeria during the Roman period, such as neo-Punic inscriptions, have been confined to the urban areas of the river valleys of the Tell, or the sites of former Carthaginian coastal settlements, as Tipasa. None have been discovered in the Kabylie where Gsell and Gavault's discoveries were made, and none in the Aures mountains or the high plains of central Algeria (southern Numidia) where most of the examples of 4th–5th century native art have been found. An alternative solution might be that the artistic revival was a revival of Berber art, in part inspired from prehistoric Berber motifs; and that this revival can be closely associated with first, the growing prosperity of the African countryside during the 3rd and 4th centuries, and secondly, with the rise of the Donatist Church as representative of the Berbers' reaction and revolt against the Latin civilization, which their masters had endeavoured to impose upon them.

The history of North African art in the Roman period is in some ways similar to the history of art in Roman Britain. In general neither the Berber nor the Celt were able to adapt classical themes to their own needs and so develop a provincial art.[7] In the first three centuries A.D. the native artist remained for the most part a bad copyist of a classical

---

[5] Augustine, *Ep.* 87, 10. *CSEL*, XXXIV, 2, p. 406. *Contra Litteras Petiliani*, II, 83, 184, pl. XLIII, col. 316. cf. Ammianus Marcellinus (ed. Loeb), XXIX, 5, 15.

[6] Augustine, *Ep.* 84, 2. *CSEL*, XXXIV, 2, p. 293, on region of Setif ' sed cum Punica lingua, cuius inopia in nostris regionibus evangelica dispensatio multorum laborat, illic autem euisdem linguae usus omnium est '. cf. *Ep.* 209, 3. See note by author on this subject in *J.T.S.*, July-October, 1942, p. 188.

[7] A notable exception is the frieze, dated approximately to the end of the 2nd century A.D., found during the excavation of the theatre at Hippo (Bone). The frieze is cut in very flat relief, and the geometric designs, which form the greater part of the ornamentation, include many which were popular with the Berbers two centuries later.

masterpiece. In the larger Roman cities his attempts to imitate Roman sculpture were passable, but further away from the main centres of Romanization his copy became increasingly barbarous. Funerary monuments, found in more remote Romano-Berber towns, show little attempt to proportion the head of the figure to its body, or to make its feet face front, or its arms repose naturally. The relief of the carving becomes flatter, until the Roman citizen, whose memory the sculptor was being paid to perpetuate, shades into the Libyan god of the previous age. It is often differentiated from the latter only by a few parallel strokes on the body to represent a toga.[8]

At the time of the Roman occupation, however, Libyan art could claim no high level of achievement Libyan carvings in flat relief in stone can hardly be said to portray living figures. Chiefs, such as Retaten, whom the native artists may have tried to represent, remain stiff and hieratic, symbols of deity rather than once living beings.[9] The Libyan attempts at decorative design were little more advanced. Simple linear ornament, such as lozenges, chevrons, rosettes, spirals and chequers were sometimes stamped on their pottery or carved on burial steles from a remote period, but there is no parallel to the genius of Celtic art at the same period. Pre-Roman Libyan art can be assessed from fairly typical examples such as an uninscribed stele from Calama, for which a date in the 1st century A.D. may be suggested. This shows a figure holding a sacrificial cake aloft in his left hand. The figure itself is represented by a series of straight lines with a pointed oval for his head. A five-pointed rosette inscribed in a circle (symbol of the sun?) and resting on his head, has been marked out with a compass. The relief is never more than $\frac{1}{2}$ inch.

Imitation of Roman methods did not wholly supersede Berber ideas during the first three centuries A.D. The art of the conquerors, however, caught hold, and by the middle of the third century the inhabitants of the high plains of Numidia were representing Saturn (Baal-Hammon) in Roman dress, whereas previously the god had only been shown in symbol or by a geometric figure.

But in the 4th century a complete change seems to have taken place. Imitations of classical art fall into disrepute in the North African

---

[8] Dr L. Carton describes some of these more grotesque Romano-Berber sculptures which he found at Thuburnica near the present Algerian-Tunisian border. *Bulletin archéologique du Comité des Travaux historiques* (=*BAC*), 1908, p. 436.

[9] A. Vel, *Recueil de Constantine*, 1905, XXXIX, 204. The statue now stands in the courtyard of Constantine Museum.

PLATE I

(A) CARVED STONE FROM HENCHIR TENTILIA, THEVESTE

(B) SQUARE PILLAR FROM CHURCH AT OUED R'ZEL (CENTRAL ALGERIA)

Phs. W. H. C. Frend

PLATE II

FRIEZE OF CAPITOL AT TIMGAD
Ph. W. H. C. Frend

PLATE III

CLAY LAMP FROM 4TH-5TH CENTURY CHAPEL, HENCHIR SEFFANE
Ph. A. Berthier

PLATE IV

KABYLE DECORATED STORAGE JARS FROM SIDI AISSA
Ph. Ofalac

THE REVIVAL OF BERBER ART

countryside. Art becomes once more the business of the village woodcarver, and mason. One might quote as an example of the reaction against classical themes a carved upright of the chancel arch from a chapel at Henchir Tentilia, some 40 miles south of Theveste (Tebessa). A funerary monument of a husband and wife in Roman costume has been disfigured, the face smashed in, and the surface bearing the inscription planed down, while on the remaining three sides finely executed geometric patterns have been carved in successive panels. The technique and the designs, which include wheels, interlacing discs, and triangles, are strikingly similar to the woodwork carvings made by the Kabyles today. Another re-used stone bearing similar carvings found in the chapel at Henchir Tentilia is shown (PLATE I, A).

Further illustrations of the skill of the Berber craftsmen in the late Roman period may be found in carvings in stone or plaster which have been discovered throughout what might be termed the ' Berber fringe ' of Roman North Africa, from Asabaa in Tripolitania to Tigzirt in Kabylie. By far the largest proportion, however, of these sculptures has been found in buildings (mostly churches) in villages in southern Numidia, the territory between Constantine and the Aures mountains. These include carved oblong slabs shaped like the false doorway of the Bled-Guitoun, from chapels at Vazaivi (Ain-Zoui),[10] on the Djebel Djaafa near Mascula (Khenchela)[11], and Henchir bou Said,[12] square, sculptured pillars from Henchir Beguer,[13] Vegesela[14] (Ksar el Kelb) and La Maison des Parrasols near Mascula,[15] and stone and plaster carvings from churches, such as Ain Fakroun,[16] Bou Takrematem,[17] Morsott,[18] Sef ed Dalaa,[19] and Henchir el Ateuch.[20] Timgad, the

---

[10] This is now in the museum at Tebessa (illustrated under ' Pilastre ' by H. Leclercq in the *Dictionnaire d'archéologie chrétienne*, 1939, column 1031).

[11] Now in the church of the Sacré Coeur, Constantine, *CIL*, VIII, 17715.

[12] P. Monceaux, *Bulletin de la Société nationale des Antiquaires de France*, 1909, p. 210. Also at Kheret el Ousfane, see S. Gsell and H. Graillot, *Mélanges de l'Ecole de Rome*, 1894, XIV, 575.

[13] S. Gsell, *Musée de Tebessa*, 1902, p. 52, figure 4.

[14] P. Cayrel, *Mélanges de l'Ecole de Rome*, 1934, LI, 133.

[15] S. Gsell and H. Graillot, *Mélanges de l'Ecole de Rome*, 1893, XIII, 499 and plate VII.

[16] *CIL*, VIII, 18742.

[17] Illustrated in A. Berthier's and M. Martin's ' Les Fouilles à Bou-Takrematem ', *Revue Africaine*, 1936.

[18] Carved cornices now in Algiers Museum, See S. Gsell, *BAC*, 1901, p. 158-61.

[19] P. Monceaux, *BAC*, 1895, p. 76-77.

[20] M. Simon, *Mélanges de l'Ecole de Rome*, 1934, LI, 167.

largest town of southern Numidia, has also produced the finest examples of 4th-century Berber art—a marble frieze carved in shallow relief which served as a façade for the base of the raised cella of the Capitol (PLATE II), and the mosaic which lined the font in the baptistery of Bishop Optatus' cathedral. The colours in which the chevron design employed by the artist have been picked out—a medley of orange, green, and blue mosaic—show a particularly high standard of taste and workmanship.[21] That these patterns were inspired by the current ideas of the Berber peasants is suggested by the fact that the chevron and rosette motif were used equally for coarse pottery ornamentation, or the decoration of interior walls of buildings in Numidian villages. Rough clay lamps and burners have been found in the churches of Henchir Seffane and Ferme Gourdon (on the plain of Bou Lhilet, north of Timgad) on which the chevron has been chipped out so as to imitate basket-work[22] (PLATE III).

A second development in Berber art of the 4th century was a reversion to sculpture in very flat relief. In this, though the technique would appear to have been the same as that employed by the Libyans, the craftsmanship of the 4th-century Berber was far superior to that of his ancestors. Examples of this type of sculpture, representing Biblical scenes, such as Balaam beating his ass, or Noah's ark, have been found at Tigzirt[23] and at Oued R'zel[24] in southern Numidia. A stone table on which fish had been carved in similar style, also from Oued R'zel, was probably used for some form of funeral feast[25] (PLATE I, B).

The designs and methods of ornamentation outlined above have remained almost the only themes of Berber art to the present day. After the Arab invasions from the 7th to the 11th century, certain purely liturgic themes connected with Christianity, such as the dove or the peacock, or the Eucharistic vase, died out, but the tradition of geometric patterns remained. It has been pointed out that the lozenges, rosettes, arcades, and draught-board patterns which characterize the stone and wood carvings of early North African Moslem art, such as those from

---

[21] cf. A. Ballu, *Les Ruines de Timgad*, Paris, 1911, pp. 40–4 (photograph published).

[22] These and many other examples of rustic Romano-Berber ceramic art are now in Constantine Museum, where they await publication by their discoverers M.M. Martin and Berthier.

[23] P. Gavault, op. cit. 17 ff.

[24] A. Berthier, ' Fouilles dans une chapelle chrétienne à l'Oued R'zel ', *Revue Africaine*, 1936.

[25] A. Berthier, ibid.

XX

THE REVIVAL OF BERBER ART

the 10th century Kharedjite buildings of Sedrata and Ouarghla, bear no relation to the designs which later became popular in the Mohammedan West.[26] They do, on the other hand, find exact parallels in the Berber art of the Christian period. An illustration of how these same patterns have survived among the Berbers today may be given by a comparison between the decoration of the pottery from Numidian village sites as illustrated (PLATE III) and that on some modern storage jars in a house in the Kabyle village of Sidi Aissa (PLATE IV). The lines of the chevron pattern on the jars have become wavy and indistinct, but they are recognizable as a degenerate copy of the art of Bishop Optatus' mosaic, and of the lamps and incense burners of the southern Numidian chapels.

In contrast to the revival of native art in the countryside during the later Roman period, art in the towns and villas of the more Romanized parts of North Africa continued to show strong classical influence.[27] The same conventions and the same mythological scenes which were popular in the second and third centuries retained their favour in the sixth. Designs became more stylized, the horror of empty space more pronounced, and representations of living forms often degenerated into magical symbols, but classical art, like its counterpart, Latin rhetoric, found in the African cities an hospitable last refuge.

The technical skill of the Berber craftsman in the late Roman period, and the rich variety of the designs which he used, might suggest the existence of comparatively prosperous communities in the North African countryside in that period There are indications that this in fact was the case. In Herodian's time the African peasant population was reputedly numerous.[28] Evidence for the increase both of the area and wealth of the African villages from the 3rd century onwards is

---

[26] G. Marçais, *L'Art Musulman de L'Algérie*, Alger, 1909, p. 4–9, plates I and II. An extremely fine example of Kabylie wood carving dated to the 14th century, in which the craftsman has contrived to find room for nearly all the patterns typical of Berber art in the later Empire, is described by Prof. Marçais under 'Note sur une Coffre Kabyle, in *Revue Africaine*, 1927, p. 92–8.

[27] This subject has been dealt exhaustively by M.M. Poinssot and Lantier. See articles on 'L'église d'el Mouasset' in *BAC*, 1925, p. 172 ff., and 'La Chapelle de l'Evêque Honorius, in *BAC*, 1932–33, pp. 787–93. Also 'Les Mosaiques de la Maison d'Ariadne à Carthage', in *Monuments Piot*, XXVII, p. 28, and 'Les Mosaiques d'El Haouria' in the *Actes du Premier Congrès de la Fédération des Sociétés savantes de l'Afrique du Nord*, 1935, p. 183–206.

[28] Herodian (ed. Stavenhagen) VII, 4, 4, ' φύσει γὰρ πολυάνθρωπος οὖσα ἡ Λιβύη πολλοὺς ἔιχε τούς τὴν γῆν γεωργοῦντας.

to be found both in Numidia, and in the neighbouring province of Mauretania Sitifensis. Almost the whole area of Mauretania Sitifensis was included in great Imperial and private estates, peopled by groups of small tenant-farmers. A series of inscriptions covering the period 190–250[29] from the settlements of these Imperial coloni, shows that the bounds of their villages were being continually enlarged, and their buildings renovated and improved. At the same time, to the south and southwest, in country now parched and almost uninhabited, new areas of settlement were being opened up. These areas, particularly round Doucen, have provided evidence for their continuing prosperity in the next century.[30]

In Numidia there are no such precise indications, but the peasant population must have been very large. On the high plains each side of the chotts which lie to the north of the Aures mountains, are the remains of over 1200 farms and villages—almost one settlement every $2\frac{1}{2}$ miles. Round each well, even though the water there is brackish, there are signs of occupation in Roman times. Though the average size of the villages is not more than 15 to 20 acres, there existed also some great areas of settlement, such as Kherbet Bahrarous or Kherbet bou Addoufen the ruins of which extend nearly 100 acres. Much of the building must have taken place in the 3rd and later centuries. Churches and storehouses, two characteristic ruins in a Romano-Berber village, often stood on new ground. At Kherbet Bahrarous the writer found coins of Gallienus resting on the virgin soil, into which the foundations of a building which comprised both church and storehouse had been dug.[31] The level of prosperity in some of these villages, especially in the territory south of Tebessa, seems also to have been fairly high.[32]

---

[29] The best commentary on these inscriptions is J. Carcopino, 'Les Castella de la Plaine de Setif, in *Revue Africaine*, 1918, pp. 1–22.

[30] J. Carcopino, 'Sur l'Extension de la Domination romaine dans le Sahara du Numidie', *Revue Archéologique*, 1924, pp. 316–25.

J. Guey, 'Note sur le limes de Numidie et le Sahara au IVe siècle'. *Mélanges de l'Ecole de Rome*, 1939, LVI, 220.

[31] The probable prototype of the modern Berber 'tighremt', except that the place of the church has been taken by the mosque. Otherwise the plan is identical.

[32] Most of the buildings were of mud and stone construction, but in some villages very carefully hewn and dressed blocks were used in what appear to be ordinary buildings, e.g. at Tebessa Khalia two miles south of Tebessa. The growth of prosperous villages in the Hauran in the 4th century may perhaps be quoted as a parallel development in Syria.

XX

THE REVIVAL OF BERBER ART

The key to the comparative prosperity of the North African village in the late Roman period is the successful cultivation of the olive. In the 4th century North Africa was as famous for its oil as two centuries earlier it had been for its wheat.³³ In the first centuries of the Roman occupation prosperity lay in the wheat-producing areas of the Tunisian and Algerian river valleys, which were also those most open to settlement and Romanization; but in the 4th and later centuries the remoter parts of Roman North Africa, the high plains of southern Algeria, and the back-country behind the ports of Leptis Magna and Tripoli where native traditions had resisted the impact of Rome, became the centres of Africa's wealth. These were the best olive-growing areas, and the social change which resulted to the detriment of the Romanized town-dweller in the wheat areas should not be underestimated. Even in the Tell native villages grew up among the ruins of the former Roman cities and olive presses were built amid the debris of bishops' palaces and fora (e.g. at Thuburbo Maius, and Djemila).

One of the most obvious signs of a Romano-Berber village in central Algeria is the remains of an olive press. At Kherbet Bahrarous there are remains of 85 presses, and at Bou Takrematem, once a *municipium*, but in the late Empire a vast rural settlement, visible traces of over a hundred presses. Excavation revealed small buildings containing one or two presses, often accompanied by a silo in which grain was stored—suggesting that each family had its own installation. Very much larger oil fabrics, some housing as many as eight presses, are to be found on the plains south of Theveste, or on the borders of Tunisia, as at Bir Sgaoun and Henchir Brisgane. On some of these Christian symbols have been cut, thus indicating a date.³⁴ The style of construction of the oil presses also suggests that most are contemporary with the churches in the same villages. These are facts which imply a coincidence between the revival of Berber art and the comparative prosperity of the North African villages in the 4th century, and this applies particularly to the high plain country of southern Numidia, which was equally a centre of North African olive production, and a centre of the African

---

³³ Among other texts bearing on this, see :—
Expositio totius Mundi et Orbis (ed. Lumbroso), p. 80–1.
' Ab hac provincia, Africae regio dives in omnibus invenitur; omnibus bonis ornata est, fructibus quoque et iumentis, et poene ipsa omnibus gentibus usum olei praestat '.

³⁴ For instance, at Henchir el Gouma, and Henchir Khadem, between Cillium and Thelepte (Kasserine). P. Gauckler, *BAC*, 1897, p. 385

artistic renaissance. Both these developments may be associated with a Berber religious movement, the Donatist Church.

From the distribution map which can be constructed of Donatist and Catholic sees, and from literary evidence which has been amply borne out by archaeological discoveries, there is no doubt that Donatism had both its origin and centre in southern Numidia and was a religion which had a particular hold over the African country populations in general. It is clear too, that the inhabitants of the villages of southern Numidia from the 4th–7th centuries were as fervently Christian as their successors are Mohammedan.[35]

The village churches are very similar and suggest a common form of cult. All contain a martyr's tomb beneath the altar, and in many there is an additional coffin alongside holding relics. Biblical texts, often relating to persecution, were painted on the white plaster which covered the interior of the building. The Donatists considered persecution by powers of darkness whether in the form of the Imperial authorities, or of their Catholic rivals—an inevitable and necessary part of the Christian's life. Donatism was above all a religion of the Holy Spirit which stressed that the act of martyrdom was the highest form of sacrifice to God, and paid great heed to literal interpretation of the Scriptures. In many churches inscriptions bearing what are known to be Donatist watchwords have been found.

It has been shown how most of the examples of 4th–5th century Berber art have been found in Christian churches, especially in southern Numidia. It would, however, probably be a mistake to consider Berber art a religious art inspired by the needs of liturgy. One might interpret it as a popular art which finds its best means of expression in a religious setting. In North Africa popular movements in any cause have generally taken on a religious form, and one would expect the art of the people to be closely associated with their religious faith. Two examples of this association between Berber art and the Donatist Church may be quoted. The mosaic in the baptistery at the cathedral at Timgad already mentioned belongs not to a 5th-century monastery as previously supposed, but to a cathedral which was built almost certainly by the Donatist Bishop Optatus.[36] The latter was a picturesque and fanatical Donatist 'Mahdi', who held sway over southern Numidia

---

[35] Each Romano-Berber village in Numidia, hitherto examined, contains not one, but five or six chapels, just as a modern North African village may contain a number of mosques and koubbas, each for a separate brotherhood.

[36] E. Albertini, *CRAI*, 1938, p. 101.

XX

THE REVIVAL OF BERBER ART

for ten years before his execution for his part in Gildo's revolt in 398. At Mascula, on two of a group of five panels decorated with patterns similar to those found on stones from Vazaivi (Ain Zoui) and Henchir Tentilia there was carved the Donatist watch-word ' Deo laudes'.[37]

Donatist dissent and an artistic revival on the part of the Berbers were by no means incompatible. Both coincided with an upward trend in conditions in the African countryside, and may have expressed a growing feeling of independence on the part of the peasant towards the once all-powerful urban landowner. Donatism was a continuation of that school of African Christians which had always seen in the new religior a weapon by which the dominant Roman civilization in Africa could be attacked. This spirit, as illustrated in the works of Tertullian, prevailed in 3rd-century African Christianity. Those who held these views only became Donatists in the 4th century when Constantine supported the more moderate pro-Roman party among the African Christians, and took economic measures to prevent the extremists ever again exerting their influence within the Church. Those who became Donatists renounced all study of Latin literature as well as the more material aspects of Roman city life, games, circus, and theatre, as had African Christians in Tertullian's and Cyprian's day. The Bible became for them what the Koran remains for their descendants, the single source of all learning.

Added to the impetus which Donatism gave to the Africans' hostility to the cultural aspects of Roman civilization in Africa, the Donatist Church provided a focus for the economic discontents of the peasants. The latter had the means of prosperity, in their olives, barley, and flocks, but a disproportionate weight of the burden of Imperial taxation fell on their shoulders. The citizens who were responsible for obtaining the quota of taxes on pain of restitution from their own estates if they failed to do so, were unlikely to be sparing on the crops of the weaker men. The wealthier landowners were able to evade their obligations, but the laws of the Codex Theodosianus relating to 4th and 5th century North Africa paint a grim picture of the sufferings of the peasants at the hands of the tax-collectors. Moreover, the latter were often leagued with the richer landowner in plots to divide up the lesser men's estates.

---

[37] Gsell and Graillot, *Mélanges de l'Ecole de Rome*, 1893, XIII, 499-501. This same war-cry has been found on a number of other similarly carved objects from Numidian churches, e.g. Vegesela, Sef-ed-Dalaa, and Henchir bou Said. Iomnium (Tigzirt) and Vazaivi (Ain Zoui) also were both undisputed Donatist sees in the early 5th century.

On three occasions during the 4th century, the African peasants rose against Roman rule. Each time, contemporaries, or writers in the following century, such as Zosimus (IV, 16) were agreed that the causes of the revolts were a combination of fiscal oppression and hatred of the larger landowners. The same areas which have produced most examples of Berber art of this period, the Kabylie, and southern Numidia, were also the centres of the risings. Each time, in 345–46, in 371, and in 397, the Donatist Church supported the rebels, while the Catholics threw their weight into the scale of Roman authority. In all these periods of revolt, the Donatists, or at least the more fanatical among them, attempted to enforce a social programme resembling the primitive communism of the Early Reformers, and to redistribute land and inheritances among the peasants.

The revival of Berber art in the 4th century must be regarded against the background of these wider developments. It is one of the symptoms of the decline of Roman culture in North Africa; one of the explanations why North Africa is not romance territory; and why the river valleys of Tunisia and Algeria are littered with the ruins of once-flourishing Roman *municipia* while the Berber village in the Aures or Kabylie has survived. How far the parallel revival of Celtic art in Britain can be associated with any such series of revolutionary movements is uncertain. There are indications of a renewed interest in Romano-British religion in the same period. Temples are built in old Iron Age encampments; there is a harking back to Iron Age technique and ornamentation in pot-making; and it is possible that the populations of the downland villages in southern England increased. But this is scanty fare. These trends cannot yet be connected up. We have the clues as to what may have happened in Britain, but the substance of the story still eludes us.*

---

* An interesting series of Libyan and Romano-Libyan votive and funerary carvings is shown by J. Guey in his 'Kriba et à propos de Kriba', *Mélanges de l'Ecole de Rome*, 1937, LIV, p. 85 ff.

XXI

NORTH AFRICA AND EUROPE IN THE EARLY MIDDLE AGES

READ 8 MAY 1954

RECENT discussions about Mediterranean trade in the early Middle Ages have tended to be based on two main assumptions. First, trade has been regarded as trade between ports in the eastern and western parts of the Mediterranean. Secondly, as a result of this view, the attention of historians has concentrated on the advance of the Arab fleets in the seventh and eighth centuries, which disrupted regular commerce and temporarily diminished the importance of the trading cities of Italy and Provence.[1]

My object in this paper is to supplement rather than to dispute that point of view. North Africa played an important and sometimes a decisive part in the policies of Rome and Byzantium down to the middle of the seventh century. Apart from its strategic importance, it produced goods which were in constant demand among the Mediterranean peoples throughout this period, and which had to be transported by sea. These included grain for Rome, olive oil for use in the public baths and for domestic cooking, cleaning, and lighting, and marble from the quarries at Simitthu (Chemtou). In the Byzantine period, camels were

[1] Of the abundant literature, see H. Pirenne, 'Mahomet et Charlemagne', *Revue Belge de Philologie et d'Histoire*, i (1922), 77–86, and 'Un Contraste économique: Mérovingiens et Carolingiens', *ibid.*, i (1923), 223–35; also Pirenne's final statement in *Mahomet and Charlemagne* (Engl. tr., London, 1939). Discussed by E. Sabbe, 'L'Importation des tissus orientaux en Europe occidentale au Haut Moyen Age', *Rev. Belge*, xiv (1935), 811–48; P. Lambrechts, 'Les Thèses de Henri Pirenne sur la fin du monde antique et les débuts du moyen âge', *Byzantion*, xiv (1939), 513–36; R. S. Lopez, 'Mahomet and Charlemagne', *Speculum*, xviii (1943), 14–38, and D. C. Dennett, 'Pirenne and Muhammed', *ibid.*, xxiii (1948), 165–90: in addition the able reviews published in the *Journal of Roman Studies* (= *JRS*), by N. H. Baynes, xix (1929), 224–35, and A. Momigliano, xxxiv (1944), 157–8.

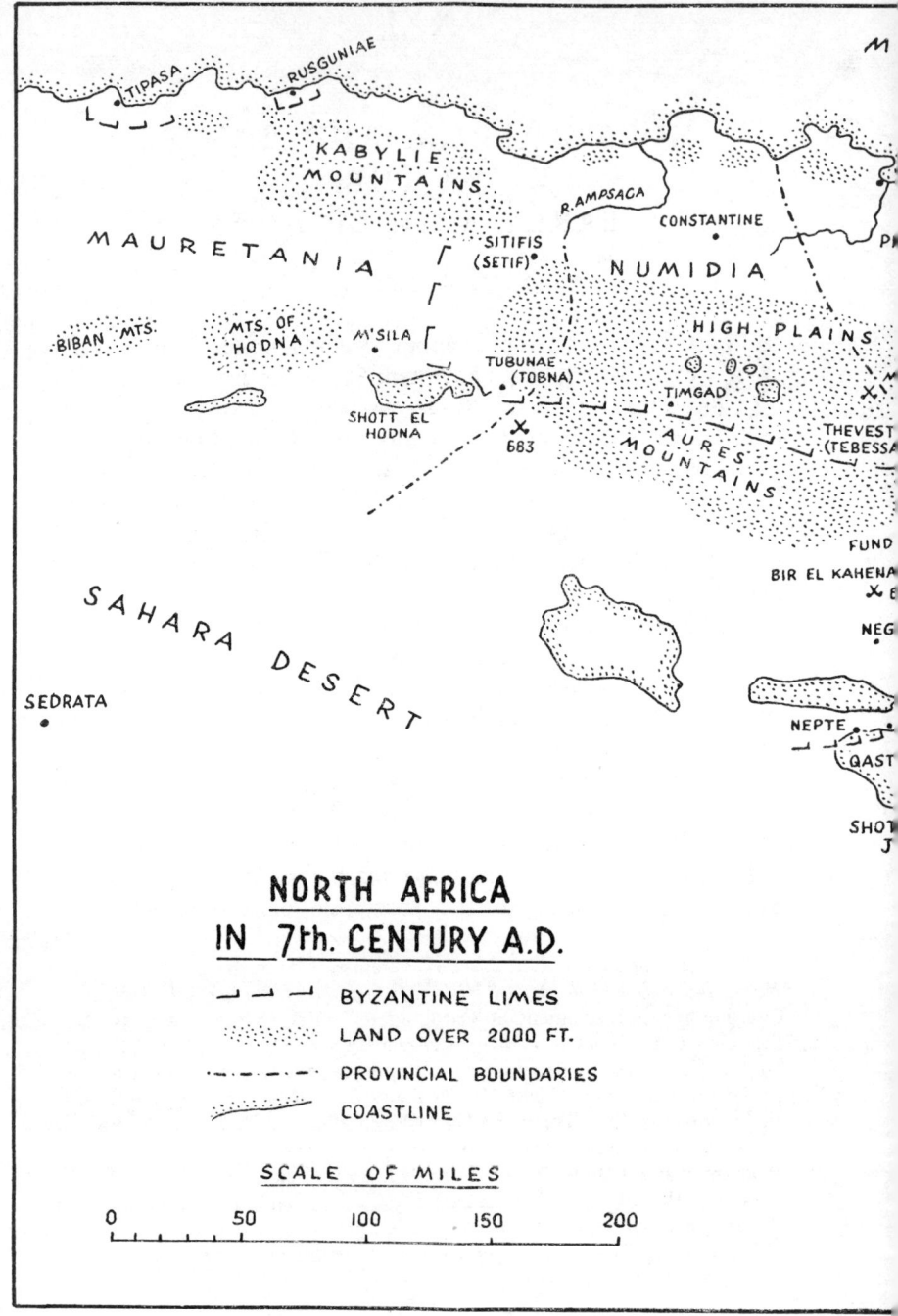

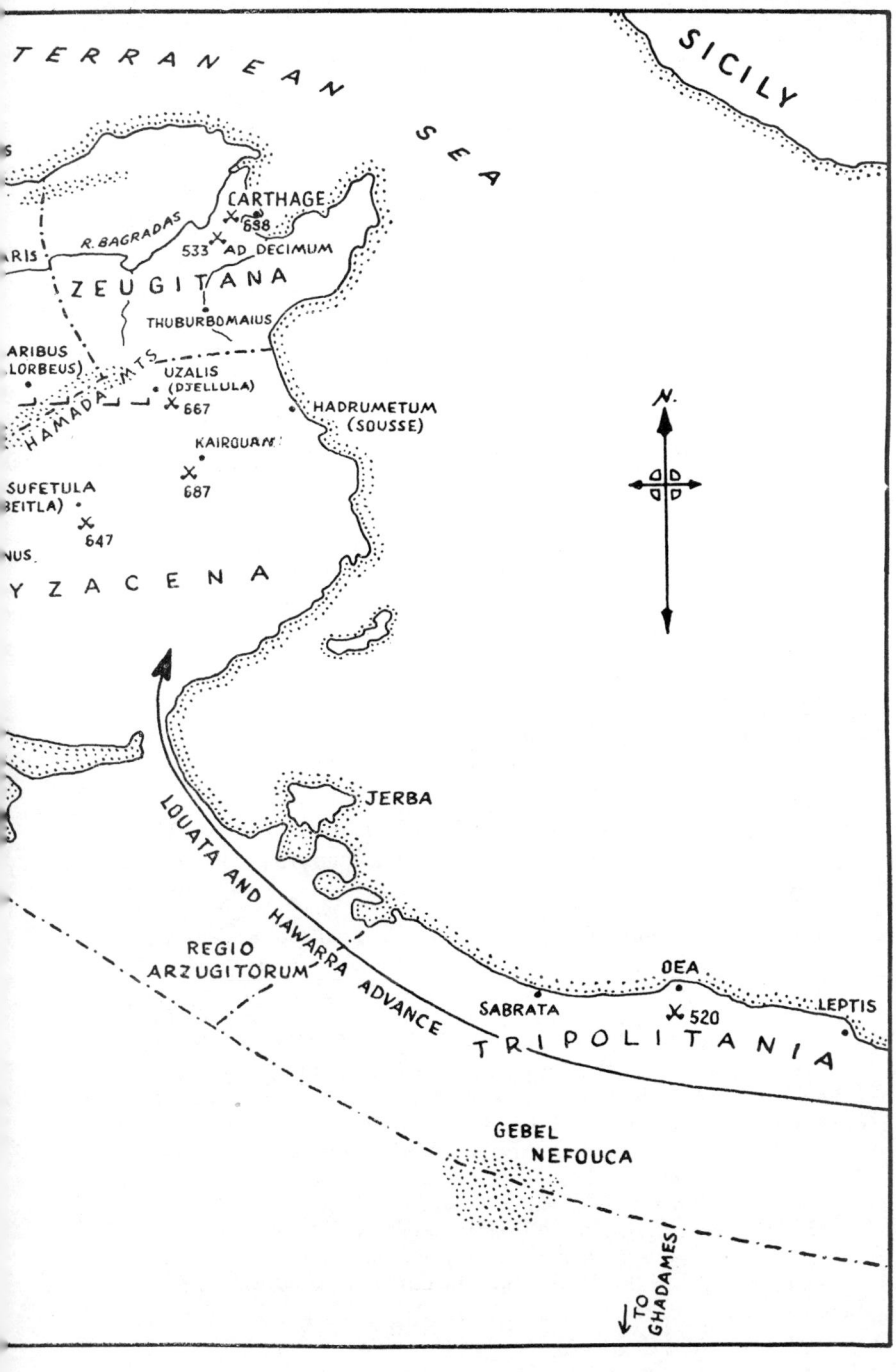

employed as draught animals in Gaul and Spain.¹ These exports, together with a teeming native population, placed North Africa in a key position among the western provinces of the Empire. It fully deserved the importance which successive emperors from Constantine to Heraclius attached to its loyalty.²

One may ask whether the depredations of the Arab fleets and the activities of the first Arab governors during the eighth century were sufficient in themselves to account for the decline of these links between North Africa and Europe. We know, for instance, from the sources used by the ninth-century Arab historian Ibn Abd al Hakam³ that even at the end of the Byzantine occupation Africa was still a vital source for the supply of olive oil to the Byzantine dominions. Two centuries later this was evidently no longer the case. In 879 we hear of a North African convoy carrying oil bound for Sicily being successfully raided by the Byzantines, but that the captured olive oil was not particularly welcome in Constantinople. In the intervening two hundred years the Byzantines had been obliged to seek for their supplies elsewhere, and the arrival of this windfall caused a glut on the market.⁴ Yet as D. C. Dennett has pointed out, neither in the Koran, nor in the sayings of the Prophet, nor in the acts of the first Caliphs, nor in the opinions of the Muslim jurists is there any prohibition against trading with the Christians or unbelievers.⁵ Naval operations in the Mediterranean by the Arabs appear to have been spasmodic and hardly calculated to disturb well-established commerce. Products from the Ummayad dominions such as papyrus from Egypt continued to reach Europe,⁶ and Venetian fabrics were worn at

---

¹ For camels, Gregory of Tours, *Historia Francorum*, vii. 35 (ed. Arndt in *Mon. Germ. Hist.*, *Scriptores Rerum Merovingicarum*, i. 315), and Julian of Toledo, *Historia Wambae*, 30 (ed. Levison in *M.G.H.*, *Scriptores Rerum Merovingicarum*, v. 525). In general, R. M. Haywood, *Economic Survey of Ancient Rome*, *North Africa* (Baltimore, 1938), and R. Cagnat, 'L'Annone d'Afrique', *Mémoires de l'Académie des Inscriptions*, xl (1916), 247–77.

² Ammianus Marcellinus, *Rerum Gestarum*, xxi. 7.2: 'Africa . . . ad omnes casus principibus opportuna'; R. Cagnat, *op. cit.*, pp. 250–1.

³ Ibn Abd al Hakam, *Futûh Ifrîqiya wa'l Andalus* (ed. and tr. A. Gateau. Algiers, 1942), pp. 44–5.

⁴ Cited from Pirenne, *Mahomet and Charlemagne*, p. 181.

⁵ D. C. Dennett, *art. cit.*, p. 168. On the desultory character of Arab naval operations in the western Mediterranean, *ibid.*, pp. 170–1.

⁶ *Ibid.*, p. 174. See also R. S. Lopez in *Cambridge Economic History of Europe*, ii. 275–7.

the court of Baghdad.[1] In North Africa itself the early Moslem governors such as Musa ben Nuçair (698–711) continued to strike a gold coinage of Byzantine style, an indication perhaps that they did not intend to obstruct commerce between their provinces and the rest of the world.

One must look, therefore, for other causes which contributed to the removal of North Africa from the European to the Middle Eastern orbit during the early Middle Ages. In the writer's view, the main factor in this process, and one which has previously been underestimated, was the impetus which the Arab victories gave to nomadism. The nomad and the transhumant gradually replaced the settled farmer as the occupier of the soil in the territories which the Arabs overran. In this process the supply of agricultural products, such as olive oil and grain on which trade between countries bordering on the Mediterranean depended, was gradually cut off. In no other area were the consequences more marked than in North Africa.

It will be recalled that from the end of the fourth century A.D. until the great Arab invasions of the seventh century, the most persistent threat which Rome (or the Vandal Kingdom in Africa) had to face along the southern and south-eastern *limes* of the empire had been confederations of nomadic tribes. These had gradually come to dominate the steppes that lay immediately beyond the Roman frontier. Ghassanids, Saracens and Arabs on the borders of Syria and Palestine, Blemmyes in the deserts on either side of the Nile valley, Louata in Cyrenaica and Austures in Tripolitania, all these were possible enemies who had either to be overawed or bribed into quiescence. They were an ever-present menace to the Byzantines, and the victory of the Arab armies all along this frontier was indirectly their victory.

These events destroyed the uneasy balance which had existed in favour of the farmer during the five centuries of Roman and Byzantine rule. Henceforth, for more than a thousand years, the nomad with his destructive flocks of sheep and goats was lord of the arid but once richly cultivated plains. The fruit and olive trees

[1] *The Arabian Nights* (ed. Lane. London, 1889), ii. 85. Cf. F. L. Ganshof, 'Notes sur les ports de Provence du VIIIe au Xe siècle', *Revue Historique* (1938), 28–37.

planted by the farmers in the Negev and Numidia were gradually cut down as firewood or nibbled away by goats. The desert returned.[1] The farmer was pushed on to the defensive whence he did not emerge until the assertion of European influences during the last century.

In North Africa the Arab invasions led to two important results. First, communications and also cultural influences which previously had centred on Rome and Constantinople now tended to flow from east to west along the inland desert routes favoured by the Arab armies. Cairo became the source of cultural and religious inspiration to the North African Moslem and has remained so ever since. From the point of view of trade, the chain of oases that stretch along the 29th parallel from Siwa to Khufra and across Fezzan to Ghadames became as important as the old-established Mediterranean ports, and the first generation of Arab leaders in the seventh century took care to impose treaties of subjection on these oasis inhabitants.[2] Secondly, the withdrawal of the Byzantine garrisons from the massive fortresses on the frontiers and in the interior of the African provinces, probably between 647 and 680, left the native farmer without adequate protection.[3] The Berber nomads moved in along the coastal plain in the wake of the Arab invaders. The sedentary population either withdrew to the mountains or fell under their domination. The landward advance of these nomadic tribes was of far greater immediate consequence in the history of North Africa than the fluctuating fortunes of the Arab and Byzantine fleets.

The course of events has been graphically described in the Berber tradition which Ibn Abd al Hakam drew upon.

> The Louata (he says) later split up and spread over this part of Maghreb (i.e. Tripolitania and Tunisia) until they reached

[1] Ibn Khaldoun, *Les Prolegomènes historiques* (tr. de Slane. Paris, 1863–8), i. 310. [2] Ibn Abd al Hakam, *op. cit.*, p. 57.
[3] The dating of this phase of the history of North Africa is obscure. There seem to have been some organized Byzantine forces in the field as late as 683, when Sekerdid the Roum is mentioned as the ally of the Berber leader Koçeila in battles against the Arabs (Ibn Khaldoun, *Histoire des Berbères*, ed. de Slane (Algiers, 1852–6), i. 211, 288). On the other hand, the important fortresses placed near the south Tunisian shotts, such as Tozeur (Thusuros) and Nefta (Nepte), seem to have been abandoned about 667 (L. Poinssot, *Bull. archéologique du Comité des Travaux historiques* (= *B.A.C.*), 1940, Séance de 27 mai, pp. v–ix).

Sousse. The Hawarra established themselves at Lebda and the Nefusa in the territory of Sabratha. The Rûm who were occupying these lands were forced to leave, but the Afariq who were subject to the Rûm remained, paying a tribute which they were accustomed to render to all who occupied their country.[1]

The Rûm were the Byzantines, and the Afariq the Latin-speaking Berbers. The great nomadic tribes of the Louata and Hawarra dominate the scene. The native inhabitants exchange subjection to a centralized and autocratic administration in favour of subjection to a nomadic host.

Let us now turn to the detail of these events, and follow out the fortunes of the native farmers who produced North Africa's most important single crop in late Roman and Byzantine times—olive oil.

The North African provinces were the chief source for the supply of olive oil to the western Mediterranean countries from the third to the fifth centuries, and they continued to be an important source until the end of the Byzantine occupation. Innumerable farms and villages containing olive presses of this period have been found all over the northern half of the African steppes. These latter extend in a broad band from the Babor and Biban mountains and the Shott el Hodna in the west as far as the Tripolitanian Gebel in the east. They include the Constantinian high plains which lie between the Aurès mountains and the coastal Atlas, and the great open expanse of central Tunisia. In Roman and Byzantine times they covered the southern part of the provinces of Mauretania Sitifensis and Numidia, practically the whole of Byzacena, and part of Tripolitania. The climate, except probably immediately south of the Aurès mountains and in some parts of Tripolitania where it has become drier, has not changed in historical times.[2] The rainfall over the most favoured areas is seldom more than twenty inches a year, and the more general average is between eight and fifteen inches. To some extent, the effect of this

[1] Ibn Abd al Hakam, *op. cit.*, p. 31. Cf. D. Oates, 'The Tripolitanian Gebel: settlement of the Roman period around Gasr ed-Dauun', *Papers of the British School at Rome*, xxi (1953), 113. The Hawarra were still in the area of Leptis in the eleventh century. See El-Edrisi, *Description de l'Afrique et de l'Espagne* (ed. R. Dozy and de Goeje, Leyden, 1866), p. 154.

[2] See S. Gsell, *L'Histoire ancienne de l'Afrique du Nord*, i (Paris, 1913), pp. 53–99, and A. N. Sherwin-White, 'Geographical Factors in Roman Algeria', *JRS*, xxxiv (1944), 1–10.

is offset by the presence of water-tables near the surface, but settled agriculture is always difficult. Drought and the salty nature of much of the soil has prevented the growth of an urban civilization based on mixed farming, such as developed in the Tunisian river valleys. This great area of country has always been the debatable land between nomad and settler. Its flatness and the vast expanses, coupled with the prevalence of drought, makes retrogression easy. Agriculture depends entirely on the natives' will to maintain the wells and irrigation channels, and that in turn depends on the amount of protection and encouragement provided by the administration.

In the first three centuries A.D. the Roman authorities applied a deliberate policy of settling the natives on the land. The movements of nomadic tribes were restricted, recalcitrants were expelled beyond the *limes*, penalties were imposed on sheep farmers who allowed their flocks to stray on to cultivated land.[1] Through decisions known as the *Lex Manciana* and the *Sermo Procuratorum* parts which had once been regarded as waste were leased to the native farmers on attractive terms.[2] By the end of the reign of Septimius Severus (A.D. 193–211) the whole of the high plains from the Hodna mountains to the gulf of Sirte had been protected from incursions from the Sahara tribes by a well-defended *limes* whose outlying forts, such as Messad, were placed at the furthest limits of the habitable steppe.[3] These measures were successful. For most of the third century Roman Africa and especially Numidia shared the distinction with Roman Britain of being a military backwater.[4]

The result was the steady growth of farming communities, living either as Mancian *coloni* on the great imperial or senatorial estates, or settled as farmer-soldiers (*limitanei*) near the forts on the frontier. Olives, whose trees drive their roots deep into the subsoil, were found to be the most productive crop, and enormous

[1] *CIL*, viii. 23956, l. 14 (Henchir Snobbeur).
[2] Best studied in Tenney Frank's two articles in the *American Journal of Philology* (= *AJP*), xlvii (1926), 'The Inscriptions of the Imperial Domains of Africa', pp. 55–73, and 'A Commentary on the Inscription from Henchir Mettich', pp. 153–70. See also J. Carcopino, 'L'Inscription d'Ain el Djemala', *Mélanges d'archéologie et d'histoire de l'Ecole française de Rome* (= *Mélanges*), xxvi (1906), 365 ff.
[3] Beautifully illustrated in J. Baradez' *Fossatum Africae* (Paris, 1949).
[4] Eric Birley, 'The Governors of Numidia', *JRS*, xl (1950), 68.

quantities were grown in places which to-day are desert. Archaeological evidence from Tripolitania,[1] Numidia,[2] and Mauretania Sitifensis[3] points to the middle or the end of the third century as the time when the villages began to expand and prosper. Their development is thus in direct contrast to that of the African towns. Their prosperity was, however, firmly based on the export of their oil, and when in about 350 the writer of the *Expositio totius mundi et rerum* declared that the province of Africa supplied the world with oil almost alone, he was not exaggerating.[4] We know, for instance, from St. Augustine that Italy depended on African oil for lighting,[5] and from other contemporary sources such as Symmachus and the *Codex Theodosianus* that this had the same importance as African wheat in the provisioning of Rome.[6]

A certain amount is known about the organization of these exports. The deliveries destined for Rome were handled by the state corporation of the *navicularii*. Evidence for eight groups who traded with African ports at the end of the second century has been found at Ostia,[7] and even earlier an inscription from Rome refers to an association of *mercatores frumentarii et olearii Afrarii*.[8] As Cagnat points out, the demands of Rome must have entailed in themselves a very large production of olive oil.[9] Landowners and the bailiffs of imperial estates in Africa seem to have benefited

---

[1] R. G. Goodchild and J. B. Ward Perkins, 'The Limes of Tripolitanus in the light of recent discoveries', *JRS*, xxxix (1949), 81–95, at p. 93.

[2] J. Guey, 'Note sur le "limes" romain de Numidie et le Sahara au IV⁰ siècle', *Mélanges*, lvii (1939), 178–248, pp. 221 ff.

[3] J. Carcopino, 'Les Castella de la plaine de Sétif', *Revue Africaine*, lxii (1918), 1–22.

[4] Ed. G. Lumbroso (Rome, 1903), p. 81; 'Paene ipsa (Africa) omnibus gentium usum olei praestat.'

[5] Augustine, *De Ordine*, i. 3.6 (Migne, *Pat. Lat.*, xxxii. 981). See E. Albertini, *Mélanges Paul Thomas* (Bruges, 1930), pp. 1–5.

[6] *Codex Theodosianus*, xiv. 15.3 (Ad Senatum, 15 April 397); Symmachus, *Ep.* ix. 55 and x. 55. See also the present writer's *The Donatist Church* (Oxford, 1952), pp. 47 ff.

[7] G. Calza, 'Il Piazzale delle Corporazione e la funzione commerciale di Ostia', *Bull. della Commissione archeologica communale di Roma*, xliii (1916), 187. On the dating, F. Walbank in *Cambridge Econ. Hist.*, ii. 47. A mosaic in the museum at Tébessa shows a galley laden with amphorae under sail, with an inscription *Fortuna Redux*.

[8] *CIL*, vi. 1625, 1626. Cf. ii. 1180. Dating probably end second century.

[9] Cagnat, *op. cit.*, p. 257. Also H. Camps-Fabrer, *L'Olivier et l'huile dans l'Afrique romaine* (Algiers, 1953), pp. 70 ff.

considerably from the export in bulk, for the exploration both of the Theveste (Tébessa) area and more recently of the Gebel escarpment of Tripolitania has revealed a close association of large-scale olive farms with lavishly-built houses often with private mausolea standing near by.[1] Those at Ghirza are an exceptionally fine example dating to the fourth century.[2] Much farther west, Madouros seems to have been one of the centres to which the Numidian olive crop at this time was sent for export.[3] The smaller producer also shared in the network of trade connections between North Africa and Europe. Oil lamps made in the comparatively unimportant settlement of Henchir es Srira in Byzacena have been found at Palermo, Syracuse and even Rome.[4] The itinerant merchant whom we learn from Synesius[5] acted as middleman between native producer in Cyrenaica and markets abroad probably had a similar rôle in North Africa. All available indications suggest that in the last century of the Roman Empire in the west, North Africa was one of the pivots of the economy of the whole Mediterranean area.

As Baynes points out,[6] the Vandal invasion of 429 brought this situation to a halt. Contemporaries such as Salvian or his African source regarded the Vandals as 'cutting off the vital channels of the Empire',[7] and for thirty-five years, from 440 to 475, the Vandal fleet was in control of the Mediterranean. The sack of Rome in 455 and the pillage of the Greek coastal towns which Procopius

[1] R. G. Goodchild, 'Roman Sites on the Tarhuna Plateau of Tripolitania', *Papers of the British School at Rome*, xix. 41–77. For the Theveste area, Commandant Guenin, 'Inventaire archéologique du Cercle de Tébessa', *Nouvelles archives des Missions scientifiques*, xvii (1909), 75–234.

[2] Illustrated by O. Brogan, *Illustrated London News*, 22 and 29 January 1955.

[3] See M. Christofle, *Essai de restitution d'un moulin à huile de l'époque romaine à Madaure* (Algiers, 1930).

[4] L. Hautecoeur, 'Les ruines d'Henchir-es-Srira', *Mélanges*, xxix (1909), 383 ff. The African abroad was proud of his title 'civis Afer negotians' (*CIL*, iii. 5230).

[5] Synesius, *Ep.* 52.

[6] N. H. Baynes in *JRS*, xix (1929), 234; also J. B. Bury, *The Invasion of Europe by the Barbarians* (London, 1928), pp. 123–4.

[7] Salvian, *De Dei Gubernatione*, vi. 12, 68; 'Postremo, ne qua pars mundi exitialibus malis esset immunis, (populi Wandalorum) navigare per fluctus bella coeperunt; quae vastatis urbibus mari clausis et eversis Sicilia et Sardinia, id est fiscalibus horreis, atque abcisis velut vitalibus venis Africam ipsam, id est quasi animam captivavere reipublicae.'

records[1] may be compared with similar activities by the Saracen fleet four centuries later. But the disruption of trade between North Africa and the rest of the Mediterranean was only temporary. Gaiseric's policy we know from the contemporary work of Victor Vitensis was directed against the Catholic Church and the senatorial landowners whom he identified with it.[2] It would be tempting to associate the decline of the coastal cities and the great olive farms of southern Tunisia and Tripolitania in these years with the effects of this policy, as well as with the raids of the nomadic Austures. But the two essentials for the maintenance of trade, the existence of an exportable surplus made available by the primary producers, and of merchants to handle it, were less seriously affected.

Archaeological evidence has added to what we know from literary sources about the condition of the people under Vandal rule. The detailed analysis of the *Tablettes Albertini*, discovered in a remote area sixty miles south of Tébessa, has provided interesting evidence for the comparative prosperity of the native farmers under the later Vandal kings.[3] They also testify to the continuity of Roman legal institutions and the Latin language at this time. The fifty wooden tablets which were unearthed are dated precisely to the latter years of King Gunthamund, A.D. 486–96. They were used as the deeds witnessing the buying and selling of small plots of land in the area. They show that at this period the district was known as the *Fundus Tuletianus*, and that its inhabitants were not petty nomads as they are to-day but *coloni* possessed of rights derived from the *Lex Manciana* which their ancestors had obtained three centuries before. In return for the payment of a rent in kind they had the right of 'freely enjoying, bequeathing and disposing of their holdings'.[4] They were

[1] Procopius, *De bello Vandalico*, iii. 22. 15.
[2] Victor Vitensis, *Historia persecutionis*, i. 4. Roman state organizations such as the *navicularii* evidently went out of business in this period. See C. Courtois, 'De Rome a l'Islam', *Revue Africaine*, lxxxvi (1942), 27.
[3] *Tablettes Albertini*, ed. C. Courtois, L. Leschi, C. Perrat, and C. Saumagne, published on behalf of the Government General of Algeria by Arts et Métiers, 1952. E. Albertini's article in the *Journal de Savants*, Jan. 1930, on the preliminary results of the discovery is still valuable.
[4] *Tablettes Albertini*, p. 84. In all the transactions the vendor is described as selling his rights to the purchaser in the formula 'ut [is] eam rem habeat, teneat, possideat, utatur, fruatur, ipse heredesve eius in perpetuum'. Cf. Tenney Frank, *AJP*, xlvii (1926), 166.

evidently not tied to a particular plot of ground. Their main assets as revealed in almost every transaction were plantations of olive trees and figs.[1] In contrast, caravans of nomads were something of a curiosity. The name *via de camellos* mentioned in one of the contracts indicates the existence of a track which these caravans would be using.[2] Their presence does not seem to have given rise to alarm. It has been pointed out that the language and legal formulae used on these records have similarities with those in use in Visigothic Gaul and Spain.[3] No more than in those countries did the presence of a Germanic barbarian kingdom break the continuity of Roman civilization and institutions.

These farming communities on the edge of the Sahara were producing olive oil which continued to be marketed in Italy in the first part of the sixth century. From Cassiodorus (*Variae*, iii. 7) we learn of the onward transhipment of cargoes of oil for filling lamps in churches from Italy to Salona,[4] and Procopius refers to communities of merchants from Constantinople living in Carthage.[5] There were also African irrigation experts resident in Rome at this time.[6] We gather too from Victor Vitensis that in the latter half of the fifth century communications between Africa and Spain were open once more,[7] and an interesting piece of evidence of how North Africa continued to play a part in the general Mediterranean economy comes from Tipasa, a small port some thirty-five miles west of Algiers. In the immense cemetery which grew up from the fourth century onwards around the tomb of the martyr Salsa were graves, attributable to the Vandal period, of travellers from Tripolis in Syria and from Italy.[8] They are reminders of the existence of long-distance travel and trade between Vandal Africa and the rest of the Mediterranean world.

In the last twenty years of Vandal rule a new factor was making itself felt in the settled areas. This was the pressure of a great con-

[1] *Tablettes Albertini*, pp. 201 ff.   [2] *Ibid.*, pp. 192–3.   [3] *Ibid.*, p. 175.
[4] Cassiodorus does not say that the oil came from Africa, but he uses the term *orcae* in which the African oil was shipped. I am accepting Pirenne's view (*op. cit.*, p. 93) that the merchant John who was supplying the bishop of Salona originally got his cargo from Africa (Cassiodorus, *Variae*, iii. 7; ed. Mommsen in *M.G.H.*, *Auct. Antiq.*, xii. 83).
[5] Procopius, *De bello Vandalico*, iii. 20. 5 and 16.
[6] Cassiodorus, *Variae*, iii. 53.
[7] Victor Vitensis, *Historia persecutionis*, iii. 29.
[8] L. Leschi, *Tipasa* (Algiers, 1948), pp. 48 ff.

federation of nomadic tribes known as the Louata, resulting from
their westward movement from Cyrenaica. It is not my intention
to add to the discussion as to when the camel became a menace to
civilized life in North Africa or when the Louata first enter on the
scene.[1] It is difficult to-day to accept the view that the camel was
actually re-introduced into Africa during the Roman occupation.[2]
It seems to have been used as a domestic beast in small numbers in
pre-Roman times, and to have continued as such, particularly in
the southern part of the country.[3] On the other hand, it would be
unwise to see in the raids of the Austurian tribesmen on Leptis
Magna and Sabratha in 364–5 a starting-point in the decline of
agricultural settlement in North Africa.[4] As one scholar has
pointed out, in Tripolitania the country remained Christian, populous and agriculturally prosperous for another century and a half.[5]
The same may also be said of the arid wastes beyond the southern
limes of Numidia.[6] This could hardly have been the case if the area
was dominated by hostile nomadic tribesmen. It seems evident
that the Vandals had had no experience in dealing with a camel-
mounted host when they rashly attacked Cabao's Louata tribesmen near Leptis Magna (*c.* 520). The defeat they suffered as a

---

[1] A study on the early history of the Louata is badly needed. They appear to have spread across the Gulf of Sirte from Cyrenaica during the fifth century until they reached the area of Leptis Magna *c.* 500. References to them have been collected by O. Bates, *The Eastern Libyans* (London, 1914), pp. 69–70.

[2] Suggested in a well-documented article by S. Gsell, 'La Tripolitaine et le Sahara au IIIe siècle de notre ère', *Mémoires de l'Académie des Inscriptions*, xliii (1933). See also the valuable discussion of the evidence by L. Leschi, *Rome et les Nomades du Sahara central* (Algiers, 1942), and E. F. Gautier's forceful pages in *Le Passé de l'Afrique du Nord* (Paris, 1937), pp. 210–14.

[3] Caesar, for instance, in *Bellum Africum*, 68.4, reports the capture of twenty-two camels which belonged to King Juba.

[4] Ammianus Marcellinus, xxviii. 6. Cf. Oates, *art. cit.* (above, p. 65, n. 1), p. 112.

[5] Goodchild, *art. cit.* (above, p. 68, n. 1), p. 65. On Christianity in Vandal and Byzantine Tripolitania, J. B. Ward Perkins and R. G. Good-child, 'The Christian Antiquities in Tripolitania', *Archaeologia*, xcv (1953), 57 ff.

[6] Late, perhaps even seventh-century Berber ruins have been located along the Oued Itel some thirty-five miles south of the *limes* at Gemellae, in country which is to-day desert (P. Blanchet, *B.A.C.*, 1899, pp. 137–40). See also J. Baradez, *op. cit.*, pp. 141–2.

result of the nomads' tactics has been graphically described by Procopius and treated as a factor which was to confront Belisarius.[1] The conclusion we might come to is that for the previous century the southern frontier zone garrisoned by native *limitanei* had continued to protect the rest of the country even though there was no longer a Roman military command.

The defeat of Thrasamund had important consequences. It marks the beginning of the long process as a result of which the Louata came to dominate the inland plains of North Africa. It showed, too, the weakness of the traditional infantry and cavalry tactics employed by the Vandals and the Byzantines when confronted by nomads. By the time Belisarius appears on the scene in 534, the Louata under their new king Antalas had been pushing their raids over the whole of the central Tunisian plain as far north as the Hamada mountains.[2]

After Belisarius, the Byzantine governors Solomon and John Troglita just managed to hold the Louata in check. But while they were able to inflict decisive defeats on the Berbers dwelling in the Aurès mountains they were never able to subdue the nomads. The Louata with their flocks and herds, their camels and their barbaric pagan rites form a permanent background to the pages of Procopius and Corippus. Moreover, the site of the battles fought by the Byzantines against them such as at Laribus (Hr. Lorbeus)[3] or near Theveste[4] and Sicca Veneria[5] show that the contested ground had become the great plain of central Tunisia. This was also one of the main olive-producing areas. Whereas Belisarius had fought the Vandals for the possession of Carthage, the military problem confronting his successors was to prevent the Berber nomads from dominating the immense and at that time fertile plain of Byzacena. We may attach a certain amount of significance to Procopius' statement that by 547 Byzacena was becoming depopulated and that some of its inhabitants were taking refuge overseas.[6] It may be at this period too that the great frontier area between Byzacena

---

[1] Procopius, *De bello Vandalico*, iii. 8. See also E. F. Gautier, *Genséric* (Paris, 1951), pp. 288–94. For the Louata's use of similar tactics against the Byzantines, Corippus, *Iohannidos*, ii. 93; iv. 598; v. 430; vi. 194; viii. 40.

[2] Procopius, *De bello Vandalico*, iii. 9, 3. Cf. Ferrandus, *Vita Sancti Fulgentii* (ed. R. P. Lapeyre), p. 30.

[3] Corippus, *Iohannidos*, iv. 22, 18. [4] *Ibid.*, iv. 21, 19.

[5] *Ibid.*, iv. 24, 7.

[6] Procopius, *De bello Vandalico*, iv. 23, 27, 28, 52.

NORTH AFRICA AND EUROPE

and Tripolitania known as the *Regio Arzugitorum* finally came under barbarian control. Its name was becoming forgotten by the time Corippus wrote (*c.* 550), and it was described as a desert.[1]

The death of Antalas seems to have brought a long respite. Archaeological evidence suggests that the natives' villages and small olive farms enjoyed a relative prosperity amid the general decay of the rest of the province. At Thuburbo Maius (Pont du Fahs) the Capitol and the forum were already in ruins when natives built their oil presses and squalid huts among the fallen masonry. The presses which were decorated with curious cabalistic symbols appear to have been their most prized possessions. Byzantine coins, including a hoard of *solidi* ending with Heraclius, were found in the ruins of one of the huts.[2] A further piece of evidence comes from Casae Nigrae (Négrine) on the edge of the Sahara one hundred miles south of Tébessa. There an *ostrakon* dated to 542–3 refers to a 'producer of oil' in the area.[3] On their side, the Arab writers on the conquest of North Africa speak of the first raiders riding through a land teeming with villages, and under the shade of olive trees all the way from Tripoli to Tangier.[4] There was a grain of truth behind this Eastern tale.

It seems clear that so long as the Byzantine administration continued to function, North Africa remained one of the main sources of supply of oil exported to Europe. This trade was both with the barbarian kingdoms and the Byzantine dominions. The importance of African olive oil to the latter in the first half of the seventh century is well attested by Arab tradition. The scene is near Sbeitla following the defeat and death of the Patrician Gregorius in 647 at the hands of the first Arab raiders. The Arabs demanded an enormous ransom, but soon to their amazement, a heap of gold coins began to pile up in front of Abd Allah ibn Saad's tent. He asked an Afariq (Latin-speaking Berber) how his people were able to pay this amount. The man scratched the surface of the ground and produced an olive stone. 'The Roûm,' he replied, 'have no

[1] Corippus, *Iohannidos*, ii. 146–8. Cf. R. G. Goodchild, *The Limes Tripolitanus* (II), *JRS*, xl (1950), 38.
[2] L. Poinssot and R. Lantier, *B.A.C.*, 1925, pp. lxxv–lxxxiv.
[3] E. Albertini, 'Ostrakon byzantine de Négrine', *Cinquantenaire de la Faculté des Lettres à Alger* (Algiers, 1932).
[4] En-Noweri (ed. de Slane, Appendix i to Ibn Khaldoun's *Histoire des Berbères*, p. 341). See also G. Marçais, *La Berbérie musulmane et l'Orient au moyen age* (Paris, 1946), p. 23.

olives themselves, and therefore they come to us to buy the oil, which we sell to them. This is the source of our wealth.'[1] The story is undoubtedly based on fact. There was a considerable quantity of gold in the hands of the natives at this period. An example is the hoard of one hundred and fifty *solidi* dating from Phocas to Heraclius Constantine (602-41) at Thuburbo just quoted.[2] The export of olive oil is the only obvious source of this wealth. Similarly, we know from Gregory of Tours that olive oil was being imported in considerable quantities into Merovingian Gaul via Marseilles throughout the sixth century.[3] Recently fragments of Mediterranean type amphorae unearthed on a Dark Age site at Tintagel, suggest that African oil may have been finding its way even farther afield.[4]

The arrival of the first Arab armies in 647 destroyed that element of security which the native farmers had enjoyed under the Byzantines. The immediate shock of their onset is perhaps indicated by the hoards of gold *solidi* ending with Heraclius which have been found in areas threatened by them, south of Kairouan, at Bou-Arada and near Carthage.[5] From the point of view of the cultivator there was little to choose between the Arab nomads and the Louata. Ibn Khaldoun noticed the similarity in the way of life of each. He says of these Berbers,

> They live in tents, they breed camels, and ride on horseback. They transport their dwellings from one place to another; they spend summer on the Tell (coastal mountains) and winter in the desert. They kidnap the inhabitants of the cultivated areas and they reject the rule of a just and regular government.[6]

It is perhaps small wonder that he records how following the withdrawal of the Byzantines the sedentaries rejected the rule of the Berber nomad queen, the Kahena, when the latter began wantonly to destroy the olive plantations in Numidia.[7] In the half century

[1] Ibn Abd al Hakam, *op. cit.*, pp. 44-5.
[2] Poinssot and Lantier, *art. cit.*, p. lxxxiii.
[3] Gregory of Tours, *Historia Francorum*, iv. 43. Also v. 5.
[4] Information from C. A. Raleigh Radford, F.S.A., who conducted the excavations.
[5] References to these hoards are given by Poinssot and Lantier, *art. cit.*, p. lxxxiii, n. 1.
[6] Ibn Khaldoun, *Histoire des Berbères*, iii. 179.
[7] *Ibid.*, i. 214. Cf. En-Noweri (ed. de Slane, p. 341).

of confusion that follows the death of Gregorius, it is clear that these nomads gradually predominated over the Byzantines and the native inhabitants.

But equally the Arabs who conquered the Kahena were a nomadic horde. Their campaigns against North Africa were conducted over immense distances from bases over five hundred miles away in Cyrenaica. Like the Kahena herself they fought for control of the plains, in particular for the broad channels of communication which traverse the continent between Constantine and the Aurès mountains, and south of these mountains along the edge of the Sahara desert. The site of the battles fought by the Arabs in this period, at Sbeitla, and Djelloula in Byzacena, Tobna southwest of the Aurès, and at Bir el Kahena on the edge of the plains of Tébessa, illustrate these aims. The old centres of settlement in North Africa, such as the Tunisian river valleys and even Carthage itself, hardly figure in the narratives of the Arab chroniclers. It is noticeable that Sbeitla in Byzacena and not Carthage is Gregorius' capital. The selection of Kairouan, isolated on a great, open plain, as the Arab capital indicated a future for North Africa which turned its back on the Mediterranean, to become instead the desert highway that linked the Arab centres of Cairo and Cordova.[1]

The Arab victories had as their immediate result the permanent control of the cultivated steppes by the Berber and Arab nomads. The advance of the Louata has already been described, but farther west other nomads such as the Matghara swept up from the Sahara to establish themselves among the villages and olive plantations which had grown up on the plain of Hodna and near Tlemçen.[2] The process by which the cultivator reverted to transhumance was slow and unspectacular. In southern Numidia one finds evidence for the gradual decay of villages rather than their violent destruction. The churches become smaller and more crudely built, and the last signs of dwellings are untidy fragments of re-used stone robbed from ruined buildings.[3] On the other hand some hill-forts, notably Tiddis fifteen miles north-west of Constantine, show

---

[1] See E. F. Gautier's excellent analysis of the campaigns fought between the Arab and Berber armies in the last half of the seventh century, *Le Passé de l'Afrique du Nord*, pp. 247–54.

[2] Ibn Khaldoun, *Histoire des Berbères*, i. 237.

[3] A. Berthier, *Les Vestiges du christianisme antique dans la Numidie centrale* (Algiers, 1942), p. 172 (decay of churches in Numidia).

traces of continued occupation until the eleventh century,[1] and similar evidence for the prolonged occupation of native villages in the Moslem era comes from Tripolitania.[2]

Near the end of the ninth century an Abbasid official, Ibn Yakoub, drew up a report on North Africa for his masters, and this shows that the country was still in transition between its Latin and Christian past and Islam.[3] Ancient Numidia was by this time inhabited by numerous nomadic tribes among which the Louata were prominent,[4] but here and there were prosperous villages and olive farms owned and peopled by Latin-speaking Christians; and there were even a few Roûmi who claimed to be the descendants of Byzantines. On the whole these were survivals, without much chance of renewal from outside. The foreign communities which he mentions were those of Persians and Arabs, and not Italians and Franks. Relations even with Sicily appear to have been subject to treaty rights rather than of free exchange.[5]

At the same time the direction and the character of North African trade were changing. We hear no more about the arrival of cargoes of olive oil in north-west Europe after the Corbie charters of 673 and 716,[6] though some undoubtedly continued to reach Adriatic countries through Venice. On the other hand, ports which had handled this trade, such as Sousse, were becoming famous for the export not of olive oil but of turbans and fabrics.[7] African oil was being sent eastwards, probably by caravan, along with almonds, saffron, nuts, leather and water bottles with which Africa was now providing the Moslem world.[8] At the very time when Carolingian Europe was tending to consolidate round the great inland waterways rather than the Mediterranean, the Berbers were themselves looking away from Europe. Some of the ports on the north coast were becoming disused, and their road links

[1] A. Berthier, *Tiddis, antique Castellum Tidditanorum* (Algiers, 1952), pp. 50–2.
[2] Goodchild, *The Limes Tripolitanus* (II), p. 37.
[3] Analysed by G. Marçais in 'La Berbérie au IXe siècle d'après el Ya'koubi', *Revue Africaine*, lxxxv (1941), 42 ff.
[4] Ibn Khaldoun, *op. cit.*, i. 233–4.
[5] Lopez in *Cambridge Econ. History*, ii. 276.
[6] Cited from Pirenne, *Mahomet and Charlemagne*, pp. 89–90.
[7] El-Idrisi, *Description d'Afrique et de l'Espagne*, p. 149.
[8] Al-Muqaddasi (writing c. 980), *Description de l'Occident musulman au IX–X siècle* (ed. and tr. G. Pellat. Algiers, 1950).

NORTH AFRICA AND EUROPE

with the interior blocked, while M'Sila on the steppes north-west of the Shott el Hodna became a flourishing centre for trade across the Sahara, and its merchants famed for their wealth.[1] In the desert itself, Sedrata the capital of the Ibadite Berber kingdom has now been revealed as a prosperous city, preserving something of the science of irrigation and artistic achievement which had characterized the African peasant in late Roman and Byzantine times.[2]

These developments may be associated with another movement which expresses clearly the change in the relations between North Africa and Europe which was taking place. All through the early middle ages Christianity was losing ground in North Africa, and Islam was in the process of becoming the predominant religion of the country.[3] So long as the Byzantines remained, the rival parties of Catholics, Donatists and Manichees struggled for pre-eminence. In 645 the Patrician Gregorius built the last dated church in North Africa on a mound outside Timgad in Numidia.[4] Next year an African council at Hadrumetum (Sousse) declared itself against the imperial *Ecthesis* favouring the Monothelete heresy. A century later, the African cultivators appear still to have been Christian, but the nomads were not. A source used by Ibn Abd al Hakam states that among the Berbers, 'most of the Beranes (sedentaries) were Christian, and a few of the Botr (nomads)'.[5] About half the Botr seem to have been Louata and the rest were composed of other nomadic tribes. This difference between the religions of the nomad and the cultivator may be traced into the Byzantine period. The native farmers including the *limitanei* were Christian, while the nomadic tribes mentioned by Procopius and Corippus were pagan. Cabao, Procopius records, was 'ignorant of the Christian god'.[6] The Louata of a generation or so later performed human sacrifices.[7] When the Arabs defeated the Berber nomads they imposed on them the *kharaj* payable by non-Moslems, under pain of

---

[1] El-Idrisi, *op. cit.*, p. 141. The merchants seem to have penetrated lands occupied by negroes and obtained gold from them.

[2] M. van Berchem, 'Uncovering a lost city of the Sahara', *Illustrated London News*, 31 Jan. 1953.

[3] W. Seston, 'Sur les derniers temps du Christianisme en Afrique', *Mélanges*, liii (1936), 101–24; Marçais, *La Berbérie musulmane*, pp. 32 ff.

[4] P. Monceaux, *Timgad chrétien* (Paris, 1911), p. 22.

[5] Ibn Abd al Hakam, *op. cit.*, p. 77; also Ibn Khaldoun, *Histoire des Berbères*, i. 215.   [6] Procopius, *De bello Vandalico*, iii. 8. 18.

[7] Corippus, *Iohannidos*, vii. 307–15; cf. ii. 109.

seizing their womenfolk if they did not pay.¹ Whether to avoid this or for other reasons the Berber nomads in their overwhelming majority accepted Islam, and by 710 were fighting under Arab leaders in Spain. For many tribes there was no intervening Christian phase. Ibn Khaldoun describes the important tribe of Sanhadja nomads in the neighbourhood of Sousse as having never been christianized.² Yet this particular area from the end of the third century until the middle of the seventh century had been completely Christian. Thus, the domination of the nomads both Berber and Arab entailed also the domination of Islam as against Christianity in North Africa. While the Arab historians never regarded the Afariq or latinized Berbers as enemies, and there is no formal proscription of Christianity, the Church became a minority religion. A slow but continuous decline set in, paralleled by the decline of the African villages. The Christian cemeteries of Ain Zara and En-Gila in Tripolitania show that it was not until the eleventh century that the religion of Donatus of Carthage and St. Augustine became extinct. Here the Hillalian invasions mark the end of the story.³

In these pages we have not been describing events peculiar to North Africa. Recent discoveries point to a rather similar development taking place in northern Syria following the Arab occupation. There too an amazingly prosperous rural society grew up between the mid-second and mid-seventh centuries in an area which until lately was almost deserted. Like their African contemporaries, these Syrian villagers were Christian and owed their prosperity to the careful cultivation of olive groves. As in Africa also, there was a tendency in Byzantine times for the regime of the single wealthy proprietor owning a large and well-built farm and oil press to give way to that of a farming community. At Qirk Bizze villas built earlier had been subdivided into tenements each equipped with its olive press.⁴ I have seen the same thing in the

¹ Ibn Abd al Hakam, *op. cit.*, p. 31. See also Marçais, *La Berbérie musulmane*, pp. 35 ff. Ibn Khaldoun, *Histoire des Berbères*, i. 214, states that the Kahena's followers (i.e. nomadic Berbers) embraced Islam after the battle of Bir el Kahena in 698.
² Ibn Khaldoun, *op. cit.*, i. 212.
³ Seston, *op. cit.*, pp. 121 ff. As late as 1140 the Aghlabids were using Christians or converts to Islam in the army and administration.
⁴ G. Tchalenko, 'La Syrie du Nord: Etude économique', *Actes du VIᵉ Congrès international des études byzantines* (Paris, 1950), ii. 389–97.

ruins of the Roman houses at Sbeitla and in the 'bishop's palace' belonging to the church of Cresconius at Djemila. We may expect evidence for similar developments on Tripolitanian sites.[1] The eventual abandonment of the Syrian sites was not due to their destruction by the Arabs, but to the more general economic changes brought about by the presence of nomads and the insecurity caused by the presence of the frontier between the Byzantine and Arab realms. The natives gradually abandoned their villages and reverted to subsistence farming and transhumance. As in Africa, failure to maintain hydraulic installations automatically involved the return of steppe conditions in which the nomad was supreme.

Thus in two widely separated parts of the Mediterranean the Moslem invasions brought about similar results. It is fair to ask why the administrations of Kairouan and Damascus allowed the situation of the cultivators to deteriorate. Probably part of the answer must lie in the psychology of the new rulers. The Arab armies were, as Ibn Khaldoun points out, plundering hordes. Their main object was booty, and they despised those who were not riders like themselves.[2] On the other hand, the barrages and irrigation channels on which the native cultivator depended for his crops needed constant maintenance, and this was only worth while in relatively stable conditions. The Romans, Vandals and Byzantines had provided this stability, even though their officials taxed the natives harshly. The Arab administration seems to have left them to the mercy of nomadic tribes,[3] and cultivator and nomad cannot occupy the same area continuously together. This is particularly the case where the cultivator's main crop is olives, whose trees take between ten and twelve years to mature. Apart from this, the break-up of rural society in North Africa during the eighth and ninth centuries was hastened by the ferocious civil wars caused by the Kharedjite schism in Numidia.[4]

[1] Sites such as Gasr ed-Dauun in Tripolitania where smaller buildings have been built in the ruins of large olive farms have been surveyed but not yet excavated.
[2] Ibn Khaldoun, *Prolegomènes* (ed. de Slane, i. 309). See also J. Schumpeter, 'Les Conquêtes musulmans et l'Impérialisme arabe', *Revue Africaine*, xciv (1950), 283-97.
[3] The Hafsids also used the Louata as collectors of tribute from other Berber tribes (Ibn Khaldoun, *Histoire des Berbères*, i. 233).
[4] See Gautier, *Le Passé de l'Afrique du Nord*, pp. 281 ff.

The relations, therefore, between North Africa and Europe during the early middle ages may be characterized as those of gradual but lasting estrangement. The clue to this situation is to be found less in the domination of the Mediterranean by the Arab fleet or in the deliberate policy of the Arab conquerors than in the progressive transformation of the way of life of most of those who had once been the primary producers. In addition, such articles as now left North Africa tended to travel by camel caravan along the oasis routes rather than by sea. These changes coincided with gradual changes in taste and outlook which were taking place in Carolingian Europe and which lessened the demand for the oil which North Africa produced.[1] As a result, the geographical factors which have always tended to shut the country off from contact with Europe, such as the high coastal mountains, the lack of navigable rivers, and limited communications between the ports and the interior, reasserted themselves. The Berbers turned their ambitions southwards to begin the great movement across the Sahara which was to lead eventually to the establishment of Moslem kingdoms in the Niger valley. In Europe the Latin Church abandoned the use of oil lamps for the humbler but equally efficient candle while the court of Baghdad enjoyed the pleasure of the trickle of that precious substance that continued to leave the olive farms of Tunisia.

[1] Lopez in *Camb. Econ. Hist.* ii. 261.

NUBIA

XXII

The Mission to Nubia:
An Episode in the Struggle for Power
in Sixth Century Byzantium

XXII

THE POLISH EXCAVATIONS AT FARAS have opened up a whole series of questions relating to the religious history of Nubia during the Byzantine period. The magnificent frescoes from the cathedral and graffiti associated with them have encouraged a series of detailed studies devoted to the liturgy and iconography of the Christian kingdom of Nobatia, and these have given rise to discussions concerning possible changes in religious allegiance by the rulers as between Monophysite and Melkite.[1] Was there, for instance, a Melkite succession of bishops which lasted between 999 and 1057 and included the Bishop Marianos (d. 1036) whose memorial has been found not at Faras but at Q'asr Ibrim?[2] Was there later on a Melkite restoration after an interval of Monophysite power?[3] These questions are not easy to answer. Regarding Bishop Marianos, for instance, his representation at Faras with his head uncovered and not wearing the Coptic *šamla* could be interpreted as pointing to a Melkite allegiance, while the emphatic description on his funerary stele that he was "orthodox bishop" and his designation elsewhere as "ἀπόστολος τοῦ Βαβυλῶν" (i.e. envoy from Babylon = Old Cairo) can be urged with equal force in favour of his allegiance to the Coptic Monophysite patriarchate at Old Cairo. Perhaps it may be worthwhile to remind ourselves of the circumstances in which Nobatia chose Monophysitism rather than Chalcedon in the first place in 542, and then to conclude by asking ourselves whether the evidence to hand shows any reason for so profound a change of allegiance.

What was happening in the Byzantine empire in the crucial years 542–543 when Justinian and Theodora sent apparently rival missions to Nubia? Was this an isolated incident or did it represent perhaps more powerful cross-currents in the political and religious life of the empire? Above all what factors lay behind the Nobatian acceptance of Monophysitism and rejection of the creed of the emperor? Our main authority for the events is John of Ephesus, a Monophysite monk who combined the confidence of Justinian and great success as a missionary in Asia Minor with that of titular Bishop of the Monophysite see of Ephesus. John records how in 541 an elderly monk named Julian in the entourage of the exiled Monophysite leaders at Constantinople persuaded the Empress Theodora that the conversion of the Nubians to Christianity was possible. The empress listened with enthusiasm. She was heart and soul in their camp, but could not keep her ideas to herself and told her husband Justinian. Justinian agreed, but made up his mind that any mission that penetrated Nubia must be orthodox Catholic and not Monophysite in persuasion. The creed of the Council of Chalcedon must be accepted throughout the whole of Christendom.[4]

There is enough evidence to show that Julian was well-informed. A year or two before, Justinian's general Narses had destroyed the shrine of Isis on the island of Philae near Aswan where the Nobatians foregathered for a yearly celebration of her cult, but Christianity had already made considerable progress in northern Nubia. The excavations of Professor Michałowski at Faras have revealed the existence of a Christian church and cemetery which originated in the

---

[1] See for instance, M. K r a u s e, Zur Kirchen- und Theologiegeschichte Nubiens = pp. 71–87 in Kunst und Geschichte Nubiens in christlicher Zeit (ed. E. Dinkler), Recklinghausen 1972, and S. J a k o b i e l s k i, Faras III, Warsaw 1972, especially pp. 143–6.

[2] See J. M. P l u m l e y, The Stele of Marianos Bishop of Faras, Bulletin du Musée National de Varsovie XII, 1971, pp. 77–84.

[3] As suggested by J a k o b i e l s k i, op. cit., p. 154.

[4] J o h n o f E p h e s u s, Hist. Eccl. IV. 6 (ed. E. W. Brooks, Corpus Scriptorum Christianorum Orientalium, Scriptores Syri III. 3, Louvain–Paris, 1935–6).

fifth century but had been overlaid by one of the royal palaces.⁵ On the island of Philae itself there was a rather crudely built church existing while the temple was still in use, and it is evident that the Monophysite Bishop Theodore of Philae had considerable contact with the leaders of Nobatian society. The speed of the success of Julian's mission once it arrived in Nobatia speaks for itself.

Many obstacles had to be overcome before that success was assured. Justinian fitted out a caravan with gifts, including gold for the Nubian court and baptismal robes for the converts. He urged orthodox bishops and civil authorities in Egypt to speed his mission on its way. But he had not counted on Theodora's boldness and cunning. She wrote to the military commander of the Thebaid bordering Nubia informing him (truthfully) that she and her husband would be sending a mission to Nubia, but added that the monk Julian would be in charge of the party! The good soldier was taken in. He accepted Theodora's instructions in preference to the emperor's which unfortunately arrived later. A richly equipped caravan was soon on its way to Nobatia. One may imagine perhaps its arrival at the ruler's palace at Faras, and its reception there. Had the Nobatians perhaps invited it beforehand? Anyhow Julian converted the king Silko, some of his nobles and the people, and even instructed them why Chalcedon was to be rejected and the One-nature creed accepted. After a few years, his work completed, he returned to Constantinople.

Justinian however did not accept defeat lightly. Julian was an old man and did not come back to Nubia. Theodore, Bishop of Philae, had his own problems north of the Nubian border, and to add to the Monophysite difficulties their patron Theodora herself died in 548. For nearly twenty years there was no renewal of a Monophysite mission in Nobatia. Meantime, the emperor's missionaries had been active further south in the kingdom of Makurrah, south of Nobatia, with its capital at Old Dongola, and by 560 that territory was as strongly orthodox and Chalcedonian as Nobatia was Monophysite. It blocked the way to Monophysite expansion southwards further down the Nile towards the kingdom of Axum.

Two factors saved Nobatia for Monophysitism, first the vigour and military prowess of King Silko, who about 550 moved across the Nile eastwards to defeat the Blemmyes and reduce their fortress of Ibrim; and the Blemmyes accepted the Monophysite faith. Secondly, the Monophysites at Constantinople at last appointed a successor to Julian. The presbyter Longinus was consecrated bishop of the Nubians by the Monophysite patriarch Theodosius shortly before the latter died in 566.⁶ He proved an even more resourceful and successful missionary than Julian. Apparently his qualities were well known in the capital, for every effort was made to prevent his leaving. Only in 568 did he succeed in escaping disguising his bald head with a wig as he crept out of the city gates, and after further adventures arrived in Nobatia.⁷

Longinus was the real apostle of Nubia. Except for three wretched years 575–578 when he found himself caught up in a web of intrigue in Egypt he remained in Nubia and his greatest triumph was the conversion of the southern kingdom of Alwah. He was invited thither by the ruler who was an ally of Nobatia, but first he had to surmount the difficult passage through Makurrah. The river was blocked to him but this time the Blemmyes were on his side. As John

---

⁵ K. M i c h a ł o w s k i, Faras, Die Kathedrale aus dem Wüstensand, Zurich 1967, pp. 28–31.
⁶ J o h n   o f   E p h e s u s, Hist. Eccl. IV. 8.
⁷ Ibid.

of Ephesus records, "But because of the wicked devices of him who dwells between us (i.e. Makurrah) I sent my saintly father to the king of the Blemmyes that he might conduct him thither (to Alwah) by routes further inland; but the people of Makurrah heard this also and look posted outs on the thoroughfares of the kingdom both in the mountains and the plains."[8] Longinus got through. Again he had brilliant success. Alwah, with its capital at Soba, was converted and within twenty years all the territory south towards Ethiopia had come into the Monophysite fold. Even in Makurrah the Chalcedonian creed was not destined to survive. Perhaps in the reign of the great Nobatian ruler Mercurios who united Nobatia and Makurrah into one kingdom in *circa* 700, the whole Nile valley south of the Egyptian border was Christian and Monophysite.

This story will be familiar, thanks to Professor Michałowski's excavations at Faras. It is worth re-telling and now placing in the context of Byzantine history as a whole. The first point to be noted is that the conversion of Nobatia was achieved as the result of a deliberate missionary policy. For us in the west, it comes naturally to think of missions to the non-believer in terms of *western* missionary expansion. But in the fifth and sixth centuries this was not the case, and the reason illustrates the profound difference of outlook that characterised eastern and western Christendom in Justinian's day. For the west, missions had often been defensive, aimed like those of Nicetas of Remesiana in the Balkans or Victricius of Rouen along the coast of the English Channel as a means of promoting the *pax romana*. Christianity was the means of taming barbarians and making them more willing to accept peaceful relations with the Roman Empire. The west never lost entirely this defensive view of missions. Even the famous missions of Pope Gregory the Great to the Arian Lombards and heathen Angles and Saxons were motivated by a desire to save as many souls as possible from the perils of the approaching end of the world.[9]

The Byzantine missions were also acts of policy, and designed to secure the goodwill and political alliance of those converted. Thus Constantine courted the Black Sea kingdom of Iberia whose geographic position made it an important buffer state between the Roman Empire and Persia.[10] The strategy, however, was expansionist. The Roman emperor in the eyes of his advisers and his subjects also was ruler of the secular world and that world coincided with Christ's kingdom. The object of the godly ruler must be to extend that kingdom and extend also the sway of orthodox Christianity even in those parts which lay technically beyond the political frontiers of Rome. The policy was made perfectly clear by Constantinus II *circa* 350 in a letter directed to the Ethiopian princes of Axum, whom Frumentius had converted to Christianity. "I think the whole race of mankind", says Constantius, "claims from us equal regard in this respect, in order that they may pass their lives in accordance with their hope, being brought to the same knowledge of God, and having no differences with each other in their inquiries about truth and justice."[11]

Constantius was writing with more than half an eye to discomfiting Athanasius, but the incident shows what was in the minds of the emperors at Constantinople. The mission to the Nubians must be seen in exactly the same context. It was part of a world Christian mission, executed through the destruction of the remains of poganism in Asia Minor and Syria on the

---

[8] Ibid., IV. 53.
[9] On the motives in the west for missions to the barbarians, see my The Missions of the Early Church, 180–700 A.D., published in Miscellanea Historiae Ecclesiasticae III, Louvain 1970, pp. 13–15 and 18.
[10] Socrates, Hist. Eccl. 1. 20.
[11] Cited by Athanasius, Apologia ad Constantium 59.

one hand, and missions down the Red Sea to the kingdom of the Himyarites and even to southern India on the other. Nobatia was ripe for conversion to Christianity. It was a border kingdom among whose subjects Christianity had made some progress. The continued existence of pagan sacrifices at Philae on Roman territory was a scandal, and the time had now come to extend to the Nubians the saving benefits of the knowledge of the Truth. On this both Justinian and Theodora were agreed. The mission to the Nubians was part of a well established Byzantine missionary strategy.

The problem arose, what kind of Christianity? And here one must mention very briefly the doctrinal issue that devided emperor and empress at the Byzantine court. In 451 at the Council of Chalcedon the bishops had decided after considerable prompting from the emperor that Jesus Christ, Word Incarnate, existed in two natures of Godhead and manhood, inseparably united, each sharing the properties or particular characteristics of the other. This formula had been arrived at through compromises. The Emperor Marcian had been determined to vindicate the position of the see of the capital whose patriarch had been humbled and outrageously treated by the patriarch of Alexandria, Dioscorus, two years before. He was also determined that the communion of Old and New Rome should be maintained. Only thus could the unity of the Roman Empire itself be upheld. The western Church represented by Pope Leo, however, insisted on the inclusion of the Two Nature doctrine in any Christological definition and that this should be binding on Christendom. The majority of the bishops at Chalcedon wanted to express the mystery of human salvation through the Christology of the great patriarch of Alexandria, Cyril (d. 444), namely that man was saved through the suffering of God in Christ incarnate. Somehow or other the whole Godhead must be involved in the salvation of mankind. The formula "in two natures" suggested that in some respects the Godhead in Christ was not complete and hence that mankind's salvation would be incomplete also. The most therefore they would agree to was that the Chalcedonian formula was valuable as a guard against the rival heresies of Nestorius and Eutyches, but not that it was the binding and unalterable legal, statement that Pope Leo required.[12] For the Egyptians who had seen their patriarchs deposed at the Council, and increasing numbers of Syrians, the formula was rejected on the grounds that there could only be one reality or nature in Christ, namely the divine nature: all His human characteristics were accepted as part of a voluntary self-emptying process (the *Kenosis*) which afforded the means by which he manifested himself to men. Christ could be "out of two natures" one, but not "in two natures" two. It was the same God-man who accepted the invitation to the feast at Cana and then performed the miracle of turning the water into wine.[13]

There is no doubt that this corresponded to the popular point of view wherever Christianity took root in the East. This explains more than any other single factor the success of Theodora's mission among the Nobatians. To primitive peoples who accepted Christianity, the attraction of the new religion was quite simply, the saving virtue of the Cross; its guarantee of salvation against demonic forces that assailed body and soul. The point had been made in heroic circumstances a few years before by one of the Christian martyrs after the fall of Najran in Southern Arabia to Jewish forces allied to the pro-Persian faction among the Himyarites. Southern Arabia

---

[12] See the account given, with references, in my The Rise of the Monophysite Movement, Cambridge 1972, Ch. I.
[13] Dioscorus' image cited by Makarius of Tkow writing *circa* 680, and quoted from E. A m é l i n e a u, Le christianisme chez les anciens Copts, Revue de l'histoire des religions XIV, 1886, p. 324.

in the century before Mahomet was the cockpit of rival Jewish, Persian and Ethiopian forces each trying to impose their rule and realigion on the people. In 523 the Christian stronghold at Najran had been stormed by pro-Persian Jewish forces. A young captive named Habsa was brought before the commander. She was asked to accept at least the Nestorian version of Christianity favoured by Persia, but she replied "You must know that not only will I not say that Christ was a man, but I worship and praise him because of all the benefits he has shown me. And I believe he is God, Maker of all creatures and I take refuge in his Cross".[14] The simple equation Christ, God was enough for many including the Egyptian bishops at Chalcedon; and that this could best be understood in One-Nature terms is clear from the crude analogy drawn by the Arab Christian leader al-Hareth in the 580's. He compared the "nature" of Christ to a bowl of the finest soup he would offer to a guest. You would not expect me, he said, to have it ruined by placing a dead rat (i.e. human nature) in it![15] Not surprisingly then, the Nobatian king, Silko, told Justinian's emissaries that though he was prepared to accept the emperor's gifts he could not accept his "wicked faith".[16] Only the Monophysite faith was truly worthy of the name "Christian".

Monophysite Christology therefore received among the Nobatians the same fervent welcome as it did among other peoples beyond the immediate control of the emperor. It was an immovable conviction and with Nobatia as an ally one may wonder why Justinian was not prepared to let matters be. There were three good reasons for this. First, however much a Byzantine emperor might be drawn personally towards a Monophysite interpretation of Christology, he could not denounce Chalcedon without forfeiting the ideal of the union of the two Romes, that on the banks of the Tiber and that on the Bosporus, and forfeiting also the rights of the see of Constantinople which had been guaranteed in the famous 28th Canon of Chalcedon. Secondly, the Monophysites also, however loyal they might be personally to the emperor, were not prepared to accept Chalcedon, and there was not room for two Churches within the framework of the Byzantine Church-State which included Christian kingdoms beyond the political frontier. Thirdly, the emperor realised that the successful conversion of Nobatia to Chalcedonian Christianity would strengthen enormously the position of Chalcedon in Egypt. Constantinople would never have to fear a Chalcedonian patriarch of Alexandria, but could be threatened again by a powerful Pharaoh like Cyril and Dioscorus had been in the fifth century.

All these issues were very much alive at the time when the conversion of Nobatia was being planned. In the west, the undreamt of progress of the Byzantine armies had reconqered first Africa, then Sicily and Dalmatia, and finally in 537 Rome itself. The Pope was once more a subject of the emperor, but the upshot had been the purge at Constantinople of Monophysite influence and the exiling and condemnation of the former Monophysite patriarch of Antioch, Severus. On the other hand, at long last the Monophysites were beginning to establish their own hierarchy. It had taken a very long time. There can be no greater mistake than to think that the Monophysite schism was an immediate reaction to Chalcedon like the Donatist schism had been to the after-

---

[14] Cited from A. Moberg (ed.), The Book of the Himyarites, Lund. 1924, p. CXXIV.

[15] Michael the Syrian, Chron. IX. 29 (ed. J. B. Chabot).

[16] John of Ephesus, Hist. Eccl. IV. 7. Silko said "If we deserve to become Christians we will follow after the Pope Theodosius [i.e. the Monophysitism of Severus of Antioch], whom because he would not accept the wicked faith of the king [Justinian] he expelled and ejected [from Alexandria]."

math of the Great at Persecution in North Africa in 312. There were riots but no altar was set up against altar in Alexandria in 451. The Monopysites were interested in the rejection of Chalcedon by the whole empire and so long as that hope remained, as it did until the death of the Emperor Anastasius in 518, there was no identifiable Monophysite hierarchy. In 482 the Emperor Zeno had written to the patriarch, bishops, monks and laity of Egypt stating that Christ must be confessed as One not Two, and though Chalcedon had not been explicity denounced, the Letter of Union or *Henotikon* was accepted by bishops both Chalcedonian and Monophysite throughout the Byzantine empire.

With the advent of Justin and Justinian and the ending of the Acacian Schism in 519 all this had changed. No less than 55 Monophysite bishops had been sent into exile and Monophysite monks had been dispersed from their monasteries[17]. By 530 the numbers of Monophysite-minded bishops in the Byzantine empire outside Egypt had dwindled practically to nothing. It was in response to this situation that Severus, the exiled patriarch of Antioch and now living in Alexandria, agreed in 531 to the ordination of lower clergy and the establishment therefore of a rival hierarchy to that of the emperor's church. At the end of 536, realising that so long as Justinian ruled there was little hope of Monophysitism becoming recognised officially, Severus took the final step of authorising the consecration of bishops.[18] In 542 the same year that saw the launching of Theodora's mission to the Nubians also saw the consecration of James Bar'adai and with him the founding of the "Jacobite" Syrian Church.[19] The dispatch of a mission to Nobatia independent of that of the emperor may by interpreted as further assertion of Monophysite independence. The Monophysites aided by their imperial patroness Theodora had not opted finally for a separate Church both within and outside the empire. This presented Justinian with a challenge to his entire concept of the imperial Church-State that he could not avoid.

Egypt moreover played a vital part in Justinian's aims. The patriarchate of Alexandria had been the main rival to the capital's claims to the leadership of Greek-speaking Christendom. Dioscorus, patriarch of Alexandria, had allowed himself to be called "ecumenical patriarch" half a century before the powerful patriarch of Constantinople, Acacius, had used this title. Alexandria, moreover, had initiated the conversion of Ethiopia in the time of Athanasius, and Christians beyond the southern borders of the empire in the Red Sea kingdoms looked to Alexandria for leadership. Somehow or other, the emperor must control Alexandria as firmly as he controlled Constantinople. For thirty years after the Council of Chalcedon, the emperors attempted to maintain a pro-Chalcedonian line of patriarchs in Alexandria. This failed, and the *Henotikon* of Zeno in 482 resulted in the acceptance of the Monophysite patriarchs who regarded themselves as the true successors of Cyril and Dioscorus. Even the religious revolution that accompanied the accession of Justin I had left the Monophysites in Alexandria undisturbed. In 537, however, a combination of events, including the reassertion of papal influence in Constantinople, the breakdown of discussions with the Monophysite leaders, and the realisation how close the capital could come to having a Monophysite patriarch itself, allied to a colleague in Alexandria, impelled Justinian to a radical change of policy. In 536 the Monophysite patriarch

---

[17] For the list see Chronicon ad ann. 846 (ed. Brooks and Chabot, Paris 1903, pp. 171-3).
[18] John of Ephesus, Life of John Bishop of Tella (ed. Brooks, in: Patrologia Orientalis 18, p. 39).
[19] Michael the Syrian, Chron. IX. 29 and see also, John of Ephesus, Lives of James and Theodore (ed. Brooks, in: Patrologia Orientalis, 19, p. 154).

Theodosius was convoked to Constantinople and deposed, and in his place Justinian appointed a Chalcedonian. Though this particular choice was a failure, the emperor persevered and in 540 a new and vigorous patriarch loyal to the emperor and his creed had been established in Alexandria. Moreover, whatever they might think privately no thought of rebellion crossed the minds of the citizens of the Egyptian capital. As the Monophysites ruefully admitted, the Alexandrians had a reputation for obeying the orders of the emperor.[20]

So next year at the moment when plans were being laid for the mission to Nubia, the situation was balanced on a knife edge. In Egypt the emperor's policy seemed to be succeeding as in all else he had set out to do. The restoration of Egypt to Chalcedonian orthodoxy was the final triumph. To extend the religion of the empire beyond Aswan to the Nubians would consolidate this victory, for here would be a Christian kingdom dependent on a Chalcedonian patriarch of Alexandria and through him to the patriarch of Constantinople. Church and state would alike be served.

For the Monophysites the situation was almost equally desperate. To lose Nobatia would compromise their already weakened position in Egypt. Perhaps Cyril could be interpreted in the manner which the emperor, no mean theologian himself, wished. Perhaps Dioscorus had been the villain that many of the Pachomian monks alleged him to be. For these reasons success in Nobatia was essential. In Theodora the Monophysites had a superb tactician dedicated to their cause. Her letter to the *dux* of the Thebaid proved to be one of the more decisive acts in the history of the Nile valley.

The results of Theodora's action have been unfolded gradually this last decade. Nobatia has been revealed as a Christian kingdom owing a good deal more to Byzantium than to Coptic Egypt. Even though Alexandria or Old Cairo remained the ecclesiastical focus for Nubia, Nubian and Greek remained the languages of Court and liturgy. Did the continuance of Byzantine influence also imply a change of religious allegiance at some time? The evidence is not conclusive.

Perhaps the memorial tablet to Bishop Marianos is a little too emphatic in its assertion of the bishop's Monophysite "orthodoxy" not to arouse suspicion. There is much research still to be done. Let this work, to which your Academy of Sciences, the West Germans, ourselves and many other nations have contributed so much not only unravel this mystery, but be a continuing bond between our peoples today.

---

[20] Severus of Ashmounein, History of the Patriarchs (ed. B. W. Evetts, Patrologia Orientalis 1, p. 467).

XXIII

The Cult of Military Saints in Christian Nubia

It is already evident that the salvage excavations undertaken by international teams in Nubia from 1963 onwards have thrown a great deal of light on the religious ideas of the inhabitants of Christian Nubia. In particular, the publication of *Faras* by Professor Kazimierz Michalowski and the studies on various detailed aspects of the frescoes by his students and Dr. Stefan Jakobielski's *A History of the Bishopric of Pachoras* (1972) have provided a framework for understanding how the Monophysite Church in Nubia was organized and what beliefs most inspired its members.

The discoveries made at Faras now await amplification from other sites. One of the most important of these latter is the cathedral-fortress of Q'asr Ibrim situated some 70 miles to the north, where the Egypt Exploration Society has been excavating since 1963. If Faras has produced the finest examples of Christian Nubian pictorial art yet known, the excavators at Ibrim have been fortunate in the number and variety of manuscripts they have found. It is clear that the cathedral at one time possessed a considerable library of liturgical, biblical and devotional works. These included some interesting fragments of eucharistic sequences, resembling the Liturgy of St. Mark, written in both Greek and Nubian, fragments of New Testaments in Nubian and Coptic and some Coptic translations of Patristic works. The devotional literature included fragments of two *Acta Martyrum*, both of military saints, namely, Saint Georgios and Saint Mercurius.

The discovery of the torn fragments of manuscript from the cathedral library on the floor of the cathedral itself, has already been reported[1], and a preliminary account of the contents of the manuscripts has been presented to international conferences[2]. Here, I would like to comment briefly on the two

---

[1] See W. H. C. FREND and I. A. MUIRHEAD, The Greek Manuscripts from the Cathedral of Q'asr Ibrim, Le Muséon, 89, 1–2, 1976, p. 43–9.

[2] The colloquium of the Commission internationale d'Histoire ecclésiastique comparée, at Warsaw, 25 June – 1 July 1978, and the Cambridge colloquium of the Society for Nubian Studies, 3–8 July 1978.

Acta Martyrum discovered and to see what relation had the Nubian cult of Military Saints to that practised in other parts of the Byzantine world[3].

Two pages written on both sides in Greek of the *Acta* of St. Mercurius were found during the excavations in January 1964[4]. The narrator is Athanasius, and he is telling his clergy (?) of his experiences as an exile under the emperor Julian, while staying at the monastery of Pachomius (Pachomius, of course, had been dead for some 15 years!). The first fragment opens with Athanasius describing how once he and Pachomius were studying (the word [?]) of God in the Scriptures, when unknown to Athanasius his companion had a vision of a angel standing by him, and pointing to a striking military figure who accompanied him. When Pachomius fails to recognize him, the angel reveals that it was none other than the general *(stratelates)* Mercurius. Pachomius asked why he was carrying a lance, and the angel replied that God had given him a spear so that he might cut down that (miscreant) Julian. A conversation between Pachomius and the angel follows (but is unfortunately too fragmentary for accurate reproduction). When the text becomes complete again *(verso* of first page), we find Pachomius explaining to Athanasius how Mercurius described his mission to him. Julian, the enemy of God was setting out to war against the Persians. »God sent me that I might strike him down because of his wickedness«, and »having been instructed, I went against him and executed justice on him as he deserved. And behold my spear *(longarikin)*. And the blood running off it is his blood. And now I have returned hither, having struck down and killed him in the midst of his great men *(magistriani)* and those of the foreigners and of the Persians.« The text again breaks off but the second page seems to be an immediate continuation of the narrative. Pachomius has now awoken and is highly delighted. Athanasius sees him laughing and thinks that he is laughing at him because of his predicament in exile. Pachomius reads Athanasius' thoughts, and in most honorific language, which occupies most of page 2 (recto) assures him that no such dishonourable thought crossed his mind, but that he had seen a vision of an angel of God standing by him and showing him the weapons of the martyr, Mercurius. Athanasius presses him for details (page 2, verso), asking him how he knew it was Mercurius. Pachomius recounts how the angel of God appeared to him, informed him how God had sent the martyr Mercurius to kill Julian

---

[3] See H. DELEHAYE, Les légendes grecques des Saints militaires, Paris, 1909, at pp. 96–101 on Mercurius.

[4] A general account is given here. The texts themselves will be published shortly (1978) by the author and his collaborators at Glasgow University on behalf of the Egypt Exploration Society in London.

and that he had shown him the spear with which he carried out the deed. The manuscript breaks off at the point where Pachomius is about to tell of his conversation with Mercurius himself.

The *Acta* were clearly in the form of a detailed narrative. They show the importance attached by the Nubian Church to the Alexandrian Patriarch, Athanasius, and to Pachomius, the founder of the Egyptian coenobitic monastic tradition. They provide a background to one of the most interesting of the Faras frescoes[5]. This is probably tenth century in date which would seem also to be the approximate period for our manuscript. It shows a figure of truly royal proportions, »wearing a kind of crown studded with coloured stones, set in pearls«, seated on a splendidly caparisoned charger adorned with rosettes of white pearls. The saint holds a long lance, with which he is bearing down on a crouching figure clothed in a white tunic. There are traces of blood on the ground and of a crown on the figure's head. A graffito written in ink under the horse's hind hooves, reads »Merkure« thus proving the identification with the martyr saint Mercurius.

A similar fresco from the church of Abd el Qadir also shows Mercurius mounted on horseback and spearing a fallen figure, which may now be presumed to be the emperor Julian[6]. Fragments of another, similar portrayal were found at Abdallah Nirqi, which van Moorsel dates to the end of the tenth century[7]. The discovery of Mercurius in similar guise in St. Antony's monastery in Egypt suggests a possible Coptic derivation for the story of Mercurius in Nubian hagiography[8].

The legend had travelled far since the emperor Julian was struck down by an unknown hand in battle against the Persians on 26 June 363. Ammianus Marcellinus' »No one knows whence«, the fatal spear-thrust came, provided ready openings for romance[9]. By 440 when the two Constantinopolitan his-

---

[5] K. MICHALOWSKI, Faras, (Wall Paintings in the Collection of the National Museum in Warsaw), Warsaw, 1974, p. 200–204, Plate 42.

[6] F. LL. GRIFFITH, Liverpool Annals of Archaeology and Anthropology (= LAAA), XV, 1926, illustration, XXXIV; and U. MONNERET DE VILLARD, Nubia Mediaevale, Cairo, 1935–57, III, Illustration CLXXVI.

[7] P. VAN MOORSEL, JEAN JACQUET, HANS SCHNEIDER, The Central Church of Abdallah Nirqi, 1975, p. 109–111.

[8] A. PIANKOV, »Peintures au monastère de Saint Antoine«, Bull. de la Soc. d'archéologie Copte, XIV, Cairo, 1958, p. 160, illustration IV.

[9] AMMIANUS MARCELLINUS, Res Gestae (ed. John C. Rolfe) XXV.3.6, »incertum inde«. Libanius believed he was killed by a Christian. For the Julian Romance in Christian historiography see TITO ORLAND, Studi Copti (= Testi e Documenti per lo Studio dell›Antichita‹ XXII), Milan, 1970, p. 87–145, and N. H. BAYNES, »The Death of Julian the Apostate in Christian Legend«, JRS XXVII, 1937, pp. 22–9.

torians, Socrates and Sozomen, were writing, it was believed that supernatural vengeance on the Apostate had played a part[10]. Byzantine legend, as represented in Pseudo-Amphilochius, *Life of Basil* (sixth century), and John Malalas, *Chronicle (Chron* XIII, Bonn ed., p. 332), fixed on Mercurius as executioner, a soldier allegedly martyred under the emperor Decius (249–251) for refusing to sacrifice to the gods[11]. There was little other relation to the Coptic/Nubian story. In place of Athanasius, we find Basil of Caesarea, and the commander of the saints who picks out Mercurius as executioner is not Christ, but the Theotokos, and the reason given for the execution is »his evil attitude towards my Son and Lord, Jesus Christ«. Basil awakes and hastens to the saint's shrine which is located outside Caesarea, and he finds the saint's body and his weapons up to then piously preserved, no longer there. Later he hears of Julian's death in battle.

An interesting link between Basil and Athanasius as the heroes of the story is provided by the writer of the *History of the Patriarchs of the Coptic Church of Alexandria,* Severus, Bishop of Asmounein, who compiled his work in the tenth century. Severus recounts the story of the slaying of Julian by Mercurius, and attributes the dream to Basil, but he sets the whole incident under the life of Athanasius[12]. At this time the Copts and even the Ethiopians praised the saint in legend[13], and the entry of the cult into Nubia from Egypt would seem to be the obvious route. If one considers that the Cappadocian Fathers do not seem to have attained the same popularity in Nubia as, for instance, St. John Chrysostom, it is easy to understand how the association of Athanasius and Mercurius was built up, while Athanasius' close friendship with Pachomius was well known.

The fragments of the second *Acta Martyrum* found in the cathedral at Q'asr Ibrim, illustrate perhaps a more direct Byzantine influence on the Nubian Church. St. Georgios is the classic military saint, associated with other heroes of the Diocletianic persecution, such as Demetrius or Theodore, or Sergius and Bacchus, legendary personages whose defiance of the emperor and consequent martyrdoms came to inspire popular veneration in epic Acta Martyrum throughout the Byzantine world but particularly in Syria and Palestine[14]. Faras produced one example, dating probably late eighth century

---

[10] SOCRATES, HE III.21.
[11] See TITO ORLANDI, op. cit., pp. 100–10.
[12] Patrologia Orientalis (ed. B. T. A. Evetts) 1907, I, pp. 419–20.
[13] See E. A. WALLIS BUDGE, Miscellaneous Coptic texts in the Dialect of Upper Egypt, 1915, p. 231ff, 256ff, 283ff and 1161ff (Ethiopian).
[14] For the spread of the cult of St. Georgios throughout the Byzantine east, see H. DELEHAYE'S »Les Origines du Culte des Martyrs, 1933, pp. 86 (Trachonitis) 175 (near Apamea),

because of the style, of a saint dressed in military costume with cloak over the right shoulder, knee-length tunic and armour-greaves and a leather belt[15]. He is holding a shield in the left hand and with the right, pierces a serpent's throat with a long spear. Unfortunately, the name of the saint is missing, as is also that of a third military figure mounted on a horse, like Mercurius, found on one of the pillars of the nave of the cathedral.

The Q'asr Ibrim fragments consist of six sides of parchment written in large Nubian-style majuscules, plus some small fragments. They are taken from the numbered pages of a codex, but judging from the size of the letters (0.55 cm) and the length even of the smaller version of the Martyrdom, the Acta could have occupied two entire volumes of Nubian.

St. Georgios has nothing to do with Egypt, and so the appearance of frescoues in his honour and Acta Martyrum underline the importance gained by the Byzantine military saints and their legends in Nubian religious life. Georgios is a Cappadocian in the army of King Dadianus (a corruption of »Diocletianus«?), a powerful autocrat who governed the world with the aid of seventy sub-kings. Georgios comes to the king's court with a view to receiving the insignia of a *comes* at his hand. He enters the royal city, but to his disgust finds it filled with statues of the pagan gods, and once in the king's presence he urges him and his lesser rulers to turn to Christianity. The king flies into a rage, orders Georgios to be tortured and eventually he dies. The archangel Michael restores him to life.

He confronts King Dadianus again, and then proceeds to perform miracles in his kingdom and baptize many of his subjects. Eventually, he comes to a great temple where there are idols representing Apollo, Heracles and other gods. These he challenges and after demonstrating their false and evil character, despatches them into the Abyss. The temple priests, however, seize and bring him bound before the king once more. In a renewed confrontation Georgios braves the king's wrath, refuses to sacrifice and is again condemned to death. Dadianus' queen, Alexandra, declares herself a Christian. She and the saint are executed along with 8,599 other martyrs[16].

---

184 (Diospolis – Lydda), 186 (Jerusalem, a monastery), 209 (Damascus, with Sergius), 213 (Edessa), 237 (Constantiople). For other Syrian sites, see WADDINGTON, Inscriptions de Syrie, 1981, 2092, 2126, 2142, 2158 and 2498. Other dedications have been discovered in Palestine and will be published by Y. E. MEIMARIS for the Hebrew University.

[15] K. MICHALOWSKI, Faras, p. 116, Pl. 14.
[16] Acta Martyrum II. Coptic, ed. J. BALESTRI and H. HYVERNAT, Paris, 1924, and translation ed. HYVERNAT, CSCO, 125, 1950, pp. 179–202. Greek texts ed. by KARL KRUMBACHER, »Der heilige Georg in der griechischen Überlieferung«, Abhandlungen der Kgl. bayerischen Akad. der Wiss., Phil. Hist. Kl. XXV. 3. 1911.

Three of the Q'asr Ibrim manuscripts relate to four distinct episodes in the saint's career. The first and most fragmentary, concerns Georgios' initial encounter with King Dadianus. He describes himself as an officer and a native of Palestine, and asks why he should be compelled to sacrifice to the gods. If Apollo sustained the heavens as the king believed, he was indeed a god, but if not . . . The king was angry and the second fragment concerns the saint's tortures after he had been ordered to be taken out of the city and tortured. The entire text of two sides of parchment is occupied by a description of a succession of bizarre tortures. The saint is thrown to the ground, lacerated, scourged with the thongs made from the entrails of an ox, and tortured by sharp nail-studded sandals being placed under the soles of his feet. The king orders Georgios to be suspended on a gibbet. Again, the saint is tortured, this time with long pointed instruments, and finally his skull is crushed by an instrument called a »crow«[17].

The Nubian text follows the Greek text of the Athens saga published by Krumbacher in 1911, very closely though with occasional changes of word (thus instead of τοὺς μώλωπας καὶ ζιβύναις ἀποξέεσθαι the Q.I. text reads, τους μωλωπας και τριχινοις ανασμηχεσθαι. The Greek is technical and, judging from other Nubian-Greek texts, far beyond the competence of a Nubian scribe to edit himself. It would follow that the Nubians were copying an independent but very similar text. The variations with the Coptic text are more numerous, the Q.I. text adding a torture with sharp points before the »crow« which the Coptic edition has omitted. A further incident preserved in the Nubian version, and not recorded in Krumbacher's »Interpolierte Normaltext«, relates to the cure of the saint's father from a fever, and Georgios' preaching of repentance to him.

The main episode, covered by two sides of the *Acta,* concerns Georgius' successful encounter with the gods Heracles and Apollo and his subsequent confrontation with King Dadianus and his minions[18]. Here, there is considerable divergence between the existing Greek, Coptic, and the Nubian *Acta.* In the Coptic, the evil spirit inhabiting Apollo's statue tries to defend himself. He had refused obeisance to Adam in the Garden of Eden and God had punished him by imprisoning him in a statue, and he called upon the saint to free him. Georgios, however, sees through this deceit, stamps his foot and the evil spirit descends to the Abyss. In the Greek *Acta,* the demon gives the

---

[17] παθηναι εν τη κεφαλη / κ(αι) το κορακι τυπτεσθαι / την κεφαλην αυτου / ωστε τον ενκεφαλον. Compare HYVERNAT, p. 182, lines 12–15; KRUMBACHER, p. 4–5.

[18] HYVERNAT, pp. 198–9; KRUMBACHER, p. 13.

same cause for his downfall but admits a long list of destructive acts against humanity, absent in the Coptic, and finally threatens Georgios with destruction. The Nubian *Acta* again follows the Greek more closely than the Coptic, and the text starts with the demon's threat to Georgios with destruction in the Abyss. The saint rebukes him, stamps his foot, the earth opens, and the evil spirit goes down »until the great day at which he would render account for the souls he had destroyed«[19].

The next episode on the other hand, follows the Coptic more exactly. The saint removes his belt, approaches the statue of Heracles and throws it down, ordering the remaining demons to flee from him if they wished to avoid his anger. The priests of Apollo, however, arrest Georgios, bind him and bring him before the king, angrily complaining about what had happened to »the great Apollo«. The king threatens »the thrice accursed« saint but tries to persuade him to sacrifice to the gods.

The frescoes and the elaborate Acta leave no doubt about the popularity of these Byzantine military saints in Nubia between the eighth and twelfth centuries. In the Church of Abdallah Nirqi, north of Abu Simbel, the frescoes, apart from the Theophany, were dominated by military figures on horseback. There, there is not only Mercurius and Theodore (?) but possibly Phoibammon and Epimachos, venerated in Egypt, Epimachos being associated with Pelusium and Phoibammon being represented as a crowned horseman in a chapel at Bawit[20]. Georgios is invoked with saints and prophets by a humble owner of a vessel from the monastery el Ghazali[21], and he is mounted on horseback at Abd el Qadir and accompanies another military saint, Demetrius, on a fresco from Abdallah Nirqi[22]. Why should this be? A suggestion arises from the association of both saints with the Archangel Michael, who appears at Faras, Ibrim, el Ghazali and on many other sites as one of the great protecting powers over the Nubian kingdom and its people. At Faras, Michael takes second place only to the Virgin and is shown on one fresco in a Nativity Scene[23] as her protector while he stands above the Angel

---

[19] καταβηθεις τα κατοχθονια / της Αβυσσου · εως της/ μεγαλης ημερον ης / δωσεις λογων περι των / ψυχων ων απολεσας · / (Punctuation and accents in the Nubian text).

[20] See VAN MOORSEL and colleagues, op. cit., p. 121–2, and 124.

[21] See P. L. SHINNIE and H. N. CHITTICK, »Ghazali – A Monastery in the Northern Sudan« (Sudan Antiquities Service. Occasional Papers, No. 5, Khartoum, 1961), p. 98 (Fig. 38, No. 86).

[22] Abd el Qadir, see U. MONNERET DE VILLARD, Nubia Mediaevale IV, illustration CLXVV, and for Abdallah Nirqi, see P. VAN MOORSEL, »Gli scavi olandesi in Nubia« (= Acta del VIII, Congresso Internacional di Arqueologia cristiana), Barcelona, 1972, p. 594, Illustrations 7 and 8.

[23] K. MICHALOWSKI, Faras, p. 31.

Gabriel at her side in a second[24]. In a third, he flanks the Virgin with Gabriel at her other side[25].

It is interesting that the galloping figure of Mercurius was identified at Faras at first as Michael. He is the human counterpart of the archangel. The latter was represented on a fresco also as mounted, the commander of the heavenly forces casting the fallen angels into hell. Invariably, he is a stern military figure, protector of governors and soldiers, guardian of the Gates of Heaven. But he is also the guardian of the military saints themselves. In the *Acta Sancti Georgii* he raises the saint from the dead and sustains and encourages him in face of King Dadianus' threats. The military saints, therefore, link the heavenly with earthly examples of Christian prowess. They become the human representatives of Michael, providing protection to the Christian armies of the kingdom of Nubia as they themselves are protected by angelic forces. The Nubian armies, it need hardly be said, in the tenth and eleventh centuries were formidable representatives of Christianity vis-a-vis the Moslem emirs of Egypt. The direct connection between the military saints and the army can be shown by an inscription on a lintel of a barracks on a site between Tripoli and Apamea in Syria[26]. It reads – Μητ(ATON) τ(οῦ) ἁγ(ίου) Λογγίν(ου) κ(αὶ) τ(οῶ) ἁγ(ίου) Θεοδώρ(ου) κ(αί) τ(οῦ) αγ(ΙΟΥ) Γεοργ(ΙΟΥ). τ(οῦ) Γλώ(ἔτος?) The military saints epitomised the military virtues and these were particularly apt in Nubia, cut off from the rest of the Christian world and often threatened with attack from its northern Islamic neighbour.

There was, however, the more general protection against militant powers of evil, illustrated by another fresco from Abdallah Nirqi, showing three military saints mounted either side of an anchorite and each spearing a dragon with his lance. On another, the donor of a fresco cries κυριλεσον (kurie elieson) invoking the aid of a giant mounted figure that dominated the scene[27]. Clearly, at this church the cult of the military saints came second only to that of Christ and His angels.

How the cult of St. Georgios centred on Diospolis (Lydda) in Palestine from the sixth century and particularly popular from that time onwards in Palestine and Syria, spread to Nubia is unknown. Abu Salih mentions several altars and churches in honour of the saint existing in Egypt in the thirteenth

---

[24] K. MICHALOWSKI, Faras, Die Kathedrale aus den Wüstensand, 1967, Tafel 64–5.

[25] K. MICHALOWSKI, Faras, Die Kathedrale aus den Wüstensand, Tafel 24–5.

[26] See R. P. MOUTERDE, Syria, IX, 1928, p. 167, Dating probably to 524–525, and used for troops on the way to defend the frontier against the Persians.

[27] P. VAN MOORSEL, art. cit., p. 594 and Illustration 7.

century[28]. One Coptic manuscript of the *Acta Martyrum* comes from the monastery of al-Baramous and dates to 1293 AD[29]. But, the surviving Nubian fragments seem at this stage to have more in common with existing Greek *Acta* than they do with the Coptic. There is a greater degree of verbal similarity between the Nubian and Greek versions. However, transmission of the cult via the Coptic Church can obviously not be ruled out, though direct Byzantine/Syrian influence as in some other aspects of Nubian religious art and liturgy seems more possible in this case. The cult of the military saints provides perhaps a further instance of the close resemblances of Nubian religious life with that of the remainder of the Byzantine world, during the Classical period of Nubian Christianity.

This contribution is dedicated to Erich Dinkler, Honorary DD of Glasgow University, whose scholarship has so abundantly illustrated how archaeological science can throw ever greater light on the New Testament and the history of the early Church, and whose enthusiasm had added so much to the study of Christian Nubia.

---

[28] ABU SALIH, ›Churches and Monasteries in Egypt‹ (ed. B. T. A. EVETTS, Oxford 1895), folios 45a, 64b, 73b, 75b, 81a, 87a and 93a.

[29] HYVERNAT, op. cit., p. XI, where other MSS are also listed.

XXIV

RECENTLY DISCOVERED MATERIALS FOR WRITING THE HISTORY OF CHRISTIAN NUBIA

CHANCE discoveries have been among the 'uncovenanted blessings' that have fallen to the study of new testament times and the early church. The finding of the Isaiah scroll by a shepherd boy in the judaean desert in 1947 led to the greatest discovery in biblical studies of all time, that of the Dead Sea scrolls and the essene monastery of Kharbet Q'mran. Similarly, the recovery of the gnostic library of 48 separate books from a christian cemetery at Nag-Hammadi, not far from Luxor, in 1946, has thrown a wholly unexpected light on the complex of beliefs and attitudes of orthodox christianity's great rival during the second and early third centuries, gnosticism. Recently, professor Morton Smith has made the boldest claims on behalf of a 'secret Gospel of Mark' used apparently in Alexandria in the second century AD. An extract from this gospel he found in the library of the monastery of Mar Saba near Jerusalem, quoted in a letter which may be attributed correctly to Clement of Alexandria circa 190 AD.[1]

Some of the discoveries made since 1960 in the area of the middle Nile once occupied by the christian nubian kingdoms have been equally surprising. In 1960 the egyptian government obtained the help of UNESCO and thence of a number of international teams to salvage as much as possible of the material remains of the successive civilisations that had occupied the stretch of the Nile valley from Aswan to the third cataract. They were destined to be flooded beneath the waters of lake Nasser formed through the building of the high dam of Aswan. The work, however, of the international teams like that of those who researched into the Dead Sea scrolls rested on a long tradition of scholarly endeavour. Long before Faras and its frescoes became famous the salient features of nubian christianity were known and many of the main sites had been surveyed.

[1] H. M. Smith, *The Secret Gospel*, (New York/San Francisco 1973), *Clement of Alexandria and a Secret Gospel of Mark* (Harvard 1973).

The reconstruction of the life and thought of any vanished civilisation depends on the historian's ability to combine literary with other forms of evidence. The progress that has been made towards understanding medieval nubian christianity has depended on there being some literary sources to which the archaeological discoveries could be related. For the conversion of Nubia to christianity, the monophysite historian John of Ephesus (died c 585) has left a near contemporary, if strongly biased, account of the rival missions sent to the court of king Silko of Nobatia, the northern of the three nubian kingdoms, by Justinian and Theodora in 542.[2] Probably christianity had already begun to penetrate Nobatia. There was a bishopric at Philae on the frontier with Egypt, and Theodora's mission may have owed something of its success to the help of Theodore, the bishop there, who was an ardent supporter of the monophysite cause.[3] The victory of Silko over the still heathen Blemmys commemorated on an inscription from Kalabscha around this date confirmed the Nubians in their choice of faith.[4]

John of Ephesus gives some impression of conditions in Nubia during the sixth century. His information about nubian history is supplemented by incidents incorporated in the account of the coptic-monophysite patriarchate at Alexandria, compiled in the tenth century by Severus of Asmounin under the title of the *History of the Patriarchs of Alexandria*.[5] Though some of the details of the intervention of the Nubians in egyptian affairs during the mid-eighth century for the benefit of the coptic patriarch Michael may be legendary, Severus left the impression of a nubian kingdom governed by powerful monarchs

---

[2] John of Ephesus, *HE*, ed E. W. Brooks, *CSCO, SS*, 3 (1924) III, iv, pp 6-8, 45-53.
[3] See L. P. Kirwan, 'Prelude to Nubian Christianity', *Mélanges offerts à K. Michalowski* (Warsaw 1966) p 126, and [W. Y.] Adams, ['Post-Pharaonic Nubia in the light of Archaeology'],2, *J[ournal of] E[gyptian] A[rchaeology,]* 51(Oxford 1966) p 172. Theodore's influence is demonstrated by a coptic text in the temple of Dendur in which the priest, Abraham, states that he set up a cross there which he received from Theodore. Abraham stresses that he did this on the orders of the nubian king Eirpanome. The date is either 22 January 559 or 574.
[4] Silko attributed his victory to 'God' (θεός) while the defeated Blemmys had to swear on their idols (εἴδωλα) to keep the peace. For the inscription see *CIG* 3, 5072 and J. B. Bury, *History of the Later Roman Empire* (London 1923) 2, p 330, note 1. Silko cooperated with the byzantine general Narses, and the date could be as early as 539, when the byzantine treaty with the nubians was abrogated. This had left open the temple at Philae for annual celebrations by the pagan nubians.
[5] Published in *PO* 1, 5 and 10.

Recently discovered materials for writing the history of christian Nubia

based on Dongola.[6] These were well capable of defending themselves against the muslim armies of Egypt and had a number of lesser kings subordinate to them. One of these rulers, king Mercurios, is now known to have been the founder of the cathedral at Faras in 707. In 836 the *History* tells of an embassy sent by king Zacharias and headed by his son Georgios to the caliph of Baghdad, which resulted in a commercial treaty between Egypt and Nubia.[7] This was an important event in nubian history for it demonstrated that Nubia counted throughout the muslim world: both rulers connected with the embassy are recorded also among the inscriptions found at Faras. It may be significant that the great period of nubian prosperity typified by the complex of churches and official buildings at Faras and the finely decorated christian pottery of the classical period of nubian art dates from this era.[8]

The later periods of nubian history are only sparsely recorded in the arab chronicles. Events, however, like the raid by Saladin's brother, Shams ed Doula on Q'Asr Ibrim in 1173, and the last known offensive operations by the Nubians against muslim Egypt, consisting of the attack on the Red Sea port of Aidhab in 1272 by king David[9], have been preserved. A generation later, however, a Fung muslim dynasty was established in the kingdom of Makuria at Old Dongola and a tablet commemorated the conversion of the church (in fact the royal palace) into a mosque.[10] It was assumed that after the death in 1323 of Kudanbes, the last known christian nubian king of Dongola, christianity declined rapidly in favour of islam.[11]

Literary evidence provided just enough outline of nubian history to make sense of the archaeological remains which confronted the antiquities services of Sudan and Egypt after the formation of the anglo-egyptian condominium in 1899. Thence to 1960 knowledge of christian

[6] *History of the Patriarchs*, ed B. T. Evetts, 1, cap xviii, *PO*, 1, p 144.
[7] *Ibid* 1, cap xx, *PO*, 10, pp 505-7. See G. Vantini, 'Le Roi Kirki (Georgios) de Nubie a Bagdad: un ou deux voyages?', in *K[unst und] G[eschichte] N[ubiens in christlicher Zeit]*, ed E. H. Dinkler (Recklinghausen 1970) pp 41-9. The journey is authenticated also in the contemporary chronicle of Dionysius of Tell Mahre: *Chronique de Michel le Syrien*, ed J. B. Chabot (Paris 1903) 3, pp 90-4. The wealth and magnificence of the nubian embassy was a matter of wonder.
[8] Abu Saleh, [*Churches and Monasteries in Egypt and some neighbouring countries*], ed and trans A. J. Butler and B. T. Evetts (Oxford 1895) p 295.
[9] Mufazzal ibn Abil-Fazail, *Histoire des sultans mamelouks*, ed E. Blochet, *PO* 10, p 375.
[10] See Adams 3, *JEA* 52 (1966) p 152. The information that the 'church' was the royal palace I owe to professor K. Michalowski.
[11] Thus, P. L. Shinnie, *Medieval Nubia* (Khartoum 1954) p 7.

nubia accumulated steadily through thorough surveys of sites and the excavation of selected areas. One major discovery was the extraordinary tenacity of the byzantine legacy, even though direct contacts between nubian kingdoms and Constantinople must have been limited to occasional trading contacts and embassies. Griffith's publication in 1913, for instance, of the first nubian documents to be discovered, revealed that the nubian language was written in greek characters but included some coptic and nubian letters to represent non-greek sounds.[12] In addition, eleventh and twelfth century inscriptions cut in comparatively good greek were found, and on some of these there were traces of byzantine commendatory prayers for the dead.[13] The *Euchologion Mega* was being used in nubian liturgy between 1000 and 1200 though it was not used in coptic Egypt. These discoveries confirmed statements by arab chroniclers that the Nubians, though 'jacobite' christians used greek as well as nubian in their liturgy.[14] Evidence also came to light of an episcopal organisation and of monasticism, though the latter was not as pronounced as in Egypt. The nubian court ceremonial and organisation was also conducted on byzantine lines as shown by the use of medieval byzantine titles, such as *Eparchos*, *Primicerios* and *Protodomesticos* in nubian texts.[15] Nubia had clearly been a cultural outpost of Byzantium which retained even more links with this aspect of its origins than other areas of byzantine mission such as Ethiopia and Armenia. By the outbreak of the second world war enough was known about Nubia for the archaeologist Ugo Monneret de Villard to collate into a comprehensive outline a history of christian Nubia from the seventh to the fourteenth century in his *Storia della Nubia Cristiana*, published in 1938.

Thus, when a large part of Nubia was threatened with destruction enough possible lines of research existed to challenge the skill of international scholarship. By far the most important site proved to be Faras,

---

[12] F. Ll. Griffith, 'Nubian Texts of the Christian period', in *AKPAW*, Phil. Hist. Klasse 8 (Berlin 1913) and in a British Academy lecture, 'Christian Documents from Nubia', *PBA* 14, (1928) especially p 14.

[13] H. Junker, 'Die christliche Grabsteine Nubiens', *Zeitschrift für agyptische Sprache*, 60 (1925) pp 111–48, and J. F. Oates 'A Christian Inscription in Greek from Armenna in Nubia', *JEA* 49 (1963) pp 161 et seq, and his conclusion that in the eleventh and twelfth centuries 'Greek was alive and widespread' in Nubia, p 171.

[14] Thus, Abu Saleh, p 272.

[15] See U. Monneret de Villard, *Storia della Nubia Cristiana* (Rome 1938) cap 20, and the writer's 'Nubia as an outpost of Byzantine cultural influence' *Byzantino-Slavica*, 18 (Prague 1968) pp 319–27.

Recently discovered materials for writing the history of christian Nubia just over the sudanese border on the west bank of the Nile. Its significance had long been realised by the Sudan antiquities department, and two large churches had already been uncovered, one of which had contained painted frescoes.[16] It was, however, the polish team led by professor Kazimierz Michalowski which discovered the cathedral below the great mound that dominated the site. Thanks to him the magnificent frescoes that covered the walls layer upon layer were salvaged and identified, and now, intimately studied, provide the means for a further and more detailed understanding than before of the religious history of medieval Nubia.[17]

First, there is the sheer magnitude of the find. Some 400 inscriptions and 169 frescoes, including palimpsests were uncovered.[18] The completion of the cathedral by bishop Paulos in 707 in the reign of king Mercurios was recorded on two fine inscriptions in greek and coptic.[19] Mercurios was already known from the *History of the Patriarchs*, and by the monophysite writer John the Deacon as king of Dongola, whom the Nubians knew as 'the new Constantine' in true byzantine style.[20] Under him the two kingdoms of Nobatia in the north and Makurrah round Dongola had united, and the Faras inscription provided further proof of his achievement and authority.

The inscriptions also proved that the cathedral had been the seat of the metropolitan at least until the twelfth century. In a niche in one of the walls was found thirty-one lines of inscription written in black ink listing twenty-seven bishops who ruled between 827 and 1169, recording the length of their episcopate in years, together with the month and day of their death. It was drawn up in greek probably originally near the end of the tenth century and then added to, and there were some entries in coptic and nubian.[21] This in itself was a discovery of the greatest importance, because it enabled an accurate chronological framework to be established without which archaeology can only deal

---

[16] F. Ll. Griffith, *Liverpool Annals of Archaeology and Anthropology*, 13 (1926) pp 66–93, recording discoveries made in four years' work, 1910–13.
[17] See [K.] Michalowski, *Faras*: [*Die Kathedrale aus den Wüstensand*] (Zürich 1967) a commendably rapid and fascinating publication of six season's work.
[18] I am accepting this more conservative estimate communciated to me by W. Y. Adams. For a higher figure of 'about 500 inscriptions , see [S. Jakobielski 'La Liste des Eveques de Pachoras'] *Travaux* [*du Centre d'archeologie mediterránéene de l'Academie polonaise des Sciences*], 3 (Warsaw 1966) p 152.
[19] [S.] Jakobielski ['Some new data to the History of Christian Nubia as found in Faras' Inscriptions',] *Klio*, 51 (Berlin/Wiesbaden) p 500.
[20] *History of the Patriarchs*, part i, cap xviii, PO 1, p 144.
[21] *Travaux* 3, pp 153–70, at p 154.

23

with approximations. At Faras, however, ecclesiastics used elaborate methods of dating, including the 'era of Diocletian' (AD 284), 'from the beginning of the world', the 'cycle of Alexandria' and 'the Ethiopian era' ('from the birth of Christ'): on the tombstones of some of the bishops of Pachoras there would be a combination of two or more eras.[22] In addition, some of the *acta* of the bishops were included on inscriptions. For instance, bishop Cyros, the fifteenth bishop of Faras, who ruled for thirty-five years, from 866-902, made considerable alterations in the cathedral and was the first bishop to be described as 'metropolitan bishop'.[23] The nubian church was shown, like its coptic neighbour, to have been monastic oriented, some bishops being described as 'abbot', and two as 'archimandrite'. Promotion from monastery to bishopric seems to have been in the ordinary course of affairs.

In addition, the frescoes commemorated some of the rulers of Nobatia and occasionally members of their families, high court officials and senior monks. All these were represented as being protected either by Christ or the Virgin or a saint, usually Michael.[24] Information derived from inscriptions associated with the frescoes established the dates of the rulers Georgios I, who as a prince had gone to Baghdad on an embassy, and who died in 920 after a reign of fifty-six years, and Georgios II (969-1002). The prominence given to the queen-mother among certain groups of royal personages suggested that a leading place was reserved to the latter in the nubian court.[25]

Furthermore, the careful uncovering of the frescoes enabled clearly defined periods of nubian religious art to be established. In the eighth and ninth centuries a style in which much use was made of violet and mauve colouring predominated, to give way to a 'white' period for the next country, a 'red yellow' style for the magnificent fresco of the youths in the fiery furnace (eleventh century) and more elaborate and garish colouring in the twelfth century. In this period the paintings have a wide-staring ethiopian look superseding the byzantine style of earlier centuries.[26]

The Faras excavations provide one of the foundations on which the

---

[22] Jakobielski, p 502.
[23] *Travaux* 3, p 159.
[24] See the fine illustrations in Michalowski, *Faras*, plates 71-90, and B. Rostkowska 'Iconographie des personnages historiques sur les peintures de Faras', *Travaux* 6 (1972) pp 196-205.
[25] See P. L. and M. Shinnie 'New Light on Medieval Nubia', *Journal of African History*, 6 (Cambridge 1965) p 270.
[26] See Michalowski, *Faras*, pp 72 *et seq*.

Recently discovered materials for writing the history of christian Nubia

story of nubian christianity will be based. Already, detailed examination of the style of the paintings has raised the question whether Nubia remained true to its monophysite origins throughout its long history. Not only the existence of byzantine liturgical sequences, but the representation of the Christ as a suckling child has suggested to some critics that there were intervals, particularly in the eleventh century, when the court accepted the chalcedonian formula that acknowledged Christ in two natures, Godhead and manhood, inseparably united.[27] So far, however, the alleged chalcedonianisms have all been found in monophysite environments, and the lack of physical evidence, such as the deliberate covering up of prominent monophysite bishops and rulers, argues against any such change.[28] Modifications in ritual and vestments there may have been, but not in the basic religious outlook accepted at the period of the conversion to christianity.

The British excavations under the auspices of the Egypt exploration society at Q'Asr Ibrim on the east bank of the Nile some fifty-five miles north of Faras, complement the discoveries from Faras. Q'Asr Ibrim was a fortress strategically placed on a high cliff overlooking the Nile. It was the seat of a bishopric and of a local ruler, probably an eparch, though in the final christian period he was known as 'Ourou Dotawo'–(king of Lower Do) in contrast to the king of Do-n-houl (= Dongola).[29] Throughout the christian era the site was dominated by a finely built stone church dedicated, we are told by the chronicler Abu Salih, to the Virgin.[30] Q'Asr Ibrim produced no frescoes. Instead it provided the excavators with a wealth of manuscript material preserved thanks to the extreme dryness of the climate. The most remarkable of these were found in January, 1964, by professor J. M. Plumley, attached to the thighs of a bishop who had been crudely buried or

---

[27] See Adams pp 172 *et seq* arguing on the basis of the melkite patriarch, Eutychius, c 890, *Annales* asserting that all Nubia was originally orthodox but transferred its allegiance to monophysitism in c 719 after the suppression of the melkite patriarchate in Alexandria, *PG* 111 (1863) col 1122D. Supported by Michalowski, *Faras* pp 91–3, but criticised, to my mind effectively by M. Krauze, 'Zur Kirche und Theologiegeschichte Nubiens', *KGN* pp 71–86, and [P. van] Moorsel, ['Die stillende Gottesmutter und die Monophysiten',] *KGN* pp 81–91.
[28] Moorsel.
[29] See, T. Save Soderbergh, *Late Nubian Sites, Churches and Settlements*; *the Scandanavian joint expedition to Sudanese Nubia* (Stockholm 1973) p 17.
[30] Abu Saleh, p 291. The fullest account to date is that by the present writer, in the *Abhandlungen des vii Internationalen Kongresses für christliche Archäologie* (Trier 1965, publ Rome 1968) pp 531–8. Also J. M. Plumley, *JEA* 50 (1964) pp 3–5.

rather deposited beneath the arch of the west crypt of the church.[31] They consisted of two paper scrolls, one in Bohairic coptic (the only Bohairic document found as yet on a nubian site), and the other, in arabic. When unrolled in the museum of antiquities at Cairo, they proved to be the consecration deeds of the dead man, giving his name as Timotheos and his see as the joint see of Pachoras (Faras) and Tilybe (Ibrim). Most important, however, was the fact that his consecration was performed by the patriarch Gabriel IV in Old Cairo, and Gabriel was in office between 1372-80. The mention too, of 'the most pious bishops who have come with him to carry out his enthronement in the church in which the bishops of the see [used to be enthroned]' shows that an organised episcopate existed in the northern kingdom of Nobatia as late as the last quarter of the fourteenth century, or fifty years later than had previously been thought.

The continued survival of nubian Christianity into the european later middle ages was indicated by another discovery. Excavating on another part of the site, the present writer found a large sealed pot which had been hidden amidst the rubble of a house and protected from destruction by a large beam that had lain across it.[32] Inside were nine leather scrolls written in the nubian language. They were of christian date, as shown by a latin type cross in the top left-hand corner of the scroll. The hand-writing in black ink was on the soft inner side of what had been probably pieces of leather garments made from gazelle skin, and it was clear and bold. It was immediately possible to distinguish a royal name 'Joel', and further research by professor Plumley has established that his kingdom was known as Dotawo, and that there was a bishop Merkcos of Ibrim, and also other officials.[33] The date, however, worked out from a combination of greek symbols and modern nubian words and related to the era of the martyrs (AD 284) appears to be AD 1464.[34] Until confirmatory evidence is discovered this must be treated with reserve. Though the scroll in question was the last to be inserted before the jar was sealed, and the leather was still supple when discovered, so late a date for an organised christian kingdom would appear to go beyond other evidence for

---

[31] Publication is expected in 1974, with commentary by professor Plumley, as an Egypt Exploration Society monograph.
[32] To be published by J. M. Plumley and the writer.
[33] See J. M. Plumley, 'The Christian period at Q'Asr Ibrim. Some notes on the MSS finds', *Acts of the Warsaw Colloquium on Nubian studies* (1972) ed E. H. Dinkler (Bonn forthcoming).
[34] *Ibid*

Recently discovered materials for writing the history of christian Nubia

organised christianity even in more remote areas of Nubia below the second cataract where its survival could be presumed.[35] There were also economic movements which led to major shifts in patterns of trade away from Nile traffic to trans-desert routes that favoured the dominance of the desert nomads against settled agriculturists such as were the christian Nubians.[36] Nubia had flourished partly because it had a monopoly of the transit trade between the Mediterranean and Africa south of the Sahara. This was steadily eroded by the desert tribes who had been converted to islam. Already by the mid-fourteenth century neither Nubians nor the Mamelouk armies from Egypt could contain this threat. It is surprising too, that while the coptic and ethiopian churches were known about in Europe and were represented at the re-union council of Florence-Ferrara 1439–45, nothing was heard of nubian Christianity at this time. It would seem unwise, therefore, for the moment, to push the survivial of christian Nobatia much beyond the first decades of the fifteenth century.

The scrolls were historical documents, and they have been supplemented by the discovery of some remarkable texts written in nubian or arabic on paper which appear to be letters to the bishop or eparch of Ibrim. A series of arabic texts studied by Mr Ahmed al Bushra at Cambridge date to c 1150–70.[37] They concern relations between the eparch and fatimid palace official who owned ships in the port of Aidhab on the Red Sea, and seems to have acted as agent for the nubian rulers by sending them goods, and selling slaves on their behalf. Their existence confirms the existence of friendly relations between Nubia and fatimid Egypt at this time. Another group of four letters, however, written a short time later, foreshadow changes towards a more aggressive policy by the Egyptians, including a demand for tribute.[38] This may well have been an issue that led to the war between the Nubians and the new ayyubid dynasty, which came into power in Egypt in 1171, that resulted in the temporary capture of Q'Asr Ibrim in 1173. Perhaps the loss or deposit of these letters may have been connected with this event.

Apart from the wealth of secular texts, there were scattered in a

---

[35] Adams believes that christianity 'probably lasted until the end of the fifteenth century on Kulubnarti island, 130 km south of Wadi Halfa', *KGN* p 150, but the churches both there and in other fortified christian sites in the same area seem to date to the fourteenth century at the latest.
[36] Thus Adams, 2, p 175.
[37] Cited by J. M. Plumley, *The Christian Period at Q'Asr Ibrim*, (forthcoming).
[38] *Ibid*

layer just above the floor of the cathedral, and hidden in tombs or under stones outside, what can only have been the remains of the cathedral library. As had been noted elsewhere,[39] these texts consisted of fragments written on vellum, parchment and paper in greek, nubian and coptic. They were often torn or charred, and some had been obviously salvaged and hidden. So far as preliminary research allows one to say, they were liturgical and homiletic pieces, and fragments of the new testament, acts of martyrs, eucharistic sequences and prayers. As at Faras, it seems that while coptic was retained as the principal language for biblical reading and patristic work, the liturgy and more popular works, such as the extracts found of acts of martyrs were in greek or nubian.

Faras and Ibrim have proved to be outstandingly important sites, but the accurate assessment of the discoveries made there depend on the study of material from a large number of other nubian sites that have been investigated in recent years. Some, like the church of Abdallah Nirqi near Abu Simbel, excavated in 1963–4 by the dutch expedition, produced frescoes rivalling those of Faras and earlier than most of the latter.[40] Apart from the leather scrolls from Q'Asr Ibrim the most important evidence for the declining years of christian Nubia has come from the desolate area in the northern Sudan, known as Batn el Hajar, where rudely constructed churches under the shadow of fortifications point to a final period of insecurity as the threat from the bedouin tribes from the west gradually increased.[41] Indeed, as with christian north Africa, the nomads seem to have proved more deadly enemies to christianity in the middle Nile valley than the hostility of muslim rulers.[42] This is obviously an important field for future research.

The discoveries which have been made in recent years on nubian sites have opened up new fields of study, particularly monophysite

---

[39] See the writer's 'Coptic, Greek and Nubian at Q'Asr Ibrim', *Byzantino-Slavica*, 32, 2 (1972) pp 224–9.

[40] Hans D. Schneider, 'Abdallah Nirqi—description and chronology of the central church', *KGN* pp 87–103.

[41] Thus E. H. Dinkler, 'Die deutsche Ausgrabungen auf den Inseln Sunnarti, Tangur und in Kulb' *ibid* pp 259–72. For the possible survival, however, of christianity in the southern kingdom of Alwah, (around Soba near Khartoum) see P. L. Shinnie, *Excavations at Soba*, Sudan Antiquities Service, *Occasional Papers*, 3 (Khartoum 1955) pp 12–13 (cites references).

[42] Thus Adams, 3 *JEA* 52 (1966) pp 150–1, for North Africa, see the writer's 'North Africa and Europe in the Early Middle Ages' *TRHS*, fifth Series, 5 (1955) pp 61–81.

Recently discovered materials for writing the history of christian Nubia

christianity. The nubian kingdoms stood midway between the Copts and the Ethiopians and were influenced by both while developing their own distinctive christian culture. It is now possible to see the eight hundred years of nubian christianity in terms of a succession of changes from period to period, and to study these in some depth. Stefan Jakobielski's work on the *History of the Bishopric of Faras*, will be a basic study of the history and administration of northern Nubia.[43] Between the tenth and twelfth centuries, when Nubia was a very prosperous area, something of the detail of its relations with its neighbours can be worked out, as well as possible developments in its religious life. Its religious art and liturgy can also be related to that of other kingdoms in the byzantine east. Old nubian as the language of a christian kingdom awaits further research and a project of a *Fontes Rerum Nubicarum* planned by the Heidelberg and Warsaw academies of science is under way.

There is, however, always need for care in handling the archaeological evidence. For instance, at Q'Asr Ibrim the discovery of the bishop's body under the arch of the west crypt has been taken sometimes as an indication of the use of the church down to the end of the fourteenth century, and that, in consequence, the scattered remains of the library found in light silt above the floor of the church must therefore be even later, perhaps early fifteenth century. A moment's thought, however, suggests the fragility of this reconstruction.[44] The bishop's body had been deposited where it lay: it had hardly been buried: only a thin covering of dirt obscured it when it was discovered lying askew and hunched up as though placed by bearers who had no time to dig a grave. It would hardly be credible in the heat of the nubian summer for services to have been conducted with the stench of a corpse emanating from the crypt only a few feet away. The deposit of the body with the scrolls attached to it is more likely to mark one of the grimmer scenes in the final era of christianity in that part of Nubia. The arch of the crypt already half filled with rubbish in the abandoned cathedral, would provide a suitable resting place for a bishop who may himself, have come to an untimely end.[45]

The nubian discoveries illustrate the variety of sources that contribute towards building up a picture of a hitherto little known christian society. They also illustrate the variety of skills required to derive the

[43] Published as *Faras*, 3 (Warsaw 1972).
[44] I owe this suggestion to professor W. Y. Adams, March 1973, though professor Plumley has since raised objections of some weight to it (July 1974).
[45] When found, one of his feet was missing.

greatest amount of information from them. In investigations spanning as much as a thousand years of history, and including material connected with the organisation, language, and liturgy of a church as well as its place in society, team work is all important. In this the polish academy of sciences under professor Michalowski have shown what can be done, and their example has been followed elsewhere on the continent. In Britain we have been slower to learn.

In this field as in many others there has been a tendency to adhere to methods of excavation and the organisation of research that have served well in the past but are now out-dated. With all the difficulties taken into account, publication of the results has been too slow and too meagre. Attitudes towards collaborative scholarship also have been over-cautious. A nubian institute on the lines of its polish counterpart would not be possible to-day owing to financial and other stringencies. If however, the rich material to hand from Q'Asr Ibrim is to be studied and nubian research in the United Kingdom linked with that proceeding apace on the continent, fresh attitudes are essential. In particular a greater combination of disciplines and institutions will have to be brought into play than hitherto.

Erich Dinkler (Hrsg.): Kunst und Geschichte Nubiens in christlicher Zeit, Ergebnisse und Probleme auf Grund der jüngsten Ausgrabungen. Recklinghausen (Aurel Bongers) 1971. 390 S., geb. DM 180.–.

Christian Nubia is a unique historical phenomenon. For nearly a thousand years, from circa 500–1500 A. D. the narrow band of fertile territory on each side of the Nile extending from Aswan to Khartoum sustained a vigorous Christian population who defied Moslem armies and Beduin raiders, and have left behind an artistic heritage that excites the wonder of scholars to-day.

The finely produced volume with magnificent illustrations edited by Professor Erich Dinkler is the result of an international conference held in the Villa Hügel at Essen in September 1969, which was devoted mainly to discussing the significance of the artistic treasures discovered by Professor Michalowski and his colleagues at Faras. In the present volume while Faras continues to dominate the scene, the scope of the twenty-five contributions by archaeologists and historians of art from Europe and the United States has been widened. It now includes the whole field of Nubian art, religion and history, while a number of new archaeological excavations undertaken in the years 1964–69 have been reported. The editor's aim has been to combine contributions on general themes with special studies in the wide context of Nubian religious, artistic and social history, and from the resulting discussions to establish what are the main outstanding problems still to be settled by further excavations.

The task ambitiously conceived in a context of world-wide co-operation among scholars has been brilliantly fulfilled. Here and there the critic might plead for greater brevity (there was surely no need to include a lecturer's statement that he was ending „to leave more room for discussion"), or for greater co-ordination of the work of the different contributors. The parallelism for instance, between the architectural remains from the great church at Q'asr Ibrim (Plates 74–77) and those from Old Dongola (Plates 130–133) deserve to be brought to the readers' attention. In general, however, particularly in the choice of illustrations and the preparations of plans and overlays, the editorial work deserves the highest praise. The publication is a landmark in the study of Nubian civilisation.

Apart from discussion of individual sites, the main themes are introduced in Professor Michalowski's opening paper, "Open Problems of Nubian Art and Culture in the light of the discoveries at Faras". That "for 500 years Faras (Pachoras) was the main artistic centre of northern Nubia" can hardly be doubted, but from what directions, asks Michalowski, came the inspiration of the three main stages of style and craftsmanship that can be discerned in the frescoes at Faras? Was it possible also, to discern a change of religious allegiance by the Kingdom of Nobatia from Monophysitism to Chalcedon with the enthronement of Bishop Joannes about A. D. 1000? What were the respective roles of the Coptic, Old Nubian and Greek languages in the Nubian kingdoms, and finally, how could various problems of chronology, for instance regarding the introduction of Christianity and the typology of the churches, be solved?

The formative influences on Nubian art are discussed in an important contribution from Professor Kurt Weitzmann, ("Some remarks on the sources of the fresco paintings of the Cathedral of Faras"). Weitzmann demonstrates convincingly that the "violet style" typical of the early period, 8th–9th century frescoes, are paralleled closely by the Bawit frescoes (6th/7th century), and that differences in detail "cannot obscure the general impression that this phase of fresco painting is a direct offshoot of Coptic art" (p. 327). This result finds additional confirmation from J. M. Plumley's finely illustrated account of the sculpture and carved woodwork found at Q'asr Ibrim. Much of this is contemporary with the building of the church probably late 7th-early 8th century, and "was influenced by Coptic art forms" (p. 133). This is true, in particular, of a fine sandstone stele representing a dove with outspread tail, similar examples of which have been found at Luxor and Armant. In the later periods of Nubian history, however, including the climax-centuries of Nubian artistic achievement circa 950–1150, direct Coptic influence seems to have been less evident, and was replaced by that of other centres such as Palestine or even the Byzantine empire itself. Weitzmann concludes carefully "that Nubia's art was not produced in isolation but that it reflects in each phase the same general trends that can be observed in neighbouring Egypt as well as in Syria-Palestine" (p. 335). While it is not easy to see how the latter area could have become a major influence even during the Byzantine reconquest of northern Syria (957–1084), the increasing presence of non-Coptic influences on Nubian painting and sculpture seems an established fact from the tenth century onwards.

Michalowski's suggestion of a return to Nubian Chalcedonian (Melkite) allegiance circa 1000 A. D. is less well founded. Dr. P. van Moorsel demonstrates convincingly ("Die stillende Gottesmutter und die Monophysiten") that the principal evidence for this, namely the appearance of the cult of Maria Galaktotrophusa at Faras at this time need not imply a change to Melkite allegiance. The fresco emphasises Mary as *Theotokos* rather than the human nature of Christ, and indeed, the representation of the Galaktotrophusa can be traced through the Gnosticising *Protoevangelium of James* into Coptic and Syrian Monophysite homiletic and liturgical work. In this respect the story of the cult of Maria Galaktotrophusa in the east seems to follow closely on that of the Assumption of the Virgin. Michalowski's further arguments based on the use of the formula Τὸ Ἐυχολόγιον μέγα on the Greek stelae of some of the Faras bishops, and Bishop Marianos' (1005–1037) title of "Orthodox bishop" can also be explained differently. The grave formula is found also with Coptic burials, while "Orthodox" was the normal attribute claimed by the patriarchs of Alexandria from Dioscorus I onwards and was used by the Monophysite chroniclers to describe clergy their own faith. An additional point originally made by W. Y. Adams and discussed here by Martin Krause, „Zur Kirchen- und Thelogiegeschichte Nubiens", is that Eutychius the Melkite Patriarch of Alexandria 933–940 claimed that Nubia was Melkite until 77 years after the Arab conquest of Egypt (i. e. until 718/19). This date, however, coincides roughly with the absorption of the kingdom of Makuria which had originally been Chalcedonian into Nobatia under King Merkurios. On the whole, excavations have confirmed the truth of John of Ephesus' account of the definitive conversion of the Nubian kingdoms to Christianity in the sixth century. As a result, Nobatia and Alwah adopted Monophysitism while the middle kingdom of Makuria opted for about a century for Chalcedon. There is no firm evidence for subsequent change to Chalcedon in the united kingdom of Nobatia-Makuria.

While reversion to Chalcedonian orthodoxy by the Nubians seems improbable, there is little doubt that Byzantine influence made itself felt increasingly in the organisation of the central and provincial administration and in the language and liturgy of the Nubian Church. The reports on individual sites included in this work throw much light on the relationship between Coptic, Greek and Old Nubian. Adams' account on the University of Kentucky's excavations at Kulubnarti (p. 141–155) records the existence of Greek texts roughly carved on door lintels, and indicating therefore a popular knowledge of that language. Dr. Detlef G. Müller reports the use of Coptic in a legal document dated to circa 1000 A. D. from Kulb (p. 245–55) and in his contribution on "Some remarks on Faras Inscriptions" Dr. Stefan Jakobielski points out that while Coptic texts are always in correct Coptic, those in Greek are often corrupted by Nubian terms. Greek and Nubian seem to be much more interchangeable and familiar languages. His conclusion that "Coptic was treated as the official language imposed by the adopted ecclesiastical rite" (p. 31) needs some elaboration. At Q'asr Ibrim Coptic was the language of the great Consecration Scroll for Bishop Timotheos dated 1372 and was used in Biblical texts and some homiletic texts (such as the fine illuminated Coptic MS of John Chrysostom's *Homily on the Four living Beasts,* found by the reviewer in

1964), but the more normal liturgical languages were either Nubian or Greek, and Nubian was used in private correspondence. Coptic indeed may have played much the same role in Nubia as Latin played in the sub-Roman Britain of Gildas, a literary language used for some ecclesiastical purposes but not the spoken language of the people. As demonstrated by the leather scrolls probably of the reign of King Joel (circa 1420) found at Q'asr Ibrim (See the reviewer's report in *Akten des VII. Internationalen Kongresses für Christliche Archäologie,* Trier 5–11 September, 1965 (pub. Roma 1968), p. 537–8) by the end of the Christian era Nubian has also become the language of the administration. Even so, one cannot afford to be dogmatic. The example of Christian North Africa with Berber, Punic and Latin in use at the same time, or of second-century A. D. Palestine with family archives including letters in Greek, Nabataean and Aramaic (See *Palestine Exploration Journal* xii, 1962, p. 235 ff. and 258 ff.) argues against the view that the presence of one language in a particular setting automatically excluded the use of others.

Of the contributions on individual sites, notable are those of Donadoni on the church at Sonqui Tino, Vercoutter on the three sites of Akhsa, Mirgissa and Sai, Schneider on the most rewarding excavation of Abdallah Nirqi just north of Abu Simbel, Hintze on Musawwarat es Sufra (excellent overlays) and the new Polish excavations at Dongola, where the large church is revealing itself as in many ways similar in size, architecture and date to the cathedral at Q'asr Ibrim. Finally, the Kentucky University excavations at Kulubnarti in 1969 provide further much needed evidence for conditions in the transition period between Christian and Moslem Nubia. The final Christian phase on this site, as at Meinarti, Sunnarti, Q'asr Ibrim and elsewhere, was characterised by the heavily fortified watchtower. These towers together with what appear to be mountain refuges on Gebel Sahaba explored by the Scandanavian expedition (p. 219–240) point to the Beduin marauder as the decisive enemy of the Christian civilization.

The concluding article, (another finely illustrated contribution), by Bruce G. Trigger moves away from Christianity to problems of Nubian landsettlement. The sites of Toshka and Arminna provide type sites where settlement can be traced from Meroitic to late Christian times, and those who would see war and invasion as the agents of migration and dispersion of populations are reminded that flood, disease and drought can be equally powerful influences on human ecology. Trigger's criticisms, however, that the excavation programmes have not been problem-oriented (p. 347) and that archaeologists failed to explore the settlement patterns of major sites such as Faras and Q'asr Ibrim (p. 378) are not well-founded. At Faras the Polish team succeeded in the herculean task of disengaging the churches and their murals and have gone a long way towards establishing a demography of the earliest Christian population. More could hardly be asked in the time available. At Q'asr Ibrim the excavators were confronted by different problems. Standing 210 feet above the Nile in 1964 the site will be preserved even after the filling up of Lake Nasser. This is true also of Gebel Adda. The need therefore is for relatively slow and careful work undertaken over a period of years. The value of both sites as a means of checking results elsewhere will increase greatly in the future, and a settlement plan of much of the area under excavation will emerge automatically.

More to the point is the criticism made by Martin Krause that, "von dem reichen, in Q'asr Ibrim und Gebel Adda ausgegrabenen Quellenmaterial gibt es z. Z. leider nur kurze Hinweise" (p. 72). On whatever grounds, the lack of adequate interim reports on Q'asr Ibrim of the type published by Michalowski in *Kush* for Faras has been a serious hindrance to scholars. Almost every topic discussed in this publication except murals would have benefitted from further publication of the discoveries from that site. Unfortunate too, is the fact that Plumley's contribution in the work under review contains mistakes which affect the readers's interpretation of the history of the site. The mosque, for instance, represents the final phase of the occupation of the cathedral and was separated from the floor of the latter by an average of 1.50 m. of occupation earth which included at least three levels of domestic occupation (See Frend, *Akten,* p. 533–4). It would be unwise to date it as early as the 16th century and thereby indicate that the cathedral was almost at once converted by the Bosnians into a mosque (p. 130). Similarly, the statement that until then there was no "intensive occupation of the fortress area" needs modification (p. 129). One of the main features of the site is the apparent alternation between wholly religious and mixed religious and secular settlement. The crowded Meroitic dwellings with their wall paintings on the north side of the church and the X-group houses on the south side provide evidence for the latter type, while from the 11th century Christian houses covered the whole area of the great forecourt of the Meroitic temple before these gave way probably in the 14th century to a watch-tower and magazines.

Nubian archaeology is a continuing saga. Like the Dead Sea Scrolls, the Nubian discoveries could hardly have been exploited so fully but for the foundations laid by the patient, piecemeal work of previous generations of scholars. Without Monneret de Villard, without Emery and Kirwan's excavation of the Royal Tombs at Q'stul and Ballana, and above all the work of the Sudan Antiquities Service up to 1956, the present generation of researchers would have lacked essential guides for their endeavours. The outlining of Nubian social structures, religion, language, church, pottery types had, however, become established by them and the vast international undertaking resulting in the exploration of scores of sites could build its results on sure foundations. This debt needs always to be acknowledged. Professor Dinkler's masterly publication, however, marks a new stage in the study of Christian Nubia. Its inspiration points the way forward to even greater discoveries in the future.

Glasgow

INDEX

Aaron,martyr: XII 130;XIII 126
Abdallah Nirqui: XXIII 157,161, 162;XXIV 28;XXV 338
Abd el Qadir: XXIII 157,161
Abel: I 29;VIII 74
Abitina,martyrs of: I 40; X 282;XVIII 38,41,44,46,47
Abraham: IX 473,474
Abu Simbel: XXIII 161;XXIV 28; XXV 338
Acacius,Acacian Schism: IV 20; XI 69 ff.;XXII 15
Acta Martyrum: XXIII 155,156, 159
Adamites: II 14;VIII 80
Adams,W.Y.: XXV 337
Adrianople: XIV 1,3
Aemilian,Vice Prefect: X 265, 270
Africa: XXII 14;XXIV 27,28; see also North Africa
Agrippinus,Bishop of Carthage: XVII 189,190
Aidhab: XXIV 21,27
Ain Ghorab: XVIII 38,43,44-5
Ain Zirara: XVIII 45
Akiba,Rabbi: XVII 185
Alaric: XIV 1,7
Alban,martyr: XII 130,143
Alexander,Bishop of Alexandria: II 9
Alexander of Lycopolis: III 6; X 2
Alexander Jannaeus,king: I 30
Alexander Severus,emperor: IX 474,475;X 268
Alexandria: I 29,37;II 5,8; III 15,23;IV 27;VIII 67; IX 476,479;X 263,280;XI 69,71,75,79;XII 131;XIV 9; XXII 13-16;XXIII 158;XXIV 19,24;XXV 337
 -Influence over Carthage: XVI 24
 -Jews in: XVII 191
 -Philosophical tradition: X 266,283;XIV 10
 -Trade: XIII 129
Alfius Caecilianus,duumvir: X 27
Alienatio: XIV 10
Alypius,Bishop of Thagaste:XIV 4-6

Amandus,presbyter: XIV 5-6
Ambrose,Bishop of Milan: II 8; VIII 60,64,69,78,81;XIV 5,6
Ambrose,friend of Origen: X 268
Ambrosiaster: VIII 74-6; XVII 191
Ammianus Marcellinus: I 25; VIII 7;XIV 3;XXIII 157
Anastasius,emperor: XI 69, 74-6,79,80;XXII 15
Anastasius I,Pope: XIV 6,7
Anastasius II,Pope: XI 75-6
Anniamus,inscription: XVI 27; XVII 190
Antalas,Berber king: XXI 72-3
Antichrist: X 285;XV 171
Antigonus Papias: XIII 125,129
Antioch: I 25,32,37: II 8,9; IV 23;VIII 62;IX 476,479; XI 71;XXII 14,16
 -Council of: IV 19;VII 61,66
 -Persecution in: X 272
Antiochus III: I 30,35;II 2
Antony,monk: I 27-8,40: II 5; III 23;VIII 79;X 267,280,282; XXIII 157
Aphraat (Aphraates): 41;III 19; XI 77
Apocalyptic: II 2,8,14;III 16; IV 24;X 286;XV 172,175
Apollinaris,Apollinarianism: XI 79
 -forgeries: XI 78-9
Apollinarii : VIII 73
Apollinaris Sidonius,writer and bishop: VII 60,72;XIV 9
Apollonius of Tyana: IX 473-5
Apostates: X 272,282
Apostles,cult of: XVIII 32 ff.
 -Sites: XVIII 32-5,49
Apostolic Succession: VI 48
Aquileia: I 26;II 10;XII 136; XIII 125,129
Arabs: XVI 34;XVIII 36;XX 346; XXI 61-4,73,80;XXV 337
Aramaic: III 15,19;XXV 338
Archdeacon: XVI 22,23,29-30
Area (cemetery): XVI 24,27,39
Arius,Arianism: II 9;VIII 59-60,70;X 264;XI 79;XII 131
Arles: XII 137,142;XIII 127

-Council of: II 10;XII 129,
  137;XIII 126,129
Arsacius,high priest: II 6;
  X 285
Art,Berber: XX 343 ff.
  -Celtic: XX 342,350
  -Islamic: XX 342,346-7
  -Nubian: XXV 336
Asceticism: III 19;XIV 4,6
Asia Minor,Christianity:
  II 1,2,7;XII 137;XIII 126
  -migrants from: XII 127
  -missions in: XXII 10,12
  -paganism in: X 278
  -sects in: VIII 80
  -also: X 266,271;XV 169
Athanasius: I 26,28;II 6;
  V 260;VIII 67;X 282,283;XI
  75;XII 131;XXII 12,15;
  XXIII 156-8
Athanasius II,Patriarch of
  Alexandria: XI 75
Atheism: VI 42-3
Augustine of Canterbury:
  XII 129-30,144
Augustine of Hippo: I 42;II 8;
  IV 21,25-6;VI 47;VIII 62-3,
  67,71,73,76;XIV 1,2,5-7;
  XVI 22,31-2;XVIII 46,48,49;
  XIX 543,549;XXI 67
  -in Carthage: XVIII 38
Aurelius,Bishop of Carthage:
  XIV 6;XVI 22,31-3
Aures mountains: XVIII 36-7,
  46;XX 343,352;XXI 72
Ausonius,poet: I 25;VIII 78;
  XII 138;XIV 2-5,9
Austures,nomadic tribe: XXI
  69,71
Axum,Kingdom of: VIII 67;XXII
  11-12

Babylon: XIV 10
  -Old Cairo: XXII 10
Bagaudae: II 10;XIII 125;XIV
  1,3,9
Baghdad: XXI 63,80;XXIV 21,24
Baptism: I 38;III 19;XV 170,172;
  XVI 21,31
  -of blood: XV 172
  -baptisteries: XVI 21
  -baptismal tanks: XII 136
Baŕadai,James: IV 27;XXII 15
Barnes,T.D.: IX 480;XVII 186,187
Basil of Caesarea: II 13;IV 22;
  VII 59,69,80;X 266,275;XIV
  5,9;XXIII 158
Basilica Majorum: XV 25-6,31,36

Basilica Restituta: XVI 23-4,
  30,38
Basiliscus,usurping emperor:
  XI 70
Bawit: XXIII 161;XXV 336
Baynes,N.H.: XXI 68
Bede: II 2;XII 129,130,144
Belisarius: XVI 23;XXI 72
Bellerophon: XII 134-5,139
Benedict of Nursia: II 12;VI 41
Berbers: X 279;XXV 338
  -art: XX 342 ff.
  -local sites: XX 345
  -become Moslem: XXI 78
  -nomads: XXI 64,65,72-4,77
Berthier,A.: IV 25
Bible: X 282;XVI 22;XX 351
  -African: XVII 188
Bignor,villa: XII 143;XIV 3
Bigua,monastery: XVI 27,31
Bir Djedid: XIX 547
Blandina,martyr: XIV 167 ff.
Bled Guitoun: XX 342
Blemmyes,nomads: XXI 63;XXII
  11,12;XXIV 19
Bollandists: VI 41
Boniface,missionary: II 11,13
Bordeaux: I 25;XIV 2
Bou Takrematem: XX 349
Brisson,J.P.: XIX 543,548
Britain: XII 129 ff;XIV 3;
  XXI 66;XXIV 30
  -art in: XX 342,343,352
  -Christianity: XII 129 ff.
  -paganism: II 10-11;XII 129 ff.
  -Pelagianism: XII 141-2;XIV 1
  -villas: XII 134-5,142-3;XIV 3
Byzacena: XXI 72,75
Byzantium,Byzantine: XVI 23,24
  ff;XXI 72,73;XXII 10-16;XXIII
  156,158,161,163;XXIV 22;XXV
  337;(see also Constantinople)
  -in Africa: XXI 64 ff.
  -churches: XVI 23-5,28,31
  -trade: XXI 61

Cabrol,F.de: VII 320-22
Caecilian,Bishop of Carthage:
  VIII 61;XVI 22,29;XIX 546
Caecilian,ruler of synagogue:
  XVII 188
Caesarea: I 32;X 265,282
Caesarea Philippi: I 31;II 1
Cairo: V 260,262;XXI 64,75;
  XXIV 26
Calama: XX 344;XVIII 48
Calderone,S.: XXI 542 n.,543
Camels: XXI 61-2,70-1,74

Carlisle: XII 131-2;XIII 125
Carthage: I 37,40;II 10;VI 40;
  VIII 58,61;IX 478;X 269-71,
  275;XII 133;XXI 72,74
-Arabs in: XVI 24,27,31-2
-basilicas: XVI 23,37-40
-Byzantine: XVI 21 ff.
-Conference of: VIII 67
-Councils in: XVI 33;
  XVIII 38
-Jews: XVI 21;XVII 185 ff;
  martyrs: XV 167 ff.
-Trade: XXI 70
-falls to Arabs: XVI 24
-monasteries: XVI 24,27,31-2
Cassiodorus: XXI 70
Celerina,martyr: XVI 25,27
Celerinus,confessor: XVIII 37
Celsus,pagan apologist: I 35 n.;
  III 17;IX 478;X 269;XV 168,
  174
Chalcedon,Council of: II 9;IV
  18;VI 39,49;XI 69,70,72,
  75-77,80;XXII 10-12,13-16;
  XXV 336-7;28 Canon of: XXII
  14
Chenoboskion. See Nag Hammadi
Christ. See Jesus Christ
Christianity,Christians: I 28,
  29,38,41;II 1;IX 470 ff;
  XXII 10-12;XXIII 159
-Anglo-Saxon: XII 143-4
-Aramaic: III 15,19
-Celtic: II 12-13;XIII 128
-Greek speaking: IV 17
-in Britain: 263-4;XII 129 ff.
-in Carthage: XVI 21 ff.
-in Gaul: XII 138-40;XIII
  126-7
-in Nubia: XXIV 26,27;XXV
  336-8
-as "atheism": II 6
-as "a law": XIX 546
-as "nazarenes": IX 478;XVI
  21;XVII 189
-Cynics and: XV 168
-women and: XIV 5
-religion of martyrdom:
  X 268
-urban cult: I 34,38;X 269
-rural cult: I 36,38;II 5
-mission: I 39;II 3-4,8;
  X 266;XIII 126-9;XIV 8
-social standing: XIII 127
-organisation: XVI 28-30
Christology: II 9;IV 27;XI
  69 ff;XXIV 25;XXII 13
Christos-Helios: X 286

Church and State: XVI 33-4
Circumcellions: I 27,28,41-2;
  II 6,8,10,14;IV 26;VII 80;
  X 284;XIV 9;XVIII 284
-agonistici: XIX 549
-pilgrims: XIX 546-7,549
-revolutionaries: IV 26;XIX
  545
-status: XIX 542-3,548
Cirta (Constantine): I 26,39;
  II 7;VIII 63;X 272,274,281
Classical literature
-Catholic attitude: VIII 77-8
-Donatist attitude: VIII 71-2;
  XX 351
-Syraic Church and: VII 72
Clement of Alexandria: I 38;
  III 15,23;IV 18;IX 479;XIV
  10;XXIV 19
-I Clement: III 22-3
-II Clement: III 18,21;V 263
-pseudo-Clementines: III 20
Commodian: X 285;XVIII 46
Confessors: VIII 58;X 267,269,
  274,280;XIII 30 n.;XIV 10;
  XV 172
-Powers of: XV 174
Constantine,emperor: I 28,41;
  II 7;V 261;VI 28;VIII 68;
  IX 474;X 277-8,286;XII 130,
  140;XIV 10;XVIII 44;XIX 546;
  XXII 12;XXIV 23
Constantinople: II 8-9;VIII
  70;XI 69,74,75,80;XVI 24;
  XXII 10-12,14-16;XXIV 22
-Council of: XI 72
-Trade: XXI 62,64,70
Constantius II,emperor: I 25,
  41; VIII 67;IX 22;XII 131,
  133,138
Copts,Coptic: I 39;II 5;IV 27;
  V 260;VIII 79;X 279-80;
  XVI 34;XIX 544;XXII 10,16;
  XXIII 155,157-8,160,163;
  XXIV 24,29;XXV 336-8
Corippus: XXI 72-3,77
Cotopices: XIX 543
Cresconius,Bishop: XXI 79
Cresconius,Donatist grammarian:
  VIII 71-2
Cuicul,See Djemila
Cynics: XV 168
Cyprian: V 261;VI 210;VIII 58,
  62,64;IX 470;X 269,271,275-6;
  XI 78;XII 137;XVI 22,33-4;
  XVIII 36-7,43,47
Cyril,Archbishop of Alexandria:
  II 6;VI 39;VIII 67,70;

Dadianus,King: XXIII 159-160, 162
Damasus,Pope: XIV 10
Damous el Karita,Church: XII 133;XVI 21,26-7,31,37;XVII 189
Daniel,stylite: XIV 7
David,Nubian king: XXIV 21
Dead Sea Scrolls,see Q'mran
Decius,emperor: II 4;VII 322; X 270;XXIII 158;see also Persecution
Defensor Ecclesiae: VIII 65-6
Delattre,R.Père: XVI 25,27-8, 34
Delphinus,Bishop of Bordeaux: XIV 5-6
Demetrius,saint: XXIII 158,161
Deo Laudes,Donatist inscriptions: XVIII 45-6; XX 351
Diatessaron: III 13;IV 18; V 263-4
Didache: I 34;V 264
Dinkler,Erich: XXIII 163;XV 336,339
Dio-Caesarea,Jews in: X 274
Diocletian,emperor: I 25,38-9; IV 21;IX 476;X 274,284; XXIII 159;see also Persecution
Dionysius,Bishop of Alexandria: I 38;III 23;IV 22;IX 470; X 265,270,275,280;XI 77-8
Dionysus,Pope: IV 22;X 275
Dioscorus,Patriarch of Alexandria: II 6;IV 22;XI 75,80;XXII 13-16;XXV 337
Diospolis: XXIII 162
-Council of: IV 22
Dispersion,see "Jews"
Djemila (Cuicul): I 26;X 279; XVI 28;XX 349;XXI 79
Dölger,F.J.: VII 321
Donatus,Donatism: I 38,41-2; II 6,10;IV 24-7;V 262;VI 40-1,49;VIII 62,65-6,71-2, 81;X 264,278-9,286;XIV 11; XVI 22-3,26,33;XVIII 38,40; XXI 77;XXII 14
-Art: XX 350
-Cemetery churches: XVI 26
-Church of the martyrs: XVIII 36,41 ff;XIX 549; XX 350
-Inscriptions: XVIII 40, 45-8;XX 350-1
-and Monks: XVI 31;XIX 542 ff.
Dongola (Old Dongola): XXII 11; XXIV 21,25;XXV 336,338
Dotawo,Nubian Kingdom: XXIV 26
Dugmore,Rev.C.: XII 144
Duin,Council of: XI 79
Dura-Europos: II 3;V 264
Durnovaria (Dorchester): XII 133-4
Duval,N.: XVI 21,31,34

Edessa: II 5;III 19,25
Egypt,Egyptians: II 14;III 15, 18,25;VI 46-7;VIII 81;IX 473; X 271,277;XXII 11,14-16;XXIII 161-2;XXIV 19,21-2,27;XXV 337
-Confessors: X 280
-Gnosticism: III 15,18,23
-Jewish Christianity: III 25
-martyrs: I 39;II 6;VI 39; XXIII 161
-monks: I 27-29;II 5;VIII 80; X 282-3;XI 76;XIV 9; XXIII 157-8
-persecution in: X 273
Egypt Exploration Society: XXIII 155;XXIV 25
Elijah: I 29;II 6;X 282
Elvira,Council of: I 39;VIII 61;X 276
Emeritus,Donatist Bishop: XVIII 41,44
Encratism: III 27-8;IV 18
Ennabli,L.: XVI 25
Ennabli,M.A.: XVI 21
Ephesus: VI 48;VIII 70;XXII 10
-Council in 431: VIII 67;XI 79
-Council in 449: II 9;IV 22; XIX 548
Ephrem Syrus: I 41;XI 77
Epiphanius,Bishop of Salamis: V 260
Essenes: II 1;III 25
Ethiopia,Ethiopians: XXII 12, 15;XXIII 158;XXIV 22,29
Eusebius of Caesarea: I 39; II 5;IV 17;VI 39,47;VIII 57, 81;IX 470,475-6;X 263,265, 272,281,288;XII 127
Eutyches archimandrite: VIII 67;XI 72,80;XXII 13
Eutychian,monk: II 6;VIII 80

Faras: XXII 10-12;XXIII 155, 157-8,161-2;XXIV 19,21-25,28; XXV 336-8
Farnborough: VII 321-3

Fatalis: XII 143
Fausta,wife of Constantine:
    VIII 69
Felicitas,martyr: XV 175;XVI 25
Felix,Bishop of Aptunga:
    VIII 63;X 272
Felix,Manichee: XVI 321
Felix,martyr: XIV 2,4,6
Felix III,Pope: XI 73
Festus,senator: XI 75
Fevrier,P.A.: XIX 546
Firmus,Kabylie chief: XX 342-3
Flavian,Bishop of Antioch:
    VIII 60
Florus,<u>praeses</u>: X 281
<u>Fontes Rerum Nubicarum</u>: XXIV 29
Fortunatus,Manichaean: VIII 71
Frampton,villa: XII 134-5;
    XIV 2
Frumentius,missionary: VIII 67;
    XXII 12
Fulgentius,Bishop of Ruspe:
    XVIII 48;XIX 547

Gabriel,archangel: XXIII 162
Gabriel IV,patriarch: XXIV 26
Gaiseric,Vandal king: XIV 2,9;
    XVI 23,34;XXI 69
Galatia: II 6,9;X 285
Galerius,emperor: X 274,286
Galilee: I 30,32
Gallienus,emperor: X 267,275;
    XX 348
Gamart,Jewish cemetery: XVI
    21,27;XVII 185-7,190
Gaul,Church in: XII 138-40;
    XIII 126-8
-Paganism: XIV 2-3
-Visigothic: XXI 70
Gavault,P.: XX 342-3
Gaza: II 7;X 274
Gelasius,Pope: VIII 61,65;
    XI 69,74-6
Gennadius of Marseilles: VII
    141
Georgius I,Nubian King: XXIV
    24
Georgius II,Nubian King:
    XXIV 24
Georgius,martyr: XXIII 155-162;
    XXIV 21
Germanus,Bishop of Auxerre:
    XII 142
Gibbon,E.: VI 42-3;XIV 1
Gildas: II 10;XXV 338
Gildo: XVIII 40;XX 343
Gnostics,Gnosticism: I 34,41;
    II 9;III 13-15,18,23;V 259;

VI 47;XV 175
God-Fearers: I 33;IV 17
Gospel of Thomas,see Thomas
Grace: XIV 6-8
Gratian,emperor: VIII 77;XII 141;
    XIV 2,3
Great Persecution: II 6;VIII 57;
    X 263 ff;XVI 22;see also
    Persecutions and Diocletian
Gregory,Byzantine general:
    XXI 73,75,77
Gregory of Nazianzus: VIII
    69,70
Gregory of Nyssa: II 4;X 266
Gregory I,Pope: VIII 61,65,77;
    XVI 24;XXII 12
Gregory of Tours: VIII 77;XII
    140;XXI 74
Gregory the Wonderworker:
    X 266,268,271,286
Gsell,S.: XVIII 45;XX 342,345
Gunthamund,Vandal King: XXI 69

Habsa,martyr: XXII 14
al Hareth,Arab Christian King:
    XXIII 14
Harnack,Adolf von: V 259;VI 45-6
Hegesippus: III 17;VI 39
Henchir Taghfaght: XVIII 41,43
Henchir Tentilia: XX 345,350
<u>Henotikon</u> of Zeno: IV 15,28;
    XI 72-3,75,78;XXII 15
Heracleon,Gnostic: III 23
Heracles: XXIII 159-61
Heraclius,emperor: XXI 62,73-4
-coin of: XXI 73-4
Hermas: III 17
Herodian: XX 347
Hierakas,Coptic ascetic: III 23;
    VIII 79
Hierocles,governor of Bithynia:
    X 267
Hilarion,monk: II 7;XIV 3
Hilary,Bishop of Poitiers:
    XII 137;XIII 128
Hilderic,Vandal King: XVI 22-3;
    XVIII 44
Hillalians,Arab tribes: XXI 78
Hinton St.Mary,villa: XII 132,
    134-5,139;XIV 2
Hippo Regius: XVI 28,32;XVIII
    49
Hippolytus: VIII 58
Historiography,Christian:
    VI 40 ff.
Holy Men: II 7;XVIII 48;see
    Monks
Holy Spirit: IV 19-20;VIII

57-8,79;XIV 10;XV 171,174;XVI
  22;XVIII 36,43-4;XX 350
Honorius,emperor: XI 141;XIV
  542
Hormisdas,Pope: XI 69-70,76,79,
  80
Hosius,Bishop of Cordoba:
  II 13

Iberia: XXII 12
Ibn al Hakam,chronicler: XXI
  62,64-5,77
Ibn Khaldun: XXI 74,79
Ibn Yakub: XXI 76
Innocent I,Pope: XIV 10
Irenaeus of Lyon: III 15;IV 17;
  V 264;XIII 126-8
Irenaeus,Count: VIII 67
Isaac,Donatist confessor:
  XVIII 43-4
Isidore of Seville: XIX 543
Isis: XV 175;XXII 10
Islam: XX 350;XXI 62,77-8

Jacobite Church: XXII 15
Jakobielski,Dr.S.: XXIII 155;
  XXIV 29
James,of Jerusalem: III 16-17;
  IV 16;VI 39,48;XVII 189
James Bar'adai,see Bar'adai
Jerome: IV 20;VIII 62,76,78;
  XIV 3-4;XXIV 19
Jerusalem: I 29-31,33;II 1;IV 16;
  VI 39;XIV 4;XVII 191
  -Temple: III 24;VI 47-8
  -Holy Sepulchre: VIII 69
  -Patriarchate: XI 71
  -Council of: XVII 189
  -Heavenly: XIV 10
Jesus Christ: I 31-4;II 1,14;
  III 13 ff;IV 16;V 262-3;VI
  38,47-8;XVII 189;XVIII 45;
  XXII 12-15;XXIII 158;XXIV 19,
  24-5;XXV 337
  -messiah: XVII 192
  -perfect martyr: XV 174
  -physician: XVIII 45
Jews,Judaism: I 29,34-5;II 6;
  IV 17,23;IX 470 ff;XIII 126
  -in Africa: VI 43,47;VIII 64-5;
    XV 167 ff;XVI 27;XVII 188
  -in Asia Minor: XVII 189
  -in Carthage: XVI 21;XVII 184 ff.
  -Dispersion: I 32-3;II 1;IV 23
  -Edessa: III 19
  -Nile valley: III 24
  -Palestine: X 274
  -Italy: XVII 191

  -anti-Christian: IV 17;X 268
  -anti-Roman: XV 168
  -pro-Parthian: IX 477
  -mission: IX 477
  -magic: IX 475
  -messianism: XV 168
  -polemic: XVII 192
  -cemeteries: XVII 185 ff.
Joannes,Nubian bishop: XXV 336
Joel,Nubian king: XXIV 26;
  XXV 338
John the Baptist: I 30-1
John Chrysostom: II 8;VIII 67;
  XXIII 158;XXV 337
John of Ephesus,(Amida): II 8;
  VI 39;XIV 9;XXII 10-11;XXIV
  19-20;XXV 337
John,Gospel of: IV 18;V 264
John,Patriarch: XI 79,81
John Talaia: XI 72,74
Jordan Hill,temple: XII 141
Judgement: X 282;XIV 4,10;
  XV 172;XVI 32
Julian,Bishop of Eclanum: XIV
  7-8
Julian,emperor: II 6;VI 39;
  VIII 66,68;X 284;XII 138;
  XIII 128;XIV 3;XXIII 157-8
Julian,monk: XXII 10-11;XXIII
  156
Julius,martyr: XII 130
Julius,pope: XI 75,78-9
Justin I,emperor: XI 69,75,80;
  XXII 15
Justin Martyr: I 34-5;II 2
Justinian: II 8;IV 20;VIII 67;
  XI 70,73,75,80;XVI 23;XXII
  10 ff;XXIV 19

Kabylie: X 275;XX 342,345,352
Kahena,Berber queen: XXI 74-5
Kairouan: XXI 74-51,79
Kharedjism: XX 347;XXI 79
Kherbet Bahrarous: XX 348-9;
  XIX 547
Klauser,Th.: VII 320,322-4;
  XIII 129
Krause,M.: XXV 337-8
Krumbacher,K.: XXIII 160
Kudanbes,Nubian king: XXIV 21
Kulubnarti: XXV 337-8

Lactantius: IV 19-21;X 273,
  275-6,281,284;XIV 10
Lampridius: IX 473-5
Language boundary: IV 20-2
Leclercq,Dom.Henri: VI 41;
  VII 320-4;VIII 79

Legacies: VIII 69-70
Leo,Pope: II 13;VII 60-1;XI 73, 76,78-80;XIV 8;XXII 13
-Tome of: XI 75-77,80
Leo I,emperor: XIV 9
Leptis Magna: XXIII 32;XX 349; XXI 71
Lérins,monastery: XII 142; XIV 8
Lex Mancia: XVIII 40;XXI 66
Libanius: I 25;II 7;VIII 68; XIV 5
Liberatus,archdeacon: XVI 24
Liberius,pope: VIII 70
Logos theology: IV 18,19;X 286
Longinus,missionary: VII 67; XXII 12
Louata,nomads: XXI 63,71-2,74, 76-7
Lucian,confessor: XVIII 37
Lucilla,opponent of Caecilian: XIX 546
Lullingstone,villa: V 263;XII 129,137,139,143;XIV 3
Luxor: XXIV 19;XXV 337
Lydney,temple: II 10;XII 140-141
Lyon,martyrs of: I 35;II 10; IX 480;X 268;XII 137;XIII 126-7;XV 167 ff.

Mabillon,Jean: VI 41-2;VII 322
Macedonius,Patriarch: XI 74,78
Macomades: XVIII 40,45
Magnentius,usurping emperor: XII 134,138
Magnus Maximus,usurping emperor: II 11-12;XII 131;XIV 3
Maiden Castle,temple: II 10;XII 141
Makurrah (Makuria) kingdom: XXII 11-12;XXIV 21,23;XXV 337
Mameluks: XXIV 27
Mani,Manichaeism: II 9;III 26; V 260,262;VIII 71;X 281;XII 141;XVI 31-2;XXI 77
Marcellinus,imperial notary: VIII 67,76;XIV 7;XVI 22
Marcian,emperor: VIII 61;XXII 13
Marcian,bishop: XII 137
Marcion: I 41;II 9;II 19;IV 18; X 268
Marculus,bishop: XVIII 38,40,47
Marcus,Gnostic: XIII 127
Marianos,Nubian bishop: XXII 10, 16;XXV 337
Marius Victorinus: IV 22;VIII 73
Marseille: XIII 127-8;XXI 74
Martin of Tours: II 11;XII 131,

139,40;XIII 128;XIV 3,5
Martyrs,martyrdom: I 26,37,39-40;II 5-6;VIII 58,80;X 263 ff; XII 130;XVI 22,25;XVIII 32 ff.
-memoriae: XVIII 32 ff.
-military: XXIII 155 ff.
Martyrius,Patriarch: XI 71
Martyrius,martyr: II 12
Masada: II 1;III 25
Mascula: XVIII 46;XX 345,351
Matthew,Gospel of: I 31;III 17, 20,23;IV 17
Mauretania: X 284;XVII 193; XVIII 32,36,46-7;XX 348; XXI 67
-Donatists in: XVIII 46; XIX 542 ff.
Maurists: VI 41
Maxentius,usurping emperor: VIII 63;IX 474;X 277,286; XII 130
Maximian,emperor: IV 21
Maximian,Donatist confessor: XVIII 43
Maximin,emperor: VI 39;X 273, 279,286
Maximus,Bishop of Turin: II 12
Medinet Madi: V 260
Melania,the elder: VIII 70
Melania,the younger: XIV 6,9
Meletius,Meletians: II 9;VIII 59,80;X 280
Melkites: XXII 10;XXV 337
Mensurius,Bishop of Carthage: IV 24;VIII 63;XVII 190
Mercurius,military martyr: XXIII 155-159,161-2
Mercurius,Nubian king: XXII 12; XXIV 21,23;XXV 337
Michael,archangel: XXIII 159, 161-2;XXIV 19,24
Michałowski,K.: XXII 10,12; XXIII 155;XXIV 23,30;XXV 336-8
Michigan University: XVI 21,31
Miggin,martyr: XVIII 42,47
Milan: VIII 66;XIV 2,4-6;XVI 34
-Edict of: VIII 59
Minor orders: VIII 58;XVI 29
Minucius Felix: XVII 186
Mishna: XVII 188,195
Modalism: VIII 70
Momigliano,A.: IX 473,76;XIV 1
Monasticism: I 27,37,40;II 5-7; III 16,25;VIII 79 ff;X 286; XIV 3,9
-Celtic: XII 143-4
-Circumcellions and: XIX 544 ff.
-Eastern: VIII 79-81;XIV 10

-North African: XVI 24,27,31-2
-Paulinus and: XIV 6
see also "Egypt" and "Syria"
Monceaux,P.: XVII 185;XVIII 32 n.
Monophysitism,Monophysites:
 II 81;IV 27;VI 49;XIV 9;
 XXII 10-12;XXIII 155;XXV 336-7
Monotheletes: IV 20;XVI 24;
 XXI 77
Montanus,Montanism: I 35-7;
 II 2-3;XIII 127;XV 172;
 XVIII 37
Montefiore,H.W.: III 14,25
van Moorsel,P.: XXIII 157;
 XXV 337
Moses: IX 475,477;XVII 191
Mosheim,L.von: VI 42-43
Moslems: XXIII 162;XXV 336,338;
 see also Islam
Munatius,Felix,Curator of Cirta:
 X 272

Naassenes,Gnostic sect: III 16
Nag Hammadi: I 41;II 9;III 13;
 V 259,263;VI 47;XXIV 19
Najran: XXII 13,14
Nazirites: III 17,25
Nennius: II 12
Nepos,Bishop of Arsinoe: III 23
Nestorius,Archbishop of
 Constantinople: VI 39;VIII
 67,80;XI 72,77;XXII 13-14
Newman,J.H.: VI 44-5
Nicaea,Council of: I 28;IV 19;
 VI 39;XI 72,78;XII 13
Nicetas,Bishop of Remesiana:
 XIV 8;XXII 12
Nicetius,Bishop: II 12,13
Nicomedia: I 25,38;VIII 69;X 274
Ninian: II 11,12;XII 129,131
Nitria: VIII 80
Nomads: XXI 63-4,69-70,72,78-9;
 XXV 336-338
North Africa,Bible in: V 262
 -Christianity: V 261;X 261,277,
 288;XVI 2-3;XVII 191,193;XXI
 78
 -Catholicism: XVIII 37,38,40,
 47;XX 352
 -Donatists,see Donatism
 -Jews: XVII 185 ff.
 -olive oil: XX 349-50;XXI 61-2,
 65-70,72-3,80
 -trade: X 277;XXI 67-9
 also: VII 323;X 277-79;XVII
 193;XXI 65-6,69;XXII 15;
 XXV 338
Novatian: II 6,9;X 275;XII 137

Nubia (Nobatia): XVI 34;XXII 10-16;
 XXIII 155-8,160,161-2;XXIV 19,22-
 3,27-9;XXV 337-9
 -Art: XXV 336
 -Languages: XXII 16;XXIII 156,
 160-1;X 63;XXV 336,337,338
Numidia: I 38-9;II 2;II 18;IV 25-7;
 VIII 63,69;X 273-4,281;XVII 190,
 193;XVIII 36,41;XX 346;XIX 549;
 XXI 66-7,76;see Circumcellions
 -Donatist preponderance: XVIII 40
 -villages: X 284-286;XX 346,348;
 XXI 75
 -art: XXI 349-50

Optatus,Bishop of Milevis: IV 25;
 V 261;VIII 62;X 272;XVI 34;XIX
 543
Optatus,Bishop of Thamugadi: XVIII
 40,46;XX 346-7,350
Origen,Origenism: I 37;II 4;III 23;
 IV 18,19;V 260,263;VI 39;VIII 58,
 76,78;IX 479;X 264-8;XII 130;
 XIV 10
Orpheus: IX 473-5
Osrhoene: IV 16;X 274
Ostia: XXI 67
Oum el Adhem: XVIII 38,46-7
Oxyrhynchus: XIX 548
 -churches in: X 280
 -*logia*: III 23,25;VI 46

Pachomius,monk: I 27-8;II 7;III 23;
 VIII 79;X 283;XIV 9;XXII 16;XXIII
 156-8
Pachoras,see Faras
Paganism: II 7-8;XIV 1
 -Celtic: II 10-12
 -Germanic: XII 129
 -Romano-British: XII 140-1
 -in Rome: XIV 1-2
Painter,K.S.: XII 140
Palestine: III 16,22;IV 24;IX 476;
 X 282;XV 168;XVII 185;XXIII 158,
 160,162;XXV 337-8
 -Jews in:II 1,14;III 25
 -martyrs: II 6;X 273
Palladius,Bishop: XII 142
Pammachius,senator: XIV 6,9
Panium,battle: I 30
Papacy: VI 401,409;VIII 61;XVIII 41;
 XXII 14
Parthia: IX 476-7
Patriarchates: II 5-7;XI 69 ff.
Patrick,missionary: VIII 67;XII 129,
 131,141
Paul,apostle: I 32-34;III 18;IV 16;
 VI 38-9,48;VIII 75;XV 1;XVIII 37;

see also Apostle
Paul,Bishop of Cirta: X 272
Paul of Samosata: X 276;XI 78-9
Paula,friend of Jerome: VIII 73, 78
Paulinus of Nola: VIII 70;XII 131,140;XIV 1 ff.
 -early career: XIV 2-4
 -asceticism: XIV 5-8
 -friendships: XIV 8-9
 -and Grace: XIV 7-8
Paulus,Nubian Bishop: XXIV 23
Paulus Orosius: IV 19,22;VI 40; XIV 1,9
Pelagius,Pelagianism: IV 27; VIII 71,74-7;XII 141-3;XIV 1,7
Pepuza: I 35;II 2
Perpetua,martyr: I 37;IX 479; XV 167 ff;XVI 21,25-6;XVIII 46,43
 -Church in honour of: XVI 25
Persecutions: I 35;XVIII 32 ff.
 -Decian: I 37;II 4;IV 25; X 264,268,270-72,285;XII 130;XIV 4;XVI 22
 -Diocletianic: II 5,6;VI 39 X 263 ff;XXIII 158;XXIV 24
 -Maximin: X 273,279-80
 -Severan: VIII 58;IX 470 ff; XV 169 ff.
 -Valerianic: X 276,274;XVI 22
 -in North Africa: XV 169 ff; XVI 21
 -in Lyon: XV 167 ff.
 -in Phrygia: X 281
Persia,Christians in: II 4; XXII 14
Peter,Apostle: III 17;VI 48; XI 73,76;XVIII 37;see also Apostles
 -Primacy: XI 77
Peter,Bishop of Alexandria: X 280
Peter,"the Faller": XI 80
Peter Mongus: XI 71-3,75,80
Petilian,Donatist bishop of Constantine: VIII 71,74;X 285; XVIII 36,41,43
Philae: XXII 10-11,13;XXIV 19
Philo: III 23-4;X 266;XIV 10
Phrygia: I 35;II 2,3,8;VI 46; XIII 127;XV 169;see also Montanism
 -Paganism in: X 278
 -Persecution in: X 281,2
Pilgrimage: VIII 80,81
Pinanus,friend of Augustine:

VIII 62,70;XIV 6,9
Plato,Platonism: IV 22;VIII 73, 81;X 265,67
Plotinus: X 267
Plumley,J.M.: XXIV 25-6;XXV 336, 338
Polycarp of Smyrna: I 34;II 3; IV 17;VI 43
Pontius,deacon: XVI 25;XVIII 41, 43
Pontius Pilate: VI 39;VIII 81
Possidius,Bishop of Calana:I 42; XII 143
Poundbury,cemetery: XII 132-4
Primian,Donatist Bishop of Carthage: VIII 63
Priscillian of Avila: VIII 78-9; XIV 3,6n.
Procopius,historian: XVI 24,31; XXI 68-9,70,72,77
Prophets,prophecy: I 33,35-6; II 3;XV 171;XVIII 36
Prosper Tiro: XII 142
Proterius,archbishop: II 6
Prudentius: VIII 73;XVIII 41
pseudo-Amphilochius: XXIII 158
Ptolemy,Gnostic: XV 175
Punic,language: XX 342;XXV 338
Pythagoreans: III 18;XIV 6;XV 173

Q'asr Ibrim: XXII 10-11;XXIII 155, 158-60;XXIV 21,25,27-30;XXV 336-38
Q'mran,sectaries of: I 30;III 17, 21,24-5;V 260;VI 47-8;VIII 65; XV 171;XXII 19
Quispel,G.: III 13,20;V 263; XVII 186,188

Ramsay,Sir W.: VI 46;X 278
Rebaptism controversy: XI 78
Redemtus,archdeacon: XVI 23,29
Reformation: IV 16;VI 40,47,49
Remnant: XIV 10
Reparatus,Archbishop of Carthage: XVI 23-4,30
Richmond,I.A.: XII 132
Romanus,confessor: X 273
Rome,Church in: VIII 65,69
 -Councils: VIII 61
 -Gnostics: V 265;XV 175
 -Martyrs: I 37
 -Persecution: IX 479;X 272
 -Primacy: XI 80
 -Trade: XXI 64,68
 -gods of: X 269
 -Greek in: XIII 126
 -Jews in: I 34

-"Romans of": XIV 1,11
  Also: X 275,277;XI 69,72-6,
    79,81;XXI 67;XXII 12-14
Rufinus,historian: XIV 4-6
Rutilius Namatianus: XIV 9

Sabbath,kept by Christians:
  XVII 189
Sacraments: VI 49;VIII 66,80;
  X 270;XII 135;XVI 30
Sahara: XXI 66,70,73,75,80;
  XXIV 25
  -oases: XXI 64
Saint Peter's,excavations: V 261
  -patrimony: VIII 65
Salona: I 26;II 10;XIII 125,128-9;XXI 70
Salsa,martyr: XVI 26;XXI 70
Salvian,presbyter of Marseille:
  IV 21;VIII 69,77;XIV 1
Samaritans: IX 473-5
Sardis,Jews in: XVII 189
Saturn,North African god: II 3;
  IV 25;X 278;XVII 193
Saturninus,confessor: XVIII 38,
  41-43
Saturus,confessor: IX 479;XV 175;
  XVI 25;XVIII 43
Sbeitla (Suffetula): XXI 73,75,79
Scapula,Proconsul: XVI 24
Scilli,martyrs: XVI 21,25;XVIII
  37
Scriptores,Historiae Augustae:
  IX 470 ff.
Sedrata: XX 347;XXI 77
Seniores: VIII 62-5;XIII 126;
  XVI 30;XVII 191
Septimius Severus,emperor:
  IX 470,476-7;X 284;XV 168,175;
  XXI 66
Serapis: II 3;X 278
Serdica,Council of: II 8,13;IV
  20,24
Sethites,Gnostic sect: II 9;II
  13;V 259
Severus,Bishop of Asmounein;
  XXIII 158
Severus,Patriarch of Antioch:
  XI 77-79,80;XIV 9;XXII 14-15;
  XXIV 19
Shenute (Schenuti) monk: II 8;
  VIII 79;XIX 545
Sheppard Frere: XII 132
Silchester,church: XII 132-3,
  137
Silko,Nubian King: XXII 11,14;
  XXIV 19
Silvanus,Bishop of Cirta: X 274

Simeon Stylites: XIV 9;XIX 545
Simon,Marcel: XVII 185,194
Simplicius,Pope: XI 69,71-2,77
Siricius,Pope: XIV 6,10
Slaves,Slavery: I 39;IV 26;VIII
  68;XIII 127;XV 175;XIX 546
Sleepless Monks: XI 73
Smyrna: X 269,271
Soba,Nubian Kingdom: XII 12
Socrates,church historian:
  II 6;IV 24;VI 69;XXIII 158
Solomon,general: XVI 24,32;
  XXI 72
Sonqui Tino: XXV 338
Sozomen,church historian: II 7,
  13;VI 39;XIV 3;XXII 158
Spartian: IX 470,476,480
Stephen,pope: XVIII 190
Stephen,proto-martyr: XV 174
  -Convent of: XVI 32
Sulpicius Severus: II 11;XII
  139;XIV 4-6
Symmachus,pagan senator: XIV
  7n;XXI 67
Synesius,Bishop of Ptolemais:
  VIII 73;XIV 1;XXI 68
Syria,Syrian: XXII 12;XXIII 158,
  162,163;XXV 337
  -Christianity in: II 1;IV 17
  -Jews: XV 168
  -monks and ascetics: I 28,29;
    III 16-18;XIV 9;XIX 545
  -merchants: IV 21;XIII 125 ff.
  -migrants: XIII 128-9
  -paganism: II 7-8
  -villages: XXI 78
Syria,Secunda: XI 76,79,80
Sudan: XXIV 23,28;XXV 339

Tablettes Albertini: XXI 69-70
Tatian: I 34;III 13,19;IV 17-18;
  V 263
Tembris Valley,inscriptions: I
  I 36;II 3;X 282n.
Tertullian: IV 18,20;V 261;VIII
  57;IX 470,478-9;X 268-9,276,
  285;XII 130;XIV 10;XV 172;
  XVI 22;XX 351;XVII 185-6,188;
  XVIII 36
  -and Judaism: XVII 188,191-3
  -and the Spirit: XVIII 36
Tertullianists: XVIII 36
Tetrarchy: IX 471,473-4;X 278;
  XIII 125
Theodora,empress: XXII 10-16
Theodore,Bishop of Philae:
  XXII 11,15;XXIII 158,161;
  XXIV 7

Theodore,High Priest: X 285-6
Theodoret,Bishop of Cyrrhus:
 II 4,7,9;XIV 9
Theodoric,Ostrogoth king:
 VIII 77
Theodosius I,emperor: II 8,10;
 XIV 3
Theodosius,Monophysite patriarch:
 XXII 11,15
Theotokos: X 79;XVI 24;XXIII 158
Therapeutae,Jewish ascetics:
 III 24
Therasia,wife of Paulinus:
 XIV 2,5-6
Theveste (Tebessa): XVII 40,42;
 XX 345,369;XXI 68,72
Thomas,Gospel of: III 13 ff;
 IV 18;V 263;VIII 65;XV 173;
 XVII 186,189
Thrasamund,Vandal king: XXI 72
Three Chapters,controversy:
 IV 20
Thuburbo Maius: XV 169;XX 349;
 XXI 173
Tiddis: XXI 75
Tigzirt: XX 342,345
Tillemont,Lenain de: VI 41
Timasius,general: II 8
Timgad (Thamugadi): I 26-7;
 V 264;X 279;XII 134;XVIII 38,
 40,45-6;XX 345-6,350;XXI 77
 -baptistery: XX 346
 -Donatist Holy City: XVIII 40
Timotheos,Nubian bishop: XXIV
 26;XXV 337
Timothy,"the Cat": XI 71,74
Timothy,Chalcedonian patriarch:
 XI 72
Tintagel: II 121;XXI 74
Tipasa: VIII 69;XX 363;XXI 70
Tipasius,martyr: XVIII 42
Traditores: X 282;XVI 22
Trier: II 10;XIII 125,129;XIV
 3-4
Tripoli: XX 349;XXIII 162
Tripolitania: XXI 67-9,71,73,78
Tyconius,Donatist theologian:
 VIII 73-5;XIX 543-549

Uppenna: XVIII 38,43,48
Urbanilla: III 18;XV 173n.

Valens,emperor: II 10;VIII 59;
 X 265;XII 141;XIV 1

Valentinian I,emperor: II 10;
 XII 133,141;XIV 3
Valentinian II,emperor: XIV 2
Valentinus,Gnostic leader:
 III 23;V 259
Valerian,emperor: I 39;X 264,270;
 see also "Persecutions"
Vandals: I 42;XIV 8-9;XVI 23,28,
 30,31,34;XXI 63,68-9,70
Vatican cemetery: IX 474;X 286
Vazaini (Ain Zoni): XX 345,351
Vegesla: XVIII 37-8,47;XX 345
Verulamium: XII 130,140,143
Victor,grammarian: X 272
Victor of Vita: XVI 23;XXI 69,
 70
Victoria,confessor: I 40;XVIII
 41,47
Victricius,Bishop of Rouen:
 II 11;VIII 60;XII 131;XIV 6,
 8-9;XXII 12
Vienne: XIII 127-8
Vigilantius,opponent of Jerome:
 XII 140
Vigilius,missionary bishop:
 II 11
Villard,Ugo Monneret de: XXIV
 22;XXV 339
Virgin Mary: XXIII 161-2;XXIV
 24;XXV 337
 -Assumption: XXV 337
 -Galaktotropheusa: XXV 337
Visigoths: XII 142;XIV 1,2;
 XXI 70
Vitalian,general: XI 74,76
Volubilis: XVII 188
Volusianus inscription: XIII
 128
Vopiscus: IX 473,475

Water Newton: XII 135-6
Wealth,Christianity and: X 285;
 XIV 7
Widows: VIII 60-1
Wilson R.McL.: III 14
Woodeaton: II 10;XII 140

York: XII 130,132-3

Zacharias,Nubian King: XXIV 21
Zacharias Rhetor: XI 74
Zeno,emperor: IV 15;XI 69-73,80;
 XXII 15
Zosimus,historian: XX 352
Zosimus,Pope: XIV 8